ECONOMICS READ

THE GLOBAL POSSIBLE

A WORLD RESOURCES INSTITUTE BOOK

The Global Possible

Resources, Development, and the
New Century

EDITED BY ROBERT REPETTO

YALE UNIVERSITY PRESS
New Haven and London

Designed by James J. Johnson
and set in Melior Roman type.
Printed in the United States of America by
Vail-Ballou Press, Binghamton, N.Y.

Library of Congress Cataloging in Publication Data
Main entry under title:

The Global possible.

   "A World Resources Institute book."
   Consists chiefly of the rev. papers from the Global
Possible Conference held at Wye Plantation in Maryland,
May 2–5, 1984.
   Bibliography: p.
   Includes index.
   1. Economic development—Environmental aspects—
Congresses.   I. Repetto, Robert C.   II. World
Resources Institute.   III. Global Possible Conference
(1984: Wye Plantation)
   HD75.6.G55 1985   363.7   85–8209
   ISBN 0–300–03382–6 (alk. paper)
   ISBN 0–300–03534–9 (pbk.)

*The paper in this book meets the guidelines for
permanence and durability of the Committee on
Production Guidelines for Book Longevity of the
Council on Library Resources.*

10   9   8   7   6   5   4   3   2   1

Contents

Figures

Tables

Foreword

In May of 1984, the World Resources Institute staged an international meeting at Wye, Maryland, to take a fresh look at global resource and population problems and opportunities. Wye, a converted farmstead in the beautiful flatlands that gird the Chesapeake estuary, may not have become another Yalta or a Bretton Woods, but something important did happen there. For the seventy-five experts and leaders from twenty countries who participated, the Global Possible Conference demonstrated that there are a host of feasible and often tested solutions to the environmental and resource issues comprising some of the most important challenges facing societies in the decades ahead. In the process, the conference produced an unusually broad assessment of global-scale resource, population, and environmental problems and the policy shifts and initiatives needed to address them.

This book contains the outcome—principally the papers commissioned for the Global Possible Conference, revised in view of the expert working sessions that took place there. Its chapters not only represent up-to-date analyses by some of the leading authorities in the fields of natural resources and population, they also impart an interdisciplinary view that reveals more than the sum of its parts. Perhaps more important, this book gives grounds for informed optimism about how the world's governments, businesses, and citizens can make headway against an array of difficult environmental challenges that, if unaddressed, threaten not only the quality of life but also prospects for sustainable development and the political stability of societies.

In the resource chapters that are the core of this volume and in the concluding agenda developed at the conference, the environmental scientists and others who prepared the analyses have taken an important step in proposing initiatives for public and private action, thus allaying the restive pessimism that stands between the world we have and the one we want. This bridge between science and informed policy, as well as that between theory and the real-world success stories recounted here, is what makes this volume especially useful.

The Global Possible Project was the first undertaking of the World Resources Institute. The institute is a policy research center created in late 1982 with a grant from the John D. and Catherine T. MacArthur Foundation to help governments, international organizations, the private sector, and others address a fundamental question: How can we meet basic human needs and nurture economic growth without undermining the natural resources and environmental integrity on which life, economic vitality, and international security depend? Independent and nonpartisan, WRI seeks to provide accurate information about global resources and population, identify emerging issues, and develop politically and economically workable proposals.

Everyone at WRI and those who wrote for and participated in the Global Possible Conference contributed in one way or another to this volume, but none more than Robert Repetto, who directed the project, edited this volume, and wrote two of its chapters. Jessica Mathews, the institute's vice-president and research director, was also a major driving force throughout the effort.

JAMES GUSTAVE SPETH, President
World Resources Institute

Acknowledgments

The Global Possible project owes much to those who joined the World Resources Institute in conceiving and carrying it out. Robert O. Anderson, Robert S. McNamara, Matthew Nimetz, Soedjatmoko, Maurice F. Strong, M. S. Swaminathan, and Russell E. Train served as convenors to initiate the project. Sound advice was contributed by members of the steering committee: William Baumol, Napier Collyns, Meinolf Dierkes, Richard Ford, Thomas Jorling, Mohammed Kassas, Edwin Martin, Jessica Mathews, Mihajlo Mesarovic, Kenneth Prewitt, Robert Repetto, Thomas Stoel, E. Casey Westell Jr., Gilbert White, and James Gustave Speth, acting as chairman. A very special debt is owed to Martin W. Holdgate, who served ably as conference chairman. The authors of the commissioned background papers contributed their expertise, as did the conference participants, who worked hard to formulate working group reports and recommendations. Thanks are also due to many other experts who drafted or reviewed materials, to Rusty Winthrop and Edward Tripp, and to the entire staff of the World Resources Institute—particularly Moira Ambrose, Alison Webb-Jones, and Wenda Wright—whose contributions made the Global Possible project possible.

CHAPTER ONE

Overview

ROBERT REPETTO

PROGRESS AND POSSIBILITY

During the twenty-two years from 1960 to 1982, world per capita income grew at an average rate of 3.5 percent per year, slightly more than doubling its original level. Yet consider two countries: Korea, a middle-income country with a per capita income in 1982 of $1,910, and Ghana, a low-income country with a per capita income of $360, less than one-fifth as high. Population density is eight times greater in Korea than Ghana—the Gold Coast—which by any standard is more generously endowed with natural resources. Over these twenty-two years, income in Korea rose on average by 6.6 percent per year, doubling and redoubling. In Ghana, income actually fell at an average compound rate of 1.3 percent over this period, leaving Ghanaians only three-quarters as well off in 1982 as they had been in 1960. But in 1960, Korea and Ghana had exactly the same per capita income.

The same enormous range of performance is evident in specific demographic, environmental, and economic trends. For low- and middle-income countries, combined, per capita food production rose by a modest 10 percent between 1960 and 1982, while overall cereal imports rose 50 percent. But, as the paper by Janos Hrabovszky points out, Asia made considerable progress while Africa fell backward. In Sri Lanka, where 16 million people inhabit an area the size of Ireland, per capita food production increased 54 percent and cereal imports were halved. But in Egypt, per capita production fell 15 percent and imports nearly doubled.

In the developing countries, excluding China, the rate of population growth remained approximately constant at 2.5 percent per year

1

over these decades. But as chapter 6 documents, this aggregate masks enormous variation. In Cuba, the rate of natural increase fell from 2.5 percent in 1960 to 1.0 percent in 1982, the fertility rate fell to replacement level, and life expectancy reached seventy-five years, the same level as in the United States. In South Africa, a country whose per capita income is nearly twice as high, the rate of natural increase rose over these years from 2.4 to 3.1 percent, life expectancy is sixty-three years (the average rate of China and India), and the fertility rate remains twice the replacement level.

In low-income countries overall, the proportion of girls aged six to eleven enrolled in primary school rose from 34 to 81 percent between 1960 and 1982 (from 25 to 58 percent if China and India are excluded). In Kenya, the increase was from 30 to 100 percent, while in Pakistan, a country with the same per capita income, the improvement was only from 13 to 31 percent.

There are similarly wide differences in rates of resource depletion. John Spears and Edward Ayensu, in their paper on forestry, cite a recent Food and Agriculture Organization (FAO) study of clearing and degradation of tropical forests, which concluded that the overall rate of clearing of tropical forests in the 1980s is about 0.6 percent per year, although there is wide variation from country to country. In the central African region, including the Congo, Zaire, and Cameroon, the rate is as low as 0.2 percent annually, while in the West African coastal nations of Ivory Coast and Nigeria, the rate may be as high as 4.0-6.0 percent. In Latin America, the rates range from 0.4 percent in Brazil, where, despite widespread clearing, enormous reserves remain, to more than 3.5 percent per year in Costa Rica, El Salvador, and Paraguay, where large-scale commercial ranches have taken over previously forested land.[1]

Countries have differed tremendously in their response to changing scarcities and costs of energy. Amulya Reddy's paper points out that in the OECD countries, total energy demand fell on average by 0.3 percent per year while gross domestic product (GDP) increased by 2.1 percent per year. Among middle-income developing countries, in which commercial energy sources are more important than noncommercial sources, energy consumption slowed from an annual rate of increase of 8.0 percent between 1960 and the first oil crisis in 1974, to an annual rate of 5.4 percent from 1974 to 1981. But growth in GDP slowed only marginally, from 6.0 to 5.4 percent, between the 1960s and 1970s, thereby implying gains in energy efficiency. In the Dominican Republic, however, production growth accelerated from 4.5 to 6.0

percent between the two decades, even though half of all export earnings had to be spent on energy imports, whereas energy consumption, which had been rising at the rate of 14.0 percent per year up to the oil crisis, subsequently fell by 1.2 percent annually until 1981. Thus energy efficiency increased significantly. Similarly, in Singapore, production growth barely fluctuated, declining from 8.8 percent annually in the 1960s to 8.5 percent in the 1970s, but growth in energy consumption fell from 9.4 percent before the oil crisis to 1.6 percent thereafter. Despite having no energy resources whatever, Singapore ended the period with a debt service burden of less than 1 percent of annual exports. By contrast, Mexico, an oil exporter, experienced a decline in GDP growth rates between the 1960s and 1970s from 7.6 to 6.4 percent, despite the oil boom, and saw annual growth in energy consumption accelerate from 7.4 to 9.3 percent after 1974. Hence Mexico ended the period in economic crisis, with debt service obligations equal to 30 percent of export earnings.

These wide variations in performance are one reason for the wide range of uncertainty in forecasts. Optimistic or pessimistic assumptions extrapolated into the future lead to very divergent predictions when the differences in performance are so great. Deforestation at 2 percent per year would result in the loss of three-quarters of present forest acreage by the year 2050, but at the rate of 0.2 percent, only one-eighth would disappear. Population projections based on the assumed continuation of past trends imply that the world's population will ultimately stabilize at about 14.5 billion, whereas projections based on diffusion of the most rapid declines in fertility observed anywhere predict an ultimate world population size just half that.

There are ample grounds in experience for both optimistic and pessimistic assumptions. The contrasts outlined above could be matched in any other realm of performance. The gap between best performance and failure is enormous. What is important is that these wide variations are attributable not to chance events or uneven resource endowments but to identifiable differences in policy orientations and actions. Korea's economic success and Ghana's struggles are due to the economic policies of the countries. Cuba's demographic transformation and South Africa's lagging transition are due mainly to differences in their social policies. The improvements in energy efficiency made by Singapore and the Dominican Republic stemmed from their energy policies and adaptation to external economic changes. Therefore, disputes between optimistic and pessimistic forecasters are implicitly disputes about future policies.

The critical issues arise not so much from modest changes in the average indicators of progress but from the wide variation in experience. That the trends, overall, have been modestly upward is of limited interest and relevance. What is important is that examples of success demonstrate how much better the record would be if the policies and actions underlying those successes were followed more universally. The failures are reminders of the probable consequences if wrong policies are pursued.

Although food production per capita rose by 10 percent in low-income countries taken together over the past two decades, it fell significantly in fifteen out of thirty-four. Although the rate of population growth in the developing countries declined overall between the 1970s and 1980s, it accelerated in almost half the individual countries. Of sixty-four developing countries for which estimates are available, one-third managed to raise the level of GDP per unit of commercial energy consumed—an aggregate measure of energy productivity—over the decade of the 1970s. Two-thirds did not. Since the record is so mixed, the important question is not the level of the average performance but how to tip the balance toward more widespread success.

This tension between success and failure continues to heighten as human power over the planet grows and becomes increasingly concentrated in the leadership of a few organizations. World war, a development of this century, now threatens the extinction of human life in a nuclear exchange of hours or even minutes. World markets for energy, food grains, and credit now supply an increasing share of world demands and are subject to disruptions originating in national decisions that have worldwide repercussions. The environmental impacts of economic activity are no longer only local in scale but are capable of altering the planet's climate and primary productivity. Large organizations dominate human events. National governments increasingly control the allocation of goods and services. In the United States, the government share in GDP has risen from about 5 percent in 1900 to over 20 percent today. In US agriculture, the 1 percent of farms that market half a million dollars' worth of product or more each year command 65 percent of all farm income. In industry, the parent companies of US multinational firms contribute 41 percent of the GDP of all corporate business. As power becomes concentrated in fewer organizations whose power grows, the future becomes more dependent on a few key policy decisions. The stakes have risen.

Those decisions need not be voyages into uncharted waters. Innovators have already gone ahead in many directions. Rapid progress consists in following quickly on the heels of the pioneers. Enormous gains in transportation and information technologies transmit innovations around the world almost instantaneously. In his paper on the historical context of current resource issues, Hugh Thomas reminds us that at the time of the Europeans' arrival in the New World, the potato had not yet reached Mexico from Peru, nor had the tea bush reached India from China. But today, the entire globe is under continuous scrutiny and surveillance.

The possibilities far exceed the actualities. The gap between the average and the leading edge is wide. In agriculture in developing countries, the "yield reserve" estimated by the FAO, based on the gap between average reserves and those obtainable through application of present-day technologies, ranges from 300 to 400 percent for various major crops, as Hrabovszky's paper points out. The gap between actual and biologically potential yields established by research stations is much larger, from 500 to 1,000 percent for rice in the tropics, for example.[2]

The potential improvement in the efficiency of energy use, just through adoption of known technologies, is enormous. In the United States, fuel use for space heating can be reduced by one-half or two-thirds in existing houses and by three-quarters in new houses through investments in insulation, storm windows, caulking, and weather-stripping. Similarly, the most efficient appliances on the market today require only one-half to one-third the energy of the average appliance currently in use, and more efficient woodstoves for the billion people dependent on for fuel can triple the usable energy derived from a load of wood as Reddy's paper indicates.

Large energy savings are possible in the major energy-intensive industries. Amulya Reddy reports that in the US chemical industry, energy efficiency rose 3.9 percent per year between 1972 and 1979 due to better "housekeeping," heat recovery, and process design. US steelmakers use 60 percent more energy to produce a ton of steel than do the Japanese, and twice as much as is required by new Swedish technologies. Moreover, technologies under development require only one-third as much energy expenditure per ton.

The gap is obvious in the transportation sector. The US automotive fleet's average mileage per gallon of gasoline in 1981 was 16, when the VW Rabbit achieved 31 and the VW diesel got 45. The 1984

Honda Civic CRX recorded 52 mpg in Environmental Protection Agency (EPA) city-highway mileage tests, and experiments suggest that almost 80 mpg can be achieved with only modest advances over today's technology.[3]

Equally impressive gains are possible in energy production. The World Bank, in conjunction with energy sector lending, has raised petroleum recovery threefold in Turkey's largest field, by introducing carbon dioxide injection techniques used previously only in advanced oil-producing countries, and has raised natural gas recovery tenfold through hydraulic fracturing.[4] These technologies are widely applicable elsewhere.

The examples can be multiplied almost indefinitely. While New Yorkers lean on their horns in daily traffic jams, Hong Kong drivers carry electronic sensors under their cars to record their entry into congested downtown areas and pay congestion fees based on their contribution to peak traffic loads. While Indian farmers, who flood their fields with water delivered through unlined canals, lose 85 percent of the irrigation water potentially available for uptake by plant roots, Israeli and California farmers using drip irrigation precisely scheduled to crop requirements use 85 percent of the water potentially available.

Thus the possibility of widespread and rapid improvement in the efficiency of resource use is not utopian. It rests on successful experience and tested innovation. To a large extent, the models are already there for adaptation and diffusion. Since the pace of technological change is quickening, the application and management of what is known is an ever-growing challenge and opportunity. In particular, institutions must adapt more rapidly to keep pace. Advances in information technology, biotechnology, energy technologies, and so on put pressure on institutions that evolved in earlier and technologically simpler times. Property rights over new ideas and technologies must be assured, and standards developed that ensure compatibility of processes and products across international boundaries, if the benefits of innovation are to be diffused rapidly.

Further, the direction of future innovation is affected by present policy. Innovation is determined by both scientific possibilities and potential economic rewards. When the price of fossil fuels rose dramatically, a flood of new products and processes for energy conservation and alternative energy supplies came onto the market. In his paper, William Vogely recounts that when cobalt prices rose in the mid-1970s, as supplies from Zaire of this supposedly critical mineral were cut off, the search for new technologies and substitutes was spurred on. Cobalt-free magnets were developed, and ceramics began to be used for turbine blades. Likewise, new processes for reducing or treating hazardous wastes emerged when they could no longer be discarded cheaply in the environment.

Hugh Thomas's historical perspective corroborates our own generation's sense that the stream of innovation constantly shifts its channel. The currents of progress quicken in countries that were backwaters, while past leaders stagnate. The European nations that forged the industrial revolution are no longer in the forefront, and Asian nations surge ahead. Finding and using the policy levers that sustain dynamism in technological and institutional innovation and channeling that energy into socially desirable directions are of critical importance in the long run.

A POSSIBLE AND SUSTAINABLE FUTURE

Disturbing visions of the human condition early in the next century are not difficult to imagine from the present situation. Population growth at the high end of the projected range, which corresponds to a continuation of current rates of decline of birth and death rates, would exacerbate already serious problems in many developing countries. The number of people in Bangladesh will double with another doubling ahead; but already more than one-third of the rural population is landless, the average size of a farmholding has declined from 3.5 acres (1.42 ha) in 1960 to 1.3 acres (0.53 ha) today, more than 40 percent of the rural poor survive on less than 80 percent of the FAO's minimum caloric intake requirement, and real wages in agriculture have fallen by 50 percent over the past twenty years.

Many more people could be exposed to the squalor of slums and the deteriorating environmental conditions of Third World cities. According to the paper by Jorge Hardoy and David Satterthwaite, the population of Nairobi, where 40 percent of the inhabitants now occupy shacks in illegal shantytowns with no piped water, sewers or drains, lighting, or access roads, would grow from one million to more than five million early next century. Uncontrolled air pollution could contribute to elevated levels of tuberculosis, pneumonia, bronchitis, and lung cancer in the industrial cities of the Third World, where respiratory diseases are already the leading overall cause of death.

The loss of agricultural land through erosion, salinization, and waterlogging could undermine the livelihood of millions of cultivators and impede efforts to raise agricultural production. Thirty-five percent of the world's land area, including significant portions of the productive regions of the Northern Hemisphere, are at risk. In the Sudan, for example, where per capita food production declined 13 percent during the last decade, the deterioration of rangelands is moderate to severe. Rain-fed croplands are increasingly afflicted by declining soil fertility and by soil crusting due to unsuitable cropping practices, leading to lower yields and abandoned farms. Irrigated lands are deteriorating severely because of poor management and siltation from upstream erosion. Deforestation is very severe, especially around the cities, contributing to further erosion and the encroachment of sand dunes from the Libyan desert.[5] These processes at work in the Sudan and other arid and semiarid regions, which destroy the productivity of an estimated 20 million hectares per year, could become more severe as pressures on agricultural land intensify.

In the industrialized world, disturbing environmental trends persist. In the United States, there are more than fifteen thousand sites in EPA's Emergency and Remedial Response Inventory at which hazardous wastes have been dumped without any controls. In addition, eighty thousand sites in the nation have contaminated surface lagoons, pits, and ponds. Tests of underground drinking water supplies in 954 cities with populations exceeding ten thousand found contamination by hazardous wastes leached from landfills and surface impoundments in 275. Despite this threat from waste that has already been dumped, more than one metric ton per person of hazardous wastes is being generated and added to landfills and surface impoundments each year, and progress in finding locations for safe disposal and treatment facilities, given local opposition, is painfully slow.

From 1950 to 1980, worldwide emissions of carbon dioxide rose at an average rate of 4 percent per year. Even energy models that forecast future increases in emissions of carbon dioxide and other "greenhouse" gases at less than half this rate predict sizable climate changes: a mean rise in surface temperatures of $3 \pm 1.5°C$ by the first quarter of next century. The implications of such a shift in temperature are uncertain but substantial, since 5°C represents the entire temperature variation of the last 125,000 years. As Schneider and Thompson explain in their paper, the consequences could include major shifts in precipitation and runoff that could imperil agricultural production in important temperate farming regions, more frequent occurrences of damaging temperature extremes, and possible rises in sea level of 2-12 feet (0.60-3.66 m), enough to cause major flooding and storm damage in coastal areas.

These scenarios are not forecasts, nor are they predictions: they are possibilities that could result from policy choices or from failure to act. They are not implausible because, in part or in embryo, they already exist. Although there are many different visions of a desirable future, none includes scenarios such as these.

There is in fact considerable consensus on what would constitute the basic elements of a more desirable future, resting in part on the physical facts of life. There is consensus that the human population must become stable, as it was for most of human existence. Rates of population growth even remotely approaching those experienced in this century are unsustainable over the next. The time it takes to reach stability, however, as well as the size of the human population at stability and the way in which stability is achieved, are critical. A balance of births and deaths with life expectancies around the world of 75 years, the current level in industrial countries, implies that crude birth rates (number of births per 1,000 population in a given year) must be below 10 per 1,000—less than one-third the current level in low-income countries.

There is further consensus that economic growth conceived and organized as an assembly line, drawing virgin materials into the production process at one end and spewing out finished goods ultimately to be discarded along with waste materials at the other, is unsustainable. The capacity of natural systems to withstand disruption, either by intrusion of wastes or by harvesting of part of the stock, is limited. Continuing expansion of these activities at anything like 4 percent per year, the rate of growth of the world economy, is impossible. George Woodwell's paper forcefully makes the case that the assimilative and rejuvenative capacities of natural systems would ultimately be overwhelmed, and the natural resource base on which we ultimately depend impoverished. Future economic growth must emulate natural productivity, recycling materials and energy to a much larger extent. There must be continual reduction in the generation of wastes and the use of virgin materials per unit of output, as well as ongoing substitution of more abundant materials for those becoming more scarce. There is a consensus that more attention must be paid to the future implications of current economic policies. This idea is summarized in the goal of "sustainable development"—a development strategy that manages all assets—natural and human resources, as well as financial and physical assets—for increasing wealth and well-being. Sustainable development, as a goal, rejects policies and practices that support current living standards by depleting the productive base, including natural resources, and that leave future generations with poorer prospects than our own.

What sustainable development is not is clear. What is not sustainable is the support of current consumption through foreign borrowing that leaves the next generation with a heavy burden of debt service obligations, or failure to maintain the quality and skills of the next generation by sufficient investment in education, or the support of current consumption levels by depletion of soils, forests, fisheries, and energy resources, so that future productivity of these resources is impaired.

At the core of the idea of sustainability, then, is the concept that current decisions should not damage prospects for maintaining or improving living standards in the future. As Kristin Shrader-Frechette points out in her essay on ethical issues, this is strikingly similar to John Locke's criterion for judging appropriations of natural resources, that such property claims should be considered valid only if they leave "as much and as good for others." This implies that our economic systems should be managed so that we live off the dividend of our resources, maintaining and improving the asset base so that the generations that follow will be able to live equally well or better. This principle also has much in common with the ideal concept of income that accountants seek to determine: the greatest amount that can be consumed in the current period without reducing prospects for consumption in the future.[6] Accountant and philosopher thus agree on the basis of sustainability.

This does not mean that sustainable development demands the preservation of the current stock of natural resources or any particular mix of human, physical, and natural assets. As development proceeds, the composition of the underlying asset base changes. In resource-rich countries, such as the United States, abundant natural resources were exploited rapidly and early on, to finance the creation of ports, roads, houses, farms, and, later, factories. Land, which was the predominant asset in colonial times, amounted to only one-third of total tangible assets by 1900 and accounts for only one-quarter now. At the same time, human capital—the valuable skills and training embodied in the population and labor force—has risen to dominate our national wealth. Depending on the means used to estimate the value of human capital, it now constitutes between 50 and 90 percent of all assets in the United States. Not only has the composition of US national wealth changed dramatically, but the increase in total assets per head has been impressive. Over the entire period, 1900-80, per capita total assets as conventionally defined (excluding human capital) rose by 1.7 percent per year, doubling and redoubling; moreover, the rate of increase of assets would be appreciably greater were the growth in human capital included, since that has doubled and redoubled on a per capita basis just since 1953.[7] This accumulation of national assets has supported a sharp rise in living standards.

Although sustainable development is compatible with dramatic changes in the asset base, some changes are irreversible and can entail serious long-run losses. There are a limited number of good storage sites for impoundment of surface waters to be used for irrigation and hydroelectric power generation. Most have already been developed. When their capacity is diminished by siltation, the sites are, for practical purposes, irreversibly lost and no longer available to meet rising demands for agricultural products and renewable energy. Similarly, when species become extinct, their potential value in scientific research, in developing improved agricultural strains or finding new pharmaceutical products, is irretrievably lost. The paper of Kenton Miller and his colleagues asserts that the million species extinctions likely to occur over the remainder of this century if strong action is not taken will eliminate options of inestimable value. Therefore, sustainable development implies that assets must be managed for the long run, taking into account their possible value in the future as well as their value now.

Sustainable development is thus a three-legged stool. Its bases are scientific realities, consensus on ethical principles, and considerations of long-run self-interest. There is broad agreement that pursuing policies that imperil the welfare of future generations, who are unrepresented in any political or economic forum, is unfair. Most would concur that an economic system and policies that consign a large share of the world's population to massive deprivation and poverty are also unfair. But pragmatic self-interest also reinforces that belief. Poverty, which denies people the means to act in their own long-run interest, underlies the deterioration of resources and the growing population pressures in much of the world and affects all. Further, the threat of destruction from military confrontation in a world of increasing nuclear proliferation is so strong and imminent that there is an urgent need to reduce conflict and its sources and to build mechanisms for cooperative, mutually beneficial approaches to world problems. Even if the chances of a nuclear outbreak in any year were only one in a hundred, the odds *against* our surviving the next century without a nuclear catastrophe would be three to one.

For the goal of sustainable development to be fulfilled, then, the Global Possible Conference declared that several critical transitions must be completed:

- A demographic transition to a stable world population of low birth and death rates
- An energy transition to high efficiency in production and use and increasing reliance on renewable sources
- A resource transition to reliance on nature's "income" without depletion of its "capital"
- An economic transition to sustainable development and a broader sharing of its benefits
- A political transition to a global negotiation grounded in complementary interests between North and South, East and West.

The results of the many assessments that provided the foundation for the Global Possible Conference suggest that such a prosperous and sustainable future is attainable. Population can be stabilized before it doubles again, with much improved health and life expectancies around the world. This will happen only if the poorer half of the world's people, who probably consume less than 10 percent of the world's output, can find productive jobs and access to land, credit, training, or other resources by which to raise their incomes; only if women throughout the world can find ways of living that do not involve early marriage and many children; and only if basic and inexpensive health and family planning services are available to all.

Agricultural production can expand to meet all future demands, including the needs of the undernourished, without exerting destructive pressures on marginal lands, water resources, or ecological systems. But this will happen only if farming systems and agricultural technologies that match land capabilities are developed and explained to the world's farmers; only if systems of incentives to farmers reflect accurately the true value of agricultural outputs and inputs and the true costs of resource use; and only if farmers and herders are not pushed onto marginal land by population growth and increasing concentration of land in the hands of a small number of owners.

Economic growth can be sustained with markedly lower energy input, and energy can be supplied by a mix of sources that do not imperil the climate or the natural environment. The buildup of carbon dioxide in the atmosphere can be contained at concentrations that limit the risk of climatic disruption, and energy services can be provided without exacerbating nuclear insecurity, international economic instability, air and water pollution, and other energy-related problems. This will happen only if energy prices and policies are structured to realize the enormous potential that exists for further energy conservation and improved efficiency in energy use, and if energy plans and decisions are based on the full costs and risks of energy alternatives.

Further, forest resources, essential to the functioning of many ecological systems and as energy and income sources for much of the world's population, can be stabilized and expanded through better management and productive investment. The loss of biological diversity can be arrested, and the potential of this enormous resource better explored and used in agriculture, medicine, and industry. Nonfuel minerals and material can be supplied over the long run at affordable prices through the efficient movement of capital, technology, and commodities in international markets. Environmental pollution can be markedly reduced and the quality of the environment preserved by more efficient resource recovery and source abatement. Cities, even in low-income countries experiencing rapid urbanization, can be made healthier and more livable if individual and community initiatives are encouraged and mobilized, and if public investments concentrate on providing basic urban services to all neighborhoods at levels that all can afford.

These goals are not expensive to achieve. In fact, they are usually less costly than the present course, and many represent the least-cost approach to the problem. Basic health and family planning services that can cut mortality and morbidity rates by half and that encourage more effective protection against unwanted pregnancies that can be provided in most Third World countries at an annual cost of $2-$4 per capita, much of which can be recovered from clients. This is less than most Third World countries are now spending on health care and less than many public health services alone spend.

Safe drinking water through appropriately designed community systems can be supplied in low-income urban neighborhoods at a cost as low as one-tenth what slum dwellers without such systems now pay to water carriers and vendors. Sanitation systems that minimize water pollution and facilitate resource recovery have been installed in Third World cities at a cost one-twentieth that of conventional sewer systems.

Development strategies that attack poverty by emphasizing employment growth; small-scale, decentralized, quick-yielding investment programs; and wide access to land, credit, technology, and other resources have resulted in faster overall growth in per capita income as well as more rapid elimination of poverty. A more equitable distribution of arable land and more attention to smallholder agriculture typically result in higher agricultural productivity, as well as greater rural employment, wider availability of food crops, and less pressure on marginal lands and forests.

Watershed protection programs that introduce appropriate mixed-farming systems to hilly areas—checking soil erosion by maintaining continuous vegetative cover and through better water control and improved animal husbandry—afford high economic returns in the form of improved productivity and income. Watershed reclamation projects in the Indian foothills of the Himalayas have yielded a direct economic benefit-cost ratio of 2.5 to 1 and have reduced sediment transport downstream by 90 percent. Similar projects in Nepal have raised the incomes of participating farmers fourfold in three years. The total returns of such projects, including reductions in downstream siltation and flooding, are even more impressive as Spears and Ayensu point out in their paper.

Energy conservation investments, despite the substantial gains that have already been made in many areas, remain the least-cost means of meeting demands for additional energy services, even before the environmenal benefits are calculated. As regards energy expansion, a recent detailed study of the options for meeting energy demands in the US Pacific Northwest through the end of this century found that the least-coast approach would be a combination of residential and industrial conservation investments and expansion of renewable energy sources (low-head hydroelectric potential), which would save $2.7 billion—15 percent of the cost of meeting demands through the best conventional supply program—and elminate the need for any additional conventional capacity.[8]

Numerous studies of the world's fisheries have demonstrated that the present catch, or a higher sustainable catch, could be achieved at less than half the present cost if the overcrowding associated with inadequate restrictions on fishing were elminated. This finding is representative of those on many common-property resources, including rangelands, forested areas, and groundwater, which are exploited not only beyond their optimal sustainable yields but inefficiently, with significant excess costs.

Maintaining environmental quality through pollution abatement costs much less. In the industrial countries, estimates of the savings that can be achieved just by applying the severest strictures to sources that can reduce damage to the environment least expensively typically amount to 40-60 percent of the present costs of pollution control.[9] However, the longer-run savings that can be achieved by combining and changing processes so as to reduce and recycle wastes instead of treating and discharging them are even more significant. One innovative company, 3M of St. Paul, Minnesota, in the last decade has reformulated products and redesigned processes to eliminate—*each year*—more than 90,000 tons of air pollutants, 10,000 tons of water pollutants, 1,000 million gallons of wastewater, and 150,000 tons of solid wastes. In so doing, 3M has saved a total of about $200 million, of which 60 percent represents annual operating and maintenance costs.[10]

Thus economic factors do not block the attainment of a more desirable and sustainable future—they favor it. The payoffs due to better management of resources are large. The present costs of switching to better policies and programs are small relative to future costs or the damages that will result if action is not taken. The industrial world is now finding that the costs of properly disposing of hazardous wastes or recycling them is small relative to the cleanup costs of inadequately regulated hazardous waste sites. The developing world is now finding that the costs of watershed protection are small relative to the costs of increased flooding and reduced irrigation and hydroelectric capacity resulting from unprotected watersheds.

This advantage is multiplied by the fact that some actions promote both better resource management and more sustainable development. Norman Myers's paper points out that promoting more rapid demographic transition reduces pressures on marginal agricultural lands as well as on cities in developing countries. Actions that promote energy conservation reduce risks of global climate change, air and water pollution, and pressures on forested areas in the Third World. Actions that encourage reforestation and protection of forested areas provide an important renewable energy source and contribute to climate regulation and to soil and water management. The elements of a program to promote sustainable development support each other and are attactive both environmentally and economically.

THE MECHANISMS FOR IMPROVEMENT: STRATEGIES
FOR SUSTAINABLE DEVELOPMENT

Strategies for dealing with the range of resource, environmental, demograpic, and economic issues that can strongly influence the attainment of a desirable future turn out to have key elements in common. There are a relatively small number of mechanisms that can be widely applied to particular situations and that, over time, will yield enormous benefits. These mechanisms are neither speculative nor utopian; rather, they have been tested and found to be effective. The following discussion identifies several key elements which stand out among the findings and assessments of the Global Possible Conference.

Attending to Basics

Many problems of resource deterioration, environmental decay, population growth, and inadequate living standards persist or worsen not because they are impossible or difficult to solve but because they have not yet been seriously addressed. One reason for this neglect is that those immediately affected have little voice, power, or economic standing. Thus, they have little ability to attract resources or attention. Yet, their problems affect everybody. Poverty and lack of opportunity or choice are among the root causes of rapid population growth, migration to overcrowded cities, wretched housing and environmental conditions that spread disease, encroachment on marginal soils and forests, depletion of coastal and inland fisheries, and other pressures on resources.

Ingenuity and resources have been lavishly applied to solving the problems and meeting the needs of the world's powerful, and there have been stunning advances. But little has been done to solve the problems and meet the needs of the urban and rural poor, landless and marginal farmers, pastoral people and forest dwellers, or Third World women. As a result, rapid advances are still to be had at relatively low cost.

A striking example was reported recently in the *Washington Post* (August 3, 1984). It concerns a team of scientists who are close to developing a vaccine for malaria, a disease that is resurgent throughout the world as the anopheles mosquito develops resistance to DDT and other insecticides. Malaria afflicts more than 200 million people annually and kills millions, including a million children in Africa, every year. The total cost of the research, much of which was supported by the US Agency for International Development, has been about $35 million over the past twenty years. This cost, spread over the number of lives likely to be saved over the next twenty years as a result of the vaccine, is probably less than a dollar per life.

The opportunities for improving resource management, environmental quality, and standards of living through low-cost and simple programs that address neglected needs of neglected populations are enormous. Low-cost health and family planning programs, emphasizing basic services and preventive care, can reduce mortality rates and raise contraceptive use rates by a factor of two within five years, as witnessed by India's Jamkhed Rural Health Project, which is discussed in my paper. These programs can be mounted for $2-$4 per person, much of which can be financed through community payments even in the poorest of villages. Yet half the population of the developing world outside China is still without ready access to these services.

In the poorer neighborhoods of Third World cities, now in appalling condition, safe drinking water, toilets, and washing facilities can be provided, drainage can be improved, and walks and entry roads can be constructed for modest sums. In Indonesia's Kampung Improvement Program and elsewhere, it has been demonstrated that communities will contribute rights of way and sites for facilities, will assess themselves to compensate households whose property is impaired, and will pay for the maintenance of water sources. Further, it has been demonstrated that much of the investment cost can be quickly recovered in higher urban property values and tax revenues. Yet, the large majority of Third World urban residents live in slums and shantytowns.

Highly successful programs in rural areas of India, China, and elsewhere have greatly improved the prospects of landless and marginal farmers by allotting them seedlings, plots of deforested wasteland, and credit to enable them to plant trees. Often, the cash yield per acre of those plantations has been higher than that resulting from the return of land to crops, and, at the same time, erosion and further deforestation have been checked. Yet, John Spears and Edward Ayensu estimate that the rate of planting for fuelwood must be increased fivefold over present levels if the acute shortage of fuelwood and fodder in many Third World countries is to be relieved.

Small-credit programs, which often amount to little more than easing government regulations over the interest rates that private banks can pay for deposits and charge for loans and infusing a small initial sum of capital, have freed low-income people starved for capital from the need to borrow from moneylenders at interest rates of 10-20 percent per month and have greatly expanded their earnings opportunities. So starved for capital are the poor in many countries that, even at interest rates 1-2 percent per month above inflation, borrowers can quickly expand their small-scale production or trading activities and markedly raise their earnings, expanding their credit lines and also permitting small-credit institutions to grow quickly from deposits and retained earnings.

As these examples show, given a chance, the impoverished will manage to help themselves. In cities, almost all construction and improvement in housing is through self-help and private initiative. In Bogota, Colombia, 60 percent of the neighborhoods in the city have evolved from illegal squatter settlements. Yet, in many countries, the poorest people in urban areas are regarded as illegal entrants. Their property rights over the shelters they build are not recognized, and their efforts to upgrade them are frustrated by authorities reluctant to acknowledge them as permanent residents. Hardoy and Satterthwaite argue, on the basis of extensive field research, that often mere legitimation of their presence and removal of impediments to their efforts, such as unrealistic building codes, can result in substantial improvements.

In rural areas, credit, extension services, and infrastructure have been directed toward larger farmers and prime lands, despite the evidence that yields and employment per hectare are usually no lower—and are often higher—on small holdings. The training-and-visit system, which has helped extension services reach smaller farmers, has resulted in impressive gains in agricultural yields and farm incomes. In the Seyhan project in Turkey, within three years of the introduction of this system, farmers had increased cotton yields from 1.7 to more than 3.0 metric tons per hectare (mt/ha). In India, farmers in regions where the system was introduced within two years, had raised paddy yields from 2.1 to 3 mt/ha and wheat yields from 1.3 to nearly 2 mt/ha. In the main, the recommendations that led to these improvements were simple, low-cost steps that were well within farmers' capabilities: better seedbed preparation and stand densities, more careful weed control, and so on.[11]

Exploiting these opportunities involves changes in approach for development agencies. There is a tendency for such agencies, both national and international, to devote the bulk of available manpower and resources to large discrete projects. Since commitments to these tend to grow as cost and time overruns occur, smaller-scale programs are disproportionately squeezed, and other opportunities overlooked. Large water resource projects are undertaken, whereas more cost-effective alternatives involving rehabilitating and upgrading existing systems, exploiting opportunities for small-scale irrigation and power development, and more efficient use of existing water resources are neglected. Major energy development projects are taken on, whereas least-cost opportunities for energy conservation, cogeneration, and other small-scale decentralized energy developments are passed over.

Correction of the balance involves, first, decentralization of more of the responsibility for program planning, finance, and execution, since no central agency can effectively develop the information required to plan and execute a program of many small components. This, in turn, implies greater reliance on markets for resource allocation rather than administrative decisions, since the latter inevitably favor large projects and large constituencies. Second, it implies involvement of community organizations to a greater degree, since many effective programs to aid the neglected depend on community action and participation. Third, and above all, it requires a change in priorities that will put emphasis on exploring least-cost options and extending basic services to all before providing more elaborate services to the better off.

Managing Common Resources

The following report by Richard Witkin is excerpted from the *Washington Post*, 6 August 1984:

> At Kennedy International Airport one recent day, 63 planes were scheduled to arrive in the hour beginning at 3:45 P.M., but the most the airport could handle, even with clear weather, was 44. At Laguardia, 80 airline arrivals and departures have been scheduled for the hour starting at 8 A.M. on the average weekday. The capacity is 68. . . . These and other examples from the Federal Aviation Administration indicate [overscheduling] is a fairly widespread problem [and has] contributed to a sharp rise in flight delays.
>
> Officials at several airlines acknowledged that they scheduled more rush-hour flights than the system could handle, saying

they were responding to competitive pressures. There are no government controls on how many flights may be put in the airline schedule.

"If we shy away from a 5 P.M. take-off, others won't, and they'll gobble up the prime time business," said Jerry Cosley, a spokesman for Trans World Airlines.

This report aptly illustrates a much larger and more widespread need: the need to manage community resources, or common-property resources, more efficiently. In this instance, the resource is airport capacity at peak hours, to which all airlines have virtually open access, since the Federal Aviation Authority (FAA) has withdrawn from regulating schedules and routes. The result, to be expected in such circumstances, is that airlines add flights until any advantage to passengers of a prime-time schedule is canceled by the probability of delays. No airline, as Mr. Cosley rightly points out, has any good reason to cut back on overscheduling. No airline is individually motivated to reduce the number of peak-hour flights, since the reduction in delays benefits mainly the passengers of other airlines.

This is a classic common-property problem. The inefficiency of the situation is obvious: thousands of travelers every day suffer delays until any advantage of flying at the preferred hour is negated. The possible remedies are also classic. Schedules could be regulated by the FAA, as they were, albeit inefficiently, in the past. Landing fees could be raised for peak-hour arrivals and departures until demand no longer exceeded capacity: the economist's favorite congestion tax solution. Or permits to land could be awarded to airlines according to some fair formula, in numbers equal to airport capacity, and made tradable among them. With a sufficient number of airlines in the running, trading would lead to an eventual reallocation of landing rights that allowed the available capacity to be used efficiently and provided compensation to airlines that relinquished their rights.

The gains that can be realized from application of this mechanism for managing a common-property resource are well illustrated by Alaska's recent success in limiting entry to its salmon and herring fisheries. Without effective controls, the fate of fisheries is essentially the same as that of airports. Fishing boats crowd in, sharing the catch, until the unit costs of the fish caught are as high as their average value and all profits are exhausted. In fisheries, however, the crowding often results in a catch greater than the reproductive capacity of the fishery, leading, especially in bad fishing years, to serious depletion or even exhaustion of the resource. In the last decade, Alaska has implemented a system that awarded a limited number of permits to fish in specific fisheries (defined by region, prey, and fishing method) to individuals, based on a complex and long-negotiated formula that seeks to balance various interests. These permits are freely transferable. Although the system is by no mean perfect, the results have been striking:

- Since the big processors can no longer refuse to deal with fishermen who demand higher prices for their catch and encourage others to take their places, fishermen's bargaining position and the remuneration they receive have improved.
- Since limited entry protects fishermen from the erosion of profit margins through overcrowding, banks have been willing to provide credit to permit-holders to finance vessel improvements and gear, and fishermen have been willing to make those investments.
- Profit margins and the incomes of participating fishermen have risen. The clearest indication has been the rise in the price of permits. In the years 1976-78, the price of Bristol Bay salmon gill net licenses rose from $2,000 to $25,000, and the current price is in the vicinity of $125,000. These prices reflect the capitalized, value of the expected net revenues from the fisheries, a value that under open access is eliminated.
- About 3 percent of permits have changed hands each year, indicating a gradual reallocation from those who, for one reason or another, cannot use the permits effectively to those who can.
- Fishermen have been willing to assess themselves collectively for contributions to expand hatcheries in the state, knowing that they and not some newcomer will reap the benefits of their contributions.[12]

Unfortunately, management of the world's common resources still resembles the situation at Kennedy and Laguardia airports more than that in Bristol Bay. The exploitation of renewable resources such as groundwater, rangelands, forests, and fisheries is virtually open access in much of the world, with serious depletion and inefficient utilization of the resource as a result. The use of the atmosphere, oceans, and other bodies of water as receptacles for waste products is virtually unlimited in many places, with concomitant risks to the environment and human welfare. Resources of global scale, such as climate and the store of genetic information contained in the world's biological diversity, are the least effectively governed.

Thus there is a great scope for improvement in the management of these resources, often through mechanisms similar to those used in Alaska. Where feasible, the creation or clarification of rights to the use of a resource is a powerful mechanism. Oyster grounds in Connecticut that are leased to individuals are ten times more productive than those in Maryland that are fished in common, because fishermen will seed individually leased beds with shellfish spat (oyster bait) for higher yields, thin and transplant the growing crop, take steps to eliminate predators, and make other improvements. Oystermen on public waters do not do these things, because the returns are not assured. Roger Revelle's paper on ocean resources points out that the world harvest of aquaculture products could be expanded thirtyfold or more if constraints on the leasing of coastal areas could be overcome and investment opportunities realized.

When permits to dispose of wastes in a public place must be purchased, or when the disposer is liable for any damages that result, firms find ways to reduce the volume and toxicity of the wastes in need of disposal. Villagers who ruthlessly cut trees in government forests for firewood and fodder will zealously nurture and protect groves that belong to them or, if community organization is sufficiently strong, to their village. Community systems of common-resource management are often highly adaptive and resilient and, too often, are undermined rather than strengthened by development efforts.

The power of these mechanisms is that they create incentives for better resource use, just as they induced fishermen in Alaska to expand hatcheries and invest in better gear. Over time, these incentives foster the innovation that is required for sustainable development. Contrast the enormous resources devoted to the development of chemical pesticides, which can be patented and marketed for profit, with the meager amounts spent on the development of biological agents for pest management, which in general cannot. From the standpoint of the individual, it makes sense to develop ways of conserving a resource or expanding its supply only if the benefits can be appropriated through enforcement of property rights.

The functioning of government agencies in the management of environmental quality and other common resources can be greatly improved. In the developing countries, by and large, the mechanisms of control are just being forged. Legal and administrative frameworks, the foundations for further research in the environmental sciences, and trained personnel are slowly being put in place. The Global Possible Conference identified international cooperation in strengthening the capacities of the developing countries for more effective resource and environmental management as highly productive.

In the industrial countries, governments have reacted to the pervasive environmental impacts of economic activities piecemeal with ad hoc and inefficient systems after the costs have become obvious. Pollution control has focused on abatement rather than resource recovery and recycling, and rational resource use is impeded by a thicket of fiscal and administrative measures that discourage private incentives. Reconsideration of these policies can yield large returns. Further, in industrial societies, new problems such as those resulting from toxic chemicals, long-distance air pollution, and risks from chronic exposure to multiple environmental hazards demands attention.

International agreements and institutional mechanisms can be developed to manage international common resources more effectively than at present. Threats of climate change, depletion of the ozone shield, impoverishment of marine ecosystems, and damage to other international resources are real. The limited successes achieved to date in the Regional Seas agreements promoted by the United Nations Environment Program and in international conventions to protect the Antarctic, regulate trade in endangered species, and limit ocean pollution show that there are potential agreements from which all parties can gain, but that better assessment of costs and risks and better mechanisms for creating and enforcing such agreements are required.

Proper Resource Pricing

The most widespread opportunity for improving resource management is also the most obvious: to treat scarce resources as scarce, not as if they were free, by pricing them at the cost of increasing their supply. Competitive markets do so, signaling buyers not to devote resources to uses that have values less than the cost of supply, signaling producers to expand supplies if they can find ways to do so more efficiently, and signaling innovators to devise substitutes that can provide equivalent services more cheaply.

The most convincing demonstration in recent years of the power of pricing to affect resource use occurred after OPEC oil producers combined to restrict output and raise prices dramatically. The consequences for energy production and use are well known. In the United States, total energy consumption fell by 2 percent between 1972 and 1983 even though GNP, in constant prices, rose by more than 30 percent. The overall efficiency of energy use, therefore, rose by one-third. Gains in other industrial countries were of similar magnitude.

Much of this gain in efficiency was achieved at remarkably low cost. In the household sector, big improvements resulted from better insulation, weatherstripping, and temperature controls that reduce the amount of energy needed for space heating and cooling. In industry, half the gains came from simple "housekeeping" measures, such as keeping warehouse doors closed and furnaces in better adjustment. Further improvements from more energy-efficient equipment and process designs will continue to accrue for decades as new equipment replaces old.[13]

Equally impressive has been the power of pricing and other economic incentives to induce innovation and investment in substitutes. Since the rise in oil prices, production of solar collectors in the United States has risen by 30 percent per year, from 1.2 to 16.8 million ft^2, and three out of five new houses incorporate passive solar collectors. Shipments of photovoltaic generators rose from nil at the time of the first oil crisis to a capacity of 5.7 MW in 1982 and have more than tripled, to 18.5 MW in 1984. Installed capacity of wind energy systems rose from 3 MW in 1980 to 300 MW in 1983 and an estimated 800 MW by the end of 1984. The use of energy derived from biomass fuels, primarily wood pellets, ethanol, and methanol, is increasing by 10 percent per year.

Thus, proper resource pricing is an enormously powerful way of inducing more efficient production and use. The potential for further gains from pricing reform are enormous. In the United States, electric utilities are beginning to introduce rate structures that charge customers more for electricity consumed during the hours of peak demand since old, high-cost generating equipment must be brought on-line or new, more expensive capacity added to meet such demand. In France, where "time-of-day rates" have been used since 1957, the electricity system's load factor has risen by only 1.5 percent per year as customers have adapted so as to reduce consumption during peak hours, and the anticipated need for 6,500 MW in additional capacity—15 percent of total installed capacity—has been avoided.[14]

Similarly, in the use of water resources, pricing reform can result in large savings and improvements in efficiency. Throughout the world, irrigation water, which accounts for 80 percent or more of all water consumption, is supplied at highly subsidized rates. Federal water projects in the United States and government surface-water projects in India and Pakistan, for example, all price irrigation water to farmers as much as 90 percent below the cost of storage and convey-ance. In all three countries, this discourages simple conservation measures, like lining channels to prevent seepage (which also contrib-utes to waterlogging and salinity) and more careful water application. Pilot projects in Pakistan have demonstrated that water losses of 40-60 percent could be readily eliminated, and that farm yields could be maintained with on-farm applications 40 percent lower if simple im-provements, such as leveling of fields, were undertaken. In Israel, where water scarcity has forced the government to adopt a strict con-servation strategy and all irrigation water is metered, allocated, and priced at increasing block rates, agricultural growth averaged 6.8 per-cent per year over the decade 1968-78, while water use per hectare of irrigated land fell 21 percent. Israeli farmers are world leaders in the adoption of drip irrigation and computer-controlled systems that lead to increased crop yields and improve water-use efficiency by as much as 30 percent.[15] Conservation, more efficient irrigation practices, and the use of water only on more valuable crops are all consequences of more rational pricing. Peter Rogers's paper on fresh water in this volume summarizes a large body of research that demonstrates that each 10-percent rise in the price of water generates about 6-percent savings in water use. Since, as we have already seen, in many coun-tries the price of water to most agricultural users is only a small frac-tion of its supply cost, the scope for conservation is clearly large.

Demand Management

Adjusting the pricing of resources promotes greater efficiency but is only one step. Examining opportunities for better use, sector by sec-tor, and the impediments to their realization results in more far-reaching and rapid improvements in resource management. Demand management, by contrast with supply management, is a relatively neg-lected approach to resource pressures. The traditional approach to scarcity has been to seek expanded supplies and production, but typi-cally there are promising ways to expand the services obtained from existing resources through changes in institutional arrangements and policies.

Industrial cogenerators of process steam and electricity, for exam-ple, typically save as much as 30 percent of the fuel needed to pro-duce these services separately. In the United States, only 5 percent of industrial electricity is cogenerated, whereas European countries cogenerate four or five times as much. Rulings under the US Public

Utilities Regulatory Policies Act that required utilities to physically interconnect with cogenerators and purchase or sell electricity at incremental cost and that clarified the regulatory status of cogeneration facilities opened the way to rapid expansion of this source of improved efficiency. Cogeneration is expected to double its contribution to industrial energy by the end of the century.

The benefits of such policy and institutional changes are large. In the western United States, water law has severely impeded improvements in efficiency and conservation. The "beneficial use" doctrine that entitles users to only such amounts of water as they can put to good use has been interpreted as implying that someone who transfers water to someone else, to whom its value is greater, must not be able to put the water to beneficial use and can therefore be stripped of rights to it. Similarly, the "appurtenancy doctrine," which holds that water rights are tied to particular pieces of land for which they were granted, has impeded users from conserving water in one irrigated field for use on another or for transfer to another user. The doctrine of "prior appropriation" has made difficult the transfer of any water to another use, no matter how valuable, if the transfer would affect water availability to another right-holder. States that have relaxed and revised such restrictions have been able to achieve greater efficiency through reallocation of water among users as demands for water change. A recent study demonstrated that a water transfer of 400,000 acre-feet per year between the Imperial Irrigation District and the Metropolitan Water District of Southern California would raise the productivity of the water by $100 to $250 per acre-foot and save $500 million in construction costs that would otherwise be necessary to bring in additional supplies.[16]

Designing for Efficiency

Natural systems of production and consumption are designed for total resource recovery. All materials and energy flows balance. By contrast, engineers usually design linear systems that grow by utilizing sources of primary materials and energy and depositing growing mountains of wastes. Sustainable development requires that designs bend from the linear toward the circular. Large improvements in efficiency result.

Advances in wastewater treatment provide an excellent example. Traditional water supply systems reach farther and farther afield for suitable supplies of uncontaminated water for growing cities. This water passes through kitchens, bathrooms, and swimming pools to sewers to treatment plants, where it is disinfected and solids and organic material are removed. The water then passes into the ocean—leaving the increasing problem of disposing of the remaining sludge.

Land treatment of wastewater uses the natural filtration of soils, the bacterial action of soil organisms, and sometimes the capability of plants to use the nutrients in wastewater directly. The quality of water that has undergone land treatment is typically equal or superior to that of effluent from tertiary treatment in conventional systems; further, there is no problem of sludge disposal, organic material and minerals in the wastewater are available as nutrients to improve soil quality or stimulate plant growth, and the treated water returns to aquifers or streams for reuse. Construction and operating costs compare favorably with conventional systems, and total costs are lower. The number of land treatment systems for municipal wastes has risen rapidly in the United States, from 571 in 1972 to 1,180 in 1982.[17] In Israel, by the end of the century, more than 30 percent of the total wastewater flow will have been recycled for irrigation or industrial use.[18]

Industrial process designers are increasingly seizing the opportunities for recycling, as restrictions on the disposal of wastes grow. Process improvements in a US Goldkist poultry plant, for example, cut water use by 32 percent, reduced wastes by 66 percent, and saved $2.33 for every dollar spent on the changes.[19] Several US companies are now recovering the methane generated in huge municipal landfills and selling it as industrial and residential fuel. In the developing countries, resource recovery is highly economical because materials and energy costs are high relative to labor costs. For example, private investors in Costa Rica, with the support of the Inter-American Development Bank, have promoted a new industry based on pulp constituting over half the weight of the coffee beans that had been discarded as a polluting waste. A drying and processing plant that costs $5 million produces chemicals and animal feeds worth $4.5 million annually. This former waste has thus been transformed into a potential resource capable of yielding products worth $150 million per year in Costa Rica alone.

Active secondary markets for all kinds of materials rest on the efforts of recyclers and scavengers. Policy and institutional changes can support resource recovery. In the developing countries, changes in policies that misguidedly attempt to stimulate industrialization by subsidizing raw materials through tax and duty exemptions can instead encourage materials conservation and recovery. In the industrial countries, tax advantages for producers of primary materials and energy can be removed with the same effects. Since secondary materials are close substitutes for virgin materials, demand over the long run is highly responsive to such policy changes.

Building Management Capability

Especially in the Third World, where other concerns have had priority and capabilities are thinly spread, there are enormous gains to be realized by strengthening management for environmental protection and resource use. This involves putting in place technical personnnel, information systems, and legal and administrative mechanisms to plan and guide resource use when market mechanisms under rational incentives are insufficient. The potential gains are large:

- Coastal countries lack means to manage fisheries within their exclusive economic zones, since data from which the allowable harvest could be estimated and systems to monitor and control fishing effort are lacking.
- In most countries, systems to control use of groundwater are lacking: information on recharge and sustainable yield, as well as mechanisms to monitor and control withdrawals, are not available for most aquifers.
- Although many countries have adopted laws and regulations to govern pesticide use, the means to enforce them and monitoring systems for early detection of adverse health effects, pest resistance, and secondary pest emergence are not in place.
- Although master plans and land-use plans have been drawn up in Third World cities, the implementation of zoning regulations is deficient.
- The management of urban services, such as solid waste collection is poor, leading to deteriorating environmental quality and affecting water quality and drainage.
- Although reserved forests and conservation areas have been demarcated, the means for controlling use of these areas by households and commercial interests are often undeveloped, along with the ecological knowledge for sustained multiple use.

In these circumstances, much can be accomplished by attention to management and administrative concerns. Modern data systems can make an enormous difference. Substantial gains in productivity are possible by reallocating expenditures toward maintenance and improvement of existing systems, away from new projects. Training, management assistance, and productivity incentives are proven tools that have wide applicability in the management of resources as well.

A powerful means of improving management is involving the people that are directly affected, in both the planning and implementation of programs. Overcentralized, bureaucratic processes fail to take advantage of local knowledge of needs, preferences, and opportunities—or of the managerial capabilities of local communities. Partnerships between the public sector and community organizations have succeeded in improving health and family planning programs, the urban environment, soil conservaton, watershed protection, community forestry, and other resource programs.

These mechanisms are not the only effective means by which substantial improvements in future welfare and resource availability can be ensured. The papers that follow and the summary statement of the Global Possible Conference identify others. The application of research and technology to critical world problems, better monitoring of resource and environmental conditions, the awakening of public opinion, and political action are also important—many would say more important. The availability of all these means reinforces the basic theme of this book, that ample opportunities exist to build a prosperous and sustainable future.

The many projections and assessments underlying the Global Possible papers have in common a widening range of outcomes as we move ahead into the next century. These increasingly divergent futures reflect primarily the consequences of different policy choices. Decisions taken now are critical because of the momentum built into the processes of global change. When carbon dioxide concentrations in the atmosphere stop increasing, temperature will continue to rise for another twenty years or more. When fertility rates reach replacement levels, world population will continue to rise for another half-century. Policies adopted now to improve the efficiency of resource use will yield results that will continue until outmoded equipment and processes are retired and will generate a continuing flow of efficiency-increasing innovations as new technologies are perfected. It is the awareness of the tremendous long-term benefits that follow from relatively small and simple steps that justifies a sense of optimism about the global possible.

NOTES

1. J. P. Lanly, *Tropical Forest Resources,* FAO Forestry Paper no. 30, (Rome: FAO 1983).

2. T. R. Odhiambo, "Biological Constraints on Food Production and on the Level and Efficient Use of Chemical Imputs," in *Chemistry and World Food Supplies: The New Frontiers,* ed. G. Bixler and L.W. Shemelt (Manila: International Rice Research Institute, 1983).

3. I. Mintzer and A. Miller, "Impact of Energy Conservation Measures and Renewable Energy Technologies on Global Emissions of Carbon Dioxide," World Resources Institute, unpublished paper, April 1984.

4. World Bank, *The Energy Transition in Developing Countries* (Washington, D.C.: World Book, 1983).

5. L. Berry, "Assessment of Desertification in the Sudano-Sahelian Region, 1977–1984" (Report to the United Nations Sudano-Sahelian Office, Clark University, Worcester, Mass., January 1984).

6. E. O. Edwards and P. W. Bell, *The Theory and Measurement of Business Income* (Berkeley: University of California Press, 1961).

7. R. W. Goldsmith, *The National Balance Sheet of the United States* (Chicago: University of Chicago Press for the National Bureau of Economic Research, 1982).

8. A. P. Sanghvi, "Least-Cost Energy Strategies for Power System Expansion," *Energy Policy* 12, no. 1 (March 1984): 75–93.

9. T. H. Teitenberg, "Marketable Emission Permits in Principle and Practice" (Paper presented at Conference on Economics of Energy and Environmental Policies, Stockholm, Sweden, August 6–10, 1984).

10. J. T. Ling, "The Impact of Environmental Policies on Industrial Innovation" (Keynote Address to International Conference on Environment and Economics, OECD, Paris, June 18–21, 1984).

11. D. Benor and M. Baxter, *Training and Visit Extension* (Washington, D.C.: World Bank, 1984).

12. A. Adasiak, "Alaska's Experience with Limited Entry," *Journal of the Fisheries Research Board of Canada* 36, no.7 (1979): 770–81.

13. R. W. Sant, D. W. Bakke, and R. F. Naill, *Creating Abundance: America's Least-Cost Energy Strategy* (New York: McGraw-Hill, 1984).

14. Y. Balasko, "A Contribution to the History of the Green Tariff: Its Impact and Prospect," in *New Dimensions in Public Utility Pricing,* ed. H. M. Trebing (East Lansing: Michigan State University Press, 1976).

15. US Congress, Office of Technology Assessment, *Water-Related Technologies for Sustainable Agriculture in Arid/Semi-Arid Lands* (Washington, D.C., 1983).

16. Robert Stavins, *Trading Conservation Investments for Water* (Berkeley: Environmental Defense Fund, 1983).

17. R. W. Crites, "Land Use of Wastewater and Sludge," *Environmental Science and Technology* 18, no. 5 (1984): 140–47A.

18. See note 15.

19. Michael Royston, *Pollution Prevention Pays* (Oxford: Pergamon Press 1979).

PART I

Vantage Points on the Future

CHAPTER TWO

The Historical Context
HUGH THOMAS

RESOURCES AND PROSPERITY

The relationship between resources and prosperity has posed some of history's most intricate puzzles. Although human history has been largely a quest for resources—a remarkably small and stable set of resources at that—many nations without resources have prospered while some with resources have not. Athens, Venice, Babylon, the Netherlands, and modern Japan have achieved brilliant successes through conquest and trade, which in part have compensated for the lack of a resource base. Thus, Athens was inspired by Pericles to acquire its Aegean empire because its hinterland, Attica, was short of farmland (as of gold) and its silver mines were inadequate to finance the commerce necessary. Eventually, the Athenian Empire spread throughout the Aegean, and the Athenian navy reached the grain fields of the Ukraine and Crimea. Similar observations might be made about all the great sea-faring nations of the past. On the other hand, Britain's preeminence in the eighteenth century, from which so much ensued, owed something to its native iron and coal, as much as and perhaps more than to the intellectual tolerance and independence of its people, its relatively large market, its fair laws, and its commercial strength.

Indeed, military empires since the time of Christ have turned out to be less those who controlled sources of raw materials than those able to impose on the suppliers their own conditions of trade. Indeed, it appears that for the two and a half thousand years after the fall of the Hittites, the dominant cultures have been those that were short of essential native raw materials and had to trade: Egypt had gold but nothing else; Athens silver but neither gold nor wheat; Babylon had no wood; Rome no wheat after the third century B.C., when her empire overseas began to be established; and Venice had nothing but ships and sailors. One of the decisive lessons of history is that commercial preeminence and military victories have as often as not gone to "have-not" peoples.

The Demand for Resources

Human history has revolved in general around the interaction of demand for, pursuit of, and access to resources. In history, as conventionally rendered, wars seem to be struggles for inheritance or territory or land or to stem from religious or racial motives. But the root cause has as often as not been covetousness of particuarly fertile valleys, specially prized grazing grounds, or desirable habitations on protected hills. From the beginning of agriculture, nomadic tribes have preyed on settled habitations, sometimes overwhelming them, sometimes being absorbed by them in the end, as was the case in China with both Yuan (Mongol) and Manchu dynasties. These wars were as much wars for resources as was Frederick the Great's seizure of the rich Austrian province of Silesia.

FOOD. Through most of history, demand for resources has not only been predominantly demand for food but has overwhelmingly concentrated on a few key crops: wheat, rice, and maize, followed by rye and barley. If historians of agriculture were to discuss these crops exhaustively, they would exclude from their histories little of importance prior to the sixteenth century. Even since then, this handful of crops represent the main themes, potatoes and sugar (from cane and beet) being the main additions. One of the most striking indications of the continuity of human activity is that the three main crops have throughout human history occupied the place they do today.

The main changes in agriculture have not been in the crops themselves but in their cultivation, distribution, and yield. Those changes, particularly in yield, have admittedly been considerable. As regards distribution, people in Europe now eat a great deal of rice and even more potatoes, crops that in origin are oriental and American respectively. America produces acres of wheat, which was Middle Eastern initially. Maize, the staple crop of pre-Columbian America, is now also that of Africa. Yet, there is continued dominance of rice in the East, wheat in Europe, and maize in the Americas.

A second characteristic of the world food scene has been the decrease in variety and growth in consistency, even the size, of any particular product. The so-called green revolution of the 1960s has intensified this trend toward a concentration on fewer products that are increasingly alike.

Many countries enjoy a relative abundance of food in comparison with the past. This does not derive only, or even primarily, from an increase in yields or an increase in the amount of land under cultivation, important though these are. The distribution system has usually been cited as the cause. It has affected large-scale as much as small-scale distribution of food, from the sea transport of refrigerated meat from Argentina and Australia, of grain from North America, and from Russia to Europe, to the daily distribution of milk made possible by railroads and trucks in modern cities.

Food supplies have always been affected by the security and reliability of transport as much as by the availability of the food itself. Before the Europeans arrived, the potato had not even reached Mexico from Peru, nor had the tea plant reach India from China. It would, of course, be impossible to feed the inhabitants of modern cities at all without modern communications. Access to food has been a direct cause of nearly every significant upheaval, the French and Russian revolutions included. Likewise, it was because of the piracy that interfered with the Roman supply of grain from North Africa that the Senate created special powers for Pompeii, a concession that in turn led directly to the Roman revolution of the first century B.C.

MINERALS. The demand for minerals, like that for food, has centered on just a few kinds. Precious metals (gold and silver) remain in top demand, even though tin, copper, and iron have also occasionally been prized for their precious quality or applications. When tin was in great demand in the late nineteenth century, primarily for food canning, the wife of the Bolivian entrepreneur Patino accompanied her husband to a mountain previously known for its silver but where tin was suspected. A find was made: "Lord: let it be tin," she is known to have prayed. Throughout much of history, precious stones have been equally sought after; and stones suitable for grinding grain to make flour were frequently carried from remote places to serve mills in grain-producing valleys. Wood, for housing, furniture, and ships, has also been transported from one remote place to another from the earliest times until now.

Consider the history of iron which is probably the most prized metal of all, so much so that Iron Ages in history have been numerous. Iron has been in constant use since its usefulness was discovered in Asia Minor about 2500 B.C. By then the art of metallurgy—the attempt to reduce metals to their elementary state and to separate them from the other elements with which they were organically combined—was 2,000 or 3,000 years old. The process was carried out in furnaces in which temperatures were high enough to set off the chemical reactions through which separation could be achieved. Copper, tin, antimony, and lead had all been used even earlier. Copper had transformed not only agriculture and war but mining itself, for coppersmiths swiftly produced tools that were of use in copper mining.

Iron is a harder metal to work than copper, since pure iron melts at a temperature about 50 percent higher than copper. Temperatures high enough to smelt molten iron for casting were not achieved in the West until at least the fourteenth century A.D. and in China until about 250 B.C. Prior to that, iron had to be beaten when red-hot into the desired shapes. For several hundred years even even that art was a secret one, confined to the Hittites, who began by making ornaments and only later made weapons. But once they began to use iron weapons, they swiftly dominated the whole eastern Mediterranean. A similar military empire was achieved by the Chin dynasty in China about 200 B.C. united China by standardizing its customs, language, script, numerals, wheels, tracks, and money in a way that still leaves its mark even today.

Iron continued to be of critical importance throughout what we now call the age of agriculture, and its use and the art of smelting spread throughout the world: even central Africa enjoyed iron engineering by A.D. 500. The acquisition of iron weapons and agricultural tools was probably behind the southward and eastward thrust of the Negro peoples of West Africa between the second and first centuries A.D. Medieval Europe was reconstructed by ironsmiths able to make iron axes to level the great forests and iron stirrups for knights in iron armor bearing iron weapons. The wars in the Renaissance further increased European demand for iron—not only for weapons, but also for cooking pots, forks, and knives for new foods; agricultural implements for new crops; and anchors for transatlantic ships. Access to iron as well as steel accounted in part for Britain's early industrial preeminence, and iron hoarding helped France, Germany, and the United States "take-off." But in no case was it the determining factor.

ENERGY. Of all resources, those producing energy cause most worry in the late twentieth century. The availability of oil (the most portable and, hence, popular fuel) has indeed seemed the most disturbing of all current international problems. Indeed, disputes over access to energy are still the most likely causes of world war.

In the remote past, people traveled far for stone for monuments, jewels for their women or temples, and wood for houses (even in the days of the pharaohs, merchants went to Lebanon for wood). But on the whole, energy was produced at home by people, animals, or water. The agricultural revolution, which started in the Middle East between about 10,000 B.C. and 8000 B.C., was marked by the beginning of a shift from human power to animal power with the domestication of reindeer, sheep, dogs, and goats. The harnessing of water followed a few thousand years later. Subsequent useful innovations such as the castration of bulls to "create" oxen, the taming of the horse and subsequent breeding of the cart horse, and the fashioning of water mills were variations on ancient themes rather than essentially new developments.

Wind power, apparently first used by the Chinese, and the use of coal for furnaces were later innovations. Some have seen in the felling of England's forests and subsequent decline in its native supply of wood the essential ingredient that led first to English exploitation of coal and then to the industrial revolution.

Coal was, as it were, iron's twin in the energy field in the industrial age. This commodity had been used in blast furnaces and in houses (for heating) in China at least since about 2000 B.C.—that is, before the establishment of any historic dynasty. No doubt it is one of the achievements of the Hsia. But in Europe, coal was rarely used until the Renaissance, except rarely to heat houses (especially in England where the shortage of wood became serious before 1500) and also in limekilns. Ironworks normally used charcoal. Coal at that time was thought to impair the quality of iron even though it was sometimes used to smelt lead, tin, and copper. The widespread use of coal was also hampered by its weight and by the lack of good inland transportation systems. Canals and railroads altered this state of affairs.

Improvement of rivers and canals in England, in imitation of

France, made possible the transport of coal, at first within a single community and then abroad. It is not clear when coal was first exported, but by the end of the seventeenth century £50,000 worth of coal a year was being exported from Great Britain to continental Europe.

Access to indigenous coal plainly helped some countries ready for industrialization (Britain, Belgium, the United States, France, and Germany) to embark on their first industrial economic development. But it was not the determining reason any more than iron was. Some countries with large coal deposits (Poland, for example, and Russia, until 1870) did not embark on industrial development. Nor did possession of coal prevent the relative decline of the industrial leader, Britain, in the late nineteenth century. (Britain's coal exports continued to increase until 1914, though her industrial position had already slipped, as measured by most usual standards, to behind those of the United States and Germany).

The use of petroleum as a source of energy began just when the Atlantic slave trade was finally drawing to an end in the 1860s, and by 1900, it had become a major source. All the same, it required great self-confidence (or perhaps naiveté) for European nations consciously to turn to oil from coal as the main energy source of their economies (as well as of their automobiles) just before or just after the First World War. The leaders who made the decisions plainly believed that they could control the places from which the oil came indefinitely (at least indirectly, as the British had controlled India), and that their navies could keep the sea lanes open for international trade, come what may. For example, Churchill's decision, as first Lord of the Admiralty, to put the British Navy's fleet on oil instead of coal was made in 1912. In the official life of Churchill and Churchill's own writing (The World Crisis, vol. 1, p. 129), it is simply noted that liquid fuel conferred advantages—speed, the possibility of refueling at sea, and benefits for the sailors ("for instance nearly a hundred men had been continually occupied in The Lion in shovelling coal from one steel chamber to another, without ever seeing the light of day, nor even of the furnace fires"). Churchill believed that all these and consequent problems could be solved by establishing enormous installations of reserve oil. Politicians did not foresee any difficulties in shifting responsibility for their fuel from coal miners (always politically unreliable) to "foreign trust." Lord Curzon, the British foreign secretary in 1918, believed that the war had been won by those who had controlled the waves for oil, and a similar theme might have been detected in the Second World War. The two superpowers that emerged in the late 1940s, the USSR and the United States, were rich in this by then especially prized natural resource.

POPULATION AND PROSPERITY

The relationships between population and prosperity is as complex as that between resources and prosperity. Despite the obvious connection between size and military and industrial power, many of the countries or city-states that have dominated human history have been small: Greece, Babylon, Rome, Spain in the sixteenth century, France in the eighteenth, Britain in the nineteenth. (I once tried to define a demographic model of the typically successful and adventurous "can-do" nation of the type of Britain in 1750 or Spain in 1490 and found that the only ones that seemed to fill the bill in 1980 were Israel and Cuba.)

Although population growth has impeded progress in China and India, the moment of peak success in many countries seems to have coincided with that of their peak fertility rate (Germany in 1871, France in 1802, Britain in 1875). Equally, the moment of demographic decline has often seemed to coincide with a time of national doubt, if not outright decline. For example, when Britain began to yield first place in industry to the United States in the 1870s, the British birth rate began to decline.

The Rising Growth Rate

For most of human history there has been a slow, if unsteady, increase in population. The figures, of course, are notoriously unreliable. J. Z. Young thought that the "very rare food-gathering bipeds" that men seemed to be in about 2 million B.C. may have numbered 100,000. At the beginning of settled agriculture, about 8000 B.C., there could have been 5 million people. About the time of Christ's birth, there were probably 200 million in the world, or a little less than the present population of the United States, of whom half were probably in China and India. In A.D. 1500, there may have been 500 million human beings. Since that time, however, world population has been growing swiftly. There were 1 billion people by 1750, 2 billion by 1900, and 4.4 billion by 1980.

The exact reasons for this change in the pace of population growth are elusive and presumably never will be much clearer. Improved food? But in the eighteenth century the population went up faster than anywhere else in Russia, which then had virtually no access to the great new American or Eastern foods (potatoes, turkeys, maize, tomatoes, and rice). Access to sugar may have been another matter, however. Improved medicine? It would be hard to establish that medicine had any effect on birth rates or death rates until the 1860s, when anesthesia, knowledge of microorganisms, and improved hygiene transformed surgery. (Oddly enough, the immediate consequence was the beginning of a decline in Europe's birth rate.) Better climate? That seems to have been a characteristic of the eighteenth century in the Northern Hemisphere, and many people have leaned toward that rather engaging explanation for the increase. Could it be that the use of spirits had a marked effect on fertility? The eclipse, though not for medical reasons, of the large killer diseases, such as bubonic plague and leprosy, may be the most likely explanation and this may have been caused primarily by changes in weather patterns. The end of the reign of the black rat, *Rattus rattus*, was of course more important than that of the Bourbons or the Hohenstaufen.

Whatever the reasons behind the rise in the rate of population growth, it has been one of the dominant forces in modern history. Population in many countries is still increasing annually at high rates. This will almost certainly continue for several generations. Nevertheless, it does look as though the peak at least in the *rate of increase* of world population was reached in about 1962. At that time, it began to decline modestly, in such a way that, with immense courage and risk to itself, the World Bank, in its annual surveys, can now envisage a zero growth rate in virtually every country in the next century.

The 1960s, incidentally, coincided with a period of hope—apparent end of the cold war, the offer of a more humane communism apparently put forward by Khrushchev, the Kennedy presidency, and the pre-Vietnam consensus in the United States.

Until the industrial revolution (or the American Revolution, for that matter), shortage of labor seemed a more potent cause of economic setback than too great a population. Indeed, until the nineteenth the economies of most advanced societies depended on imported labor. (In societies where slaves were not used, serfdom or corvées or other disciplined forms of labor organization were in effect.) Babylon, Egypt, Greece, the Indus civilizations, and the Middle Kingdom all depended on slaves. So did poor city-states such as Athens, which in many other ways were freer than most of the world today. Despotisms such as Egypt differed only in degree from Athens.

Vast numbers of Negro slaves were also carried to the Middle East and the Mediterranean throughout the Middle Ages. The special value of West African people—Negroes were, of course, indigenous in what is now Nigeria—was immediately recognized by the Portuguese. Indeed, it was this recognition that gave rise to the famous Atlantic slave trade, in which all European peoples with possessions in the Americas became engaged ultimately. Until the end of the seventeenth century, however, the trans-Sahara trade was probably equal to the more notorious Atlantic trade.

Since the Atlantic slave trade ended in the 1860s, advanced countries have all felt ambivalent with regard to the import of labor. Most have succumbed to the desire for cheap service offered by access to poor populations, whose size has recently been increased by the use of Western medicine and transport of whom is now so easy. Latin American immigrants in the United States, Turks in Germany, North African Arabs in France, and Indians, Pakistanis, and West Indians in England all provide cheap labor as slaves did in the past—and as Spaniards did in Europe before 1973. In the future, with the likelihood of a continued shortage of cheap labor on the one hand and a persistent awareness of national or ethnic distinctiveness on the other, this ambivalence may be greater than ever. In the eighteenth century, clever men, such as Montesquieu (whose other reflections on, say, the part of geography or climate in history still seem pertinent), believed that population was generally declining. There is little trace of that idea now (though there were one or two panics in the 1930s associated with the names of Hogben and Charles). On the contrary, since Montesquieu's time, the general increase of the stock of humanity has grown at what seems certain to have been, at least considered in aggregate, an unprecedented pace.

The effect of population growth on resources of all sorts has been of vast consequence, negative and positive. The tremendous increase of population in China in the seventeenth, eighteenth, and nineteenth centuries was the main cause of its impoverishment and the chaos that beset it in the late nineteenth and early twentieth centuries. China changed from being able in the late eighteenth century to look with scorn at would-be commercial partners from Europe to exhibiting a sickening subservience. The increase in rural population in Russia (despite a steady decline in the proportion of the population living on the land) in the era between the emancipation of slaves in 1860 and the First World War was a major cause of the Bolsheviks' success in 1917-18. Population pressure still seems something of an obstacle in such countries as India, Indonesia, and Nigeria. Rapid population growth is a background cause for the current crisis in Central America.

Increasingly, intelligent lay people attribute to population pressure many, even most, historical problems, from the invasion of the Vikings to the African slave trade, from Japanese adventurism in the twentieth century back to that of Rome in the third century B.C. But in this they may have gone too far. China's huge population may explain the failure of China to take full advantage of her technological superiority over the West during the early Ming dynasty. At the same time, a population decline was no doubt a critical reason for the collapse of Rome and probably for that of Greece after 400 B.C.

Avoidance of a high birth rate is all very well, but in a generation or two, countries that have attained zero growth in population or are in decline, such as most European countries, may be experiencing real anxiety. What, one wonders, would be the future of Germany, even of the German language, if the combined population of the two Germanies in 2014 were to be less than what it was in 1914? And what of a world in which the population of Mexico City alone (70 million inhabitants) might be larger than, say, that of any European nation by 2050, as seems very likely?

IMPLICATIONS FOR THE FUTURE

The question that lay people most often put to population experts is whether the past bears any relation to the present, and, if so, how. Statesmen look back, as Truman and Kennedy did, for a historical precedent for their problems. So do ordinary men and women. A second question is whether the past affords any guide to the future, one that is scarcely satisfied by recalling satirist Philip Guedalla's comment that, while history does not repeat itself, historians repeat one another. Yet another question is whether judgments on modern economic preoccupations—standards of living, income levels, food consumption per capita—bear any relation to those of the past if put beside such scant evidence as there is. Statistics are, after all, very inadequate for the present, and for the past, they are often nonexistent, despite economic historians' efforts over the past hundred years.

Historians sometimes reply to such inquiries defensively by questioning what "the present" actually is and when it began. It might be argued, for example, that the world has been living in a state of permanent crisis since 1945 (the Hiroshima bombing, or the end of the

Second World War), or 1917 (the Russian Revolution), or 1914 (the outbreak of the First World War), or, more scientifically, since Watt's invention of the steam engine in 1764, or since Abraham Darby first smelted iron in 1720, or even since the discovery of the Americas in 1492. Others might argue that the real crisis of today began in the late 1960s, when the Soviet Union began to rival the United States in nuclear weapons.

The question of weapons may seem to some a decisive point. Certainly modern weapons, particularly nuclear ones, are far more lethal than they were in the past. But casualties in modern wars, as a percentage of men involved in the battle concerned, often look modest in comparison with the past. Also, deaths from epidemics in most tropical wars up to the Spanish-American War of 1898 far exceeded deaths in combat. In these respects, the "past" lasted until the First World War. Indeed, only in the 1930s did people realize that wounds are better treated if left open to the air.

Whichever of these judgments is viewed as true in the future, one prediction can surely be made: our descendants, if any, will not know us by any name we would recognize. The "medieval people" in the title of G. C. Coulton's books, did not know themselves to be living in the Middle Ages; Leonardo did not think that he would be called a "Renaissance man" (the word *Renaissance* was an invention of Michelet) any more than Cicero knew himself to be an orator of antiquity. Depending on what happens next, we may find that our times are (1) the last before the general recognition of the United States' global political hegemony, inaugurating an age of universal plenty; (2) the waiting room to Soviet world power; (3) the last age of relative stability before the outbreak of universal crime, vandalism, and terror; or, (4) the last days before the breakdown consequent upon an exchange of nuclear weapons on a large scale, which could lead to any of the first three alternatives.

There are, no doubt, other possible scenarios for the future, equally utopian, equally catastrophic, or more so. All these scenarios, however, are basically political. That fact indicates, perhaps, the major contrast between our day and the past. The second key fact is our society's international nature.

The Politicization of Society

The authority of governments in general over their populations has been enormously extended by technology and improved communications. Both of today's superpowers were made nations by railroads in the nineteenth century. "Imagine Genghis Khan with a telephone," Tolstoy is believed to have said. Governments often delude themselves into thinking that they can organize and plan the societies that they rule: this illusion is shown by the colossal black economies of both the Communist and Western societies and no one quite knows whether it is good or bad. Even so, comparing the present with the eighteenth century, it would immediately seem to someone from that ebullient, inventive, and tolerant age that all countries, even the United States, had today surrendered to the illusions of an overmighty government, the same illusions that two hundred years ago were mocked as characterizing (and ruining) France under Louis XVI. Remember that Edmund Burke in *Thoughts on Scarcity* (1795) explained the French Revolution as deriving from overgovernment: "The leading vice of the French economy was in good intention ill-directed and a restless desire of governing too much. The hand of authority was seen in everything and in every place."

Another centralizer of our time is the information explosion. Almost everywhere, television, radio, and the press make what is believed to be happening as important as, and sometimes more important than, what is actually happening. Mass media make for mass emotions. The spirit of the multitude is permanently present. This, too, assists politicization.

The politicization of the framework in which we live is the most striking of all our innovations. It extends to education and to policy toward the aged, even the dead. It affects sport and art. Paradoxically, politicization may be more intense in free than in totalitarian societies, even though the latter ceaselessly aspire to control all available information in the interests of a fixed political system. For in such closed societies, there is really no politics worthy of the name; it has been subsumed in the general cause held to motivate all. So the result of totalitarianism is often total cynicism concealed by a mask of total participation.

A study of the breakfast habits of Western people, with their appetite for tea, sugar, coffee, bacon, eggs, marmalade, salt, pepper, bread, and so on, and their preference for stainless steel cutlery and china, could indeed be made an entire history of the modern world. But—and here is the political element—the ability of Western people to reach and maintain such standards depends on the political judgments of others. The responsibility of a US president or a Soviet secretary-general of the Communist party has no precedent. Never has power been so narrowly concentrated. At the same time, though, the sea lanes through which consumer goods travel have to be kept open by political will—nothing else.

The Internationalization of Society

The internationalization of our society is the next point to notice. The average person (so useful to talk about, so difficult to envisage) even in a backward country is cosmopolitan compared with one in a relatively rich nation in, say, the sixteenth century, if tastes in dress, foods, drinks, and culture are the yardstick.

The famous passage in Keynes's *The Economic Consequences of the Peace* about the dependence on international trade of the average person before 1914 should be recalled:

> What an extraordinary episode in the economic progress of man that age was which came to an end in August 1914! The greater part of the population, it is true, worked hard and lived at a low standard of comfort, yet were, to all appearances, reasonably contented with this lot. But escape was possible for any man of capacity or character at all exceeding the average, into the middle and upper classes, for whom life offered, at a low cost and with the least trouble, conveniences, comforts, and amenities beyond the compass of the richest and most powerful monarchs of other ages. The inhabitant of London could order by telephone, sipping his morning tea in bed, the various products of the whole earth, in such quantity as he might see fit, and reasonably expect their early delivery upon his doorstep; he could at the same moment and by the same means adventure his wealth in the natural resources and new enterprises of any quarter of the world, and share, without exertion or even trouble, in their prospective fruits and advantages; or he could decide to couple the security of his fortunes with the good faith of the townspeople of any substantial municipality in any continent that fancy or information might recommend.

Before about 1500, it was impossible to speak in any way of world problems. Before 1492 there was no sustained contact between the New and Old worlds. There had been little contact between Europe and China for the previous thousand years. Africa was a dark continent for Europeans despite the constant shipment of slaves across the Sahara to Mediterranean buyers. Indeed, it remained so until quinine enabled others to follow David Livingstone's route across the center of the continent. But since the extaordinary information explosion of this century, especially since 1945, there are few parts of the world whose dramas are easily hidden (the exceptions being Russia and China, where vast tracts of country are, if anything, less easy to reach now than they were a hundred years ago).

The Past Indicative?

"The past is another country," wrote L. P. Hartley at the beginning of *The Go-Between*, his best-known novel. Yet, the more we look at the past with realistic eyes, the less certain this epigram seems. Most of the ways that we look at resources have precedents, even our anxiety at the prospect of being cut off from essential sources of supply. For the fear of nuclear war as we move toward A.D. 2000, there is even the precedent of the expectation that the world would end in the year 1000.

CHAPTER THREE

On the Limits of Nature

GEORGE M. WOODWELL

What are the limits of the earth for support of man? How can we establish a pattern of use of the earth that keeps many possibilities open for the future, a pattern of development that is sustainable?

The underlying problem is growth in the human population, a growth sustained by development of new technology that allows more intensive use of resources and expansion into untouched realms of the earth. At each stage of technological development, there is an optimum size of population that offers the highest standard of living. Below that population size, the potential of the available technology is not realized; but as economic, social, and political forces push populations above the optimum, resources are degraded progressively. The pattern is fundamental, a framework within which the effects of the biotic impoverishment of the earth now under way can be reviewed.

The world's most important resources are biotic—the plants and animals that maintain the biosphere as a habitat suitable for life. The continued expansion of the human enterprise in its current mode is reducing both the number of species and the flux of energy through biotic systems. The special focus in this discussion is biotic diversity and the necessity for strong steps to assure that human activities do not contribute to loss of species locally, regionally, or globally. Equal attention is given to primary productivity, especially to net primary production, whose global total is being reduced by the cumulative effects of man. The net effect is to diminish the capacity of the biosphere to support life, including human life.

The solution, if there is one, must recognize that detailed management of the biosphere is beyond human capacity at the moment; since the biosphere is dominated by natural communities whose function is poorly known. The most practical steps seem to be those that limit human intrusion: (1) steps toward closing man-dominated systems such as cities and agricultural and industrial activities to the point where their net effects on the biosphere approximate those of the natural systems they have replaced; and (2) zoning segments of the biosphere to maintain diversity at all levels.

These are large steps. They will require substantial innovation, scholarship, technology, and engineering in both government and politics. They present a major challenge in the reindustrialization of the western nations and in further development of technology and government elsewhere. But they offer a system for living on a finite earth.

The earth is obviously finite; its resources limited. But the questions of how large it is and what the limits might be for the support of man are not as easily answered as the concept of a finite earth might imply. Complexity enters at every turn. Mineral resources such as copper and iron, commonly considered finite and nonrenewable, enter cycles of use and reuse that given them long if not infinite lives. Living resources such as forests and fish, normally considered renewable, are destroyed, often irreversibly, when used intensively. And man himself changes. What was unacceptable to one generation may become the norm for the next. The question of the limits for the support of man, at first sharp and reasonable, loses clarity under scrutiny; what seems finite becomes infinite, and what should be infinite becomes finite. And the entire frame of references shifts with human adaptation to a new circumstance. Nonetheless, there are limits although the limits may not themselves be unitary, stable, and finite.

The question of how many people the world can support is unanswerable in a finite sense. What do we want? What purpose is served by the poverty and political chaos in nations attempting to support the world's densest populations: India, China, El Salvador, and soon much of Africa. Fewer, many fewer, are supported at the standards of living of North America and Western Europe. And even then, industrialization threatens global changes from carbon dioxide and other gases and regional if not global changes from a diversity of other toxins and toxic effects.

Are there global limits, absolute limits beyond which we cannot go without catastrophe or overwhelming costs? There are, most certainly. The most clearly defined limits might be similar to those anticipated from nuclear war: darkness and cold for weeks to months over the hemisphere and, possibly, the world, in addition to the effects of the heat, blast, and ionizing radiation. The extinction of *Homo sapiens* is within the realm of possibility (Turco *et al.*, 1983; Ehrlich *et al.*, 1983).

Short of nuclear war, a surge of volcanism, or some other cataclysmic event such as that of 65 million years ago when many species seem to have become extinct (Alvarez *et al.*, 1980, 1982), I would estimate that the most serious transition now under way is the destruction of biotic resources, a series of irreversible changes in the habitat of man. The changes follow curves and extract a cost in terms of compensation, replacement, or repair of environmental systems and in the quality of life. The increments of change seem small and are difficult to measure. They are, nonetheless, identifiable and quantifiable.

In the following pages I will discuss, first, the transitions in standard of living that commonly follow both technological innovation and growth in population. The pattern of these transitions offers insight into changes in human status due to biotic impoverishment and helps to show why there is no single point, no easily identified threshold, beyond which life becomes impossible. Such a threshold exists, of course, but it is beyond our present ability to determine. Second, I have set forth the two major changes that are part of biotic impoverishment. Finally, I suggest a pattern of use based on the assumption that intensive management of the biosphere is probably impossible, and that the best course is to limit the extent of human intrusion, difficult as that might be.

STANDARD OF LIVING AND THE DILEMMA OF GROWTH

Few will deny that the division of a resource among an increasing number of people produces a diminished per capita share. When the resource is large, division means little, but as the actual or potential per capita use approaches the per capita share available, competition develops. But even at this point, the increment of additional competition per capita for the addition of one or several new competitors is small, and it is easy to deny the fundamental relationship as Julian Simon has chosen to do (1977). Denial is based on the proposition that since the growth of population in the Western world has been accompanied by an expansion of resources through industrialization; standards of living have improved and will continue to do so.

The relationships among these factors are easily misinterpreted, as they have been by Simon, on the basis of fragmentary data and apparent, but misleading, correlations. We might, I suppose, draw a graph that shows the relationship between some measure of standard of living on the ordinate and density of population on the abscissa. The shape of the curve would be determined by the technology available at any moment. In a hunting and gathering culture, curve A of figure 3.1 might describe the relationship, and the optimum is at some point where teams can work together. A larger number of people results in impoverishment due to overuse of the resource, but there is always room for one more at a very low and diminishing standard of living.

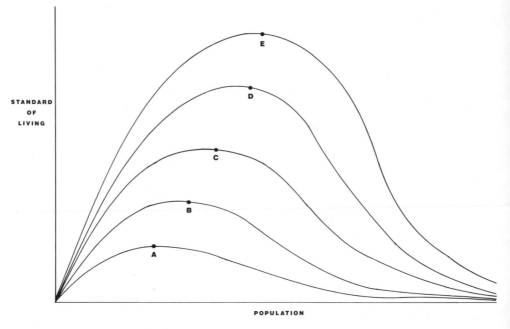

FIGURE 3.1. Relationships between some measure of standard of living and density of population for different levels of technological development.

The introduction of agriculture, an obviously necessary innovation, itself in part the product of growth in population beyond the resources available, might move the relationship to curve B, with a higher standard of living possible for more people. Industrialization might move the curve to C, then D, the median standard of living increasing with each new development in ways of exploiting resources more efficiently. The curves help to define the limits.

Commercial pressures are all in one direction, toward more people and a larger market. Nor is there any guarantee of counter-pressures to keep population from rising beyond the peak that can be supported at a particular standard of living or to assure that technology is not lost and that a sudden drop from one curve to another does not occur, such as would result from nuclear war. We form governments to lay down rules under which resources can be used but not destroyed.

The important point about these curves, borrowed from a lecture by F. Smith at Woods Hole several years ago, is that they help to explain the confusion that so commonly surrounds the relationships between numbers of people, industrialization, and standard of living. There is always room for more people, but at some maximum the standard of living is lowered by each addition. At one end of the curves, there is an obvious advantage in having enough people to work together in marshaling the resources required to develop better conditions for life; at the other end, pressures developed on the downward slopes may help stimulate the new level of technology required to start the next curve. Population, of course, is not the only factor driving these changes. Inequalities in the distribution of resources, political corruption, depletion of resources, and other factors all work together to force change. The topic has been examined extensively by economists (see, for example, Repetto and Holmes, 1983).

How many layers of technology can be piled on earlier layers? There are limits, of course. Lester Brown and his colleagues at the Worldwatch Institute have shown that Western society is on the downward slope of these curves for many resources (Worldwatch Institute, 1984). The assumption is that technology will be devloped to solve the problems, but technology is simply a way of expanding the access of an individual to resources; it may not change the underlying base. The chain saw, for instance, makes wood available at a fraction of the labor involved in using an axe and hand saw, but it does not increase the area or rate of growth of forests. The question is, how large is the underlying resource that we tap, ever more efficiently, with larger numbers of people who have a progressively developing technology?

THE BIOTIC RESOURCE: RENEWABLE BUT FINITE

Species

Life occurs in a limited space on earth—and nowhere else. The thin skin of the earth, a few miles thick, extending from the tropics to the poles and centered on sea level, supports all the life we know. The conditions, too, are limited in general by temperature, light, nutrients, the availability of water, and other factors. Within the biosphere, there are several million different kinds of organisms, sufficiently different one from another to be called species. The total may be 10 million or 30 million or more if all the microbes are counted.

The species are not independent, free-standing units of life. Each is the evolutionary product of an evolving environment, dependent on its own special circumstances of time and place and on physical, chemical, and biotic conditions. No species has come into being without these connections to the rest of the world or without selective pressure exerted over thousands of generations and unimaginable stretches of time.

The interactions where they are known, are fundamental: the microbial populations of the human intestine, for instance, if disturbed, can suddenly become personally and intensely significant. So, too, the microbes of the human skin perform a special function, as do the symbiotic fungi growing on the roots of pines and the nitrogen-fixing microbes of the Leguminosae and probably many other plants. Species do not exist alone; the common state of nature is symbiosis, living together for mutual benefit. The examples, such as the dependence of plants on insects—even birds—for pollination, are as many and diverse as life itself. Wherever we look we find more instances, more diversity, and more subtle interconnections among species.

The biota continues on its developmental path, slowly if measured in terms of human time, but nevertheless inexorably moving toward greater specialization, more branching of the evolutionary tree, increased dependence piled upon dependence, and more species living in a more diverse and complex enviroment. The tropical forest is commonly thought to be the ultimate in evolutionary expression, but the coral reef might vie with it in the eyes of some. A hundred species of tree per hectare is common in a moist forest of the Amazon, so many in fact that it is difficult to find two individuals of the same species. The mere identification of species is a major challenge, awkward even for the expert.

But are they important, all those species? Could we live without them? The age of the dinosaurs passed 65 million years ago, and we seem not to suffer thereby. Why should we worry about the loss of lesser species now? How many could we lose without there being a problem?

These questions are not more explicitly answerable than the question, how many people? Ehrlich and Ehrlich (1981) addressed the issue in detail. They identified direct economic values of the species to man, indirect benefits of maintenance of the environment, and a combination of interests that fall in the category "compassion, aesthetics, fascination and ethics."

None of these items, however elaborated, provides an absolute limit; the erosion of biotic resources proceeds by increments, each apparently small enough to be acceptable at the moment. Cumulatively, however, the landscape becomes impoverished, less capable of supporting any life, including that of man. The search for an absolute limit is no more useful here than elsewhere; there is always the possibility of further compromise in standard of living, further erosion of the potential of the environment.

But the compromise is in earnest; species lost cannot be replaced. The irreversibility of such change concerns us. And the fact that species do not exist alone means that the loss of one species threatens others. The demise of the American chestnut, *Castanea dentat*, caused by a fungus disease, *Endothia parasitica*, imported from Europe, sped the demise of the wild turkey of the eastern forests, thereby removing an important source of food for a host of other animals, including man. Furthermore, human life was made slightly less attractive, deprived of a fast-growing shade tree, a source of easily worked wood, and a fruitful component of forest, field, roadside, yard, park, and hill.

Other organisms are connecting links between the environment and man, channels through which solar energy passes from light into radiant heat to be diffused ultimately into the black cold of space. In the biosphere, a small fraction of the incident energy is caught for a short time and passed through myriad conduits in support of living systems. In the process, mineral elements are captured and mobilized—carbon, nitrogen, phosphorus, sulfur, calcium, magnesium, iron—and a host of trace elements, each essential for some biochemical function.

The product of the evolution and continued interaction of species over time is the biosphere. While no single species may be essential to its normal functioning, all species together are the driving force that maintains it. If we have to ask which part of the biosphere is most important, species A or B, oceans, estuaries, forests, lakes, savannas, tundras, or tropical reefs, the answer might well be equivocal. Which part of a watch is the most important when all parts are required for normal functioning? And yet, some parts have a greater influence on its operation than others. For the biosphere, forests loom large in any calculus involving numbers of species or any measure of functions such as total photosynthesis, respiration, or annual flux of carbon, nitrogen and sulfur. Forests are the major reservoir of biotic diversity globally, and moist tropical forests are probably far and away the richest locations in terms of species per unit area. They are so rich in fact that the very idea of an endangered species there is absurd. Yet if one species is endangered, scores, perhaps thousands of others in the same area face the same threat. The rich primate fauna of the coastal forests of eastern Brazil is now near extinction due to the destruction of these forests, but the primates are simply one of the more conspicuous taxa known to be in trouble; hundreds, perhaps thousands of other taxa, conceivably including whole genera yet unnamed, have probably already been lost as the forests have disappeared in the wake of human intrusion.

The effects of the expansion of human influence globally take many forms, from changes in the chemistry of the environment that are sometimes subtle, such as the acidification of rain, to the wholesale scarification of the earth to put in roads and expand agriculture. One of the most spectacular examples of this latter process is in the Brazilian state of Rondonia in the southwestern Amazon Basin. Here, by governmental plan and with international aid, many thousands of square miles of forests are being cleared to make way for settlement and agriculture. The rate of development has been rapid. Figure 3.2 shows two satellite images, taken five years apart, of the same area around Brazilian route 364. A recent study by my colleagues and I (1984) reports that the clearing seen in this area, 14 percent of Rondonia, represents the replacement of 220,000 ha (2,200 km²) of tropical moist forest by agriculture or pasture.

Here we have the classical dilemma: an expanding human population with aspirations for personal independence, opportunity, and wealth, all focused on the need for a place in the sun, a piece of land, with the potential for photosynthesis turned to personal support. The aspirations are reasonable, but the resources are limited and declining rapidly. One of the resources is simply space, but space is biotic diversity; and diversity is both opportunity and essential function in maintaining habitat. Reason would dictate an overt effort at preserving the inherent diversity of localities, accepting the fact that we live in a matrix of natural systems that will continue to dominate the biosphere, continue to operate at little or no expense to society as long as the basic function of the matrix is maintained intact. Violated, the costs to man in maintenance accumulate.

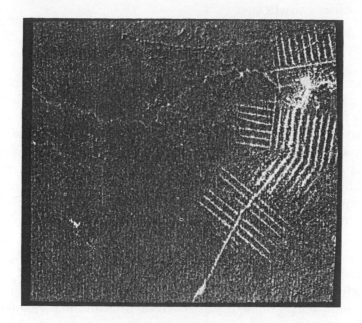

FIGURE 3.2a. INPE LANDSAT scene 176173-125857 from 21 June 1976, Rondonia, Brazil. Grid patterns in this area of about 185 x 185 km are roads and cleared forests within INCRA colonization areas.

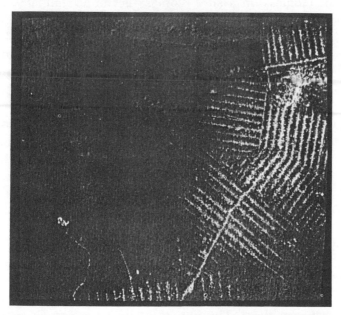

FIGURE 3.2b. INPE LANDSAT scene 281137-133031 from 17 May 1981 covering the same area as in Figure 3.2(a). Extensive new forest clearing is evident by comparison.

Primary Production: The Energy of Life

The corollary of diversity is primary production, the fixation of energy into forms usable by living systems. In the modern world, most of the energy fixed is solar energy, and fixation is through the reduction of carbon dioxide to carbon compounds by photosynthesis. Some of that energy is used immediately in support of the metabolic processes of the plants that fix it; some, however, is accumulated. This excess is called by ecologists net primary production. It is the source of energy that supports all animals and all organisms of decay. It is also the source of all accumulations of organic carbon on earth, such as the biomass of soils, the mass of wood, bark, and roots in forests, the peat of swamps and bogs, and the ancient deposits of coal and oil. Human food from agriculture, forests, or plants from the sea is net primary production; animal protein is one or more levels higher up on the food chain, but is, nonetheless, derived from the net production of plants.

Ecologists differentiate between net primary production, usually expressed on an annual basis, and the standing stock of carbon compounds or biomass on a site. Biomass is the accumulated standing stock; net production is the annual increment.

Net primary production is directly measurable and has been measured systematically for the major natural and man-dominated communities of the earth. These measurements have been summarized in table 3.1, drawn from an appraisal by Whittaker and Likens (1975). The data were those thought to apply to the world of 1950. More recent appraisals based on later studies of forests around the world have produced lower estimates of total biomass and higher estimates of net primary production on land. Ajtay *et al.* (1979), for instance, estimated biomass on land as 1,244 x 10^{15}g/yr. Olson *et al.* (1983) have suggested similar quantities for the world of 1980, but the analyses of various types of vegetation are not directly comparable among these studies, and the later studies have not included reappraisals of the oceans.

Differences also occur in the classification of vegetation, the areas of each type of vegetation, the mass of organic matter per unit area, and the primary productivity per unit area. There is little basis for judging between them. The important point is that on such a vital matter as the size of the biotic resources globally there is little data and much uncertainty.

The standing stock of organic matter in plants, not including the humus of soils, the peat of bogs, and the dissolved organic carbon of

TABLE 3.1. Global net primary production and plant biomass.

	Area (10⁶ km²)	Net primary production (dry matter)			Biomass (dry matter)		
		Normal range (g/m²/yr)	Mean (g/m²/yr)	Total (10¹⁵ g/yr)	Normal range (Kg/m²)	Mean (kg/m2)	Total 10¹⁵ g
Tropical rain forest	17.0	1000–3,500	2,200	37.4	6–80	45	765
Tropical seasonal forest	7.5	1000–2,500	1,600	12.0	6–60	35	260
Temperate forest:							
evergreen	5.0	600–2,500	1,300	6.5	6–200	35	175
deciduous	7.0	600–2,500	1,200	8.4	6–60	30	210
Boreal forest	12.0	400–2,000	800	9.6	6–40	20	240
Woodland and shrubland	8.5	250–1,200	700	6.0	2–20	6	50
Savanna	15.0	200–2,000	900	13.5	0.2–15	4	60
Temperate grassland	9.0	200–1,500	600	5.4	0.2–5	1.6	14
Tundra and alpine	8.0	10–400	140	1.1	0.1–3	0.6	5
Desert and semidesert scrub	18.0	10–250	90	1.6	0.1–4	0.7	13
Extreme desert — rock, sand, ice	24.0	0–10	3	0.07	0–0.2	0.02	0.5
Cultivated land	14.0	100–4,000	650	9.1	0.4–12	1	14
Swamp and marsh	2.0	800–6,000	3,000	6.0	3–50	15	30
Lake and stream	2.0	100–1,500	400	0.8	0–0.1	0.02	0.05
Total continental:	149.0	—	782	117.5	—	12.2	1,837
Open ocean	332.0	2–400	125	41.5	0–0.005	0.003	1.0
Upwelling zones	0.4	400–1,000	500	0.2	0.005–0.1	0.02	0.008
Continental shelf	26.6	200–600	360	9.6	0.001–0.04	0.001	0.27
Algal beds and reefs	0.6	500–4,000	2,500	1.6	0.04–4	2	1.4
Estuaries (excluding marsh)	1.4	200–4,000	1,500	2.1	0.01–4	1	1.4
Total marine:	361.0	—	155	55.0	—	0.01	3.9
Full total:	510.0	—	336	172.5	—	3.6	1,841

Source: Wittaker and Likens, 1975.

the oceans, provides one measure, albeit a crude one, of the total amount of life on earth. The estimates range between about 1,200 and 1,800 x 10^{15} g, a factor of 1.5. The greatest uncertainty lies in knowledge of the area of forests. There is a significant discrepancy between the area of the earth that could potentially be forested and the actually forested area. Fires and grazing have permanently deforested major segments of the earth. China, India, Great Britain, the Levant, and the Mediterranean Basin, among other regions, were deforested centuries, even millennia ago, and have been heavily grazed since. Now, rapid growth in the human population, especially in the tropics, is bringing further destruction of forests in hitherto undisturbed areas such as the Amazon Basin, Southeast Asia, and central Africa. The best guesses as to the extent of the current destruction and the area of forest remaining are based on careful review of the published data (Spears and Ayensu, ch. 10; Woodwell et al., 1983; Houghton et al., 1983). More accurate appraisals are now possible using several techniques of remote sensing, outlined in detail by Woodwell et al. (1984). (See also Woodwell, 1984.)

The standing stock of plants globally in 1980 was probably about 1,200 x 10^{15} g of dry organic matter (Olson et al., 1983). This total is an estimate of the total amount of life on earth—that is, the total standing crop of living things. The fact that animals have not been included is irrelevant; their mass is so much smaller than the mass of plants that including all animals as well as man would not change this sum at all.

The magnitude of net primary production obviously varies greatly around the world. The highest productivities may be generated in agriculture by the very intensively managed triple or quadruple cropping in the moist tropics using hybrid or other specially produced crops. This type of agriculture is not common, since it requires intensive management, large contributions of energy in the form of manpower and fossil fuels, fertilizers, irrigation, and usually the chemical control of pests. Globally such man-dominated communities are small in area and of minor significance. Most agriculture does not fall in this extraordinary realm.

The important figure in this analysis is the magnitude of the global flux of net production. It is currently estimated at about 175 x 10^{15} g dry organic matter annually (table 3.1). More than two-thirds of this total is on land; the remainder, about 55 x 10^{15} g, is marine. The rates of production are high for forests, estuaries, and marshes, but the total production is affected heavily by the extensiveness of the various communities. Forests dominate because they have both high rates per unit area and occupy large areas globally.

The process of impoverishment, which will be described below, reduces the flux of net production. A change from forest to pasture or agriculture commonly reduces the net production per unit area by 50 percent or more. The destruction of forests and their replacement by shrubs usually reduce not only the diversity but also the net production, and therefore the potential for supporting life.

Here again is the great dilemma of management, the conflict between the immediate demands of a swollen human population for the diversion of primary production into human food and the clear need to preserve the potential of living systems for the maintenance of the biosphere as a rich and versatile habitat. The problem is even more immediate. We might ask what fraction of the earth's total primary production is used directly by man for food. The answer includes all of agricultural production, of course. Because most of the world's remaining natural grasslands and savannas are grazed commercially, the ecosystems, including lakes, streams, and the oceans, are also harvested for protein. This harvest has remained constant for 10 out of the last 15 years at 70 million metric tons (mt). In 1982 it rose slightly to about 77 million mt (FAO, 1982). The increase reflects a substantial intensification of effort in fishing. There is, apparently, little basis for expecting a further doubling of the yield of fisheries under present systems of management. Most of the net primary production that can be diverted to man's use is already being diverted. The quantities of net production globally are listed in table 3.2 The estimated sum is

TABLE 3.2. Net primary production devoted to human food in 1980.

Net primary production	Dry organic matter $(10^{15}g)$
Agriculture	9–27
Grasslands, grazing lands, savannas	19
Aquatic systems	56
Total	84–102

Sources: Whittaker and Likens, 1975; Olson *et al.*, 1983.

84-102×10^{15} g based on the most recent appraisals for terrestrial systems and the Whittaker and Likens (1975) appraisal for aquatic systems. The estimate is crude. It includes only food and does not take into account fiber, including lumber, pulp, and other natural products. Nor does it include other uses of natural vegetation as reservoirs of biotic diversity for stabilization of drainage basins or for other functions in maintaining the human habitat.

Clearly, no other single species has ever reached the point where such a high fraction of the earth's biotic potential was being diverted to support it with food and fiber. What is the limit? Again, it is elusive. The destruction of forests, toxification, and the processes of impoverishment are reducing the global total of net production. The very expansion of agriculture, necessary for support of the expanded human population globally, reduces the total net production globally while diverting a higher fraction of the residual to human food. At some point, deforestation of a river valley extracts in erosion, siltation, loss of water, and loss of control of water flows a cost to society that exceeds the capacity of an impoverished populace to repair. Such a point is an obvious limit, but the human circumstance that leads to that point is difficult to measure and even more difficult to prevent. Changes of this sort are now global and accelerating. They can be measured as local, regional, and global declines in primary production and as a shift in the flux of net production toward an increased use by man for food. Normal functions of nature in maintaining the biosphere fall out of the calculus as the demands for immediate needs for food increase.

CURRENT TRENDS

The current trend globally is toward progressive, chronic disturbance, both chemical and mechanical, as a result of increased human interference. Disturbance is now becoming global whereas before it was regional. One important possibility is a warming of the earth due to the accumulation of carbon dioxide and other infrared-absorbing gases in the atmosphere. The warming is expected to be sufficient to change climatic zones, to displace forests and agriculture, and to raise sea level, all within decades (NCR, 1983). At the same time, industrial toxins circulate globally in air and water and affect biotic systems. These substances not only enter human food chains and ultimately contaminate them, they also affect the biosphere.

Disturbance, whether it is a sudden change in climate, the introduction of a toxin that is then chronically present, or repeated mechanical disruption, causes a series of changes in biotic systems that have been defined as biotic impoverishment. Initially the changes involve a reduction in the complexity of the structure of natural communities: for example, a forest becomes less diversified by losing certain species of trees. Later, if the disturbance continues, it may lose all its trees. Still later, tall shrubs disappear, and the vegetation consists of low shrubs and hardy herbs. Examples include such well-known vegetations as the mawuis and garigue of the Mediterranean Basin, the blueberry barrens of eastern Maine, and the pocosins of the southeastern coastal plain of the United States. Further disturbance drives the impoverishment farther to a plant community in which hardy, low-growing annuals dominate. Species have been lost, primary productivity is diminished, and the residual community, although it may be highly diversified, is made up of small-bodied, rapidly reproducing species that are the weeds or insect pests of garden and roadside. Strangely enough, diversity, measured as numbers of species per unit area, may fluctuate through this series of transitions. Deforested lands that have been heavily grazed for decades to centuries may have a very high diversity of low-growing herbaceous plants. I have observed deforested and heavily grazed areas in Minas Gerais in Brazil where one square meter supported as many as forty species of such herbs. A similar observation was made by Whittaker on the long-deforested hills used for grazing goats in Israel (Whittaker, 1977 a, b).

Similar transitions occur within the animal community. Larger-bodied, longer lived species are lost in favor of smaller-bodied, rapidly reproducing forms. Impoverishment leads to communities in which hardy insect populations, rodents, and scavenging birds survive alongside weeds and insects of the garden (Woodwell, 1970; Holzner et al., 1983).

The patterns of impoverishment are well known and are developing rapidly in both aquatic and terrestrial systems. They lead to a biosphere that is less capable of supporting life, including people. The trends arre clear enough; most are reversible, at least in the early stages, but become irreversible quickly as species are lost, habitat changes, and toxins and toxic effects accumulate.

WHAT CAN WE DO?

The ecologist sees the biosphere as the product of the interactions of discrete units: forests, fields, marshes, estuaries, river drainages, lakes, oceans, and continents, all of which function together to support life. Each unit has a biotic structure that can be measured and defined. The structure develops with time and is vulnerable to disturbance. It also has a metabolism that is related to structure: it grows as a forest develops, for example, and shrinks as the forest is destroyed. Each unit accumulates and recirculates essential nutrients in patterns that are commonly cyclic, and each is in constant interaction with other ecosystems: forests with lakes and streams, streams with coastal waters, estuaries with both land and sea and so on. The normal operation of the biosphere is dependent on the normal operation of its parts, not species alone, but whole units of the earth's surface. The normal function is biotic, follows simple rules, and requires no tinkering by man. Disturbed chronically, problems accumulate. Current trends are toward the destruction of these systems, toward drastic alteration of their function, and toward equally drastic changes in the biosphere that will diminish its habitability for man.

Is it possible in a finite world to support an expanding human enterprise that has industrial potential and continued aspirations for wealth, especially when that world is characterized by an apparently fragile series of biotic systems vulnerable to both minor physical and chemical disturbance? Or is the impoverishment of India the model for the world as a whole? What is possible, if we act in recognition of what is happening?

The immediate need is to preserve the normal function of biotic systems that are the basic components of the biosphere. Preservation of the physical, chemical, and biotic integrity of those systems is paramount. Obviously, there must be room for man—for cities, suburbs, industry, agriculture, forestry, and fisheries. But man's activities, if they are to be sustainable, must not exceed close and finite limits and impair the normal function of the natural ecosystems they have in part replaced. The simplest solution is to make man-dominated systems mimic natural systems in their effects on the biosphere of the particular place.

The purpose seems simple, but the challenge is large. It is the challenge of closing man-dominated systems. Success will require much innovation in technology, science, politics, and government. The need, however, is clear enough, rooted in ancient biblical principles fixed in English common law (Humpstone 1972): *Sic utere tuo, ut alienum non laedas.* (Use what belongs to you in such a way that you do not impair rights of others.)

Such a principle precludes one nation's fouling the air or water of another. It seems to be the only fair basis for managing shared resources among neighbors, states or nations; it is a fair basis in law as well as in physics, chemistry, and biology.

Control of the ins and outs of man-dominated systems is but one step in the ascent toward reason in the management of the biosphere. The second comes in the recognition that some finite ratio between disturbed and undisturbed natural systems would be appropriate to assure the preservation of both biotic diversity and the normal function of the biosphere. Disturbance is not absolute: varying degrees are possible, even desirable, to assure a place for species that occur only as a part of successional communities or those maintained by periodic fire. But the point is to recognize the need to control the use of the surface of the earth to assure that biotic diversity is maintained.

Here again, innovation is needed, in scholarship, management of land and water, including the seas, and in government. Fundamental questions remain: What is the ratio of disturbed to developed areas, locally, regionally, globally? How large must preserves be to retain plants? birds? mammals? fish populations? Can we develop ways of harvesting natural populations without destroying them or impairing the normal function of their ecosystems?

The questions are not new. They have become newly acute, however, presenting a novel, different kind of challenge to those planning reindustrialization and the further development of technology in the less-developed parts of the world.

Innovations are possible. As insights accumulate, there will be evidence occasionally that certain activities, for example, the detonation of nuclear weapons within the biosphere or the control of pests with persistent toxins, are simply not feasible in a shrinking world. There is no requirement that every technological innovation, every chemical, and every potential activity of man be indulged. Some are proscribed; others will be.

We cannot manage the biosphere in detail. It manages itself, and in an ideal world we would preserve the circumstances in which that self-management can continue with no cost to the human enterprise. Why not accept that objective as one of the guiding principles, perhaps the central principle, of the wave of industrialization now sweeping the world, driven in part by the advances in computers? What better way is there to accept the reality of a finite but renewable earth?

REFERENCES

Ajtay, G. L., P. Ketner, and P. Duvigneaud. 1979. Terrestrial Primary Production and Phytomass. In *The Global Carbon Cycle*, SCOPE 13, ed. B. Bolin *et al.*, pp. 129–81. Chichester: John Wiley & Sons.

Alvarez, L. W., W. Alvarez, F. Asaro, and H. V. Michel. 1980. Extraterrestrial cause for the Cretaceous-Tertiary Extinction. *Science* 208:1095–1108.

———. 1982. Iridium anomaly approximately synchronous with terminal Eocene extinctions. *Science* 216:886–88.

Ehrlich, P. R., and A. H. Ehrlich. 1981. *Extinction: The Causes and Consequences of the Disappearance of Species*. New York: Random House. See especially p. 305.

Ehrlich, P., J. Harte, M. A. Harwell, P. H. Raven, C. Sagan, G. M. Woodwell, J. Berry, E. S. Ayensu, A. H. Ehrlich, T. Eisner, S. J. Gould, H. D. Grover, R. Herrera, R. M. May, E. Mayr, C. P. McKay, H. A. Mooney, N. Myers, D. Pimentel, and J. M. Teal. 1983. Long-term biological consequences of nuclear war. *Science* 333:1293–99.

FAO. 1982. *Yearbook of Fishery Statistics*. Vol. 55. Rome: FAO.

Holzner, W., M. J. A. Werger, and I. Ikusiam, eds. 1983. *Man's Impact on Vegetation*. The Hague: W. Junk. See especially p. 370.

Houghton, R. A., J. E. Hobbie, J. M. Melillo, M. Moore, B. J. Peterson, G. R. Shaver, and G. M. Woodwell. 1983. Changes in the carbon content of terrestrial biota and soils between 1860 and 1980: A net release of CO_2 to the atmosphere. *Ecological Monographs* 53(3):235–62.

Humpstone, C. C. 1972. Pollution: Precedent and prospect. *Foreign Affairs* 50:325–38.

NRC. 1983. *Changing Climate*. Washington, D.C.: National Academy Press. See especially p. 496.

Olson, J., J. A. Watts, and L. J. Allison. 1983. *Carbon in live vegetation of major world ecosystems*. Report for US Department of Energy TR004 DOE/NRB-0037. Washington, D.C. See especially p. 152.

Repetto, R., and T. Holmes. 1983. The role of population in resource depletion in developing countries. *Population and Development Review* 9:609–32.

Simon, J. L. 1977. *The Economics of Population Growth*. Princeton: Princeton University Press.

Turco, R. P., O. B. Toon, T. P. Ackerman, J. B. Pollack, and C. Sagan. 1983. Nuclear winter: Global consequences of multiple nuclear explosions. *Science* 222:1283–92.

Whittaker, R. H. 1977a. Animal Effects on Plant Species Diversity. In *Vegetation Fauna*, ed., R. Tuxen, pp. 409–25. Vaduz: J. Cramer.

———. 1977b. Evolution of species diversity in land communities. *Evolutionary Biology* 10:1–67.

Whittaker, R. H., and G. E. Likens. 1975. The Biosphere and Man. In *Primary Productivity of the Biosphere*, ed. H. Lieth and R. H. Whittaker, pp. 305–28. New York: Springer Verlag.

Woodwell, G. M. 1970. The effects of pollution on the structure and physiology of ecosystems. *Science* 168:429–33.

Woodwell, G. M., ed. 1984. *The Role of Terrestrial Vegetation in the Global Carbon Cycle: Measurement by Remote Sensing*. SCOPE 23. Chichester: John Wiley & Sons.

Woodwell, G. M., J. E. Hobbie, R. A. Houghton, J. M. Melillo, B. Moore, B. J. Peterson, and G. R. Shaver. 1983. Global deforestation: Contribution to atmospheric carbon dioxide. *Science* 222:1081–86.

Woodwell, G. M., J. E. Hobbie, R. A. Houghton, J. M. Melillo, B. J. Peterson, G. R. Shaver, and T. A. Stone. 1984. *Changes in the Area of Forests in Rondonia, Amazon Basin, Measured by Satellite Imagery*.

Worldwatch Institute. 1984. *State of the World, 1984*. New York: W. Morton. See especially p. 252.

CHAPTER FOUR

An Economist's View of Natural Resource and Environmental Problems

ROBERT DORFMAN

The task of economists with respect to natural resource and environmental policy is to provide a framework within which the data provided by experts in other fields can be viewed and the social implications drawn. Economists can only repeat, without quite understanding, what geologists, ecologists, public health experts, and others say about physical and physiological facts. Their craft is to perceive how economics and people in general will respond to those facts.

It must be emphasized that the analysis of these responses, though predicated on secondhand knowledge, is critically important. What is happening and what is going to happen to our natural resource base and our environment depend not only on the facts of nature but also on human responses to them. The efficacy of any policy that may be adopted depends as much on how it affects human behavior as on how it is intended to influence natural phenomena. Judgments about the desirability of different policies are based on judgments about how they affect people's welfare. All these are matters that economists study and that they have come to treat with some sophistication.

The following discussion relates facts only insofar as necessary —others can speak to these facts with much more authority. Rather it bears down heavily on social interpretation. It is hoped that it can contribute some necessary unifying threads to the discussion of natural resource and environmental problems. Inevitably, such discussion dismembers unified problems into manageable segments to the neglect of both their basic unity and the fact that the same principles of human response apply to all of them.

One unifying thread has been mentioned already; that is, how people react to problems related to natural resources or the environment. This depends on what they know about the problem, what options are open to them, and what their motivations are. These things deserve attention whether we are dealing with deforestation, acid rain, or whatever.

One widespread and important factor is how much things cost. Often the most effective way to get people to exercise their ingenuity in economizing on the use of a resource is simply to make it expensive. Sometimes the best way to persuade people to stop desecrating their environment is to widen the alternatives open to them. These and other expedients appear in different guises in different contexts.

Therefore, the discussion is divided roughly in accordance with the kinds of information and incentives that are appropriate. The major division is between natural resource problems and environmental quality problems. The natural resource section is subdivided according to renewable or nonrenewable resources. In the environmental section, problems of planning and evaluation are discussed first, then problems of implementation, which are subdivided further according to whether the environmental problem occurs in an industrial nation, a less developed nation, or transcends national boundaries.

The first distinction, between natural resources and the environment, is not an easy one. For example, is a forest a natural resource, or a part of the environment, or both? It is both, as most people use the terms; these categories are not mutually exclusive. If we were legislators, we might have to define these words more precisely, but for our present purpose hairsplitting is not in order. Whether a particular item is to be regarded as a natural resource or an environmental feature, or a human artifact for that matter, depends on the problem under consideration and on the point of view being taken. A graded and drained field is a human artifact to the farmer who invested in it, a natural resource to the economic geographer, and part of the environment to the ecologist. For working purposes we can be satisfied with the crude distinction that a natural resource is something that can be altered in quality but not diminished in quantity. We shall consider natural resources first.

NATURAL RESOURCE PROBLEMS

The first distinction to be made in discussing natural resource problems is that between exhaustible and self-renewing resources. Exhaustible resources are typically of geologic origin, and any amounts consumed will be replaced on a geologic time scale, if at all. Any amount used is gone forever for all practical purposes. Self-renewing resources are typically biological, and the amounts harvested will be replaced by natural forces rather quickly, within limits. But there are borderline cases. Groundwater is one example—left to itself, a depressed water table will rise in a few years or decades. Another is a climax forest—the biological processes that generated it may take millennia and, indeed, may never be repeated. Again, fine distinctions are unnecessary.

There is a paradox. Exhaustible resources are never totally exhausted. The general rule is that as a deposit is worked, the successive units of the resource become increasingly expensive to extract, until finally the deposit is abandoned with much of the resource still in place. Typically, an oil well is capped with 50-60 percent of the original oil still in the reservoir. It is said that there is still gold in Vermont, but the ore is of such poor grade that it is not worth extracting even at current high prices.

On the other hand, self-renewing resources can be annihilated. Simple mention of the passenger pigeon and the American buffalo establishes that. Thus, exhaustible and self-renewing resources present quite different problems of resource management.

Exhaustible Resources

Economists have an elegant theory for the use of exhaustible resources. It is frequently attributed to Harold Hotelling, but the main lines were presented by Lewis Gray about a generation earlier. The basic theory has several variants. The one discussed here is not quite the simplest, but it is the simplest that has empirical relevance.

The theory concentrates on the behavior of a mine-owner, who may be an entire nation. At any time, the owner has to decide how much to extract, taking into account the fact that the more extracted right away, the greater will be the cost of each unit extracted in the future. The reasoning is a bit subtle but is essentially as follows. Suppose that in any month the owner should extract one unit less than he is now planning and make it up the next month. Then in the current month he would sacrifice the net profit on one unit at this month's price. In the second month two things would happen. First, he would gain the net profit on one unit at the second month's price. Second, the net profit on every unit extracted in the second month would be increased because the reserves in place at the time that unit was extracted would be one unit greater, thereby reducing extraction cost.

It would be advantageous to cut back the first month's output if the sum of these two effects on the second month's profits were greater than the first month's sacrifice accumulated at interest for a month. Similar reasoning applies to the option of increasing production in the first month. And the current plan is just right if the price is increasing just quickly enough that no shift in either direction is advantageous.

To continue, if the price were not increasing, or were increasing only slowly, all producers would be induced to increase their current output to obtain their profits now rather than later. But the increase in current output would reduce the going price, while its effect on future prices would be, if anything, to increase them, because the reserves available for the future would be reduced. Hence, the market behavior would be to accelerate the increase in the price, and the process would continue until prices were growing quickly enough that producers were content with their current rates of production.

This theory thus leads to the conclusion that, left to itself, the market for any exhaustible resource will generate a path of gradually increasing prices. Further, if the prices at any two dates are compared, the price at the later date, the net of extraction costs discounted to the earlier date, will equal the price at the earlier date, also net of extraction costs. Moreover, to the extent that the price of a unit of a resource, net of extraction costs, measures the social benefit of extracting that unit, this price path reflects the fact that the resource is being extracted at just the rate that a wise, beneficent planner would recommend.

Of course, the gradual increase in price will be an inconvenience to future generations. It will induce them to use the resource more sparingly, to extract and process it more carefully, to reclaim and recycle it more extensively, and to substitute other, somewhat less suitable resources for it if they are cheaper. That is as it should be. The inconveniences in the future are offset by the advantages in the present of using the resource at the rate induced by the price path, if the discount rate that generates the market behavior reflects the relative social evaluation of present and future net benefits.

There is some empirical confirmation for this theory, but not much. When the oil-exporting nations abruptly increased their prices, inducing a reduction in worldwide consumption, all the other producers increased their outputs as much as possible, just as the theory predicts. But the main prediction of the theory, that the prices of exhaustible resources would rise faster than prices in general, was not supported in this case. It is easy to think of reasons for this. The basic one probably is the great continuing advances in the technologies of finding, extracting, and processing exhaustible resources, accompanied by the development of substitutes for expensive minerals. Another important reason is the notorious instability in the price of raw materials, which fluctuates so much that producers are reluctant to forego current profits for uncertain gains in the future.

So the theory, though perhaps correct in principle, merely points to one consideration, the effects of which may be swamped in practice by other considerations. For predictive purposes the theory has a poor record. Prescriptive purposes—telling us how fast exhaustible resources ought to be extracted—are another matter, although they depend on similar reasoning. The essence is to recognize that every unit of an exhaustible resource that is extracted confers an immediate social benefit, the extent of which is measured by the price that people are willing to pay for the unit less the cost of the resources used to extract it. It also imposes costs on the future, their extent being measured by the increase in the cost of extracting future units because of the reduced amount of the resource in place. The proper balance between present and future is struck when the immediate benefits are just balanced by the deferred costs.

The problem lies in the estimation of the deferred costs. They have to be assessed from the point of view of the present, since our future selves and our descendants cannot express their views. This assessment is a difficult task for several reasons. One has already been mentioned: the impossiblity of foreseeing technological improvements in the production and use of a resource or the development of substitutes for it. A second is the problem of "discounting." Today's needs always seem more urgent than the future's. To some extent this habit of discounting the future is justifiable, since the future will be more technically adept than the present. It will also be richer, in the sense of having larger stocks of productive capital to work with and therefore more ample flows of most consumable goods. Justifiable or not, we always do it, so the question arises as to how much we should discount future consequences of current actions. This question is important and has generated an enormous literature, but it is far from being resolved. In this circumstance, the best way to contend with a practical problem of exhaustible resources is to estimate the consequences of applying a wide range of discount rates. It may turn out that the rate of extraction will be influenced strongly by the rate of discount that is applied. Then the decision is thrown into the realm of judgment. But the analysis that leads to such an indecisive result is not futile. One man's good judgment is another man's folly. Where there are differing judgments about social decisions, it is important to clarify the source of the difference. If different opinions about proper extraction policy arise from differing opinions about the proper rate of discount, then that is the issue on which public debate should be focused. If agreement is unobtainable, as is generally the case, it is nonetheless helpful to know what people are disagreeing about and where they stand.

A third problem is associated with the concept of reserves. Reserves are, in fact, a kind of bugbear. Geologists make estimates of the amounts of various minerals in the earth's crust. For example, there are about 2×10^{18} metric tons (mt) of aluminum. But nearly all of this enormous quantity is in such low concentrations or otherwise unavailable that for practical purposes it might as well not be there. So the significant quantity is the amount in usable deposits. Although usable deposits is not a geological concept, we rely on geologists to estimate it. The US Geological Survey makes estimates for a number of conceptual quantities such as "proved reserves," "inferred reserves," or "recoverable resources," which are distinguished by the degree of confidence that geologists have in the actual existence of the deposits and by their judgment of the economic practicality of extracting the minerals. Those estimates are interesting but of little value in formulating extraction policies. As we have noted, deposits are invariably abandoned before they are exhausted, because the cost of further extraction has risen. For policy purposes, there is a need for estimates of the cost of further extraction from the best deposits remaining after various quantities have been mined. Such estimates require a knowledge of both geology and mining economics, and just plain future vision. They are extraordinarily difficult to make and can rarely be made with much confidence.

The final problem that deserves mention is this. To ascertain the desirable current rate of extraction of an exhaustible resource, we need to know the costs that any choice will impose at future dates. But future costs will depend on the rate of extraction at the time. We seem to be caught in a bind of circular reasoning: to know the proper rate at one date, we need the answer to the same question for all future dates. Happily, the problem is not so much circular as simultaneous. The proper current rate of extraction cannot be estimated without forecasting the whole course of extraction until an inevitable day when costs have risen so much that further exploitation of the resources costs more than it is worth. Then the resource is exhausted from an economic point of view, though geologically a great deal remains in place. Charting this proper course of extraction, where every year along the way present benefits are balanced against future costs, is a difficult technical problem, but solvable within the limits imposed by the problems of prediction and discounting mentioned before.

Things now stand as follows. To establish the proper rates of use of any exhaustible resource, we must make necessarily tenuous projections of future uses and future extraction and processing costs and agree on an appropriate discount rate. With those data we can calculate the proper rate of extraction currently and in the future. Simultaneously, we can calculate the future course of prices for the resource, since the price at any time must equate the amount demanded with the proper rate of extraction. The prices that obtain at present and that will obtain in the future are, in fact, the key to the problem. If the price of a resource could be made to follow its proper course, the amounts of the resource extracted and used would automatically allocate its use over a time in the best way possible. This theory maintains that for any exhaustible resource, there is a course of prices that will induce producers, all trying to exploit their deposits as profitably as possible, to extract the resource at the socially optimal rate. Further, though this course of prices is difficult to estimate, by making use of the available pertinent knowledge, we can make estimates that will be the best attainable guides to policies for use and conservation. But now there is another difficulty to be faced: If we knew the socially optimal price path, how could we implement it?

Most of the critical exhaustible resources are traded in world markets. They are extracted, typically, in both industrial and developing countries. The industrial countries are generally net importers and depend on imported raw materials for their industries. They have a great stake in rational allocation of resource use over time. The developing countries also depend on the resource as a way of paying for current imports and storing wealth with which to finance their own development. Optimal allocation over time is a secondary concern to them;

high prices in the immediate future are more important. Management of resources is particularly complicated in developing countries, where both the nation itself and multinational mining companies participate according to elaborate contractual arrangements. There is little basis for expecting the international markets thus created to generate socially optimal prices. Institutional arrangements for coordinating the policies of the mining companies and the nations with the deposits are lacking, but there is no lack of conflicts of interest.

In these circumstances, the outlook for implementing any farsighted plan for extracting nonrenewable resources in a way that will service the interests of all the countries concerned is dim indeed. The only expedient appears to be to alter the structure of the markets so that they induce more satisfactory performance. I will suggest one way in which this might be done.

One notorious problem in the markets for exhaustible minerals is that the prices fluctuate erratically, quite unlike the smooth evolution required to induce optimal rates of extraction. These fluctuations are harmful in many ways: high prices contribute to inflationary pressures in the importing countries, whereas low prices exacerbate foreign exchange problems and generate unemployment in developing countries. Whether prices are high or low, their variability interferes with the process described above; decisions about the rate of extraction become dominated by short-run speculative considerations instead of a long-run concern for how best to allocate use over time.

One expedient for moderating these fluctuations and some of their consequences is rarely used. It is a type of loan that an international lender, either an international agency or an institution like the National Westminster Bank, might make to a developing country when the price of a mineral export is depressed. The loan would be secured by a mortgage on a stated amount of the still unmined deposit. The amount of the loan per unit would be a fraction, say one-half, of the long-run value of the resource-in-place calculated by means of the theory discussed above. The loan would be retired in, say, quarterly instalments, each payment being the amount secured by the ore extracted in the previous quarter plus accumulated interest. Such loans would ease the pressure on a developing country to maintain production when the price of its resource was depressed and would also reduce the amount extracted at times when the social value, as indicated by the price, was lower than the long-run socially optimal value. To the extent that it succeeded in reducing the volume produced during troughs in demand, it would also moderate the violence of the price fluctuations.

Surely many other devices are available for improving the performance of the international markets in exhaustible commodities. We shall have to continue to rely on the markets, however, to control the rate of extraction of exhaustible resources, and this is not altogether a bad thing. Properly performing markets reflect the assembled knowledge and judgment of the people who are in the best position to assess the present and future values of the resource, who have a canniness that central planners cannot be expected to equal. The important thing is that the markets should not be dominated by speculative or narrowly acquisitive motivations.

Of course, we do not know at present which markets are performing well and which are inducing excessive rates of mineral extraction. The only way to find out is to gather the pertinent data, apply the normative theory, and compare the actual course of prices and extractions with the socially optimal one. This is no mean task, but the stakes are so high that studies of this kind would be worthwhile for at least some of the more important minerals such as copper, nickel, and tin.

Self-renewing Resources

The problems presented by self-renewing resources are different from those presented by exhaustible resources. For one thing, there is a real possibility that the world's stock of a self-renewing resource will be depleted permanently and irretrievably. Nevertheless, there is a close kinship in the conflict, present in both cases, between the enticements of immediate harvesting and the awareness that large current harvests increase the costliness of future harvests.

This awareness has given rise to the doctrine of "maximum sustainable yields," which is a good starting point for discussing the complications introduced by self-renewal. The doctrine is based on the "logistic law of population growth," which holds that any environment or habitat has a maximum carrying capacity for each species that inhabits it. When the population of any species is small in relation to the carrying capacity for it, the population grows rapidly in terms of percentage but slowly in terms of absolute mass, simply because the number of individuals growing and reproducing is small. As the population increases, the percentage growth rate declines (in part because food becomes harder to find and predators become more numerous), but the growth rate in absolute numbers and weight increases—up to a point. After that point, the decrease in the percentage growth rate overcompensates the increase in numbers to which that percentage is applied, and the growth rate in terms of absolute population becomes smaller and smaller as the carrying capacity is approached.

The maximum sustainable yield is the absolute growth rate at that critical point at which the population is growing most rapidly. For if the harvest taken each year is equal to the natural annual amount of growth, the population will remain stationary, and that size of harvest can be sustained indefinitely. Without appraising this ecological theory, it can be stated empirically that it appears to apply to some species and not to others. However, it is often maintained that the population of any economically significant species should be allowed to grow to the level at which the natural rate of growth is fastest and then be held at that level by an annual take equal to the maximum sustainable yield.

The doctrine may be ideal from the point of view of the species in question, but from a social or economic point of view, there are at least three things wrong with it. First, it takes no account of the cost of harvesting. Whatever the species may be—fur-bearing animals or fish or teak or truffles—it is generally cheaper to find and capture any given number the more numerous they are in the particular area. It follows, then, that if the population were held at a level somewhat greater than the one that affords the maximum sustainable yield, the saving in the average cost of harvesting would be greater than the value of the (slight) decrease in the sustainable yield.

The second defect in the maximum sustainable yield theory is complementary to the first. The doctrine ignores the fact that the social value of units of any commodity falls when the supply increases. Thus, if the population of a commercial species were held somewhat above the level of the maximum sustainable yield, the annual harvest would be reduced but the value of the units forgone would be lower than the value of those harvested and the average cost of harvesting would be reduced, for the reason just explained. It can be shown, in fact, that there is always a sustainable yield somewhat smaller than the maximum that gives rise to a perpetuity of social benefits that is preferable to the one corresponding to the maximum sustainable yield.

The third defect is somewhat less obvious. It is that this doctrine and almost any policy based on maintaining a constant harvest in perpetuity ignores the cost of attaining the population at which that harvest can be sustained. Consider the "socially optimal sustainable yield," the yield that takes into account the effect of harvest size on the average harvesting cost and the social value of each unit harvested. Suppose that the current population is smaller than the one at which the socially optimal yield can be sustained. Then, for the population to grow to the optimal level, the current harvest must be reduced below the sustainable take, thus reducing current social benefits. That reduction is the cost.

On the other hand, if the current population is at least equal to the one at which the socially optimal yield can be sustained, the current harvest and social benefits can be increased, although it will not be possible to harvest the optimal sustainable yield thereafter. It turns out, nevertheless, that the temporary increase would be worthwhile, since the current gains would outweigh the future costs. In a nutshell, it is not best to maintain the socially optimal sustainable yield even if you are in a position to do so. Economists will recognize the analogy between this finding and the distinction between "the golden rule of economic growth" and the "modified golden rule."

We conclude that all policies based on constant annual harvests are socially wasteful. The socially optimal policy has to be deduced from an analysis similar to the one that applies to exhaustible resources, but amended to allow for the natural replenishment of the population. The result of such analysis is almost inevitably a recommendation against harvests that remain the same year after year.

So much for the economic theory of self-replenishing resources. It has been discussed here largely to discredit the maximum sustainable yield doctrine, but now its limitations must be emphasized. All the principles of economically optimal harvesting are derived from some variant of the logistic growth assumption that the growth of a natural population depends primarily on its own numbers. But this is rarely, if ever, the case. The growth of a population is likely to be influenced at least as strongly by the abundance of its food, its competitors, and its predators, of which human beings are usually only one. Often the dominant influence on the growth of a population is a subtle change in its environment such as a slight change in water temperature or acidity, or a variation in the amount or timing of rainfall. Thus few natural populations grow in accordance with logistical laws, and harvesting policy, within wide limits, is an ineffective way to control population growth. On the whole, the best way to sustain a population is to control the factor that influences its growth most strongly. This is frequently the extent and condition of the population's habitat. Even if no one had ever hunted the American buffalo, there would not be millions of them roaming the western plains today. Acid rain has eliminated the trout from many lakes despite determined efforts to limit the annual catch. And so on.

Although limits on harvesting cannot be relied on to maintain a population at a desired level or constrain its growth to a desired path, uncontrolled harvesting can reduce a population to the critical level below which reproduction fails to compensate for natural mortality. There is a strong tendency for just that to happen to commercially valuable species. Animals and plants in the wild are common property—that is, no one's property—so fishers, hunters, and gatherers do not feel that they have much influence over the size or costs or even the existence of future harvests. Sensibly, they take what they can now, instead of leaving it for someone else to reap. Occasionally, common-pool problems afflict exhaustible resources also, but they are much more prevalent with regard to renewable resources.

Probably the most ominous instance of the common-pool problem today is the overuse of forests and rangelands in the developing countries. Free access to forests and ranges has been part of the way of life in those countries, at least since the invention of slash-and-burn agriculture. With the growth of human populations, the practice has become more destructive than the resources can bear. Garrett Hardin's "tragedy of the commons" is being enacted on Java, in the Sahel, in the Amazon Basin, and in many other parts of the world.

Coping with this deeply ingrained practice is difficult. Direct control is futile; the intruders are too numerous and the control apparatus too feeble. Besides, to the extent that controls are effective, they impose cruel hardships. The only effective approach seems to be to make available satisfactory and competitive substitutes for the goods and services now provided by the open lands: fuel and building materials to protect forests, alternative forage or crops to protect grazing lands, and so on. The roles of central governments and international agencies would then be twofold: first, to provide the substitute commodities needed to make life tolerable without incursions into fragile areas of the environment; and second, to provide strong incentives to local authorities—village elders, panchayats, and the like—to protect and reclaim the forests, grazing lands, and other natural resources in their districts. Such efforts, if widespread, would make greater demands on the budgets and administrative apparatus of the developing countries than they could meet. Programs would therefore have to be concentrated on the most severely threatened localities and, even then, given adequate support by international agencies.

ENVIRONMENTAL PROBLEMS

Natural resource problems shade imperceptibly into environmental problems, as the discussion of common pools may have suggested. After all, the environment consists of resources, some, such as the air we breathe, of supreme importance. The rough distinction adopted here is that natural resource problems relate to the quantity and environmental problems to the quality of the resources that constitute the environment.

Environmental problems, then, concern the quality of our shared surroundings—terrestrial, aquatic, and atmostpheric. In some interpretations, they concern both man-made and natural components of the environment. But this is another difficult distinction. The natural features will be emphasized here, although without paying much attention to the boundary between them and human artifacts.

It has been conventional to divide environmental problems according to whether they related to the condition of the air, land, or water. Fortunately, that division seems to be falling into disuse. The same principles apply to all three, since they are all common pools, and the conditions of the three are intimately linked. The classic example is sulfuric emissions into the atmosphere, most measures to reduce which generate nasty sludges that must be disposed of either on land or in water. The land-air-water distinction will therefore not be used much here. Instead, the discussion will be organized around two aspects of environmental protection programs: planning or appraisal, and implementation.

As used here, *planning* means deciding on the goals to be achieved in specific situations, whereas *implementation* means deciding on the means to be used to attain those goals. The two are not really separable. Planning requires knowledge of the means available, since they affect the costliness and even the practicability of attaining various goals. Implementation, of course, requires knowing what is to be achieved. But it is best to talk about one thing at a time, and planning is discussed first.

Planning Problems

Planning, then, is the selection of goals—for example, the level of dissolved oxygen to be attained in a waterway or the rate of emission of sulfur oxides to be permitted in a region. It is always a compromise among evils and, in practice, amounts to a form of benefit-cost analysis.

Although benefit-cost analysis is a banner to some people and a red flag to others, it is unavoidable. To choose among courses of action, one must compare the advantages and drawbacks of the permissible alternatives. Since this must be done, it is best done consciously and systematically.

Nevertheless, the use of benefit-cost analyses is a subject of controversy, and the results are regarded with skepticism. This low esteem is well-merited, for few analyses can command respect or confidence. As a result, most have come to be paper exercises, undertaken for the record, while actual decisions are made without the guidance accorded by careful analysis of their consequences.

There are numerous reasons for this costly and unsatisfactory state of affairs. A half-dozen of the leading problems that can be corrected will be discussed below.

ABSENCE OF STANDARDS. It is not too much to say that every benefit-cost analysis is ad hoc, an exercise in the analyst's judgment and ingenuity. Every analyst goes about this work in a distinctive way and, in general, carries out each task differently. This state of affairs has numerous disastrous consequences. The analogy that comes to mind is auditing, in many ways a similar enterprise. How much confidence would financial reports deserve if every auditor had wide latitude to define the various classes of assets and liabilities and to devise valuation assumptions? That is essentially the situation with benefit-cost analysis.

The burden placed on readers of these analyses is excessive. They must search through the footnotes in the appendixes to the annexes to find out what the innocent sounding words really mean. More often than not they discover that the definitions are inappropriate and the assumptions implausible. But that is not all. Environmental plans have long histories during which diverse alternatives are supposedly evaluated. Each time one of the alternatives is studied, it is done differently, using different assumptions and definitions. To make use of these reports, frequently thousands of pages in total, the details of what was done have to be rooted out, and rough-and-ready adjustments have to be made to render them at all comparable. It is a task to be approached not without dread. Policymakers might do better relying on "trained intuition," or "expert judgment," or "wise experience."

Clearly, planning will not be effective while these conditions persist. There have been attempts to deal with the problem. Both the Organization for Economic Cooperation and Development (OECD) and the United Nations Industrial Development Organization (UNIDO) have sponsored handbooks on the conduct of benefit-cost analysis, and numerous government agencies have issued manuals and guidelines (for example, the Water Resources Council of the United States). The extent of their effectiveness is indicated by the fact that more than ten years after the OECD and UNIDO reports were issued, nothing has changed, and for good reason. Both were scholarly, subtle, general, abstract, demanding of data, difficult to apply, and, above all, unenforced. In fact, both contain disclaimers assuring the reader that they have no official status. As it happens, neither deals explicitly with environmental problems.

There is need for some influential agency or group of agencies concerned with environmental problems to set forth specifications for benefit-cost evaluations and to require that studies submitted to, or generated by, the agency conform to them. That is not easy in the present state of the art. To be useful, the specifications would have to be explicit and detailed. Undoubtedly, several formats would have to be permitted, to allow for differences in the scale of the appropriate analytic effort, in the availability of data, and in the nature of the problem. Preparing such a document will require difficult negotiations and some experimentation. The effort would certainly not be worthwhile if the need were not so urgent. But considering the amount of effort now devoted to preparing benefit-cost analyses of doubtful usefulness and questionable validity, it would be a sure winner.

The promulgation of acceptable standards is only first step, though a major one. The standards would have to be brought up to date from time to time as experience and knowledge accumulated. Most important, any benefit-cost analysis invokes numerous assumptions—about population growth, trends in price levels and interest rates, and other matters. For comparability of studies, therefore, standard sets of assumptions would need to be prescribed. They need not pretend to precision and in fact should not. The important thing is that they impose uniformity and be reasonably plausible.

For these purposes, some continuing organization or institution must be established. It is hoped that such an institution and its standards would in time acquire the authority of the Institute of Certified Public Accountants and similar organizations. No other single development could do as much to advance the practice and usefulness of benefit-cost analysis.

NEGLECT OF DISTRIBUTIONAL EFFECTS. At least nine out of ten benefit-cost studies adopt the time-honored procedure of adding up benefits and costs "to whomsoever they may accrue." This alone is enough to disqualify them as guides for making practical decisions. Decisions about environmental policies are—and ought to be—political decisions. Their effectiveness depends ultimately on public acceptance. Under any form of government, the officials who make the decisions must be alert to the reactions of the constituencies to which they owe their positions and influence. Analyses that omit the effects of policies on relevant population groups—farmers in the affected region, workers in the affected industries, richer and poorer nations, the poor wherever they may be—thereby leave out the very information that is or should be most significant to the people who make the decisions. A major concern of political decision-makers is to get that information. If it is left out of benefit-cost analyses, they will get it from other sources, ignoring the analyses in the process.

Practical politicians and administrators often point out that it is indiscreet to be explicit about who benefits and who pays for environmental measures, that it can lead to nothing but dissension. It can be countered that it is impossible to hide the fact of distributional consequences and that it is far better to admit them openly than to leave a vacuum to be filled by tendentious claims.

UNPERSUASIVE TREATMENT OF NONMONETARY EFFECTS. Environmental problems are undoubtedly the most difficult field of application of benefit-cost analysis. This is because the major benefits and many of the costs have no natural monetary values: examples are protection of public health, preservation of natural areas and wildlife, improvement in air quality, reduction in urban noise levels. There have been endless efforts to put dollar values on these things and equally endless debates about those efforts. The very propriety of trying to place dollar values on such ultimate goods has been challenged. The problem is built in and it is also inescapable. It has been pointed out many times that every decision involving an environmental problem entails an implicit or explicit judgment about how much we ought to be spending on the goals that it is designed to achieve.

Since there is no generally accepted way of assigning monetary value to many of the benefits that motivate environmental programs, benefit-cost analyses will not be persuasive if their conclusions depend on monetary values selected by the analyst. Instead, estimates of the physical results (for example, number of untimely deaths averted, number of hectares preserved, increase in the level of dissolved oxygen) should stand at the heart of the analyses, so that the reader can judge whether the results are worth the cost according to his or her own scale or values.

The reader will often be helped if the physical results are translated, after they are presented, into monetary equivalents by applying a plausible range of values to those results. Occasionally this translation will show the cost to be so small or so great as to force a decision but the analyst has no right to presume this.

NEGLECT OF UNCERTAINTY. The future is always uncertain, but never more so than when attempting to foresee the benefits and costs of environmental interventions. We know painfully little about the effects of human actions on environmental or ecological conditions, or about the way in which people respond to programs intended to alter their behavior with respect to the environment. Thus, the effects of environmental programs cannot be predicted with any accuracy, and it is pretense to behave otherwise. Yet that is the almost invariable practice. It is standard for benefit-cost analyses to present point estimates of decreases in death rates, increases in net social benefits, and the like, with no indication of how uncertain those estimates are.

No reader, of course, takes those estimates literally, but neither does he have a basis for judging how skeptical he should be about them. It is the responsibility of the analyst to provide such a basis, by indicating the ranges within which there is good reason to believe the true values lie. Lip service is often paid to this dictum in qualifying phrases and footnotes, but that doesn't help the reader much or instill much confidence. The analyst should recognize that these ranges define the limits of his knowledge and should base his reasoning and his interpretation on them rather than on fictitiously precise point estimates. Most important, the tables that summarize the results of an analysis should emphasize the ranges that are believed to include the true values rather than follow the current, misleading practice.

This aspect of benefit-cost analyses has an important link with the implementation problems to be discussed below. The choice of implementation strategy often depends on where the uncertainties lie. For example, one of the critical choices may be whether to rely on economic incentives or to impose direct regulations. Poor information about the private costs of abating emissions will produce less confidence in estimates of the effects of economic incentives than in those of the effects of regulations. On the other hand, if the major uncertainties relate to the beneficial effects of abatement, then the economic and administrative advantages of economic incentives will loom large. Information about the reliability of the various estimates in a benefit-cost analysis is therefore critically important to the design of an implementation plan.

INADEQUATE ATTENTION TO ALTERNATIVES. There are always a number of potential responses to an unsatisfactory environmental condition—in fact, often more than one can conceive of, much less analyze. The possible alternatives differ in the amount of protection they afford and in their cost, side effects, and methods of implementation. Sound planning requires, first, identifying a variety of plausible responses to a problem, though a complete listing is out of the question. Second, it requires that the identified alternatives be assigned a price tag and compared incrementally—that is, that each alternative be compared with the one whose costs are just below its own so that readers can see what improvements are bought with the additional expense.

SUPERFICIAL TREATMENT OF COSTS. So much effort is generally expended in estimating the benefits of environmental protection measures that cost is relatively neglected. But this neglect can be costly. For example, when the use of a dangerous pesticide is banned or restricted, farmers are likely to resort to some other pesticide that may also be dangerous. The dangers imposed by the second pesticide are one of the costs of restricting the first, and they should be taken into account. Again, when tall stacks were recommended as a means of dispersing the sulfur dioxide generated in congested areas, the effects of long-distance transport were not taken into account. We are now worrying about them, a bit late. Many other examples could be cited of adverse but foreseeable side effects that might well have influenced environmental decisions. It is a mistake to assume that the visible expenses of implementation are the only costs of environmental policies.

ALLOWANCE FOR DEGREE OF EFFECTIVENESS. Finally, benefit-cost studies invariably take it for granted that the policies studied will be executed with 100-percent faithfulness by all concerned. Alas, life isn't like that. Emissions, for example, are never abated by quite as much as a plan calls for; endangered species continue to be trapped and gathered despite determined efforts to protect them; and so on. Benefit estimates should not presume 100-percent efficiency in execution; the actuality may be far lower.

Thus far the discussion has concentrated on some technical aspects of planning, which is where the most pervasive and serious shortcomings lie at present. There are naturally, substantive issues as well, at least one of which should be mentioned.

No planner leaves costs, in the narrow dollars-and-cents sense— entirely out of account in environmental planning, although sometimes the United States pretends to do so. However, one implication of these costs is rarely taken into account, perhaps because it is so unpleasant. It is that some countries and communities can afford more protection than others. Many countries adopt American or German environmental standards to avoid the onerous task of establishing their own. The World Health Organization has recommended some uniform environmental standards as guides to individual nations. All such blanket proposals are misguided. In environmental matters, as in education, nutrition, health care, and so on, sound planning requires that aspiration levels be adapted to available resources. In any country, the stricter the environmental standards the greater the resources that will required to attain them, and the less the resources that will be available for other urgent needs such as health care and developmental investments.

The poorer countries of the world confront tragic choices. They cannot afford drinking water standards as high as those to which the industrial countries are accustomed. They cannot afford to close their pristine areas to polluting industries that would introduce technical know-how and productive capital and thereby earn urgently needed foreign exchange. They cannot afford to bar mining companies from unexploited regions. Nor can they afford to impose on those companies antipollution requirements that are as strict and expensive as those in richer industrialized countries. They should always realize that environmental protection measures are financed out of the stomachs of their own people, since the multinationals cannot be made to pay for them. It follows that every country, and particularly the poorer ones, has to choose its own environmental standards, adapted to its needs and resources.

These remarks apply to global pollutants, particularly carbon dioxides, as well as to local and regional pollutants. The richer countries are beginning to cut back on globally polluting emissions. The poorer countries can say, justly, "You fellows have increased the carbon dioxide concentration in the atmosphere by at least 12 percent. Now it's our turn." Is there any really satisfactory response to that? The world can neither stand by complacently while India, China, and the others pour carbon dioxide into the atmosphere, nor can it expect them to desist. A partial response would be for a consortium of the richer countries to subsidize the more expensive fuels and processes that would permit poorer countries to expand their production of energy with small emissions of carbon dioxide than they could otherwise afford.

Implementation Problems

Implementation is concerned with the means for attaining goals. The central difficulty of implementation is that governments cannot abate injuries to the environment directly; they must induce other people to do so. Thus, implementation amounts to the choice and administration of instruments that will induce people to cut back on polluting behavior. It is no less than an application of the art of government to a particular field.

One would not, therefore, expect implementation to be a simple matter, and it is not, though surprisingly little systematic thought has been given to it. The choice of instruments to be used in attaining any given environmental goal depends on many things, including three that will receive special attention here: the nature of the activities that cause the damage, the people who engage in polluting activities, and the array of instruments available to the government. All these variables are different in developing countries than modernized countries, and pollutants that traverse national boundaries cannot be controlled by the ordinary instruments of government at all. These three causes therefore are dealt with separately, beginning with environmental impairments specific to industrialized countries.

INDUSTRIALIZED COUNTRIES. It is easy to take for granted the progress that has been made by the industrialized countries. Drinking water and urban waste ceased being transmitters of infectious diseases three or four generations ago. More recently, the atmospheric concentrations of particles and sulfur oxides have been diminishing in most industrialized countries. But other problems have come to the fore. New harmful substances that conventional treatments do not eliminate are being released into the atmosphere and public waters, and new hazards presented by some conventional pollutants are being recognized. In addition, the hazards of land disposal of urban and industrial wastes are becoming evident, as are the dangers of open-sea disposal.

The implementation problems presented by release of pollutants into the air and public waters are entirely conventional. The new pollutants, like the old ones, are unwanted by-products of industrial activities, with major contributions from automobiles and space heating. Such activities cannot be conducted without generating undesirable waste products. From the generator's point of view, the most efficient way to dispose of the waste is to release it and allow the air or water, as the case may be, to carry it away. This time-honored method of disposal is also efficient from the social point of view to the extent that waste products are harmless when sufficiently diluted. However, since frequently they are not harmless, questions arise: Are the producers acting efficiently from their own point of view, generating too much waste? Are they releasing too much? The benefit-cost analyses already discussed are designed precisely to answer those questions.

If the answer to either of those questions is yes, then the implementation question is how to induce the generator to act in a socially acceptable manner. The answer in any instance depends on circumstances—for example, on who the generator is. We will consider industrial and commercial polluters first.

The instruments applicable to industrial and commercial polluters are classed under the two broad headings of regulations and economic incentives. If regulations are used, firms can be expected to respond grudgingly and to comply in the most economical way possible from their own point of view. This is frequently not the most economical way from the social point of view, because regulations are inherently blunt instruments. They must be designed so that violations can be detected easily and unambiguously, and they cannot make fine distinctions. As a result, regulations typically either require or prohibit some easily observable behavior, which is not likely to be the behavior that abates the pollution most efficiently from anybody's point of view. This is why so many regulations require the installation of equipment for end-of-pipe treatment of waste flows, though it is well known that simply having the equipment on hand does not guarantee that it is used or used effectively, and that end-of-pipe treatment is frequently not the efficient way to abate polluting discharges. The presence of equipment for waste treatment can be checked easily, but its effective use is harder to observe, and the desired result, the reduction of polluting discharges, much harder still. Designing pollution control regulations therefore requires considerable ingenuity and technical expertise to attain an efficient compromise between effectiveness when the regulations are complied with and ease of enforcement. The problems are aggravated by the politics of the regulatory process. The industry that will be subject to the regulation is sure to press for regulations that are economical from its point of view and, if possible, difficult to enforce.

Further, circumstances differ, so that a regulation that is reasonable and effective for some firms in an industry is ineffective or unduly onerous for others. Therefore, a practice called segmenting has developed, in the United States at least. The firms in an industry are divided into classes by size or some other criterion, and different regulations are imposed on each class. Segmenting somewhat reduces the bluntness of the regulatory instrument but still without making it very sharp, and it introduces a new complication, that of defining the classes. There is no need to recount the litigation that ensues when a firm with 102 employees in one month demands to be classified according to the 98 workers it claims it "normally" employs. Even with segmenting, no regulation can be attuned to each firm's circumstances. In addition, segmenting greatly reduces the effectiveness of regulations. The firms that qualify for the most lenient treatment are likely to be the smaller ones, located in the most congested places, where their discharges are most harmful.

Indeed, a pervasive inefficiency of most such regulations is that they are designed to reduce discharges rather than the harm that the discharges inflict. A plant in an isolated location with ample diluting water is required to go to the same expense as one in a densely populated place with only a thin stream to carry its waste away. Several studies, relating to both atmospheric and aquatic discharges, have shown that abatement costs could be reduced by 25 percent or more without reducing the amount of protection afforded by taking such considerations into account, but it is difficult to do so.

The other major class of instruments is economic incentives, which may take the form of subsidies for abatement or fees for discharging or variants on those themes. Let us right away dismiss the subsidy approach. Aside from the administrative problem of establishing the base level of discharge to be used in computing the subsidy, subsidies have the perverse effect of transferring some of the social cost of pollution from the industry that generates it to the general public, thereby encouraging production of the very pollutants they are intended to abate.

We are left then with fees for discharging and with variant schemes such as expensive discharge permits. As compared with regulations, discharge fees are exquisitely sensitive to the special technology of each polluting firm and lead it to reduce its discharges to the optimal extent and to do so in the most efficient possible way. For this reason, economists typically advocate the use of fees and zealously cite studies that show the great savings that could be attained by relying on fees instead of regulations to secure a given level of abatement. Polluting industries generally object to the use of fees, despite the greater discretion they afford, pointing out that fees cost them more than regulations that would achieve the same amount of abatement, because they must bear both the cost of abatement and the cost of the fees on the discharges that remain. This contention is entirely correct. By the same token, fees, more than regulations, tend to discourage firms from entering the industry, thereby making it more concentrated than is socially desirable. The trouble is that, for the reasons already recited, there are no regulations that will do the same job.

The advocacy of fees has been seriously marred by the fact that it is generally based on an unfair comparison. Fees levied on discharges are compared with regulations designed to be monitored easily. If the regulations were imposed directly on discharges, leaving the firms free to use their own discretion in deciding how to abate them, they would attain virtually the same level of economic efficiency as fees. It is overlooked that control by fees presents the same monitoring problem as control by regulation. A fee levied on operating without a prescribed end-of-pipe treatment plant is little more efficient than a regulation requiring such a plant. The ostensible difference in efficency arises from a difference in the point at which the control is presumed to operate.

Practical experience with fees is limited, but such experience as there is shows them to be powerfully effective. Much of that experience relates to liquid discharges. Some of it is inadvertent, as when treatment charges are levied on waste delivered to public treatment facilities. Invariably it is surprising to see the alacrity with which industries reduce the amounts of pollutants they discharge once a fee is levied that makes abatement worth their while.

What has been said here far from exhausts the points that have been raised in the continuing debate over economic inducements versus regulatory controls. But enough has been said to indicate that the difference does not appear to be as vast or as vital as the contending parties often maintain. On balance, there is some advantage in the use of fees, largely because they are easier to administer and because direct monitoring of discharges seems to be almost always feasible, whichever approach is taken, by using carefully designed sampling methods.

Discharge fees are not able to control discharges by individuals operating automobiles or home heating plants or garbage disposers, all of them significant sources of pollution. There are too many individuals, all too long accustomed to unrestricted discharge of their wastes. The only feasible control here lies in the equipment used. This is the strategy used in controlling automobile exhausts, and it is sound. It can be implemented either by direct regulation or by imposing license fees on equipment that does not meet specified discharge standards. The only basis for choice appears to be administrative convenience.

The really difficult problems relate to some quite different forms of pollution that were, surprisingly, overlooked in the early days of concern for environmental protection. They are the disposal of solid wastes and of toxic and otherwise hazardous wastes. Solid wastes traditionally were deposited in municipal or industrial dumps, which were unsightly but thought to be otherwise innocuous. Dangerous substances used to be generated in relatively small volumes and were dealt with ad hoc, often simply by making the disposer liable for any damages that might result. Altogether, the hazards imposed by these forms of waste were largely unrecognized until recently.

The industrial nations now realize that things are already pretty far out of hand. Many substances deposited in sanitary landfills have been leached into groundwater. In addition, in congested areas, many of the established landfills are reaching capacity, and there are few if any available sites for new ones. Chemicals too toxic to be discharged into waterways were formerly also deposited in dumps or, illegally, along roadsides. That is now recognized as an extremely hazardous practice, but it continues.

These problems relate to the law of the conservation of matter, hazardous or not; the waste has to go somewhere, and there does not seem to be any place to put it. Toxic chemicals present an additional problem. They frequently are generated in a dilute, but insufficiently dilute, mixture along with harmless substances. Removing them from the mixture so that they can be handled with the care they require turns out to be technically difficult as well as expensive. Generators would naturally much prefer just to throw the whole mixture away.

I regard the disposal of solid wastes and toxic substances as the most urgent environmental problem now confronting the industrial nations, but I have no tidy solutions. A good deal can be accomplished by not throwing so much away: by making things more durable, using less elaborate packaging, and recycling waste materials. Some incentive could be provided by increasing the charges for disposal and making them proportional to the volume of waste, but unfortunately this also provides an incentive for illegal disposal. Any tight system for controlling waste disposal would require elaborate record keeping. This is not practical for household and commercial waste and is difficult for the toxic by-products of industry because of the problem of estimating the amount that was generated. So I have to conclude lamely that a solution, or a battery of solutions, will have to be sought. There is opportunity for a number of worthy research projects.

DEVELOPING COUNTRIES. It is an illusion to think that environmental problems afflict only rich countries. On the contrary, they are more severe and more ominous in poor countries. Water is no longer a carrier of infectious disease in the industrial countries, but that is hardly true of many of the poor ones. The air in Cairo and Mexico City is dirtier than any rich country would tolerate. And the poor countries suffer from many environmental threats that are peculiar to themselves. To be sure, it would be inappropriate for poor countries to aspire to the environmental standards of richer countries—poverty means doing without. But hardly any country is so poor that it has to endure waterborne epidemics, pandemic intestinal worms, or massive soil erosion.

An important aspect of both planning and implementation in developing countries is that the instruments available for implementing plans are much weaker than those in industrialized nations. The civil service is not of the same quality, statistical and other records are scanty and unreliable, and communication is slow and difficult. In many developing countries, the arm of the central government does not extend effectively much beyond the limits of the major cities, and civil unrest is not far away. Major capital investments have to be financed from external sources, meaning that policies and plans are not entirely under the government's control.

These limitations dictate a good deal of modesty. Plans must be simple to understand and administer. Programs for implementation must be designed so that misunderstanding and negligence are easily detected. And, whatever precautions are taken, only partial effectiveness can be expected. Most important, however many the urgent needs, the administrative apparatus must not be stretched too thin. Only a few of the urgent problems in a few localities can be handled at any one time. The rest will have to wait, and it is small comfort to remark that the people are used to waiting.

The typical developing country contains both a modern and a traditional sector. The issues presented by the modern sector are much like those encountered in the industrial countries, though, as just noted, the instruments available are far less adequate. The issues presented by the traditional sector are entirely different, since this sector consists largely of farmers plus some artisans and small merchants, none far from subsistence level. These people are very hard on their environment; they have no choice. They have to cultivate every accessible bit of land, gather every available twig of wood, poach all the game they can, dispose of wastes in any way they can. Neither regulations nor taxes can reach them, since folkways are stronger than "law-ways," and need is stronger than either. These problems have already been referred to in the context of natural resource management, and the same remarks apply here.

The key to controlling environmentally harmful activities in the traditional sector is to provide effective alternatives and simultaneously to provide economic incentives to the community, rather than to the individual, to protect and restore the environment. Only then will governmentally imposed penalties, either charges or legal sanctions, have any chance of being effective. It is important to enlist the cooperation of community leaders because only they, and not the formal government apparatus, are in a position to influence and monitor the behavior of the community's members.

I do not minimize this task or the financial and administrative resources required to perform it. That is why I said earlier that the central government's plans have to be very selective, to the neglect of many urgent problems. It is better to succeed at a few enterprises than to make passing attempts at many.

INTERNATIONAL AND GLOBAL PROBLEMS. We are ascending the ladder of difficulty. Pollution that crosses national boundaries is the most difficult of all to control. There are no instruments available and there would be no one to wield them if there were. The matter was discussed, naturally, at the lengthy Law of the Sea Conference, and Part XII of the draft convention is devoted to it. According to this, the signatory states accept the obligation to protect and preserve the marine environment; undertake to pass laws and enter treaties designed to minimize the release of harmful pollutants into international waters by their nationals; agree to cooperate in monitoring the marine environment, to promote research on marine phenomena, to publish findings of the research, and so on. No agreement seems to have been reached on any specific problem, and no organ was established to keep track of performance with respect to these provisions. This upshot is symptomatic. International pollution is controlled only by the consciences of the individual nations and the pressures that nations can exert on their neighbors.

Neighborly pressures are effective up to a point. The United States has agreed to limit the amount of salt introduced into the Rio Grande and is negotiating with Canada over the transport of sulfates and sulfur oxides from the Midwest to eastern Canada. In Europe, West Germany has accepted responsibility for controlling the quality of the Rhine where it enters the Netherlands. There are many other examples. These bilateral agreements fail, however, where the responsibilities and the damages are more difficult.

The two most ominous current problems of this sort are the increasing concentration of atmospheric carbon dioxide and the depletion of the ozone layer. There appears to be no way to deal with either of these problems in the absence of a competent international organization or authority. The experience with the Law of the Sea Conference and at the Stockholm Conference on Environmental Problems underscores the difficulty of establishing any such institution, given deep-seated conflicts of interest. Nothing can be done until the urgency of the problem is appreciated by all or nearly all the nations that contribute to it. Moreover, these global environmental problems appear to result from insidious, slow-acting, and irreversible processes. To be effective, correctives have to be initiated before severe damage is visible to the naked eye.

The first step, then, toward averting irremediable damage to the global environment is to obtain persuasive indications of impending impairments before they occur. Such indications can come only from a system for monitoring the state of the world environment, operated by an authoritative and widely respected organization. There is no such system at present, not even on the part of the United Nations Environment Programme, the obvious agency for the undertaking. In 1986 the World Resources Institute, in cooperation with the International Institute for Environment and Development, is planning to initiate annual reports on the state of the environment. This will be an important beginning, but whether those organizations will have the resources needed to maintain surveillance over the world's environment remains uncertain.

Assuming that a global monitoring system detects a serious hazard, the second step is to do something about it. Corrective measures will undoubtedly require sacrifices and self-denials on the part of many nations, which will not be forthcoming until they, individually, see themselves threatened. Under such circumstances, nations are capable of great sacrifices for a common goal, as countless military alliances have demonstrated.

Under such pressure, then, I can see the possibility of an alliance for global protection. To operate, such an alliance would first have to ascertain the highest level of global emissions or other insults that the environment can tolerate without crippling damage. Then it would have to determine the total national emissions implied by reasonable plans for economic growth. To reconcile these two figures would undoubtedly require reducing the growth aspirations of selected nations, allowing for higher growth rates in developing countries than in the developed nations.

Thus, national quotas for harmful emissions could be established. Compliance could be monitored as part of the continuing surveillance of the global environment, and infractions punished by imposing discouragingly heavy fines on nations that exceed their quotas. The fines could be enforced, if need be, by liens on the violators' property within the territories of other members of the alliance. The alliance might also make grants-in-aid to selected developing countries to help them achieve their growth rates within the constraints imposed by the quotas. Flexibility could be introduced by permitting nations to sell or donate portions of their quotas to one another. All this, I am persuaded, can be achieved if the peoples of the world are really convinced that they face a common danger and that the required sacrifices are being shared equitably. But not otherwise.

CHAPTER FIVE

Environmental Ethics and Global Imperatives
KRISTIN SHRADER-FRECHETTE

In 1969, U Thant, secretary-general of the United Nations, warned that inhabitants of the world "have perhaps ten years left" to improve the human environment. If environmental problems are not addressed soon, he said, then they will have reached such staggering proportions that they "will be beyond our capacity to control."

Although the task of improving the environment is an urgent one, it does not lend itself to short-term solutions or quick technological fixes. Long-term global policies, if they are to be successful, require long-term changes in perceptions. If our global physical environment is not to be degraded, then we must alter our conceptual environment. And in altering our conceptual environment, ethics, or moral philosophy, plays a major role. This is because ethics helps determine the decisions we make. The way people answer ethical questions affects the way they live their lives. To a great degree, ethics determines, for example, whether to have an abortion, invest in a weapons-producing company, or become a vegetarian. For this reason, the worst environmental pollution is perhaps mind pollution, and the rarest global resources are well-thought-out ethical principles.

If a healthy conceptual and ethical environment is a necessary condition for a healthy physical environment, then one way to help the planet would be to analyze, and if necessary amend, the various value systems undergirding policies relevant to human and environmental well-being. Such analysis would reveal that we often pay lip service to ethical values, such as equal opportunity, but follow policies that logically presuppose denial of those same values, or that we laud particular ethical goals but sanction decisions that preclude achievement of those goals.

The purpose of this essay is twofold: first, to lay out the major ethical presuppositions and policy consequences of alternative positions in a number of questions of environmental ethics, and second, to provide brief arguments for some of those positions. The three major ethical issues discussed are each at the root of controversy over a variety of problems regarding global environmental policy. These issues are (1) the ethics of distribution and whether goods should be distributed on the basis of egalitarian, utilitarian, or libertarian value schemes; (2) the locus of planetary values, and whether individual freedom should take precedence over group welfare, or vice-versa; and (3) the frame of reference from which one decides questions of global environmental policy, and whether it should be anthropocentric or ecocentric.

THE ETHICS OF DISTRIBUTION

Many of our most pressing environmental problems, especially those of resource allocation and depletion, concern how we should cut the world pie, both among and within generations. Should we distribute planetary resources and environmental well-being according to principles of, for example, equality, entitlement, or utility? Do members of future generations and citizens of Third World countries deserve equal opportunity to compete for the goods of the earth—for example, land, coal, oil? Or, should we say that the present generation is entitled to certain resources, by virtue of property rights and that they can use them as they wish, regardless of the needs of future generations and today's poor? Or, finally, should resources be allocated so as to maximize utility, regardless of whether the alleged rights of various minorities are violated? Whether one considers issues such as immigration policy or the supposed duty to feed the indigent who cannot feed themselves or the alleged obligation not to impose on future generations any pollution-induced health risks greater than those imposed at present, the primary ethical question is how we should distribute environmental quality and natural resources.

A Case Study: Land and Resource Distribution

According to a recent US government-funded land ownership study, Appalachia is in many ways like a captive colony ruled by powerful coal interests. For example, 80 percent of the mineral hectares and 75 percent of the surface hectares in the study are owned by absentee landlords. Most of these lands and minerals are concentrated in the hands of only a few corporations. Of the top fifty private owners, forty-six are corporations.[1] The sixty government-funded researchers, who worked for two years on the study, drew a number of startling conclusions:

1. That the greater the concentration of land and mineral wealth in the hands of a few, and the greater the degree of absentee ownership, the less money generated by coal production remains in the counties giving up their resource wealth.
2. That little land is owned by, or accessible to, local people.
3. That because of the above, many ills plague Appalachia: inadequate local tax revenues and services, an absence of economic development and diversified job opportunities, losses of agricultural lands, insufficient housing, a lack of locally controlled capital, and a rate of out-migration proportional both to corporate ownership and to concentration of land and mineral wealth in the hands of a few.[2]

They argued that the concentrated absentee ownership of mineral-rich land was the cause of virtually all the social and economic ills besetting Appalachia, and that land reform was a necessary, although not a sufficient, condition for correcting these ills.[3]

If the researchers are correct, both about the causes of Appalachian ills and about at least one necessary remedy, land reform, then there are important ethical grounds for limiting the property rights of Appalachia's corporate absentee landlords. But according to libertarians, those who believe that distribution should be based on entitlement, these property rights should not be limited, except in cases in which fraud was involved in the acquisition of property and transfer. Even if one assumes that no fraud was involved, however, a case can be made for land reform and for a nonlibertarian distribution of Appalachian property. Making such a case requires accepting two claims of the authors of the study. Consider the following argument:

1. Concentrated absentee ownership of Appalachian coal land leads to a concentration of political, legal, and economic power in the hands of the owners.
2. Such concentrated political, legal, and economic power limits the voluntariness of land and other transactions between large owners (holders of power) and others.[4]
3. Apart from legitimate reparation or punishment, whenever so-

cial institutions interfere with the voluntarism of transactions, they thereby limit the background conditions necessary for procedural justice.

4. Whatever restricts procedural justice should be avoided.
5. Concentrated absentee ownership of Appalachian coal land should therefore be avoided.
6. But to avoid such ownership is to specify an egalitarian, rather than a libertarian or utilitarian, ethic of distribution.

Although there is not space here to defend this argument properly, several brief considerations will at least render it plausible. Premises (1) and (2) depend on the view that monopolies tend to reduce the freedom of market transactions, and that property generates inequality, which menaces liberty. Land economists, in particular, have explicitly noted how concentration of rural land in the hands of a few owners leads to monopsony (owners' control of wages), the absence of land for development, the lack of a diversified economy, and the absence of local capital.[5] These factors in turn mean that if persons without comparable resources and the concomitant power engage in economic transactions with those having land and power, then often the transactions cannot be said to be wholly voluntary. And voluntarism, like the existence of a free, competitive market, is a background condition for procedural justice.[6] This means that to provide conditions for procedural justice, as a consistent libertarian is bound to do, is to provide conditions for voluntary transactions. But if the Appalachian researchers are correct, to provide conditions for voluntary transactions, one needs to limit concentrations of land whenever failure to do so would be at least partially responsible for limiting voluntarism. To limit concentrations of Appalachian land, however, is to prescribe a nonlibertarian, egalitarian principle. Hence, libertarians cannot consistently claim both that they support the requirements of procedural justice and that it is unethical to subscribe to principles of egalitarian justice.

Applying the tenets of this Appalachian example to problems of planetary pie slicing, it is reasonable to argue that, whenever concentrations of wealth, natural resources, or environmental quality are distributed in such a way as to limit the voluntarism of individual or global transactions, then to provide conditions for greater procedural justice or more fairness in the transactions, the land must be redistributed. At root, this argument consists of a rationale for generating the conditions necessary for equal opportunity and fair play. It explains a very puzzling insight of Gandhi, who claimed that, "Whenever I live in a situation where others are in need. . .whether or not I am responsible for it, I have become a thief."[7] A hard saying? Yes. But perhaps he is right, especially if the background conditions for procedurally just exchanges are taken into account. If someone else's need is so great that he is not free, in some minimal sense, in the choices he makes, then the transactions in which he takes part may not be procedurally just. But suppose I continue to live prosperously and to be involved in procedurally unjust transactions with another person. If I do not attempt to create the background conditions for just exchanges, I might accurately be termed a thief, relative to the disadvantaged person. Likewise, if industrialized countries continue to live prosperously and to be involved in procedurally unjust transactions with Third World countries, and if they do not attempt to create the background conditions for just exchanges, then, as countries, they are thieves.

Distribution: Egalitarian, Utilitarian, or Libertarian?

As the Appalachian example reveals, there are powerful arguments for accepting egalitarian ethics for distribution of global resources and environmental well-being. The predominant practice of most countries, however, appears to be to follow either libertarian or utilitarian ethics of distribution.

Put most generally, the egalitarian position is that all human beings, within and among different generations and countries, share a social contract according to which all are to be treated as morally equal.[8] There are at least two reasons for believing that all humans share a social contract. First, they possess the two essential characteristics of moral personality: a capacity for an effective sense of justice and a capacity to form, amend, and pursue a conception of what is good.[9] Second, individuals and national societies are not self-sufficient but exist within some scheme of social cooperation.[10] Because all humans have moral personalities and exist within schemes of social cooperation, so the argument goes, they should all be accorded equal treatment, including equal opportunity, as moral persons.[11]

In response to the kind of contractarian-egalitarian argument just sketched, a utilitarian is likely to adopt one or more of several strategies.[12] He might argue, for example, that while he does not wish to see vast numbers of the present poor starve to death, and while it is not desirable for current generations to impose their carcinogenic,

mutagenic, and teratogenic pollution on future generations, nevertheless, it does not make sense to adopt a principle of equal opportunity
or equal treatment with respect to all persons of all nations and all
generations. This is because a utilitarian typically believes that more
human suffering is caused by following principles of equal treatment
and equal opportunity than by attempting to maximize the well-being
of all. He also maintains that the right to equal treatment and equal
opportunity is not absolute because, if it were, it might delay social
improvement.[13] Hence, on utilitarian principles, he might deny the
alleged right to equal treatment to great numbers of the present poor
on the grounds that ignoring their welfare will enable society to
achieve greater social improvement over the long term. A central presupposition of this view is that there are ethical grounds for
sacrificing the welfare of significant numbers of human beings for the
sake of the rest; hence there can be no in-principle obligation to fulfill
alleged mandates of equal treatment.

Although libertarians would agree that there is no ethical basis
for principles of inter- and intra-generational equity requiring equal
treatment of all persons, their reasons for denying such principles are
quite different from those of utilitarians. Unlike utilitarians and egalitarians, libertarians would claim that the key question posed by problems of resource allocation is not what particular distributions should
achieve and whether they should provide equal treatment or optimal
social improvement. Rather, the key issue is whether someone is entitled to a particular distribution quite apart from whether that distribution promotes equality or social improvement. For them a distribution
is just, not if it meets some alleged social or individual need, but if it
arises from another just distribution by legitimate means—for example, legal entitlement.[14] In other words, for libertarians it is ethically
sufficient that a distribution be procedurally fair—that is, accomplished without force, fraud, theft, or enslavement—in terms of the
historical conditions by which it came about. If it is procedurally fair,
then the precise nature of the resulting distribution or end state, and
whether it meets alleged social needs or goals, is irrelevant. Hence, according to this view, there is no moral imperative to provide equal
treatment, either to the present poor who seek a redistribution of planetary resources, or to the members of future generations, unless present holdings were acquired by force, fraud, theft, or enslavement.
And, of course, the question of the circumstances of acquisition are
primarily a matter for factual, not ethical, determination.

Grounds for Accepting Egalitarianism

Some of the main differences among these three positions come down to their respective concepts of individual rights, community, and procedural (versus substantive) justice. Egalitarians and libertarians, for example, are willing, in principle, to speak of individual, inalienable human rights, whereas utilitarians, in principle, are not. As a consequence, acceptance of a utilitarian scheme (for global and intergenerational distribution of resources and environmental well-being) entails the possibility that the resulting allocations will be matters of mere expediency. Even utilitarians admit that a consequence of accepting their view is that every individual would not be protected, even in principle, from capricious or expedient denials of justice.[15] This is because utilitarians are bound to maximize the happiness of humankind as a whole, which means ignoring alleged rights, especially of minorities, whenever the latter stand in the way of achieving this goal. For my part, this consequence alone is sufficient grounds for rejecting utilitarian ethics. I take it as given that there is a moral imperative to recognize individual human rights, especially those of minorities, even when it is not convenient to do so. For those who do not share this assumption about individual rights, however, utilitarian distribution schemes are viable options.

If we reject utilitarianism on the grounds that it allows for violations of minority rights, then, we are left with egalitarianism and libertarianism. One of the most basic presuppositions separating proponents of these two ethical schemes is that libertarians do not assume that human beings are essentially social and community-oriented beings, whereas most egalitarians take human beings' social and communal nature and their roles in some sort of social contract for granted. Because libertarians have an essentially individualistic view of the moral person, it is not surprising that they deny the existence of distributive principles based on the needs or interests of others. In fact, without some sort of presupposition as to the essentially social nature of human beings, one could not consistently argue that a particular end-state distribution was desirable. Hence, given their individualistic presuppositions, it is perfectly consistent for libertarians to make justice simply a matter of guaranteeing that transactions among individuals are nonfraudulent and not imposed by force.

Apart from consistency, however, the obvious question is whether this ethical assumption is correct. Are human beings not essentially social? Are they not members, by virtue of their common humanity, of a single global and intergenerational community? Again, although there is no space to defend the claim here, it seems obvious that we are essentially social and communal, and that we need each other both physically and spiritually if we are to achieve the full wealth of what it is to be human. Hence, at the level of their ethical presuppositions, it makes sense to reject utilitarian distributions because they allow for violations of minority rights and to reject libertarian distributions because they presuppose a radically individualistic conception of the human person. Because egalitarian distributions fall victim to neither of these errors, they are, in principle, more justifiable.

Problems with Egalitarianism

One of the main problems with egalitarianism, and with the egalitarian argument presented in the Appalachian case study, of course, is that it is often difficult to specify in a concrete case when the requisite conditions for equality and procedurally just transactions have been met. The important fact about the Appalachian argument, however, is that it is not socialistic. It does not require that persons receive the same share, or the amount that they need, but only that distributions be such as to ensure a free, open, competitive market and voluntary economic exchanges. Admittedly it is difficult to deterine when these conditions for voluntarism have been met and what sort of circumstances might enable them to be met. But even a cursory look at the current global distributions of resources and environmental quality and at the ways in which members of present-day generations (through resource depletion and pollution) have preempted the choices of future generations suggests that much is askew, and that changes must be made in distribution patterns if the conditions for procedural justice are to be met.

One of the main objections to such a radical call for redistribution of planetary resources according to egalitarian considerations is that it is unrealistic. It might be claimed that contractarian-egalitarian views of ethics, grounded on a communitarian conception of the moral personality, are plausible only as part of a theory of global justice. Such a theory would provide for institutions at the international level that would compensate for uneven distribution of natural and cultural resources among people and states.[16] Since there is no theory of global justice that provides for such institutions, goes the objection, then more egalitarian planetary pie slicing cannot be required until it can be achieved institutionally.

The answer to this objection, however, is that although one may not at present have the necessary institutions to redistribute global resources, one nevertheless is bound to help create the background conditions and institutions necessary for such a redistribution. The extent to which one is "bound," however, admittedly invites considerable argument. The precise nature and degree of one's obligations to help create institutions necessary for more equitable distributions need to be established by careful ethical analysis.

There is at least one way to approach this problem, though, and to respond to the person who quite reasonably protests, "Look, I have my own life to lead and my own children to raise, and I ought to be free of the demand that I promote egalitarian, contractual relations of distribution and the necessary conditions for such distributions."[17] In other words, there is a reasonable way to respond to the person who claims, quite correctly, that he cannot possibly be successful at, much less be obliged to be a hero at, providing equal opportunity and promoting background conditions for procedural justice. Clearly there is an upper bound to what can be said to be required of persons and nations striving for more egalitarian planetary relations. What conditions might describe this upper bound? First, individuals clearly have a right to pursue their own commitments, apart from the sacrifices that appear to be demanded by impersonal global morality. Obviously, however, to be a consistent egalitarian, one should not forgo a chance to do great good for others merely to avoid a trifling sacrifice for others.[18] Likewise, a nation should not forgo a chance to do great good for the people of other nations merely to avoid a trifling sacrifice for itself. Second, individual sacrifices appear to become more burdensome and hence less of a moral imperative when they set us, either individually or as nations, at a disadvantage relative to others who have sacrificed less. Conversely, individual sacrifices appear to become less burdensome and more of a moral imperative when they set us at no great disadvantage relative to others who have sacrificed less.

Shue's distinction between the scope and the magnitude of justice also provides some clues as to the upper bounds on the costs required to achieve the distributions necessary for procedurally just transactions.[19] With respect to scope, everyone may have rights and duties grounded in global justice, because we may all be said to share a social contract within which these rights and duties may be specified. This does not mean, however, that the magnitude of the duties imposed is the same for all of us. A population having some specific duty, for example, is likely to be much smaller than a population bearing the correlative right, for example, to free, open, competitive transactions. This means in turn that just because one claims that principles of justice are global rather than national in scope, one is not obliged by virtue of that admission to claim that the magnitude of one's obligations is any greater. Why not?

The main reason why the magnitude of one's duties to reallocate resources does not necessarily increase merely because the scope increases (that is, because the number of persons who have rights to such allocations increases) is that there are a number of considerations that limit one's obligations to bring about redistributions. These considerations likewise make egalitarian global ethics more practical and more capable of realization. One such limiting condition, in addition to the two already mentioned, is that those with duties to transfer wealth, natural resources (such as land), or environmental quality, have no less right to these things than that guaranteed by the minimum rights of those to whom transfers are to be made. This principle is obvious on the grounds of consistency. A fourth limiting condition is that justice should require only what normal, nonheroic persons are capable of being convinced that they should do. In other words, it should be possible to convince persons with normal self-interest that they should act in accordance with the authentic demands of justice; if at least some persons (having normal self-interest) cannot be so convinced, then it is questionable whether the proposed standard of justice is legitimate. This is because one is bound to do only what it is possible to do. In other words, our planetary pie slicing must satisfy principles acceptable to humans, not angels.

A fifth limit on the costs that can be demanded in order to achieve the distributions necessary for procedurally just transactions is also a function of the degree of coercion required to bring about redistribution. Redistribution requiring either bloody revolution or totalitarian enforcement is highly questionable, primarily because of the cost in both lives and civil liberties. "Sometimes an unbloody half loaf is better than a bloody loaf."[20]

Two Principles to Guide Egalitarian Policymaking

In addition to the objection that egalitarian global ethics unrealistically requires humans to live as martyrs and to bear great costs imposed by the alleged demands of justice, another likely complaint is that there are no clear and precise criteria for specifying what is required in an egalitarian framework. Admittedly this is a powerful objection. There is no algorithm for how to be moral in all situations. If there were, our world would be far less troubled by conflicts of rights and arguments over what might be done to achieve the greatest good in a particular situation. Unless we are unrelenting and insecure dogmatists, our moral judgments must require just that—judgment, based on philosophical analysis. The discussion so far has been an attempt to lay out some of the more compelling arguments for egalitarian schemes, some of the more important necessary conditions for arriving at an ethical redistribution, and five significant limits on the costs that can be demanded in order to achieve distributions necessary for procedurally just interactions. One necessary condition is that the costs of enforcement not significantly outweigh the benefits of redistribution, but, of course, implementing this necessary condition itself requires both ethical analysis and value judgments.

Two other important criteria for assessing obligations with regard to planetary redistribution are what may be called the principle of prima facie egalitarianism and the principle of everyone's advantage. The point of the first principle is to put the burden of proof on the person who wishes to discriminate with respect to equal opportunity. The principle is simply that, in the absence of arguments to the contrary, one should assume that providing equal opportunity to compete for natural resources and environmental quality is required of individuals and of nations. There are at least four reasons why the presupposition should be in favor of equal opportunity:

1. All human beings have the same capacity for a happy life.[21]
2. Free, informed, rational people would agree to the principle.[22]
3. It provides the basic justification for other important concepts of ethics and is a presupposition of all schemes involving justice, fairness, rights, and autonomy.[23]
4. Equality of treatment is presupposed by the idea of law; law itself embodies an ideal of the same treatment for persons similarly situated and an ideal of equal opportunity for all persons willing and eligible to compete for certain goods.[24]

Although a clear line between relevant and irrelevant reasons for discriminating between equal treatment and equal opportunity is not evident in every case, the principle of prima facie egalitarianism requires that, unless there are contraindications one should not discriminate. In deciding whether a particular argument is a sufficient basis for discrimination, at least one consideration comes to mind. This is the principle of everyone's advantage, the principle that providing unequal opportunity or unequal treatment among persons is justified only if the discrimination works to the advantage of everyone.[25] (This principle is not equivalent to the Pareto criterion, since the word *advantage* is not employed here in a purely economic sense.[26]) For example, one might justify reverse discrimination in favor of blacks on the grounds that in certain instances it works to the advantage of everyone, including whites. Advantages might include more integration of the races and greater understanding and social cohesion as a result.

Admittedly, drawing the conclusion that it would be to everyone's advantage to discriminate in a particular manner rests on a chain of tenuous causal inferences. In spite of the obvious practical difficulties in judging whether a particular instance of discrimination will contribute to everyone's advantage, this principle appears to be the most promising theoretical candidate for an ethical criterion to determine acceptable discrimination. This is because almost any other principle would be open to the charge that it sanctioned using some people as a means to the ends of others.[27]

Because human beings may not be used as a means to some end, a principle that we take to be self-evident, fulfilling the principle of everyone's advantage is a necessary condition for justifying discrimination against various particular persons, all of whom are protected by a contractarian-egalitarian ethical scheme. It is also a sufficient condition, since presumably any legitimate grounds for opposing discrimination (for example, the existence of certain rights) would be equivalent to the claim that the discrimination did not serve the authentic advantage of everyone.

Now that we have specified a necessary and sufficient condition for justifying discrimination with respect to equal treatment and guaranteeing equal opportunity, it is obvious that, although there are individual rights to equal treatment, these rights are not absolute. But if individal rights to equal treatment and to equal opportunity are not absolute, then it is reasonable to ask whether there are also limits on other alleged individual, inalienable rights, such as the right to determine the number and spacing of one's children or the right to use whatever natural resources and environmental quality one is capable of purchasing.

THE LOCUS OF CONTROL: INDIVIDUAL AUTONOMY
VERSUS GOVERNMENT COERCION

The question of limits on individual freedom and autonomy raises a whole host of issues in environmental ethics. Does government have the right to ration or to limit use of natural resources, thereby limiting individual freedom to obtain these goods in otherwise morally acceptable ways? Do individuals have the right not to have cancer inflicted on them, or does government have the right to sanction dangerous levels of polluting emissions and effluents on the grounds that further industrial controls are not cost-effective? Who has the right to control the number and spacing of children, the state or the potential parents? In the name of the common good, does the government have the right to control pollution, even when there are no demonstrable negative effects on the persons or property of other citizens? Does government have the right to institute land-use controls and other allegedly environmentally desirable actions if the actions limit property rights? Whether about population, pollution, use of natural resources, planning, or zoning, each of these issues focuses on the problem of control. Does the individual have the right to reproductive freedom or to autonomy in the use of his property, for example, or does the state, following its mandate to protect the common good, have the right to control population, property rights, and uses of natural resources?

A Case Study: Pollution Control

Suppose a person claims that he has an absolute right not to be inflicted with cancer.[28] (This can easily be argued on the grounds both that persons have a right to informed control over the conditions that might lead to their incurring serious harm, and that there is a general absolute prohibition against killing innocent people, especially when the harm comes about as an unintended but foreseeable and controllable effect of what someone else does.) Suppose, further, that he lives next door to company X, and that the company allows vinyl chloride emissions from its stacks to pollute the air surrounding the plant and to increase nearby residents' chances of contracting cancer of the liver and other organs. Suppose, finally, that the person contends that his right not to be inflicted with cancer overrides the company's right to use its property as it pleases. The issue here is indeed one of individual autonomy (the company's right to its property) versus government control, since presumably the government has determined that the company's vinyl chloride emissions are within acceptable limits, or "as low as is practicable," and in conformity with government standards for public exposure to that carcinogen. Does the government have the right to say that, for the sake of the public good, some small number of cancers induced by company X are acceptable? Does the state have the primary right to control levels of pollution, or do individuals have the right to say that no risk, however small, should be imposed on them without at least their consent and their being compensated? The answer to this question lies in the fact that one's right to control something ends where another person's right begins. In the case of the person exposed to vinyl chloride emissions, the relevant observation is that the company's right to do what it wishes with its property ends where the individual's strong, or absolute, rights begin. What morally relevant considerations might reveal where one right ends and another begins?

Presupposition in Favor of Rights of the Individual

One morally relevant consideration is whether the two rights in conflict are rights of the same degree of importance. Most people would probably say that the right of an innocent person not to be killed by cancer from an industrial smokestack is more important than the company's right to use its property as it wishes. They would argue that the right of an innocent person not be killed is a strong, or absolute, right, whereas the right to use one's property however one chooses is only a weak right.[29] However, it is not so simple.

A second morally relevant consideration is the degree of probability associated with the respective harms against which the two rights are alleged to serve as protection. The right of an innocent person not to be killed protects against a cancer risk. Although statistically, casualties will result from any above-threshold exposure to a carcinogen, the risk to different persons is a function of many factors such as their medical history, genetic makeup, and health habits. Hence, especially with current government pollution standards, a given individual can never know whether he will contract cancer because of his exposure to particular industrial emissions. The industry, on the other hand, may know with certainty that if it is forced to control its emissions further, it will sustain great losses. We would then have a situation in which we were weighing whether it is more important to give primacy to a strong right (not to be killed) so as to avoid a possible evil (contracting cancer) or to give primacy to a weak right (to one's property) so as to avoid a certain evil (property losses).[30] Although the admittedly low probability of inflicting cancer makes resolution of this case more problematic, it still seems that the presupposition should be with the individual and his right not to have his life put at risk, for several reasons. First, the right of the innocent not to be killed is a strong right, one not subject to revocation on purely utilitarian grounds, whereas property rights are only weak rights, which are subject to limitation on such grounds. Even if an opponent maintained that the strong right not to be killed is inapplicable here because only a probability of death is at issue, nevertheless it can be argued that there is another strong right involved. This is the right to informed control (so far as is possible) over the conditions relevant to one's incurring serious harm. This is a strong right for at least three reasons. First, its recognition is essential to personal autonomy. Second, it is necessary for one's well-being. Third, its recognition is required as an effective guarantee of the right not to be killed, since it is often impossible to tell (because of the probabilities and synergisms involved) when allegedly insignificant emissions are enough to cause death.

A second reason why the presupposition should be with the individual rather than the property owner is that although the latter may be causally and morally responsible for a neighbor's cancer, the neighbor is neither causally nor morally responsible for the alleged ill effects of stricter pollution controls. In other words, even if it is alleged that the company cannot afford stricter controls for vinyl chloride emissions, and that stricter controls would limit the company's profits and cause numerous workers to lose their jobs, thereby jeopardizing their family stability, the pollution victim is not responsible for these consequences. Hence, it should not be argued, on some utilitarian calculation, that it would be preferable to allow the carcinogenic emissions so as to preserve the workers' jobs. Such an argument is invalid because of the principle of intervening action: "Whenever there is a causal connection between some person A's doing some action X and some other person C's incurring a certain harm Z, this causal connection is 'negatived' or removed if, between X and Z, there intervenes some other action Y of some person B who knows the relevant circumstances of his action and who intends to produce Z or who produces Z through recklessness."[31] In other words, since X is not sufficient to cause the harm Z, and only another action Y is sufficient, then there is no causal connection between X and Z, and hence the agent A is not responsible for the harm Z. In the vinyl chloride case, two workers lost their jobs because of stricter pollution controls, then it follows from the principle of intervening action that it is not the person requesting pollution controls, the victim of the vinyl chloride emissions, who is morally and causally responsible for the loss of jobs in company X. Perhaps this responsibility lies instead with the plant-owners, who did not streamline their operation in other cost-effective ways, or with stockholders who were unwilling to take a lower profit margin to save jobs. Either of these groups could be held causally and morally responsible for the intervening action resulting in the loss of jobs. Hence, it is not correct to argue that the right of government to promote the common good (by preventing job losses) supersedes the right of the individual not to be inflicted with cancer, if there is no causal or moral connection between recognition of the individual right and the job losses.

Amenity Rights

Another morally relevant consideration in the conflict between the autonomy of the property owner (the company) and the governmental duty to protect the public against the infliction of cancer is that of amenity rights. Even if the company's rights should take primacy over the public's rights, the problem does not end there. This is because there are reasonable grounds for arguing that the social costs represented by the emissions should not go uncompensated. Even if the company were allowed, on some justifiable ethical grounds, to continue its present level of emissions, one could argue that an innocent person should not be forced to absorb the noxious by-products of the activity of others.[32] Moreover, even if amenity rights were not said to be rights in the strong sense, there would still be grounds for their recognition and for the company's compensating citizens when they were violated. One reason is that amenity rights, such as the "right to a livable environment,"[33] are necessary if government is to guarantee the recognition of other rights, like the right to equal protection and the rights to life, liberty, and the pursuit of happiness. It would be nonsensical for someone to recognize the strong right of an innocent person not to be killed but to refuse to recognize the amenity rights that would control harm short of killing. Recognition of amenity rights "is necessary to insure equality of rights and freedom."[34] Moreover, if amenity rights were recognized, then persons would be prohibited from causing any spillovers for which they were unable to compensate others. For too long, people have been robbed of free choice regarding such things as safe, quiet, and attractive surroundings. If these rights are not recognized, then markets will not flourish in an orderly fashion, the real costs of goods will be misrepresented, and private enterprise will be more likely to ignore the welfare of the public. In other words, amenity rights would provide industry with an incentive to attempt to protect society from the ill effects of its actions.

Yet another reason for implementing a theory of amenity rights is that it would probably give rich and poor alike more equal access to desirable environmental quality. Without recognition of these rights, only the rich are able to afford to avoid certain spillover effects. In other words, "The richer a man is the wider is his choice of neighborhood."[35] But if amenity rights were recognized, then living in an environmentally desirable neighborhood would not be largely a function of a person's ability to pay for enough land to insulate himself from many noxious externalities. Recognition of amenity rights would have favorable distributive effects on the welfare of society. It would enhance the environment generally and most of all would help the poor, who have borne the worst effects of faulty schemes for the distribution of resources.

Of course, it is not possible in a short essay to provide principles for deciding every case in which individual autonomy is set at odds with government control in matters regarding the environment. Each case must be argued on the basis of analysis of the specific circumstances. However, the discussion has provided several important distinctions among rights, as well as several necessary criteria for adjudicating conflicts between individual autonomy and the alleged public welfare. It is important to note that these distinctions, as well as the previous ones concerning problems of global distribution, have all been formulated in terms of human rights and principles of equal opportunity or distribution for human beings. They betray the fact that classical ethical reasoning, especially in the West, is unmistakably anthropocentric. The human-centered character of ethical analysis leads one to ask whether, if our global environmental problems are to be solved, we do not need an ecocentric, rather than an anthropocentric, basis of analysis. Might such an ethics be possible? And if so, what might it be like? And how might it enable us to address problems such as global pie slicing and the resolution of environmental conflicts?

ANTHROPOCENTRIC OR ECOCENTRIC ETHICS?

To challenge the anthropocentric presuppositions of classical ethics is to call into question the whole way we have thought about right and wrong in the West. Perhaps E. F. Schumacher is correct in arguing that our traditional economic institutions have misled us about ethics and have condoned mores and morals that constitute "an act of violence against nature which must almost inevitably lead to violence between men."[36] Perhaps Lynn White is correct in alleging that our Christian traditions have erred in destroying animism and in supposedly sanctioning an absolute human right to dominate nature.[37] Many writers such as Schumacher and White have concluded that traditional ethical theories do not take adequate account of planetary well-being, and that a new ethics, an environmental ethics, is required to provide a theoretical basis for taking into consideration the needs and interests of nature, rather than merely the needs and interests of humans.[38]

Biologist Wayne Davis, for example, has argued that "the time has come when we must all develop respect for the air, water, land, and the living things thereon. We are all dependent upon the same life-support system of Earth and must protect it if we are to survive. I hold these truths to be self-evident: All living things are created equal and are interdependent upon one another."[39] Pursuing a slightly different line, attorney Christopher Stone has argued for the recognition of the legal rights of natural objects on the grounds that, in principle, legal rights have been, and can be expanded to include inanimate things.[40] A historian at the University of California has become well known for his belief that "rocks have rights," and Australian philosopher Peter Singer has become the recognized international authority on the question of animal rights. Singer has argued, quite persuasively, for an end to "speciesism" and for recognition of animal rights on the grounds that, since animals suffer, there can be no moral justification for refusing to take that suffering into account in our ascription of rights.[41] When one looks at the ways in which humans have ignored the well-being of ecosystems, have cruelly practiced factory farming, and have paradoxically accorded legal rights to ships, for example, but not trees, one wonders if something is not amiss in our approach to ethics in terms of anthropocentric "business as usual."

A Case Study: Property Rights in Natural Resources

Even in terms of classical anthropocentric ethics, our environmental actions are highly questionable. Further, good utilitarians, bent on ignoring distributive equity but maximizing the well-being of all persons of all generations, would have to admit that present policies of pollution and resource depletion cannot possibly be justified on the grounds that they optimize the welfare of all persons, especially members of future generations. Similarly, our current views of property rights, allegedly derived from the views of John Locke, are woefully inconsistent with classical criteria for generating and transferring ownership. In fact, if we really accepted Locke's views, we would see that it is ethically impossible at the present time to accord humans property rights in natural resources such as land or minerals. Why is this so?

Locke had a labor theory of property. He maintained that whatever a person takes out of the state of nature and mixes his labor with, he makes his own property. He held, further, that people have property rights to as much as they "can make use of to any advantage of life before it spoils," but that "whatever is beyond this, is more than his share and belongs to others."[42] The one proviso that Locke made is that there be "as much and as good left in common for others."[43] Locke believed that this proviso could easily be fulfilled, since there were vast lands in the world and relatively few inhabitants,[44] and since he held that labor "puts the greatest part of value upon land, without which it would scarcely be worth anything."[45]

Of course, the crucial point in Locke's theory is whether appropriation of property such as land worsens the situation of others.[46] As long as global population was small and unexplored lands extensive, there was likely to be "enough and as good left in common for others." But it is doubtful that contemporary theorists are correct if they defend Locke's theory of property rights and argue that his proviso can be met. How can one own and use vast amounts of land, oil, or coal, for example, and yet claim that "as much and as good" is left for others?

The whole point of Locke's reasoning is that the earth is given in common to all people, past, present, and future, and that people deserve to have property rights in what has been created by their labor. To the extent that contemporary theorists fail to recognize that one cannot have property rights in what one's labor does not create and in resources when one's ownership does not leave "as much and as good" for others, then to that degree are their allegedly Lockean justifications of private property in natural resources inconsistent with current patterns of ownership. Hence, even on traditional anthropocentric grounds it is not clear that it is ethical for humans to claim to have Lockean property rights over land, water, air, minerals, and other natural resources,[47] when enough and as good will not be left for those to come. But if so, then many of our global problems arise not because our anthropocentric ethics errs but because we do not practice the Lockean ethics we preach.[48]

Two Views of Environmental Ethics

Generally when thinkers propose adoption of a new, environmentally oriented ethics, they are defending one of two possible approaches, an "expanded-rights view" or a holistic view based on ecosystemic considerations.[49] Proponents of the expanded-rights view see the new environmental ethics as another "liberation movement," but for flora, fauna, and rivers instead of for blacks and women only.[50] Proponents of the ecosystemic view believe that what makes our actions morally right, or good, is the way they affect ecosystems.[51] Although I have great empathy for proposals for a new environmental ethics, especially one based on ecosystemic considerations, both types of proposals seem to me to suffer from fatal conceptual flaws.

"EXPANDED-RIGHTS" VIEW OF ENVIRONMENTAL ETHICS. Consider first the expanded-rights view of environmental ethics, according to which rocks and rivers, as well as sentient beings, are said to hold rights. If such an expanded-rights view proposes merely that the class of rights-holders be enlarged to include all beings that can feel pleasure, pain, or joy, then, of course, there is nothing problematic about accepting such a view. Nor is this new. Bentham, in spelling out his utilitarianism, long ago stipulated that each sentient being, not merely each person or human, was "to count for one and none for more than one."[52] His reasoning was that insofar as a being could suffer, it was worthy of consideration, a point of view accepted by a number of moral philosophers,[53] as well as by most contemporary thinkers. People generally agree that it is wrong to mistreat animals or imbeciles, not because they are moral persons but because they suffer, and needless suffering is to be avoided.[54]

Insofar as the expanded-rights position calls for including beings that are not sentient in the class of rights-holders, then it is both new and problematic. Although stirring appeals for recognition of the inherent value and inalienable rights of all beings have been made, much of the apparent persuasiveness of the expanded-rights claim will not hold up under rational scrutiny. For one thing, the position often relies on calls to end "human chauvinism" and thus aligns itself with every group that has wished to end some "-ism," whether racism, sexism, or speciesism. But merely to call for an end to human chauvinism is to beg precisely the question at issue. Why should human chauvinism, or better, sentient chauvinism, be ended? What must be proved is that there is a nonanthropocentric reason for ending it. From a moral point of view, it is unclear why one should respect a thing—for example, a rock or a river—if it experiences no pain, elation, or suffering.[55] What is it about nonsentient things that deserves our respect? Why, apart from anthropocentric considerations, should poison oak have rights? Why, other than for anthropocentric reasons, should one not dump toxic wastes in places where they will pollute groundwater?

Of course, there are sound anthropocentric reasons why persons should not destroy rare plants or despoil landscapes. I, too, believe that one should revere all things.[56] My reason for this belief, however, is not that rocks or rivers have rights but that needless destruction bespeaks human callousness, myopia, and perhaps greed, all of which are wrong on anthropocentric grounds. The point of view of the expanded rights theorists appears to be that there is some other, inherent, nonanthropocentric reason for not picking flowers or destroying rocks. But such a notion of inherent value is puzzling. What would it mean to say that everything has rights.[57] How then, would any action be possible that did not "harm" something? If everything had equal status and there were no sentient or human chauvinism, then would there be a realistic way to adjudicate controversies over rights? Perhaps controversies within an expanded-rights position would be resolved by some sort of survival of the fittest, some natural selection process? Or, if this were too savage, then, perhaps humans would be prohibited from killing the staphylococcus bacteria infecting them, and the staphylococcus bacteria would be prohibited, on grounds of bacteria chauvinism, from killing humans. But if rights claims are thought to entail correlative obligations on others, how could allegedly free human beings have rights that obviously unfree bacteria were obliged to respect? What could a right mean in such a situation? Moreover, would there not be something conceptually awry in according inherent value to all sorts of things, like rocks, and at the same time, alleging that there was nothing special about being alive, or sentient, or intelligent?[58]

Yet another problem with the expanded-rights position, insofar as it calls for recognition of the alleged rights of nonsentient beings, is that it fails to take into account that all values are necessarily values for us; there is no such thing as a value in and of itself, without a valuer. If nonsentient beings cannot have values, what would it mean to assert their value?[59] How can one visit good or evil on something that has no thoughts or feelings, even in a potential sense, as does a human zygote or a comatose person? (Of course, within many theological and mystical perspectives, things do have intrinsic value. The point of proponents of the expanded-rights view, however, seems to be that they can provide a rationalistic, analytic, naturalistic argument for their appeal to expand the class of rights-holders, and that they do not see their position as mystical or theological.) The problem is that their position povides no conceptual or nontheological rationale for extending the range of moral relevance, short of question-begging appeals to inherent value.

Other difficulties with the expanded-rights position have to do with conceptual problems of individuation, interspecies comparisons of utility, and justice among nonhumans.[60] Although such problems are not an indication that extension of the class of rights-holders is prima facie undesirable, they do illustrate that the burden of proof should be on the proponents of the expansion. As it is, one is left wondering what sort of method might be possible for assessing the newly recognized rights claims, and how those claims might be adjudicated, especially in the context of claims by older, sentient, rights-holders. Such worries are not without merit, since even among humans, who are said to be equal as moral persons, there are unbelievably difficult controversies over rights. Among all beings, however, the complications would seem to be so horrendous as to raise the question of whether expansion of the class of rights-holders is capable of being worked out in terms of criteria for making decisions about permissible actions. This suggests that, although expansion of the class of rights-holders may be desirable as a personal moral ideal, it is unlikely to be defensible as a rationally justified ethical obligation.

ECOSYSTEMIC VIEWS OF ENVIRONMENTAL ETHICS. The ecosystemic versions of environmental ethics fall victim to the same sorts of problems as the expanded-rights positions. According to proponents of holistic environmental ethics, recent industrial history is a biotic hemorrhage, to be remedied by judging all human action in terms of their effects on all the ecosystems of the planet. According to this view, whatever promotes ecosystemic well-being is said to be good and right, whatever jeopardizes it to be bad and wrong. A basic problem arises, however: why consider a whole that is not a conscious, sentient being? What reasons are there, apart from human well-being, for ascribing moral worth to some ecosystemic whole?[61]

In response to such questions, a proponent of ecosystemic ethics is likely to respond that the earth has a beauty, a balance of nature, that is inherent in it. But the problem with such a response is that these are values that the earth and its ecosystems have only as objects of consideration by conscious, sentient human beings. It is not clear that the earth has these alleged properties apart from some viewer or valuer. Hence, it is not clear that there is some nonanthropocentric basis for affirming an ecosystemic ethics.[62] Moreover, even if there were inherent value in ecosystems, apart from human or divine ascription, it is not clear what this might be. Presumably the purpose of affirming an ecosystemic ethics would be to provide a value system according to which actions could be judged right, or good, if they promoted the well-being of the planet. But what might it mean to help or hinder the well-being of the biosphere or to maintain some balance of nature? Ecosystems regularly change, and they regularly eliminate species. After all, the dinosaurs are gone! It is unclear how contemporary proponents of ecosystemic ethics can claim some nonanthropocentric, theoretical justification for their repeated claims that humans should not wipe out species, when nature does this herself. (Of course, for clearly anthropocentric reasons, I do not believe species should be destroyed by humans. But it is a different matter to claim that species should not be destroyed for their own sake.) Why is the elimination of species by humans different from their elimination by natural selection? How can it be wrong for humans to do what nature does if the only grounds for alleging wrongness are theories about maintaining a balance of nature? It is generally admitted that the balance of nature is not a static thing. This being so, it is unclear how proponents of ecosystemic ethics can maintain that certain ecological changes are good whereas others are not. The difference cannot be merely that what happens naturally is good and that what happens through human interference is bad, for this would be to sanction a purely stipulative definition of ecological and moral goodness and badness.

Perhaps the main difficulty besetting ecosystemic ethics is that it somehow derives an ethical *ought* from a scientific or ecological *is*. In other words, some natural characteristics of ecosystems are taken as normative, as things that should be preserved. It is widely held by moral philosophers, however, that one cannot legitimately deduce some moral duty from an existing state of affairs.[63] The mere existence of a thing is not a justification for what should be. Thus the interference of ecosystemic ethicists from *is* to *ought* must be mediated by value judgments—for example, preserving diversity is good. But to the extent that the tenets of ecosystemic ethics rest upon value judgments, then to that same extent they are open to question. One such question is why a different, but equally plausible, value judgment should not be made. Moreover, it is at least conceivable that one particular value judgment, one presupposing great species stability, might appear plausible within a short time frame, but that another, presupposing great variation in the appearance and disappearance of species, might appear plausible within a longer time frame.

The problem of specifying criteria for a balance of nature is as much a central conceptual difficulty for ecosystemic ethicists as it was for medievalists to specify criteria for what was "natural," and hence allowed, under natural-law ethics. Many who are allegedly expert in natural-law ethics claim that homosexual acts and acts of contraception are unnatural and hence unethical, and their claims continue to cause controversy in the world of moral philosophy. It is difficult to see how proponents of ecosystemic ethics could avoid similar difficulties with respect to specifying what is natural or healthy for an ecosystem or in keeping with the balance of nature.

Environmental Ethics and Moral Ideals

The point here is not to argue that natural-law ethics or ecosystemic ethics are incorrect but rather, in resurrecting difficulties with the terms *natural* and *healthy*, to point out that correctness is not a sufficient condition for the workability of an ethic in preventing environmental harm or in providing a basis for the adjudication of court cases. Natural-law ethics and ecosystemic ethics simply won't "play in Peoria"; they involve too many value judgments and problematic presuppositions to provide a clear foundation for either law or action. That is why our current, crude system of allegedly according equal rights to humans and of adjudicating rights conflicts on the basis of simplistic principles of equal treatment has been as effective as it has been. Its anthropocentric simplicity has been a bonus in implementation and enforcement.

It is one thing to have a theory of what is right but another to have a procedure for guaranteeing that right decisions will be made. It is one thing to have moral culpability but another to have a conviction by a jury. Likewise, it is one thing to have a theory of environmental ethics but quite another to have a procedure for guaranteeing that environmentally sound ethical decisions will be made by owners, corporations, and juries. Hence, although it may be true theoretically that some kind of ecosystemic ethics should be adopted, it is far from clear that there are procedures and associated criteria for specifying in a noncontroversial and enforceable way which actions are in accord with such an ethics.

Where does this agnosticism about the merits and workability of an environmental ethics leave us? Actually, not in a bad position. It could easily be argued that even if one does not adopt some new environmental ethics, one can make great progress in promoting environmental, global well-being simply by taking seriously some of the old ethics. As the earlier example about Lockean property rights illustrates, once we are ready to practice what we preach about equal rights (for all generations), about optimizing the welfare of all persons of all nations and generations, and about ensuring that "as much and as good" resources are left after we have claimed our property rights, then our planetary behavior will have to change rapidly and radically. We will have to grant equal rights to all persons of all nations and all generations, and we will have to optimize the utility of all persons of all nations and all generations. We will have to be sure that "as much and as good" natural resources are available to everyone before we attempt to claim our alleged property rights. Moreover, even without ecosystemic ethics, if we loosened our rigid notions of property and really adopted Lockean criteria, then we would be unable to find ethical grounds for harming the earth, because it would not be ours to harm, but only to use, leaving "as much and as good" for others.

POLICIES AND THEIR IMPLICATIONS

Admittedly, it has not been possible here to provide ethical principles for deciding each case of environmental controversy involving inter- and intra-generational distributive equity, individual autonomy versus the common good, and anthropocentric versus ecocentric norms. Each case must be adjudicated on the basis of a number of ethical subprinciples and on analyses of the specific rights claims involved. This is a task to which researchers should address themselves in the future. In this paper, however, I have provided a number of philosophical distinctions that will be useful in such analyses and have argued for several necessary conditions for ethical resolution of conflicts. In a few cases, I have taken a stand for particular ethical stances that require important policy changes.

In discussing inter- and intra-generational distributive equity, several principles have been set forth:

1. Contractual-egalitarian ethics provides a sounder basis for slicing the planetary pie than utilitarian and libertarian ethics.
2. Planetary distributions are ethically suspect if they preclude procedurally just transactions and interactions.
3. There are limits to the redistributive sacrifices required by global egalitarian morality, and to the degree of coercion that can be tolerated.
4. Among criteria for assessing the desirability of following principles of equal treatment in a particular situation are the principle of prima facie egalitarianism and the principle of everyone's advantage.

As a consequence of accepting these four principles, at least two policy conclusions follow:

1. Land reform is required in a number of countries to provide necessary conditions for procedurally just transactions and interactions.
2. Various forms of discrimination should not be permitted, on the grounds that they are inconsistent with the principle of prima facie egalitarianism and that of everyone's advantage.

Discussion of the problem of individual autonomy versus government control argues for acceptance of at least two principles:

1. Strong rights, such as the right of the innocent not to be killed, can never be superseded by utilitarian considerations about the greater good, but only by rights of comparable importance held by other persons.
2. Weak rights, such as the right to one's property and the right to purchase whatever environmental resources one is able, can be superseded by utilitarian considerations about the greater good and, in a case of conflict, are always trumped by strong rights.

As a consequence of these two principles, at least two policy conclusions follow:

1. Government has a strong right to restrict all forms of pollution, even when such restriction inhibits property rights, since government's mandate arises from the strong right of individuals not to be killed and the strong right to informed control over conditions likely to lead to serious harm.
2. Whenever violations of amenity rights are not prohibited, people should at least be compensated for these violations.

In discussing whether to accept an anthropocentric ethics or an ecosystemic ethics, three principles were advocated:

1. Expanded-rights views of environmental ethics are neither old nor controversial when they propose admitting sentient beings to the class of rights-holders, but they are both new and controversial when they propose admitting nonsentient beings too.
2. Although they may be correct in some theoretical sense, systems of ecosystemic ethics are not feasible because of difficulties associated with defining what is "natural," "healthy," or in keeping with the "balance of nature."
3. Many environmental problems could be solved if we practiced the anthropocentric ethics we preach (egalitarianism, utilitarianism) rather than searching for an elusive nonanthropocentric ethics.

On the basis of these three principles, the following three conclusions are drawn:

1. Because of problems of individuation, comparison of interspecies utility, and justice among nonhumans, the class of rights-holders should not be extended beyond sentient beings.
2. Because there are no clear criteria for judging actions according to whether they contribute to ecosystemic well-being, ecosystemic ethics should not be adopted.
3. We should attempt to implement the radical consequences of accepted anthropocentric (egalitarian and utilitarian) theories before attempting to formulate some new environmental ethics.

If sound ethical policy for the planet were merely a matter of recognizing principles such as those outlined above, then global environmental problems might be more tractable than they are. As it is, however, solution of these problems requires putting these principles into practice. We must implement an egalitarian ethics for inter- and intra-generational distribution; we must adopt a new framework of amenity rights for justifying government control over private property; and we must abandon the notion that we can hold title to natural resources if "as much and as good" is not left for those who will come after us. In short, if we wish to end our environmental and ethical malaise, we must live as if we really believe ourselves to be essentially social beings. Saying that we are our brothers' and sisters' keepers is not some pious statement left over from a bygone religious era. It is a statement of fact about what it is to be human. Until we see this, we, our ethics, and our global policies are unlikely to succeed.

NOTES

1. J. Egerton, "Appalachia's absentee landlords," *The Progressive* 45, no. 6 (June 1981) 43; hereafter cited as Egerton, "Landlords." The government study is by J. Gaventa and B. Horton, cochairs of the Appalachian Land Ownership Task Force, *Land Ownership Patterns and Their Impacts on Appalachian Communities: A Survey of 80 Counties,* vol. 1, pp. 25–59, 210–11; (Washington, D.C.: Appalachian Regional Commission, 1981), hereafter cited as Task Force, *Land Ownership.*

2. Task Force, *Land Ownership,* esp. pp. 210–12.

3. Task Force, *Land Ownership,* p. 212. See Egerton, "Landlords," p. 44, for quote from M. Clark, director of the Highlander Center, New Market, Tenn. See also E. Moss (of the Natural Resources Defense Center), *Land Use Controls in the United States* (N.Y.: Dial Press/James Wade, 1970), pp. 235–36; hereafter cited as Moss, *Land Use.*

4. See notes 1–3 above.

5. See, for example, K. Griffin, *The Political Economy of Agrarian Change* (Cambridge, Mass.: Harvard University Press, 1974) pp. 225–33; idem, *Land Concentration and Rural Poverty* (New York: Holmes and Meier, 1976); and W. J. Samuels, "Welfare Economics, Power, and Property," in *Perspectives of Property,* ed. D. Wunderlich and W. Gibson (University Park, Penn.: Pennsylvania State University, Institute for Land and Water Resources, 1972), pp. 140–41.

6. End-state principles provide reasons for a *particular* distribution of goods, whereas historical, or procedural-justice principles describe fair or correct methods for arriving at any distribution, regardless of what it is.

7. Cited in D. Goulet, *The Cruel Choice* (New York: Athenaeum, 1971), p. 133.

8. See C. R. Beitz, *Political Theory and International Relations* (Princeton, N.J.: Princeton University Press, 1979); hereafter cited as Beitz, *PTIR.* See also J. Rawls, *A Theory of Justice* (Cambridge Mass.: Harvard University Press, 1971); hereafter cited as Rawls, *Justice*; and Henry Shue, *Basic Rights: Subsistence, Affluence, and American Foreign Policy* (Princeton: Princeton University Press, 1980); hereafter cited as Shue, *BR.* Finally, see C. R. Beitz, "Cosmopolitan ideals and national sentiment," *Journal of Philosophy* 80, no. 30 (October 1983): 591–600; hereafter cited as Beitz, "Cosmopolitan"; and Henry Shue, "The Burdens of Justice," *Journal of Philosophy,* 80, no. 30 (October 1983): 600–08; hereafter cited as Shue, "Burdens."

9. J. Rawls, "Kantian Constructivism in Moral Theory," *Journal of Philosophy* 77, no. 9 (September 1980): 515–72, esp. pp. 521, 525; and Beitz, "Cosmopolitan," p. 595.

10. Beitz, *PTIR,* pp. 129–36, 143–53, makes this point; see also idem, "Cosmopolitan," p. 595.

11. This, of course, does not mean that there are never morally relevant grounds for discrimination among persons, but merely that, when morally relevant considerations

are equal, then the treatment of persons should also be equal. In this regard, see my *Risk Analysis and Scientific Method* (Boston: Reidel, 1984) ch. 3; and R. S. Dworkin, *Taking Rights Seriously* (Cambridge, Mass.: Harvard University Press, 1977), p. 273; hereafter cited as Dworkin, *Rights.*

12. For a good argument for the equivalence of act and rule utilitarianism, see D. Lyons, *Forms and Limits of Utilitarianism* (Oxford: Clarendon Press, 1967). For a summary of arguments on both sides, see M.D. Bayles, ed., *Contemporary Utilitarianism,* (New York: Doubleday, 1968).

13. See J. S. Mill, *Utilitarianism, Liberty, and Representative Government* (New York: Dutton, 1910), pp. 58–59; See also J. J. C. Smart, "An Outline of a System of Utilitarian Ethics," in *Utilitarianism: For and Against,* ed. J. C. C. Smart and B. Williams (Cambridge: Cambridge University Press, 1973) p. 72, hereafter cited as Smart, "*Utilitarianism.*"

14. Robert Nozick, *Anarchy, State, and Utopia* (New York: Basic Books, 1974). pp. 151–53.

15. Smart, "*Utilitarianism,*" p. 69.

16. See Beitz, "Cosmopolitan," p. 597.

17. See Thomas Nagel, "Ruthlessness in Public Life," in *Mortal Questions* (New York: Cambridge University Press, 1979), p. 84.

18. See Peter Singer, "Famine, Affluence and Morality," in *Philosophy Now,* ed. K. J. Struhl and P. R. Struhl (New York: Randon House, 1980), pp. 485–88, esp. p. 487.

19. Shue, "Burdens," pp. 602 ff.

20. Shue, "Burdens," p. 607.

21. W. T. Blackstone, "On the Meaning and Justification of the Equality Principle," in Blackstone, *The Concept of Equality* (Minneapolis: Burgess, 1969); hereafter cited as Blackstone, *Equality.*

22. See the previous note. J. Rawls, "Justice as Fairness," in *Philosophy of Law,* ed. J. Feinberg and H. Gross (Encino, Calif.: Dickenson, 1975), p. 284 also makes this point; hereafter cited as Rawls, "Fairness," and Feinberg and Gross, *POL.*

23. For arguments to this effect, see M. C. Beardsley, "Equality and Obedience to Law," *Law and Philosophy,* ed. Sidney Hook (New York: New York University Press, 1964) pp. 35–36; hereafter cited as Beardsley, "Equality." See also Isaiah Berlin, "Equality," in Blackstone, *Equality,* p. 33; W. K. Frankena, "Some Beliefs About Justice," in Feinberg and Gross, *POL,* pp. 205–51; M. Markovic, "The Relationship Between Equality and Local Autonomy," in *Equality and Social Policy,* ed. W. Feinberg (Urbana, Ill.: University of Illinois Press, 1978), p. 93; hereafter cited as Markovic, "Relationship," and Feinberg, *Equality.* See also Rawls, "Fairness," pp. 227, 280, 282; and G. Vlastos, "Justice and Equality," in *Social Justice,* ed. R. B. Brandt (Englewood Cliffs: Pretice-Hall, 1962) pp. 50, 56 hereafter cited as Vlastos, "*Justice,*" and Brandt, *Justice.*

24. J. R. Pennock, Introduction to *The Limits of Law,* Nomos 15, Yearbook of the American Society for Political and Legal Philosophy, ed. J. R. Pennock and J. W. Chapman (New York: Lieber-Atherton, 1974), pp. 2, 6; hereafter cited as Pennock and Chapman, *LL.*

25. See Rawls, "Fairness"; Charles Fried, *Right and Wrong* (Cambridge, Mass.: Harvard University Press, 1978); and Alan Donagan, *The Theory of Morality,* (Chicago: University of Chicago Press, 1977). See also S. I. Benn, "Egalitarianism and the Equal Consideration of Interests," in *Equality,* Nomos 9, Yearbook of the American Society for Political and Legal Philosophy, ed., J. R. Pennock and J. W. Chapman (New York: Atherton Press, 1968), pp. 75–76. See also W. K. Frankena, *Ethics* (Englewood Cliffs, N. J.: Prentice-Hall, 1963), pp. 41–42.

26. I am grateful to Toby Page, of the California Institute of Technology, for pointing out the question of whether the principle of everyone's advantage is identical with the potential Pareto criterion. There appear to be two reasons why they are not the same.

First, the principle requires that everyone's advantage be served in fact, and that compensations be made if everyone's advantage requires it. The Pareto criterion, however, does not require that the compensations actually be made. Second, the principle defines *advantage* as overall welfare (including well-being aside from economic criteria), whereas the Pareto criterion defines it in a purely economic sense. As was pointed out (in notes 1–3), serving everyone's advantage might include according to everyone rights to equal concern and respect. Such rights, however, do not fall within the scope of the Pareto definition of *advantage*.

27. W. K. Frankena, "The Concept of Social Justice," in Brandt, *Justice*, pp. 10, 14.

28. See Alan Gewirth, *Human Rights* (Chicago: University of Chicago Press, 1982), pp. 181–96; hereafter cited as Gewirth, *Rights*.

29. See Dworkin, *Rights*, p. 191. See also Gewirth, *Rights*, p. 226.

30. See Gewirth, *Rights*, pp. 187ff.

31. Gewirth, *Rights* pp. 183–84. See also H. L. A. Hart and A. M. Honore, *Causation in the Law* (Oxford: Oxford University Press, 1959), pp. 128ff., 195ff., 292ff.

32. For arguments to this effect, see E. J. Mishan, *Technology and Growth*, (New York: Praeger, 1969), pp. 38–39; hereafter cited as Mishan, *Technology*. See also idem, *The Costs of Economic Growth* (New York: Praeger, 1967), pp. 55, 128–29. Finally, see my *Nuclear Power and Public Policy*, 2d ed. (Boston: Reidel, 1983), pp. 127–29.

33. See W. T. Blackstone, *Philosophy and Environmental Crisis* (Atlanta, Ga.: University of Georgia Press, 1974), pp. 29–38; hereafter cited as: Blackstone, PEC.

34. Blackstone, PEC, pp. 29–31.

35. Mishan, *Technology*, p. 41.

36. E. F. Schumacher, *Small is Beautiful* (New York: Harper and Row, 1973), p. 57; hereafter cited as Schumacher, *Small*.

37. See Lynn White, "The Historical Roots of Our Ecologic Crisis," *Science* 155 (10 March 1967): 1203–07; for a critical analysis of White's views, see my *Ethics*, pp. 19–20.

38. Some of those who believe that we need a new ethics to deal with the environment are W. H. Ferry, "Must We Rewrite the Constitution to Control Technology?" in *Technology and Society* (London: Addison-Wesley, 1972), pp. 15, 19; and K. A. Manaster, "Law and the Dignity of Nature," *Environment Law Review 1978* (New York: Clark Boardman, 1978), p. 4.

39. W. H. Davis, "The Land Must Live," *Environment Action Bulletin* 3 (July 15, 1972): 5, 7.

40. C. D. Stone, *Should Trees Have Standing?* (Los Altos: William Kaufmann, 1974).

41. See P. Singer, "Animal Liberation," *New York Review of Books*, section 20 (April 1973): 17–21; hereafter cited as Singer, "Liberation." See also T. Regan and P. Singer, eds., *Animal Rights and Human Obligations* (Englewood Cliffs, N.J.: Prentice-Hall, 1976).

42. John Locke, *Second Treatise of Government*, paragraphs 25–31.

43. Ibid., para. 27.

44. Ibid., para. 36.

45. Ibid., para. 43.

46. Robert Nozick, *Anarchy, State, and Utopia* (New York: Basic Books, 1974), pp. 174–76.

47. L. C. Becker, *Property Rights* (London: Routledge and Kegan Paul, 1977), p. 109, presents a similar argument.

48. See John Passmore, *Man's Responsiblity for Nature* (New York: Charles Scribner's Sons, 1974), also W. K. Frankena, "Ethics and the Environment," in *Ethics and Problems of the 21st Century*, ed. K. E. Goodpaster and K. M. Sayre (Notre Dame, Ind.: University of Notre Dame Press, 1979), pp. 3–4; hereafter cited as Frankena, "Ethics," and Goodpaster and Sayre, *Ethics*.

49. Admittedly it is an oversimplification to speak merely of the "old" ethics and the "new," or "ecosystemic," ethics. See Frankena, "Ethics," pp. 5–15.

50. See notes 55 and 56. See also Holmes Rolston, "Is There an Ecological Ethics?," *Ethics* 85, no. 2 (January 1975):101; hereafter cited as Rolston, "Ecological."

51. See A. Leopold, "The Land Ethic," *A Sand County Almanac* (New York: Oxford University Press, 1949), pp. 201–06; C. D. Broad, *Five Types of Ethical Theory* (New York: Harcourt Brace, 1930) p. 283; T. C. Williams, *The Concept of the Categorical Imperative* (London: Oxford University Press, 1968), pp. 22, 121; Henry Sidgwick, *The Methods of Ethics*, 74th ed. (New York: Dover, 1966), p. 420; Thomas Colwell, "Ecology and Philosophy," in *Philosophical Issues*, ed. J. Rachels and F. Tillman (New York: Harper and Row, 1972), p. 360.

52. Singer, "Liberation," expressly quotes Bentham.

53. G. J. Warnock, *The Object of Morality* (London: Methuen, 1971), pp. 148ff.

54. Frankena, "Ethics," pp. 5, 10.

55. Frankena, "Ethics," pp. 11, 13, makes a similar point.

56. See A. Schweitzer, *Civilization and Ethics*, 3d ed. (London: A. C. Black, 1949), p. 344.

57. Rolston, "Ecological," p. 101.

58. Frankena, "Ethics," p. 13, makes a similar point.

59. Frankena, "Ethics," p. 14, makes a similar point.

60. See K. E. Goodpaster, "From Egoism to Environmentalism," in Goodpaster and Sayre, *Ethics*, p. 29.

61. Frankena, "Ethics," pp. 14–15, raises the same question.

62. A similar point is made by Frankena, "Ethics," p. 15.

63. See G. E. Moore, *Principia Ethica* (Cambridge: Cambridge University Press, 1951) p. 20; W. H. Bruening, "Moore and 'Is-Ought'," *Ethics* 81, no. 2 (January 1971); 143–49; W. K. Frankena, "The Naturalistic Fallacy," *Mind* 48, no. 192 (October 1939): 467; and J. H. Olthuis, *Facts, Values and Ethics* (Assen: Van Gorcum, 1969), pp. 28–34.

PART II

Issues and Opportunities

CHAPTER SIX

Population, Resource Pressures, and Poverty
ROBERT REPETTO

POPULATION TRENDS AND PROSPECTS

What Is Happening?

If historians in the distant future are able to look back at the twentieth century, they will undoubtedly write about population change as one of its most remarkable features. Our generation is witnessing the flood crest of population growth. Already in this century, world population has increased threefold. From tens of thousands of years in neolithic times and hundreds of years at the start of the industrial age, the time required to double the population has shortened in this half of the twentieth century to just thirty-five years (see table 6.1).

Only since World War II has the population growth in the poor countries begun to outpace that in the rich countries, and only within the last decade has the population of the Southern Hemisphere (Africa, Oceania, Latin America, and South Asia) exceeded that of the North (North America, Europe, USSR, and East Asia). These dramatic changes have provoked much concern about the pressures that population growth exerts on world resources and living standards.[1] If current growth rates continue for a few generations more, the carrying capacity of the earth will be greatly exceeded.

This Malthusian perspective represents a shift in the way population growth has been regarded. During the 1930s and 1940s, a more widespread fear was that the slow population growth foreseen for the postwar period would not provide sufficient stimulus to the industrial

TABLE 6.1. Population projections (above) and annual rates of growth (below) for the world and major regions, UN medium variant.

	Total population (billions)					
	1980	2000	2025	2050	2075	2100
World	4.43	6.12	8.20	9.51	10.10	10.18
More developed areas	1.13	1.27	1.38	1.40	1.42	1.42
Less developed areas	3.30	4.85	6.82	8.11	8.68	8.76
Africa	0.47	0.85	1.54	2.17	2.51	2.59
Latin America	0.36	0.57	0.87	1.10	1.22	1.24
North America	0.25	0.30	0.34	0.36	0.38	0.38
East Asia	1.18	1.48	1.71	1.77	1.76	1.76
South Asia	1.40	2.08	2.82	3.20	3.31	3.28
Europe	0.48	0.51	0.52	0.51	0.50	0.50
Oceania	0.02	0.03	0.04	0.04	0.04	0.04
USSR	0.26	0.31	0.36	0.38	0.38	0.38
World	1.70	1.39	0.82	0.36	0.10	−0.03
More developed regions	0.68	0.40	0.15	0.07	0.02	−0.01
Less developed regions	2.04	1.64	0.96	0.41	0.11	−0.03
Africa	3.00	2.77	1.70	0.84	0.31	−0.03
Latin America	2.38	1.92	1.25	0.52	0.20	−0.06
North America	1.04	0.62	0.32	0.22	0.06	0.03
East Asia	1.24	0.89	0.33	−0.03	−0.04	0.01
South Asia	2.17	1.53	0.77	0.30	0.01	−0.04
Europe	0.34	0.15	−0.08	−0.08	−0.00	0.01
Oceania	1.44	0.92	0.64	0.19	0.07	0.00
USSR	0.93	0.60	0.38	0.16	−0.00	−0.06

Source: Population Division, "Long Range Global Population Projections," *Population Bulletin* no. 14 (New York, 1983).

world economy, which would lapse back into depression and economic stagnation. Few expected the brief postwar baby booms in the combatant nations or the rapid gains in life expectancy in the poorer countries. Antibiotics, DDT and immunizations, combined with improvements in transportation, communications, and food supplies, have increased life expectancy by five years each decade and population by more than 2 percent per year in the developing world.

As dramatic as these channnges have been, they are overshadowed by the downturn in the world population growth rate that occurred in the early 1970s. Annual growth touched 2 percent per year but has subsequently fallen back. The significance of this change is not that it relieves population pressures in this century: the increase in actual numbers will continue to rise from about 84 million per year now to almost 90 million per year in the year 2000. Its significance is that it reverses a rising rate of population growth that began way back in pre-history. At this moment we are watching the flood crest pass.

The flood has not been contained by the checks that Malthus thought likely: famine, war, and pestilence. It is later marriage and falling fertility within marriage that have reduced growth rates, even as mortality continues to fall. Modernization and rising living standards have provided the checks, not poverty and resource limits.

Each year the world adds the population-equivalent of a new Mexico, mostly in the poorer countries. These increases have strained the abilities of economies in the developing countries to provide employment, to increase agricultural production, and to make the investments needed if expanding cities are to function. Yet, living standards have been rising in almost all countries. Per capita agricultural production, school enrollment and literacy, the fraction of the population with access to safe drinking water, life expectancy, and per capita income have all been increasing. The rapid growth of population has enormously complicated the task of raising living standards but, clearly, has not precluded success.

Demographically, the developed world has become more uniform while the developing world has become more diverse. In the former, birth and death rates are low and similar, and differences among nations, regions, and classes are for the most part small. For the developed world as a whole, replacement fertility has been reached. In several countries, the current generation of parents will not have sufficient children to replace themselves, and population size may start to decline.

In the less-developed world, considerable divergence in population growth rates has emerged. Africa, the Arab Middle East, and much of Central America continue to have high birth rates, and their population growth rates have been rising as mortality declines. (In Kenya, the rate of natural increase exceeds 4 percent per year, which means a doubling of population size in eighteen years.) In these regions, fertility is higher than it was anywhere else *before* the beginning of the decline. Only the United States, which was the country with the highest fertility in the nineteenth century, started the transition with birth rates at such a level.

Social and economic conditions in these high-fertility countries vary considerably, from the poverty of much of sub-Saharan Africa to the wealth of some oil-producing countries. The importance of cultural factors in sustaining high rates of population growth is apparent.

Yet, in a few countries, such as Tunisia, Egypt, Mauritius, and some of the smaller Persian Gulf states, birth rates have fallen significantly.

The belt of high fertility and rapid population growth continues eastward across central Asia, mainly (but not entirely) through areas of Moslem culture, and includes southern Russia and northern India, along with Afghanistan, Pakistan, and Bangladesh. Birth rates have fallen rapidly, however, in the Punjab, a region of vigorous agricultural growth and modernization.

Countries of South and Southeast Asia are in demographic transition, but at speeds that vary considerably. Sri Lanka, the Indian states of Kerala and Karnataka, and Singapore started early and have gone furthest. In Indonesia and Thailand, birth rates have fallen rapidly within the past decade, largely because of successful family planning programs. Elsewhere in the region, birth rates are also declining but since death rates are also falling, the decline in population growth is only moderate.

In China, home to almost a quarter of the world's people, and in other East Asian countries, birth, death, and growth rates have all fallen precipitously. China, a low-income country, now has rates characteristic of the industrial nations.

In South America, considerable diversity has emerged. Rapid fertility declines have occurred in the past fifteen years in Chile, Colombia, Guyana, and Brazil. In other countries—Bolivia, Ecuador, and Peru, for example—the declines have been slow or nonexistent; overall, population growth rates have declined somewhat but remain high.

In Central America, birth rates have fallen rapidly in Costa Rica, many of the Caribbean islands, and more recently, in Mexico and Panama. Cuba has demographic characteristics like those of an industrial country. In other countries of the region—Guatemala, Honduras, and El Salvador—birth, death, and growth rates have remained extremely high.

In many of the countries that have only recently entered a state of demographic transition, the pace of the decline in fertility has been much faster than in countries that started earlier. Birth-rate declines in these countries have exceeded 1.0 percent per year, compared to rates of change of 0.25 - 0.50 in Europe, Japan, and the United States during their transition periods.

Cultural differences partly explain the variations that have emerged, but economic differences and policy factors are also important. Most countries that have experienced rapid fertility declines have made vigorous efforts to bring modern means of birth control within reach of the entire population and have pursued economic policies that have brought social and economic change and opportunities to the large majority of the population. Countries that have done neither have experienced less change in fertility and population growth.

Figures 6.1 and 6.2 show the demographic variation among countries and the correlation between birth and death rates. Both the levels and recent trends run parallel from country to country. Belts of high mortality run across Africa and Central Asia and through tropical Latin America. Rapid reductions in mortality have occurred in East Asia, especially China, where life expectancy rose from forty-one to sixty-seven years between 1960 and 1981. However, unlike the recent trend with regard to fertility, the pace of mortality decline has apparently slowed in the last decade, especially in Latin America and South Asia.

All over the developing world, cities are growing rapidly. The urban population is doubling in less than twenty years, more than

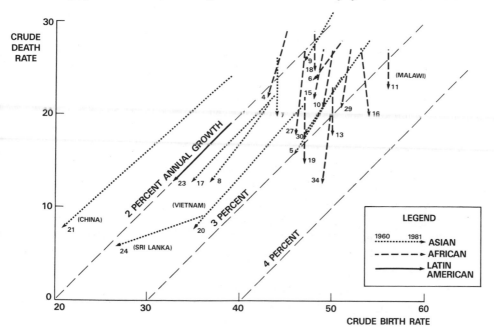

FIGURE 6.1. Crude birth and death rates (per 1,000 population) for low-income countries, 1960–81. Key: 4, Chad; 5, Bangladesh; 6, Ethiopia; 7, Nepal; 8, Burma; 9, Afghanistan; 10, Mali; 11, Malawi; 13, Uganda; 15, Upper Volta; 16, Rwanda; 17, India; 18, Somalia; 19, Tanzania; 20, Vietnam; 21, China; 23, Haiti; 24, Sri Lanka; 27, Sierra Leone; 29, Niger; 30, Pakistan; 34, Ghana.

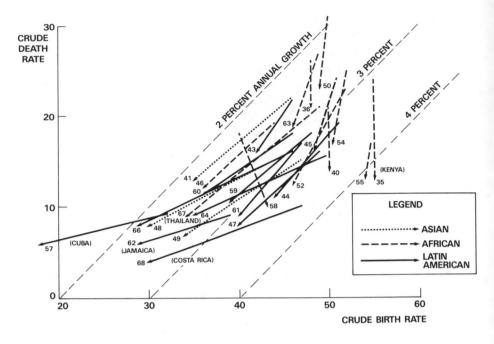

FIGURE 6.2. Crude birth and death rates (per 1,000 population) for middle-income countries, 1960–81. Key: 35, Kenya; 36, Senegal; 40, Liberia; 41, Indonesia; 43, Bolivia; 44, Honduras; 45, Zambia; 46, Egypt; 47, El Salvador; 48, Thailand; 49, Philippines; 50, Angola; 52, Morocco; 54, Nigeria; 57, Cuba; 59, Guatemala; 60, Peru; 61, Ecuador; 62, Jamaica; 63, Ivory Coast; 66, Colombia; 67, Tunisia; 68, Costa Rica.

twice as fast as the population as a whole. About half this increase is the result of migration from rural areas. Most migrants end up in the largest cities. In 1950, only 18 percent of the urban population of the Third World lived in cities with more than a million inhabitants. By 1980, 35 percent did. Similarly, the percentage of the urban population that lived in cities with more than five million inhabitants grew from 2 to 14 percent. The number of people living in these largest cities increased over these thirty years by 15 percent per year, as more and more cities exceeded the five-million mark. The world's huge cities are increasingly in the developing countries. Sao Paulo, which in 1990 will be the world's fourth-largest urban area (behind Tokyo, Mexico City, and New York), was smaller in 1975 than Manchester, Detroit, or Naples. London, the world's second-largest urban area in 1975, will in 1990 be smaller than any of eleven Third World cities, including Seoul, Jakarta, and Cairo.

Urbanization patterns vary considerably among countries and regions. Two-thirds of all Latin Americans are urban dwellers, compared to one-quarter of all Africans and South Asians. Higher incomes, highly concentrated rural land ownership, and industrial development oriented toward substitutes for materials that would otherwise have to be imported are the main reasons for the greater urbanization of Latin America.

Overall, the world has become much more densely populated in this century. The population is younger and more likely to be urban, poor, and nonwhite. In most parts of the world, however, these changes have been accompanied by improvements in living standards.

What Is Likely to Happen?

The United Nations' current medium projection of world population (table 6.1) is based on the assumptions of rapid fertility declines to replacement levels in all regions and continuing gains in life expectancy. These assumptions imply a world population of 6.1 billion in the year 2000, 8.2 billion in 2025, and 10.2 billion by the time population growth ceases completely, by the end of the twenty-first century. Ninety-five percent of this growth would take place in the developing countries. By 2050, the population of Africa would be four times that of Europe, and that of South Asia would be greater than that of the entire Northern Hemisphere including China.

In the developing areas, the labor force would grow faster than the total population until 2050. The size of the working-age population in the developing countries would triple over this period. By 2025, it would surpass the current population of the world. This represents an enormous increase in the number of people needing employment. Most jobs will have to be in the nonagricultural sectors, since the urban population in developing countries will probably rise five- or six-fold between 1980 and 2050, and urban migrants are disproportionately job-seekers in their prime working years.

Yet the UN projections indicate that the rural population will rise by at least another billion people by the middle of next century, despite out-migration. In many already densely populated rural areas, pressure on land resources will intensify, and per capita land availability in rural areas is likely to fall by about one-third.

However specific these numbers may seem, they are very uncertain. They do not take into consideration the real possibility of disaster. Nuclear war could destroy most of the present population. Catastrophes of this magnitude are not unprecedented. The indigenous peoples of the Americas and much of Oceania, for example, were virtually eliminated by disease after contact and conquest by Europeans.

The limitation of projections, which are informed extrapolations of current trends, is that they miss the turning points. Projections made during and after World War II all proved too low, because they missed the rapid postwar declines in mortality in the developing countries. More recent projections have all been too high, since they missed the rapid declines in fertility.

The uncertainty lies in the developing countries, and, more specifically, in about twenty countries in which most of the growth will take place. The advanced countries are, in the aggregate, too small and too close to stability for errors in forecasting their future vital rates to make much difference to the accuracy of the foreecast of total world population. The developing countries, by contrast, have large populations. Their birth and death rates are high and often quite different, so that many different trajectories of decline and convergence are plausible. Almost 40 percent of the population of the Third World is under fifteen years of age, and its fertility rate in adulthood will make an enormous difference. For this reason, the government of China at present feels compelled to push young couples toward having one child only, because so many people born during the baby boom of the 1960s are now reaching childbearing years.

What happens now and in the near future to birth rates (and, to a much lesser extent, death rates) in the developing countries has enormous consequences for the future population of the world. Each birth adds to both the population now and the potential source of future births. The medium UN projection is close to one based on the assumption of replacement fertility by the year 2025. Should replacement level be reached twenty years later, the ultimate world population would be 2.8 billion larger; should it be reached twenty years earlier, the ultimate population would be 2.2 billion smaller.[2] The difference arising from this variation of forty years is greater than the present population of the world.

Of course, the assumption that fertility will ultimately settle at replacement levels may not be valid. Fertility has declined to levels well below replacement level in all of northern and western Europe and shows no signs of returning, despite official support for childbearing and family welfare. The birth rates that result from the individual decisions of several hundred millions of couples bear no necessary relation to what demographers say. Projections that assume fertility settling at levels below replacement imply that world population will be 7.2 billion at the end of the twenty-first century and slowly declining.[3]

This range of demographic possibilities shows the significance of the wide range of demographic profiles illustrated in figures 6.1 and 6.2.[4] Countries can be found in every region and at every level of income with low birth and death rates and rapid declines. Other countries can be found with high and almost constant rates. These differences reflect developmental patterns and past policies. Governments of countries and regions lagging in the demographic transition have paid little attention to population issues or to the persistence of large numbers of households untouched by social or economic change.

By the same token, the wide range of urban patterns now observable in various countries suggests that there are many plausible urban futures. The rate of urban growth and the extent to which the urban population will be concentrated in the principal cities will depend predominantly on the macroeconomic policies pursued by national governments.

CLARIFYING THE ISSUES

What are the objectives of population policy?

The objective is not the stabilization of population as an end in itself but rather the improvement of human welfare. It is important to recognize that for most households and individuals, given the conditions of their lives, the desire for relatively large numbers of children has been natural and reasonable.

As all the developing world did until recently, the world's poor lose one of every four children before maturity. As a result, the typical nuclear family in the Third World contains only five members. It is self-employed on a farm or in a household enterprise, or its members depend on casual labor earnings, or both. Because it operates close to the margin of subsistence, additional family members are welcomed as workers who can help to reduce the insecurity and uncertainty of life and livelihood.

Throughout much of the world, women's security and status are linked with their children and their role as mothers; for women whose other outlets and opportunities are limited, early marriage and early childbearing make sense. Indeed, for many, there are no other choices. Later, if these women wish to limit or terminate childbearing, the interest of males or the network of relatives often opposes them. As recently as two generations ago in the United States, when mortality rates were as high as they are now in the developing world and when few women worked outside the home, typical American couples wanted four to six children, the same range most couples in the high-fertility countries of the Third World want now. It is the small-family norm of one or two children that is novel and that, until recently, was confined to a small affluent part of the world.

Social controls over fertility have been the rule in human societies, through restrictions on marriage and sexual activity, frequent abstinence, prolonged breastfeeding, contraception, abortion, and infanticide. Lack of mechanisms for controlling fertility has never been as important as lack of motivation. In the West, low fertility was achieved before the pill, the intrauterine device, vasectomy, tubal ligation, and menstrual regulation became available. Women born in the United States in the years 1905-15, whose prime childbearing years coincided with the Great Depression had the lowest fertility of any cohort of American women so far.

However, as modernization proceeds, a shift from social to individual control over fertility occurs. Contraception within marriage replaces a more diffuse control over family formation, the length of the breastfeeding and postpartum infertile period, or the elimination of unwanted children. Because cultural change with regard to individual contraception occurs unevenly, many couples, especially those without much education and still embedded in traditional communities, find themselves with unwanted children or facing high risks of unwanted children. Shortening or eliminating the breastfeeding period, a practice that accompanies modernization, adds to this risk by shortening the interval between births. There are hundreds of millions of households without information about, and access to, modern means of family planning. The best evidence of this is the tens of millions of unsafe, often illegal, sometimes fatal abortions that are performed yearly around the world. There are also hundreds of millions of women with little choice but to marry early and raise their children because of their lack of education and restricted social and economic opportunities.

Closely spaced births that begin when the mother is young and continue until she is in her late thirties or forties entail considerable health risks to both mothers and children. In low-income populations, the length of the interval between births is a prime determinant of the new baby's birth weight, which in turn is the main determinant of its chances for survival. Close spacing also puts the older child at risk of malnutrition if weaning is advanced by the arrival of another infant. High fertility greatly increases the health risks for mothers as well because of complications of pregnancy and poor nutrition. In addition to such public health concerns, there are other good reasons for official national and international attention to population issues. Individual households fail to take into account the effects of their decisions, individually small but powerfully large in the aggregate, on the community and the entire globe. These neglected effects may reverse the benefits households foresee in having larger families: to the individual, many sons may mean many earners and greater security; to the entire community, it may mean only more unemployment, stagnant real wages, and greater educational burdens. If the outcome of millions of individual decisions is rapid population growth, the distribution of income between present and future generations and between rich and poor will probably be adversely affected.

In the West, there is a long history of government intervention in individual reproductive decisions, including restrictions on who can have children and what means can be used to control fertility. Incentives and disincentives have been used to influence family size, usually in an attempt to raise fertility. However, it is not a question of population policies being promoted or imposed by the West on the people of the Third World. The large majority of Third World governments have adopted policies designed to ensure that couples have ready access to contraceptive means and information so as to achieve lower rates of population growth. More than 90 percent of the people of the Third World live under governments committed to such policies.

Though stabilization of the population is imperative from any long-sighted perspective, and though there are strong reasons for government attention to population issues, coercive policies toward individual reproduction are not justifiable. Noncoercive measures that will rapidly reduce population growth and improve the welfare of those affected are available. There are policies to cushion the consequences of population growth during the period of stabilization. Naturally, one nation cannot define coerciveness for another with different political and social traditions, but there is a recognizable difference between policies that expand people's options and those that explicitly or implicitly use the threat of penalty to alter people's behavior.

How Does Population Growth Affect Resources and the Environment?

The increase in population has put natural resources and the environment under pressure in many regions. Agriculture in the poorer countries has expanded at the expense of forest and fallow land, and, where soils are poor and unstable, at the expense of the land itself. The rising demand for energy in rural areas, in the absence of programs to expand supply, has stripped many countrysides of vegetation and crop residues. In the expanding cities, congestion and the flow of wastes have overwhelmed the inadequate planning and infrastructure.

If population continues to rise as projected, resource pressures will probably become more taxing, because, in some important respects, the unexploited resource base is reduced. The costs of bringing new lands under cultivation and developing new energy resources will become higher in real terms. However, the population pressures on resources vary widely by country and region. In much of Latin America and Africa, natural resources are substantial relative to the current and projected populations. In South Asia, China, and elsewhere in East Asia, scarcities of land, water, and energy resources are much greater. Many of the regions experiencing population pressure are those, like Bangladesh and the island of Java, where natural productivity is high, and relatively dense populations have been supported throughout history.

The relationship between natural resources and population is determined by technology and social organization. In agriculture, for example, a recent elaborate FAO study of regional carrying capacities has demonstrated that the population that can be fed is determined mainly by the degree of agricultural intensification achieved.[5] Sub-Saharan Africa and China, two low-income regions currently straining to achieve self-sufficiency, can intensify agriculture further with available land and water resources, thereby improving the diets of increasing populations.

Historically, intensification of agriculture and higher yields have been the response to increasing pressure of population on available land. The spread of irrigation, the wider use of manures and the reduction of fallow, and the change of cropping patterns are typical responses.[6] With the modern technology now available, rapid increases in yield are possible through farm research and extension, distribution mechanisms for inputs and products, and adequate incentives to promote rapid diffusion. New technologies on the horizon promise significantly greater potential for yield increases.

For the most part, the issue of population-resource balance is a global question, not a regional or local one. Migration and international trade in commodities, including foodstuffs and fuels, have always been the response to regional differences in resource and population densities. The establishment and expansion of the world economy rested largely on international trade driven by such differences.[7] The historically important trade in grain from the Baltic, iron from Scandinavia, furs and timber from the New World, and silks and fine muslin from the East all reflected different balances between population and resources. The growth of international trade in the twentieth century has been even more rapid than the growth of population, and many countries with totally inadequate natural resources—Japan, Korea, Singapore, for example—have used international trade to achieve outstanding success in improving living standards. The rate of exploitation of both renewable and exhaustible resources has increased. Yet, resource prices do not signal more severe scarcities. Aside from oil prices fixed by cartel, the market scarcities of natural resources and primary commodities have remained steady.

These points should not obscure the connection between living standards and the local population-resource balance. Transportation costs and other barriers to trade in basic commodities like grains and fuels are substantial. Moreover, a substantial fraction of the world's population consists of subsistence farmers little tied to the market economy or unskilled laborers with narrow employment opportunities. Thus, among low-income and lower-middle-income countries, those countries that, in the FAO study, have populations exceeding their estimated carrying capacities have, as a group, significantly higher infant-mortality rates than do other countries at their income level.

Population growth contributes significantly to pressures on resources and the environment, but it is only one factor, and probably not the most important.[8] Thus, while slower population growth will help safeguard the resource base, it is certainly not enough and not even the most critical change needed.

It is projected that worldwide economic expansion in the industrial countries will continue to be the largest source of additional demand for minerals, energy resources, industrial wood, and many agricultural products. Even for cereals, the industrial and newly industrializing countries are expected to account for nearly half the rise in demand over the balance of this century. Much of this increase will be used for animal feed. In the Third World, about a third of the growth in demand for cereals is expected to come from improvements in per capita incomes, and two-thirds from the rise in population. In the aggregate, therefore, population growth in the Third World will contribute only a minor part of the worldwide increase in demand for cereals.

Commercial exploitation, often to meet foreign demands, has frequently led to resource depletion and the destruction of potentially renewable resources. The beaver of North America, the prime hardwoods of the Philippines, and the whales of the North Atlantic are but a few of the well-known victims. Commercial exploitation is likely to lead to depletion whenever high profits can be made from sales of the accumulated stock of a resource that reproduces slowly; whenever property rights over a resource are uncertain, so that conservation is not in the interest of a single proprietor; or whenever new technologies make the costs of exploitation insensitive to the level of the remaining stock.

Although the pressures of poverty and rapid population growth on resources are intense, abundance more frequently than scarcity has been the context of massive resource destruction. Abundance encourages the idea that resource destruction entails no permanent harm, whereas perceived scarcity evokes social mechanisms to limit and regulate resource use. Historical examples abound, especially from the United States and other areas of relatively recent settlement.[9] More recently, tropical deforestation has proceeded rapidly in such sparsely populated areas as the outer islands of Indonesia, the Amazon basin, and central Africa. Clearly, serious damage to resources can take place without population pressure.

The most important step to preserve the resource base is the creation, or oftentimes the re-creation, of effective social controls over exploitation, whether market or subsistence. The lack or breakdown of effective controls is related in complex ways to population growth, which can overwhelm the social institutions and traditional mechanisms evolved by communities for resource management or can lead to regions being opened up for commercial exploitation without adequate institutional safeguards. But strengthening the controls will do more to reduce resource and environmental damage than will slowing the rate of population growth.

The problem of inadequate controls is broader than the problem of "the commons," which is often identified as the critical issue. Not only are common-property institutions consistent with sustainable resource use, community control over fragile environments has a long and successful record in resource management. The "tragedy of the commons" never occurred in England, where the custom of the manor governed use of community pastures and woodlands, nor has it ever occurred in the many other societies where strong social controls regulated the use of common resources.

Inadequate social control includes market exploitation under inappropriate institutions, property rights, and price incentives. It includes inadequate regulation by responsible government agencies and the absence of effective community institutions and processes for management of the resource base. Seizing the numerous opportunities to remedy these deficiencies would improve the prospect for resource conservation more than a faster reduction in the rate of population growth.

Population pressure on resources is often the result of restricted access to resources, not of an overall imbalance. Most of the rural population is crowded onto small holdings (less than two hectares) that occupy a small fraction of total agricultural land, often less than 5 percent. Oftentimes, these small holdings are on erosion-prone hillsides with relatively infertile soils or in areas where rainfall is uncertain. It is misleading to describe the resource degradation that results when marginal farmers misuse marginal lands as a consequence of population pressure, when, in reality, it is a consequence of the gross inequality in access to resources between the rich and the poor.

Frequently, poverty precludes effective resource use. Poor households cannot afford to leave their land in fallow, despite the progressive loss of fertility otherwise. They cannot afford to forgo the current crop to plant tree crops, although that would preserve their land and income. They cannot afford to spend the off-season constructing terraces and conservation works and forego the wage earnings on which they depend. Low-income households usually lack alternatives, even though they know that their practices are undermining the resource base.

It is a mistake to regard population primarily as a problem that results in pressure on resources. People are also a resource. The most serious wastage of resources in the world today is the wastage of lives through illness, premature death, poverty, and lack of opportunity.

THE MECHANISMS FOR IMPROVEMENT

Effecting Demographic Change

The measures that can lower birth and death rates are similar, since they both are considerably higher among lower-income groups and respond readily to social and economic changes that benefit low-income households. Both fall as women acquire literacy and other skills. Both respond to programs that make health and family-planning services and information accessible to households in need. But once moderate living standards are attained, neither fertility nor mortality is very sensitive to further gains. Both the pattern of birth rates and life expectancy among nations[10](figure 6.3) and the statistics of individual households illustrate this.

Although uncertainty remains about what most strongly influences the number of births and deaths as households emerge from poverty, there is little uncertainty that households are able to invest more heavily in the well-being of their children, assume greater control over their environment and their lives, and gain access to more

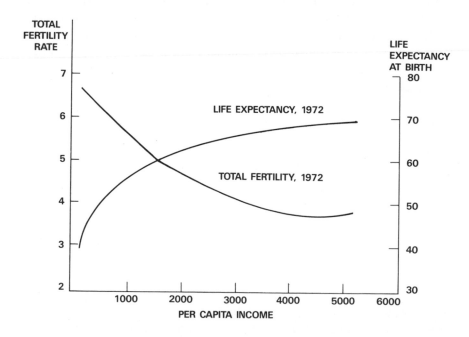

FIGURE 6.3. Relation of fertility (per 1,000 population) and life expectancy (years) to per capita income ($) in the developing countries, 1972.

institutions outside the family. Rapid demographic change depends heavily on social and economic development that alters the outlook and circumstances of the large majority of households. In every region and at each level of development, those countries where birth and death rates are relatively low and where demographic change began early are those where development has affected the broad majority of households. Those countries where birth and death rates are relatively high and where demographic change was retarded are those where social and economic improvement has benefited only a small minority of the population.

It may seem a counsel of despair that the means of accelerating demographic change is the reduction of poverty, but in fact, much can be done. Poverty is not a resource problem. China and Sri Lanka, very poor countries, have largely eliminated malnutrition and other manifestations of extreme want, which remain widespread in much richer nations. The resources required to eliminate extreme poverty are not large. According to World Bank estimates, for example, the food grains required to eliminate malnutrition would amount to only 2-3 percent of world output if they could reach the populations in need of them. The Republic of Korea, which thirty years ago was called "an international basket case," has achieved a level of income equal to the low end of the European range, despite a severe deficiency of natural resources. The important measures required to reduce poverty are known, and known to work.

Before examining specific mechanisms to accelerate the decline of birth and death rates, it is worthwhile stressing that these declines are closely connected. In most developing countries, up to half of all deaths are of infants and children under the age of five. Lowering birth rates reduces mortality in several ways. First, reducing the number of pregnancies at both young and advanced ages saves lives, since such pregnancies put both mothers and infants at higher risk. Second, longer intervals between births reduces nutritional stresses, both on the earlier children who may be breastfed longer and get more maternal attention, and on the mother. This results in higher birth weights and lower perinatal mortality for subsequent children. Third, eliminating births that are not strongly desired results in improved child care, and this is one of the most important determinants of child survival in an essentially unhealthy environment.

Conversely, when infant and child mortality rates are lowered, parents are more strongly motivated to plan births and have smaller families. Also, when infant mortality is low, the breastfeeding period (an important way of spacing pregnancies and protecting infants' health in communities where contraceptive use is low) is not cut short by the infant's death. These interconnections explain why there is considerable correlation between birth and death rates.

MECHANISMS FOR ACCELERATING MORTALITY DECLINES. Eighty percent of all deaths are in the Third World. Death rates have fallen quickly there, but the cause of the decline has been considerably different from that responsible for the earlier decline in the advanced countries. In Europe and America, most of the decline in death rates, both in general and from specific diseases, took place *before* there had been significant scientific advances in the understanding and treatment of disease, before the development of effective chemotherapy or immunization.[11] Reduced mortality resulted from improvements in nutrition, housing, hygiene, and sanitation.

In the Third World, the opposite has been true. Rapid gains in life expectancy have been achieved through the application of medical techniques developed in the West: immunization, the use of antibiotics and other medicines, and the control of disease carriers through the use of DDT and other pesticides. These gains preceded significant improvements in living standards, but they account for most of the decline in mortality since World War II.[12]

As a result, the pattern of the remaining mortality differs markedly from that observed in the West at the same level of life expectancy. Infant and child mortality accounts for a much higher share of the total, with respiratory and diarrheal infections compounded by malnutrition involved in most deaths. The reason the proportion is so high is that a child's survival depends so heavily on the adequacy of the immediate environment, including diet and the quality of care received. Usually, the child who dies has suffered from a whole series of infections that have progressively weakened bodily resistance.

For this reason, mortality rates, especially of the young, are very much higher among the poor, the uneducated, and the rural population. Typically, in countries without well-developed primary health care networks in rural area, infant mortality rates are 50-100 percent higher in the countryside than in the cities. In most countries, infant and child mortality is twice as high if the mother is uneducated or illiterate as it is if she has completed primary school.[13] This striking differential persists even among households with the same income, although poor households in general experience much higher mortality rates than those that are better off. Consequently, in countries where poverty is widespread, whether because the distribution of income is unequal or because per capita income is so low, the excess of infant and child mortality is pronounced. Children are the victims.

Striking reductions in mortality have been achieved in the past decade or two by countries that have improved economic and educational standards for poor households and implemented programs to improve their basic health services and environmental conditions. In China, for example, infant mortality rates are estimated to have fallen from 165 per 1,000 live births in 1960 to 71 in 1981. Deaths from infectious, parasitic, and respiratory diseases have been much reduced by strenuous efforts to improve water supplies and sanitation, to eliminate disease sources to provide all households with basic health services, and to ensure minimally adequate food supplies to all. The Chinese health system has emphasized preventive measures and health promotion, as well as extensive use of paramedical personnel and community health promoters. Important health benefits have also followed the substantial advances in education and the longer intervals between births that have accompanied the fall in the birth rate. Life expectancy in China exceeds that of Brazil, where income per capita is five times as high. China has achieved this with a level of spending on health of only about $4 per person per year.[14]

Where rapid gains in reducing mortality have been achieved, improvement in the educational and social status of women has been a key. The mother is the basic health worker in all societies. She is the first to detect illness or a faltering of growth in the child. She sees that the child receives adequate nutrition and looks after his hygiene, administers simple treatments at home, and ensures that the child receives immunizations and early medical attention when he is sick. The better-informed and educated woman is markedly more successful in caring for the child. Often, her care makes the difference between life and death.

People who understand health problems are constantly amazed at how easy it is to achieve further rapid and substantial improvements in health and life expectancy through simple and well-understood measures that do not require a large expenditure of funds or the availability of highly trained personnel. In both the advanced countries and the Third World, these gains can be realized by shifting emphasis toward health promotion and preventive measures. Especially in the Third World, the creation of effective networks of basic health facilities to provide elementary services to all households is a necessary step.

As UNICEF and other agencies have stressed,[15] the knowledge and the technical means to reduce illness and death sharply are readily available:

- providing oral rehydration packets locally, and instructing mothers on simple home-mixed rehydration doses
- monitoring the weight of infants and small children through the use of growth charts, and providing remedial measures when growth falters
- expanding immunization programs to inoculate children or mothers against tetanus, diphtheria, tuberculosis, measles, whooping cough, and other significant infectious diseases
- providing prenatal and postnatal care, emphasizing nutritional supplements for undernourished pregnant and lactating women, and promoting breastfeeding
- supplying family planning services and information
- educating and training women regarding the importance to family health of sanitary treatment of food and drinking water, of safe disposal of excreta, of washing hands before meals, and other simple preventive steps.

These are elements of a successful, inexpensive health service that has demonstrated dramatic results.

These measures can be applied only if health workers and basic supplies are readily accessible to all households, and especially to poor households. To create this broad accessibility, successful programs have:

- created facilities in villages and urban neighborhoods using paramedical personnel, with referral to, and supervision from, district or subdistrict medical centers
- expanded outreach to the household, using workers recruited from the local community
- worked with and through such local organizations as mothers' clubs
- integrated services at the local level and decentralized many aspects of program management.

Many countries have responded to the World Health Organization's call for expanded primary health care networks by extending programs of this kind. Yet, much more remains to be done. An estimated 75 percent of households in the Third World do not have ready access to even these basic health services, and deaths of tens of millions annually from easily preventable or treatable illnesses reflect this.

The problem is not one of resources. Effective services can be operated for $2-$4 per capita per year, and it has been shown that beneficiaries can and will bear a substantial part of the cost. Indeed, many poor households now pay more than that for ineffective health care. In most Third World countries, public and private health expenditures combined exceed this amount; in many, the public health budget alone does. Effective basic health services for all could be provided within present expenditure levels in many countries *if* inefficient patternns of spending and inappropriate health systems were revised.

Typically, these inefficient systems (1) overemphasize inpatient curative services rather than health promotion and preventive programs; (2) spend excessively on the overdeveloped upper end of the referral pyramid, central hospitals; (3) rely excessively on physicians to provide direct medical attention rather than to supervise paramedical workers; (4) concentrate personnel and facilities in high-income urban areas; (5) spend wastefully on supplies, pharmaceuticals, and equipment. These points also characterize health systems in many advanced countries.

Reorienting health services requires, first of all, a commitment on the part of national leadership to the development of primary health care for rural populations. It requires extensive changes in training programs: many more community health workers and paramedical personnel are needed, and physicians should be trained to act as public health supervisors and leaders rather than solely as clinicians and medical specialists. Academic institutions, international organizations, and national governments can contribute to these training programs.

It requires redirection of health expenditures, whether financed by foreign assistance or internal sources, away from expensive clinical facilities and equipment in urban hospitals and toward primary health care. It requires simplifying and standardizing the pharmacopoeia, making procurement more cost-effective, and making basic drugs and supplies, including contraceptives, available in the community. In many countries, reforming the drug supply system could lead to enough savings to finance a whole primary health care system. It also requires a reorientation in the way health systems are financed to ensure that the better off pay for health services, including the costs of water supply and sanitation, so that public funds can be conserved to provide basic services for the poor.

Community health programs do not have to be organized and operated by government agencies. There are outstanding examples of privately organized programs, some of them largely self-financed, that have successfully met the needs of the poorest and demonstrated the feasibility and promise of new approaches. The Comprehensive Rural Health Project in Jamkhed, Ahmednagar District, one of the poorest regions of Maharashtra in India, is one of many examples. Client payments meet 75 percent of recurrent costs. Table 6.2 shows the results of the first five years of the project's operation. A substantial expansion of private community health programs of this type, with the support and cooperation of public health services and external financing sources, could accelerate the attainment of basic health services for all.

In most developing countries, the private-sector provider of Western-style medicine has served the urban middle and upper classes because the poor, especially in rural areas, cannot afford to pay for such treatment. The private sector's activities have sometimes been dangerous, as in the promotion of infant formula, which some Third World countries have now classified as a prescription drug because of the risks attendant on bottle feeding in those conditions. To bring the skills and resources of the private sector to bear more effectively on the massive health problems of the poor, more cooperative programs with public health agencies are needed. There are many such programs that could be broadened and expanded: subsidized sales of oral rehydration packets and contraceptives through widespread commercial distribution networks, use of private communications channels for health education, production of medical supplies, and sponsored research on tropical diseases. Health ministries can make better use of the strengths of the commercial sector. Often, faulty policies provide inappropriate incentives, and lead to poor results; the overprotection of in-country pharmaceutical production by Third World governments, for example, results in the marketing of too many and too expensive proprietary and prescription medicines.

Institutions in the more advanced countries can make important contributions. Foreign assistance can be directed toward the expansion of primary health care and away from programs using expensive technologies to serve the urban elite. International cooperative training programs can help in redirecting medical education. By far the largest share of resources for biomedical research is available and expended in the advanced countries, only to a small degree on the problems that result in most of the world's sickness and death. Funding

TABLE 6.2. Jamkhed Rural Health Project, India: Comparison of
project and nonproject areas.

	Project area		Nonproject area
Measure	*1971*	*1976*	*1976*
Population surveyed	1,490	1,491	1,405
Percentage of children under five immunized	<1	84[a]	15
Infant mortality rate (per 1,000 live births)	97	39	90
Percentage of pregnant women receiving prenatal care	<0.5[b]	78[c]	2
Crude birth rate (per 1,000 population)	40	23	37
Percentage of eligible couples practicing family planning	2.5	50.5	10

Source: D. Pyle, Voluntary agency managed projects delivering an integrated package of
   health, population, and nutrition in Maharashtra, India, *Services* (New York:
   Ford Foundation, 1979).
[a] In 1978 it was 98 percent.
[b] Percentage for all women.
[c] In 1978 it was 96 percent.

for research on malaria, filariasis, schistosomiasis, and other tropical
diseases, which kill or incapacitate millions annually, amounts to
about $0.05 per case. Because so little has been done, much remains
to be achieved, and the payoffs are large. The partly serendipitous discovery of oral rehydration, using a simple blend of water, glucose, and
salts, has been called the century's most significant medical break-
through. Other major breakthroughs are attainable in the development
of a malaria vaccine and of improved heat-stable vaccines for other
diseases and in better prevention and treatment of illnesses that affect
millions. A large and sustained increase in the level of funding for research on widespread health problems of the Third World is needed
to build long-term research programs and to attract the career interests
of scientists.

   In the advanced countries, significant further reductions in morbidity and mortality are also readily and cheaply available. It has been
estimated that a typical American male in his late forties would add
eleven years to his life expectancy if he stopped smoking, drank alco-

hol only in moderation, exercised regularly, and ate less, especially less animal fat. Not even the discovery of a cure for cancer would have a comparable impact.

Cigarette smoking, for example, accounts for 90 percent of deaths from lung cancer in men under the age of sixty-five and 30 percent of all cancer deaths, 75 percent of deaths from bronchitis and emphysema, and 25 percent of deaths from heart disease. In women, smoking contributes heavily to miscarriage and perinatal mortality. Its overall health consequences dominate those off all airborne environmental pollutants, which industrial countries spend billions of dollars annually to control. Worldwide tobacco production continued to grow during the past decade, as did exports from the advanced countries. Cigarette smoking is becoming increasingly widespread in the Third World and is a distinct threat to health.

The private and public costs of tobacco, alcohol, and high cholesterol consumption are in the hundreds of *billions* of dollars per year. Excessive cholesterol intake is particularly unfortunate, in view of the large and rapidly growing share of world grain production devoted to animal feed. One-third of the world's population suffers health impairment from undernutrition while the wealthiest 10 percent suffers from excessive dietary intake. Significantly higher excise taxes on tobacco, alcohol, and high-cholesterol food products would help; so would more stringent regulation of advertising, greater educational and informational expenditures by public health agencies to discourage heavy use of those products, and the removal of direct and indirect subsidies to producers.

ACCELERATING FERTILITY DECLINES. In the discussion of fertility change in the developing countries, there has often been a false dichotomy and unnecessary debate about the respective influences of "development" and family planning programs. The two are complementary, and *both* contribute to changes in the birth rate. Rapid fertility decline depends both on strong motivation and on access to suitable means for fertility control.

Widespread socioeconomic change and opportunity is a key factor in strengthening motivation, largely because it shifts the perceived costs and benefits of fertility limitation.[16] New aspirations and alternatives for women are especially important. There is overwhelming evidence that increased education, increased participation in the economy outside the home, increased control over finances, and in increased status within the home are all associated with lower fertility, because they either delay marriage or lower marital fertility or both. No other change exerts a more powerful and predictable influence over the pace of fertility decline.

Improvements in the survival chances and the opportunities available to children raise parents' child-rearing costs but at the same time motivate parents to educate their children to take advantage of those opportunities. Often, as parents see that there is something to gain as well as something to lose in the decision, smaller families result.

Once established, new social norms for smaller families, family planning, and increased school attendance and new roles for women are diffused throughout societies. But the pace is slower if large segments of the population experience no economic improvement or increased opportunity, since their continued high fertility will be a brake on the overall decline.

The provision of supplies, services, and information through strong family planning programs has helped broaden access to the means of birth control. Not surprisingly, family planning programs increase contraceptive use and reduce fertility rapidly where the social and economic conditions are conducive, but they can also make a difference where the conditions are unfavorable. For example, pilot programs in urban areas in Bangladesh supported by the Pathfinder Fund raised contraceptive use rates to an average of 50 percent of eligible couples in a country where less than 12 percent nationally use contraceptives, the crude birth rate is 47 per 1,000, and the population growth rate is still rising.

Successes like these reflect significant innovations in family planning programs. In the early days, most programs were clinic-based. Their outreach to rural areas and people unlikely to use clinic services was limited. Most concentrated on recruiting new acceptors rather than fulfilling clients' continuing needs for contraception and maternal and child health care. They offered a narrow range of methods and operated in isolation both from local community institutions and from commercial channels. Theirs was a medical, not a social change, paradigm.

Significant innovations in program design and delivery over the past decade or so have included:

- community-based programs making use of local workers and paramedical personnel to visit couples, stock and resupply contraceptives, and provide basic health and birth-control services to a much wider segment of the population

- subsidized commerical sales of conventional contraceptives to broaden availability further
- expansion of the range of birth-control mechanisms available
- greater involvement in program administration of agencies other than the health ministry, including local governmental and nongovernmental bodies.

These innovations have been partly responsible for rapid gains in both acceptor rates and improved continuation rates in a number of countries, and recent fertility declines have been rapid. In Thailand and Indonesia, strong programs have exploited the complementariness of basic health and family planning services by adding immunizations, prenatal care, and growth-monitoring of infants to the repertoire of family planning workers. Experience to date shows that while more intensive effort costs more, it results in a broader coverage and higher rates of continued use. Program costs per continuing user in the range of $10-$20 per year do not rise sharply.

Much more remains to be done to extend family planning services. At present, perhaps 25 percent of married women of reproductive age in Third World countries are protected, about 150 million people. Of the unprotected, a large fraction does not have ready access to supplies and information. If replacement fertility in the Third World is to be reached by the year 2015, an ambitious but possible goal that would lead to the stabilization of world population at about nine billion in the second half of next century, almost a billion couples will need to be using contraceptives effectively by 2015. This implies something like a 6.5-percent annual rise in the number of users. To expand the availability of services at this pace will require continuing increases in funding, recruitment and training of personnel, organizational efforts, and the strong support of governments, international agencies, and nongovernmental bodies. Traditionally, foreign assistance has accounted for half the financial resources of family planning programs in the Third World, but in recent years, aid has stagnated in real terms. Additional resources are needed.

There are certain regions where population growth rates are high, severe poverty is widespread, actual or potential pressures on resources are serious, and the availability of family planning services is deficient for the great majority of the people. Much of sub-Saharan Africa falls into this category, as do parts of Central and South America, West and South Asia. The World Bank has projected population levels at the time of stabilization to be 430 million for Bangladesh, 411 million for Pakistan, 244 million for Ethiopia, 112 million for the Sudan, and 127 million for Kenya. The governments of many such countries have come belatedly to realize the demographic prospects facing them and the possible consequences. Most now support the diffusion of family planning services. Priority in program assistance should be given to these countries.

Clearly, the expansion of services is not sufficient; the motivation to use them is essential. However, there is evidence of latent demand. Data from the World Fertility Survey suggest that most Third World women over the age of thirty want no more children. A substantial fraction of those under thirty, perhaps one-third, want no more children, and a larger fraction want to delay the next conception. Of all these potential users, the majority is not currently practicing contraception.[17] But pilot programs have demonstrated that a substantial fraction of these women will become users if sufficient outreach and attention are brought to bear.

Improved means of fertility control have also made a strong contribution. Low-dose oral pills, intrauterine devices of improved design, and simplified procedures for abortion and for male and female sterilization became available in the 1960s and 1970s and are today the most widely used mechanisms for birth control. While strongly motivated couples can make do with inconvenient methods, new and improved means increase the likelihood of continued successful use in a population of potential users who vary in goals, constraints, and preferences.

Current research focuses on pills and intrauterine devices that have low risks and side effects, contraceptive implants and injectables, improved barrier methods not tied to the timing of intercourse, long-term reversible methods, and improved methods for predicting the ovulatory period. Although the potential payoff from such research continues to be high, in recent years, funding sources have diminished the level of support. Funding should be increased.

Access to means of birth control can be improved by removing restrictions on the availability of sterilization, abortion, and contraceptive information and supplies. In many countries there are special needs, such as contraceptive counseling and services for adolescents, that are not being met. Unintended pregnancies in this age-group often lead to the interruption of plans for education and work, to early marriage and continuing high fertility, or to abortion and its medical and psychological consequences. Rapid modernization, urbanization, and social change are undoubtedly leading to more sexual activity among adolescents in all countries. Usually the older generation is reluctant to acknowledge this or to seem to acquiesce by providing access to contraceptives.

Policymakers are also reluctant to acknowledge the prevalence of abortion or to seem to sanction it through the removal of legal and other barriers. Yet abortion is widespread even in countries where it is illegal. An estimated 55-70 million abortions are performed in the world each year, one for every two or three live births. Where access to abortion has been relatively easy, it has reduced unwanted births by backstopping contraceptive failures and has usually been followed by more efficient and effective contraception. The effect of restrictions is only to deny abortion to poor and uneducated women and to increase the number of high-risk abortions performed under inadequate conditions by poorly trained personnel.

This discussion of health and family planning programs leads to three general conclusions. First, enough knowledge is available both on the technical means for reducing illness and regulating fertility and on the design and operation of programs to make these means accessible to all. Second, widespread evidence has shown that application of this knowledge leads to rapid declines in birth and death rates. Third, much more can be done, at reasonable cost, to make these services available to hundreds of millions still without them. A concentrated effort now would have a dramatic impact on the world's demographic future.

Implications for Development Policy

Services are only half the story. The other half is accelerating social and economic improvements in the lives of those whose birth and death rates remain high. The means of improvement are known. Highly complementary mechanisms to alleviate poverty, reduce mortality and fertility rates, slow urban migration, and relieve pressures on the environment are available. They promote two goals: improving the prospects of low-income households and expanding the opportunities for women. These goals are linked, both because the means are similar and because throughout the world a large percentage of households headed by women are poor households.

IMPROVING THE PROSPECTS OF LOW-INCOME HOUSEHOLDS. Three important mechanisms to alleviate poverty are available: acceleration of employment growth, redistribution of assets, and adoption of a development strategy that builds from the bottom up. Experience shows not only that all three are effective but also that they are feasible since they have been accomplished.

Accelerating employment growth in the Third World through a more labor-intensive development strategy. Faster employment growth is the most effective way to reduce poverty. Most of the poor are in the labor force and have nothing to sell but their labor. Lack of job opportunities is the main constraint on people's earnings. Faster growth of jobs will draw women into employment because women work in the more labor-intensive sectors. It may slow urban migration, much of which is due to the search for employment. It will reduce resource and environmental pressures by lowering materials and energy inputs per unit of output while raising the labor input. Labor-intensive development minimizes these pressures by reducing the flow of physical resources in the creation of income.

In most countries, accelerating employment growth requires changing development policies that have typically failed to generate sufficient jobs to keep up with the growth of the labor force, let alone absorb the slack. There are success stories that point the way. Taiwan and Korea, for example, followed economic policies that rapidly raised employment in both agriculture and industry. As surplus labor was eliminated in those countries, real wages rose rapidly, and young women joined the labor force in large numbers. There are four significant ways in which governments can accelerate employment growth.

Establishing Appropriate Factor Prices. One reason why employment growth is slow, even in countries in which GNP has grown rapidly, is that many Third World countries pursue policies that make capital artificially cheap and encourage capital-intensive production. Many, for example, provide tax concessions and tax holidays linked to the amount of capital investment rather than to output or employment and make available low-interest loans for the purchase of equipment. Because economic policymakers mistakenly equate investment with development, they commit investment resources to capital-intensive projects that generate few jobs, while farms and small-scale enterprises that provide most jobs grow slowly and are starved for investment funds. Examples abound: arterial highways are built, but not feeder roads; large-scale water projects are constructed, but not small-scale irrigation works and local distribution and drainage systems; funds are poured into large state farms, and smallholder agriculture is neglected. This bias stems partly from the overcentralization of planning, project development, and budgeting. It is often exacerbated by similar biases in foreign assistance agencies.

Governments that reverse these policies find employment growing much more quickly. Multilateral aid agencies and the governments of advanced countries can help by phasing out subsidized credit tied to the purchase of equipment and by providing development assistance to a greater extent through program lending (which covers operating as well as capital costs) and structural adjustment loans linked to the pursuit of agreed policies and development strategies.

Redirecting Government Programs. Several countries, Indonesia among them, have achieved quick increases in output and employment from implementation of a large number of dispersed, small-scale, attractive projects by decentralizing some planning and budgetary authority to regional and local governments. For programs like these to work, administrative ability at local levels must be strengthened, funding must be flexible and capable of expanding with program capabilities, and considerable attention must be paid to program supervision and evaluation. Aid agencies and Third World governments can accelerate employment growth by putting more emphasis on small-scale decentralized programs.

Liberalizing Trade Regimes. The comparative advantage that most Third World countries already have in labor-intensive activities will increase as growth of the labor force continues in the Third World and virtually ceases in advanced countries. The basis and need for international trade will expand, as will the potential gains for all parties. Temperate-zone agriculture will continue to produce surpluses and have an increasing comparative advantage in cereal and livestock products. Potential trade in these commodities and in energy products will rise, owing to disparities in resources and population growth rates. This trade, as well as the Third World's ability to pay interest and amortization on their capital imports, depends on the export of labor services at an increasing rate, either directly as migrants or indirectly in the form of labor-intensive processed goods. In most industries, the experience of the past two decades is that Third World countries that have pursued trade-oriented strategies have been able to expand output and employment rapidly, without causing serious economic disruption in importing countries. This trade is mutually beneficial, since exports to the Third World have risen in step, and the exchange has expanded real income and contained inflation on both sides.

But despite these examples, most Third World governments have severely discouraged labor-intensive exports by excessive protection of domestic markets and import-substituting industries, overvalued exchange rates, and heavy taxation of export industries and agriculture, which is labor-intensive and usually contributes heavily to exports. There is now an enormous and convincing literature documenting these practices and their unfavorable consequences.[18] They have been shown to discourage the growth of exports, agriculture, and small-scale industries, which are all labor-intensive and the source of much employment. The import-substituting industries serving the domestic markets that these policies foster tend to cluster around the largest cities, the biggest markets, thus increasing the amount of migration. The export industries that are discouraged, often based on agriculture or primary raw materials, tend to be more dispersed.

Liberalization of North-South trade promises mutual gains and requires mutual efforts. Discussions of the "new international economic order" emphasized "concessions" to the developing countries and accomplished little. Progress is likely to be based on the realization that countries almost always gain when their trading partners reduce trade barriers *and also* when they themselves reduce trade barriers. Preferences in favor of Third World products are worth little compared with the benefits of a general and mutual reduction of trade barriers. Negotiations on this principle would lead to more progress in the liberalization of North-South trade.

The advanced countries and the Third World are interdependent. In recent years, high real interest rates, a severe international recession and plummeting commodity prices, and rising protectionism have devastated the developing countries. But the indirect effects on advanced countries like the United States, which sends 40 percent of its exports to the Third World, have also been substantial. Hundreds of thousands of jobs have been lost as the Third World has been forced to cut back on its purchases, and the stability of the international financial system has been threatened by the difficulties this economic situation has created for the Third World in servicing its debt.

More than any other measure, the progressive elimination of quantitative restrictions on simple labor-intensive manufactures, textiles and apparel, footwear, and the like, would benefit low-income countries. Simplification and standardization of border requirements, codification of safeguard procedures, and more recourse to compensation and retraining for workers displaced by imports, rather than trade restrictions, would all encourage Third World exports. Reducing tariff rates on products from Third World countries and eliminating tariff escalation on the various stages of processing would enable these countries to expand employment by exporting processed instead of raw materials. At the same time, consumers in advanced countries would benefit from lower prices, and dynamic export industries in advanced countries would expand as Third World economies grew more quickly.

Increasing Capital Flows to Low-Income Countries. Increasing international migration from low-income countries partly reflects the immobility of international capital. Even with labor-intensive development, low-income Third World countries need more investment than they can finance out of domestic savings to create new jobs for the increasing labor force. Although the flow of external assistance to the poorest countries rose considerably in the 1970s, middle-income countries continued to receive most of the public and private capital that flowed to the Third World. Private capital flows went overwhelmingly to a relatively short list of such countries, like Brazil, Mexico, and South Korea.

Employment would rise and poverty would be overcome more rapidly if risk-spreading and risk-reducing mechanisms were expanded so that more private capital was invested in low-income countries. Such mechanisms include more co-financing between official and private lenders, expanded insurance facilities, and the expansion of institutions to act as financial intermediaries for lending to low-income countries.

Until export growth in the poorest countries improves, however, their ability to absorb more capital on commercial terms will be limited. There is an obvious need, documented by the Brandt Commission, the International Monetary Fund, the World Bank, and other bodies, for an expansion of the resources available for compensatory finance, structural and balance-of-payments adjustment lending, and concessionary finance to the poorest countries. An increase of International Development Association subscriptions by the US government would by itself allow capital flows to the poorest countries to expand substantially.

Adopting a development strategy that builds from the bottom up. The essence of such a strategy is that development programs be designed to ensure that a minimal level of services reaches all households before public resources are spent to provide superior services to middle- and upper-income groups. This implies that public funds be used to establish minimum services for all, and that private resources be tapped to satisfy demands for higher-quality services for the better off. This solution has worked successfully in some countries in health, transport, education, and other sectors. In education, for example, private schools and universities often satisfy the demands of middle and upper classes for more or sometimes better education than the state can provide. Alternatively, when there are compelling reasons to develop unified sources of supply, as with urban utilities, the better off can be made to pay the full long-run marginal costs of the services they use, or more, while public resources are used only to ensure that minimal needs are widely met.

By contrast, many governments use their limited resources to provide subsidized services to middle- and upper-income groups that could and would pay the full cost and then find it difficult to extend these services to the much larger goup of low-income households. Concentration on services for the better off also implies concentration of services in urban areas. Subsidized schools, health facilities, communications, and transportation are markedly better in cities. This urban bias pulls migrants away from the rural areas.

This does not imply that services must be supplied to low-income groups free of charge. Often governments that have tried to do so have either been unable to finance investment programs because of the heavy burden of subsidized services or have found that financial constraints limit the provision of even basic services to just a fraction of the population. "Free but unavailable" is the too-common response to the poor seeking access to public services. Yet, experience demonstrates that basic services can be provided at costs that almost all households can bear. These services are often superior to those otherwise available to poor households and cheaper than those the poor often buy in the marketplace. If programs are well designed to provide minimal but effective services in cost-effective ways, it is usually possible to recover a large fraction of the costs from the beneficiaries, however poor.

A telling example is that of small-credit programs. Usually these are subsidized through lending-rate ceilings that require monetary authorities to inject funds that cannot be obtained through the banking system. At these subsidized rates, only a small fraction of potential borrowers can be accommodated, usually borrowers with sufficient influence and resources to obtain favorable treatment. Meanwhile, the vast majority of poor households continue to borrow from unofficial capital markets at interest rates two to three times as high. By contrast, successful unsubsidized small-credit programs have shown themselves capable of growing rapidly with only a small initial infusion of capital, by profitably accepting deposits, servicing extremely small short-term borrowers, many of them self-employed women, and charging rates that are much lower than those that would otherwise have been available to the poor.

This bottom-up approach could be applied to research efforts as well. By far the greatest fraction of resources available for research is devoted to the problems and needs of the better off. We have seen this to be true in biomedical research. In agriculture, little research has been carried out on the potentialities of dry-land cropping or the subsistence crops of the poor—cassava, millet, and pulses, for example. In energy, little research has been devoted to improving fuelwood species and growing systems, to Third World applications of solar energy, or to other energy problems of the poor.

Third World governments and development assistance agencies can do much more to build development programs from the bottom up. Reviews of fiscal and financial policies, projects and program design, and development priorities would turn up many opportunities for change in almost all countries and sectors.

Redistributing assets: reform of land tenures. In many countries, the concentration of land ownership is extreme. Twenty percent of the rural population may be landless, and half the farmers, with the smallest holdings (usually under two hectares), may occupy only 3 or 4 percent of the total agricultural area, whereas 10 percent of farmers with large holdings, often consisting of thousands of hectares, occupy half to three-quarters of the total area. These large estates tend to include much of the level and well-watered bottom lands, whereas the subsistance holdings include many areas marginal for sustained cropping.

Typically, the large holdings are used less intensively. A smaller percentage of arable land is put under crops, and on the cropped area, labor inputs are less and yields often lower than on small holdings.[19] More of the large holdings are used to produce nonfood crops and commodities for export. Under such conditions, tenurial reform would dramatically reduce poverty. Greater access to land would improve the productivity of the poor and provide additional employment opportunities. The flood of impoverished rural migrants to the cities would be reduced. And, since small holdings typically produce more subsistence food along with cash crops, the local availability of food would improve. More intensive use of the better soils and wider access to them would reduce pressure on marginal lands that deteriorate rapidly when repeatedly cropped by poor subsistence farmers.

Naturally, land redistribution evokes intense political resistance and has been accomplished only when the traditional power structure has been disturbed, either by external forces or through internal upheaval. Yet, land reforms carried through in South Korea, Taiwan, Japan, and elsewhere have resulted in productive, innovative, and efficient small farms. It has been repeatedly shown that, in the medium term, the higher productivity of suitable lands under more intensive use creates real gains in output that facilitate the transfer of land ownership. It is not a zero-sum game.

Opportunities for constructive programs of tenurial reform, land redistribution, and increased land productivity do exist. If potential smallholders had access to long-term credits at reasonable interest rates, in general they could buy land from large holders at the capitalized value of its income yield. If these transfers were accompanied by accurate surveys and title registration so that the holders were assured that they would reap the benefits of investments in land improvement, there would be further productivity gains. In many countries, with additional investment in plot consolidation, land leveling, installation of water-management systems, and other infrastructure that can best be installed over a wide area, much greater gains would be realized.

Although it seems quixotic even to contemplate land reform by other than revolutionary means, a program like that outlined above would be a highly productive use of national and international resources, with enormous long-term implications for resource management, employment and income, and the reduction of poverty. While international agencies such as the World Bank and bilateral agencies such as the US Agency for International Development have stated policy commitments to support such initiatives, in fact, little is being done, and much more could be attempted.

IMPROVING THE POSITION OF WOMEN. The critical, often underestimated, contribution of women to development has been documented in recent years. Women play the crucial role in safeguarding the family's health and the children's survival, likewise in the regulation of fertility. Women have important roles in resource management and environmental preservation. In many countries, they take the lead in cropping decisions and farm operations, especially for subsistence crops. Women commonly supply the fuel for household use. Among the poor, basic household survival often depends on the contribution of women.

Obviously, the measures outlined above to improve the status of the poor are of prime importance to women, much more important, in fact, than special "women's programs." In Third World countries, as in the advanced nations, a large fraction of poor households are headed by women and are neglected by development programs both because they are poor and because they are headed by women.

The two critically important and closely related ways to improve the position of women both depend on strong leadership and government support, because progress depends largely on changes in social attitudes and expectations. Nonetheless, nongovernmental organizations, women's groups, and international agencies have made, and will continue to make, important contributions.

Expanding educational opportunities. Educated women are more effective basic health providers and family planners than their uneducated contemporaries. Education and training are critical in expanding the labor market opportunities for women and in increasing their productivity in self-employment. Directly and indirectly, they lead to later marriages and delayed childbearing.

In the past twenty years, great strides have been taken in schooling for boys and even more so for girls. Among low-income Third World countries, female primary school enrollment as a percentage of the number of girls between six and eleven has risen from 34 to 80 percent; in the lower middle-income countries, the percentage has risen from 56 to 91 percent. There are countries in which the rise has been extremely rapid: in Laos, from 16 to 88 percent; in Nepal, from 1 to 53 percent; in Tanzania, from 18 to 98 percent; in Kenya, from 30 to 100 percent; in Iraq, from 36 to 110 percent; and in Libya, from 24 to 119 (figures exceeding 100 percent reflect the attendance of some five- and twelve-year-olds).

In many countries, relatively fewer females are enrolled in school because relatively more drop out. Girls leave school to help with household work, to care for younger siblings, or sometimes to marry. Strong public campaigns directed at parents, the commnity, and the schools have been effective in reducing the attrition rate for girls.

In deciding whether to keep their daughters in school, parents are more sensitive to distance and cost than they are with boys, perhaps because they feel more strongly their obligation to educate sons. Programs to build additional primary and junior secondary schools in local communities have the effect of raising female enrollment. Lower educational costs at the primary level, including the provision of textbooks, supplies, and uniforms, are also effective. At secondary and higher levels, scholarships for girls can increase participation.

Deliberate measures are needed to open and reserve educational opportunities for females in institutions that train workers for technical and managerial occupations in the modern economy, from which women have largely been excluded. In particular, many Third World countries would do well to employ more women as teachers and instructors beyond the lowest grades of primary school so as to provide girls with role models. Teaching materials could also be purged of gender stereotypes that fail to encourage educational and career aspirations of females.

These are elements of successful programs to accelerate the education of females. In addition, because there are so many young women who have already dropped out of school, informal educational programs, organized in the community through mothers' clubs, cooperatives, and other associations, can be effective.

Finally, the rise in educational participation and the expansion of employment opportunities for women are closely related. The experience of successful countries has been that, as parents see the benefit of educating their daughters further, they become increasingly willing to do so.

Expanding employment opportunities for women. Women make up a large fraction of the labor force in all countries, whether or not this is reflected in the official statistics. If their work is outside the modern sector of the economy, it is often excluded from the statistics by the definition of labor-force participation. But their participation is especially high in agriculture, small-scale trade, agricultural processing, and light manufacturing and services. Overall, it is much higher in the traditional than in the modern economy, in the small-scale than in the large-scale sector, and in the labor-intensive than in the capital-intensive sector.

Employment opportunities for women expand rapidly when these sectors expand rapidly. For this reason, female employment grows fast if the overall development policy favors employment growth and labor-intensiveness. The sectors that employ women in large numbers thrive in relatively open, competitive market economies in which prices and costs are not distorted, and monopolized sectors are few. In these economies, the barriers between large and small enterprises, modern and traditional enterprises, are weak. But these sectors—agriculture, light manufacturing, petty trade, finance, and services—do not prosper when inputs, credit, foreign trade, and prices are regulated by government agencies, even agencies ostensibly bent on fostering them. In such countries as South Korea and Taiwan, despite long traditions of social discrimination against women, employment of women has risen rapidly within relatively open, labor-intensive development patterns.

The importance of the demand for labor cannot be underestimated. Culturally rooted patterns of gender segregation in labor markets break down readily in the face of changes in the demand for labor. The emphasis of policy, initially at least, should therefore be on reducing barriers to entry to areas of employment, rather than on ending wage discrimination. From the employer's perspective, women workers are then attractive, because they offer lower labor costs. Where there is considerable labor surplus, there is an inevitable trade-off between more rapid gains in wage rates for women and more rapid gains in employment. The latter does more to improve living conditions for low-income women, because the earnings they can obtain through more rapid employment growth, even with wage discrimination, are superior to what they would have otherwise.

In addition to these macroeconomic policies, specific steps are important to remove discriminatory barriers women face as borrowers, property owners, and workers. Many governments have made progress in amending discriminatory provisions in legal codes and revising administrative practices and policies that impede the advancement of women. Nongovernmental organizations have effectively advocated change and have established pilot programs to broaden opportunities for women. The role of business enterprise is critical, since recruitment, promotion, work practice, and compensation policies can actively encourage or discourage the pariticipation and advancement of women. Increased efforts by all parties would yield large returns in the pace of social, economic, and demographic progress.

Not enough is known to permit anybody to estimate the effects of the implementation of these proposals. Neither the effects or measures that improve poor households' socioeconomic conditions nor those of wider availability of health and family planning services can be estimated accurately. However, the rapid declines in birth and death rates in countries that have carried out the substance of these proposals demonstrate that, if carried through as a worldwide development strategy, they would result in more rapid demographic change than even optimistic forecasts now envisage—and in rapid reduction of the burden of poverty and disease afflicting most of the world.

NOTES

1. R. S. McNamara, "Time bomb or myth: the population problem," *Foreign Affairs* 62, no. 5 (Summer 1984):489–511.

2. T. Frekla, "Long-term prospects for world population growth," *Population and Development Review* 7, no. 3 (September 1981):489–511.

3. UN Population Divison, "Long-range global population projections," *Population Bulletin* 14, New York, 1983.

4. Data are taken from the World Bank, *World Development Report 1983* (Oxford: Oxford University Press, 1983) table 20, p. 186.

5. FAO, *Potential Population-Supporting Capacities of Lands in the Developing World*, Technical Report of Project Int/75/P13 (Rome, 1982).

6. E. Boserup, *The Conditions of Agricultural Growth* (Chicago: Aldine-Atherton, 1965).

7. D. North and R. Thomas, *The Rise of the Western World* (Cambridge: Cambridge University Press, 1973).

8. R. Repetto and T. Holmes "The role of population in resource depletion in developing countries," *Population and Development Review* 9, no. 4 (December 1983): 609–932.

9. W. Cronon, *Changes in the Land* (New York: Hill and Wang, 1983).

10. World Bank, *World Development Report, 1984* (Oxford: Oxford University Press, 1984).

11. T. McKeown, *The Modern Rise of Population* (New York: Academic Press, 1976).

12. S. H. Preston, "Causes and Consequences of Mortality Declines in Less Developed Countries During the Twentieth Century," in *Population and Economic Change in Developing Countries*, ed. R. A. Easterlin (Chicago: University of Chicago Press for the National Bureau of Economic Research, 1980).

13. UN Department of International Economic and Social Affairs, *Levels and Trends of Mortality Since 1950* (New York: Unipub, 1982).

14. World Bank, *China: Socialist Economic Development*, vol. 3, *The Social Sectors* (Washington, D.C.: World Bank, 1983).

15. J. Grant, *The State of the World's Children* (Oxford: UNICEF, 1984).

16. R. Repetto, *Economic Equality and Fertility in Developing Countries*, (Baltimore: Johns Hopkins University Press for Resources for the Future, 1979).

17. D. Nortman, "Measuring the unmet need for contraception," *International Family Planning Perspectives* 8 (September–December, 1982):125–34.

18. A. O. Krueger, *Foreign Trade Regimes and Economic Development: Liberalization Attempts and Consequences.* (Cambridge, Mass.: Ballinger, 1978).

19. W. R. Cline and R. A. Berry, *Agrarian Structure and Productivity in Developing Countries* (Baltimore: John Hopkins University Press 1979).

CHAPTER SEVEN

Third World Cities and the Environment of Poverty

JORGE E. HARDOY and
DAVID E. SATTERTHWAITE

As cities grow in size and population,[1] and as they come to house an increasing proportion of the Third World's people, problems arise at three different levels of the environment. The first can be called the internal environment—the environment of the home and its immediate surroundings.[2] The second is the environment that cities provide for their inhabitants—for instance, in terms of air and water quality. The third involves the regions in which cities are located and the extent to which city-based activities, drawing on limited resources such as fertile land, fossil fuels, and fresh water, create environmental problems for the wider region.

Later sections discuss ways in which citywide environmental problems and problems relating to productivity, housing, and control of land use might be addressed. Separate attention is given to the role of nongovernmental organizations and international agencies in solving these problems. Since the term *city-linked environmental problems* encompasses so much and the term *Third World* so many nations, most of which have a considerable diversity of cities within their boundaries, only a somewhat impressionistic sketch can be given here. In the West, it is largely through the efforts of individual activists, citizens' groups, and nongovernmental organizations that attention has been drawn to environmental problems. Few such groups exist in the Third World, although their number and influence are growing. Funds are not available, however, to support them in organizing sustained programs. Thus, the examples of environmental problems given here cannot be considered the "worst cases," since the latter are frequently not documented. Sources of information for this paper include publications of citizens' groups based in the Third World. (See the list of references which follows.)

Western researchers who look at how environmental problems relate to health and living conditions tend to focus only on the presence of some pollutant or pathogen. But in the Third World, lack of income and inadequate diet in poorer households are perhaps the root causes of both poor health and the inability to secure better housing and living conditions. Although the lack of drains and piped water in a shantytown may be the main cause of the high incidence of typhoid, diarrhea, and dysentery, the toll taken by such diseases may be greatly exacerbated by inadequate food intake because of inadequate income. Inadequate income is also the major cause of poor, overcrowded housing conditions, since in most cities, people's access to what might be termed the minimum acceptable standard of accommodation is governed by their ability to pay, not their needs.

What are regarded in the West as the great city-based environmental problems—air and water pollution derived from factories, automobile exhausts, and lack of sewage treatment, for example—are usually not the major environmental problems in Third World cities. Although these problems do have serious effects on human health in Third World cities, they are usually less serious than the problem of poverty and the low priority given by city, state, and national governments, as well as the private sector, to tackling poverty's underlying causes and its appalling consequences. This paper will concentrate on the environmental aspects of poverty, however, without discussing how the incomes of the poor might be improved, even though inadequate and often unstable income is usually the main reason for the environment of poverty in which so many Third World city dwellers live.

URBAN GROWTH

During the last hundred years, there has been an unprecedented growth worldwide in urban populations and in the concentration of population in large cities and conurbations. Underlying this trend has been the growth and development of an increasingly integrated and city-based world economy. As national economies and people's livelihoods become less dependent on an agricultural base, urban centers, cities, and metropolitan areas replace farms, villages, and transient seasonal settlements as the main location of human activity.[3] World production, trade, and communications take place within an increasingly interlinked network of cities. The labor force associated with these activities must live nearby, so residential areas are in or close to such cities. Only a tiny privileged elite can work in these centers and commute from houses in quiet suburbs or rural areas.

Although the Third World's rural population little more than doubled between 1920 and 1980, its urban population grew from about a hundred million to almost a billion in the same period. In 1980, about 60 percent of this urban population was in cities of 100,000 or more, while some 33 percent lived in cities of a million or more. Table 7.1 gives some idea of the differences between Third World regions in terms of urbanization and population concentration in large cities. But, because of the way it is laid out, it gives little idea of the enormous diversity in degrees of urbanization and in rates of urban population growth between nations within each continent, and indeed between regions within nations.

Going on alongside this process of urbanization has been the settlement of large areas that only forty or fifty years ago were either uninhabited or only sparsely populated. The search for new farmland and pasture and for timber and nonrenewable mineral resources has provided the impetus for the rapid colonization of new land, both through government programs and through spontaneous, uncontrolled population movements. Examples can be seen in Bolivia, Ecuador, Amazonia, eastern Peru, southeastern Venezuela, Patagonia, southern Nepal, and parts of Indonesia and Malaysia. Some of the more rapidly growing cities are those emerging as administrative, service, or processing centers in these newly settled areas. Such cities are Manaus in Brazil, Santa Cruz in Bolivia, and Ciudad Guyana in Venezuela, as shown in table 7.2.

Although most Third World inhabitants still live outside urban areas, and only a small proportion in Africa and Asia live in large cities, the economic and political role of cities is inevitably larger than that suggested by the size of their populations. It is in cities and their wider metropolitan areas that the production and sale of nonagricultural goods, services, and information are concentrated. They are the centers of political and economic power and of consumption. The investments of national governments in infrastructure, services such as piped water, education, health, and subsidized housing usually favor

TABLE 7.1. Population of urban areas and different-sized cities in Africa, Asia, and Latin America.

Population in Urban Areas

	1950		1980		2000	
	no. (in millions)	%	no. (in millions)	%	no. (in millions)	%
Africa	31.8	14.4	133.0	28.9	345.8	42.5
Latin America	66.3	40.6	240.6	64.8	466.2	75.2
East Asia	108.9	16.0	359.5	33.1	622.4	45.4
South Asia	107.4	15.5	329.8	23.1	790.7	34.9

Population in cities of 100,000 or more inhabitants

	1950		1980		2000	
	no. (in millions)	%	no. (in millions)	%	no. (in millions)	%
Africa	14.0	6.4	86.2	18.7	249.1	30.6
Latin America	30.7	18.8	157.8	42.5	354.9	57.3
East Asia	64.2	9.5	229.8	21.1	431.2	31.5
South Asia	49.0	7.1	204.8	14.4	538.9	23.8

Population in cities of 1 million or more inhabitants

	1950		1980		2000	
	no. (in millions)	%	no. (in millions)	%	no. (in millions)	%
Africa	3.5	1.6	36.5	7.9	154.6	19.0
Latin America	15.3	9.7	101.3	27.3	232.2	37.5
East Asia	31.1	4.6	131.9	12.1	261.5	19.1
South Asia	17.9	2.6	105.9	7.4	328.2	14.5

Population in cities of 5 million or more inhabitants

	1950		1980		2000	
	no. (in millions)	%	no. (in millions)	%	no. (in millions)	%
Africa	0.0	0.0	7.5	1.6	58.3	7.2
Latin America	5.2	3.2	50.6	13.6	147.5	23.8
East Asia	12.5	1.8	58.1	5.3	125.2	9.1
South Asia	0.0	0.0	45.2	3.2	190.7	8.4

Source: Figures are taken or derived from those quoted by Philip M. Hauser and Robert W. Gardner, "Urban Future: Trends and Prospects," in Population and the Urban Future (New York: Fund for Population Activities, 1980).

Note: East Asia statistics include Japan.

city rather than rural or small-town inhabitants. So do subsidized food prices, import substitution policies, taxes, and macroeconomic policies in most cases. In most Third World nations, the trend toward increased centralization of decision making within national governments has reinforced the political and economic dominance of national capitals and, as a result, has weakened state (or provincial) and city governments.

THE HOUSING ENVIRONMENT

The housing environments of lower-income groups in Third World cities are among the most degraded and unhealthy living environments that exist. Between a quarter and a half of the inhabitants of most cities live in grossly substandard housing. In this discussion, low-income housing in Third World cities is divided into squatter settlements, illegal subdivisions, subdivided inner-city housing, custom-built slums, and boarding and rooming houses, although these categories are an oversimplification. Most housing in these categories shares two characteristics. One is a lack of readily available drinking water, sewers (or other systems for hygienic disposal of human wastes), garbage collection, and basic measures to prevent disease and provide primary health care; thus many diseases and physical disorders are endemic—diarrhea, dysentery, typhoid, and food poisoning. The other is crowded, cramped conditions, which often means that communicable diseases such as tuberculosis flourish, usually aided by low resistance due to malnutrition. Household accidents are also common, which is perhaps not surprising considering that five or more persons often live in one room and there is little chance of protecting the occupants (especially children) from fires, stoves, and kerosene heaters. Thus, inadequate incomes combine with substandard shelter to provide totally degraded internal environments.

It is possible to generalize about the most fundamental cause of these conditions—namely, that access to "minimum-standard accommodation" is open only to those with sufficient money, and this is more than many (or most) city inhabitants can afford. But generalizations about solutions are far more difficult because of the great diversity in people's needs and priorities.

If individuals or households find minimum-standard accommodation beyond their financial means, they must make certain sacrifices to bring down the price. And this usually means foregoing environmental quality in housing. Other items maybe are more important for survival—for instance, food, children's education, or a second-hand

TABLE 7.2. Examples of cities that have experienced
rapid population growth.

	1950		No. of in habitants (in millions)	
			Most recent estimate	Projection for 2000
Mexico City	2.45		16.0 ('82)	31.0
Sao Paulo (Brazil)	2.45		12.49 ('80)	25.8
Bombay (India)	3.34		8.0 ('82)	16.8
Jakarta (Indonesia)	1.45		6.18 ('77)	15.7
Cairo (Egypt)	2.5		8.5 ('79)	12.9
Delhi (India)	1.74		5.2 ('79)	11.5
Manila (Philippines)	1.78		5.5 ('80)	11.5
Lagos (Nigeria)	0.27	('52)	4.0 ('80)	10.5
Bogota (Colombia)	0.61		3.5 ('77)	9.6
Nairobi (Kenya)	0.14		0.83 ('79)	5.3
Dar es Salaam (Tanzania)	0.15	('60)	0.9 ('81)	4.6
Greater Khartoum (Sudan)	0.18		1.05 ('78)	4.1
Amman (Jordan)	0.03		0.78 ('78)	1.5
Ciudad Guyana/San Feliz de Guyana (Venezuela)	0.128	('70)	0.41 ('80)	1.20
Nouakchott (Mauritania)	0.0058	('65)	0.25 ('82)	1.1
Manaus (Brazil)	0.11		0.51 ('80)	1.1
Santa Cruz (Bolivia)	0.059		0.26 ('76)	1.0

Source: Jorge E. Hardoy and David Satterthwaite, *Shelter: Need and Response, Housing, Land and Settlement Policies in 17 Third World Nations* (New York: Wiley, 1981); and UN *Urban, Rural and City Populations 1950–2000* (as assessed in 1978) (Population Division, Department of Economic and Social Affairs, 1980).

Note: Accurate statistics for city populations are difficult to obtain, and different sources give different estimates. For instance, another estimate for Manila in 1980 puts its population at well over 7 million, much larger than the 5.5-million figure listed here. Also, official statistics or estimates rarely state whether the figure is for a specified city area or includes developments that have sprawled beyond city limits. Some of the population growth reported between 1950 and the mid-1970s is due to new, wider, metropolitan area boundaries. Population projections for the year 2000 are based on extrapolation of past trends, which are often a poor guide to the future. But rarely are data available to provide more accurate projections, based on considerations such as the city's economic prospects, compared with those of other areas, the nation's economic prospects, and anticipated changes in population growth rates.

sewing machine to allow a member of the family to earn additional income. Each low-income individual or household will have to make compromises with regard to size of accommodation, the terms under which it is occupied, suitability of site, housing quality, location, and access to infrastructure and basic services. For example, to bring down housing costs, a household of five might forego space and live in one room or sacrifice secure tenure and piped water to live in a self-constructed house on illegally occupied land. To delineate the possibilities for improving the housing environment of such people, it is necessary to comprehend their diverse needs and priorities. One must also understand their present circumstances, and this requires the exploration of complex questions such as the legality of the site or house they occupy, and the terms under which the occupants are there—that is, are they nonpaying guests or legal or illegal tenants, sub-tenants, or owners.

Thus, it is difficult to generalize about needed action. It is possible to make a broad distinction, however, between those living in illegally constructed houses (or shacks) and those living in poor and overcrowded houses or apartment blocks, the construction of which was legally approved. People living in illegally built housing are often said to live in shantytowns,[4] whereas those living in legally built but inadequate housing are said to live in slums.

The appendix at the end of this chapter gives some idea of the proportion of certain city populations forced to live in shelters on illegally occupied or subdivided land. Those people are often referred to as squatters, although this is misleading, since many live in illegal subdivisions that are managed by the landowner or occupant. They are illegal because they were not authorized by the city and are usually contrary to the city plan (where one exists). The difference between squatting and living in an illegal subdivision is significant, since housing in an illegal subdivision is generally more expensive but may have some infrastructure provided by the developer. The "owners" or "tenants" in such subdivisions may be relatively well-off compared with most squatters, and their chances of obtaining legal tenure and publicly funded infrastructure are generally better.

Many shantytowns grow up on sites ill suited to human habitation because the land is cheap or free. Examples can be seen on hills prone to landslides in Rio de Janeiro (Brazil) and Caracas (Venezuela), on sandy desert in Lima (Peru), or on land prone to flooding or tidal inundation or under water as in Guayaquil (Ecuador), Recife (Brazil),

Lagos (Nigeria), Delhi (India), and Bangkok (Thailand). In Mexico City approximately 1.5 million people live on the drained lake bed of Texcoco. This land is subject to dust storms in the dry season and becomes a bog when it rains. Its use for housing developments is illegal. Yet these "colonies populares," in common with many others in and around the city, were built because more suitable sites within the economic reach of lower-income groups were not available.

The occupants of shantytowns generally organize the construction of their own houses and, to save money, often help build them. Low-income groups choose such sites or sites around industrial or residential dumps because the land is unsuitable for commercial development. The worse the environmental conditions, the more likely that the landowner will allow them to stay. But environmental problems in such shantytowns are compounded by the fact that they are illegal. City authorities do not feel obliged to provide them with water, drainage, sanitation, public transport, and primary health care. Indeed, it is not uncommon to find water being sold out of tankers by private concerns for ten to twenty times the price charged by municipalities for piped supplies in middle- or upper-income residential areas. These illegal settlements are not isolated or small-scale phenomena. They house tens or even hundreds of thousands in most major Third World cities. Construction in such settlements remains the main source of new city housing in the Third World.

In most cities, many low-income people live in older and usually more centrally located buildings. These have some of the characteristics of Western inner-city slums. The buildings often once housed relatively well-off families. As these households moved to the suburbs, their houses or apartments were subdivided, so that today several families live in a space previously occupied by only one. Rarely have sewerage or piped-water facilities been improved to cope with the greatly increased use. The facades of the historic centers of many older cities often hide poor and overcrowded housing conditions.

"Custom-built" slums have also been constructed by the private sector in many cities. These were usually built when migration into a city was particularly rapid and in places where public controls did not inhibit their construction. They were profitable investments because single rooms were let to households, but provisions for piped water, washing facilities, and sanitation were generally inadequate. Examples can be seen in Latin American cities such as Buenos Aires, Rio de Janeiro, Montevideo, Havana, and Mexico City. They were designed and built to house immigrant workers and often provided high

returns on the capital invested. The "slum gardens," or "slum tenements," of Colombo in Sri Lanka, originally built by businesses, colonial corporations, and real estate developers, today house around one-
fifth of the city's population, although their construction ceased in the
late 1940s. Similarly, Bombay's "chawls," one-room tenements that
now house about one and a half million people, were built between
1920 and 1956 by factory owners and landowners for a growing working class. Hong Kong has examples of more recent "custom-built"
slums constructed by the private sector between 1955 and the late
1960s. It was not unusual for fifteen to twenty people to live in a
three-room apartment in these slums.

In the last twenty to forty years, many governments have enacted
laws limiting the rent that slum property owners can charge, so the
owners have put little or no investment into upkeep or improvement.
It is not uncommon to find leaking roofs, crumbling wall plaster, and
rotten window and door frames. Many households live in one room
with no window. There are also frequent reports of such inner-city
housing collapsing. Fifteen percent of Bombay's population lives in
eleven thousand buildings that are on the verge of collapse.

Although most lower-income people find accommodation in a
slum or an illegal settlement, others resort to more desperate solutions. One is simply to sleep on the streets or in some other public
space, as an estimated 100,000 - 500,000 people do in Bombay. Another alternative is to rent a room or a bed in cheap hostels or
rooming houses. Perhaps the cheapest are the "hot-bed" hostels in
Calcutta, where six males per room rent beds by the hour so that at
least two people working different hours can use one bed each day.

Inner-city slums were often the first source of cheap housing in
growing cities before the rapid growth of illegal shantytowns provided
alternatives. The history of shantytowns is perhaps as old as the history of cities. But even with increasing urbanization and the growth of
large cities, their extent was initially limited by poor public transportation and working days of ten hours or more which meant that people had to live close to their work. Over time, improved public transportation, shorter working hours for some of those with stable jobs,
and the location of factories and other enterprises outside the central
city made less centrally located shantytowns a viable alternative.

Shantytowns today usually house many more people than inner-
city slums. As certain cities have grown to unprecedented size and
the journey to work has come to take three or more hours of a worker's day, there are signs that new inner-city slums are being created

and old ones further degraded. However, few potential shantytown sites remain within reach of centers of employment, and the demand for housing is such that even shantytowns have become sufficiently commercialized to exclude the poorest groups. Because of the world recession and the economic problems of most Third World nations, an increasing number of people find themselves needing to live close to central city districts. They cannot afford the time or money for the daily journey from shantytowns on the periphery. Whereas many city inhabitants suffered from inadequate wages or lack of a stable income in the 1960s and 1970s, income-earning prospects are generally even worse today and affect a higher proportion of the population. So the demand for living space in inner-city districts grows and brings with it increasing pressures on dilapidated inner-city dwellings.

THE CITY ENVIRONMENT

Citywide environmental problems such as air and water pollution might be assumed to be less pressing in the Third World than in the West for two reasons. First, a smaller proportion of the population lives in cities. Second, cities are less industrialized; in 1980, the Third World (excluding China) accounted for half the world's population but only 11 percent of its industrial production. Rural and agriculturally based environmental problems such as deforestation, soil erosion, loss of topsoil, water pollution, and deaths and disability from biocide use (and misuse) might seem more urgent, even though, as described later, some of these problems bear also on cities. Thus, the problems of growing industrial and citywide needs for water, its subsequent pollution and disposal, and air pollution and solid-waste disposal might be assumed to be less urgent than in the more urbanized and industrialized West. But again, the aggregate picture hides the fact that there are hundreds of Third World cities or metropolitan regions with high concentrations of industries. Nations such as China, India, Mexico, Brazil, and South Korea figure prominently in tables of the world's largest producers of many industrial goods.

Third World cities and urban regions with high concentrations of industries (especially heavy industries) suffer pollution problems comparable to those experienced in Europe, Japan, and North America. Industrial production has grown rapidly in many Third World nations in the absence of effective planning and regulation. More than thirty-five Third World nations recorded annual average growth rates for industrial production of 5 percent or more during the

1960s and 1970s. The more rapid the growth, the more serious the problem is likely to be in that few governments have had much interest in controlling industrial pollution. Also, industrial production is often concentrated in one or two regions within each nation, and government efforts to decentralize industrial development away from these areas rarely steered new industrial plants outside the wider city region. Similarly, in cities with large concentrations of motor vehicles and traffic flows too great for existing road networks, air pollution from internal combustion engines presents problems comparable to those in the West. The major cities of richer Third World nations have ratios of automobile ownership to population comparable to those of many Western cities. And even where the ratio is lower, narrow, congested streets and old and poorly maintained vehicles with higher levels of polluting emissions can make the problem significant.

Local climatic conditions can also exacerbate the problems. Thermal inversions are common in the winter in northern Chinese cities. Certain Southeast Asian cities have long periods in the year with little wind to help disperse air pollution, and, with high concentrations of automobiles and an abundance of sunshine, photochemical smog becomes an increasing problem. As in the West, Third World city environments present the familiar litany of problems associated with lead, mercury, cadmium, oxides of nitrogen and sulphur, petroleum hydrocarbons, particulate matter, carbon monoxide, polychlorinated biphenyls, and asbestos.

Documentation of environmental problems in Third World cities is too poor to indicate where problems are most acute or even to suggest the magnitude of the effects on health. However, the limited documentation on air and water pollution and solid-waste disposal gives grounds for concern. The discharge of mercury-contaminated wastes into bodies of water has received much publicity because of the hundreds of deaths and disabilities it caused in Minamata, Japan. Likewise, serious problems of the type known in many North American water bodies have also been noted in Bangkok, Thailand; Perai, Malaysia; Bombay, India; Managua, Nicaragua; Alexandria, Egypt; Cartagena, Colombia; and in various Chinese cities. Significant build-ups of mercury, lead, cadmium, copper, and chromium have been reported recently in almost every industrializing nation in Southeast Asia. Thirteen children were recently reported to have died of mercury poisoning in Jakarta, Indonesia, after eating fish caught in the waters of Jakarta Bay tributary. One of the problems is that since governments in "the North" started enforcing more stringent regulations, production in certain "dirty industries" has increasingly been transferred to the Third World to cut costs. For instance, there is a trend toward relocation of asbestos manufacturing industries from the United States to Brazil and Mexico, among other Latin American countries. Asbestos textile imports into the United States from Mexico, Taiwan, and Brazil grew rapidly between 1969 and 1976, and Taiwan and South Korea have been displacing Japan as a source of asbestos textiles for the United States as new regulations on this industry have been introduced in Japan. There has been a comparable transfer of production by Japanese and North American subsidiaries in other dirty industries to Taiwan, South Korea, the Philippines, and Thailand. Arsenic production, lead refining and battery manufacture, metal smelters, and biocide production are among the industries in which this transfer is increasingly taking place. When allied to increasing local dirty industry to meet local and regional demands, this has serious implications for the health of Third World city populations both now and in the future. The lessons learned in the West over the last fifteen to twenty years on the enormous health costs associated with certain uncontrolled industries seem to go unheeded by government and are often being ignored by the industrial sector.

Mercury pollution in Managua illustrates this problem. In 1980 an investigation by Nicaragua's new government found that Electroquimica Pennwalt (Elpesa), an affiliate of a Philadelphia-based multinational, was responsible for mercury contamination of Lake Managua, from which drinking water for the capital city is drawn. The lake, more than 1,000 km² in size, had also been a major source of fish for city inhabitants. In addition, an examination of workers at the factory revealed that 37 percent showed evidence of mercury contamination. The workers had not been warned about possible hazards, even though the level of mercury in the air at the factory was found to be twelve times the safety level recommended by the US National Institute of Occupational Safety and Health.

Reports from China in 1980 and 1981 noted very high cadmium and mercury concentrations in rivers and underground waters. For instance, organic mercury pollution in the Songhua Jiang downstream of Jilin, an industrial city that became a major center for the chemical industry after the 1949 revolution, reached concentrations of between 2 and 20 mg/l. This is between two thousand and twenty thousand times the maximum recommended concentration in water and waste directives of the European Economic Community.

However, the health hazards due to heavy metals are probably more localized than those of other pollutants. In almost any Third

World city, environmental problems such as smog or smoke, inadequate provision for garbage collection and disposal, open sewers (or no sewers at all), inadequate drainage, and noxious and polluted waters are usually all too evident. But there is surprisingly little detailed documentation of the levels of nitrogen oxides and sulfur oxides in the air, the extent to which specific bodies of water are polluted by sewage and industrial effluents, or the capacity at specific sites to absorb and break down those pollutants.

In India, environmental problems tend to be better documented than they are elsewhere in the Third World. A recent report cites the following examples of air and water pollution in Indian cities.[5] Bombay, with its great concentration of population and heavy industry, probably suffers more than India's other metropolitan areas. One study compared the health of residents in two major industrial areas, Chembur and Lalbaug, with that of residents in a cleaner suburb, Khar, in 1977-78. People living in the industrial areas suffered from a much higher incidence of chronic bronchitis, tuberculosis, skin allergies, anemia, and irritation of the eyes. The rate of worker absenteeism was much higher, particularly in Lalbaug's textile mills, and there was a notable rise in the number of deaths from cancer in Lalbaug. In other Indian cities, domestic fires are a major cause of air pollution. One estimate suggests that domestic fuel burning generates about half of Delhi's air pollution. An estimated 60 percent of the residents of Calcutta suffer from respiratory diseases related to air pollution.

Bombay, Delhi, and Calcutta also have major water-pollution problems, problems they share with most other Indian cities. Much of India's surface water, even in large perennial rivers such as the Ganges, is polluted. Of India's 3,119 towns and cities, only 8 have full sewage disposal and treatment facilities; 209 have partial facilities. The River Ganges alone carries the untreated sewage of 114 cities, each with 50,000 or more inhabitants. DDT factories, tanneries, paper and pulp mills, petrochemical and fertilizer complexes, rubber factories, and a host of others use the river to get rid of their wastes. The Hooghly River, which branches off the Ganges, passes between Calcutta and Howrah and receives untreated wastes from more than 150 major factories and raw sewage from 361 outfalls.

In China, the industrial sector is the dominant consumer of fossil fuels, and its heavy concentration in about twenty cities, most of which use coal in outdated furnaces and boilers, ensures high levels of air pollution. Although total fuel combustion by households is small by comparison, the burning of raw coal in millions of small inefficient stoves is a major source of air pollution in the colder parts of the nation. In Beijing, as in Delhi, domestic fuel combustion is a major cause of air pollution. Lung cancer mortality in China is four to seven times higher in cities than in the nation as a whole, and the difference is largely attributable to heavy air pollution.

The Brazilian city of Cubatao, near Sao Paulo and the port of Santos, has long been known as the Valley of Death. It is a city of heavy industry. The extraordinarily high incidence of stillborn and deformed babies, of tuberculosis, pneumonia, bronchitis, emphysema, and asthma, and the high infant mortality rate are all linked to the high levels of air pollution. Many of those who work in the city live in shantytowns built on stilts above swamps. Hundreds, perhaps thousands of the inhabitants of one such shantytown are reported to have been killed in late February 1984 after a pipeline carrying gasoline leaked into the swamp under the shantytown and then caught fire.

Alarming levels of airborne lead and carbon monoxide have been noted along busy roads in Kuala Lumpur, Calcutta, Rio de Janeiro, Lagos, and Ibadan, and in Zimbabwe. The problem of lead pollution in many Third World countries is made worse by government policies that permit a much higher lead content in gasoline than in Western countries. Major air and water pollution problems have also been documented in Manila, Bangkok, Mexico City, Sao Paulo, Rio de Janeiro, Jakarta, and several major cities in South Korea.

It is not only the largest cities or those with a concentration of heavy industry that suffer serious environmental problems. So do many cities with weak industrial bases and relatively few automobiles. Problems in these cities are caused by poor drainage, lack of sewers or other hygienic methods of disposing of human wastes, lack of planning controls to ensure, for example, that industries are located downstream and downwind of city inhabitants, and the lack of regulation (or its enforcement) of industrial air pollutants and liquid and solid wastes. Just one or two agricultural processing, chemical, pulp and paper, or beverage factories can seriously pollute a river. Just one cement plant or one thermal power station burning high-sulfur coal or oil can create serious air pollution.

Recent examination of environmental problems in Cameroon shows some of the problems faced by cities that do not have concentrations of population and industry on the same scale as the largest Third World cities. The estimated population of Douala is nearly 500,000, and of Yaounde more than 300,000. Both cities have major

environmental problems linked to uncontrolled effluents from industries, inadequate means for disposing of household sewage, and a
large proportion of low-income inhabitants who have no alternative
but to build shelters illegally on sites poorly suited to safe, healthy
housing. In residential areas with no garbage collection, rubbish heaps
build up on streets and sidewalks and become breeding grounds for
rodents and disease sources. During rains, floating garbage often col-
lects at bottlenecks and causes flooding. The waterways, polluted by
sewage, industrial effluents, and runoff from higher ground, flow
through some of the poorest residential areas. In Yaounde, wastes
from a beer factory heavily pollute the Mfoundi River. As in most cities, lower-income people suffer most, since they are forced to occupy
the most dangerous and polluted sites. It is no surprise to find that
low-income "spontaneous settlements" have grown up in valleys and
marshy areas infested with mosquitoes. Even in smaller cities with between 50,000 and 100,000 inhabitants, environmental problems are
not necessarily mitigated by small size.

REGIONAL IMPACTS

As the major centers of production and consumption, cities demand a
high input of resources—water, fossil fuels, land, and all the goods
and materials that their populations require. Cities are also major centers for resource degradation. For instance, water used by cities is returned to rivers, lakes, or the sea at a far lower quality than that originally supplied. These effects on the environment are called regional
impacts and can be divided into those arising from cities drawing on
resources from the wider region and those arising from city-based activities that affect the wider region.

The first of these categories can only be outlined, since the impos-
sibility of isolating city-based environmental problems from the
broader economic, social, and spatial conditions is evident. City-
based demand for fuelwood, for example, is often partially met by
preempting supplies formerly used by rural inhabitants. Deforestation, and the soil erosion that usually accompanies it, may be considered rural problems, but these processes can be intimately linked to
urban demands for fuelwood or charcoal. Furthermore, the soil erosion that comes with deforestation destroys the livelihoods of rural
people, forcing them to migrate to the city. Erosion can contribute to
floods that devastate large areas downstream, including cities. Demand for electricity in cities can also cause environmental problems

for rural areas. Through the preemption of agricultural land or the introduction or exacerbation of waterborne or water-related diseases, large hydroelectric dams affect the rural environment even though the electricity is consumed mostly in the cities.

Within each nation or region there are also complex population movements linking rural areas, towns, and cities. Migration can have a major impact on the population growth and demographic structure of cities and thus on city environments. It may result from high population densities in rural areas, shortages of arable land, declining soil fertility, increased commercialization of agriculture and of agricultural land markets, inequitable patterns of land ownership, and exploitative landlord-tenant relations. Such factors are likely to be cumulative and mutually reinforcing. Cities feel the effects of migration directly, and their growth as centers of demand for rural produce can in turn contribute to the commercialization of agricultural land markets, which pushes still more people off rural land. Furthermore, the livelihood of rural artisans frequently is destroyed or damaged by the increasing availability of mass-produced goods made or distributed by city-based enterprises. These conditions, together with the concentration of public and private productive investment in relatively few cities, have contributed to rapid net migration into most cities of the Third World. Most Third World cities affect the environment of their wider region in three distinct ways: by uncontrolled physical expansion, waste disposal, and air pollution. Uncontrolled physical expansion impinges on what might be termed an immediate hinterland around a city. As the city expands, agriculture in this area disappears (or stagnates) as land is bought by people or companies in anticipation of a change from agricultural to urban use. The lack of effective public control of such changes in land use or of the profits that can be made from them encourages unplanned and often illegal urban sprawl. Lack of other high-return investment opportunities helps fuel such land speculation.

This uncontrolled physical expansion has important environmental consequences. One is that the haphazard development of peripheral lots, many of which remain undeveloped or only partially developed, ensures that the pattern of development is too dispersed for cost-effective provision of roads, water mains, sewers, and social services. In Sao Paulo, where large tracts of land remain undeveloped because of the capital gains accruing to owners from speculation, the urbanized area could accommodate a two-thirds increase in population without further physical expansion. There are hundreds, even thousands, of hectares of vacant land in and around cities such as Manila, Bombay, Delhi, and Bangkok. These and many other Third World cities and their hinterlands present the paradox of extreme over-crowding and chronic housing shortages (because housing sites are too expensive for most people who live in the cities) and acutely inadequate infrastructure and services amid vast amounts of vacant or only partially developed land.

A recent study of the effects of uncontrolled physical expansion in Colombia revealed the underuse or deterioration of recently extended utility networks at the same time that speculators are causing urbanization to spread uncontrolled to the nation's most agriculturally productive land.[6] Such loss of productive land is also apparent in many other nations, since cities often develop in or close to the best agricultural land. In Egypt, more than 10 percent of the most productive farmland has been lost to urban encroachment in the last three decades, much of it through illegal squatting or subdivision, while at the same time prime sites within cities remain undeveloped. Since 1900 the urban area of Delhi (including New Delhi) has grown by a factor of nearly thirteen, eating into surrounding agricultural land and absorbing more than a hundred villages. This unplanned and uncontrolled expansion has been accompanied by an increase in the use of fertile topsoil to make bricks.

A consequence of this uncontrolled city growth is the destruction or degradation of the natural landscape and thus of open spaces for recreation. Use of land for this purpose is crucial to the urban environment but is forgotten since it has no explicit economic function. Recreation might be judged less urgent than housing, but to ignore it now deprives city dwellers, both now and in the future. Once an area is built up, it is difficult and expensive to create open space. Contamination of lakes and seashores, which diminishes their recreational value, is also common. Coastal cities dump untreated sewage in the sea. Such dumping is the main cause of polluted beaches in Montevideo, Rio de Janeiro, and along the northern coast of Venezuela, near Caracas. Pollution is often so severe that beaches have to be closed to the public, thus eliminating the major recreational areas easily accessible to lower-income groups.

The disposal of city wastes can have an environmental impact stretching beyond the immediate hinterland. Damage or destruction of fisheries by effluents from city-based industries is increasingly common. Pollution threatens the livelihood of millions of river fishermen in India where, in a 158-km stretch of the Hooghly River, the average fish yield in polluted zones is only about one-sixth that in unpolluted zones. In Malaysia, water pollution has destroyed the livelihood of many river and lake fisherman, and inshore fishermen report serious declines in catches in waters affected by industrial effluents and oil. Other fisheries severely damaged by industrial effluents are in Lake Maryut, Egypt; the Han River, South Korea; and Rio de Janeiro's Guanabara Bay. In China, fisheries have been damaged in the Li Jiang River in Guilin, in Hangzhou Bay (near Shanghai), and in the Wujin Country's portion of the Grand Canal.

River pollution from city-based industries and untreated sewage can lead to serious health problems in downstream settlements. The Bogota River, for example, is contaminated by effluents from the city of Bogota, the site of Colombia's largest concentration of industries and a city of nearly five million inhabitants. At the town of Tocaima, 120 km downstream, the river has an average fecal bacteria coliform count of 7.3 million, making it unfit for drinking or cooking. (A fecal coliform count gives the number of baterial colonies per 100 ml of water, and less than 100 is considered safe to drink.) In a village close to Tocaima, the river was reported in 1980 to be black and, despite its distance from Bogota, to smell of sewage and chemicals. Nearly all the children in that village had sores or growths on their skin from swimming in the river.

Regional impacts of this sort extend to international bodies of water. On the shores of the Persian Gulf, a small, shallow, salty, and almost landlocked sea, rapid urban and industrial growth endangers one of the world's more fragile ecosystems. Although the major source of marine pollution is oil discharged from tankers, raw sewage and industrial wastes from rapidly expanding coastal cities also have a considerable impact, as do desalination plants along the coast.

The third kind of regional environmental impact relates to air pollution. Damage to vegetation or falling crop yields often provide the first evidence of harm. In China, reports in 1978 noted that heavy industrial air pollution in Lanzhou, a major city and industrial center, had destroyed fruit trees and damaged crops and livestock in nearby villages. Vaclav Smil's book *The Bad Earth: Environmental Degradation in China* (p. 121) suggests that many similar instances of environmental damage are not reported and that considerable damage to plants and livestock must also occur near coal-fired power stations, refineries, and chemical works with no (or only rudimentary) controls. Smil's point is valid for most other Third World nations where the industrial sector has grown rapidly. In the Samsoon plains of

South Korea, once an important rice-producing area, damage is attributable to power, petrochemical, and fertilizer plants, copper and zinc smelters, and oil refineries. Problems with acid rain, caused by industrial emissions, which figure so prominently in the West, have also begun to be reported in certain urban areas in the Third World, including Shanghai, China; Petaling Jaya, Malaysia; and Cubatao, Brazil.

There is increasing concern that large cities, especially those growing most rapidly, will overtax the "beneficence of nature," which provides and then purifies air and water and yields cheap and easily exploitable energy sources. This concern is heightened by a look at projections for the year 2000 and beyond. Today there are numerous examples of environmental stress, and these seem likely to multiply as cities expand.

TACKLING CITYWIDE PROBLEMS

The last fifteen years' experience in the West has shown that polluting emissions can be controlled, given resources and political will allied to appropriate legislation and its enforcement. Many new industrial-plant designs eliminate or reduce polluting wastes or recover and recycle process chemicals that were formerly dumped. A substantial reduction in the emission of pollutants is possible in most industrial operations for a small fraction of production costs. Indeed, in many cases, industries actually cut costs or increase profits at the same time that they reduce polluting emissions. Wastes from agricultural processing industries, among the major sources of pollution, have been shown to be valuable feedstocks for other industrial operations. For instance, bagasse (sugarcane waste) is commonly used as fuel in sugarcane mills, as an ingredient in animal feed, and in the production of certain building materials. The Cuban Research Institute for Sugarcane By-Products has developed a process for turning bagasse into high-quality newsprint at reasonable cost. In many Third World nations, this could replace newsprint imported at high cost. Other organic residues can be used as feedstocks for the manufacture of animal feed, packing materials, chemicals and pharmaceuticals, fertilizers, fuel, food, and construction materials.

In Third World cities, as in Western cities, air pollution problems due to internal combustion engines can be greatly reduced by use of more efficient engines and lead-free gasoline. Regulation of private vehicles and efficient public transportation services can also help, and this can be done without resorting to such expensive measures as new subway systems. Less congested and more efficient transportation systems can be brought about at relatively low cost by a judicious mix of taxes and physical restrictions on private automobiles, improved facilities for other commonly used forms of transportation (from trains and buses to communal taxis and rickshaws to bicycles and walking), and better traffic management. The transportation system of the Brazilian city of Curitiba was greatly improved by a bus system that included exclusive express busways, which were integrated into improved citywide, district, and neighborhood bus services.

New designs for power stations burning coal or heavy oil can greatly reduce sulfur oxide emissions and increase the efficiency with which such fuel is converted into electric power. Some Third World nations would benefit from the introduction of "cleaner" technologies as they build or expand their industrial base. Many modern and rapidly expanding industries (such as electronics) do not demand the high consumption of natural resources or produce the amounts of air, water, and land pollution associated with, say, the steel industry. Furthermore, many Third World cities, especially those in the richer nations, are finding that services account for a high proportion of new jobs, and this implies fewer problems with pollution and resource consumption.

However, Third World governments are inhibited from acting on pollution problems for various reasons. Most serious is governmental concern for expanding industrial production, with little or no concern for social or environmental side effects. Although most Third World governments have established national environmental agencies in the last ten years, few have set up the institutional structure to implement a sustained and effective environmental policy. Leonard and Morell, (1981) note that the enforcement of environmental regulations in the Third World is "a relatively haphazard process, depending heavily on the political power of those who violate the regulations and on the extent to which the government is under pressure to take action to stop pollution and environmental degradation. Enforcement is arbitrary at times, in ways which appear to have more to do with political considerations than concern with the environment" (pp. 302-03). Ad hoc action in response to specific localized problems and pressures—for example, to a group of fishermen complaining about industrial effluents damaging their livelihood—is far more common than coherent, sustained programs of regulations and enforcement.

It is difficult for citizens' groups in these countries to play a role similar to that of such groups in the West, since there are few funds to sustain a continuous campaign of activism and education, and governments seek to repress (or at least discourage) their work. And of course, it is still more difficult for citizens' groups to play a major role in societies ruled by nonrepresentative governments.

Particularly relevant also is the economic crisis confronting most Third World nations. If a government's main concerns are the survival of the national economy (or its own survival) and avoiding additional unemployment, the formulation of new environmental legislation or the implementation of existing legislation is unlikely to be given high priority. There is still a strong fear that enforcing pollution controls creates unemployment, even if in most instances, there is little substance with which to back this claim. The export earnings of most Third World nations are substantially smaller than their import bills. Foreign exchange is limited, and machinery and equipment usually accounts for between a quarter and a third of all merchandise imports. Following the Western example for reducing industrial pollution may mean expensive imported add-on equipment or completely new industrial-plant designs. Even if the add-on equipment is not expensive, the foreign exchange cost will discourage its installation. With foreign exchange so scarce, numerous other goods will be judged of higher priority than such equipment, as controls are put on imports. And although many governments are encouraging the development of their own industry to reduce their almost total dependence on technology imported from Europe, the USSR, or North America, in few Third World nations does the industrial sector have the capacity to make such equipment.

The notion that environmental quality and pollution control are luxuries, at least with regard to city-based industries, is slowly being eroded. Attitudes toward the cost of safe and hygienic disposal of sewage and household waste and the provision of safe water supplies seem more rigid, however. National and city governments frequently claim that these are too expensive. But the claim is based on the installation of systems designed to Western standards. There are various low-cost alternatives to conventional waterborne sewage systems and sewage treatment plants that are more effective and hygienic than the standard pit latrine or bucket latrine systems. World Bank research involving field studies in thirty-nine communities in fourteen nations found a wide range of such sytems that could be implemented to match local physical conditions, social preferences, and economic resources. Several of these options had a total annual cost per household (including both investment and recurring costs) of between only one-tenth and one-twentieth that of conventional sewage systems. Most required lower volumes of water than conventional systems, and some required no water at all. Further, it is possible to install one of the lowest-cost technologies initially and then to upgrade it over time.[7]

Inexpensive improvement in the quality and availabilty of water supplies is also possible and can actually reduce present costs for water, considering that shantytown residents must often buy water from vendors. A piped-water system can often provide a more economical and accessible water supply. Lower-income groups in Lima, Peru, purchase water from vendors at three times the price paid by those whose houses are connected to water mains, despite the fact that their daily water consumption is less than a sixth that of those with piped water. If the daily expenditures now made to water carriers were invested in a piped-water supply, greatly improved services could be provided.[8] But major improvements are needed in most Third World nations in skilled manpower and in investment capacity of municipal governments. The trend has been for power and funds to be increasingly concentrated at higher levels of government. Unless city governments are strengthened, other needed changes will also be difficult to implement—from the enforcement of environmental legislation to the efficient collection of garbage, management of solid-waste sites, and improved traffic management.

Much could be done if national governments gave higher priority to these essential aspects of improving city environments, and if local governments had the manpower and funds to invest in appropriate systems, maintain them, and recover costs. A serious constraint is the illegality of many of the neighborhoods where improved water supplies, sanitation, garbage removal, and public transportation are most urgently needed. Government agencies are unwilling to make public investments in these locations, since it would imply official recognition of the residents' rights to be there. The importance of giving legal tenure to occupants of illegal settlements as well as of providing much-needed infrastructure and services is discussed in the next section.

Of course, citywide problems would be lessened if city populations grew more slowly. Slowing the flow of migrants is often suggested as a way of alleviating the environmental problems of large cities. But to slow migration, better employment opportunities must exist in other locations. This in turn implies the diversion of capital investment into productive activities, infrastructure, and services to locations other than cities, so as to provide better alternatives for potential migrants to cities. The reasons for rapid migration to the cities in most Third World nations have been the heavy concentration of private and public investments in cities over the last thirty years and the forces at work in rural areas that dispossess peasants and landless workers of their livelihood. The rapid growth of cities and metropolitan areas like Lagos, Amman, Manila, Cairo, Sao Paulo, Jakarta, Mexico City, Lima, Dar es Salaam, and Nairobi over the last three decades and the contribution of migration to their demographic growth are hardly surprising when one notes the extent to which these cities concentrate their entire national industrial, commercial, and service base and how they have been the main beneficiaries of public investments.

These trends are unlikely to change rapidly in the immediate future. Returns to private capital remain higher and more certain close to or within major cities. At best, firms locating there pay only a small part of the costs that their operations generate in terms of increased migration and increased demand for land, water, services, and infrastructure. Even if it is no longer the largest cities that are growing the most rapidly—which is the case in many Third World nations—there is little sign of major flows of private captial to productive activities in small towns and rural areas, although this would help slow migration to cities. Even if the flow of city-bound migrants could be diverted to smaller towns or rural areas through better economic opportunities, the populations of most Third World cities would still grow rapidly from natural increase. Indeed, in many cities, natural increase already plays a more significant role than migration in population growth.

TACKLING HOUSING AND LAND-USE CONTROL

Unless lower-income groups secure adequate and stable incomes no strategy to improve their environment can have a lasting impact. Many Third World nations, especially the poorest, face fundamental constraints here that relate to the relationship of their economies to the world market, constraints that are far beyond the scope of this paper. But it is important to remember that housing environments cannot be expected to improve in nations with poor or bankrupt economies.

Actions that most national governments can take to alleviate at least the worst aspects of the degraded home environments of the poor can be divided into two categories: those to ensure more appropriate and affordable new houses and those to improve existing housing. To increase construction of low-cost housing, government priority should be to boost the supply and reduce the cost of all elements in what might be termed the minimum-standard house: a site with reasonable access to centers of employment or income; building materials; infrastructure such as pavements, roads, and water, electric and waste-removal service; services such as public transportion, education, and health care; and credit for house construction or improvement.

Boosting the supply and reducing the cost of appropriately located housing sites is perhaps the first priority. Public authorities must ensure that legal alternatives to squatting and unauthorized subdivisions are as cheap and conveniently located as their illegal competitors and that infrastructure and services are provided. This is a precondition for lessening the environmental destruction caused by cities' uncontrolled physical growth, as described above in the section on regional impacts.

The choice of location for the government's legal, affordable alternative housing is as critical as the housing itself. Lower-income people cannot afford to be too distant from their sources of income or from family and friends. But, because of the cost of land, government-sponsored low-cost housing projects are often far from the major sources of employment for unskilled or semiskilled workers, so that people living in such projects frequently abandon them and return to squatting.

There are many ways to achieve the needed public control of land use. Each nation already has traditions of land tenure and public rights on which control can be built. In rapidly growing cities, public authorities may have to acquire land themselves, at least temporarily, to ensure that individuals, public bodies, nonprofit housing cooperatives, and the like can obtain land for houses and community facilities. To avoid tying up capital in a "land bank," a public agency could have a rolling program such as exists in Tunisia for land acquisition, development, and disposal. A study of housing, land use, and settlement policies in seventeen Third World nations found that those governments that had come closest to meeting needs for low-income housing were those with strong and effective controls on urban land markets and who were not afraid to intervene to ensure that cheap, conveniently situated land sites were allocated to housing for low-income groups.[9]

Numerous public controls or inefficient policies can hinder housing construction. Official standards for mininum plot sizes are often unrealistic and simply push the cost of the cheapest legal plot beyond the ability of most households to pay. The paperwork, time, and expert advice needed to obtain permission to build is often unnecessarily expensive and burdensome, especially for lower-income groups. Building codes and norms set unrealistic standards. Obtaining a loan requires collateral that those most in need do not possess. The purpose of all building and planning regulations should be to encourage better-quality living environments and thus ensure that minimum standards of health, safety, and access are met at minimum cost in both time and money.

Government support of the efforts of lower-income groups to build and improve their own housing is often referred to as the self-help approach, even though it implies a much higher degree of government involvement than most current policies. It is also a different kind of involvement from that of most governments today. During the 1970s, many governments initiated measures to increase the supply of low-cost housing or expanded measures begun in the 1960s. After these practices were recognized as destroying the only kinds of housing that many could afford, however, slums and illegal settlements were bulldozed less often. An increasing number of governments subsequently supported "serviced site projects" where, to reduce costs, households were supplied with only a housing plot with basic infrastructure and services. But in only a few nations did these initiatives boost the supply of housing and reduce costs enough to have much impact, although one or two individual projects may have succeeded. Government agencies must move beyond supporting only various dispersed projects. Instead, working to boost the supply and reduce the cost of all housing elements, they should provide the institutional framework and the infrastructure for greatly expanding housing construction.

This suggests the need for fundamental changes in government practices. City and metropolitan governments must be strengthened to enable them to undertake such tasks—tasks that require manpower, legislation to provide suitable powers, and a financial base. Yet, as noted earlier, most Third World nations are moving in the opposite direction. This recommended approach is no more than the application at a national and citywide level of principles that have formed the basis for the most successful Third World city housing projects. Such projects have been based on working with slum or squatter communities in determining their needs, funding improvements to infrastructure and services, and providing cheap serviced plots for construction of new houses. Projects in which the people themselves played a major role in design and implementation and in managing the construction or upgrading of houses have usually worked far better than government programs that sought to build houses *for* the poor. Public housing estates, even when subsidized, usually turn out to be too expensive, badly located, and inadequately designed.

Indeed, many rapidly become slums. Ambitious public housing projects frequently incur enormous cost and time overruns. In Kenya, for instance, only 8 percent of the low-cost units for 1974-78 had been completed by 1979, and on average they cost five times the amount anticipated. The massive public housing program planned for Nigeria in its 1975-80 plan suffered a similar fate. In most Third World nations, public housing programs have produced only a tiny proportion of the needed units and only at excessively high unit costs. If large subsidies have to be given for each unit, relatively few can be built. And those that are built rarely benefit the poor. In Indonesia, as in many other nations, civil servants and military personnel get priority access to new public housing. Even if lower-income groups do receive subsidized public housing, they frequently find it in their interest to (illegally) rent or sell it, since the income this provides is more valuable to them than the subsidized house. Many of the more successful projects of the last twenty years have in fact been sponsored by religious groups and charities. Their collective impact, however, like that of most government policies, is tiny compared with the scale of the problem and the speed with which it is growing.

The self-help (as opposed to public housing) approach has been used by some governments as an excuse for doing little or nothing. But many poor people cannot afford to construct part (or all) of their houses. Their survival often depends on more than one of their members (including children) working long hours. The fact that many income-earning activities are in the so-called informal or unrecorded sector means that the workers are often characterized as unemployed or underemployed when in reality they are overemployed, working long, underpaid hours. Thus, government policies must understand the range of housing needs among the poor within each city and the differences in skills, resources, and incomes that different households can bring to bear in helping solve their own housing problems.

The potential difficulties should not be underestimated. Land speculators and associated financial interests will oppose many of these changes. But, with or without public support, the so-called informal sector will dominate housing construction in most major Third World cities. Governments' effectiveness in aiding self-help can be measured by the rate at which the housing environment of poor households and communities improves. At present, many governments' claims that they are increasing support for self-help projects are no more than an attempt to legitimize their inaction.

To this program for boosting the supply of new housing must be added programs to improve existing residential environments. Many governments have adopted programs to upgrade low-income neighborhoods rather than bulldoze them. The Kampung Improvement Programme in Indonesia, initiated in Jakarta and later extended to many other cities, is one such program. Similar programs in Dar es Salaam, smaller cities in Tanzania, Lusaka, and Zambia, and several Indian cities, among others, have demonstrated that the environment in low-income areas can be considerably improved at relatively modest per capita costs.

It is difficult to generalize about what should be done because circumstances differ. The need to improve water supply and provide for garbage removal and sanitation is almost universal. So, too, is the need to provide health care and education. Granting (or regularizing) tenure in illegal settlements is often to be recommended, since it reduces fear of forcible eviction and gives people the security they need to invest in improving their houses. Once an illegal settlement is legalized, it is also in a stronger position to demand public provision of infrastructure and services. But great care must be taken in giving tenure to ensure that it is those in need who benefit. In many shantytowns, there is extensive landlordism, so simply granting tenure to those claiming ownership may not benefit the actual occupants. Indeed, it is likely to increase the price of rented accommodations to the detriment of the poor.

There are similar complications in trying to improve inner-city housing. Those living in tenements subject to rent control may not be able to afford to contribute to the costs of improvements. Moreover, if governments help fund improvements, owners can increase rents. Although in theory rent control could be applied to improved properties, in most cases it is ineffective, either because the owner demands extra payments on the side or because the tenant sublets the property, thereby excluding it from rent control. Lasting improvements to inner-

TABLE 7.3. Links between health and improvements in the physical environment.

Health problems	Action at household level	Action at neighborhood or community level	Action at city or district level	Action at national level
Contaminated water—typhoid hepatitis, cholera dysenteries, diarrhoea, guinea worm, etc.	Protected water supply to house; hygienic water storage within house.	Provision of water-supply infrastructure. Knowledge and motivation in community to use it.	Plans to undertake this and resources to do so.	Ensure that local government units have the financial and technical base to undertake these measures. Also that official norms and standards in use in all infrastructure are appropriate to needs and to the resources available.
Human waste disposal—potential for this to contaminate water/food or come into contact with human/disease vectors.	Adequately designed and maintained latrine/toilet that matches physical conditions, social preferences, and economic resources.	Needed mix of technical advice, installation equipment, and its servicing and maintenance (mix dependent on technology used).	Plans to undertake this plus resources. Manpower and financial base to service and maintain.	
Disposal of waste water and garbage—to get rid of stagnant pools and household wastes, which attract disease or disease vectors.	Adequate provision for drainage of wastewater and provision for space to store garbage safely (e.g., dog/rat proof stores).	Provision for drainage infrastructure.	Regular removal or provision for safe disposal of household wastes and plans plus resources for drainage.	
Diseases related to inadequate personal hygiene and lack of washing facilities—trachoma, skin and fecal-oral disease.	Adequate water supply for washing and bathing. Provision for laundry either at house or community level.	Health and personal hygiene education for children and adults. Perhaps laundry facilities if not in house.	Support for health education and public laundries.	Technical and financial resources to support educational campaigns. Coordination of housing, health, and education ministries/agencies in this.

Problem	Household-level support	Community-level support	Financing/resources	National/citywide support
Disease vectors or parasites living in house structure with access to occupants/food/ water, e.g., rodents, vectors for Chagas disease and leithmaniasis.	Support for improved house structure, e.g., tiled floors, protected food storage areas, roofs/walls/floors protected against disease vectors.	Technical advice and information; part of adult/child educational program.	Loans for upgrading house. Cheap and easily available, building materials.	Ensure building codes and official procedures for approving house construction or improvement are not inhibiting these actions. Support for nationwide availability of building loans, cheap materials (where possible based on local resources), and building advice centers. Production of technical and educational material to support this.
Health problems related to overcrowding, inadequate size, structure—respiratory diseases, stress, household accidents, etc.	Technical and financial support for house improvement or extension.	Technical advice on improved ventilation; education on overcrowding-related diseases and accidents; recreation and play space.	Loans (including small ones with flexible repayment) to build advice centers, etc.	Technical/financial support for nationwide system of hospitals, health care centers, dispensaries, etc., and nationwide availability of needed drugs and health-related goods. Production of primer.
No access to curative/preventive health care/advice.	Availability of simple primer on first aid/health.	Primary health care center and easy availability of health related goods.	Small hospital and resources to support lower-level centers.	
House sites subject to landslides/floods as result of no other land being available for poorer groups.	Regularize tenure if dangers can be lessened and basic services provided; otherwise offer alternative site.	Action to reduce dangers and encourage upgrading or offer alternative sites.	Ensure availability of safe housing sites that lower-income groups can afford.	National legislation and financial and technical support for intervention by local and city governments in land market—to ensure this is possible. Training institutions to provide needed manpower for all levels.
Illegal occupation of site or illegal subdivision with disincentive to upgrade and lack of service.	Steps to regularize tenure and provide basic services.	Work with community to provide basic infrastructure and service and incorporation into "official" city.	Support for incorporating illegal subdivisions into the city.	
Nutritional deficiencies and lack of income.	Preventive action to reduce work burden. Support for income-generating activities within house.	Ensure availability of vegetable plots? Food/vitamin supplements? Support for commercial/industrial operations.	Ensure space is left for vegetable plots and for commercial enterprises in settlements.	Structural reforms and other measures to improve the economic base of the poor.

city slums will probably require either joint ownership of the building by the occupants or the vesting of ownership in some official body. But here, as in most government housing programs, if only a small proportion of the housing stock is improved, better-off households are likely to push out poorer households, whatever controls public agencies try to devise.

Thus, it becomes apparent that government action to improve housing and living conditions in Third World cities has to be undertaken within a broad strategy involving many coordinated efforts and activities. Table 7.3 summarizes the kinds of actions that need to be coordinated at household, neighborhood, city, and national levels to address health problems commonly associated with housing for low-income groups. Individual housing projects, however successful, can have only limited impact. Broader, more fundamental changes are needed. For instance, it makes little sense to attempt to improve health conditions by installing piped water if no provision is made to improve santitation and remove wastewater. Similarly, a network of primary health care centers can do little to better the health of its clients in the absence of safe water and adequate garbage disposal. Thus, the priority for Third World governments must be to concentrate on what is often termed the enabling role—that is, providing the institutional, regulatory, and financial framework to respond to the needs of lower-income groups and to boost the supply and reduce the cost of all the components that go into making an adequate housing environment.

THE ROLE OF NONGOVERNMENTAL ORGANIZATIONS AND INTERNATIONAL AGENCIES

Most of the research on Third World cities has been done by teams from universities and nonprofit research groups based both in the Third World and the North and by certain multilateral and bilateral agencies, especially the World Bank and the US Agency for International Development (USAID). Certain governments and foundations from northern countries have also actively promoted research and training by teams based in Third World nations. Among the subjects investigated during the 1960s and 1970s were: how squatter communities form and develop and how they organize themselves, urban land policies, aided self-help and services site schemes as alternatives to public housing, social structures, and migration flows. More recent studies have focused among other things on small and intermediate urban centers, spatial biases in economic and national development plans, regional economies in relation to settlement patterns and regional markets, the informal sector and survival strategies for the urban poor, the commercialization of housing and land markets, and rental accommodation in unauthorized settlements. Research (and knowledge) is still weak on the role and capacity of local governments, on local and regional power structures, on urbanization costs, on the links between health and people's habitat, and on the roles of community organizations and the poor in the construction of Third World cities. Research on children and the city, the views of the users of cities on their cities, and the roles and needs of women, especially in community projects, is practically nonexistent.

However poorly Third World governments understand their cities, there is enough knowledge for them to make good decisions if they are willing to act. As distinct from other fields of activity by international and national nongovernmental organizations (NGOs), that of human settlements does not have the voices (or perhaps the leadership) that exist for such issues as population, the environment, and energy, subjects of considerable interest in northern nations. The history of well-established NGOs in the Third World has largely been an offshoot of initiatives launched outside the Third World.

Habitat, the United Nations Conference on Human Settlements held in Vancouver in 1976, awakened sufficient interest to hope for a drastic change of attitude from governments and agencies. But despite the interest shown at the time by certain governments, and despite several promising policies and programs, the situation today is deteriorating rapidly. Hopes that an NGO movement in the Third World would spring from Vancouver have not been realized. Criticism as well as support of government activities has come from various groups, but none has had the range of activities, the information system, and the networking abilities of NGOs in the North. Citizens' groups, mostly consisting of squatters and slum dwellers, have been at the forefront of the criticism of governments, essentially motivated by their struggle to secure the land they have appropriated or to receive water, transportation, sanitation, garbage collection, schools, and health centers. In their periodic clashes with governments, these groups have often been supported by technical groups from political parties, professional colleges, universities, and research groups. Roman Catholic and Protestant church groups have helped to organize community organizations and to develop entire self-help or rehabilitation projects that involve technical assistance, training, credit, and special programs leading to better health and food. Women often play key roles in these efforts, frequently as leaders of community organizations and programs. Local and national associations of shantytown dwellers have been formed. Their political impact has been or could be enormous, but their concern for the human habitat is limited largely to their own immediate needs. Governments frequently allow them to act, but within limits, as long as they do not criticize economic policies and employment policies—in other words, the policies that are at the root of poor housing conditions.

Why have NGOs concerned with human settlements not developed more strongly in the Third World? Barbara Ward, a leading figure at the UN conference in Vancouver, talked about the general lack of interest in this field, the complexities of finding even the most basic solutions to major national or international political problems, and the death of world leaders truly committed to improving the environment of poverty in the Third World. Perhaps a different type of NGO is needed. Undoubtedly, a new approach to the understanding of urban problems has to be developed. Cities in the Third World are increasingly being built by the people themselves, without official assistance or credit, and outside official plans, norms, and standards. Governments and agencies, politicians and technocrats should have the humility to learn from the people themselves. The users of the cities, the millions of self-trained builders who live and work in them, have experience, priorities, and suggestions that may well clash with those of middle-class technocrats. But these inhabitants have a pragmatic and realistic view of their problems and needs. Professional colleges, research groups, and interested citizens could and should work with them, establishing active groups with a broader and more realistic view of the developing city. Quite possibly, a less elitist type of movement could emerge, one that could bridge the gap between the trained mind and the self-made builder in an effort to rethink the Third World city.

Formally trained urban planners have had little success. It is true that their knowledge and activities have been limited by the poor quality of most local administrations and by a lack of political support to enforce legislation and to modernize cadastral surveys and local tax systems. But it is also true that trained planners have little or no contact with low-income groups. They may have good analytical training, but they are generally poor social organizers. In fact, young architects, engineers, social activists, clergymen, and members of charity and political organizations have been more successful in helping low-income groups. There is room for theoretical as well as empirical planners in the Third World, but the essential need is for social organizers and pragmatists.

Multilateral and official bilateral aid agencies have also given a low priority to tackling "the environment of poverty." An analysis of the sectoral lending of fifteen multilateral agencies from the date of their foundation up to the late 1970s showed that less than 2.5 percent of their aid went to urban projects such as upgrading slum and squatter housing, low-cost housing, and site and service schemes. Water supply and sanitation received around 5.5 percent of the aid. In all, the number of people who have benefited from multilateral aid for construction or shelter over the last twenty years equals little more than one percent of the Third World's urban population. Bilateral aid agencies also assign a low priority to this area. Various reasons can be suggested for this. One is the difficulty of implementing projects that improve the living environment of lower-income groups. It is much easier for an aid agency to administer the construction of a dam or a bridge, for example. Furthermore, large infrastructure projects can mean contracts for Western consultant and construction firms, and the power of these and other private sector interests to influence bilateral aid programs should not be underestimated. Finally, the low priority that aid agencies give to such projects mirrors the low priority that Third World governments themselves give to them.

Certain aid agencies are showing greater commitment to improv ing housing and living conditions of lower-income people. In the 1970s and early 1980s, the World Bank has shown increasing interest in supporting programs to upgrade slum and squatter housing and for site and service schemes, even if these still represent a small percentage of its total aid. Their evaluations of the successes and limitations of their projects, along with the detailed empirical work of researchers in Third World cities, have considerably expanded our knowledge of the problems and possibilities of improving the housing environment of lower-income groups. Our understanding of the possibilities for improving water supply and sanitation and the costs and benefits of the various options has been increased by research into more appropriate technologies.

Aid agencies are also beginning to appreciate the limitations inherent in giving support to selected projects only rather than helping to build the institutional and financial framework to allow Third World governments to address the problems themselves. The next step, by far the most important, is to put this knowledge into practice and to do so guided by the needs and priorities of the people these intitiatives are designed to reach.

In the Third World, as elsewhere, the environmental problems of cities cannot be separated from those of the region or nation in which they are located. Cities inevitably form part of a national and regional structure of production. They draw on a wider region for natural resources (and usually for labor) and thus have environmental impacts far beyond their own boundaries. Since cities are the major centers of nonagricultural production and of political and economic power, city-based decisions and activities affect whole nations. In particular, the disposal of wastes arising from such activities often has serious environmental consequences for the wider region.

Environmental problems within the city and its immediate hinterland can be examined on three different geographic scales: in the home or workplace, citywide, and regionally. Environmental problems within the home or workplace take the most serious toll on human health. Many inhabitants of most cities have to make sacrifices in environmental quality because even minimum-standard housing is too expensive. To find affordable accommodation, they have to forgo easy access to piped water and basic services or security of tenure or sufficient space (or all of these). Their inadequate and unstable incomes, together with inadequate public provision of water, sanitation, and primary health care and a largely uncontrolled land market, produce dangerous and degraded living conditions. Often, environmental conditions in the workplace are no better than those in the home, with no effective protection for the labor force from toxic (or otherwise dangerous) pollutants. These, combined with inadequate lighting and ventilation, inadequate wages, and inadequate protection from machines and excessive noise, also take an enormous toll on human health.

Problems relating to air and water pollution and to solid-waste disposal are often more serious in Third World cities than in Western cities. Although the Third World is less industrialized and urbanized than the West and per capita consumption of natural resources is much lower, there are still hundreds of cities with high concentrations of industries that have little or no provision for pollution control or for the safe disposal of industrial, household, and human wastes. Many cities have sufficiently high concentrations of motor vehicle traffic that, in combination with old and poorly maintained engines and poor local environmental conditions, air pollution can reach dangerous levels. Even in smaller cities, lack of infrastructure and services and of environmental regulations (or enforcement thereof) can ensure a polluted environment despite the smaller concentrations of people and industries.

Although polluting emissions can often be reduced at relatively low cost, prospects for their reduction are hindered by Third World nations' lack of an industrial and technological base to manufacture pollution-control equipment. During the current recession, governments facing serious economic problems and foreign exchange shortages are unlikely to import the needed equipment or to take the needed regulatory action.

In the immediate hinterland of most cities, lack of control over land use and lack of legal, affordable alternatives to shantytowns create a haphazard, sprawling pattern of development too dispersed to permit cost-effective infrastructure and services. These conditions also promote illegal housing developments on dangerous land sites, unnecessary sprawl over prime agricultural land, and the destruction or degradation of the natural landscape with little or no provision for public space.

Many nations have the resources to tackle most of these problems, and virtually all could alleviate the most serious problems. But the most fundamental environmental problems cannot be tackled unless city governments have the necessary power, resources, and skilled manpower. They have to have the ability to intervene in the urban land market so as to guarantee a sufficient supply of cheap, serviced plots for housing. They have to have the resources and manpower to greatly improve and extend basic infrastructure and services. And in the longer term, it is essential that they deal with the more fundamental causes of the environment of poverty.

But to eliminate poverty is beyond the ability of many Third World countries. Many nations have such small populations and so few resources that they do not appear to be economically viable. The economies of other nations are so interrelated with the world economy that their future is closely linked with the economic recovery of the industrialized world and with the perhaps distant possibility that regional Third World economies will complement each other.

If our forecasts are correct, the already drastic situation of the human environment in Third World cities will continue to deteriorate. So what can be done? The obvious inclination is to tackle the most urgent things first. The basic knowledge is there, but the political will is not, since the nonelected governments that rule the majority of Third World countries seldom need to pay attention to citizens' pressures.

It is interesting that the recently elected government of Argentina has decided to reduce the military budget and allocate funds thereby saved to health, education, and housing. Perhaps the only financial resources for improving the environment of poverty that can be made rapidly available are those that can come from a substantial reduction in military budgets. Unless such decisions are made, there does not appear to be a second step that even in the best of cases can moderately expand present approaches. Most of the Third World's urban problems are not new, but they have been accentuated by economic problems and the rapid growth of cities.

The most poorly understood and the most underused natural resources are human resources. Governments and experts have suddenly recognized the potential for lower-income groups to organize the construction of their dwellings, and, in recennt years, some have encouraged projects based on community or family self-help. But without a broader view of what a family must contribute in time and resources to build a house while struggling for survival, and without a clearer understanding of the type of conurbation that isolated projects such as these will produce, it is difficult to foresee the type of human environment that will evolve. After all, even these aided, legalized, and serviced self-built urban environments are growing far less rapidly than illegal settlements.

The question, then, is how to create an urban environment that will take less time, energy, and money to build and manage, and that will be more conducive to social exchanges, while it helps the population to make a living. Certain things could be done immediately. Access to land, to building materials (through loans without collateral or through cooperatives or other intermediary groups), and a respect for community organization are basic preconditions. Although there might not be much order in such a process, the adoption of such preconditions would be an initial step toward a more just distribution of some of the key elements in the construction of a city.

There does not appear to be much hope for the developing city unless participatory democracy is adopted and reinforced. Participatory democracy means building a nation, a society, a city from the bottom up. The city is a human invention that is reinvented by a great number of individuals, family and community decisions, and impulses not subjected to official plans, norms, and standards. The developing city is increasingly becoming an illegal city built by the efforts of people, many of whom were born, will live, work, and die without a record. A positive step would be to understand these processes, to interpret more flexibly the meaning of illegality—in land tenure, employment, and housing construction—and to find ways of better integrating the legal and illegal sections of cities. The rich and the better off employ contractors to build their neighborhoods, thereby demonstrating their status in society. But for the poor, building a self-help community is an exercise in optimism and hope aimed at removing them and their families from a life of deprivation in a squatter settlement. In cities that grow but do not develop, people are reacting to public indifference. Governments and technocrats could learn from their experience. Those who now have the power to influence the characteristics of developing cities could learn many essential things from the people who live there. Most of these people are women and children, and their views and priorities with regard to the house, the street, the school, the shop, the health center, and the workshop must provide the guidelines for the basic social elements on which a city is based.

APPENDIX

Housing and living conditions in selected third world cities

NOUAKCHOTT (Mauritania): Estimated population of at least 250,000 in 1983. The city's population has grown rapidly from 5,800 inhabitants in 1965. Most of the population has been housed in illegal shanty/tent settlements or on the 7,000 plots distributed by the government. About two-thirds of the population lives in largely self-built communities, and more than two-thirds lacks direct access to water. Water often has to be bought from merchants with no guarantee as to its purity and at a price of up to a hundred times that paid by households with piped water.

GUAYAQUIL (Ecuador): Estimated population of more than 1 million in 1980. On the edge of the commercial center, inner-city slums (*tugurios*) accommodate up to fifteen people per room in appalling, overcrowded, and unsanitary conditions. Much of the city's rapid growth in population since 1930 has been housed in squatter communites built over tidal swampland close to the city center. By 1975, this area, known as the *suburbios*, contained about three-fifths of the city's population. Most of the *suburbios* consist of kilometer upon kilometer of small, incrementally built bamboo and timber houses standing on poles above mud and polluted water.

MEXICO CITY (Mexico):   Estimated population of 16 million in 1982. At least 7 million people live in some form of uncontrolled or unauthorized settlement. Until the 1940s, most lower-income people lived in rented rooms in custom-built slums (vecindades) or in what was middle- or upper-income housing but is now subdivided. Since the late 1940s, most of the new low-cost housing has been in unauthorized settlements developed in one of two ways. Either landowners or real estate companies sold illegal subdivisions, or land allocated to rural communities under the long-standing agrarian reform has been illegally subdivided and sold. Either way, occupants' tenure is insecure since the subdivisions contravene offical regulations and infrastructure, and service standards are well below official norms. The land sites are often ill suited to housing because of rocky, steeply inclined land, instability of subsoil, or dry, dusty land.

DELHI (India):   Estimated population of more than 5 million in 1982. A report in 1982 stated that 1.3 million people live in slum areas in or close to the historic city, and 600,000 or more live in more than 1,380 squatter settlements ("Jhuggi-Jhompri clusters"). In addition, 700,000 live on unauthorized camping sites ("Jhuggi-Jhompri colonies"), which is where squatters were moved after being forcibly evicted from public lands. Most of the households in these settlements exist with grossly inadequate water supplies and little or no provision for the sanitary removal of household and human wastes and for basic community services for primary health care, for example.

Source: Nouakchott from Serge Theunynck and Mamadou Dia, "The Young and the Less Young in Infra-Urban Area in Mauritania," African Environment 14–16:206–33 (Dakar: ENDA, 1981). Guayaquil from Caroline Moser, "A Home of One's Own: Squatter Housing Strategies in Guayaquil, Ecuador" in Urbanization in Contemporary Latin America, ed. Alan Gilbert and Jorge E. Hardoy (New York: Wiley, 1982), pp. 159–90. Mexico City from Priscilla Connolly, "Uncontrolled Settlements and Self-Build: What Kind of Solution?" in Self-Help Housing: A Critique, ed. Peter M. Ward, 141–74 (Mansell, 1982). Delhi from P. Shrivastav, "City for the Citizen or Citizen for the City," Habitat International 6, no. 1/2:197–207 (1982).

NOTES

1. Cities are here assumed to be settlements with substantial concentrations of population and nonagricultural employment that play a significant role in their nation's economy. Thus, the paper's focus is on environmental problems associated with Third World nations' larger urban centers. No range of population size can be specified, in that

an important city in a poor, predominantly rural nation with a small population could have no more inhabitants than a relatively unimportant town in a richer, more urbanized, more populous nation.

2. Environmental problems associated with the workplace, which is also at this level, are not covered. Environmental hazards to human health from workplaces ranging from factories and commerical institutions down to small backstreet workshops and from work done in the home are of great relevance, of course, but space limitations make it impossible to include them.

3. In certain areas in the West, a decreasing proportion of the population lives in metropolitan centers or urban areas, but this transition has usually taken place in relatively urbanized areas where only a small proportion of the labor force works in agriculture.

4. The word *shantytown* can be misleading, in that such a town can develop into a high quality residential area with piped water, sewers, and public services, if the inhabitants obtain legal tenure.

5. Centre for Science and Environment, 1983 (see References for graphic details of this and subsequent citations).

6. Sierra, 1977.

7. The World Bank has produced a series of publications that describe in detail these various options. These are summarized in Kalbermatten *et al.*, 1980.

8. Briscoe, 1983.

9. Hardoy and Satterthwaite, 1981.

REFERENCES

A full list of references used in preparing this paper can be obtained from the Human Settlements Programme, IIED, 3–4 Endsleigh Street, London, W.C.1. Listed below are the publications that provided the examples quoted in the notes and most other examples cited in the text.

Urban pollution and its control

Bolletin de Medio Ambiente y Urbanizicion. Quarterly bulletin available from IIED, c/o CEUR, Ave. Corrientes 2835, 7 piso, (1193) Buenos Aires, Argentina.

Centre for Science and Environment. 1983. *State of India's Environment 1982: A Citizen's Report,* available from C.S.E., 807 Vishal Bhawan, 95 Nehru Place, New Delhi, Delhi 110019, India.

Leonard, H. J., and D. Morell. 1981. The Emergence of environmental concern in developing countries: A political perspective. *Stanford Journal of International Law* 17(2):281–313.

Sahabat Alam/Friends of the Earth Malaysia. Annual reports and other publications, available from S.A., 37 Lorong Birch, Penang, Malaysia.

Smil V. 1984. *The Bad Earth: Environmental Degradation in China.* New York: M. E. Sharpe.

UN Environment Programme. Quarterly bulletin *Industry and Environment* available from 17 rue Marguerite, 75017 Paris, France.

Housing conditions, urban sprawl, and related policy

Angel, Archer, Tanphiphat, and Wegelin, eds. 1983. Land for Housing the Poor. Singapore: Select Books.

Briscoe, J. Water supply and health: selected primary health care revisited. In *Proceedings of International Conference on Oral Rehydration Therapy*. Washington, D.C.: USAID, June 1983. *Also in American Journal of Public Health*, September 1983.

Hardoy, J. E., and M. R. dos Santos. 1983. *Impacto de la urbanizacion en los centros historicos latinoamericanos*. Lima: UNDP/UNESCO.

Hardoy, J. E., and D. Satterthwaite. 1981. *Shelter, Need and Response; Housing, Land and Settlement Policies in Seventeen Third World Nations*. New York: Wiley.

Kalbermatten, J. M., D. S. Julius, and C. G. Gunnerson. 1980. *Appropriate Technology for Water Supply and Sanitation; A Summary of Technical and Economic Options*. New York: World Bank.

Sarin, M., ed. 1980. *Policies Towards Urban Slums: Case Studies in Seven Cities*. New York: United Nations (ESCAP Region).

Sierra, S., and P. Javier. 1977. *Transformacion en el sector urbano*. VI Congreso Interamericano de Vivienda, Interhabitat.

Turner, J. F. C. 1976. *Housing By People; Towards Automony in Building Environments*. London: Marion Boyars.

Ward, P. M., ed. 1982. *Self-Help Housing: A Critique*. London: Mansell.

CHAPTER EIGHT

Agriculture: The Land Base

JANOS P. HRABOVSZKY

Although the world's food comes predominantly from the land, controversy surrounds attempts to define the role of land in relation to other factors in food production and to assess the possibilities for sustaining increased food production without seriously depleting land resources. Undoubtedly, the world's land resources are under pressure to produce more goods and services for an expanding and richer population. Disagreement arises in part because of extreme variations in both land types and agricultural systems. Thus, generalizations about the causes and remedies of land abuse must be made with utmost caution, and specific solutions must be found for specific problems.

WHAT ARE THE MAIN ISSUES?

Estimates of future demands for food and of the food production system's ability to meet this demand vary widely. Population growth is still rapid and will take decades to stabilize. Demands for feed grains in middle-income countries are also growing rapidly, adding to resource pressures in an increasingly interlinked global ecological and socioeconomic system. Increases in production will come mainly from higher yields, but the environmental side effects of modern production technologies are becoming apparent. The relevant question is how much higher would the world's food bill be if optimal conservation measures were applied.

The Record on Production

Responding to rapidly rising demands, world food production has reached higher levels since World War II than ever before, although there is considerable variation among regions and countries (see table 8.1). As a result of the differential growth in per capita food production and in changes in income, the balance of cereals trade has shifted. Developing countries and countries with centrally planned economies have become major importers of cereals, while Europe is becoming a net exporter. Three exporters—the United States, Canada, and Australia—had by 1981 increased their share of world cereal exports to 64 percent. Underlying such trends is an increase in the share of cereals fed to animals.

Despite these shifts, developing countries still have a positive trade balance in agriculture. However, the 106.5 percent positive agricultural trade balance of 1980 represents a sharp drop from the 1976 figure of 144.3 percent.

The production record is mixed in developing regions. In Africa, the forces undermining self-sufficiency in food include rapidly rising

TABLE 8.1. Agricultural production and food production, total and per capita, for major regions of the world, 1979–81 averages as percentages of 1970 levels.

Regions	Total agriculture	Total food	Per capita food
World	129	129	106
Developed market economies	124	124	112
Developed centrally planned economies	115	115	107
Developing countries:	137	140	105
Africa	122	123	90
Latin America	143	146	111
Near East	136	141	104
Asia and Far East	140	142	112
Asian centrally planned	141	141	116

Source: FAO, *FAO Production Yearbook* (Rome, 1981).

population in all countries, political instability in many, and the combination of slow technological change and migration from rural to urban areas in most. In the Near East, food production is growing by almost 4 percent per year. But this impressive gain does not match the explosive demand for livestock products and other food. Many countries in Latin America have ample land resources and major unused production capacity, but production is held back for want of effective demand. In other countries of the region, resource constraints and high population growth have led to a decline in per capita food production.

Asia has shown marked progress in per capita food production, in part because the region has already passed the period of peak population growth. Here, agriculture has benefited from increased investments, technological change, and increased use of modern means of increasing yield. At the same time, India and Bangladesh still contain a large proportion of the world's underfed people and lack the resources needed to increase food production and industrial development.

Trade in food has been growing faster than production or consumption. In developing countries, food exports have grown much more slowly than food imports, and regional differences are sizable. The Near East and Africa have shown the largest increases in imports. Asia has managed with the least, but per capita calorie intake levels remain low in most countries.

Despite differences in agricultural production growth rates, developing countries share certain tendencies. First, population pressures have contributed to higher-than-average growth rates by both increasing demand and expanding the agricultural labor force. Second, wars or civil upheavals have frequently been responsible for production growth rates well below the rate of growth in demand for agricultural products. Of the forty-five African countries with populations exceeding half a million, thirty-two have experienced lower growth in production than population. Of these, eleven have undergone major political upheavals in the last decade. By contrast, only one of the countries that managed to increase domestic per capita food production was war-torn. Third, the availability of land has not been closely connected with the rate of growth in production. Many of the countries with large undeveloped land reserves show only moderate or slow growth in agricultural production, probably because they have oil or mining revenues as a buffer or because they lack the infrastructure needed to open up new lands. In most countries where per capita land resources are meager, opportunities to increase food production by intensifying land use overshadow resource constraints.

China is noteworthy for the major agricultural reforms now under way. Given China's mixed record with experimental agricultural policies, current reforms of the production and incentive systems could substantially increase production. The rising demand for livestock products, however, could further boost China's demands on the world grain markets.

In the developed world, recent agricultural production growth has also varied strikingly from country to country. The major exporters of grain—the United States, Canada, and Australia—have increased agricultural output by about 3 percent per year. In Western Europe, under the influence of the European Community's Common Agricultural Policy, which keeps prices above world market levels, agricultural production increased by 1.7 percent during the 1970s, while demand grew more slowly because of slow growth in population and income and low-income elasticity in the demand for food. In Eastern Europe, production growth varies widely, being slowest in Poland and the USSR and fastest in Hungary and Romania. In general, growth rates in these countries were lower in the last decade than in the previous one. But food consumption has been growing rapidly under subsidized prices, and serious shortages have recently emerged as higher demand for livestock products has exerted great pressures on feed supplies and invited reliance on the world feed grains market.

Nutritional Levels and the Unequal Distribution of Food

In developed countries, more than enough calories are available to meet the population's needs, and, in fact, most malnutrition results from overeating. By contrast, in many developing countries, average caloric intake is only marginally above the minimum requirement for a normal active life (see table 8.2).

Caloric intake as a percentage of the minimum requirement improved only slightly between 1969-71 and 1977-79 in developing countries. Even with these increases, two of the four developing regions had intakes below requirements, and the margins in the other two regions (9 and 13 percent) do not afford the lowest-income groups an adequate diet, given that income-distribution patterns are highly skewed. The least-developed countries have low and declining per capita food supplies.

TABLE 8.2. Daily per capita calorie supply in relation to requirements, food production, and food imports in developing countries, as percentages of 1969–79 levels.

	Daily per capita calorie supply as a percentage of requirements			Indices of 1977–79 per capita			
	1969–71	1974–76	1977–79	Daily calorie supply	Food production	Volume of food imports	Volume of food exports
Developing market economies	95.2	94.4	97.4	102	103	153	104
Africa	93.3	93.2	93.6	100	89	160	64
Latin America	107.7	107.8	109.0	101	107	155	114
Near East	102.0	108.0	113.2	111	105	218	105
Far East	92.3	90.2	94.1	102	106	113	133
Asian centrally planned economies	90.2	97.0	101.1	112	113	162	88
Total, developing countries	93.5	95.4	98.8	106	106	156	105
Total, least developed countries	87.7	83.2	82.6	94	92	107	56

Source: FAO, The State of Food and Agriculture (Rome, 1981).

Clearly, more food will be needed to feed growing populations. But increases in supply alone cannot conquer hunger and malnutrition. There is growing evidence that a large proportion of the world's hungry starve not because of a general food shortage but because households have insufficient access to food-production resources or insufficient income to purchase food. In India in the late 1970s, favorable monsoon conditions combined with strong production policies, led to a 20-million-ton increase in the grain harvest. But the poor had no money to buy the surplus, much of which went into government storage, in part to keep prices from collapsing. Making food available at little or no cost to the poor is one way to improve their diets. The main options[1] are selectively subsidizing so-called inferior cereals[1] and the other staples of the poor and providing food at subsidized prices through special outlets or through rationing. The costs of these operations are better covered by general government revenues than by forced purchases from surplus-producing farmers at below-market prices.

The central task, however, is to raise the income of the poor. Increases in average income overall will not end hunger soon enough, so special programs are needed to generate income just for the poor. One of many alternatives is to change land ownership rights so as to improve income for small farmers and landless agricultural workers, who make up the majority of the hungry. But the political and social hurdles to land reform are enormous. Many developing countries fear a drop in food production, and others (especially in Central America) are governed by allies of the larger landholders. Significantly, an analysis of income distribution in India indicates that numerous other policy measures would improve income distribution just as much as a moderate redistribution of land. Such measures include favoring smallholders in irrigation development, supporting livestock production by smallholders, and, above all, generating enough nonagricultural income opportunities to reduce pressure on the agricultural labor market, thus permitting agricultural wages to rise substantially.

Hunger and malnutrition stem partly from fluctuations in the output and availability of food. Periodic famines plague areas with low and highly variable rainfall. To reduce fluctuations in food supply, one option is to increase the proportion of products grown on irrigated land with assured water supplies. Alternatively, reserves of stored food can be used to overcome production shortages, though they are expensive and hard to manage nationally. A third option is to rely on the world food market to offset domestic shortfalls. But although the World Bank's Food Facility program was created to widen such opportunities, price variations will be large in the absence of significant world carryover stocks, now that an attempt is being made to stabilize large US inventories.

Technological change and modern knowledge of nutrition afford opportunities to improve upon traditional dietary patterns. People who migrate from rural areas to the city need help in choosing nutritionally sound diets from the different and unfamiliar types of food they encounter there. Such guidance is especially important in feeding weaned infants. Nutritional education, mainly for women, through extension services, can help low-income populations make the best possible use of the foods available.

Many of the intestinal infections and parasites common in tropical environments sharply reduce a person's ability to digest and assimilate food. Because such infections commonly come from unhygienic drinking water, it is estimated that improving water supplies would contribute much more per dollar spent than any other measure to improve nutrition.

Long-Term Projections of Food Consumption and Production

With regard to the world's long-term food supplies, predictions range from mass starvation and extremely high food prices to rising demand matched by rising production. The doomsayers' arguments rest on four assumptions: that the world is running out of agricultural land, that modern high-input technology is incompatible with long-term, sustainable production systems, that developing countries will not be able to come up with highly productive, sustainable production systems in time to avert large-scale starvation, and that population increases combined with income growth are leading to impossible demands for energy and nutrients. In 1969, the US National Academy of Sciences has reported that "ten billion people by about 2050 . . . is close to (if not above) the maximum that an *intensively managed* world might hope to support with some degree of comfort and choice."[2] At the other extreme are studies that have assessed global capacity to provide food for future populations and have put the upper limit of the world's carrying capacity at 150 billion[3] or at US consumption standards, at 47 billion.

Between these extremes are such analyses as the FAO's *Agriculture: Toward 2000*,[4] which examines world agricultural development for the remainder of the century. This and a follow-up study focused on the year 2030 indicate that substantial potential to extend cultivation and raise yields will exist beyond 2030. The FAO and the International Institute for Applied Systems Analysis (IIASA) corroborate this estimate in recent assessments of the population support capacity of land resources in developing regions.[5] According to IIASA's Global Interlinked Agricultural Model System,[6] world food prices will rise only slightly if present policies are continued to 2000, while the average caloric intake in developing countries would improve somewhat, and economic demand in the developed world would be fully met.[7] In my opinion—and I was a member of the FAO and IIASA/FAO teams —these two studies represent the most realistic estimates available.

The wide divergence between the findings of these various analyses stems from numerous factors. Estimates of the amount of arable land and its potential productivity, for instance, depend largely on the type and level of agricultural technology assumed. Similarly, the level of general development assumed (or projected) to support agriculture influences the forecast. In addition, estimates of potential and actural damage to land, water, genetic, and other production-related resources vary.

Will Agricultural Land Become More Scarce?

Historically, humankind has extended cultivated areas before intensifying land use. This choice made sense, since, whenever population density was low, human labor, not land, was the scarcest agricultural production factor. Unfortunately, the longer-term historical perspective on agricultural land use is often forgotten in today's heated debates over land use and degradation. Substantial evidence indicates that in Western Europe, a much larger share of land was under crops in the Middle Ages than was cultivated in later centuries. Today, Europe's arable land is shrinking primarily because land has been taken over for cultivated grasslands and for forests.

Similarly, in North America, a considerable amount of land has been taken out of cultivation since the land frontier was closed in about 1900, especially in the Northeast, the Southeast, and the cut-over lands of the Great Lakes region. In the postwar period, supply-control policies of the soil bank type have influenced this trend, but much of the land taken out of cultivation has been transferred to grassland and forest use under the influence of technological change. Mechanization has made sloping and other hard-to-work land marginal, and new technologies have made prime land much more productive. Land-use developments elsewhere in the developed world parallel those in Western Europe and North America.

The degree to which the developing world is using its potentially cultivable land well varies considerably by country (see table 8.3). At one extreme, seventeen countries, the populations of which make up nearly half the developing world's people (excluding China) were using fully 95 percent of their potentially cultivable land in 1975. At the other extreme, twenty-nine land-abundant countries with 15 percent of the world's population were using only 15 percent of their potentially cultivable land. Together, these countries possess nearly 60 percent of the world's cultivable land.[8]

Most of the countries where pressure on land resources is high fall into one of three groups. The first group consists of Asia's major alluvial high-rainfall monsoon areas—the Ganges-Brahmaputra Basin and the Southeast Asian rice-growing areas of the great rivers, among others. Here, permanent lowland rice cultivation, much of it irrigated, has enabled high-density populations to evolve, thus creating pressures for full use of all suitable land. The second group is made up of the cradles of civilization, the low rainfall savannahs where early man found food or raised crops and livestock and where diseases and pests were manageable and the climate favorable. This group includes the Sahel and large parts of arid Asia and Latin America. The third group of countries in which few land reserves remain to be developed includes the young volcanic highlands of the tropics and semitropics: the Himalayas, Java, parts of the Philippines, the East African highlands, the Andean and Central American highlands, and others. Here, a favorable climate, including desirable rainfall patterns, combines with naturally fertile soils; the population density is high; and the land is commonly overused despite the world's most impressive hillside terracing.

In the developed countries, as well as in developing countries with no land reserves, production can be increased significantly only by intensifying land use with appropriate technologies in areas where intensive use does not lead to deterioration. In parts of the developed world where land use is already extremely intense, new economically sustainable technological systems are needed. In many developing countries demand is growing fast, technological and institutional development has not kept pace, and serious land degradation and food supply problems have emerged.

TABLE 8.3. Arable land: Availability and use in developing countries.

	Number countries	Share of population, 1975 (percent)	Potential arable area, 2000 (million ha)	Arable area in use as % of potential arable area		Arable area in use per capita (of total population)	
				1975	2000	1975	2000
Ninety developing countries	90	100	1,843	40	50	0.37	0.25
Africa	37	16	676	30	39	0.64	0.39
Far East	15	59	335	79	87	0.23	0.15
Latin America	23	16	693	25	39	0.54	0.45
Near East	14	9	139	63	67	0.47	0.26
Low-income	40	64	846	45	53	0.30	0.20
Middle-income	50	36	997	34	47	0.48	0.34
Land-abundant[a]	29	15	1,103	15	26	0.57	0.49
Land moderately abundant[b]	23	22	309	55	71	0.39	0.27
Land-scarce[c]	21	17	160	82	95	0.39	0.23
Extreme land scarcity[d]	17	46	271	95	97	0.28	0.17

Source: FAO. Agriculture: Toward 2000 (Rome, 1981).

[a] Land-abundant cultivating up to 40 percent of potential arable land.
[b] Land moderately abundant: cultivating from 41 to 70 percent of potential arable land.
[c] Land-scarce: cultivating from 71 to 90 percent of potential arable land.
[d] Extreme land scarcity: cultivating over 90 percent of potential arable land.

Future Influences on Demand for Lands

Future effective economic demand for land-based services, dominated by food demand, will depend on population growth, income growth, and urbanization. Although long-term estimates are uncertain, a composite estimate indicates that population and income growth for 1980 to 2000 will be slightly slower than in the past. If these rates materialize, in the year 2050, population in the developed world will stabilize at 1.4 billion and that in developing countries at 7 billion (see table 8.4).

The effect of population growth on increasing demand for food can be up to four times greater than that of income in the developed countries as a group, because income elasticity of demand is very low. In developing countries where population growth and income growth are rapid and a large share of additional income would be devoted to food consumption, the share of population-induced growth in demand for food equals roughly 60-70 percent of total growth in demand for food. Within overall demand for food, commodities like sugar, vegetable oils, fruits, vegetables, and, above all, livestock products will account for a larger share of total food consumption (see figure 8.1).

The transition toward higher consumption of livestock products in low-income nonpastoral societies is slow, starting as it does from

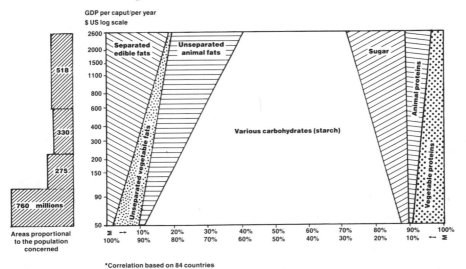

FIGURE 8.1. Calories derived from fats, carbohydrates, and proteins as percent of total calories, in terms of the income of countries, 1962. *Source:* FAO, Indicative World Plan, preliminary report (Rome, 1969).

TABLE 8.4 Estimates of ranges of growth in population, income, and food demand (percent per year).

	Population	Per capita income	Food demand (total)
World	1.8–2.0	1.4–3.3	2.5–3.3
Developed regions	0.4–0.6	1.0–3.0	0.5–0.8
Developing regions	2.1–2.3	2.0–4.0	3.0–4.0

Source: FAO, International Bank for Reconstruction and Development, *Global 2000*, IIASA's Basic Linked System, Food and Agricultural Project Model.

an extremely small base. But once it gathers momentum, it becomes a major driving force in the allocation of land. In developed countries, this transition is largely completed. Indeed, milk consumption is already declining in some high-consuming countries.

The composite estimate of economic demand put forth here would probably increase the per capita caloric intake of Third World people by 10 to 15 percent. Providing all the world's roughly 450 million hungry and malnourished people with an adequate diet would require an additional 20-30 million tons of cereals directed exclusively to the hungry. Practically speaking, a transfer of 50-80 million tons of grain is probably needed to eliminate hunger globally. In the years to 2000, agricultural output of developing countries must be increased by 3.0-3.7 percent per annum to meet all demands.

The growth in demand for food can be translated into a demand for agricultural land. In developed countries, about 95 percent of recent agricultural growth has come from increases in yield or land-use intensity. This figure could well rise to 98 percent, since any expansion of cultivated areas will be limited to North America and Oceania. In the developing countries, past increases in output have averaged about 2.8 percent per year. Roughly, 1.0 percent has come from expansion of cultivated areas, and the rest from increased yields. Globally, therefore, 21 percent of the increase in agricultural production came from increases in agricultural land. Most likely, this ratio will drop in the developing world as some countries make better use of their potentially arable land. If the contribution of increased cultivated acreage to the growth in agricultural production were to decrease to approximately 15 percent of the total production increase, the cultivated area would need to grow by 0.4-0.5 percent per year, up from about 0.25 percent in the 1970s. As reported in *Agriculture: Toward 2000*, an estimated 0.9 percent annual growth rate in arable land would be feasible in the ninety countries studied.

More land is also needed to produce nonfood crops, which today are grown on about 10 percent of the cultivated area. A special case is biomass grown for fuel-grade alcohol or other fuels, the demand for which has subsided in the 1980s as a result of the slowdown in energy prices. But technological breakthroughs in, say, the commercialized conversion of cellulose into alcohol could increase pressure on land resources. Similarly, fuelwood production in many developing countries may require increased land area (as it has recently in China), possibly at the expense of food production.

The third, and possibly largest, additional pressure would come from the use of agricultural food production capacity to feed animals. Today, about 40 percent of all cereals are used as animal feed. In developed countries, the share is 65 percent; in developing countries, it averages 20 percent; and in the poorest nations only 2-5 percent of the grain crop is fed to animals. In middle-income countries, consumption of cereal has increased by about 3 percent annually for food and 5 to 6 percent for feed.

Competing with the demand for more agricultural land are demands for land for housing, transport, industrial, mining, commerce, and recreation. Some demands can be accommodated by multiple uses of land, others cannot. In many cases, land-use regulations may make the difference. Although the overall record is far from clear (for example, in the United States), it is certain that most of the area used for urban purposes is not coming from prime cropland but from lower quality land. The FAO estimates that, in developing countries, requirements for nonagricultural land were only 1.5 percent of the total land in 1975 but by 2000 will be 2.8 percent.

Increasing Supplies of Agricultural Commodities

Two major opportunities exist for increasing the amount of land cultivated or harvested annually. One is to bring new land under the plow. The other is to grow more crops each year on the same piece of land. The total amount of potentially arable land on the earth is now a matter of consensus.[9] Most estimates are in the vicinity of 3.2 billion hectares—equivalent to about 25 percent of all ice-free land areas. Of this total, about half is under cultivation. The largest undeveloped arable reserves lie in the developing countries, though in the developed

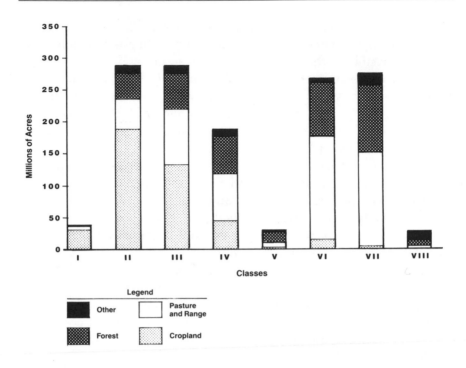

FIGURE 8.2. Land capability and land use, 1977. *Source:* US Department of Agriculture, *Program Report and Environmental Impact Statement Review Draft: Oil and Water Reserves Conservation Act* (Washington, D.C., 1980).

countries substantial acreage now under grass or forest has the potential for growing crops. Table 8.5 shows the ratio of existing and projected populations to the potential carrying capacity of lands in the developing regions, under three different levels of technology. Figures greater than 1.0 indicate that available land can support a larger population than the present or projected populations. The various countries require significantly different levels of technology to feed their populations from domestic production by the year 2000. Of the ninety countries considered, twenty-five could reach this goal even with a low level of technology, once all their land is brought into production. For twenty-eight countries, the intermediate level of technology is necessary, and for eighteen the highest level if they are to feed themselves. Nineteen countries will not be able to meet their food requirements under any scenario of technological change. This group includes five high-income oil exporters, three countries with substantial nonagricultural resources, and one middle-income country that lives off sugar exports. The remaining ten countries, of which four are low-

TABLE 8.5. Regional population-supporting capacities as ratios of 1975 and projected 2000 populations in developing countries.

Level of technological input	Africa	Central America	South America	Southeast Asia	Southwest Asia	Total
1975						
Low	3.0	1.6	6.0	1.1	0.8	2.0
Intermediate	11.8	4.2	24.3	3.0	1.3	7.0
High	34.4	11.6	58.1	5.1	2.1	16.8
2000						
Low	1.5	1.5	3.7	1.4	0.7	1.6
Intermediate	5.5	2.8	14.1	2.4	0.9	4.3
High	15.9	6.5	33.3	3.5	1.3	9.7

Source: FAO, Land, Food and Population, conference paper (Rome, 1983).

income, will contain 60 million people by the year 2000 and will be hard pressed to import all the food they need.

Besides the 744 million ha used for agriculture in 1980, an additional arable area of 196 million ha could be brought under cultivation in developing countries by 2000. In both percentage and absolute terms, the Near East and the Far East have the least room for expansion (9 and 13 percent, respectively), and Latin America (with 52 percent) has the most. Africa's maximum potential for expansion is 25 percent (see table 8.6).

Except for arid lands rendered fit for cultivation by irrigation, all "new" agricultural lands would come from present forest or grassland (probably half from each). The approximately 100 million ha from forests (an estimate in accord with FAO's recent assessment of changes in tropical forest resources) represents about 5 percent of the forested area in developing market economies in 1980 and excludes areas with slopes steeper than 14 percent.

TABLE 8.6. Arable land development in developing countries,
            by regions (ninety developing countries).

	Arable land (million ha)		Increase	
Ninety developing countries	744	936	192	26
Africa	204	256	52	25
Far East	264	297	33	13
Latin America	191	290	99	52
Near East	85	93	8	9

Source: FAO, Agriculture: Toward 2000, (Rome, 1981).

When grassland is converted to cropland, the best grazing areas are usually lost, and lower-rainfall or steeper grasslands, many of which are already overgrazed, come under even greater pressure. Worldwide, a growing share of the feed for domestic animals comes from land used to grow cereals, from fodder crops, and from cultivated grasslands.

In developed countries, the opportunities for expanding arable areas are much more limited. Europe is seeing a slow reduction in its arable land. The United States has about 16 million ha of high-potential land available for conversion to cropland and another 40 million ha of land with medium potential. Both increases would be mainly at the expense of meadows and grassland.[10] In Canada, possibilities for expansion are limited, and in Japan, where all suitable land is already used, cities are overtaking arable land. In Australia and New Zealand, arable land could be expanded substantially, but in both countries, major changes in the price ratio of crops to livestock products would be needed to make conversion economically viable.

Overall, the world could add around 250 million ha to its cultivated land area by 2000. Apart from North America and Oceania, all growth would take place in developing countries, mainly in Latin America and Africa, in areas with high rainfall. Potentially, anthropogenic changes in climate could influence these estimates, but despite a popular misunderstanding, there is no convincing evidence that the macroclimate either will or will not be altered as a result of deforestation. Scientists are also divided on the issue of carbon dioxide accumulation and its potential effects on agriculture. Until more firm scientific evidence becomes available, the "agnostic" position taken by the World Meteorological Organization at the World Food Conference in 1974 may still be the most reasonable.

The quality of land reserves is often considered lower than that of the land now under cultivation, since people usually develop the most productive areas first. Over time and with technological change, however, the relative productivity of various types of soils and lands has changed significantly, because many problems related to fertility, disease, and pests have come to be managed successfully. A major change has occurred, for instance, in the value of low-rainfall savannah land in relation to that of high-rainfall areas with poorer soils. The control of both human and animal diseases also influences land productivity. Control of malaria in the Indian *terai* opened up large areas to intensive cultivation. But in Africa, infestations of the tsetse fly and the river fly constrain the development and use of more than half the land which harbors 80 percent of the production potential. Control of both pests is feasible, but the mechanisms have ecological side effects that need to be considered carefully.

In *Agriculture: Toward 2000*, the FAO tried to quantify the differences in quality between old cultivated land and the areas that would be brought under cultivation by 2000. On the basis of relative yield levels for different classes of land and types of crop, a productivity index was calculated for all land types (four rain-fed and two irrigated) and another one for nonirrigated land. These rough indicators did not support the assumption that new cultivated lands have lower productivity potential, except in Latin America.

Most of the world's low-rainfall areas are fully used, if not overused, and low moisture availability in these areas limits yields except on irrigable land. Potentially the most productive unirrigated lands in the developing world are high-rainfall lands currently under permanent tree-crop cultivation. For these lands to be brought under annual crops, high-yield sustainable systems that successfully control erosion and manage soil fertility will be needed. Agro-silvicultural approaches (including the development of schemes for combining annual cultivation with permanent tree crops) hold considerable promise for overcoming constraints on productivity.

Major underused land resources in tropical Africa and Latin America are the seasonally flooded alluvial zones. Permanent rice cultivation on these lands makes the most sense, but flood control and, in many cases, drainage systems will be needed first.

Excluding the tropical high-rainfall areas, a sizable share of the land reserves in the better-rainfall areas of the developing countries are on sloping land. Without better soil-conservation measures and appropriate cultivation systems (including agroforestry and physical works), these lands will fall prey to soil erosion and degradation.

The Cost of Bringing New Land under Cultivation

The cost of bringing new land under cultivation needs careful assessment, since costs and benefits vary greatly with the type of land to be developed and the type of development required.[11] To make light-rainfall savannah land productive may require no more than clearing away light bush and creating drinking-water points. At the other extreme is land that cannot be used without stone terracing and fully developed waterways. Regardless of land type, the density of forests to be cleared influences land-development costs significantly, as does the degree of land leveling, flood control, and drainage needed (see table 8.7).

Overall average costs also depend on the mix of land types involved. Estimates reported in *Agriculture: Toward 2000* place overall costs for development of rain-fed land at US$620/ha in 1980 prices. Land development costs were estimated to be 5.6 percent of the investment for primary agriculture in the ninety developing countries included in the study. The marginal cost of developing new land probably will not rise much as the area of cultivated land expands in

TABLE 8.7. Costs of developing land for rain-fed cultivation
(in US$ (1980)/ha).

Light savannah	90
Heavy savannah	440
High-rainfall forest	1,230
Surface drainage and flood control	1,400
Terracing with stone supports	3,000

Source: FAO, Agriculture: Toward 2000 (Rome, 1981).

countries (such as Brazil, Sudan, or Zaire) where only a small share of
the potentially arable land is in use and where most new unirrigated
land development will take place. In countries where land reserves
are small, however, marginal costs are likely to be high.

Two opposing examples shed more light on the problems of land
development. Malaysia has been engaged in large-scale land development and settlement for the last twenty years or so. The Federal Land
Development Agency (FELDA) manages a national program that develops approximately 20,000 ha annually, mainly for oil palm and some
rubber production. Settlers are employed by FELDA as laborers while
the land is being developed and take possession of their farms only
when the trees have reached maturity. They have to pay back a large
share of the total development costs, though the government bears
some of the infrastructural expenses. Costs per hectare are relatively
high, but so are returns. The cornerstones of this highly successful
program are careful land assessment, construction of appropriate
infrastructure, tight management of production even after farmers
have taken over the farms, centralized agricultural processing, and
credit on favorable but not oversubsidized terms.

In the same region, Indonesia's long-term transmigration project
has met with much less success. The program's objective is to help In-
donesians from overpopulated Java resettle in the underpopulated
outer islands. Most settlers come from heavily populated areas where
intensive irrigated rice cultivation is practiced on extremely scarce
land, but their experience counts for little in their new situation,
where labor is short and rain-fed land abundant. Land-use capability
studies, production systems, land-clearing operations, and ongoing
production and marketing support have been deficient. Expanded
marketing opportunities, research in and initiation of growing cash

crops suited to conditions on the outer islands, and better planning
and implementation are needed.

Increasing the Intensity of Arable Land Use

Raising land-use intensity is a direct substitute for developing new
land. In general, cropping intensities (expressed as the ratio of harvested to arable land times 100) are strongly influenced by the demand for output, the climate, and the soil quality on the one hand and
by the availability of production inputs on the other. In unirrigated
areas, the annual distribution of precipitation bears a positive correlation to cropping intensities up to a point.

In developed countries with low winter temperatures, double or
multiple cropping is rare. In milder climes, such as in the Mediterranean Basin or in the southern half of the United States, however, double cropping could be increased. In the drier, cooler parts of North
America and in Australia, fallowing is an integral part of small grain-
production systems. Although fallowing helps conserve soil, manage
moisture, and control weeds and diseases, fallow areas have been reduced in recent years. In Australia, the shift reflects the wider use of
specific legumes as part of cereal rotation. In North America, the use
of a break crop (such as rape) has replaced fallowing, and cereal rotations have tightened.

Developing countries have major opportunities for increasing
cropping intensities (see table 8.8). Yet, claims that production can be
increased inexpensively by increasing cropping intensities do not
withstand careful scrutiny. Substantial inputs and investments are required, especially once cropping intensities have reached 150 percent
or so. To achieve intensities above this level nationally is rare and

TABLE 8.8. Cropping intensities, present and future, by region.

	Africa	Latin America	Near East	Asia and Far East	Total 90 countries
1980	55	62	68	108	77
2000[a]	65	66	80	121	85

Source: FAO, Agriculture: Toward 2000 (Rome, 1981).

[a] Where land is scarce, cropping intensity is high and projected to grow slowly. Underlying these differences is a difference in the share of irrigated land in the total, which is
much higher for the Near East and Asia (27 and 37 percent) than for the ninety developing countries (16 percent).

difficult. So far, only China (150 percent), Taiwan (165 percent), Bangladesh (155 percent), and Egypt (190 percent) have passed the 150-percent mark.

Increasing Agricultural Yield to Save Land

The main source of increased population in both developed and developing countries will be higher yields. This can be seen as a form of saving land by relying more on inputs other than land. Two key questions are whether the rapid increases achieved in the last thirty years can be projected into the future, and how reliance on a high-yield strategy will affect chemical, biological, and energy- and water-related impacts on the environment.

In the developed countries, farmers and researchers have taken great strides toward maximizing biological yields, but in developing countries, average yields are far below the maximum biological and economic potential. Equally important is the speed at which yields are increasing. In the developed market economies, technological change and governmental financial support have led to yield increases of approximately 2 percent annually in the last thirty years. In developed countries with centrally planned economies, progress has slowed noticeably in the last five to eight years as inputs and investments have grown tighter and technological opportunities have diminished. To reverse this slowdown, incentives for more effective performance at the farm level and for greatly increased research will be required.

In the developing countries, opportunities to increase yields are attractive. The gap between average yields from 1974 to 1976 and potential yields indicate a possibility of up to fourfold production increases (see table 8.9). The large differences that exist between land types reflect either strong constraints on yields (for example, natural floods) or difficulty in raising already high yields (for example, in fully irrigated areas).

In China, new efforts under the "responsibility system," combined with a willingness to provide more manufactured inputs and investment goods for farming, an improved pricing system, and redoubled emphasis on formal agricultural research and technical training are likely to boost yields dramatically. In most African countries, stagnant or declining yields reflect general political instability, lack of improved inputs or incentives to use them to increase production, pricing systems that favor urban consumers over farmers, and lack of institutional support for technological change.

TABLE 8.9. Yield reserves for cereals in developing countries by land classes[a] and by crop, above, and potential yield[b], as percent of actual yields 1974–76, below.

	Ample rainfall[c]	Low rainfall[d]	Naturally flooded[e]	Fully irrigated[f]	Partially irrigated[g]	Problem area[h]	All developing countries
Wheat	1,156.0	530.0	1,320.0	2,075.0	1,541.0	672.0	1,288.0
Rice	1,534.0	—	1,606.0	3,059.0	2,232.0	1,099.0	1,947.0
Maize	1,402.0	953.0	854.0	3,296.0	1,957.0	957.0	1,377.0
Barley	1,473.0	655.0	1,471.0	1,798.0	1,434.0	850.0	1,156.0
Other cereals	978.0	455.0	815.0	2,676.0	1,636.0	580.0	735.0
Wheat	302.8	377.1	227.3	289.2	227.1	372.0	290.7
Rice	221.6	—	230.2	228.8	257.6	254.8	256.5
Maize	356.6	157.4	351.3	229.1	306.6	418.0	348.6
Barley	339.4	229.0	203.9	278.1	265.0	352.9	308.2
Other cereals	511.3	307.7	184.1	224.2	305.6	431.0	409.1

[a] According to FAO's Agriculture: Toward 2000 project data.
[b] Potential yields reflect a known technology that is applicable to the area considered.
[c] Rainfall providing 120–270 growing days, soil quality very suitable according to FAO's agro-ecological zones project classification.
[d] Rainfall providing 75–120 growing days, soil quality very suitable, suitable, or marginally suitable according to FAO's agro-ecological zones project classification.
[e] Land under water for part of the year and lowland nonirrigated paddies.
[f] Equipped for irrigation, suitable drainage, and not suffering from water shortages.
[g] Equipped for irrigation but lacking drainage or reliable water supplies or with low quality and reliability of distribution.
[h] Areas in which rainfall provides more than 270 growing days and soils are all qualities, and areas with 120–170 growing days but only marginally suitable soil.

In Latin America, especially where land reserves are still abundant, extending agricultural cultivation often makes more sense than increasing yields. In Asia and the Near East, on the other hand, the call is mainly for reliance on yields to increase production. There have been widespread efforts both to foster effective national research, as well as extension systems for the application of such research, and to build up a service structure to bring the needed inputs within reach of farmers. Some of the outstanding successes of the green revolution have taken place in these regions. Similarly, cash crops for export, such as rubber, oil palm, coconuts, tea, and bananas, have seen major yield increases.

Overall, progress in cereals other than rice, wheat, and maize will be more difficult. Although dietary preferences and a lack of new technology work against the production of such crops as millet and sorghum, in large parts of semiarid Africa no other cereals will grow. Unfortunately, research on these crops (as well as on pulses and oilseeds) has been much less productive than that on major cereals, mainly because the yield-constraining factors are more severe and there are plant-protection problems that resist easy solutions. A complicating factor for research is the large number of minor cereals and the great variety of conditions under which they are grown.[12]

Most analysts of future agricultural developments estimate increases in yield by extrapolating current technological trends. But the present level of research may not be sufficient to ensure the continuation of this rate of progress.[13] In addition, recent research is aimed not only at increasing yields but also at minimizing the environmental and social side effects of new technologies. Thus, to maintain growth in yields, additional support may be required for research.

One role of fundamental research is to extend the range over which inputs can be used without risking major declines in their response. Where no major natural constraints stand in the way, crop production research should be aimed at maximizing economic yields by matching high-input agricultural systems with high-yielding varieties. Where natural, economic, or institutional barriers exist, a strategy based on more moderate yields and inputs seems appropriate. Indeed, many developing countries have taken this direction in modernizing agricultural production.

A third strategy appears applicable where natural constraints such as low precipitation or poor soil conditions limit yields. Here, the main approach should be to reduce risks by developing low-input technology that still makes full use of limited natural resources. Minimum tillage, fallowing, and drought-, pest-, and disease-resistant varieties combined in optimal crop rotations make up the best production packages for such areas.

A frequently debated point is whether there will be breakthroughs in genetic engineering research and what effect they will have. Breakthroughs in direct gene transfer, for example, or in the transfer of the symbiotic nitrogen-fixing capacity of leguminous crops to cereals could indeed increase production or reduce costs. It is estimated that fifteen to twenty years are needed for those advances, and that the major technologies in widespread use by 2000 will be those that are now being tested.

Water is made available to crops through either precipitation or irrigation. Improved traditional and modern technologies are available for making optimal use of precipitation. Many of these are aimed at reducing runoff, increasing storage in the soil, and achieving maximum usable plant output from the available moisture through soil and water conservation measures.

Additionally, irrigation has made large contributions to increases in the world's agricultural output in both developed and developing countries (see table 8.10). It is used to increase yields; to make them more secure; to allow production of high-value crops that have large water requirements in areas of limited precipitation; and to help bring about higher cropping intensities and thereby greater production per unit of arable land.

In recent years, the overall costs of irrigation have risen more sharply than those of other agricultural inputs and investments. The greater sophistication of new irrigation schemes, the dearth of additional sites in which extensive irrigation can be conducted more economically, and the extremely high costs of irrigation in the Near East and Africa account for the sharp increases. But whereas small-scale fully developed irrigation systems may cost US$12,000-15,000/ha, India is building major gravity-fed systems at costs of approximately US$2,500-3,000/ha and shallow tube-well systems for as little as US$5-6/ha. In most countries, government subsidies will be needed to build irrigation systems, but in the long run, the expense is justified in countries with limited land resources.

Irrigation development has brought problems as well as benefits. Salinization and alkalinization degrade the soil, and such waterborne diseases as schistosomiasis and malaria are also associated with irrigation. Furthermore, many irrigation systems have never fulfilled the

TABLE 8.10. Main irrigated areas of the world, 1980.

Country or region	Million ha	Share of arable land (%)
China	46.0	46.3
India	39.4	23.2
Pakistan	14.3	70.0
Indonesia	5.4	27.6
Rest of Asia (developing)	11.8	20.0
Near East	18.8	21.5
Africa	2.6	1.7
Latin America	14.2	8.8
Japan	3.3	67.6
United States	22.0	11.5
Soviet Union and Eastern Europe	17.5	6.2
Rest of OECD	16.7	3.4
World total	212.0	14.6

Source: FAO, Production Yearbook, 1982; and FAO, Agriculture: Toward 2000.

original expectations of increased crop yields and have become serious financial burdens.

Improvements needed to avoid these problems and to make better use of water resources for irrigation include:

- better planning of irrigation development, including antisalinization measures
  use of water-saving irrigation techniques in arid and semiarid locations
- pricing of water to provide incentives to economize
- improved management of irrigation systems.

Energy requirements for agricultural production are increasing faster than agricultural output everywhere in the world. In developed countries, however, the share of commercial energy used for actual production amounts to only 3.5-4.0 percent of all energy use in the economy, whereas energy use in the processing, marketing, and preparation of food equals 13-15 percent. In developing countries, agricultural production accounts for between 3 and 9 percent (with an average of 4.5 percent) of all use of commercial energy, but the postharvest component accounts for 15-20 percent.[14]

The significance of the postharvest food system in energy consumption in developing countries becomes even more striking when noncommercial energy sources are considered. In many oil-importing low-income developing countries, the postharvest phase (mainly cooking) may account for 90 percent of all energy use in the food system. Even if calculated in "oil replacement units," which take relative fuel efficiencies into account, cooking still claims more than 50 percent of total energy use. Thus, in countries where fuelwood is scarce, fuel shortages pose problems at least as serious as those of securing food supplies.

High-yield, high-input agriculture is often criticized for its heavy dependence on imported manufactured chemicals, and thus for creating unmanageable financial burdens for developing countries. Often, this criticism is coupled with a plug for replacing a good share of these inputs with biomass (including organic fertilizers) or human and animal labor. Although farmers could make more efficient use of local materials, the demands for plant nutrients and power are outstripping biomass supply. In many countries with high people-to-land ratios, all biomass resources are already in use. (Even in China, where biomass is used optimally, more than half of all plant nutrients applied to the soil come from inorganic sources.) Nearly all organic manures produced in developed countries are already in use.

The inappropriate use of chemical fertilizers is unquestionably dangerous, and alternative techniques (including split-dose applications and precision placement combined with the use of slow-release material) are well known. Only economic considerations slow their adoption. In Europe, recent increases in fertilizer prices have created incentives for more efficient use, and evidence suggests that yields have not declined with the lower applications.

Probably the most serious environmental side effects of high-input agriculture stem from the use of chemicals in plant protection. Near-exclusive reliance on chemical means for controlling plant diseases and pests and the often indiscriminate application of these chemicals have led to significant problems as pests have developed resistance to these chemicals. As resistance has built up, less persistent and more selective but much more poisonous materials have been used. These pose grave hazards to nontarget species and to human life, and their manufacture, transport, handling, and application require extreme care.

The alternative to protecting plants primarily with chemicals is reliance on integrated plant protection systems that involve breeding resistant varieties, using bioagents for pest control, appropriate rotations, timing cultivation and protection operations precisely, and using chemicals judiciously. Although such practices hold promise, they will require substantial additional research, support systems, and educational efforts. Meanwhile, reduction of subsidies to farmers on pesticide purchases would encourage more conservative application.

In the drive for high yields, another problem of environmental degradation has arisen. As concentration on a narrow genetic base of breeding materials has increased, genetic variety has diminished, and the danger of major collapse under disease or pest attacks has increased. Yet, although the issue of breeders' rights has sparked controversy, preliminary steps have been taken to preserve the genetic base. Both international and national gene banks for plant genes and some animal genes have been set up, and a draft international agreement on breeders' rights is being discussed.[15]

Diminishing Land Supplies

The conversion of agricultural land to other uses is an issue that requires much more careful collection and evaluation of data before sound quantitative statements can be made. Many factors could influence the rate of conversion either positively or negatively, including government regulations. In laissez-faire systems like that of the United States, regulation is difficult. In European countries, where government involvement is regarded as necessary, zoning and land-use regulations that are well thought out and implemented are effective.

Losses of land from deterioration result from misuse, which manifests itself as chemical, physical, and biological degradation. The three most widespread causes of deterioration are water erosion, wind erosion, and salinization, although acidification is also important.

Soil erosion is most common on desert fringes and low-rainfall savannahs, in hilly areas, and in tropical areas of high rainfall and leached soils—three of the most fragile environments. In Europe, erosion problems tend to be more severe in the south, where strong seasonal precipitation, relatively frostless winters, and poor management combine. Fire and overgrazing often add to the problem. Damage is mitigated by the concentration of intensive agriculture on flat lands and some by reforestation on steep land, where cultivation has been abandoned. In northern and central Europe, much of the sloping land is under grass or forest and is better managed. In eastern Europe, erosion problems are worse because of the centralized management of economies and the lack of individual private interest in land conservation.

In the United States, it has been claimed that extreme damage and impending disaster are unmasked by higher fertilizer use, but the evidence is inconclusive. Vociferous claims that agricultural wealth is being washed away at great speed into the Gulf of Mexico seem to be overstated and to ignore the large variations in the ecology of the United States[16] However, large fluctuations in agricultural prices and incomes probably do lead to maximizing short-run profit and neglecting land conservation. Although the US Soil Conservation Service has made major headway against soil erosion, better local assessment and better-tailored erosion prevention programs and conservation incentives for farmers are needed to solve current problems.

In low-rainfall areas in developing countries, erosion and desertification stem from increasing demands for cropland, grazing land, and fuelwood supplies. Population growth feeds these demands. In the Sahel, for instance, the age-old conflict of cultivators encroaching on the living space and land resources of pastoralists has led to overgrazing. During the inevitable drought years, there are excessive losses of vegetation, animals, and, in the absence of aid, human life.

Similar problems exist in much of the Near East. The region's oil wealth has spurred rapid urban development and created new income opportunities for rural people. But at the same time, mechanization has led to the cultivation of high-risk areas, frequently with serious losses of permanent grass cover and soil. Antiquated land-use rights systems based on livestock ownership and communal grazing rights exacerbate the problem, though to call it a "tragedy of the commons," as some have done, is an exaggeration.[17] In many societies, including those that inhabit the alpine regions of Europe, systems of regulated grazing for communally owned grazing lands have evolved. In Syria, the traditional *hema* grazing-regulation system has been combined successfully with control of cultivation in grazing zones and the creation of communal fodder and feed reserves.[18]

In hilly areas (including parts of the eastern African highlands, the Himalayas, and the Andes), population pressure has forced farmers to cultivate steeply sloping land with little or no fallow periods, thus creating serious erosion. The damage from clearing steep sloping land for cultivation is worsened by subsequent pressure for more grazing areas, which in turn prevents forest regrowth on land abandoned by cultivators. Some analysts link this denudation to growing needs for fuelwood and timber, but evidence from Nepal shows that pressures for land to raise crops and produce livestock are greater.

Salinization and alkalinization, threats to irrigated land in low-rainfall areas, can be prevented by appropriate drainage systems and proper water and salt management. Techniques for combating these problems are known, but they make the construction and management of irrigation systems more expensive and require discipline and organization.

Probably the most fundamental problem in putting a stop to resource deterioration is that the social and institutional structures within which technological change and production increases must take place are unable to respond to the increasing demand for agricultural products. In the past, the usual growth in demand in developing countries was about 1 percent, which could be met by gradual extension of the cultivated area, modest technological change, and a growing labor force operating within a slowly evolving institutional structure. But today, when demand is growing at 3 percent or more annually, new technology must be applied, which in turn demands major institutional changes. A complicating factor is that it is difficult to transfer institutional solutions from the outside, whether from the developed West or East, because such changes require careful experimentation, adaptation, and integration with traditional institutions.

Land-Use Implications of Livestock Development

Grasslands cover nearly 70 percent of the world's agricultural land (80 percent if arable land used for feed and fodder production is included). Although much of this land is unsuitable for producing food for direct human consumption, much of it may be potentially arable under certain conditions, and therefore it constitutes a considerable land reserve.

The future may bring even heavier use of agricultural land to support animals, given that most people around the world demand more livestock products as their incomes rise. Since the world's grasslands are gradually declining, the growing livestock population will depend increasingly on feeds grown on arable land—witness the relative growth in the share of meat from poultry and pork and the increasing share of cultivated feeds in the diets of productive dairy cows and fattened steers. The combined effect of these trends, which are especially visible in developed and middle-income countries, is to exert serious pressure on the world's agricultural production capacity. At the same time, however, feed grains provide a reserve for direct human consumption, provided the market mechanism is capable of shifting supplies adequately when total availability is low.

Can these trends toward a growing reliance on arable land for animal feed be reversed? Certainly, grasslands could be expanded, thereby relieving pressure on arable land, but only to a limited degree. The amount of grazing land in the developing countries has not grown for a long time and is, if anything, diminishing. New technology has become available, however, to expand the carrying capacity of grassland. One promising development is the use of tropical legumes to improve grazing land. More generally, in the developed world, the productivity of existing grasslands has risen significantly, with better grazing systems, increased fertilization, overseeding with more productive species in better-rainfall areas, wider use of improved lea rotations, and reductions in animal morbidity and mortality. In developing countries, gains of this sort have been limited, and socioeconomic conditions dictate that improvements will be gradual at best, but the scope for increased productivity is large.

The further development of livestock production will also be strongly influenced by government actions that affect prices. In the developed countries outside Oceania, livestock production is subsidized, and import restrictions protect the more lucrative markets.

MECHANISMS TO IMPROVE LAND USE, INCREASE YIELDS, AND RAISE PRODUCTION

To intensify agriculture, two fundamental institutional ingredients are needed: new technology, together with the inputs and investments needed for its application, and incentives for farmers to apply them. The need for improved technology requires that national research systems in both developing and developed countries, as well as the network of international agricultural research institutes, be strengthened.

Brazil and India both possess outstanding examples of large, effective agricultural research systems. The success of these programs is attributable to a cadre of well-trained researchers, the willingness of governments to allocate the financial support necessary to develop and maintain the systems, a strong and carefully conceived organizational form that suits the national administrative and political economic system, and some outside support.

In developed countries with market economies, agricultural research systems have suffered setbacks as financial resources have become limited and agriculture has lost ground in the competition for funds. In developed countries with centrally planned economies, agricultural research has improved as a result of depoliticization and attention to the need for improvement in agricultural production. In these coutries, technological innovation is seen as a more appropriate approach than economic incentives.

As the global agricultural research system evolved and as the national research systems in developing countries became stronger, it was recognized that the objectives of international agricultural research centers needed to change. The move is away from developing specific plant varieties or complete technologies and toward greater support for national agricultural research systems in activities where the comparative advantages of the international institutes are the strongest.

Increased effort will be required to test and adapt appropriate new technologies locally and to teach farmers how to use them. In the past, problems have arisen when a strong extension service has not received enough new research results to be able to offer new technologies to farmers, or when good research results were available but the facilities for extending them to farmers were limited. Thus, growing attention is being paid to institutional arrangements and planned programs that better integrate these two functions.

The successful extension efforts in both developed and developing countries have been those based on grass-roots organizations of farmers. The results of the improved communications and multiplier effects that such organizations afford are well demonstrated in Taiwan and Korea. In addition, the training-and-visit system now used in many Asian countries has been successful, especially in large-scale irrigation schemes.

Infrastructure development is another precondition for the technological change needed to boost agricultural production. The availability of physical infrastructure for irrigation, supplies, and marketing the increased yield must all be ensured if production is to grow quickly enough. Estimates from the *Agriculture: Toward 2000* study indicate that gross investments in agriculture in developing countries must increase by about 3.6 percent annually to reach an annual volume of US$107 billion (1975 values) by 2000. As large as this sum appears, however, it represents a reasonable share of expected agricultural income and national savings.

Much of the new technology will remain unused unless farmers have incentives to apply it. Such incentives must take account of three interlinked factors. The first is relative agricultural prices, which must be high enough to permit the profitable use of purchased inputs and to induce farmers both to use their labor and land optimally and to invest in on-farm improvements and equipment. In developing countries, government policies aim at lowering relative agricultural prices, in part to generate investment funds and government income and in part to keep a better organized and more vociferous urban consumer population contented. In developed countries, government policies keep domestic prices above world price levels to support farm incomes. Gradual and judicious removal of trade barriers for agricultural commodities under more liberal price policies would be beneficial in both cases.

Second, policies for production incentives also need to take into account fluctuations in prices. Reduced fluctuations have incentive effects comparable to increased average prices, and minimizing variability is often a less costly policy that may also have other benefits such as increased food security.

Third, better incentives will have to come from improved land and water tenure. Many tenurial arrangements discourage tenants' performance. In most developed market economies, they pose no fundamental problems, and market operations are expected to bring about an equilibrium price between ownership and the rent of land. In the developed countries with centrally planned economies, the socialization of agriculture has furthered social justice and redistributed political power, but the new agrarian organizational forms have frequently performed poorly because agricultural workers lack incentives. There are indications that a major rethinking of this issue is taking place in many Eastern European countries.[19]

For developing countries, few generalizations about tenure can be made. Undoubtedly, the greatest inequalities exist in Latin America. The Near East has recently seen major changes in land tenure, however. In most African countries, tribal land ownership coupled with rights to individual use are the norm, and the arrangement is quite egalitarian. In most Asian countries, small farms predominate, though inequalities in land ownership are serious, and the percentage of rural people who are landless is rising.[20]

The main aim of land reform has been social justice and the creation of new rural power structures. However, the records of post-reform economic performance are mixed. Much depends on the institutional forms and policies adopted after the reform. Almost certainly, agricultural production in developing countries would increase if rural people were given a greater role in planning and implementing development programs. Such a move would serve to focus programs more directly on fulfilling perceived needs and would foster more active participation.

Mechanisms to Reduce Losses of Arable Land

In developing and developed countries, marginal land can be successfully managed for long-term sustained production only if present pressures on those lands are reduced. One way to do this is by more intensive use of resilient lands, combined with the use of fragile lands for forests, grasslands, and other less demanding purposes.

In developed countries, arable land is lost primarily through encroachment by urban areas and degradation both from agricultural abuse and nonagricultural pollution. To reduce conversions of land from agricultural to other uses in developed countries, appropriate mechanisms are zoning and land-use regulation combined with taxation. But to make them work, substantial political backing and popular support are needed.

The main mechanisms for reducing land losses incurred through agricultural activities are soil and water conservation programs and efforts to minimize land and water pollution from inappropriately used agrochemicals. Sound research, financial incentives, and education of farmers, together with increased public awareness, could substantially reduce such soil losses. Training programs in soil and water conservation are especially important since few farmers recognize the potential of such measures for increasing yields.

The key issues in land degradation due to nonagricultural pollution are control issues, of acid rain, chemical poisoning in the vicinity of major industrial waste emission points, and water pollution. To combat these threats to agricultural land, well-wrought and stringently applied legislation is needed.

In developing countries where much new land will be brought under cultivation, all-out efforts are necessary to ensure that the new lands are suitable for cultivation, and that the proposed cultivation systems are appropriate. Effort is needed to ensure that complex systems for irrigation or major flood control or drainage are planned so that all potential risks of degradation are evaluated during project design. Further effort is needed to ensure that farmers are organized and taught how to construct and maintain land-improvement works, including soil and water conservation systems and appropriate cropping patterns.

Further, it is of utmost importance to generate nonagricultural employment and income-earning opportunities for rural people who would otherwise be forced to try to eke out a living through the cultivation and eventual ruin of submarginal lands. Such opportunities could come from multiple uses of resources, as in agrotourism, agrosilviculture, handicrafts based on farm or forest materials, and aquaculture in suitable locations. Part-time farming is providing benefits in both developed and developing countries. The need is for policies that promote industrialization and improvement of living conditions in rural areas and towns.

SUCCESS STORIES

The following discussion is intended to counterbalance any impression left by the preceding analysis that the task of reducing hunger and at the same time husbanding resources is too difficult to tackle. Examples of successful programs at the macro, national level are presented, not just at the local level.

Intensifying Production and Reducing Pressure on Fragile Resources

By intensifying the use of the most productive lands, three of the world's most populous and densely populated regions—Europe, China, and India—have taken great strides in increasing agricultural production. In Europe, the trend has been toward greater use of areas that can support intensive agriculture and the easing of pressure on those that cannot. Much marginal land has been taken out of production, adding 7 percent to its forested area between 1970 and 1980. But while productivity on Europe's best lands is reaching new highs, the changes needed to improve resource conservation are modest compared to the changes that have led to high productivity.

In China, the denudation of marginal hilly lands which have been used to grow food is now being reversed. Afforestation programs involving millions of small locally managed plantations show signs of success. Decentralization, provision of economic incentives, and the supply of agricultural inputs promise further increases in yield.

India's major push to develop irrigation and increase the use of fertilizer has helped to feed a population that grew from 368 million in 1950 to 684 million in 1980, at the same time keeping food prices reasonably low. While the green revolution has been accused of spawning many social ills, blame should be laid not at the doorstep of new technology but upon political power structures and skewed land distribution. Without greatly increased yields of wheat and (to a lesser extent) rice, hunger in India would have been much more serious and widespread in the last fifteen years than it has been. Indeed, if India could eliminate electrical power shortages, it could probably go further still, feeding its poor and becoming a net exporter of food from its irrigated lands. So far, boosts in agricultural productivity have enabled India to subsidize food for the urban poor and to build up a large industrial base. Although life for India's poor and malnourished is still appalling, at least the means for improvement are available, largely because of intensification of agricultural production on irrigated land.[21].

Increasing Off-Farm Employment

Although unemployment plagues many developing countries, between 1970 and 1980 the nonagricultural labor force in developing countries grew by 52 percent, from 34 to 42 percent of the total labor force—a remarkable feat. Outstanding successes in increasing off-farm employment have occurred in three Asian industrializing countries: the Republic of Korea, Taiwan, and Malaysia. In all three, the approach has been to build industry on a strong and dynamic agricultural foundation. Outward-looking economic policies and rapidly expanding exports also contributed strongly to their success.

Land and Water Management

Two traditional land- and water-management schemes have been successfully used in Indonesia and the Phillippines: terracing and irrigation. In both countries, terracing represents an adaptation to sloping land and to the use of young, fertile, volcanic soils. Both schemes have persisted for hundreds of years and have adapted well to the use of modern cash inputs. Because rice paddies retain a large percentage of the rainwater, erosion is minimal. Moreover, the system allows for crop rotation involving dry-season crops and works well within the traditional context of labor-intensive production.

Other successful land-management schemes include the time-honored soil-conservation and land-use regulation mechanisms employed in central and northern Europe. The combination of arable land, cultivated grasslands, and planted forests yields high-value produce, entails only minimal erosion, and helps balance the landscape.

Japanese water-management systems for rice cultivation have made optimal use of limited water supplies and have integrated water management with crop-growth and weed-control systems. Similarly, they demonstrate how government and farmers can work together to achieve high irrigation efficiencies. (The record of industrial water use in Japan is less impressive, and water pollution has become a serious problem.)

The lessons of China's long-standing land-use system are that a dense population can be fed from a fertile but limited land base, and that special attention to maintaining soil fertility by recycling organic materials pays off. But while China's lowland management has been outstanding, some of the country's sloping lands have been abused during periods of stress, including the Cultural Revolution. Nevertheless, the overall success achieved in intensifying land use is impressive.

Combating Malnutrition

Whereas India has successfully supported its urban poor with subsidized food through ration shops, Sri Lanka, by means of a free rice ration system, has improved the diets of its poor significantly, though food has been wasted in the process, and problems in raising domestic food production and financing the program have held gains down. Greater success was achieved in China by communal sharing of a large part of total food supplies and communal keeping of local food reserves, but China's rising standards of consumption and the diversification of the economy indicate that a new approach involving more personal responsibility in production and more personal choice in consumption is needed.

These representative success stories force three conclusions on agricultural planners and decision-makers. First, there are no magic solutions or cure-alls. Second, overcoming many of the problems discussed in this paper requires doing what is already being done, but doing more of it and doing it better. Third, all important improvements and actions involve certain costs and negative side effects, though there is every reason to believe that humankind will respond to the serious challenges ahead with inventiveness and flexibility.

AGENDA FOR IMPROVING AGRICULTURAL LAND USE

The diverse issues discussed so far provide an agenda for development and maintenance of agricultural land use. The following proposals relate to the assessment, development, and wise use of land resources.

The proposals are based on the World Soil Charter, adopted by the Twenty-first Session of the FAO Conference in November 1981. The charter establishes principles for using the world's land resources optimally, improving their productivity, and conserving them for future generations. It also calls for a commitment on the part of governments, international organizations, and land-users in general and provides guidelines for action. These guidelines cover three main areas: assessment of land resources and land-use planning, soil management and fertilizers, and land conservation and reclamation. The proposals that deserve the highest priority are as follows.

Assessment of Land Resources and Land-Use Planning

Soil surveys and land evaluation provide the foundation for most of the actions needed. Soil-survey coverage is poor in most developing countries, and a gradual selective approach is needed, given the constraints on time and resources. Little is known quantitatively about the magnitude or the impacts of land losses and degradation. Land evaluation and assessment of land-use potential based on an agroecological approach, together with an assessment of present use, will thus have to provide the main resource—capability inputs for land-use planning. More generally, land-use planning should be carefully adjusted to local conditions and tied in with agricultural and overall planning. It should also be cast in analytical units that are compatible with administrative and management units, so that decision-makers can make ready use of the data.

EXPECTED BENEFITS. Although these actions by themselves provide no direct benefits, they are crucial to sound land development, land improvement, and optimal land use.

ACTORS. Most land-use assessment and planning must take place initially at the national and subnational levels. Surveys and assessments, for instance, must be undertaken by specialized organizations, but bringing together planners, land-users, and land-use regulators is crucial for success. At the grass-roots level, compliance with plans and regulations will occur only if the people who stand to gain or lose help make the plans.

International organizations and bilateral aid can foster these activities   and   underwrite   the   development   of   standardized methodologies, as well as training. Developing nations need help especially in obtaining and using remote sensing and other modern survey technologies and tools for analyzing large volumes of data.

Soil Management and Fertilizer Use

To promote integrated plant nutrition and soil structure management systems, priority action is needed on the optimal combination of organic and inorganic fertilizers, including special measures to reduce losses of plant nutrients. Used improperly, fertilizers can cause pollution problems or become "bound," so that they are not available to crops. Further attention is also needed to make full use of the nitrogen-fixing capacity of plants. Four types of agricultural areas deserve special attention:

• Tropical high-rainfall areas, which represent a large share of the new lands to be brought under cultivation
• Irrigated areas, where potential is high and farmers already use large amounts of fertilizers
• Nonirrigated high-capacity areas where intensification is being pushed to high levels
• Areas where natural conditions are constraining but minimum-input systems hold promise.

EXPECTED BENEFITS. At present, only about 30 percent of the plant nutrients applied in inorganic fertilizers are taken up by crops. A one-third increase in efficiency at present levels of use could save 10 million tons of plant nutrients annually, at a commercial value of about US$6 billion. Savings of even a small fraction of this amount would be significant: 10 million mt of nitrogen, potassium, and phosphorus could produce around 80 million mt of additional grain, enough to eliminate undernutrition in the world.

ACTORS. The circle of actors in soil management and fertilizer use must be quite wide and must include people engaged in research, manufacturing, and application. Research is needed into plant nutrition, soil chemistry and physics, and agronomy; into manufacturing processes to improve, for example, slow-release fertilizers; as well as into engineering to improve the cost efficiency of machinery. Research on manufacturing processes and engineering could be better carried out by private large-scale producers, but public incentives could help steer them in the right directions. Additional basic and applied research must include large-scale trials and adaptations conducted under various ecological and socioeconomic conditions to ensure local applicability. In short, international, bilateral, and national research systems need to be involved. One option would be for the FAO to take on a coordinating and interest-creating role.

At the national level, the local trial and adaptation system will have to be widely dispersed and well coordinated. It must also provide opportunities for effective feedback to the more basic research systems on the one hand and to extension services on the other.

Conservation and Land Reclamation

To reduce current damage and prevent new damage to the land, users, administrators, and legislators need to understand the extend of current losses, the short- and long-term consequences of these losses, and the types and costs of preventive and curative measures available. In most developed countries, such information is being disseminated, but in most developing countries, systematic assessment has not even started.

Once ongoing damages have been assessed, a program in harmony with other land-use planning activities needs to be drawn up to establish executive bodies and the legislation that, along with financing by public and private sources, can create a base for agricultural change. During this stage, major efforts are needed to capture land-users' interest in and agreement with program proposals. In many cases, pilot and demonstration programs are needed to foster better understanding by local people.

Implementing any soil conservation and watershed management program will involve activities that are by nature communal or public and others (mainly on-farm) for which private individuals must take responsibility. (Here, legislation may be effective in forcing or inducing compliance with program requirements.) So great are the differences between various political and rural organizational systems, however, that presenting a worldwide blueprint is impossible.

Finally, any program of soil conservation and watershed management will have to feature maintenance components, performance monitoring, and activities for holding land-users' interest in conservation.

EXPECTED BENEFITS. Short-run production increases from reduced losses of soil moisture and plant nutrients, reduced longer-term losses of top soil and workability of the land, and a reduction in downstream damage all stem from conservation and land reclamation. Reliable worldwide estimates do not exist, but two examples offer starting points for calculating benefits. The FAO's recent study on population support capacity shows that unchecked soil erosion in developing countries could reduce the area of rain-fed cropland by 18 percent, production of rain-fed land by 29 percent, and total potential by 19 percent.

ACTORS. Initial action on conservation and reclamation is mainly a job for governments and local autonomous development agencies, though internationally active multilateral and bilateral agencies can help increase awareness of the problem. Later, when the problem is recognized, they can support such programs and help poorer countries secure additional funding from international sources.

International and bilateral agencies can also provide technical aid in programming and implementation, as well as research and training for program staff. ("Food-for-work" schemes are one option through which food aid could be used effectively. The World Food Program is already active in such activities and more resources could be earmarked.) Research should emphasize increased local testing and adaptation, rather than fundamental research, which is more plentiful.

Reducing Pressure on Marginal Areas

Given rising demands for agricultural products, pressure on marginal areas can be reduced only if full use is made of areas that can withstand intensive use. Two priority areas are the development and application of new technology for sustainable high-level production in suitable areas and the provision of alternative income opportunities for those who are currently forced to overuse marginal land.

To meet the requirements of long-term sustainability, high-yield, intensive agricultural systems need technological development in four areas. First, breeding efforts should focus on highly productive disease- and pest-resistant varieties with a broad genetic base and short growing seasons. Second, disease-, pest-, and weed-control systems that require only minimal use of chemicals should be developed. Third, appropriate power-input systems based on human labor, as well as draft and mechanical power, must be developed for use within tight rotational systems. Finally, even though agriculture requires energy and other resources from outside the agricultural production system, full use of all locally, internally available inputs should be made first.

Alternative income-earning opportunities for farmers on marginal land could come either from agriculture on other land or from nonagricultural sources. Often, the best way means of raising earnings is to distribute land more equitably among farmers and the landless through land reform, thereby improving opportunities for people to partake of the benefits of the intensified use of good land. As regards nonagricultural employment, the ideal solution is to greatly increase rural industrialization, combining it with tourism, handicrafts, and other potential sources of income. At a minimum, urban industrialization should be as labor-intensive and capital-extensive as circumstances allow, so as to spread higher urban incomes more equally among the population.

EXPECTED BENEFITS. The chief benefits of reducing pressure on marginal lands would be the increased opportunities to bring marginal lands into use in ways that match their production capabilities and to conserve limited but locally important production capacities for future generations. Land reforms could bring with them greatly increased social justice and, through economic multiplier effects, more buoyant development. They could also increase agricultural production over the long run.

With improved technology in high-productivity areas would come direct, high payoffs. Indeed, there is substantial evidence of high agricultural returns from research oriented toward areas of high potential response to inputs. Ideally, when combined with land reform, both income distribution and production increases could be achieved.

ACTORS. Major land reform, virtually always a painful and difficult task, is within a country's or government's decision-making sphere. But outside influences can militate strongly for or against it. Technical aid and financing should be made available to countries that decide to carry out land reforms but need extra resources to do it. In particular, international food aid should be made available to tide countries over the short-run declines in domestic production that occur while reform is carried out. Although international organizations have yet to act on this proposition, the World Bank has already extended loans for carrying out agricultural improvements in conjunction with land reforms. As stressed above, beneficiaries of land reform must receive support in the form of new technology, investments, and inputs so that they can make optimal use of their new land rights. In this regard, the FAO and other international organizations could help develop implementation programs for land reforms.

Special research efforts to support high production in responsive areas need to be placed within the framework of agricultural research in general. Practically speaking, this means strengthening all components of the worldwide agricultural research system.

In the developed countries, where resources allocated to agricultural research have declined, priorities must be reversed, since developing countries will need much more outside support if they are to build up their agricultural research systems. Some need basic systems, while others need highly specific, high-quality support in narrowly defined areas. Here, international agencies such as the FAO (which for a number of years has sadly neglected its potential role in supporting research in developing countries), UNESCO, and other UN agencies, as well as numerous bilateral organizations, could do more. In particular, waning support for international agricultural research centers under the Consultative Group on International Agricultural Research should be restored and increased, pending the results of the current study of their impact.

The developing region that requires the most urgent practical research results is Africa, where per capita agricultural production has declined, and pressures on land resources could lead to the most widespread damage. It is also in Africa that national agricultural research systems are the least developed, and where many countries are too small to develop effective research systems of their own.

The Potential Payoffs

Quantifying the potential payoffs of such a wide-ranging set of actions as those presented here is difficult, but a number of recent studies contain estimates of the benefits of certain components. The impact of the performance scenario proposed can be inferred from a comparison of the A scenario in the FAO's *Agriculture: Toward 2000* with the "trend scenario." For the ninety countries studied, output growth equals 3.8 percent per year in the A scenario and 27 percent per year in the trend scenario. Dietary intakes would be 156 calories per day higher, and the number of hungry and malnourished people would drop to 242 million from 387 million. (Even under the more optimistic scenario, major income- and food-distribution schemes would be needed to solve the nutritional problems of the most disadvantaged.) While such improvements would not free the developing world from the need to import food from developed countries, it would slow the present growth in food imports greatly and would double export earnings from agriculture.

The main messages of this review, then, are that much can be done to increase agricultural production to the levels required, and that technological changes needed for greater resource conservation are neither large nor difficult to achieve. At the same time, the unprecedented growth in demand for agricultural products warrants more attention and resources than it has been getting. Moreover, even if resources are increased, they will be effective only if incentives to farmers and to the institutions that guide and serve them are improved. These improvements must be initiated at all levels—by international organizations, national governments, subnational bodies, and farmers themselves.

NOTES

1. "Inferior cereals" are those which are replaced when incomes increase (for example, millets and sorghum, versus rice and wheat).

2. US National Academy of Sciences, Committee on Resources and Man, *Resources and Man* (San Francisco: Freeman, 1969).

3. H. Linneman et al. *Contributions to Economic Analysis no. 124: Model of International Relations in Agriculture* (Amsterdam: North Holland Publishers, 1979).

4. FAO, *Agriculture: Toward 2000* (Rome: FAO, 1981).

5. FAO, UN Family Planning Organization, and IIASA, *Potential Population Supporting Capacities* (Rome: FAO, 1983); and P. Harrison, *Land, Food and People* (Rome: FAO, 1984).

6. K. Parikh and F. Rabar, *Food for All in a Sustainable World* (Laxenburg, Austria: IIASA).

7. IIASA, draft of a report of the Workshop on Food and Agriculture, Laxenburg, 1984.

8. These figures and the table are from the FAO study *Agriculture: Toward 2000*, which did not include China but did include ninety developing countries that contain 97 percent of the developing world's population outside of China.

9. Although forest and grassland make up 83 percent of the land being used in nonurban areas, the value of their output is dwarfed by that of production from arable land, so the focus here is land used for food production. Arable land is defined to include permanently cropped areas, areas temporarily assigned to crops and meadows, and market and kitchen gardens, as well as land temporarily in fallow or idle. Harvested or cultivated area refers to the area of crops grown in a year on a specific area. Cropping intensity is defined as the ratio of arable to nonarable land times 100.

10. See notes 5 and 6.

11. One central issue is whether all infrastructural costs incurred in land development should be included. In general, they should be included at the project level but not

at the planning or allocation level, since the absolute size of the population (not its location) determines overall infrastructure costs.

12. Breeding and other technological changes affecting yield under marginal conditions have enabled many crops to be grown outside their traditional growing areas. Indeed, the wheat belt has moved much closer to the tropics, soybeans both closer to the tropics and into higher latitudes, and maize into cooler climates with shorter summers.

13. V. Ruttan, "Can productivity growth in agriculture be continued? "Minnesota Agricultural Economist 621 (July, 1980).

14. FAO, Agriculture: Toward 2000; and idem, Energy Use in the Post-Harvest Food System of Developing Countries (forthcoming).

15. FAO, "Plant Genetic Resources," report of the director-general to the FAO conference held on 25 August 1983.

16. See the more sober assessment presented in USDA, Program Report and Environmental Impact Statement (RCA, 1980).

17. See S. Sandford, Management of Pastoral Development in the Third World; and H. Jahnke, Livestock Production Systems and Livestock Development (New York: Wiley, for Overseas Development Institute, 1983).

18. FAO, Syrian Arab Republic National Range Management and Fodder Crop Production Program (Rome: FAO,1980).

19. A useful analysis of the history of socialist transformation of Hungarian agriculture is described in F. Donath, Reform and Revolution (Budapest: Corvina Press, 1980).

20. The material provided for the World Conference on Agrarian Reform and Rural Development, held by the FAO in 1979, offers much detailed information on tenurial conditions, programs, and achievements. The report of the conference contains a summary.

21. Y. Vygas et al., India 2000. (Ahmed Abad, India: Indian Institute of Management, 1979).

CHAPTER NINE

Fresh Water

PETER P. ROGERS

ROLE OF WATER IN DEVELOPMENT

Although the saying attributed to Auden, that "few have died from lack of love, many have died from lack of water," is literally true, love probably plays a much greater role in development than water does. But while the technical literature tends to place water above all the other chemical compounds with which humanity deals, water as a commodity is only important insofar as it helps humankind reach its aspirations for, say, love, beauty, or a better economic life. Only by seeing water in these terms can we rationally assess the resource base and plan for its wise use.

Water is a commodity. It is an input into other processes. It is also consumed directly by people and animals. Water, in short, is not an end in itself. This seemingly obvious point warrants emphasis, since most people understand water this way, as individuals, but treat it differently when they make collective decisions about its use. Perhaps the problem is that water is commonly perceived as a common property resource, when for many uses it is an exclusive economic good. People customarily but mistakenly regard water as a free good to be used or wasted at will.

Because water was long considered in this way, assessing the demand for water in its technical economic sense is difficult. All too often, water is viewed as a "need," and the amounts "needed" are projected into the future. Naturally, if water has been wasted, then projecting more such waste leads to huge requirements for water and to seeming conflicts with its availability.

Most people live in the well-watered parts of the world, which is no surprise given that the current world population distribution reflects settlement patterns that developed at the beginning of the Neolithic era. More surprising, however, are the recent rates of population increase in the tropical less-developed countries that are not considered to be well-watered. In countries such as Chad, Mali, and Kenya, the population's water requirements have not yet exceeded the average supply of water, but the variability of supply is such that the actual supply has been barely equal to or even less than the minimum requirements.

Typically, water "demand" is estimated by extrapolating current water use (by type of use) in proportion to projected levels of population and economic growth. Unfortunately, such projections ignore the economic fact that consumer and industrial demands reflect the price of a resource, a population's income level, and other factors.

Water is used in virtually everything people do. No other material is used as widely by industry. Energy production uses water both directly and indirectly. Water provides the basis for fishing and outdoor recreation. It is an important medium for transportation, cooling, irrigation, and waste disposal (see table 9.1). Of particular note here is the magnitude of the water requirements for irrigation. In a developing country where an urban dweller uses 7-15 m3 and a rural dweller, 2-4 m3 for domestic purposes, as much as 830 m3 of water per person is used to produce the rice he eats each year. Thus, to improve the diet to, say, half a ton of grain equivalent per capita per year could require as much as 1,700 m3 per capita per year in agricultural water use.

Demand for water has generated some of the largest construction projects ever undertaken, as well as weather-modification schemes. Such activities drastically change the underlying ecosystems, and many have unintended impacts on aquatic systems as well. More generally, water has become one of our most abused resources. Waste disposal and the improper management of water projects have led to highly unfortunate results, including the spread of schistosomiasis, a debilitating infection affecting an estimated 200 million people worldwide. Even activities not classified as water development projects may alter aquatic ecosystems detrimentally. For instance, the soil and nutrients lost in agricultural and construction activities are transferred to lakes and streams, where, along with other things that humans have put into water supplies, they can convert once-valued streams and lakes into bodies of water that are sources of disease, poisons, and little else.

TABLE 9.1. Typical rates of water use for selected activities.

Industry	Range of flow, m³/mt of product	m³/ha
Canning:	50–70	—
Green beans	15–20	—
Peaches and pears	15–20	—
Chemical:		
Ammonia	100–130	—
Lactose	600–800	—
Food and beverage:		
Beer	10–16	—
Bread	2–4	—
Meat packing	15–20	—
Milk products	10–20	—
Pulp and paper:		
Pulp	250–800	—
Paper	120–160	—
Textile:		
Bleaching	200–300	—
Dyeing	30–60	—
Electric power production		
Cooling water	—	190 (l/kwh)
Irrigation:		
Cotton (Okla. US)	29,000	9,900
Rice (tropical climate)	5,000	15,000
Wheat (Okla., US)	4,000	8,100
Corn (Colo., US)	600	4,000
Municipal, commercial, and public service	*l/capita/day*	*m³/capita/year*
US (average 1983)	453	165
Boston (1978)	883[a]	
Frankfurt, Germany (1978)	151	
Developing countries piped water (1963)	120–240	
Developing countries standpipe (1965)	20–40	7–15
Nairobi (1968)	154	

[a] Includes substantial losses in the system, possibly up to 40%.

THE FRESHWATER ECOSYSTEM

In an ecosystem, everything is connected to everything else. Freshwater ecosystems tend to be more difficult to analyze and understand than terrestrial ecosystems, however, because chemicals and nutrients are transported by water through a highly complex process.

One way to visualize the freshwater aquatic ecosystem is to consider the hydrologic and nutrient cycles. The hydrologic cycle accounts for the passage of water through the lithosphere and tropo-
sphere (see figure 9.1). Aquatic ecosystems exist wherever water is
concentrated in this cycle—in lakes, rivers, marshes, oceans, soil
moisture, and groundwater. In a sense, the freshwater ecosystem is a
natural machine, a constantly running distillation and pumping system. The sun injects thermal energy, which, together with gravity,
keeps water moving. Although this water cycle has no beginning or
end, the oceans are the major source, the atmosphere is the delivery
agent, and the land is the user. In this system, no water is lost or
gained, save for that small amount removed from the water cycle as
either hydrogen or oxygen during chemical reactions. But the amount
of water available to the user may fluctuate on account of variations in
either the source or, more usually, the delivery agent. Large fluctuations in the atmosphere and the oceans produced deserts and ice ages,
and even now, smaller local alterations in the hydrologic cycle produce floods and droughts.

Evaporation, condensation, and precipitation make up the three
most important stages of the hydrologic cycle. The atmosphere ac-
quires moisture by evaporation from oceans, lakes, rivers, and damp
soil, and by transpiration from plants in processes referred to as
"evapotranspiration." Air currents transport water vapor over large
distances. Condensation, cloud formation, and precipitation may then
occur. During precipitation, some evaporation occurs in the air but
much of the water reaches the ground, water surface, or vegetation. Of

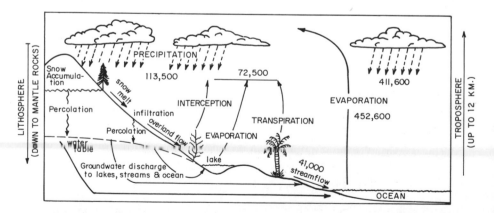

FIGURE 9.1. Hydrologic cycle showing approximate magnitudes of components in km³.

the precipitation that reaches the vegetation, some is held by the canopy and eventually evaporates again, and some will run down, drip from the canopy, or be shaken off by the wind and eventually reach the ground. Of the water that reaches the ground, some will infiltrate the surface, some will accumulate in surface depressions, some will begin to move over the surface, and some may percolate through deeper layers and enter the groundwater system, where it may be held for long periods. Water in some of the aquifers under the Sahara, for example, is millions of years old—essentially a nonrenewable resource.

Climatic conditions influence life on earth and shape the physical and biological environment, which in turn influences the state and composition of the atmosphere. In other words, strong interactions and feedback loops exist between the various components of the ecosystem. Human activities are influenced greatly by weather and climatic conditions, and man can purposefully or inadvertently modify weather, climate, the moisture cycle, and such geochemical cycles as the carbon cycle (an alteration that leads to excess buildup of carbon dioxide in the atmosphere).

The atmosphere's vapor content is directly related to air temperature, and both are greatest in summer and at low latitudes. Exceptions include the deserts of the tropics, where there is little rainfall because, along with other mechanisms, the slow descent of air in high-pressure systems hinders the ascent of air and, hence, the precipitation process. High rates of evaporation and the characteristics of tropical rainfall pose particular problems. Where rainfall is seasonal, water availability is limited at certain times of year and, in some cases, precipitation also varies greatly from year to year (particularly in the semiarid tropics), which can pose problems for agriculture and other development.

Variability in precipitation has great significance in ecosystem stability. The precise nature of the impact depends on many factors and defies generalization, but in semiarid areas variability can be devastating. Worldwide, average annual rainfall varies from almost zero in some deserts to over 10,000 mm in parts of Hawaii. At Iquique in the Chilean desert, no rain fell for one fourteen-year period, whereas at the other extreme, 22,000 mm has been recorded in a single year at Cherrapunji in India. In the Sahel region of Africa during the late 1960s, a decrease in rainfall of 20-50 percent over a six-year period seriously harmed agriculture, livestock, inland fisheries, and national economies, with many social and political ramifications.

A similar drought now seems to be occurring in southern Africa. Yet the causes of such droughts are not known. Whether the decrease in rainfall represents an irregular fluctuation or part of a long-term climatic change is not understood.

THE RESOURCE BASE

Considering the enormous amounts of water in the hydrosphere, it is difficult to understand how there could possibly be a scarcity of water. Nevertheless, the water available for human use on a sustained basis in the earth's populated regions is uncomfortably close to potential "needs" of the twenty-first century, an indication that the process of moderating those needs should begin immediately.

The most comprehensive of the studies of world water balance are those of L'vovich (see table 9.2). He estimates total annual precipitation to be 525,100 km³ (1 km³ = 264.2 x 10⁹ US gallons; the annual average flow of the Colorado River at Yuma, Arizona, is about 12

TABLE 9.2. Annual world water balance.

Elements of water balance	Volume (km³)	Depth (mm)
Peripheral land area (116.8 million km²):		
Precipitation	106,000	910
Runoff	41,000	350
Evapotranspiration	65,000	560
Enclosed part of the land area (32.1 million km²):		
precipitation	7,500*	238
evapotranspiration	7,500	238
Oceans (361.1 million km²):		
Precipitation	411,600	1,140
Inflow of river water	41,000	114
Evaporation	452,600	1,254
The globe (510 million km²):		
precipitation	525,100	1,030
evapotranspiration	525,100	1,030

Source: M. I. L'vovich, World Water Resources and Their Future, English trans. ed. R. L. Nace, p. 56 (Washington, D.C.: American Geophysical Society, 1979).
*Including 830 km³m or 26 mm, of runoff.

km³). Compared with this, worldwide diversion for human use in 1970 was about 3,500 km³, and based on this level of use, an estimated 5,800 km³ is contaminated by anthropogenic pollution. Unfortunately, most precipitation—411,600 km³, or 78 percent—is over the oceans and hence is not readily available for human use. Of the remaining proportion, only 41,000 km³ is available annually as surface or groundwater runoff and of this amount only 14,000 km³ is available as stable runoff;[1] the rest goes directly into the sea as flood runoff. Of the 14,000 km³, 5,000 km³ is available only in sparsely inhabited

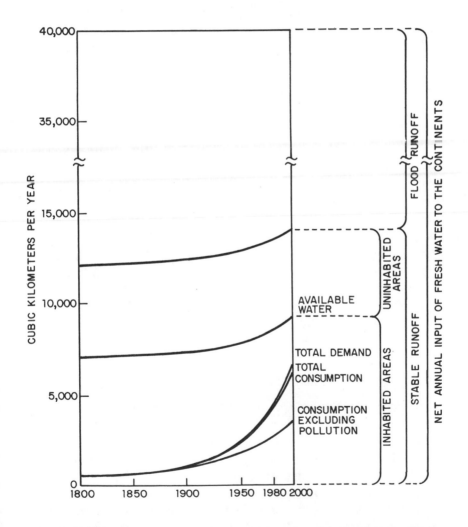

FIGURE 9.2. Global water supply and demands. *Source:* Ambroggi, 1980.

regions, and thus, only 9,000 km³ is readily available for human use. The ratio of use (including dilution of wastes) to readily available resources, then, is in the range of 38-64 percent instead of the 1 percent that would be the case if use were compared to total precipitation.

The amount of water stored in the global hydrosphere is three orders of magnitude larger than the annual precipitation. Total fresh and saline water (including water vapor) in the hydrosphere is estimated at 1,454 million km³. Of the total 84.4 million km³ of fresh water, approximately 60 million km³ is groundwater, 24 million km³ is in ice sheets, 280,000 km³ is in lakes and reservoirs, 85,000 km³ is in soil moisture, only 1,200 km³ is in rivers, and only 14,000 km³ is in the atmosphere at any time. This means that the entire amount of stored atmospheric moisture is recycled every ten days, and the storage in rivers is changed every eleven days.

Although there appears to be no scarcity of the current resource in aggregate, if use were doubled over the next twenty years and nothing were done to increase the stable runoff, water scarcity could become quite serious (see figure 9.2). Moreover, the aggregate resource position disguises many serious instances of scarcity, even at the current level of human use, at national or regional levels. For example, Africa's runoff per unit area is only about one-fifth that of South America and half the world average. This is because of lower precipitation and higher evapotranspiration than in other parts of the world. On a per capita basis, however, it is Asia that has only half the world's average water availability, and Africa is almost exactly at the world average of 8,562 m³/person/yr. Despite its low runoff per unit area, Oceania has six times the world's per capita level because of its low population. Latin America has almost four times the world's average per capita supply of water.

THE BASIS FOR ESTIMATING DEMANDS ON THE RESOURCE

The economic theory of scarce resources originally articulated by Ricardo and Malthus in the nineteenth century does not really address the complexity of water as an economic resource. Water can be considered as both a renewable and a nonrenewable resource—the former on a global and often on a local scale, particularly where supply is from rainfall and rivers, but the latter in areas that rely on groundwater supply in excess of both the natural rate of replenishment and surface water such as lakes and rivers which have been permanently contaminated by pollution.

Some attributes of water make economic theories of common-property resources difficult to apply strictly. There are the well-known external effects of pollution, for example, in which water use by one person or group affects that of another further downstream. By contrast,in areas of overabundance, water use can be a public good, for consumption by one person does not impair consumption by another. But, certain economies of scale in providing water supplies lead to natural monopolies. External effects, use as a public good, and monopolies make the existence of reliable private water markets questionable. Thus, conventional economic analysis must be modified greatly before it can be applied to water development.

Demand for Fresh Water

Demand for fresh water is a function of specific water uses and of users' characteristics. For a particular use in a particular climatic region, the demand for fresh water should be a function of both the user's income (or asset structure) and the price of water. Indeed, for all uses except domestic, the price should be the governing determinant of water use, other things being equal. Unfortunately, most studies of water use and demand either have not found statistically significant income and price effects or have not looked for such effects and have reported needs rather than demands.

Many studies assessing the economic demand for water have concentrated on municipal water and agricultural use, giving less attention to the demand for recreational and transportation use, flood control, wastewater management, and cooling water. Since almost all these studies have been based on data from North America, caution needs to be exercised in generalizing these results to the rest of the world. Even in the United States, these demand studies have not been widely employed for controlling water use and forecasting demand. For example, the most recent national water assessment by the US Water Resources Council (1978) takes a "requirement" approach rather than an "economic demand" approach in making water-use forecasts to the year 2000.

Municipal Demand for Water

The economic demand for water is commonly agreed to be a function of the price charged regardless of whether or not the supply is metered, the nature of other supply restrictions, the income and other socioeconomic characteristics of the users, and local climatic and cultural factors.

Price is expected to influence the demand for water negatively—that is, higher prices lead to lower consumption; in economic terms, this means that the price elasticity is negative. The studies of water demand mostly agree with the expectation of a negative price relationship with consumer demand. Moreover, they agree that water demand is relatively price inelastic. The range of typical values for the price elasticity in the studies is from -0.15 to -0.70, which means that with a 10-percent increase in price, the demand for water would drop by between 1.5 and 7 percent. Many planning studies ignore the fact that water is, indeed, price-responsive, and this leads to a casual approach to pricing that reflects engineering costs of supply rather than social values. Where marginal costs are greater than average costs, the average-cost pricing recommended by most water authorities and endorsed by professional bodies such as the American Waterworks Association can lead to serious misallocation of resources.

Water meters also provide a way of limiting demand. In the United States, studies comparing metered with unmetered use indicate that metering results in substantially less water use. Most of this difference is in water used outside the house—for example, for watering lawns or washing cars. Lawn watering by metered users was only 45 percent of that by unmetered users. The introduction of meters also seems to lead to a permanent adjustment to lower water use. A thirteen-year study in Boulder, Colorado, showed that domestic and lawn-watering uses were 65 and 51 percent, respectively, of what they had been before metering. In a similar study of apartment dwellers in Israel, where there was no lawn watering, the metered use was 75 percent of the unmetered use for carefully controlled and matched households.

Restrictions such as bans on outside use of water are typically assumed in North America to reduce water use to about 85 percent of normal use. These restrictions are typically imposed during droughts or summer peak-demand periods.

One form of water restriction commonly employed in the developing countries is the provision of only an intermittent supply during the day or over the year. This is a very effective way of limiting demand (although wealthier customers build their own storage works on the roofs of their houses and increase the demand during the time of supply). It is not recommended on public health grounds, however;

for, when the supply is interrupted, the pressure in the distribution system drops, and instead of leaking out of the pipes, water leaks in, bringing bacterial and other contamination with it. Moreover, temporary residential storage devices may be additional sources of contamination. Often, although a city puts high-quality, contaminant-free water into the system, heavily contaminated and potentially dangerous water comes out of the spigot in houses or at standpipes.

Household income and size appear to be the most important socioeconomic determinants of municipal demand for water. Generally, the wealthier a family, the more water it uses. Studies in the United States indicate a typical income elasticity in the range of $+0.3$ to $+0.5$. With a 10-percent increase in family income, the quantity of water used would increase by between 3 and 5 percent. The increase in use with family size (persons per household), sometimes called "people elasticity," has a typical value of about $+0.40$. In other words, if the average size of a household increases by 10 percent, water use would increase by 4 percent. Other characteristics, such as the median age of heads of households, appear as a factor in some studies and have small effects that are often unpredictable. Generally, these effects would not be considered in predicting demand unless there were strong a priori reasons for including them.

Obviously, characteristics of the housing stock and of household appliances using water are important. For example, lower water use has been observed in new housing developments than in older houses. Reduced demand can thus be achieved by modifying building codes. Also, energy-efficient appliances for washing clothes and dishes tend to use less hot water and hence reduce total water use. Shower heads and faucets in new developments are fitted with flow-restriction devices, and toilets have smaller tanks.

Conscious adaptation of pricing mechanisms to limit water demand and to produce marginally efficient economic solutions has not been followed widely. Recent developments in the United States, however, show some marked improvements in conserving water when marginal-cost pricing is followed. The experience of several cities in the Southwest is that wherever cities moved toward marginal-cost pricing, there were large savings in water consumption. Comparison of use rates and amounts paid in Boston and Frankfurt (see table 9.1) gives an indication of the magnitude of potential water savings. Boston pays $0.26/m^3$ ($1.00/1,000 gallons), Frankfurt $0.75/m^3$ ($2.82/1,000 gallons). Bostonians use on average several times as much water as residents of Frankfurt (taking systemic losses into account).

Water costs in the developing countries are typically in the same range as those in the developed countries. In Surabaya, Indonesia, for example, piped water costs $0.168/m^3$ ($0.63/1,000 gallons), and vendors sell water from standpipes at $0.36/m^3$ ($1.35/1,000 gallons). Water use from piped supply ranges from 100 to 150 liters per capita per day, and from vendors, averages 20 liters per capita per day. Based on a standard of no more than 4 percent of income being spent on water, 16 percent of Indonesia's urban population would be unable to consume 30 liters per capita per day even at the rate of $0.48/m^3$ ($0.18/1,000 gallons).

In East Africa, the cost of water and its use in urban and rural areas varied markedly. The cost of unpiped water in towns averaged $0.49/m^3$ ($1.85/1,000 gallons) with an average use of 2.59 liters per capita per day. The cost of water sold from standpipes, which in some cases included transportation costs, reached $9.46/1,000 gallons. Piped water in medium-density cities cost $0.20/m^3$ ($0.76/1,000 gallons) for a per capita use of 25 liters. These data indicate that there is indeed a downward-sloping demand curve for water, and that the slope of the curve is likely to be flat, suggesting an elastic response to price. A middle-income worker in Nairobi, however, may spend as much as 8 percent of his or her income on water, more than such a worker typically spends on fuel, transportation or household equipment. Unfortunately, using water pricing as a conservation mechanism for domestic supply in developing countries is thus very regressive in socioeconomic terms.

Agricultural Demand for Water

In many countries the agricultural demand for water dominates the total demand. In the United States, agriculture accounts for 83 percent of the annual total water consumption. Hence, small changes in the agricultural demand can free large quantities of water for other uses. It is important that irrigation water be used efficiently. Most analyses of water requirements for irrigation begin with a fixed figure for the amount required per acre of land. This involves two problems. First, there is a difference between the "biological optimum" and the "economic optimum." The latter considers not only the biology of the plants being irrigated but also the cost of all other inputs and outputs.

Even if the economic optimum for a crop is known, however, a second problem may arise: the farmer always has the option of switching to some other crop or cropping system if the costs of one of the inputs, say water, should change radically. What is needed, then, is a demand curve for water for individual farmers over a full range of crops.

Unlike municipal water, irrigation water is not a final consumption item, but an intermediate production item for crops. This makes the direct economic evaluation of the demand curve much more difficult because of the variety of productive uses of water even on one small farm. Agricultural economists have solved this problem by computing "derived" demand curves, based on what would be optimal use of water on a given farm at a given price. Typically, linear programming models are used to estimate these derived demand curves. Recent work in the United States shows a wide range of estimates for the price elasticity of irrigation water, from -0.3 to -2.0 at high price ranges. All the studies show a decrease of the elasticity as the price of water increases. Experience in California shows that with increasing prices, efficiency in the use of irrigation water rises rapidly. Also, as water costs rise, the cropping pattern shifts to more water-efficient or more highly valued crops.

Pricing of irrigation water is of critical importance in irrigation management, but it appears to be handled badly by governments throughout the world. For example, supplies of irrigation water from the proposed Auburn Dam in the Sierra foothills near Sacramento, California, will cost about $63/acre-foot. But the US Bureau of Reclamation is proposing to average this new supply cost into the total regional supply costs, raising the average cost from $5 to $18/acre-foot. But to justify the new project on strict economic criteria, the irrigation water must be worth at least $63/acre-foot or the dam should not be built.

Noneconomic approaches to irrigation prices seem to be endemic around the world. In India the water rates for rice irrigation have dropped from between 9 and 10 percent of the gross value of the crop in the year 1900 to between 2 and 3 percent today. These low rates have resulted in extremely inefficient uses of water and serious financial difficulties for the irrigation agencies, leading to deferred maintenance with subsequent deterioration of systems.

In regions where costs for irrigation water are high, however, a variety of interesting adaptations have occurred. In areas of the United States where farmers pay more for irrigation water (particularly groundwater that they pump themselves), water is used substantially more efficiently than in other areas with surface water, often government-supplied—more than 65-percent efficiency compared with less than 45 percent (US Department of the Interior [1978]). In India, areas with irrigation largely from tube wells significantly outperform other areas. At least two factors are at work here: (1) farmers control the amount and timing of their use of tube well water much more than they do that of surface water, and (2) the incentive to economize is strong, since the prices farmers pay for water as an input are higher and more directly perceived than water rates charged on a per acrefoot basis.

Industrial Demand for Water

Even though it accounts for between only 5 and 10 percent of the current water used globally, industrial use is nevertheless an important component of overall use—and its subsequent abuse, since a disproportionate amount of toxic contaminants are introduced into the aquatic ecosystem from industrial effluents. In the United States, 90 percent of industrial water is used for cooling. The major water-using industries, in order of use, are food products, pulp and paper, chemicals, petroleum, and primary metals.

By 1975 US industry as a whole had achieved a recycling rate of 2.2—that is, the water brought into the plant was used on average 2.2 times before it was discarded—and about 90.5 percent of the original water withdrawn was returned to the surface-water system. Winje (1982) reported that West Germany had a similar recycling rate, and Japan a rate of 1.5. Based on projected recycling rates, he predicts that by the year 2000 both Japan and West Germany will have higher demands per capita for industrial water than the United States.

The large amounts of water used by industry for heating and cooling are at the heart of the problem of estimating industrial demand. The many technical substitution processes available for water conservation in industry all have different costs and performance characteristics. An industrial firm's demand for water in a particular use is a function of the price. The firm uses water as an economic input in such a way that a decrease in the use of water may cause it to need to use other, more costly inputs. the value of the water is then given by the added cost of these other inputs.

By examining a firm's production technologies, it is possible to compute the derived demand function for water in such a way that the firm will choose the optimum mix of inputs at each price level for water; thus the quantity of water needed can be ascertained. A demand curve for a fossil fuel electricity-generating plant in the United States would show that, at a low price for water, the plant would employ "once-through" cooling, using as much as 50 gallons/kWh of electricity generated. As the price increased to $0.05/1,000 gallons, the optimal behavior of the power producer would be to switch to a cooling tower, which would reduce the demand for water to about 0.8 gallons/kWh—almost two orders of reduction of magnitude. If the price of water were to rise to $8.00/1,000 gallons, then a dry cooling tower, with effectively zero water use, would be the optimum technology.

After calculation of the derived demand, the response to changes in water price could be estimated for individual industries as a whole. The important point in the example above is that a fivefold increase in price leads to a fiftyfold reduction in use. The sharpness of the response should thus lead to extreme caution in projecting "needs" for industrial water. In countries such as the United States where water has been severely underpriced, there is good potential for introducing these known technologies. For countries in which the price is already high, many of these innovations are in place, and there may be little potential for improvement.

Demand for Instream Water Uses

The demand for in-stream needs, such as navigation, flood protection, recreation, fisheries, and pollution control, is much more difficult to estimate because many of these fall in the public sector. This means that the quantity demanded by one user does not impair the use of the resource by others. For navigation and recreation, this is true until congestion causes consumption by some to impair use by others.

By estimating the benefits of reducing flood losses, it is possible to compute the marginal damage-avoidance benefits for investments in flood control. This is essentially the demand curve for flood prevention.

For recreational uses of water, an ingenious approach called the Hotelling-Clawson–Knetsch method can be used to estimate the economic demand. Essentially, this method relies upon travel costs as a measure of willingness to pay for recreation. It was used by the Texas Water Plan to estimate the recreational benefits of each of thirty-two reservoirs. Future benefits of these reservoirs, judged by present worth, ranged from $4 million to $22 million. The method could also be applied directly to in-stream recreational benefits. In many developed countries, benefits from recreation are potentially as large as benefits from all other uses.

ROLE OF WATER IN HEALTH

The demand that water be of high quality depends mainly on its role in the transmission of disease. The relation between water and health has been understood, to some extent anyway, since at least the time of Frontinus, the water commissioner of Rome in 97 A.D., but the exact relation is not well understood even now. A recent World Bank report said, "Other things being equal, a safe and adequate water supply is generally associated with a healthier population."

Diseases in which water is a significant factor are commonly broken down into five categories:

1. Waterborne diseases—cholera, typhoid, and infectious hepatitis.
2. Water-washed diseases—scabies, yaws, trachoma, and bacillary dysentery.
3. Water-based diseases—schistosomiasis and guinea worm.
4. Water-related diseases carried by insects—yellow fever, malaria, dengue, and sleeping sickness.
5. Diseases related to fecal disposal but not much affected by water directly—hookworm and clonorchiasis.

Many water-related diseases can be spread or introduced into areas as a result of development of water resources. The classic case is the spread of schistosomiasis in Africa and Asia after the introduction of irrigation. Schistosomiasis currently infects more than 200 million people worldwide. Eggs passed in urine or feces produce a ciliated larva, called a miracidium, which hatches on contact with water and develops further as a parasite in snails. The schistosomes enter human blood vessels through the skin when it is exposed to the contaminated water and eventually reach the bladder or intestines where they reach sexual maturity. The worms live for several years and are capable of laying several hundred eggs per day. The disease tends to be debilitating rather than fatal in most cases. Other diseases related to irrigation include malaria, filariasis, yellow fever, onchocerciasis, and sleeping sickness.

Schistosomiasis and other waterborne diseases such as typhoid and infant diarrhea can be reduced by only 60-70 percent at best, because other modes of transmission are not affected by improving the supply of potable water. Guinea worm disease (dracunculiasis), on the other hand, which afflicts 20-40 million people worldwide, is particularly vulnerable to a concerted eradication program because it is transmitted exclusively by water.

Many other health-related problems have been introduced by new agricultural practices. For example, many chemicals used in agriculture, particularly chlorinated hydrocarbons, accumulate in animal tissues and thus enter the food chain. High concentrations of fertilizer in water supplies have been known to cause blood diseases.

The International Drinking Water Supply and Sanitation Decade (1980-90) has set as its objective "clean drinking water and sanitation for all by 1990." This is certainly an ambitious goal, since an estimated 86 percent of the world's rural population currently lacks an adequate water supply, and 92 percent lacks adequate facilities for waste disposal. To meet the UN goal, the World Bank estimates that 2,400 million people would have to be serviced, leading to capital investments of $50,000 million for water supply and six to twelve times that much for sewerage. Based upon studies in eight cities, the World Bank estimated that the investment costs per household would range between $650 and $4,000, and that the annual cost of the service would be $150-$650/household/yr. It seems doubtful, however, that a very large fraction of total family income could be spent on such programs even if it could be justified economically. (The actual per household costs are in the same range as those for the same services in the industrialized countries, where they constitute only a small percentage of annual family income.)

However, these massive costs need to be viewed in the light of the potential health benefits of such programs. These are difficult to establish. Empirical studies of the relation between water supply and health may conclude either that communities or individuals with better health status are healthier because of the quality of their water supply, or that a healthier community has taken steps to improve the quality of its water supply. Such studies are often limited by failure to take into account different conditions between experimental and control communities.

Health professionals believe that the benefits of protected water supplies are large and must be directly related to the size of the investments. They point to the significant improvements in public health that coincided with the widespread introduction of protected water supplies and wastewater treatment facilities in the industrialized countries. Recent statistical analyses indicate that a simple linear model probably does not apply. In its place has been proposed a "threshold-saturation" theory that takes into account three variables: health status, socioeconomic status, and sanitation level for various populations in sixty-five developing countries. The theory suggests that for countries at the lower end of the socioeconomic spectrum, there is a threshold below which investments in community water supplies and excreta disposal facilities alone do little to improve health status. Conversely, at the higher end of the socioeconomic scale, a point of saturation is reached, beyond which further significant health benefits cannot be obtained by investments in conventional community sanitation facilities.

If it could be further validated, this theory would have important policy consequences for the expenditure of funds for water and sanitation. It suggests that in poor countries a single-purpose program, such as the provision of safe drinking water, by itself may not sufficiently reduce exposure to sources of infection to produce measurable results. In such settings, broad-spectrum programs involving various areas of santitation, nutrition, education, and primary health care, coupled with general efforts to encourage economic and social development, need to be combined with programs to supply drinking water. Although most countries are involved in these other programs, it is difficult to integrate them with water investment programs. At the other socioeconomic extreme, the theory also implies that the marginal benefits of programs to improve water supplies and sanitation systems are not likely to justify the expenditures.

From an investment point of view, then, the countries at the socioeconomic middle level look like the best option. The equity implications of the theory may not be attractive, but for those involved in making decisions, the theory is illuminating. All of the above would also hold true, of course, of regions within countries. This tends to moderate policy implications, from giving more to those who have on an international scale to favoring the more successful regions within a particular country.

However, a review of the data on health-related costs and benefits due to water supply protection in East Africa leads to essentially the opposite policy conclusions. It is estimated that in Kenya, Tanzania, and Uganda, between 49 and 55 percent of all water-related diseases could be eradicated by reasonable water supply investments. Extrapolating these rates of disease reduction to hospital admissions and outpatient treatments, and taking into account the limitations of the data, leads to the conclusion that the health costs that are preventable range between $24,453,000 and $3,700,000 per year, or between $0.871 and $0.132 per capita per year. Whether protected water supplies (and the concomitant sanitation programs) can be provided for per capita costs in this range remains a question. The capital cost of a rural pipeline in East Africa would be about $4.00 per capita, or between $0.84 and $0.67 per capita on an annual basis. For urban water supplies, the cost might range between $1.87 and $1.25 per capita per year. These costs are far below the World Bank estimates referred to above, and, of course, they do not include the necessary santiation programs. One example of improvements in water supply only was the sinking of more than half a million tube wells in Bangladesh for village water supply without a concentrated and integrated sanitation program. This program has not led to commensurate improvements in the health of the rural population.

This is not to say that the situation is hopeless. In Patna, which has the reputation of being the dirtiest state capital in India, a nongovernmental organization set up public baths and toilets, and more than 25,000 people who previously defecated in the streets now use these facilities. A fee of 10 paise (1 US cent) is charged men who can afford to pay. Women and children are allowed to use the facilities free. Together with the user fee and a 50-percent capital subsidy from the government, the latrines and baths break even. But, the cost is still $3.65 per year per capita, a lot higher than the estimated benefits. Other successes with latrine programs are reported in Sri Lanka, and in Calcutta and Gujarat State in India.

FOUR MAJOR WATER-USING COUNTRIES

China, India, the United States, and the USSR, stand out as countries that currently consume large quantities of fresh water or will do so in the near future. Not surprisingly, these are the four nations with the largest populations. Jointly they account for 2,281 million people, or 49 percent of the estimated 1982 world population, and 44.7 million km^2 or 32 percent, of the total land area of the globe. Consequently, any discussion of the use of water resources is likely to be highly influenced by the behavior of these four nations, which can serve as development models for other countries.

It is instructive to compare the water problems and policies of these four countries. The countries differ radically in economic development and in political and social organization. What organization is appropriate at each level of economic development? How does political organization and ideology influence the range of problems and their policy outcomes? Which issues are common to these countries? Which are different? What accounts for the differences and similarities? There is not enough information available to answer all these questions, but marshaling the comparative data that are available can help structure approaches to these questions and help assess their implications for the more than 160 other countries in the world.

Table 9.3 shows that the four countries account for anywhere from 61 to 70 percent of the world's total irrigated land, depending on the source of the estimate. India leads the world with 56.6 million ha irrigated, and China has 46.6 million ha. These two countries alone account for 54 percent of the world's total irrigated land. Both India and China have only about 0.1-0.2 ha of cultivated land per capita, whereas the USSR and the United States have, respectively, 0.86 and 0.71 ha per capita. Hence, China and India are in need of agricultural intensification. Both countries also have considerably less available runoff than the USSR and the United States. In each of the four countries, irrigated agriculture consumes by far the largest amount of water. Therefore, conservation strategies should aim at small improvements in the efficiency with which these large quantities of water are used.

China

The hydrology and climate of China are dominated by the monsoon, which leads to highly seasonal rainfall, with 70-80 percent of the annual rainfall occurring between June and September. The distribution of rainfall within the country is also uneven, ranging from 100-200 mm in the northwest to 1,000-2,000 mm in the southeast. Moreover, in northern China, there are large differences between years. The average annual runoff of all the rivers of China is $2,600 \times 10^9$ m^3, however, the base flow is only 700×10^9 m^3.

China has abundant water resources. In runoff, it ranks fifth in the world after Brazil, the USSR, Canada, and the United States. But nearly three-quarters of the runoff escapes unused to the ocean. To take advantage of this resource, China is proposing major inter-basin transfers to link the Yellow River (Huang He) with the Yangtze River

(Chang Jiang). The Yangtze (annual flow of 1,000 km³), which flows through a region with abundant water resources, could export water north to the Yellow River (which has an annual flow of only 47 km³), as much as 30 km³ during dry years.

In the North China Plain, silt deposition blocks drainage and causes extreme flooding. China has a long history of irrigation (since as early as 252 B.C.), navigation canals (since 486 B.C), and large flood-control works (since the third century B.C.). Chinese water experts claim that the historical record shows one major flood or drought disaster nearly every year during the 2,155-year period from 206 B.C. to 1949—1,029 heavy floods and 1,056 severe droughts were recorded over that period (Weizhan, 1980). Chen (1980) claims that, through extension of embankments and the building of reservoirs for controlled flooding, the flooding from the major rivers is now essentially under control.

By the end of 1978, 84,000 reservoirs had been built in China, with a total storage capacity of 400 x 10⁹ m³. Recently, in the arid and semiarid areas of northern China, rapid groundwater development has taken place, with more than 2.2 million pumped wells.

As can be seen in table 9.3, China has a relatively small area of cultivated land per capita. This has greatly influenced the strategy used by the Chinese water planners, who have emphasized irrigation over other forms of water development. Fully 36 percent of the cultivated land is irrigated. More than 50 percent of the total agricultural sector investments in 1982 were targeted for irrigation and drainage.

These two items, known collectively in China as water conservancy, have made a major contribution to the growth of agricultural production. By the end of the 1970s, the irrigated area was 53 percent greater than it was in the mid-1950s and included nearly 50 percent of the cropped area. The improved and expanded irrigation made it possible for China to capitalize on the potential of new high-yielding crops and on the increased availability of fertilizer. The facilities were largely in place in many of the provinces of central and southern China during the 1950s, and expansion has taken place mostly in the North China Plain, where tube-well irrigation systems have made possible large gains in wheat production, normal rainfall in this area being unable to sustain a high-yielding wheat crop. Although investment and expansion of irrigation continues, the Chinese are moving cautiously. Most current projects are low-cost and small-scale, and large capital-intensive projects such as the proposed Yangtze diversion have been delayed. China is now on an increasing-cost part of the

TABLE 9.3. Comparison of four large water-using countries.

	China	India	USSR	US	Total	% Global
Pop[a] x 10³ (1982)	1,055,304	723,762	269,994	232,464	2,2 81,524	49
GNP/capita (1979 dollars)	452	170	4,667	10,212	—	—
Land area (ha x 10³)	9,599,990	3,287,585	22,402,177	9,363,114	44,652,866	32
Net cultivated land area (ha x 10³)	127,500	142,220	232,500	167,141	44,652,866	32
Cultivated land per capita (ha)	0.12	0.19	0.86	0.71	—	—
Irrigated cropland[b] (ha x 10³)	46,690	56,600	10,000 (30,000)	22,541	135,830 (155,830)	61 (70)
Runoff[c] per capita (m³)	2,949	2,355	16,385	10,137	—	—

Total withdrawal (m³/day x 10⁹)	1.339[d]	1.028[e]	0.790	1.701	4.858
% irrigation	0.93	93.0	51.1	33.5	45
% public-utility water	2.2	1.0	4.4	7.5	—
% industry	4.7	0.7	}31.1	10.0	—
% steam electric	n/a	1.8	}	48.8	—
Total consumption (m³/day x 10⁹)	n/a	0.605	0.445	0.378	—
% irrigation	n/a	95.8	72.0	83.0	—
% public utility	n/a	0.5	1.8	7.1	—
% industrial	n/a	0.11	}3.1	5.0	—
% steam electric	n/a	.02	}	3.3	—

[a] *Statistical Abstract of the United States, 1982–83* (US Department of Commerce, 1983).

[b] Source for the Soviet data in parenthesis is from Van der Leeden, *Water Resources of the World* (Port Washington, N.Y. Water Information Center, Inc., 1975), p. 311. The US data is for 1977 and is taken from Frederick and Manson, "Water for Western Agriculture" (research paper, 1982). The data for India is for 1980 and taken from Abie et al. (1982). The China data is for 1979 and is taken from Weizhan (1983) and USDA, *China: Review of Agriculture in 1981 and Outlook for 1982* (1982). The FAO Production Yearbook for 1977 gives the following figures for 1976: China, 85,200 ha x 10³; India, 34,400 ha x 10³; US, 16,550 ha x 10³; and USSR, 15,300 ha x 10³.

[c] S. Friedman, "World Water Availability and Demand" (memo IBRD, 19 May 1983).

[d] Z. Weizhan, "Prediction of Water Needs in China" (Wuhan Institute, Wuhan, China, 1983).

[e] M. C. Chaturvedi, *Second India Studies: Water* (Wuhan Institute, Wuhan, China, 1983).

supply curve for irrigation and is already suffering from problems related to overexploitation of groundwater. This is particularly true in the vicinity of Beijing and Tianjin, where there is serious conflict between irrigation and other demands for water. Over the next few years, however, large gains are expected from emphasis on management and low-cost improvements of existing systems.

China also suffers from serious water pollution near its large cities and industrial complexes and will need to invest more in facilities for water-quality management. Rivers, particularly the Yellow River, are notoriously silt-laden, and great care has to be taken in the development of water-storage projects so that they do not fill up with silt.

India

India has the second largest population in the world. Although rain is plentiful over most of the country, the climate is dominated by the monsoon, and rain is therefore concentrated in a few months. In many areas, the onset of the monsoon is uncertain, so farmers need supplemental irrigation even during the supposedly rainy season to ensure that crops survive. When India's population reaches almost a thousand million by the turn of the century, water availability will be reduced to 1,900 m^3 per capita per year from the current runoff of 2,355 m^3 per capita per year (and an estimated 867 m^3 per capita per year diversion at present). This reduces the availability of water to about twice the actual amount that would indicate possibly serious water shortages in drought years, limit the expansion of economic development, and certainly restrict irrigation development. Chaturvedi (1976) claims that the situation is even tighter, that the total ground- and surface-water development potential in India is 92.70 million ha-m (927 x 10^9 m^3) per year, which would account for use of all available water by about the year 2005.

India, like China, has a long history of water resource development, with documented irrigation as early as 300 B.C. The Delhi sultanate, and later the Moguls, engaged in large-scale irrigation works (some of the canals were more than 180 km in length) in northern India from 1350 until 1750. During the nineteenth century there was tremendous growth in irrigation works, and by 1900 irrigation facilities covered more than 4.04 million ha. Currently there are 34.6 million ha under surface irrigation and 22 million ha irrigated from groundwater.

Recent economic studies have shown the superior performance of groundwater systems, particularly those in the private sector, over surface irrigation systems. A recent World Bank publication also discusses the economic returns to investment in irrigation in India. It summarized the data on the anticipated and actual rates of return for private groundwater investment and public surface-water projects. For the groundwater projects, the actual rates were everywhere somewhat lower than, but very close to, the anticipated returns (in the range of 20-50 percent for tube wells and 15-50 percent for dug wells and pumpsets). The report also says that two large surface projects, Pochampod and Kadana, had rates of return of 14 and 12 percent, respectively, and that two completed major irrigation projects in Rajasthan had rates of return in the 13-14-percent range.

More than four million open wells were fitted with traditional water-lifting devices in 1971, and there was probably a similar number of wells in existence in 1951, whereas the number of power pumps in operation rose from 85,000 to more than 2.75 million in the same period, and the number of public tube wells from 21,000 to about 300,000. (This is a 19-percent annual rate of growth for pumpsets and a 17-percent growth rate for tube wells.) It was estimated that by 1971, modern water lifts raised 38 million acre-feet of groundwater, and traditional lifting devices 27 million acre-feet.

The Sixth Full-Year Plan of the Indian Planning Commission noted the disparity between the tremendous expenditure on irrigation (between 11 and 14 percent of total public-sector expenditures in recent Five-Year Plans (FYPs) and 12.47 percent in the sixth FYP) and the rate of agricultural production. The plan noted that irrigated land should yield four to five tons of grains per hectare, whereas the current yields averaged less than two tons per hectare. Partly because of these poor yields, irrigation projects were unable to recover even working expenses, and the planning commission estimated an annual deficit of $330 million (4.27 billion rupees) per year. It claimed that these deficits were due mainly to delays in completing many of the projects—in some cases projects are still not completed after more than fifteen to twenty years. Another reason given was delay in using the actual irrigation potential created. The plan allocated 121.6 billion rupees ($9,400 million) to irrigation, command-area development, and flood-control items. Of this, 69 percent was to go to major and medium projects, and only 14 percent to minor irrigation (typically groundwater) projects.

Based upon the sixth FYP, annual expenditures for water resources development in India are $4.3 x 10⁹ per year. India devotes
53 percent of its annual water expenditures to irrigation and drainage,
20 percent to hydropower, and only 18 percent to municipal and industrial water supply. See table 9.4, which shows the distribution of
the annual expenditures by water activity for each country. These priorities could be questioned, given the lack of performance in the public irrigation sector and the pressing needs for rural and urban water
supplies. It appears that India should concentrate on developing existing surface systems, perhaps by increasing groundwater storage,
and encourage rapid exploitation of groundwater resources.

USSR

The USSR is particularly richly endowed with water resources and is
second only to Brazil in availability of water per capita. The annual
precipitation is 10,860 km³, giving a total runoff of 4,350 km³. The total availability of what L'vovich (1979) calls stable runoff is 1,300
km³/yr, or 16,384 m³ per capita, compared with the world average of
8,562 m³ per capita. However, the country's population and industry

TABLE 9.4. Expenditures for water resources development.

	China	India	USSR	US
Average size of annual program, $ x 10⁹ᵃ				
1980–2000	0.537ᵇ	4.3ᶜ	6.8ᵈ	43ᵉ
Municipal and industrial	—	18%	20.5%	23%
Irrigation and drainage	—	53%	56.2%)	
			)	
			)	
Waterways and transport	—	0.6%	0.6%)	) 18%
Flood control	—	4.8%	3.4%)	
			)	
Pisciculture	—	1.7%	1.5%)	
Hydropower	—	20.4%	12.2%)	
Water-quality management	—	0.2%	—	58%

ᵃ Based upon an exchange rate of 1 ruble = 1 US dollar = 10 rupees = 2 yuan.
ᵇ Based upon the 1983 *Chinese Statistical Yearbook*, 3.412 x 10⁹ yuan for the entire 1982
agricultural and forestry sector; water conservancy was 52%.
ᶜ Based upon public-sector capital expenditures during the Sixth Five-Year Plan.
ᵈ Water-quality management is included.
ᵉ Includes federal, state, and local expenditures plus an estimate of private expenditures.

are concentrated in areas of low availabilty of water. For example, 80 percent of the population lives in regions that have only 40 percent of the country's water supply.

The data on irrigated agriculture are conflicting. L'vovich gives the total irrigated area as 10 million ha, but other estimates range between 28 and 30 million ha. This gives a range of between 4.3 and 12.9 percent of the 232 million ha of net cultivated land. Problems in estimating the actual areas irrigated may arise because of salinization of the soils. This is a major problem in the USSR, where 40 percent of the total irrigated area is considered salinized. Gustafson (1974) reports that for every three acres of new irrigation, one previously irrigated acre is abandoned. From 1961 to 1969, and increase of 1 million ha irrigated in central Asia led to an increase of only 95,000 ha in the total. Projections from 1967 data show an upper limit of 75 million ha of irrigated land, or that 32 percent of the total farmed land will be irrigated in the future.

In the USSR, major attention has been paid to problems of environmental quality associated with the use and development of water resources. Recently, for example, huge schemes that would change the direction of major Siberian rivers (from flowing north into the Arctic Ocean to flowing south) have been abandoned largely on the basis of the large potential environmental impacts of these projects. There is also concern over pollution from industries in both heavily and lightly populated parts of the country.

Estimates of the investments in water resources in the USSR are not readily available. Gustafson (1974) reported a rough estimate of $6.8 billion per year (a $205 billion program from 1970 until 2000). But this is probably too low, since investments in irrigation alone were already $6.1 billion by 1975, implying an annual program of $10 billion by now. Investments in hydropower have been of major importance historically in the USSR. By 1970, however, the proportion of water resource expenditure on hydropower had declined to almost half its 1955 level. Table 9.4 shows that the bulk of the Soviet expenditure for development of water resources will go to irrigation, drainage, and reclamation, which seems a reasonable approach.

United States

The consensus of the water experts is that the United States does not face a crisis in water resources. This does not mean, however, that there are not likely to be serious dislocations and disruptions in some parts of the country during the next fifty years. These regional disruptions make the issue very complex and the conflicts arising from them nearly unresolvable, given the current political and institutional approaches to the problem of water resource development.

In any area of endeavor, it is important to know the current situation before hazarding projections. But the data for assessing the current status of irrigation in the United States, as for other countries, are poor and inconsistent. Estimates of irrigated acreage by several agencies for various dates in the mid-1970s vary from 41 to 61 million acres (16.6 to 24.7 million ha). Similar variations exist in the estimates of the amounts of water used in irrigated agriculture, and in projections for the future. Such descrepancies advise caution about placing too much emphasis on detailed quantitative analysis based on any one data source. For example, 1977 projection of the US Water Resources Council (1978) of irrigated acreage in the year 2000 is 8 million acres (3.2 million ha) less than the amount claimed in the US Department of Agriculture's 1977 *National Resources Inventory.* Some of the differences may be accounted for by the use of different spatial units and reporting systems, but the largest discrepancies may be due to major difficulties in distinguishing full irrigation from supplemental irrigation not used every year.

All the projections, however, are substantially greater than the 32 million acres (13 million ha) recommended by the Center for Agriculture and Rural Development (1975) as the "least-cost" level of irrigated agriculture needed in the year 2000 to meet the expected domestic and export demand for food and fiber. In 1977, about 61 million acres of cropland and pasture out of a nationwide total of 546.9 million acres, or 11 percent, were irrigated.

Table 9.5 shows the Water Resources Council estimates of US withdrawals and total consumption by use for 1975 and of projections for 1985 and 2000. The table is important for an understanding of the water resources problem in the United States. Note the tremendous asymmetry between agriculture and manufacturing; the agricultural sector, which contributed only 3 percent of the GNP, used 83 percent of the nation's water, whereas manufacturing, which contributed 27 percent of the GNP, used less than 6 percent of the total water consumed in 1975.

Of the total amount withdrawn, 24 percent is groundwater. Since 1950, the bulk of the expansion in irrigation has been based on groundwater sources. This strategy has some serious drawbacks, indicated by overdrafts (excess withdrawal over annual recharge of the

TABLE 9.5. Total withdrawals and consumption of water, by functional use, for the United States (millions of gallons per day).

Functional use	Total withdrawals			Total consumption		
	1975	1985	200	1975	1985	2000
Fresh water:						
Domestic:						
Central (municipal)	21,164	13,983	27,918	4,976	5,665	6,638
Noncentral (rural)	2,092	2,320	2,400	1,292	1,408	1,436
Commercial	5,530	6,048	6,732	1,109	1,216	1,369
Manufacturing	51,222	23,687	19,669	6,059	8,903	14,699
Agriculture:						
irrigation	158,743	166,252	153,846	86,391	92,506	
livestock	1,912	2,233	2,551	1,912	2,233	2,551
Steam electric generation	88,916	94,858	79,492	1,419	4.062	10,541
Minerals industry	7,055	8,832	11,328	2,196	2,777	3,609
Public lands and others[a]	1,866	2,162	2,461	1,236	1,461	1,731
Total fresh water	338,500	330,375	306,397	106,590	120,545	135,080
Total saline water[b]	59,737	91,236	118,815			
Total withdrawals	398,237	421,611	425,212			

Source: US Water Resources Council, *Second National Water Assessment*, vol. 1, p. 29.
[a] Includes water for fish hatcheries and miscellaneous uses.
[b] Saline water is used mainly in manufacturing and steam electric generation.

aquifer) in the range of 4-95 percent in regions of high irrigation growth in the West. Frederick and Hanson (1982, p. 82) estimated that groundwater mining (overdraft) exceeds 20 billion gallons per day, or 22.4 million acre-feet per year in the western states. The data indicate that enough water to irrigate about 7 million acres (2.8 million ha) at average current rates of water use is mined from the aquifers. Clearly, this is not a long-term proposition.

One of the unintended impacts of the implementation of the Clean Water Act in the United States has been a reduction in the demand for water by industry and commerce. Since they have been required to treat their effluents or to pay someone else to treat them, industries have started to reduce the amount of water withdrawn and, wherever possible, to reduce the amount of water consumed. There is already, therefore, a substantial economic premium on industries to adapt in order to reduce their demand for water. The Water Resources Council (1978, vol. 2, p. 36) estimates that freshwater withdrawals by manufacturing industries in the year 2000 will be reduced by 62 percent relative to the 1977 figure of 51.2 billion gallons per day.

With an annual expenditure of about $43 x 10^9 for water resources, the United States spends perhaps four times as much as the USSR in this area. It is interesting to note, however, that the bulk of the US expenditures are on water-quality management (58 percent) and only 18 percent on irrigation, drainage, waterways, flood control, and hydropower. The other large consumer of funds is municipal and industrial water supplies (23 percent). These expenditures reflect a mature water economy in which irrigation, hydropower, flood control, and so forth are already in place for the most part, and hence the shift in concern to quality.

Lessons to be learned

The four countries discussed include a mature capitalist economy, a mature socialist economy, an undeveloped socialist economy, and an undeveloped mixed economy. All have large infrastructures of irrigation works, surprisingly enough dominated by the government in each case. With regard to investments, the United States has largely turned away from more irrigation development, and the bulk of the expenditures are for environmental-quality management—water pollution control—and to a lesser extent municipal water development. This is not unexpected. The United States has developed an agricultural system that is extremely efficient (in a technical, not necessarily an economic sense). Indeed, it has been shown that the United States really needs only half the irrigated acreage it already has in order to produce in an economically efficient manner all the agricultural products it could use and export by the year 2000. The actual figure of $150 per capita spent per year in the United States on water pollution abatement amounts to about one quarter of the GNP per capita of China and more than half that of India. These sums, by the way, are largely what the government forces the private sector to pay to meet environmental standards—an example of a capitalist system attempting to make up for a classic case of "market failure."

In the USSR, pollution problems are becoming equally severe, but the resources to deal with them are not available. The USSR is forced to spend the bulk of its water resource funds on irrigation to counteract trainfall in the nation's growing regions. The unevenness of the USSR's grain output, more than the actual levels, has been the cause of great concern to Soviet planners. Large-scale additions to the irrigated areas should stabilize production. Besides introducing new irrigated areas, the USSR must also allocate large resources and skilled management to reclaiming salinized irrigated land and returning it to high productivity levels. As in the United States, Soviet investment in irrigation leads to regional conflicts within the country.

China, perhaps only because documentation is considerably more scarce than for the other countries, appears to be the best organized and targeted. The bulk of its effort is toward developing and maintaining its irrigation and drainage system. Subsidiary concern is for more flood control and for maintenance of existing flood-control systems. Production from irrigated Chinese agriculture shows that the systems are working well, certainly producing twice as much as similarly irrigated crops in India. This means that the rest of the agricultural infrastructure must be functioning equally well to maintain the irrigation system's effectiveness. It is being done at high cost, however, since more than 50 percent of the investment funds in the agriculture and forestry sector go to water conservancy.

India, as a mixed developing economy, seems to be suffering for its ideological ambivalence. Despite the private sector's impressive performance in agriculture irrigated by tube wells, state governments are devoted to extending large surface-water developments or large publicly owned tube-well systems, with the goal of bringing 107 million ha under irrigation. Unfortunately, there seems to be no government awareness that 56.6 million ha might be ample for India—if it were producing at Chinese, or Taiwnese, or Philippine levels. Re-

cently, major attempts have been made at command-area development, to bring existing irrigated land up to some reasonable level of
performance. However, most of the surface irrigation works, which
water a total of 34.6 million ha, have no effective storage in the system and are essentially diversions of flood-flow systems. Thus, when
the water demands of the crops are highest, the water available to the
diversion system is lowest, the quality of irrigation provided is extremely poor, and yields are likewise poor.

India, like China, is beginning to suffer severe environmental
problems near large urban complexes. So far, the costs of conventional waste treatment have been too high to justify the expenditure.
In the near future, however, some ares may require large-scale adjustments to production systems or large outlays for pollution abatement
and control. Both China and India are using wastewater for irrigation
as a practical solution to the problem.

The lessons to be learned by other countries from these four cases
are rather simple. The first is that ideology is a poor guide to the types
of environmental problems that can be expected; affluence, or relative
affluence, may be a more useful guide. Population, land area, and
water availability certainly determine to a large extent the relative em-
phases that irrigation and environmental amenities should be given.
Another lesson is that countries can be heavily engaged in developing
irrigated agriculture and at the same time heavily engaged in elaborate
pollution-control activities, as is the USSR. Since the four countries
considered range from the energy-rich (the United States and the
USSR) to the energy-poor (India and China), other countries should
realize that oil is a poor direct substitute for water. Apart from drinking water, it is almost always more economical to import water-
intensive products (for example, agricultural products) than to produce them at home from petroleum-based desalinized water.

ROLE OF MULTINATIONAL AGENCIES

From their very beginning, multinational and bilateral agencies have
been heavily involved in supporting development and construction of
water projects. It would be very hard to estimate how much these
agencies have invested in water resources since 1948. Table 9.6 shows
in relation to their total lending the 1983 lending for water projects by
the World Bank and the International Development Association, the
Asian Development Bank, and the Inter-American Development Bank.
Interestingly, water projects account for 17 percent of the World

TABLE 9.6. Lending programs in water resources by major development banks.

Sector	World Bank, US$ x 10^6	IDA[a] (1983) % of total lending	ADB[b] US$ x 10^6	(1982) % of total lending	IADB[c] US$ x 10^6	(1982) % of total lending
Irrigation and drainage	1,029.9	7.1	308.7	19.1	92.6	3.3
Hydropower	662.7	4.6	198.6	12.3	515.9	18.8
Water supply and sewerage	810.9	5.6	96.3	5.9	381.3	13.8
Total for water projects	2,503.5	17.2	603.6	37.3	989.8	36.07
Total for all lending	14,477.0	100	1,614.6	100	1,744.0	100

[a] World Bank, Annual Report 1983 (Washington, D.C.: The International Bank for Reconstruction and Development, 1983).
[b] Asian Development Bank, Annual Report 1982 (Manila: Asian Development Bank, 1983).
[c] Inter-American Development Bank, Annual Report 1982 (Washington, D.C. Inter-American Development Bank, 1983).

Bank's total and about 37 percent of the other two banks' totals. If the 1983 spending is typical, then some $4 x 10^9$ per year is available for water projects from these agencies. In the World Bank's program, irrigation and drainage are the largest water items, followed by water supply and sewerage. The Asian Development Bank has a much larger relative emphasis on irrigation, followed by hydropower. The Inter-American Development Bank has just the opposite emphasis: its largest programs are in hydropower, followed by water supply and sewerage, with irrigation and drainage receiving less than one-tenth of the total amount. The regional banks clearly reflect the needs as perceived by their constituent countries.

In addition to these international banks, various other multilateral and bilateral organizations are involved in supporting water resources development. Most of the funds they make available, however, are in "software"—research, management, training, planning, and implementation—rather than direct investment. This does not mean that these funds, although an order of magnitude smaller than those of the international banks, are not important. They may be crucially important for the users of water programs. Hence, the combination of this software aid with the development loans of the banks should be aggressively pursued by the international lending community.

Even though annual loans in the range of $4 x 10^9$ sound large, they are small in relation to the actual financing requirements, the bulk of which will have to be met from domestic resources. Indeed, India alone has an annual program of this size. If the financing needs are roughly proportional to population, then the actual level needed for the entire developing world could be more than $20 x 10^9$ per year, and this for a fairly minimal growth of facilities and infrastructure.

FORECASTING USE

Unlike many other natural resources, particularly nonrenewable mineral resources, water is unique in that human actions can change the resource base, in some cases increasing it, in some reducing it. These effects can be global or regional, and resource shifts may be temporary or permanent. The following are examples of increasing the resource base:

1. Inter-basin transfers. One widely used and recommended method is to transfer water from another basin, either within

or outside the country. At a cost, this can increase the local availability of water.

2. Use of low-quality water. In some areas, brackish water of low quality may be used for irrigation if the cropping pattern or drainage system is adapted. Waters of this type could also be used for some commercial and industrial processes—cooling, for example—thereby freeing up higher-quality water for applications that absolutely need it.

3. Overdraft on pumping groundwater. Serious overdrafts of groundwater resources are already occurring in many areas of the world, particularly in the western United States. A conscious policy to decrease these overdrafts could be instituted.

4. Water harvesting. Various local practices and land-forming techniques can change the amount of runoff from a given amount of precipitation. These techniques are the subject of research and development by various national and international agencies, including the International Center for Research in the Semi-Arid Tropics, located near Hyderabad, India. Such techniques are already used in many arid regions of the world and could be introduced, at a cost, in other arid regions.

5. Weather modification. Serious attention has been paid during the past fifteen years to various weather-modification techniques for increasing precipitation. This is now moving from the experimental stage to practical application and could become important during the next twenty years. Extensive data in the United States suggest that winter orographic cloud seeding leads to a 10-30 percent increase in snowfall. Because evaporation is proportional to the surface area of the snowpack, a 10-percent increase in snowpack area may result in a more than 10-percent increase in runoff. Questions that must be studied carefully are these: Does cloud seeding increase local precipitation at the expense of precipitation in neighboring areas, or does it increase the total supply? What are the environmental consequences?

6. Desalinization. Desalinization is a well-established technique that will probably always be too expensive for producing irrigation water but is already in use for potable and some industrial water supplies in many Middle Eastern countries.

7. For use in irrigated agriculture, there are at least three methods of increasing the availability of water:

   a. Changing the efficiency of water application. Farm application efficiencies in many countries now average less than 50 percent. These could be increased to 85 percent by changing the techniques of water application. This means that a farmer could increase his irrigated area by more than 50 percent with the same amount of water.

b. Changing the cropping pattern. In many areas, cropping patterns reflect a plentiful supply of cheap water. As water availability decreases, and as costs increase, farmers could shift to crops, such as sorghum, wheat, or soybean, that require much less water than crops such as rice.

c. Reducing the rate of application. There is no fixed application rate or duty for water applied to an irrigated crop. The biological optimum and the economic optimum rarely coincide, and there is no real reason why they should. Farmers could reduce water application and search for economically efficient rates of application. This obviously requires careful management of the entire farming system, particularly salinity control, and is therefore not without cost.

There is great uncertainty about increasing water supply in some areas and decreasing it in others because of the buildup of carbon dioxide in the atmosphere. It is known that the increase in atmospheric carbon dioxide over the last century (more than 40 parts per million [ppm] out of a current average of 334 ppm) is due to the burning of fossil fuels. The rate of increase can be expected to at least maintain its current rate (from 315.8 ppm in early 1959 to 334.6 ppm in January 1978) of about 0.94 ppm per decade into the immediate future or until such time as a global switch to nonfossil fuels takes place. What are not so certain are the consequences of this buildup. There is increasing evidence, however, that it will lead to small changes in temperature, depending on latitude. These temperature effects could themselves lead to marked changes in precipitation and runoff. For example, Revelle (1982) shows that for an annual precipitation of 300 mm, as in upper Colorado, a 2°-C increase in temperature could lead to a 35-percent reduction in runoff. Further, because of increasing temperatures, large increases in precipitation in the high northern latitudes and decreases in the lower latitudes are predicted. For the Colorado Basin at about 10° latitude, there would probably be a 15-percent decline in precipitation. Thus, several results from the temperature effect could lead to a 50-percent reduction in the runoff of the Colorado River.

Of course, there would be some big winners if this happened. Both Canada and the USSR would have much better temperatures and precipitation for grain harvesting, and other northern regions could be similarly helped. In northern Africa, the average flow of the Niger, Chari, Senegal, Volta, and Blue Nile rivers would increase substantially; they would receive a 10-20-percent increase in precipitation and only a small increase in temperature. Other areas could be severely affected by greatly decreased flows—for example, the Huang Ho in China, the Anu Darya and Syr Darya in the prime agricultural areas of the USSR, the Tigris-Euphrates system, the Zambezi, and the Sao Francisco in Brazil.

In table 9.7, L'vovich compares present (ca. 1970) and future (2000) consumption of irrigation water. He forecasts an increase from 190 to 500 million ha for the area irrigated (substantially higher than the FAO's 1981 estimate of only 148 million ha for ninety developing countries by the year 2000).[2] His forecast is based on the assumption that irrigation will have to provide 40 percent of the incremental grain supply necessary to feed 6.3 x 10^9 people by the year 2000.

Table 9.8 gives L'vovich's forecasts for all types of water use but assumes that all sewage is recycled. The table shows that even though the amount of water required for all human needs would merely double the withdrawal, it would triple the consumption. This approaches

TABLE 9.7. Consumption of water to irrigate food crops.

	Period		Type of water in future	
	At present	In future	Clean water	Recycled sewage
Area of irrigated land (millions of ha)	190	500	425	75
Duty of water, m³/ha				
water taken from sources	13,000	8,500	9,000	6,000
irrecoverable consumption	9,000	7,700	8,000	6,000
Total annual water consumed (km³)				
water taken from sources	2,500	4,250	3,800	450[a]
consumptive use	1,900	3,850	3,400	450[a]
Grain yield				
Total harvest (millions of tons)	570	2,000	1,700	300
Tons per ha	3	4	4	4
Water consumption per ton of grain (m³)	3,300	1,900	2,000	1,500

Source: M.I. L'vovich, *World Water Resources and Their Future*, English trans. R.L. Nace, p. 56. (Washington, D.C.: American Geophysical Union, 1979).
[a] Sanitary sewage.

TABLE 9.8. Present and future expenditures of water resources (km³).

Types of Use	Water taken from source	Irrecoverable consumption	Discharge of sewage
At present			
Water supply (all types)	600	130	470
Irrigation agriculture	2,800	2,100	700[a]
Ordinary (nonirrigation) agriculture	500	500	0
	0	0	
Hydropower and navigation	170	160	0
Fishery and sports fishing	65	15	50
Total	3,625	2,405	1,220
In Future			
Water supply (all types)	1,500	1,050[b]	0
Irrigation agriculture	3,950	4,000[a]	400[c]
Ordinary (nonirrigation) agriculture	1,200	1,200	0
	700	700	
Hydropower and navigation	500	500	0
Fishery and sports fishing	175	85	90
Total	6,825	6,335	490

Source: M. I. L'vovich, World Water Resources and Their Future, English trans. ed. R. L. Nace, p. 56 (Washington, D.C.: American Geophysical Union, 1979).
[a] Including 450 km³ of sewage used for irrigation.
[b] Excluding 450 km³ of sewage used for irrigation.
[c] Some polluted water returned after irrigation.

the 9,000 km³ that is currently safely available on an annual basis (see figure 9.3). However, the amount is no longer only 9,000 km³, because additional storages were assumed. The new available stable runoff is now 17,500 km³, and the same margin of safety that we currently have would still obtain. It should be stressed that this forecast does not include large water conservation gains due to pricing and other policies.

PRIORITIES AND AN AGENDA

Several conclusions emerge from this review of the resource base and the uses of fresh water.

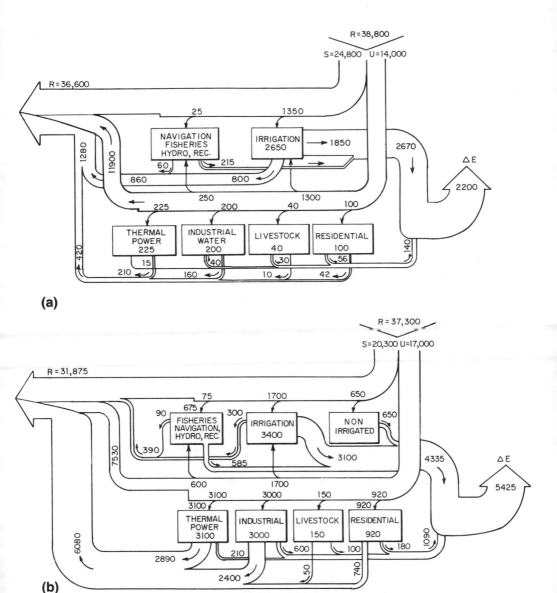

FIGURE 9.3. Water balance in 1970s (a) and the future (b). *Source:* L'vovich, 1974. Key: R = total runoff, S = unstable surface runoff, U = stable runoff resources, ΔE = unrecoverable consumption (evapotranspiration); all units are km³.

1. At a global level, available supplies of fresh water will be adequate until well into the next century, even under the current, fairly wasteful patterns of use.
2. In some regions and countries, the current and projected rates of water use (that is, without effective conservation and other national water policies) are likely to put severe stress on the supply of fresh water.
3. There are typically large differences between the average amounts of water available over a year and the amount that can be expected on a sustained basis, such as 95 out of 100 years. In many cases, less than half the annual average amount of water can be relied on.
4. Irrigated agriculture is by far the largest consumer of water in the world today and is likely to remain so over the next few decades.
5. Irrigated agriculture, as it is currently practiced in most countries, uses water extremely inefficiently. Large savings of water are possible for small investments in irrigation technology and management.
6. The groundwater storage potential is at least as great as the surface-water storage potential and is available at significantly lower costs.
7. In many countries, the efficient use of water resources is hampered by institutional and legal arrangements governing water use. This is particularly true of the development of groundwater resources. In some countries, the absence of freely operating markets in water rights leads to inefficient water use. In other countries, water-control bureaucracies are incapable of adjusting quickly to potential resource conflicts, such as shortfalls in water supplies for surface irrigation.
8. Growth of large industrial bases in developing countries rapidly leads to water-pollution problems. These problems can be as severe as those in the developed countries and may be worse in such small, densely populated countries as South Korea, Singapore, and Taiwan.
9. The costs of providing adequate water and sanitation facilities may be prohibitively high and could place an undue burden on the economic development of many countries. The expected benefits of providing such facilities apparently are exceeded by the costs in most low-income, developing countries.
10. Investment funds available from the major development banks appear to be inadequate to meet potential requirements during the next two decades. The available resources may be

as little as one-fifth of what is needed to ensure an easy transition to the new water economy of the twenty-first century.

11. Most countries lack effective policies for integrated water resource management. Evidence suggests that consistent pricing of water between different sectors of use could lead to major water savings.

12. The level of development and the relationship between the people and the land is more important in determining water use than a nation's particular ideological or political system.

There are three types of water problems to be faced. The first is self-inflicted and is caused by irrational waste of resources. The second consists of problems that can be described but for which there are no solutions or none that are currently economical. The final type is problems that are amenable to study and analysis and are responsive to government policy and investment strategies.

For the first type, it may be difficult to distinguish between the self-inflicted elements and the real limits of the resource. For example, little has been said about the problems of toxic contamination of water in many parts of the world, notably in the United States. This is a classic case of a "self-inflicted wound." By relying more on the laws of the marketplace than on the laws of physics and chemistry, the United States has created a nightmare of contamination—most of its drinking water supplies contain toxic chemicals. The cost of cleaning up the more than 15,000 abandoned dumpsites in the United States is estimated at $10-40 \times 10^9$. For self-inflicted problems such as these, the lesson for other countries is clear—don't do it! Since the cost of handling wastes according to scientific principles is low, they should be handled in this way, and the consumer should be willing to pay the small increase in cost. The misuse of irrigation water in some countries is another example of a self-inflicted problem. In the United States, for example, many farmers are heavily subsidized to irrigate crops in water scarce regions.

The second type of water problems, those that are real but about which little can be done, now includes erosion in upland areas and desertification in extremely arid regions. Both are serious problems with known solutions. When it can be shown that the problems have been caused by increases in population pressure on the land resources, people can be encouraged not to live in or use these regions. The alternative, extensive control of erosion and runoff, is not usually economically feasible. Where desertification and erosion are due largely to such natural forces as changing climate, friable soils, and volcanic action, it is unlikely that people can do anything to mitigate these effects. The solution is to avoid water development in those regions or in downstream reaches that are heavily influenced by them. If downstream development cannot be delayed or postponed, then planning for controlling the sediment in the man-made structures is all that can be done.

The world community focuses on real problems that can respond to government action. Three items in this category should be on the agenda of countries and multinational bodies. First and foremost, each country should immediately prepare a rational analysis of its fresh-water uses. Such studies are a prerequisite for estimating future demands for water. Only when data on "economic" demand have been derived can the impact of pricing policies on the curtailment of the demand be predicted and conflicting claims by different sectors and regions be assessed. Most countries have designated lead agencies to make plans for integrated water development. These plans have rarely been comprehensive enough, however, agencies with vested interests in constructing large water projects are unlikely to take much interest in water conservation, which will lead to fewer, rather than more, projects. Given that national analyses are likely to lead to proposals for reallocating investment funds and water rights, it is important that the agency, or agencies, carrying out the plans receive the political support needed to counteract the influence of interest groups wedded to the status quo.

Second, rational water-pricing policies would have the largest potential impact of all government policies. Not only would rational policies lead to conserving water in current uses, they would also lead to reassessment of the wisdom of carrying out that particular activity at all. If water is priced to reflect its scarcity value in arid countries, for example, it is unlikely to be used for irrigating grain crops. There is no reason why every country should grow food grains. Indeed, international trade in such crops will help redistribute water (in the form of grain) from the well-watered regions. Arid and water-short nations should reevaluate food grain self-sufficiency as a national goal. No country is charging the full scarcity price of water, and it is extremely difficult to price water reasonably once it has been underpriced. In most countries, too many vested interest groups already exist and will fight to maintain the status quo.

Third, major attention should be given to stabilizing water supplies. The task is to capture surface runoff each year and to stabilize the inter-year variation in water availability. This can be done by providing more storage capacity. L'vovich claims that a tripling of storage capacity will be required by the turn of the century. But how can such large quantities of storage be afforded when surface storage costs about \$120 million per km^3 (Ambroggi, 1980)? An additional 3,000 km^3 of storage would cost more than \$360 x 10^9, probably much too large an expenditure over the next few decades. One feasible alternative, proposed by Ambroggi, is to exploit underground storage; the cost of underground storage is considerably less (estimated between \$30 million and \$50 million/km^3). To recover the water, fairly expensive pumping energy costs may be incurred. Nevertheless, underground storage may be the only way to afford the large quantities of storage required. The cost could be kept as low as \$100 x 10^9, or about \$5 x 10^9 per year over the next two decades. This is within the realm of possibility, given current expenditures. It may turn out, however, that if the real economic costs of water are charged to water users, the actual demand for water will not rise so high and that all the required storage could be supplied from substantially smaller areas.

Development of water resources is not an end in itself. If we continue to waste water, serious problems will follow. If we start to take a rational approach to the problems now, we should have ample resources well into the next century. The choice is ours.

NOTES

1. Stable runoff is the part of the runoff that comes from underground flow into rivers (sometimes called base flow or sustained or fair-weather runoff). This is a conservative estimate of available water, since it ignores seasonal diversion and storage possibilities. Seasonal storage in surface impoundments is likely to remain small, while the potential for groundwater recharge from seasonal peak flows is potentially as large and much less expensive. L'vovich estimates the 1974 surface capacity at 1855 km^3/yr with a maximum of 5,500 km^3/yr. Potential groundwater storages of a similar range—3,000–5,000 km^3/yr—are predicted.

2. The FAO estimate did not include the People's Republic of China. Hence, at least another 60 million ha could be added to give a year-2000 figure of 210 million ha.

REFERENCES

Ambroggi, R. P. 1980. Water. *Scientific American* 243(3):101–16.
Center for Agriculture and Rural Development. 1975. "Documentation of the national water assessment model of regional agricultural production, land and water use, and environmental interaction." Mim-

eograped. Iowa State University, Ames, Iowa, December 1975.

Chaturvedi, M. C. 1976. *Second India Studies: Water.* Macmillan Co. of India.

Chen, D. 1980. The economic development of China. *Scientific American* 243(3):152–65.

FAO. 1981. *Agriculture: Toward 2000.* Rome: FAO.

Frederick, K. D., and J. C. Hanson. 1982. "Water for western agriculture." Research paper from Resources for the Future, Washington, D.C.

Gustafson, T. 1974. "Organizational adaptation to stress: A study of water resource development in the US and the USSR." Ph.D. dissertation, Harvard University, 1974.

L'vovich, M. I. 1979. *World Water Resources and their Future.* Translation by the American Geophysical Society, edited by Raymond L. Nace.

Revelle, R. 1982. Carbon dioxide and world climate. *Scientific American* 247(2):35–43.

US Department of Agriculture. 1982. *China: Review of Agriculture in 1981 and Outlook for 1982.* Washington, D.C.: Economic Research Service, Supplement 6 to WAS-27.

US Department of the Interior, Interagency Task Force. 1978. *Irrigation Water Use and Management.* Washington, D.C.

US Water Resources Council. 1978. *Second National Water Assessment,* vol. 4. Washington, D.C.

Weizhen, Z. 1980. *Irrigation and drainage in China.* Wuhan, China: Wuhan Institute of Hydraulic and Electric Engineering.

————. 1983. *Prediction of Water Needs in China.* Wuhan, China: Institute of Hydraulic Engineering.

Winje, D. 1982. "Entwickining des Haushalts—and Industriewasser verbrauchs in der offentlichen Wasserversaugung." Mimeographed.

CHAPTER TEN

Resources, Development, and the New Century: Forestry

JOHN SPEARS and EDWARD S. AYENSU

ROLE OF FORESTRY IN DEVELOPMENT: CAUSES OF FOREST DESTRUCTION

Forests cover one-third of the land area of the world. Annual world production of forest products exceeds US$150 billion, and global trade amounts to more than US$50 billion. Forests play a significant role in economic development: they protect watersheds and the natural environment as well as providing innumerble products vital to man. They provide subsistence, shelter, and employment, as well as resources for the development of other sectors. They comprise the most biologically diverse, readily convertible, and potentially self-regenerating natural store of biological wealth on the planet. Most important for developing countries, in which agroforestry farming systems are widespread, they have a positive impact on food production. If all the shrubs, trees, and forests in developing countries were elminated overnight, food production would decline by at least 20 percent, in part because of the disruptive impact on irrigation water and fodder supplies. Moreover, if fuelwood were no longer available, large additional quantities of animal dung and crop residues would be burned instead of being plowed back into the land, used as crop mulch, or fed to animals. Removal of all forest cover would lead to increased desertification and loss of scarce agricultural land. Figure 10.1 illustrates some of the numerous ways in which forests contribute to human welfare and development.

FIGURE 10.1 The role of forests. *Source:* World Bank Policy Paper on Forestry (Washington, D.C.: World Bank, 1978).

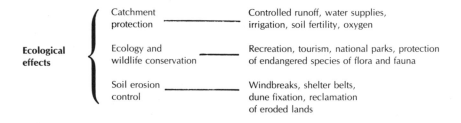

Ecological effects

Catchment protection	Controlled runoff, water supplies, irrigation, soil fertility, oxygen
Ecology and wildlife conservation	Recreation, tourism, national parks, protection of endangered species of flora and fauna
Soil erosion control	Windbreaks, shelter belts, dune fixation, reclamation of eroded lands

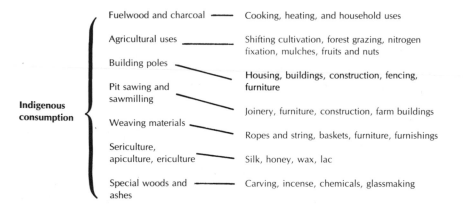

Indigenous consumption

Fuelwood and charcoal	Cooking, heating, and household uses
Agricultural uses	Shifting cultivation, forest grazing, nitrogen fixation, mulches, fruits and nuts
Building poles	Housing, buildings, construction, fencing, furniture
Pit sawing and sawmilling	Joinery, furniture, construction, farm buildings
Weaving materials	Ropes and string, baskets, furniture, furnishings
Sericulture, apiculture, ericulture	Silk, honey, wax, lac
Special woods and ashes	Carving, incense, chemicals, glassmaking

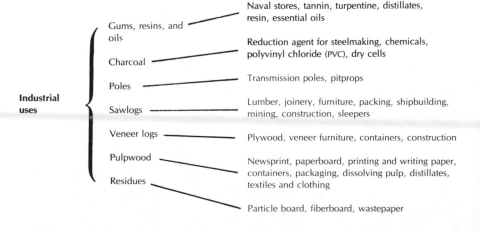

Industrial uses

Gums, resins, and oils	Naval stores, tannin, turpentine, distillates, resin, essential oils
Charcoal	Reduction agent for steelmaking, chemicals, polyvinyl chloride (PVC), dry cells
Poles	Transmission poles, pitprops
Sawlogs	Lumber, joinery, furniture, packing, shipbuilding, mining, construction, sleepers
Veneer logs	Plywood, veneer furniture, containers, construction
Pulpwood	Newsprint, paperboard, printing and writing paper, containers, packaging, dissolving pulp, distillates, textiles and clothing
Residues	Particle board, fiberboard, wastepaper

Forestry Issues in Developed Countries:
Forestry in a Stable Resource Situation

The forested area of the developed countries has stabilized and in some cases actually increased during this century.[1] The fundamental reason for this is that economic development and the creation of job opportunities in the industrial and other sectors have encouraged wholesale migration of rural populations to cities and towns, with the result that there has been a sharp reduction in the number of people dependent on agriculture. In the United States, for example, a farming population of less than 2 percent produces most of the food Americans consume, as well as a substantial surplus for export. As agriculture and livestock production have become concentrated on the more productive lowland soils, so pressure on forested uplands has decreased. This same pattern of development has occurred throughout North America, Europe, and Japan.

Given a reasonably stable forest resource base, the attention of forest policy planners in the developed world has focused on how to increase the productivity of these resources and to ensure domestic self-sufficiency, particularly in industrial roundwood supplies. The main issues have been getting more out of a given volume of wood at the lowest possible cost and making more effective use of forest waste products. During the last twenty-five years, there has been a significant shift toward use of reconstituted wood-based panels (particle board, plywood, and medium-density fiberboard) both for furniture manufacture and for construction, and a decline in the per capita consumption of solid lumber.

The concentration of populations in cities and towns has heightened awareness of the role of forests and parks as amenity and recreational outlets. The most popular form of recreation in Denmark, after watching TV, is visiting forest national parks.

The techniques for natural forest resource management and conservation are well proven, and reasonably stable institutional arrangements for forestry development have emerged in most industrialized countries. The forests of Germany, France, and other European countries, for example, have been under sustained-yield, controlled management for more than 500 years. With rising standards of living and disposable income, most of the governments of industrialized countries have become aware of the need to broaden the range of forest management objectives to embrace concepts of multiple land use.

Forestry Issues in Developing Countries: The Impact of Deforestation

By contrast, forestlands in the developing countries have declined by half and are continuing to be encroached upon at the rate of some 11 million ha/yr, primarily for agricultural settlement (see table 10.1). Some 150 million ha of tropical watersheds are threatened by overgrazing and soil erosion; most of that area is seriously degraded. The consequences are increased flooding, sedimentation of dams and reservoirs, disruption of irrigated agriculture downstream and loss of crops, land, and human life. The lives of some 500 million people have already been affected by such events.

Tropical rain forests, which account for 60 percent of the forested area lost annually, comprise the most biologically diverse ecosystems on earth, containing nearly half the world's known plant and animal species. A single hectare of the Amazon tropical rain forest may contain up to 230 tree species; whereas only 10-15 species occur in the typical hardwood forest in temperate regions.

A broad array of industrial, pharmaceutical, and other products are derived from tropical rain forests. They include essential oils, exudates, gums, latexes, resins, tannins, steroids, waxes, esters, acids, phenols, alcohols, edible oils, rattans, bamboo, flavorings, sweeteners, spices, balsams, pesticides, and dye stuffs. These products serve in the manfacture of many items used in daily life by populations of the Western world, including foods, polishes, insecticides, sedatives, cosmetics, and even golf balls.

Tropical rain forests are the earth's main repository of naturally occurring drugs, with a greater percentage of alkaloid-bearing plants than any other biome. In northwest Amazonia, for example, more than 1,300 plant species have been employed by Amerindians as medicines and narcotics. In Southeast Asia, traditional healers use 6,500 different plants as treatments for malaria, stomach ulcers, syphilis, and other assorted disorders, and as sedatives and emetics. Fourteen hundred plant species of tropical forests are believed to offer protection against cancer. In 1960, a person suffering from leukemia faced a one-in-five chance of remission, but now, thanks to two drugs developed from the rosy periwinkle (a moist tropical forest plant), the chance of survival is four times that. Worldwide sale of these drugs now totals more than US$100 million a year.

By the turn of the century, many of the unique genetic resources and products derived from tropical rain forests will be threatened with extinction because of the anticipated loss of a further 100 million ha of forest.

TABLE 10.1. Deforestation in closed and open tree formations in developing countries, 1981–85.[a]

Region	Closed forests (in thousand ha)					Open forests (in thousand ha)		All tree formations (in thousand ha)	
	Productive		not productive	All					
	undisturbed	exploited and managed		area	percent	area	percent	area	percent
Tropical America (23 countries)	1,299 (79)	1,867 (142)	1,173 (88)	4,339 (309)	0.64	1,272	0.59	5,611	0.63
Tropical Africa (37 countries)	226 (1)	1,032 (4)	73 (2)	1,331 (7)	0.61	2,345	0.48	3,676	0.52
Tropical Asia (16 countries)	395 (7)	1,278 (17)	153 (6)	1,826 (30)	0.60	190	0.61	2,016	0.60
Total (76 countries)	1,920 (87)	4,177 (163)	1,399 (96)	7,496 (346)	0.62	3,807	0.52	11,303	0.58

Source: FAO. forestry paper no. 30 (Rome, 1982).

[a] The term *deforestation* denotes the total clearing of natural tree formations (closed and open) for agriculture, including shifting cultivation, and other uses. Clearing of natural tree formations (not previously altered by agriculture) for shifting cultivation is also included in deforestation, although there is a regrowth of a secondary woody vegetation ("forest fallow"). The figures in parentheses show the part of the total deforestation corresponding to coniferous forests. The difference between the figure in parentheses and that immediately above it is practically equivalent to the deforestation of closed broad-leaved formations, since bamboo forests account for only 0.3 percent of total deforestation.

Fuelwood shortages already exist in some fifty-seven developing countries[2] and affect more than a billion people, causing them to burn about 400 million tons of animal dung a year. If instead of being burned, this could be used to improve soil fertility, cereal grain production, for example, could be increased by some 20 million tons a year.

As a result of past overcutting of industrial forests and inadequate investment in forest management and new plantation resources, twenty-three developing countries now import manufactured forest products valued in excess of US$50 million a year (in ten countries, they exceed US$200 million), despite the fact that twenty of these countries have climatic and ecological situations that are well suited to fast-growing industrial tree plantation crops.

In a further fourteen countries that depend to a significant degree on foreign exchange derived from tropical hardwood exports as a source of development capital, the more valuable species are being "mined" and will soon run out. Within the last decade, two such countries (Nigeria and Thailand) that were once major timber exporters have become large-scale net importers. Other countries such as the Ivory Coast are following the same path.

The Causes of Deforestation

The principal causes of deforestation include historical patterns of land settlement and development of commercial agriculture, both of which have led to skewed land distribution, expanding population pressure, a relatively low level of agricultural productivity in many developing countries, and rural poverty. The people most vulnerable to these trends are the poor of the world; their search for the basic requirements of food and fuel often forces them to hasten the destruction of their own environment.[3]

Population Pressures on Forestland. Today, there are some 200 million people living in tropical forests. The only hope for forest protection in the short term lies in land reform, which could help relieve further pressure on upland range and forestlands, and in massive agriculture, rural development, and forestry projects located in or adjacent to critical areas of tropical rain forest. Forest-dwelling populations need a viable alternative to an ecologically destructive way of life.

GRAZING, FUELWOOD, AND COMMERCIAL LOG HARVESTING. Other major causes of tropical deforestation have been grazing, the gathering of fuelwood at a rate that far outstrips the sustainable production from natural forests and savannahs, and extensive commercial logging. Some logging operations take out of the standing crop a few valuable species representing a very small proportion of the total volume and then move on to a new area. The road systems abandoned by logging companies encourage spontaneous agricultural settlement, often in areas where infertile acidic soils underlying the forest are incapable of sustaining annual food cropping, and after a few years, settlers are obliged to migrate to new parts of the forest.

FAILURE OF FORESTRY TO INTEGRATE WITH DEVELOPMENT IN OTHER SECTORS. Other contributing factors include the past preoccupation of forestry development planners with industrial forest management objectives, failure by the forestry establishment to be concerned with rural people, and a lack of integration with planning in agriculture, energy, health, and other sectors. The important links between forestry and food production are frequently overlooked (and rarely quantified) in national development plans. In health programs, the need to protect forests to maintain a sustained flow of safe drinking water is ignored. In the energy sector, the role of fuelwood is frequently accorded minor treatment compared with that of other commercial energy resources such as oil, gas, and coal, even though in twenty-six developing countries, fuelwood accounts for more than two-thirds of all energy consumption, and in all developing countries combined, it accounts for more than 80 percent of all wood use. In Nigeria, for example, which is the second largest supplier of oil to the United States, fuelwood accounts for 85 percent of rural energy consumption.

LOW LEVEL OF PAST INVESTMENT IN FORESTRY. Partly because of competing claims for scarce development capital, the forestry sector in most developing countries has failed to attract long-term private-sector investment and has rarely been allocated the development capital needed to adequately protect and expand the forest resource base. In eighty-three developing countries, current planned allocations for forestry development and protection of watershed and tropical forest ecosystems amount to less than 2 percent of combined government expenditures for agriculture and energy. They amount to about

US$250 million of all Official Development Assistance (ODA) for agriculture and energy development. This is less than one-fifth the level of investment needed for a viable program to protect and expand forest resources in developing countries (see the final section of this paper).

REMEDIAL POLICIES FOR CONTAINING DEFORESTATION:
SUCCESSFUL EXPERIENCES

To save the remaining forests in developing countries, a much greater effort than in the past will have to come from outside the forestry sector. Key programs are as follows:

- A vigorous program to assist upland populations in producing their own fodder and fuelwood, in moving toward stall feeding of animals, in securing access to improved seeds and other inputs needed to improve agricultural productivity and rural incomes, and to dicourage them from using steep forestland as rangelands.
- Intensified agriculture and rural development programs to assist some of the 200 million people living within or near the tropical rain forests in adopting sustainable farming systems, so as to take pressure off imminently threatened forest areas. We recommend that at least 100 million ha, or 10 percent of the world's remaining 1 billion ha of tropical rain forest, be set aside as scientific preserves, protected from all forms of human and livestock encroachment.
- Intensification of agricultural and forestry-related research in tropical forestlands, with special effort directed toward developing sustainable farming systems combining tree and food crops for parts of the developing countries' vast areas of marginal and agricultural wastelands.
- Accelerated land-reform programs that could provide some of the developing world's smallholders and landless people with an alternative to simply encroaching upon forests.
- Greater efforts and political commitment to channeling future agricultural settlement into nonforested areas. Development loans to finance extensive cattle ranching, for example, in tropical rain forests should be considered only where a sustainable pasture management system has been introduced.

Of course, implementing most of the above recommendations will depend on action by national governments through a political process that foresters can only marginally influence. The prospects for saving watersheds and tropical rain forests would be greatly improved, however, if national governments could be persuaded to incorporate more systematic consideration of watershed and forest protection issues in their economic development plans. Much could be achieved merely by *reallocating* priorities and resources so as to link development policies in agriculture, energy, and other sectors with protection of specific watersheds and tropical forests that are threatened by population pressures.

Land Reform

Historical patterns of development that have given rise to skewed land distribution underlie many of the problems in forestry today. Strong political commitment by national governments to pursue policies of land reform leading to more equitable land ownership would, in the short term, do more to relieve pressure on forestlands than any other single policy intervention or any conceivable level of investment in forest resource development.[4]

Although improving access to land is perhaps the most important priority for social change in most developing countries, it is nevertheless the most difficult of all social reforms to put into practice. Without sustained political commitment and adequate financial resources, it is unlikely to succeed. Nevertheless, the history of land reform in countries such as Korea, Japan, China, and Hungary offers guidelines for future attempts.

Scope for Intensification of Agriculture outside Forestlands

Three main sources of additional crop production could help take the pressure off further forest settlement. First, there is still considerable potential for expanding agricultural land without further forest encroachment. Globally, a quarter of the ice-free land is potential farmland, and only about half of that is currently being farmed. In the developing countries, 750 million ha was being farmed in 1980, which is less than half of the total potential arable area of about 1,800 million ha. About a quarter of the developing countries' projected food production to the year 2000 could come from expansion of existing arable lands. A further 14 percent could come from increases in cropping intensity (for example, double cropping of rice), and through crop diversification. By far the greatest contribution, however, 60 percent, can be expected to come from increases in yields.[5]

In summary, effective land-reform programs, diversion of agricultural settlement to nonforest lands, and measures aimed at increasing the productivity of existing farmlands, particularly through increased crop yields, are the three most important nonforestry initiatives that will affect the fate of the forests. Close integration of agriculture and forestry planning could help to identify critical zones adjacent to threatened forest areas, in which land-reform programs and intensification of agricultural productivity could help to relieve pressure.

Successful Watershed Rehabilitation Projects

INDIA. The relatively warm climate and high rainfall of India's Himalayan slopes readily support vigorous growth of trees, shrubs, and grasses capable of supplying local needs for firewood and forage. Although much topsoil has been lost from eroded slopes, there is a capacity for recovery, even where only pockets of soil lie between exposed rocks. Even the ravine lands (estimated at between 2 and 4 million ha) have been shown to be capable of restoration, both physically and biologically, at a positive cost-benefit ratio. A review of sixteen years' worth of reclamation studies of ravine lands that had been reduced to wasteland by cutting for firewood and overgrazing indicated that reforestation of these gullies successfully controlled erosion, while the output of fuelwood, building poles, and cut grass had more than paid the costs of the reclamation work, the cost-benefit ratio being 1 to 1.9.

Key lessons from these and similar experiences in other countries are as follows:

- There are known technologies for rehabilitating destroyed watersheds.
- Investment in such technologies can show a positive cost-benefit ratio within a reasonable length of time.

NEPAL. The Phewa Tal watershed in Nepal has a population of approximately 10,000 people, with farm sizes of 0.5-1.0 ha per family on steep terraced hillsides. Much of the watershed is severely overgrazed and scarred by landslides. Improvement plans with a positive cost-benefit ratio were proposed in 1977, and the Forest Department decided to work by persuasion. In a series of neighborhood meetings, a project team proposed that free-range grazing cease, and that farmers accept employment planting vigorous forage grasses in the eroded gullies and trees for firewood and forage on the steep wastelands above the terraces. The headmen of seven out of ten wards rejected these propsals outright, but in the three wards that accepted, progress was rapid.

Successful plantations of Nepalese alder, which benefits from nitrogen-fixation symbiosis, are growing vigorously and pruning of these fast-growing alders provides firewood. Elephant grass in the gullies is giving good forage, thereby permitting stall feeding, and there is now surplus grass between the trees to be sold to neighboring wards. The soil in the area is so exhausted from continuous cropping that farmers do not sow unless they can apply manure. But the extra manure from the stall feeding of all livestock provides for a winter wheat crop on terraces that previously remained bare between the summer crops of hill rice. With stall feeding, too, buffalo have become useful on land too steep for them to graze. By trading three scrub cows that yielded half a liter of milk each per day for one buffalo yielding four and a half liters, farmers gain the opportunity to sell the bull calves for meat (religious laws forbid the slaughter of bovines).

Several practical lessons emerge from the experience in Nepal:

- The trigger was the availability of funds to pay the farmers to plant vigorous forage grasses as a prelude to stall feeding.
- The changes were popular with the women because the labor of cutting and carrying fodder over short distances was less than that of searching steep hillsides to gather manure scattered by grazing livestock.
- The change to complete stall feeding, as a community decision, was effective, and neighboring wards respected the boundaries; thus fencing proved unnecessary.
- Foresters needed special training in growing and managing firewood and fodder species in cooperation with farmers, since traditional methods of land preparation, spacing, and pruning for timber trees proved inappropriate.

Water supplies, high on the hillsides, were critical, a point that is of great significance. Hill farmers will carry fodder to their livestock, but when water is to be found only downhill, the animals must be driven down to it. Building stone-walled stock tanks lined with plastic sheeting to protect high-level springs and using versatile plastic piping to bring water by gravity from sources higher in the mountains are practical solutions already demonstrated in the Phewa Tal watershed project. These techniques require only modest capital input and await assistance for general application around the valley.

Protecting Tropical Rain Forests in Malaysia:
An Example of Sound Land-Use Planning

Under the Jengka Triangle Land Settlement Project, which covers about 120,000 ha in the state of Pahang, Malaysia, a comprehensive land-use survey carried out in the early 1960s led to the conclusion that about 40 percent of the total area was suitable for large-scale agricultural tree crops such as oil palm, and that 60 percent of the forest located on steeper slopes and along river banks should be permanently protected. A plan was drawn up for settlement of some 9,000 farming families and cultivation of about 40,000 ha of oil palm and rubber. The urban development included the establishment of three new villages and extensive infrastructure.

Analysis of the results of the project some fifteen years later indicates that incomes of the 9,000 families settled in the first phase have shown a fourfold increase in real terms. Settler turnover rates in the communities are low (less than 2 percent) and the village communities are expected to remain stable.[6] Of greater significance, about 80,000 ha of forest that was excluded from agricultural settlement is still there today and is not being subjected to pressure from local farmers.

Important lessons have been learned from this and similar agricultural tree-crop farming projects such as those in Java, the Kandy Gardens of Sri Lanka, and the mixed forest garden/orchards of Central America:

- Careful land-use planning before settlement can help to channel agricultural development onto flatter lowlands and away from river banks and steep slopes.
- Agroforestry crop combinations are an ecologically acceptable alternative to natural forest for protection of soil and water resources. However, planting of agricultural tree crops such as oil palm, rubber, coconut, and coffee may frequently be constrained by market limitations.
- Improving farm income and the quality of life can encourage people to settle in permanent villages and thereby help to relieve pressure on the remaining forest.

Meeting Future Fuelwood Requirements

Whereas fuelwood accounts for less than 15 percent of total wood use in the developed world, in the developing countries it accounts for more than 80 percent. Of the estimated 1.5×10^9 m^3 of fuelwood produced annually in the developing countries, half is used for cooking, 35 percent for heating, and the balance for agricultural processing and other applications.[7] The search for fuelwood and the excessive harvesting of fuelwood trees in relation to their regeneration capacity have been significant causes of deforestation in many developing countries, in some fifty-seven of which there are now shortages of fuelwood.

Such shortages prevail in Africa, primarily in the arid and semi-arid areas of the Sahel, in the Himalayas and the hills of southern Asia, and within Latin America, mostly in the Andean Plateau and the arid areas of the Pacific coast. Some 150 million people in developing countries live in provincial urban centers that are experiencing major fuelwood deficits.

The prospects for meeting future demands for fuelwood in developing countries are alarming. Approximately 2,000 million people depend on fuelwood and other organic fuels for their daily domestic energy needs. In 1980, some 1,150 million people were estimated to be living in areas of increasing fuelwood scarcity, where needs were being met at the cost of depleting existing resources. On the basis of trends in population growth, depletion of forest resources, and afforestation, nearly 2,400 million people could be facing severe fuelwood shortages by the year 2000 (see table 10.2).

Increasing scarcity of fuelwood has a profound impact on rural life. It takes a significant proportion of every working day for the women and children of a family to collect the fuelwood (and fodder) needed by the household. People in some parts of West Africa—some areas of the Upper Volta, for example—now have only one instead of the customary two cooked meals a day, and in some areas of Senegal, quick-cooking cereals (rice) are replacing more nutritious foods (millets). Farmers in the uplands of Nepal increasingly grow only those vegetables that can be eaten raw. In cold climates, the mortality of older people and small children increases when houses can no longer be heated adequately. In addition to these immediate effects of the fuelwood crisis on the poor, the burning of dung and crop residue to make up the deficit limits the potential for increasing agricultural productivity in the future.

Policy options for tackling the fuelwood crisis

There are three major categories of action that can potentially affect the availability of fuelwood supplies:

TABLE 10.2. Populations experiencing a fuelwood deficit (in millions).

| | 1980 | | | | | | 2000 | |
| | Acute scarcity | | Deficit | | Prospective deficit | | Acute scarcity or deficit | |
	total population	rural population	total population	rural population	total population	rural population	total population	rural population
Africa	55	49	146	131	112	102	535	464
Near East and North Africa			104	69			268	158
Asia and Pacific	31	29	832	710	161	148	1,671	1,434
Latin America	26	18	201	143	50	30	512	342
Total	112	96	1,283	1,053	323	280	2,986	2,398

Source: FAO Fuelwood supplies in the developing countries. Forestry paper no. 42 (Rome, 1983).

- Conservation practices that help to reduce the overall demand for fuelwood—for example, manipulation of fuel prices (use of subsidies to encourage use of alternative fuels) and the introduction of improved end-use or conversion technologies (cookstoves, charcoal kilns).
- Substitution of other sources of energy—for example, solar, biogas, minihydropower, wind. More modern substitutes include liquefied petroleum gas, natural gas, kerosene, and electricity.
- Actions that increase the availability of natural resources—for example, planting trees on farmlands and village woodlots to protect existing forests and improve their productivity.

The scope for subsidizing fossil fuel prices as a means of conserving forest resources or affecting fuelwood consumption is limited. Subsidy policies place too great a burden on national budgets. More than 75 percent of fuelwood used in the developing countries is collected free. When wood is no longer available, people burn dung or crop residues instead. Pricing policies therefore have little impact on rural fuelwood consumption. Although rural electrification is a potential substitute for fuelwood used in lighting, in many parts of the developing world the cost of rural electrification on a large scale is too high for it to be a realistic option.

Perhaps the most important single cause of switching from fuelwood is continued migration, both seasonal and permanent, from rural to urban areas. In many developing countries, urbanization rates are twice the rates of overall population growth. But unfortunately, urbanization has not always relieved pressure on the rural environment or on rural energy supplies. The fuel most commonly used by the urban poor is charcoal, which is cheaper than fuelwood to transport to distant urban markets. However, the shift to charcoal usually increases pressure on rural forest lands. Urbanization involves some movement toward energy sources more convenient than wood, but in general the tendency has not significantly affected overall wood-based energy consumption. This is partly because the capital cost of switching to more convenient alternative fuels is frequently too high for many urban immigrants.

There has been a significant effort in recent years to bring about the diffusion of small-scale renewable-energy technologies that could lead to decreased fuel consumption. Opportunities for use of wind power, biogas, alcohol, briquetted agricultural wastes, minihydropower, and other renewable sources of energy are widespread. Actual adoption, however, is inhibited by financial and managerial problems and by the enormous logistical problems of bringing about technological change among thousands of dispersed and often isolated villages. In the long run, a switch to other renewable sources of energy clearly offers the best prospect of reducing pressures on forest resources; but in the short run, they cannot be expected to make a major impact on the fuelwood needs of developing countries.

Because of the constraints on adoption of policies aimed at conservation of fuelwood or its replacement by other fuels, it is clear that, for the immediate future, protection of existing forests and establishment of new fuelwood resources must remain high priorities for national governments of many developing countries. To ensure a reasonable degree of self-sufficiency in fuelwood supplies for the one billion people who are currently experiencing fuelwood shortages, the 1981 UN Renewable Energy Conference recommended at least a fivefold increase in current global fuelwood reforestation rates—that is, an increase from the current planting equivalent of 0.5 million to some 2.5 million ha/yr. In many smaller African countries, up to a twenty fold increase in present planting rates would be necessary. In Sahel-zone countries, the prospects for achieving this level of reforestation are poor, and continued dependence on the burning of crop residue or dung is almost inevitable, albeit at the cost of agricultural productivity.

Unlike industrial timber, which can be economically transported relatively long distances, fuelwood must be grown on the farm or adjacent to the village where it will be used. The number of trees needed to meet a family's domestic requirements can be small (fewer than a hundred, depending on the age at which they are harvested). Farmers are usually interested in planting trees for a wide variety of end uses, including production of fruit, fodder, building poles, and provision of shade, in addition to fuelwood. There are many tree species that can produce such a wide range of products.

In most developing countries, 50 percent and sometimes as much as 90 percent of the population lives in rural areas. A high proportion (probably more than 75 percent) of reforestation efforts in developing countries for the next fifteen years need to be directed toward farmlands and agricultural wastelands outside government-controlled forest reserves, in marked contrast to the reforestation policies that prevailed in most developing countries throughout the 1960s and early 1970s. During that period, the main priority was given to industrial forestry management.

Commercial Forms of Wood Energy

As a consequence of rising oil prices, much attention has been focused on the potential of wood gasifiers, dendrothermal power generation, and wood-based alcohol fuels. In some countries—for example, Brazil and the Philippines—large-scale programs based on these technologies are already under way.

Successes in Producing Fuelwood and Wood-based Energy

SOUTH KOREA. The Republic of Korea's Village Fuelwood Program, begun in the early 1970s, was intended mainly to establish and tend fuelwood blocks to provide for village needs. Three hundred thousand hectares of village woodlots were established in about 11,000 villages, and 600,000 ha of preexisting fuelwood blocks were brought under more intensive management.

The Korean government initiated efforts to improve fuel efficiency in the traditional ondol heating/cooking system. A new ondol (under-floor heating) developed at the Forest Research Institute and expected to decrease fuelwood consumption by 30 percent is now in widespread use. The sale of fuelwood, particularly to city residents, has been prohibited. This has helped to reduce pressure on local village supplies and to reduce the incentive for illegal cutting for fuelwood sales. Several key factors contributed to the success of this program:

- The villagers were committed to rural development and had a long tradition of community spirit directed toward the improvement of living standards.
- Fuelwood plantations yielded fuelwood and a cash crop after the second year. Climatic and ecological circumstances are highy favorable for fast-growing fuelwood trees.
- For ten years, the government exerted strong pressure on small private landowners to afforest nonagricultural land. In addition, the fuelwood program received strong and effective supervision by a specially created Village Forest Authority.[8]

SENEGAL. The Senegal Fuelwood Production Project started in 1979 to address the problems of meeting urban fuelwood needs has involved the mechanized development of 3,000 ha of fuelwood plantations in the Bandia National Forest near the towns of Dakar and

Thies. The project is using fast-growing *Eucalyptus* species; mechanized land preparation is necessary to rip through the deep laterite soil pans. The plantations are growing well and are already producing small-sized fuelwood from lopping of branches.

Successful implementation of the project to date is attributable to the following:

- Thorough research and planning before the project began ensured location of the plantations on the most suitable soils.
- Efficient technical management, such as weeding and harrowing, reduced water competition from herbaceous vegetation and permitted the trees to grow rapidly.
- A good organizational structure ensured timely planting and incorporation of Senegalese expertise in fuelwood plantation management. An extensive training program emphasized nursery operations, diesel mechanics, equipment operations, soil management, and technical forestry.

Remedial Policies for Industrial Forestry

In many developing countries, forest resources are being mined of the more valuable species, and some are facing rising import bills for forest products that they should be able to produce themselves more cheaply than the countries in temperate zones from which they import. Consequently, there is a trend toward restriction of forest areas allocated to foreign logging companies and attempts to reduce log exports in favor of domestic processing. These practices are allied with efforts to tighten administration of logging concessions, strengthen timber taxation policies, make more effective use of existing resources by widening the range of species used, and promote reforestation with farm-growing trees.

Tropical hardwoods are an important source of export revenue for about fifteen developing countries. Exported hardwoods exceed US$8 million a year in value and are the fifth largest nonpetroleum export commodity from developing countries. For this reason, environmental proposals aimed at protecting the welfare of tribal populations, for example, or creating biotic reserves are frequently overridden by political and economic pressures to increase timber-derived revenues. Moreover, far tighter arrangements are needed to ensure that a reasonable proportion of the taxes derived from logging virgin forests is plowed back into compensatory forest management or reforestation programs.

Current logging methods, particularly in the Southeast Asian dipterocarp forests, take about 60 m^3/ha out of the 300-400 M^3 of standing volume. They often leave behind a mass of logged-over vegetation, skid tracks, and exposed landings, and these can contribute significantly to soil erosion.

To ensure more effective use of existing forest resources, manufacturing processes in both developed and developing countries are making better use of waste residues—for example, through pulping processes that make use of a wide range of species. Vigorous attempts are being made to broaden the range of species that can be grown commercially and to remove and market those that now have low commercial value. In tropical countries, literally hundreds of so-called secondary hardwoods, which constitute the bulk of the forest resource, are not used either because the timber is soft and rots easily or because it is very hard and costly to process. In addition, many individual species occur in such limited quantities that commercial logging companies do not harvest them.

In the past, logging in the tropical rain forest has been highly selective. In West Africa, for example, more than 80 percent of past log removals consisted of fewer than 10 high-value species out of more than 150 species in the forest. This "creaming," or "high-grading," amounts to mining, since it is not yet possible in most tropical rain forests to sustain the original composition of the forest by silvicultural management.

Much effort has been spent over the last fifty years in testing tropical-forest management systems that would sustain and increase the proportion of higher-value species. Techniques such as "line" and "enrichment" planting (the planting of higher-value species to fill in the holes left in the forest canopy after logging) are being tested, and research in this area is a high priority.[9]

The need to create supplementary industrial wood resources in countries without a significant natural tropical forest area has focused attention on the potential for introducing industrial plantations of fast-growing species. More than 7 million ha of such plantations have already been estalished in the developing countries.[10] Planting is currently proceeding at the rate of about 0.5 million ha/yr, and at the current rate of progress, the total area of industrial plantations in the developing world (excluding China) will be on the order of 15 million ha by the year 2000.

The experience that has been gained with species such as *Albizzia, Leucaena, Gmelina, Tectona, Triplochiton, Terminalia, Maesop-*

sis, *Pinus, Eucalyptus,* and *Acacia* indicates that these plantations are capable of yielding five to ten times more merchantable wood per hectare per year than natural forests can be expected to produce under extensive management systems. Moreover, they offer the prospect of relatively short rotations (5-10 years for fuelwood and pulpwood and 20-25 years for sawlogs), compared with much longer rotations (50-100 years) for natural tropical forests and for coniferous forests in temperate regions.

Examples of Successful Industrial Forestry Policies and Reforestation Programs

CAMEROON. During the last ten years, the government of Cameroon has introduced various measures aimed at more effective control of timber concessions and more effective collection of timber taxes. Examples include raising of export and internal taxes on all log exports and introductions of tax assessments related to free-on-board value of logs (to reflect the higher value of better-quality export species), limiting maximum concession areas, stipulation that at least 60 percent of all wood cut on concessions has to be processed locally and requiring all concession-operators to submit annually a logging and roadway plan and to accept limitations on maximum road gradients. In addition, specific logging conditions (removal of obligatory species, use of low-grade material, and working of areas by controlled annual felling, subject to inspection by forestry officers) were introduced into all timber-use contracts. Since the introduction of such legislation, there has been an improvement in the collection of taxes, in the proportion of local processing, and in forest road standards.

CHILE. Since 1950, Chile has established more than 750,000 ha of mainly *Pinus radiata* industrial plantations that are already satisfying domestic demands for industrial wood and sustaining the export of some 2 million m^3 of logs and lumber and 500,000 tons of chemical pulp and newsprint per year. If planting continues at the current rate, by early next century Chile could be exporting as much wood as Finland does today.

Three main elements contribute to the success of the Chilean afforestation program:

- The Chilean government introduced tax incentives for tree planting, most of which has been carried out by the private sector.

- Climatic and ecological conditions are suited to plantation forestry.
- Cheap land is available.

ZAMBIA. Within the last fifteen years, the forest department of the Zambian government has created enough industrial plantations (on 45,000 ha) to satisfy its domestic needs beyond the year 2000. The program is successful for the following reasons:

- A well-conceived and well-managed research program (which cost less than US$5 million) clearly demonstrated the potential for growing pines and eucalyptus and paved the way for an investment of about US$50 million in industrial plantations of fast-growing species.
- High standards of plantation maintenance and fire protection were maintained.
- There was a sustained political and financial commitment to the forestry program by the government throughout the fifteen year development period.

By 1980 the potential output from these plantations was more than sufficient to meet Zambia's anticipated domestic demand for wood. Current investment is directed toward consolidation of management and further development of the wood-using industries needed to make effective use of this resource.

THE GLOBAL POSSIBLE: AN ACTION PROGRAM
FOR THE FUTURE

Notwithstanding the magnitude of the task ahead, we are encouraged by the fact that several developing countries with high rural population densities have already demonstrated that a sustained effort can, within a period of one or two decades, produce enough fuelwood, timber, and other forest products to satisfy localized domestic needs, ensure protection of vulnerable watersheds, and, in some cases, sustain an export trade in forest products. China and Korea provide outstanding examples of programs for meeting acute domestic needs for wood and wood products. With regard to satisfying future industrial wood needs, achievements of countries such as Brazil, Chile, Zambia, Malawi, Kenya, Madagascar, Angola, Fiji, Swaziland, Zimbabwe, and Portugal, are particulaly noteworthy.[11]

In rural afforestation programs, forestry can be complementary to—and need not be competitive with—agriculture. The long-proven agroforestry farming systems in the tropics point the way. Much of the tree planting now taking place in the tropics is a spontaneous response by farmers, communities, and private companies to increasing scarcity of forest products and to rising market prices. Forestry as a potential area of investment for small farms and communities will become even more profitable in the coming decade. The examples of successful forestry policies and programs cited in the previous section indicate that possible solutions to deforestation exist, and that there are precedents on which to build. What is needed is a concerted international program to multiply such projects throughout the developing world on a scale large enough to ensure that tropical deforestation is brought under control before the turn of the century. In this section, we recommend an action program covering five main areas:

- Rehabilitation of deforested watersheds
- Preservation of threatened tropical forest ecosystems
- Fuelwood and multipurpose tree planting
- Industrial forestry
- Strengthening of forestry research education and training.

The following discussion gives tentative orders of magnitude of the level of financing needed to carry out this program (US$5 billion a year, of which 60 percent would be agricultural and 40 percent forestry-related investment) and a broad indication of the likely economic and environmental payoffs that could be anticipated. Table 10.3 groups developing countries according to their needs for investment in agriculture and forestry. A summary of investment costs and of the anticipated environmental and economic payoff is given at the end of this section.

Rehabilitaton of Deforested Watersheds

About 150 million ha of watersheds in developing countries are being seriously degraded by pressure from increasing population and livestock, overgrazing of upland range and forest areas, overcutting for fuelwood, increased sedimentation, flooding, and disruption of downstream irrigated agriculture. We recommend international support for a sustained program of watershed rehabilitation in the most seriously affected watershed areas of thirty-two countries (see table 10.3).

In the longer term, the most effective way to restore watersheds will be by reducing the number of people living in the upland areas; this could happen, eventually, if economic development could increase the productivity of the land and provide more job opportunities in the lowlands. Once population pressure is lifted from the poorer mountainous areas, they can be maintained through sustainable agriculture. However, in the short term, there is little prospect of this happening in most developing countries on the scale needed to relieve pressure on forest, soil, and water resources. The only practical way to proceed is to provide farmers and others living in these watershed areas with the technical support they need to improve farm productivity and adopt soil conservation measures.

Despite the scale of the problem, given the necessary political commitment, much more could be done to at least prevent the current situation from becoming worse. Enough is known about appropriate farming systems, soil conservation, irrigation, fodder production, reforestation, and flood control to justify immediate action to contain degradation. A multifaceted approach to rehabilitation and maintenance of watersheds is necessary, combining means to improve agricultural productivity with measures to minimize erosion and flooding and to rehabilitate the land.

Watershed projects directly affect people. Hence, the key to securing people's participation in such projects lies in a better understanding of their perceived needs and, in particular, of local land tenure and other practices regarding the use of land. This implies that project development must include sociological studies to define the incentives needed to elicit cooperation.

In establishing appropriate farming systems for these areas, one of the most commonly encountered problems is that excessive numbers of livestock are kept on the land. A strategy to reduce the density of livestock should aim, primarily, at improving the draft power and milk production of fewer and better-quality animals. This can be achieved in several ways: by improving the quality of fodder produced, encouraging stall feeding, introducing improved animal stock, and providing effective marketing systems.

Communal grazing lands, grasslands, and degraded forestlands may need to be closed temporarily to allow natural grasses to regenerate and to permit planting of fodder trees, such as acacias to feed goats. Closure of rangelands and regulation of upland grazing, however, may conflict with sociological and religious attitudes, especially in Africa and Asia, where the number of livestock exceeds the carrying capacity of the land. Further, compensatory payments may be necessary for families temporarily excluded from upland grazing areas that are being restored.

TABLE 10.3. Priority countries for agriculture forestry sectoral investment aimed at containing deforestation (1986–2000).

	Rehabilitation of deforested watersheds	Intensification of agricultural productivity to reduce pressure on threatened forest ecosystems	Fuelwood and multipurpose tree planting		Industrial forestry
Africa	Ethiopia	Madagascar	Botswana	Lesotho	Nigeria
	Lesotho	Cameroon	Benin	Madagascar	Cameroon
	Madagascar	Ivory Coast	Burundi	Mali	Congo P.R.
	Mozambique	Liberia	Cameroon	Malawi	Gabon
	Kenya	Zaire	Chad	Mauritania	Ghana
	Tanzania		Comoros	Mozambique	Ivory Coast
			Gambia	Nigeria	Liberia
			Guinea	Niger	
			Ethiopia	Reunion	
			Kenya	Rwanda	
				Senegal	
				Somalia	
				Sudan	
				Tanzania	
				Togo	
				Uganda	
				Upper Volta	
				Zaire	
				Zambia	
Asia	Bangladesh	Burma	Bangladesh		Burma
	China	Indonesia	India		China
	Indonesia	Malaysia	Indonesia		Indonesia
	India	Papua New Guinea	Nepal		Korea
	Pakistan	Philippines	Pakistan		Malaysia
	Nepal	Thailand	Philippines		Pakistan
	Thailand		Sri Lanka		Philippines

	Philippines / Sri Lanka	Thailand / Vietnam	Papua New Guinea / Thailand
Europe / Middle East / North Africa	Algeria, Morocco, Tunisia	Morocco, Tunisia, Turkey, Yemen A.R., Yemen P.D.R.	Algeria, Morocco, Portugal, Tunisia, Yugoslavia
Latin America / Caribbean	Bolivia, Brazil, Colombia, Costa Rica, Ecuador, El Salvador, Guatemala, Haiti, Jamaica, Mexico, Nicaragua, Panama, Peru, Trinidad and Tobago	Bolivia, Brazil, Chile, Colombia, Cuba, Dominican Republic, El Salvador, Ecuador, Guatemala, Haiti, Jamaica, Mexico, Paraguay, Peru	Belize, Bolivia, Brazil, Colombia, Costa Rica, Ecuador, El Salvador, Guatemala, Haiti, Honduras, Mexico, Nicaragua, Panama, Peru, Venezuela

Note: Based on recommendations of the Commission on National Parks and Protected Areas, International Union for the Conservation of Nature, 1981.

In permanent cropping areas, annual fodder species such as winter oats or legumes may be introduced as a second rotational crop. Fodder trees, pasture grasses, and legumes may be planted on "bunds" (earthen levees), on risers of terraced farmlands, near houses, and in other marginal land plots. Programs will need to be established to encourage farmers to improve the productivity of their cattle by trading surplus bullocks and low-grade cows for improved breeds.

Where a high proportion of the population in a catchment area depends on crop-based agriculture, the productivity of the land can be increased by improved cultivation practices. These include plowing on the contour, preparing smoother seedbeds, timely sowing of seeds, increasing plant cover, and using improved seed, fertilizers, and pesticides. To arrest sheet erosion on steep slopes, farmers should be encouraged to plant fruit trees on the contour, to mulch them, and to interplant trees with legumes and pulses. In some places, fodder-tree farming, bamboo plantations, or planting grasses such as bhabar grass, might be more appropriate. In many situations, some activities can be undertaken by paid, landless workers. This will reduce the likelihood of their extending food-crop production onto steep, erosion-prone slopes.

Reforestation can be encouraged by establishing nurseries to provide trees and fodder grasses for planting. Plantations can help to supply fuelwood, fruit fodder, and commercial timber, and if appropriate planting methods are used, to conserve the soil. Fencing may be needed around protected forest areas. Natural regeneration of shrubs and trees should be encouraged, and logging tracks and access roads upgraded.

Further investments will be needed in most catchment areas to prevent erosion and flooding. Inexpensive, technical measures for this purpose include construction of levees, bench terracing, runoff disposal drains, retaining walls, and farm ponds to encourage improved water-harvesting practices and stall feeding.

Organization and management proably represent two of the most complex aspects of any watershed project, mainly because of the large number of institutions involved in an integrated program and also because of the intricacies of the socioeconomic issues involved in ensuring farmers' participation in the design and implementation of a project. Many of the failures of past rehabilitation programs have been the result of technocratic planning that did not include adequate consultation with local people.

Every catchment area is different, with individual determinants of costs, but some generalization is relevant. Planning should treat the watershed as a single unit. There has been an ongoing attempt to concentrate intervention on the more critical components, such as fodder supplies, on-farm soil conservation, fuelwood planting, and animal husbandry or range improvement in order to produce the maximum impact on deteriorating conditions in the shortest time at the least cost. By concentrating on such measures, watershed rehabilitation can be achieved at a reasonable cost (something on the order of US$250 to US$350 (1983) per hectare).

Without detailed surveys of individual watershed areas, it is impossible to provide more than tentative estimates of the likely cost of a tropical watershed rehabilitation program. As a working hypothesis, based on a preliminary assessment of the extent of deforested watersheds, we have assumed that 150 million ha of damaged catchments is in urgent need of treatment, and that direct government investment for rehabilitation of at least 50 percent of that area would be necessary to restore vegetative cover, protect the soil, and help regulate stream flow. We assume that this would be the minimum level of government support needed to trigger voluntary adoption of similar measures by farmers and communities in other parts of the watershed (as happened in the Phewa Tal project in Nepal described in the previous section). Assuming that rehabilitation would be spread over fifteen years, and assuming an average cost of US$300 per hectare, the total cost of a rehabilitation program would be on the order of US$1.5 billion per year.

The benefits of such a program would be both direct and indirect. They would include general improvement in the quality of life for some 30 million families residing in watershed areas, increased agricultural production and farm income, generation of income from the sale of both agriculture and forestry products, and the restoration of existing forests. Rehabilitation would, indirectly, increase the lifespan of irrigation and power works (mainly outside the watershed) by reducing silting. By reducing peak floods, chiefly outside the treated watersheds, it would decrease the loss of life and property and increase the productivity of downstream agriculture. A preliminary estimate indicates that some 500 million people live within the downstream command areas of the 150 million ha of watershed recommended for rehabilitation.

Intensification of Agricultural Production in Areas
Adjacent to Threatened Tropical Rain Forests

As a first step toward the creation of a minimum target area of 100 million ha of scientific reserves, the twenty-six countries identified by the Commission on National Parks and Protected Areas of the International Union for the Conservation of Nature (see table 10.3) should be assisted in carrying out more systematic ecological surveys aimed at identifying areas of the tropical rain forest that are biologically unique and that should be preserved. These surveys would include examination of flora and fauna, scientific and ecological studies relating to likely end uses, and studies of the complex interactions that sustain these ecosystems.

A systematic survey should be undertaken of the potential for channeling future population settlement into nonforest lands, intensifying agricultural productivity on existing farmlands along the forest fringe, and introducing land-reform and employment programs that could provide job opportunities for people living within these watersheds. Sustained family planning policies could also, in the longer term, play a vital role in helping to reduce rural population pressure on natural resources.

Where suitable soils underlie forestlands, forest dwellers should be assisted to adopt proven agroforestry farming systems based on greater use of tree crops such as oil palm, coconut, rubber, cocoa, tea, and coffee, and of fruit, fodder, nut, pole, and timber species either intercropped with agricultural crops or planted around homesteads and along farm boundaries. Key inputs would include improved seeds, fertilizer, agricultural credit, and sustained extension advice. Examples of successful implementation are the agricultural tree-crop plantations and smallholder tree farms in the prevailing agroforestry farming systems of Java, the Kandy Gardens of Sri Lanka, and the forest garden/orchard farms of some Central American countries.

A preliminary assessment suggests that of the 200 million people living in or adjacent to tropical rain forests, about 10 percent (equivalent to some 5 million families) reside in or around biologically unique ecosystems that have been recommended for scientific preservation either by national or international environmental and scientific agencies. These people should be the main target group for the kind of program outlined above. In carrying out such a program, priority should be given to development of roads, schools, clinics, and other social services that would improve the quality of life of forest-dwelling people and enable them to settle in more permanent communities, as was done, for example, in the Malaysian Jengka Project.

Intensified agriculture and forestry research should be undertaken to support such developments. Key areas of research include the potential of green manuring through the introduction of perennial mulches and the planting of live hedges of leguminous species, trials with minimum and zero tillage, improving the quality of seed and ensuring timely availability of improved seed, appropriate seed dressing and inoculation, needs for fertilizer, particularly the potential for reducing artificial fertilizer requirements by more intensive use of green manure crops, and appropriate soil conservation practices, with particular attention to the use of mulch and farmyard manure.

The investment costs for this agricultural tree-crop/forestry settlement program would be on the order of US$1.3 billion per year spread over fifteen years, based on the assumption of settling five million families at a cost of about US$3,750 per family, which includes provision for upgrading social services and access roads. This estimate also assumes investment of some US$25 million per year in scientific research and management of the protected forest areas.

In addition to the main objective of relieving pressure on some 100 million hectares of tropical rain forests, the program would ensure enhanced rural incomes and improvement in the quality of life for forest-dwelling families. Failure to implement the program could lead to extinction by the turn of the century of many plant and animal species that have the potential to contribute to human welfare. For example, more than a quarter of the world's pharmaceutical drugs, including some that are used to treat diseases such as leukemia and other cancers, come from tropical forest plants.

Fuelwood and Multipurpose Tree Planting

We recommend a three-pronged approach to the planting of fuelwood and multipurpose trees and concentration of this aproach on the fifty-seven countries listed in table 10.3:

- conservation of existing resources through such improved end-use technology as charcoal manufacture and more efficient stoves
- continued research and development of alternative sources of renewable energy such as solar, biomass, and minihydropower
- creation of new fuelwood resources.

For reasons cited earlier in this paper, there are formidable constraints to be overcome in relation to the first two of these items, and dramatic progress in these areas cannot be anticipated in the coming decade. Nevertheless, these two approaches could yield important benefits at the household and village levels over time, and for that reason, we urge that intensive research be continued, backed up by sustained pilot-scale trials of alternative technologies. Every effort should be made to involve local communities in these promotional programs and to mobilize the interest of the private sector in manufacturing and distributing more efficient wood-using devices.

To guarantee an adequate supply of fuelwood equivalent for the one billion people who are already experiencing a scarcity, and to bring economically accessible areas of natural forest under more intensive protection and management, current fuelwood planting rates would have to be increased at least fivefold between now and the year 2000, implying average annual planting of about 5 billion trees during that period. At least 75 percent of this will need to be individual tree or woodlot planting on farmlands and wastelands outside government forest reserves, and about 25 percent should be near urban townships to provide raw material for wood-burning processing plants (for example, dendrothermal power generators or gasifiers). The main thrust of this program should be toward encouraging the spontaneous interest of farmers and local communities in multipurpose tree planting. The role of government agencies should be to ensure the availability of necessary inputs such as seedlings, water supplies, credit, and extension services.

Industrial private-sector participation should be encouraged, particularly in the development of plantations for energy supply purposes. The leasing of government forestland to private companies interested in long-term farming is one option here. The rising market prices for fuelwood (and also for poles, pulpwood, and other forest products) should be used as the trigger for securing farmer and local community interest in rural tree planting.

It would be impractical to try to achieve a fivefold increase in fuelwood planting immediately. For the next three to five years, the main emphasis should continue to be on the creation of rural infrastructure (for example, tree nurseries) and an appropriate institutional and policy framework (for example, testing alternative incentive mechanisms for securing local support, strengthening extension services, and establishing credit programs for tree farmers). These would prepare the way for much larger-scale fuelwood programs in the 1990s. Based on such approaches and, particularly through the involvement of local people, countries such as Korea and India have demonstrated that a fivefold increase in fuelwood planting can be achieved at least in some localized areas.

The level of investment needed to meet this objective would be about US$1.0 billion per year for the next fifteen years, based on an assumed planting of 5 billion trees (the equivalent of about 2.5 million ha/yr) over the next fifteen years at an estimated cost of US$250 per hectare and investment in protection and more intensified management of natural forests. This cost could be significantly reduced if small farmers and local communities could be involved in raising seedlings and in planting fuelwood on their own holdings, using their own family labor (less than two days' work is needed to establish a hundred trees).

The proposed program makes no provision for development of other sources of renewable energy, such as solar and minihydro-power, because many private-sector, multilateral, and bilateral aid programs are already supporting such efforts, and funding is not a serious constraint.

Industrial Forestry

For the next two decades, we urge adoption of an industrial forestry action program with three major objectives:

- Strengthening of legislative, fiscal, and administrative policies aimed at ensuring more effective management and use of existing forest resources through a combination of improved end-use efficiency, less wasteful logging, greater use of secondary species, more effective control of the practices of logging companies, increased domestic processing as opposed to log exports, and more equitable taxation.
- Accelerated investment in industrial forest management and reforestation with fast-growing useful species in those countries that are facing increasing import bills for forest products (particularly lumber and pulp and paper) from the industrialized countries.
- An intensified program for forest management and reforestation of medium- to high-value hardwood species. The program would help to ensure that those tropical countries that depend heavily on foreign exchange earnings from wood-based industries or log exports would be able to sustain and expand these in the future.

Effective introduction of policy interventions such as those just cited will depend to a large degree on government political commitment to including appropriate measures in timber-use contracts awarded to logging companies. The contracts should require, for example, that logging operations be excluded from sensitive ecological areas such as steep slopes along riverbanks, conform to standards of road gradient and culvert installation, make a conscious attempt to widen the range of species harvested as opposed to "creaming" high-value timbers, and ensure domestic processing of an agreed percentage of log output within a given time period. These things might be encouraged, for example, by volume-based charges on all logs, together with a rebate based on the output of processed products.

The approaches of governments to the setting of forest taxation levels should be consistent and include such features as a simple escalation clause to adjust charges annually. Charges might be linked, for example, to a price index. A formula approach to price setting might be introduced, taking into account factors such as logging investment. Where competition among forest-industry firms exists, open-bid or sealed-bid auctions are recommended.

The establishment of public log markets in a few suitable locations to involve the government in planning and supervision of logging operations and transportation could provide guideline log prices that could be used in stumpage appraisal. Effective market intelligence on the prices of logs and processed products, combined with closer monitoring of contract rates and costs of logging and trucking, will provide a better starting point for stumpage appraisal procedures.

To bring existing forests under more intensive management and to ensure sustained yields in the future, techniques include so-called zero treatment (other than protection) where, as in many West African countries, the range of salable species can be expected to increase as domestic markets for construction-grade lumber expand. Other possibilities include timber-stand improvement management systems for thinning out poor trees and preserving the best. Such systems show promise in various Southeast Asian forests, including those in the Philippines and Malaysia.

Because of the relatively low level of productivity of extensive forest management systems and the fact that the remaining natural forest in many countries is too small to supply domestic market needs, let alone sustain an export trade, increasing emphasis should be placed on fast-growing, short-rotation industrial species. It is in this area that most of the new industrial forestry investment will be needed over the coming decades.

We recommend concentration of industrial forestry investment on those thirty-two developing countries listed in table 10.3 that are either importing or exporting forest products valued at more than US$50 million a year.

A reasonable degree of self-sufficiency in industrial wood should be achievable within fifteen to twenty years in twenty of these countries, given strong political commitment to this objective and allocation of adequate resources. About 70 million ha of natural forest will need to be protected and more intensively managed, and the area of new industrial plantations needed is on the order of 13 million ha—that is, annual planting of about 900,000 ha. That would represent nearly a doubling of the current rate of industrial reforestation in these countries.

The cost of doing all this is on the order of US$1 billion per year. This estimate is based on the assumption that some 900,000 ha/yr would be planted at an estimated cost of about US$1,000 per hectare, and that about US$100 million per year would be invested in improved protection and management of existing natural forest. The success of programs to establish fast-growing industrial plantations in Brazil, Chile, and Zambia and the fact that world timber prices are expected to increase in real terms at between 1 and 2 percent per year over the next fifteen years[12] provide reasonable assurance of a positive return on this investment.

In the long run, the major benefits would be a saving in the order of US$10 billion per year in the import bill of developing countries and the creation of many additional forestry and forest-industry jobs.

The payoff of the export-oriented forestry program would be the assurance that the fourteen countries that now depend heavily on timber-derived foreign exchange earnings for economic development could sustain those earnings into the next century at a minimum level of US$5 billion per year. If such an investment program is not implemented, foreign exchange revenue from timber exports will decline sharply after 2000, and many persons now employed in forest industries will have to find jobs in other sectors.

Protection and management of 70 million ha of natural forest and establishment of 13 million ha of additional plantations would also have an indirect environmental benefit in that they would promote conservation of soil and water resources and preservation of wildlife and would provide forest recreational areas for urban populations.

The Role of Forestry Research: Promising Areas for the Future

The success of a global forestry action program on the scale envisaged above could be greatly influenced by incorporating appropriate forestry research. There is growing international awareness of the need to shift the emphasis of forestry research in developing countries toward sociological and basic scientific research aimed at increasing biological productivity of fuelwood and multipurpose trees for use in rural areas. Further emphasis should be placed on conservation research, particularly for preserving biological diversity and reducing energy consumption.

We recommend that a concerted effort be made in the coming decade to concentrate forestry research on topics that will have the greatest impact on agricultural productivity and rural incomes, the productivity of fast-growing species, and the preservation of biological diversity both in tropical rain forests and in dry-zone forests. Forestry research should also be concerned with emerging technologies such as wood-based fuels, which in the long term, could be of great significance to developing countries that have favorable ecological conditions for biomass production.[13]

Research that has led to the greatest gains in agricultural productivity is also likely to be of particular significance to forestry. Among the highest priorities will be sociological research aimed at testing attitudes of farmers and communities toward tree planting, genetic research on selected provenances and clones of more promising existing and new species, applied research aimed at introduction of faster-growing plantation species in place of slow-growing indigenous trees; cultural techniques such as plowing, clean weeding, and fertilizer application, and research into methods of controlling pests and diseases of forest trees.

Research into vegetative propagation methods and tissue culture that can lead to productivity gains on the order of 50 percent over the parent material could substantially reduce the level of investment required for creation of new forest resources.

Research aimed at finding optimal approaches to intensive biomass plantations is in progress in many countries. Critical problems in this field are the possible depletion of soil nutrients by intensive monoculture cropping and harvesting and the most economical appplication of fertilizers to compensate for this depletion.

Research aimed at improvement in the techniques for monitoring forest areas (for example, via LANDSAT images) could provide a better basis for forestry sectoral planning. These research topics are indicative only. We recommend a systematic country-by-country review of research needs. Major efforts should be made to strengthen national forestry research capabilities in all developing countries. This can be achieved in part through initiatives such as those of the new International Union for Forest Research Organization program for supporting developing countries' forest research and through closer links with the Consultative Group for International Agriculture Research institutes.

Forestry Education and Training

To sustain an action program on the scale advocated in this paper, it is axiomatic that there will need to be ongoing investment to strengthen forestry education and training at all levels. The main challenge for almost all developing countries is that of restructuring traditional forest service agencies. In the past, these have been concerned primarily with policing and protecting government-owned forest reserves. By the turn of the century, a major additional task will be to provide technical extension support for thousands of small farmers, village communities, private-sector companies, and nongovernmental organizations on whom the main burden of rural reforestation will rest.

Several countries, such as Korea and India, have already created special village or social forestry departments. Other countries are introducing extension-related topics into existing forest administrations. To effect this transition implies a major change in forestry training curricula to give greater emphasis to socioeconomic and agriculture-related subjects. New and imaginative approaches are needed to involve small farmers, and particularly women, in the creation of village-level institutions for forest protection and development.

In the future, there must be closer coordination than has existed in the past in manpower planning for the agriculture, forestry, and energy sectors. More effective collaboration is also necessary in implementation of agroforestry extension programs.

Summary of Investment Requirements:
Environmental and Economic Payoff

The estimated annual cost of an action program aimed at meeting the objectives set in this paper is on the order of US$5 billion, of which

TABLE 10.4. Recommended annual forestry sector investment, 1986–2000.

Action program	Annual level of investment (US$ billion)	Environmental and economic payoff
Watershed rehabilitation	1.5	Rehabilitation of 150 million ha of degraded tropical water-sheds. Reduced flooding, sedimentation, and loss of down-stream crops. Enhanced incomes for some 30 million people already residing in these watersheds and for 500 million living downstream.
Protection of threatened tropical rain forest ecosystems through increased agriculture productivity and strengthening of scientific research	1.3	Conservation of biological diversity and protection of 100 million ha of tropical rain forest. Sustainable income and improved quality of life for some 20 million tribal and forest-dwelling people.
Fuelwood and multipurpose tree planting in farmlands and agricultural wastelands	1.0	Assured fuelwood supplies for 1 billion people. Avoidance of burning of animal dung and crop residues which can be used instead for increasing agricultural productivity.
Industrial forestry and intensification of management in natural forests and establishment of industrial plantations	1.0	Import savings valued at US$10 billion per year and sustained forest-product exports beyond year 2000 valued at US $5 billion per year. Sustained forest industrial employment. Indirect environmental benefits through protection of soil and water resources.
Forestry research, education and training	0.5	Strengthened national forestry research and institutional capability, particularly in the areas of social and energy forestry.
Total annual investment	5.3[a]	

Note: These figures are approximations based on experience in past development projects and take into account what is known about the forestry situation in the priority countries. They need to be refined by more in-depth country-by-country analysis, preferably linked with sectoral strategy studies.

[a] US$1.7 billion of this amount would be needed from Official Development Assistance sources.

60 percent would be related to agriculture and 40 percent to forestry. The environmental and economic payoffs from this investment are summarized in table 10.4.

Although the dollar amounts may seem daunting, some of the investment could, as stated earlier, be secured by reallocating existing agricultural and energy resources if national governments were to give a higher priority to agriculture, energy, and rural development programs for the coming two decades and to the needs of poor people already residing in upland watersheds and tropical forestlands. The current emphasis being given to watershed protection in the Himalayan Range and the special action programs for forest-dwelling tribes illustrate the kinds of effort that are needed.

Assuming that one-third of the required investment is met from Official Development Assistance (ODA) sources, the US$1.7 billion a year needed would represent about 10 percent of current combined ODA support for the agriculture/energy sector. A high proportion of that investment would directly benefit the rural and urban poor and would contribute to increased food production.

NOTES

1. R. Redjo and M. Clawson, *Global Forests* (Washington, D.C.: Resources for the Future, 1983).

2. FAO, *Fuelwood Supplies in Developing Countries* (Rome: FAO, 1983).

3. World Bank, *Forestry Sector Policy* (Washington, D.C.: World Bank, 1978).

4. J. C. Westoby, *Halting Tropical Deforestation, The Role of Technology* (Washington, D.C.: US Congress, Office of Technology Assessment, 1984).

5. FAO, *The State of Food and Agriculture: Toward 2000* (Rome: FAO, 1980).

6. World Bank, *Projection Completion Report, Malaysia Tengka Project* (Washington, D.C.: World Bank, 1981).

7. M. Arnold and J. J. de Jongma, *Fuelwood and Charcoal in Developing Countries* (Rome: FAO, 1978).

8. F. Wadsworth, *Forestry Management and Plantation Technologies to Improve the Use of Converted Tropical Lands* (Washington, D.C.: US Congress, Office of Technology Assessment, June 1982).

9. J. Lanly and J. Clement, *Present and Future Forest Plantation Areas in the Tropics* (Rome: FAO, 1979).

10. J. Spears, "*Tropical Reforestation: An Achievable Goal?*" (Paper prepared for a meeting of the British Association for the Advancement of Science, April 1983).

11. L. Hamilton, *Land Use Planning Technologies to Sustain Tropical Forests and Woodlands* (Honolulu: East-West Center, 1983).

12. World Bank/FAO, *Forestry Research in Developing Countries, Time for a Reappraisal* (Washington, D.C.: World Bank/FAO, 1981).

13. R. Noronha, *Sociological Aspects of Forest Project Design* (Washington, D.C.: World Bank, 1980).

CHAPTER ELEVEN

Issues on the Preservation of Biological Diversity

KENTON R. MILLER, JOSÉ FURTADO,
CYRILLE DE KLEMM, JEFFREY A. MCNEELY,
NORMAN MYERS, MICHAEL E. SOULÉ,
and MARK C. TREXLER

The biological diversity of the earth's species and of their genetic materials represents an abundant stock of natural resources that serve our material welfare in many more ways than we realize. This natural resource capital pays dividends to our economies, in part by providing aquatic material for agricultural, medicinal, and industrial products whose commercial value is measured in billions of dollars per year. As used in this paper, the term "biological diversity" refers to all life forms, with their manifold variety, that occur on earth. It includes not only species, but subunits of species, such as races and populations, all of which possess their own characteristic attributes. Thus, the concept of biological diversity is much broader than is suggested by the sum total of the earth's 5-10 million species. But unless we take steps to safeguard this stock of unique natural resources, the biological capital will swiftly go to waste, depriving future generations of options for even greater benefits.

Species are disappearing at an unprecedented rate. Right now, at least one of earth's five to ten million species is becoming extinct every day (Ehrlich and Ehrlich, 1981; Frankel and Soulé, 1982; Myers, 1979 and 1984; National Research Council, 1980; Soulé and Wilcox,

1980). By the end of this century, we may well lose a million species, and by the end of the next century, we are likely to witness the elimination of a sizable share of the planetary complement of species. This will amount to an irreversible loss of unique natural resources. Whereas many forms of environmental degradation can be reversed, the extinction of a species is final. Even when a species is not reduced in numbers to an extent that qualifies it as "threatened," it may lose so many of its subunits that much of its genetic variability is eroded.

Biological impoverishment is not usually caused by the deliberate overexploitation of species. In virtually all cases, it results from the degradation or destruction of a species' habitat by some human activity such as agriculture. Indeed, although biological diversity contributes to such vital human activities as the production of food, fiber, and energy, those activities, along with the population growth, are the source of is depletion.

Fortunately there is much scope for practical and immediate action to confront the challenge of depletion of biological diversity. We can take initiatives to:

- Launch a consciousness-raising exercise to bring the issue to the attention of policymakers and the public at large.
- Design national conservation strategies that take explicit account of the values at stake.
- Expand our network of parks and reserves to establish a comprehensive system of protected areas.
- Undertake a program of training in fields relevant to biological diversity, to improve the scientific skills and technological grasp of those charged with its management.
- Work through conventions and treaties to express the interest of the community of nations in the collective heritage of biological diversity.
- Establish a set of economic incentives to make species conservation a competitive form of land use.

THE IMPORTANCE OF BIOLOGICAL DIVERSITY

Biological diversity is the foundation upon which human civilizations are built. Thousands of species of plants and animals supported the development of early societies, providing the basis for the evolution from hunting and gathering subsistence to agricultural and industrial levels of organization. The concentrated development of corn, wheat, rice, potatoes, and a few other species set the stage for the shift from agricultural to industrial societies.

For several reasons, biological diversity remains vital to human society. First, modern technology, whether agricultural, medical, or industrial, has in no way supplanted the need for the continued availability of a wide range of genetic material. The experience of recent years has repeatedly underscored the importance of maintaining a broad pool of genetic resources. As the green revolution progressed during the 1960s, for example, scientists found that to avoid increasing vulnerability of crops to pests and disease, the new superstrains had to be crossed back to other cultivated and wild strains to develop particular kinds of pest resistance or particular environmental adaptations.

In 1970, to cite a famous occurrence, 70 percent of the seed corn grown by US farmers owed its ancestry to six inbred lines. When a leaf fungus blighted cornfields from the Great Lakes to the Gulf of Mexico, America's great corn belt was threatened. The disease eliminated 15 percent of the entire crop and as much as half the crop in several states of the South, pushing corn prices up by 20 percent and causing losses to farmers and increased costs to consumers worth more than $2 billion. The damage was halted with the aid of various kinds of blight-resistant germ plasm with a genetic ancestry that derived from Mexico.

Not only are genetic resources important for crop species, but hundreds of cases have been documented concerning the medical or industrial value of plant and animal species. It is estimated that in 1980 in the United States alone, the overall value of plant-derived drugs and pharmaceuticals was more than $16 billion. There is also no doubt that thousands of other valuable uses of particular species remain to be found. The fact is that we have never been able to predict the genetic combinations in which species may be valuable.

The second reason for the importance of biological diversity is that, of the 250,000 plant species on earth, only one in ten has been investigated in even a cursory way to assess its utilitarian benefits, and only one in a hundred has been examined in detail—that is, in terms of its subunits and their genetic spread. Little attempt has been made to appraise the potential of the animal kingdom with its millions of species. Hence, there is great scope for systematic exploitation of biological diversity, provided we maintain the resource until we can bring to bear our technological capacity to make use of it.

This is all the more significant in light of the emergent field of genetic engineering. Scientists need as much genetic variability as possible if the new technology is to fulfill its promise. Genetic engineers are no better than the materials they work with, and this places a premium on maintaining a broad array of genetic reservoirs in the wild. To cite a leader in the field, William Brill of the University of Wisconsin, "We are entering an age in which genetic wealth, especially in tropical areas such as rain forests, until now a relatively inaccessible trust fund, is becoming a currency with high immediate value." In agriculture alone, it is estimated that prospective breakthroughs in genetic engineering will generate products worth some $50-100 billion per year well before the end of the century, through contributions to new vaccines, hormones, bacterial feeds, anabolic steroids, pesticides, nitro-fixed osmoregulation and nitro-fixed cereal enzymes, and so on, to achieve a quantum jump in our capacity to feed a hungry world.

Thus, in the words of Thomas Eisner of Cornell University, the loss of a single species amounts not merely to "the loss of one volume from the library of nature, but the loss of a loose-leaf book whose individual pages, were the species to survive, would remain available in perpetuity for selective transfer to other species."

Imagine, for example, the excitement of the first group of neolithic humans when they discovered the art of smelting iron ore and of fabricating crude tools and weapons. Then imagine how these people would have reacted to the suggestion of some prophet that someday this iron would make it possible to build a self-propelled conveyance. The idea of an automobile would have been inconceivable when no models for motors existed. It took thousands of years for civilization to evolve the sciences and technologies to accomplish such a feat. Similarly, it will be a long time before scientists are able to produce a complex gene that can give an organism a new biochemical capability. This is because the difference between determining the nucleotide sequence of an existing gene and inventing a new gene that codes for an enzyme with a novel function is of about the same order of magnitude as the difference beween smelting ore for arrowheads and building an airplane.

The genes in wild species have been evolving for millions or even billions of years. They represent solutions to problems that have never even been imagined by biologists. Because it will probably be hundreds of years before human science can afford—if it ever can—to dismiss this heritage, it would be foolish to allow further attrition in genetic diversity.

A third indicator of the importance of biological diversity is that the agricultural revolution was the basis for the industrial revolution in the temperate world. Many efforts aimed at promoting the development and industrialization of tropical countries have ignored the crucial importance of such an agricultural base. Although it is tropical plants that in many cases laid the foundation for the highly successful agriculture of temperate regions, the development of a wide range of potentially useful crop plants uniquely adapted to tropical environments has been largely ignored. The conservation and sustained exploitation of the planet's biological diversity offers tremendous potential for addressing the problems of hunger and overpopulation.

In sum, any reduction in the natural resource stocks represented by biological diversity reduces our ability to respond to new problems and opportunities. The concept of genetic resources applies to much more than the tiny fraction of biological diversity that we have exploited to date. It encompasses the entire range of genetic variability available to the world (also in domesticated versions of species and their subunits such as food crops and livestock). Were we to confine our attention to those forms of biological diversity that we have already learned to exploit, we should be missing the forest for its first few trees. To the extent that we cannot be certain what needs may arise in the future, it is essential to conserve the genetic resources with which to meet them.

Fortunately, public discussion of biological diversity is moving away from questions of why we should protect it and toward questions of how best to undertake the task. Natural scientists generally agree that the loss of biological diversity, with all that entails in foregone economic opportunities, is the paramount environmental issue we face today. Moreover, the importance of conserving biological diversity is being recognized in certain official circles, as witness such statements as the Stockholm Conference Declaration of 1972, the UN Charter for Nature of 1982, and the proceedings of the US Department of State Biological Diversity Conference of 1982.

STATE OF SCIENTIFIC AND TECHNICAL KNOWLEDGE

Scientific and technical knowledge concerning biological diversity is surprisingly deficient. For example, we can only guess at the number of species that exist on the earth. To date, scientsts have identified about 1.5 million species of animal life, together with about 250,000 species of higher (vascular) or flowering species of plant life and about 800,000 lower species of plants (Ehrlich and Ehrlich, 1981; Myers, 1979 and 1983; National Research Council, 1980). At the present rate of inventorying species, we shall have identified hardly more than 2 million by the year 2000. Estimtes suggest that, as a minimum, some 5 million species may share the planet, but the total could well be 10 million. Indeed, recent research postulates as many as 30 million insect species in tropical forests alone.

With regard to the distribution of species, scientists believe that the tropics harbor at least two-thirds of all species, even though they cover only one-third of the earth's land surface. More specifically, it is believed that at least 40 percent of all species occur in tropical forests, a biome that is being depleted rapidly. Out of a total of only 10 million km^2 of tropical forests, some 75,000 km^2 are being destroyed each year, and a further 100,000 km^2 are facing gross disruption and degradation.

A consensus is emerging within the scientific community to the effect that the extinction rate is now a good deal higher than it would be under purely natural conditions—that is, under conditions free of man's disruptive impact. Of course, there have always been natural extinctions. Of all the species that have occurred since the emergence of life 3.6 billion years ago, at least 90 percent have disappeared. Yet the extinction rate of the past does not remotely compare with the rate that is anticipated for the coming decades. For example, it appears that the average natural rate of extinction ranges from 2 to 4.6 families of species per million years, rising to an average of 19.3 families of a species per million years during the five prehistoric episodes of mass extinction (Raup and Sepkoski, 1982). By contrast, the next century may witness the demise of 50 families of plants—one quarter of all plant families—together with many associated animal (mainly insect) families.

The extremely restricted range of many species, especially in the tropics, makes them particularly susceptible to extinction. At least one in ten tropical forest species, for example, is restricted to a very limited range, whereas other species are characterized by ecological specializations that make them especially vulnerable to even moderate disruption of their habitats.

Whatever the numbers, distribution, and rates of extinction of species, there remains the major concern of their conservation. Aside from the few economically important species represented in collection, the vast majority of species will be maintained or go extinct in the cultured or wild landscape. The outlook for survival is unclear. It appears certain that large numbers of species will become extinct within the immediate future without our gaining even the most rudimentary knowledge of their nature, range, ecology, and other basic attributes.

Given the progressive depletion of tropical forests, among other ecological zones of the tropics, it is imperative that we take steps immediately to increase our knowledge of tropical species. Until we learn more about the main concentrations of species, especially those with a high level of endemism, we will not know where best to establish protected areas as genetic reservoirs or the principal safeguard for threatened species. The pool of taxonomists and systematicists who study organisms in this richest biological zone amounts to a mere 1,500. That number needs to be increased by a factor of at least five if we are to identify new species faster than they become extinct. Great Britain, with 1,800 plant species, has more than 2,000 botanists and other professionals seeking to improve our basic scientific understanding of the plant kingdom, while Colombia, with perhaps 40,000 plant species, has only a small number of botanists.

Similarly, we know all too little about how to design protected areas: how large they should be, or with what configuration. Neither do we know how to manage protected areas so that they can function as genetic preserves. We do not know, beyond some scant indication, which categories of species harbor the greatest genetic variability, and we have barely made a start on the economic application of genetic resources.

These severe constraints notwithstanding, we should recognize that we do possess sufficient knowledge to allow us to manage biological diversity far better than we do at present. That we do not make better use of our knowledge is, in part, the result of shortcomings in conservation policies and planning, an area with much room for innovative advances.

INSTITUTIONAL INADEQUACIES

In essence, our institutional systems have served to promote the expansion of the human ecological niche. Regrettably our niche has expanded far more rapidly than the ability of our economic and political institutions to adjust. Institutions that earlier posed no threat to natural environments have themselves become factors in promoting rather than controlling environmental degradation. Thus, a major challenge is to adapt our institutions so that they reflect the fundamentally transformed human niche.

Although the importance of biological diversity is increasingly recognized by national and international bodies, there has been little progress in translating this acceptance into action. The problem of diminishing diversity ostensibly stems from patterns of general misuse and overuse of resources, degrading and even destroying natural environments. Examples abound in agriculture, forestry, and fishing, among other fields. As long as deforestation and desertification proceed apace, together with other environmental impoverishment such as disruption of watershed systems, biological diversity will continue to decline.

But these depletive processes are not the root causes of the problem. They are only symptoms, and as such they offer little guidance on how we should design better policies for conservation of biological diversity. Reforestation is not the simple solution to deforestation that it appears to be. The key question is, Why are forests being cut down? Similarly, we should ask, Why is agricultural land often degraded? Why do many development projects make nonrenewable use of natural resources? The answers to these questions must come from an examination of economic and political factors.

Biological diversity, everybody's heritage, is treated as nobody's business. However much humankind may regard species and other forms of biological diversity as its estate, it has no effective way to express this interest through ownership. An individual can own a cow, and ownership enables and encourages that person to take care of the cow and induces others not to use or misuse it. But wild species are not subject to readily identifiable property rights. They are subject to the law of capture, applicable only when removed from the wild. For centuries, the marketplace, along with the law, has served to formulate and consolidate the rights of private property. Common property—notably species, but also the atmosphere and large bodies of water—has suffered by default. This situation did not matter much until recently. But now that common-property resources are depleted and endangered through misuse and overuse, the institutional mechanisms that should safeguard them are found to be inadequate.

Species are treated as common-property resources in two basic ways. First, the intrinsic value of a species is indivisible. If the chimpanzee (like the atmosphere and the oceans) brings benefit to one person, it brings benefit to all. Second, since the species has no effective owner, it is subject to open-access exploitation: any individual can exploit the chimpanzee for private gain or exploit the chimpanzee's habitat for agriculture and other purposes. Consequently, exploitation of the resource is almost always wasteful, and safeguards are almost always lacking.

Thus, when biological diversity is endangered or depleted, it is less the result of human shortsightedness and prodigality than it is a reflection of the status of species and their habitats as common property. This is notably true of tropical forests. Clearing of forests brings immediate profits to a limited number of individuals. Hence the benefits to each are concentrated and appreciable. By contrast, protection of species within these forests brings benefits that may extend over a far longer period of time but will be spread among many beneficiaries and thus will be diffused. Given the way society's institutions weigh the choice, it is the short-term benefit that prevails.

Economic systems have been slow to reflect the value of biological diversity. Since its exhaustion has not been considered likely, the resource has not generally been assigned a value, and efforts to preserve it have been viewed as economically irrational. This puts conservation at a serious disadvantage, especially when economic evaluation—through such methods as cost benefit analysis—has been used to assess alternative exploitation strategies for natural environments.

In addition, there is the well-known problem of the tragedy of the commons. A group of people working toward a collective goal may not reach it, despite their best intentions, if the benefits of their effort cannot be withheld from those people who do not contribute. In many cases, each individual may rationally come to the conclusion that he or she is best off letting everyone else contribute to the effort, because he or she will get the benefits anyway: the free-rider syndrome. The result is often that the unanimously desired outcome is not achieved. The preservation of biological diversity, a collective good, is hampered by these common-property and free-rider problems.

Thus, it is not surprising that the biological diversity and genetic resources of the world are subject to major and irreversible losses. Our economic system, which should, theoretically, guide resource use and conservation decisions, is failing with respect to biological diversity and genetic resources. Our social institutions, notably political systems, are also failing to ensure sustained management of the human niche.

A political commitment to confront the problem of the reduction in biological diversity could generate important spin-off benefits. A concerted campaign based on cost sharing could help to articulate the common interest of nations. An expanded strategy to safeguard species and their genetic resources might encourage governments to adopt a more collective approach to other common issues. In short, measures to safeguard species could, by promoting a consciousness of the unity of humankind, be a solid step toward securing a sustainable ecological niche for our species.

Our current international system is characterized by many free riders. A limited number of countries, primarily the developing nations in the tropics, are the repositories of resources that provide considerable benefits to the entire world. These countries could provide even greater benefits as progress is made in fields such as genetic engineering, *if* these resources are still there when they are needed. The fact that those countries that most desperately need to take action to preserve these resources are also those least able to afford the financial expenditures required greatly complicates the situation.

It is in the interest of all countries to recognize the fundamentally self-destructive nature of many societal institutions that affect biological diversity, for the destruction of these ecologically essential and economically valuable resources poses a threat to all countries. Those temperate countries that possess the technologies to convert raw genetic resources into valuable products will also lose a great deal through the destruction of these resources. It must be stressed that the protection of biological diversity and genetic resources is not a zero-sum transaction. We are not faced with one country having to give up part of its wealth in favor of another. Instead, we are faced with a situation in which all nations will be ecologically and economically better off if these resources are protected. Given the distribution and characteristics of the resources, cooperation is required to ensure their protection.

Other approaches have also been used to protect resources that share with biological diversity and genetic resources the characteristics of common property and public goods. In the case of marine fisheries, which in many cases have been exploited to the point of commercial extinction, national economic sovereignty has been extended to 200 miles (322.58 km) to provide governments with the incentive for acting to conserve them. In the case of clean air, international law makes any damage done by one country to another country's air illegitimate; this principle has been upheld in the courts (though not necessarily implemented in practice). What lessons can we derive from our experience with fisheries and clean air that can be applied to the more complex problems of biological diversity?

THE SEARCH FOR PROGRESS, A CONTEXT FOR ACTION

Is there room for optimism, a possibility for stemming the loss of biological diversity? Measures that set the stage for action in the immediate future are already being implemented.

The goals of conservation activities as defined in the *World Conservation Strategy* are as follows:

1. To maintain essential ecological processes and life-support systems (such as soil regeneration and protection, recycling of nutrients, and cleansing of waters), on which human survival and development depend
2. To preserve genetic diversity, on which depend the breeding programs necessary for the protection and improvement of cultivated plants and domesticated animals, as well as much scientific advance, technical innovation, and the security of the many industries that use living resources
3. To ensure that any utilization of species and ecosystems is sustainable.

Above all, the *World Conservation Strategy* postulates that conservation and development are two sides of the same coin: conservation cannot succeed without development, and development cannot be sustained without conservation.

Some thirty nations from all regions of the world have taken steps to integrate existing knowledge and experience through the development of a national conservation strategy (NCS), a detailed plan for conservation action within that particular country. An NCS is developed by teams of local and invited international experts from related disciplines and interests. Typically, team members come from governmental agencies for planning, finance, and natural resources and from nongovernmental organizations with interest and expertise in environment and development.

Although a global approach to planning under varied conditions is not anticipated in the short run, actual experience already points to the importance of strategic approaches to the management and use of natural resources (International Union for Conservation of Nature and Natural Resources, 1984). Of particular relevance to the problem of biological diversity, the NCS experience suggests that:

- Those resources or particular sites that under current practice exert limitations or form obstacles to achieving the objectives of development must be identified explicitly.
- These resources must be analyzed in terms of both ecosystem

and development needs to determine options for improved management.

- Projects should be formulated to remove the major limitations or obstacles.
- Project formulation and implementation should be carried out in ways that generate the widest possible support from governmental and nongovernmental agencies and public participation.

In a way, biological resources are analogous to information resources. Information is obviously a valuable resource, yet it is characterized by major free-rider problems. If the original providers of the information are not paid for their work, they have no incentive to continue, and the amount of available information shrinks dramatically. This was realized long ago, and methods have been devised to protect the resource through such mechanisms as copyright regulations and royalty payments. While the information itself is not viewed as being owned in a proprietary sense, steps have been taken to encourage the provision of information by paying for its use. The situation with respect to genetic resources that are already being exploited or are understood to be exploitable is fundamentally similar, but mechanisms to ensure that the resources continue to exist have not been developed.

Many countries have developed conservation legislation and institutions for conserving natural resources. Such measures include zoning legislation or plans for rural areas and national and international legislation to protect certain areas, to control the use and trade of specified species of wild flora and fauna, and to promote international cooperation. For example, the rural zoning controls in European countries provide a mechanism to protect genetic diversity within the overall cultured landscape. More than 3,000 national parks and protected areas now maintain well over 400 million ha in 90 percent of the world's biogeographic regions. Eighty-seven countries are now party to the Convention on Trade in Endangered Species of Wild Flora and Fauna.

Focussing specifically on current options for the maintenance of biological diversity, the 1982 World Congress on National Parks, held in Bali, Indonesia, examined 120 prepared case studies from various regions. A total of more than 500 scientists, managers, and other specialists examined the status of protected areas and the links between biological conservation and sustainable development. The case histories clearly demonstrated the feasibility of protecting discrete, well-chosen areas for specific purposes. They showed that where the rationale for the design and location of reserves included ecological, economic, and social analysis, the goals and means for biological conservation and rural development were not necessarily incompatible. In many cases, the sustainable production of food, medicines, water, and primary fiber materials in rural areas was shown to be dependent upon the ecosystem services derived from reserve management of a portion of the region.

An action plan developed by the Bali congress calls for the implementation of ten concrete recommendations. These are based upon the learning of the past decade and can be pushed forward quickly. In essence, the Bali action plan calls for establishing a world system of terrestrial and marine protected areas within the decades 1982-92.

Managerial quality needs to be improved to ensure the appropriate use of scientific knowledge. Approaches to management of national parks, sanctuaries, forests, and monuments must be reassessed to ensure that biological conservation is given explicit status as an objective. The human capacity to manage protected areas requires major support. The relationship between management and economic development of protected areas warrants the attention of economists. Support services needed for the management of protected areas include improved monitoring and data management, international cooperation, and global efforts to promote fieldwork.

The search for solutions must be carried out with caution. Current world trends of expanding poverty and increasing loss of biological diversity will apparently continue for some time, and political and economic problems defy simple solutions. Yet, recent experience suggests that there is a range of practical steps that can be taken to coserve a significant share of the world's biological wealth.

AGENDA FOR ACTION

In this section, six areas of action are proposed to increase the awareness of high-level decision-makers and the general public concerning the relationship of biological diversity to development, and feasible measures for conserving biological diversity in the present and promoting private investment in the work that lies ahead are mapped out. In each of the six areas, the specific problem to be addressed is defined, solutions are suggested, and ideas for implementation are given.

These are first steps, to be taken immediately while there are still opportunities to retain wild reserves. Parallel efforts must also be made to prepare the agenda for subsequent action on the more complex issues involved in maintaining the biological diversity of the cultured landscape and the seas.

Real awareness of the value of biological diversity and the resources to which it holds the key is rare among both the general public and policymakers. Even such fundamental links as those between biological diversity and such necessities as food, health, energy, and industrial development are poorly understood. Without all the relevant facts and principles at their disposal and without some corresponding measure of awareness in the audience to when they address themselves, even the most sympathetic policymakers will find it hard to press the case for conserving genetic resources.

Action 1: Global Publicity Campaign

The first thing that is needed, then, is a global publicity campaign to raise general consciousness of the value and importance of biological diversity and what its loss could mean to individuals and to society as a whole. Who could take charge of such a campaign? The community of nongovernmental organizations already active in tackling environmental conservation issues is a natural choice for preparing and managing such an initiative as long as it has a firm nucleus to support and coordinate its efforts. The Environmental Liason Center, the International Union for Conservation of Nature and Natural Resources (IUCN), World Wildlife Fund (WWF), and several other more regional or local organizations could, by combining their efforts, provide an effective steering influence for such a campaign. Campaigns of this sort already under way include those focused internationally upon conservation of tropical forests, whales, and the seas, as well as mineral exploitation in Antarctica, which is the subject of growing debate. Nationally, such campaigns have promoted community action on soil and water conservation and on family planning. Funds will be needed to help originate and distribute effective documentation, to stage regional events, and to undertake baseline research and policy analysis.

Who can provide these funds? Foundations and other bodies already dedicated to environmental conservation, such as WWF, the Sierra Club, and environmental education centers around the world, have the capacity to support such work. It is also likely that major new funding sources can be tapped for such a campaign. Somewhere between the individuals who contribute to the campaigns of WWF and those who belong to politically active organizations like the Sierra Club, there is almost certainly a large group of people, including many scientists, who may not belong to any organized conservation group but who would participate in efforts expressly aimed at addressing the fundamental human problem of preserving biological diversity.

Second, a major world event or public demonstration should be staged to draw the attention of policymakers to the problems arising from loss of biological diversity and to the links between such loss and vital human concerns such as hunger, population pressures, energy, shortages of raw materials, and environmental degradation. Such an event would be designed to demonstrate broad public support for policymakers in the difficult decisions that they need to make. A recognized center of excellence in world policy affairs, preferably in the tropics, might organize this event. The funds needed to finance it could be raised in part from those industries that rely on genetic resources for their future viability.

The proposals that have been made thus far to increase awareness would create greater public concern that adequate conservation measures be taken wherever a clear need arises. Business executives and other policymakers could, if better informed of the problem, make decisions affecting living resources with much greater care and feel justified in insisting that the biological impact and after-effects of every new enterprise are fully evaluated before the first step is taken. Most important, these activities could foster a new spirit of a willingness among policymakers to consider natural resource problems in their full biological and social perspective and to feel a part of efforts to find solutions, rather than regarding conservation as a threat or an impediment to progress.

Action 2: Conservation Strategy Planning

Practical step-by-step guidelines for securing and maintaining biological diversity in a particular country or region are lacking. Under pressure from overwhelming human demands for relief from poverty or famine, for example, it is hard to find ways to remove logistic and institutional obstacles to resource conservation planning while pressing on with sustainable development projects that support biological diversity.

National, regional, and sectoral conservation strategies need to be formulated to enable countries to determine for themselves what is to be done both locally and overall to achieve sustainable development. Safeguards must be built into this process for the proper maintenance of biological diversity, so that options for future development are not foreclosed.

This planning process should recognize the need for networks of protected areas to guarantee the well-being of premium biological zones or ecosystems. It should include a review of policies relevant to conservation and use of genetic resources and should aim to relieve pressures that lead to loss of species and habitats worthy of conservation.

In developing countries, collaboration with established development aid agencies can be sought when preparing conservation strategies and raising the funds to see them through. In developed countries, the planning can be financed by governmental and non-governmental organizations concerned with environmental or natural resource issues. In either case, emphasis should be placed on the integration of home-based teams drawn from an entire range of related organizations and disciplines. From their own special and local knowledge, these teams can fit their plans for action to the needs of the region.

An example of a national conservation strategy can be drawn from India. The Environmental Ministry of the Prime Minister's Office called for the formulation of a conservation strategy to give particular attention to India's outstanding plant diversity. Of India's 15,000 plant species, some 3,000-4,000 are considered to be threatened. Many of these are the wild relatives of economically important commercial plants, including citrus plants and strains of wild rice. Up to 90 percent of all medicines used domestically come directly from plants, many of which are found only in the wild and in increasingly short supply. The strategy process began with a national analysis in which IUCN's Commission on Environmental Planning and Conservation Monitoring Center participated and progressed to the formulation of a series of projects. Specific lines of action included a nationwide survey of the status of plants, wild-plant propagation at the village level, assistance to botanical gardens, rural plant production gardens, research on tissue-culture conservation methods, and economic analysis of the impacts of pending large-scale investment projects upon plant life.

At present, thirty-two countries in many parts of the world have published or are preparing national conservation strategies to help them solve conservation problems in a determined and integrated manner. The strategies give attention to questions of policy and law, institutional coordination and cooperation, practical management, appropriate training, and the many other components of a balanced push toward sustainable development.

Strategic conservation planning, when it becomes an element of national planning, also provides a means for instantly identifying productive investment opportunities and for evaluating a range of investment options. The strategic approach makes natural resource conservation a part of the overall exercise of decision making and action in a country or region. It streamlines the general effort, rules out duplication and waste, and delineates a route that all can follow.

Action 3: Global Network of Protected Areas

Nations have already made substantial investments in land, finance, and institutions to provide protection for critical natural areas. Even so, gaps remain in the network of protected areas in many of the major biogeographical realms. Of the world's 193 biogeographical provinces, 16 lack protected areas, and another 33 contain fewer than 5 protected areas each or less than 100,000 ha total of protected area. It is not clear whether the existing protected areas and the way they are managed match the objective of maintaining biological diversity as defined in this paper. On the basis of current data, we estimate that a truly comprehensive network of protected areas would require a minimum of 10 percent of the world's land area. Although such a large portion would appear at first to be unjustifiable, the vital role of selected natural reserves managed so as to ensure a constant stream of environmental services should not be underestimated. Investments in such areas will help maintain the viability of the other 90 percent. Also, the reserves will help maintain the more limited but important biological diversity found throughout the cultured landscape.

The first step toward establishing such a network should be the reinforcement of regional efforts to analyze the terms, aims, and suitability of the present coverage of protected areas in relation to the conservation of biological diversity. The IUCN's Commission on National Parks and Protected Areas has begun this analysis at the regional level throughout the world. Data is stored and processed at the

Conservation Monitoring Center. Major gaps have been identified by regional teams. Gaps of particular concern as regards preservation of biological diversity include the tropical grasslands and savannahs of Australia and Brazil, the warm deserts and semideserts of Argentina, northern Africa, and some islands, lake systems, and Mediterranean-type forests throughout the world.

Guidelines have been provided to governments for promoting the selection of sites and the management of protected areas. However, the next step in the process requires detailed surveys and field analysis by teams of local and international biologists, management specialists, and planners. Proposals for new sites to bridge the gaps between existing protected areas can then be formulated. Subsequently laws can be written, management plants prepared, and buffer zones established to harmonize the reserves with rural development.

These latter steps need international support and assistance. The FAO, the UN Environment Program (UNEP), and UNESCO have provided limited support for these types of efforts in the past. The UN Development Program (UNDP) should be encouraged to consider these activities as they relate to developmental programs. Several major nongovernmental organizations and universities are collaborating with private landowners and public management agencies to identify gaps and prepare site proposals. Such collaborations should be encouraged.

As a second step, management of existing protected areas should be harmonized with the aim of conservation of biological diversity, involving genetic diversity both within and between species. Most national parks and other types of reserves were established and are currently managed for purposes laid down some time ago and often do not specifically take into account conservation of genetic resources. Conflicts between management objectives can arise, and individual protected areas need to be studied to minimize these conflicts. Such studies can be carried out in most cases by the agencies already responsible for the protected areas, with support from local universities for biological analysis and other research.

Third, management plans should be prepared for all protected areas. Methods and procedures for management planning that take specific account of biological diversity are widely available from IUCN, FAO, and many national agencies.

Some countries will need financial and technical assistance to prepare management plans. Support can be looked for from the World Heritage Convention, development projects supported by UN organizations, and the conservation projects of WWF and other conservation interest groups. Much more important in monetary terms, however, is the potential for support from governmental and intergovernmental aid and development agencies. Such support must always be perceived as a contribution to development, as well as a contribution to the conservation of biological diversity.

This is an area in which technical cooperation among developing countries—that is, a South-South exchange—is particularly relevant. Many developing countries now have enough expertise to be able to provide assistance to neighboring nations at low cost. Such assistance generally results in advice that is valuable in the local context.

Fourth, regional consultation and cooperation with people living in lands close to key protected areas should be an established feature in the management of those areas. Such programs in the buffer zone provide a useful way of achieving a balance between the needs and expectations of local people on the one hand and the national and global requirements for conservation on the other. The Man and the Biosphere Program of UNESCO is attempting to demonstrate ways to collaborate with local people and meet their needs for water, food, firewood, employment, and other necessities. Such techniques could be extended to all important protected areas so as to minimize boundary conflicts and to harmonize area management with local social and economic realities. In most cases, such cooperative and consultative efforts can be financed as part of regular rural development projects funded by local and national governments. Development aid agencies need to accept such work as an essential link between meeting basic human needs and securing the future of genetic resources.

Research is needed to determine how biological diversity can be maintained in multiple-use areas along with all the other goals involved, including logging and mining. Although much experience and technology exists to guide those extracting timber or minerals from multiple-use reserves, little work has been done to illuminate the right management approach for avoiding loss of biological diversity as a result of these practices. Funding for such research could reasonably be expected from interested resource-users, such as timber and mining companies. The research effort will also require the support of universities and research centers.

Protected areas provide one practical approach to ensuring the conservation of genetic resources and biological diversity. Actions designed to establish a global network of areas representing the world's tremendous variety on land and sea and to keep them safe from internal and external threat can provide the global community with a reasonable expectation of safe transfer of the genetic heritage to future generations. Out of this natural capital, we shall be able to draw genetic materials to improve foods, medicines, and industrial chemicals. As a result of establishing protected areas, many other benefits will accrue to society, including the maintenance of watersheds, a renewable supply of products and services from multiple-use areas, and a range of social, cultural, and ethical benefits. These other benefits will often carry the cost of investments and running expenses of protected-area managements. That same network of areas will supply opportunities for research and monitoring in natural habitats, locations for regional and global cooperation in research programs such as Man and the Biosphere or the Global Environmental Monitoring System, and the training of local scientists and managers.

Despite all these benefits, the network described cannot by itself achieve conservation of biological diversity. Many other items will need to be added to the agenda for action in the near future. But, in the short run, protected areas can be established while options still exist. Beyond this, the very lack of rural development, particularly in lands surrounding protected areas, is perhaps the greatest threat to the safety of these sites on which society will rely so heavily once the remaining unprotected wild lands have been converted to agriculture and other uses.

Action 4: Human Capacity for Management

There is a universal shortage of trained personnel to carry out the tasks necessary for the conservation of biological diversity. Tropical foresters, geneticists, agronomists, conservation administrators, taxonomists, managers of protected areas, and many other kinds of specialists are badly needed. Without the human capacity to deal with the key tasks involved, solutions to the problem of conserving biological diversity will not be possible.

First, university programs should be strengthened to prepare more and better specialists in those fields where academic education can help, such as genetics, taxonomy, resource management, administration, forestry, and ecology. Educational institutions should be helped to institute or maintain departments relevant to such skills. Although much thought and discussion must still go into the detailed design of curricula, the basic concepts have already been developed in several model institutions, such as the Missouri Botanical Gardens, the School of Natural Resources of the University of Michigan, New Zealand's Lincoln College, the College of African Wildlife Management in Tanzania, and the Forestry Faculty in the National Agrarian University of Peru. Financing for expanded university programs should come from national budgets, national academies of science, national science boards, and related industrial interests.

Second, mid-level training programs should be strengthened to prepare personnel for the required fieldwork. These requirements have already been defined in many regions in the course of studies undertaken by the UN organizations, development aid agencies, and conservation groups. Many specific actions have been suggested, but recommendations lie unheeded. The project sponsored by the US Agency for International Development (AID) to examine training needs in Latin America is a case in point. In 1979, AID anticipated an investment of $8 million for training in research and management of natural resources and the environment in the Latin American-Caribbean region. Under contract through the US Department of the Interior, WWF established a team of twelve experts, mostly from the region, to examine the status of training during an eight-month period. A model was proposed to AID with the endorsement of regional organizations and political leaders. Basically, it called for a large-scale program to support and enhance the existing network of institutions within the region. Unfortunately this proposal, which was developed by local authorities and carried local political support, was never implemented by the expected donor agency. The $120,000-study remains on the shelf. Past and present training activities have been sponsored by FAO, UNEP, UNESCO, UNDP, IUCN, and WWF, among others. These institutions have considerable experience in operating such courses.

Solid academic education in such fields as genetics, resource management, forestry, taxonomy, and ecology can be expected to result in wiser decisions and more appropriate management of natural resources. In the absence of such education, progress in conservation and development will be hampered by inability to identify potentially useful materials, to manage critical areas to produce timber and other commodities in a manner that is sustainable, and to underwrite decision making with good science. Similarly, middle-level training will enhance custodial management of the key resources under protection in designated areas and the manpower to provide extension services to people living in lands adjacent to protected areas. To develop this human capacity is a precondition of an effectively managed network of protected areas.

Action 5: International Conservation Law and Policy

Many international legal instruments, including conventions and treaties, have been formulated to encourage and steer international cooperation in conservation. Many of these instruments have not yet fully realized their worth because of the lack of consistent commitment to them by governments or because of failure to provide sufficient funding for implementing them. In most cases, there is a lack of information on how the legal instrument in question is actually being implemented. Research on the implementation of these laws and policies, although conceptually and analytically difficult, is very important.

First, recruitment efforts to encourage participation in international conservation treaties should be increased. Governments need to be made aware of their responsibilities in this respect, for many are now unaware of the existence or relevance of these instruments. Scant attention has been given to the benefits that governments can gain from such international cooperation. Efforts to promote international conservation instruments should include preparatiion and dissemination of printed material describing the important characteristics of each instrument. Correspondence with, and personal visits to, the appropriate officials could provide a considerable boost for the international conservation effort.

Second, international conservation treaties should be promoted. Few conventions give rise to serious conservation programs because of a lack of financial support from party states. The legal and policy provisions in these instruments should be followed up more rigorously to secure the goal of conserving biological diversity. Governments need to be made aware of the activities carried out under the terms of international instruments and to secure their financial contribution so that the work can be continued. When governments see the benefits of employing such instruments as means for international cooperation, they will surely regard them more favorably.

Support for these two activities requires the cooperative efforts of various organizations. For example, the Convention on Trade in Endangered Species of Wild Flora and Fauna (CITES) has an active secretariat now fully funded by participating countries. It is a success story on how governmental and nongovernmental actions have established an effective mechanism for cooperation in conservation. UNEP and IUCN established the basis for the development of the CITES secretariat by providing field information and lobbying where necessary. By the end of 1985, it is anticipated that CITES will be operating as part of UNEP, having taken its rightful place among the key international conservation institutions. Similar cooperative efforts are needed to push the Convention on Protection of the World's Natural and Cultural Heritage, the Wetlands Convention (Ramsar), the Migratory Species Convention (Bonn), and others.

The payoff from international agreements will consist of an institutional framework and incentives to guide and promote cooperation among nations on conservation matters of mutual concern. Such legal instruments enable states to make expenditures for exchange of experts and information, sponsor trans-border studies, develop global research and data-handling methods, and draft common plans of action.

Action 6: Economic Incentives

At present, most genetic resources are traded at little or no cost. For this reason, even though users themselves recognize their value, genetic resources are treated by many other people as worthless, and few perceive the need for an economic incentive to safeguard them. If the right to use genetic resources could be bought and sold through the marketplace, all the people profiting by such commerce would plainly be moved to protect their interests by fostering the gene supply in as many forms as possible.

There are many obstacles to designing systems for attaching a market value to genetic resources, and these obstacles exist at both national and international levels. But without a firm system of economic incentives, it is difficult to see how we shall get away from common-property management of genetic resources with all its liabilities.

If a workable market pricing system for genetic resources could be devised, society would be part way toward making the conservation of genetic resources a competitive form of land use. At best, this would be only a partial solution, however, the other part depending upon greater public awareness and appreciation of the important "environmental services" and the ethical considerations related to biological diversity. Market behavior will ultimately be set by the values people assign to the resources.

The first step toward establishing effective economic incentives is the further investigation of the economics of biological diversity. A trust fund should be endowed to assist those countries (particularly tropical developing countries) that harbor rich genetic reservoirs but do not possess the financial means to carry out effective conservation programs. A royalty system might be designed to generate funds to support such efforts. Not all revenues generated through a royalty system need to go into the trust; a significant portion, like any other state-owned commodity revenue, would go directly to the nations from which the genetic resources originate. The apportionment would be fixed under the terms of a treaty or agreement to establish the legal framework for conservation of, and trading in, genetic resources. But, as indicated in the previous section on international legal instruments, lawmaking is not by itself the answer to problems in safeguarding genetic resources.

Many other issues would have to be resolved before a system of incentives could become operational. Establishment of the basic concept of a gene market, however, would constitute a major advance in conservation of genetic resources. Perhaps chief among the controversial factors in such efforts currently under way within the FAO and elsewhere is the relationship between the country of origin of genetic materials and the country within which a product is elaborated and commercialized. Any major initiative will have to contain, among other things, two key provisions: (1) that the nations in which the resources are found have the opportunity to develop their own capacities to store material, screen wild material for potential uses, and develop products, and (2) that the same nations receive economic incentives to protect and manage species and areas of critical importance to a sustainable flow of their genetic resources.

A system of economic incentives for conserving genetic resources will be difficult to devise in principle and equally difficult to implement in practice. Herein lies the biggest problem, the greatest challenge, and the most creative prospect for making genetic resource conservation pay its way in the long term. If we are daunted by the prospect of such a scheme, let us consider the ultimate difficulty of living in a world that otherwise will lose a large portion of its biological diversity. Such a world would contain reduced opportunities to find new materials for improving our food, medicines, fiber commodities, and industrial chemicals. New options for renewable energy could be lost. The human capacity to study and understand natural ecosystems would be curtailed.

To the extent that biological impoverishment implies further de-forestation, desertification, and accelerated erosion, such a future world would have lost fundamental ecosystem services related to water flow, nutrient recycling, soil regeneration, weather and possibly climate stability, and flood control. The aesthetic dimension of such a world would be poorer—and a bit of humanity would be lost in the process.

The problem of maintaining biological diversity, of preserving the living wealth of the planet and making it available for sustainable use, has technical, economic, and political dimensions. Solutions are not to be found in any single dimension. Moreover, the lack of scientific knowledge and the obstacles posed by economic and political aspects of social institutions suggest that no easy answers can be found in the short run.

With growing human populations and rapidly changing land uses that tend to convert wild lands and homogenize cultured landscapes, the need is urgent to take action to conserve species and critical natu-ral areas within the framework of strategy plans. Building on the con-siderable network of existing protected areas, a practical program of action can be developed to identify gaps in the system, improve the management of existing areas, and train managers and other personnel.

The network of protected areas can be complemented by laws and policies to enable nations to cooperate on matters of mutual concern, which may require mutual support. Meanwhile, increased efforts to develop economic incentives require immediate action because con-siderable creativity and innovation will be needed to generate practi-cal solutions.

Ultimately, it will be increased awareness by both the public and decision-makers that will establish the values needed to ensure that conservation measures are implemented. Experience in recent educa-tional campaigns and in national conservation strategies, management of protected areas, training programs, and CITES suggests that there is cause for cautious optimism.

REFERENCES

Ehrlich, P. H., and A. H. Ehrlich. 1981. *Extinction*. New York: Random House.

Frankel, O. H., and M. E. Soulé. 1982. *Conservation and Evolution*. Cambridge: Cambridge University Press.

IUCN. 1984. *National Conservation Strategies*. Gland, Switzerland: IUCN.

———. 1980. *World Conservation Strategy*. New York: Unipub.

Myers, N. 1979. *The Sinking Ark*. Oxford: Pergamon Press.

———. 1983. *A Wealth of Wild Species*. Boulder, Colorado: Westview Press.

———. 1984. *The Primary Source*. New York: Norton.

NRC. 1980. *Research Priorities in Tropical Biology*. Washington, D.C.: National Academy of Sciences.

Raup, D. M., and J. J. Sepkoski. 1982. Mass extinctions in the marine fossil records. *Science* 215:1501–03.

Soulé, M. E., and B. A. Wilcox, eds. 1980. *Conservation Biology*. Sunderland, Mass.: Sinauer Associates.

CHAPTER TWELVE

Energy Issues and Opportunities

AMULYA K. N. REDDY

The growing use of energy sources worldwide has frequently led to reliance on foreign sources and to deleterious impacts on the environment. These strategic and environmental consequences were long neglected. However, the gravity of the environmental risks has now become clear, and the oil price shocks of 1973 and 1979 have highlighted the strategic vulnerability of external dependence. After almost a decade, the trauma of the energy crisis seems to have diminished, but the crisis remains and, if underestimated, will again intensify.

The close connection between various global problems requires that energy problems be solved without aggravating problems in other areas. Unfortunately, conventional energy strategies have tended not to do this. The strategy for societal survival is not to look upon energy as an end in itself but to focus on the uses of energy and the services that energy performs. *Energy must be an instrument for the achievement of the global goal of a sustainable world.* This means that, in the developing countries, need-oriented, self-reliant, and environmentally sound development becomes the goal of energy strategies. And in the developed countries, the goal is economically stable, environmentally safe, and strategically secure societies. With this orientation, energy can be turned into a powerful genie to serve the general welfare.

ENERGY ISSUES

The Crisis of Energy Carriers

The ascendancy of oil worldwide is a comparatively recent phenomenon associated with the modern phase of industrialization. The availability of cheap oil gave rise to a belief that the future would be a bigger and better version of the past. In late 1973, however, for the first time, the oil-exporting countries gained control over the price of oil and, through an embargo, created such a scarcity and panic in oil markets that they were able to raise the world oil price threefold. A combination of three factors made this possible: (1) the increased consumption of oil, particularly by the industrialized countries, (2) the plateauing of oil production in the United States, and (3) the resulting dramatic shift in dependence on the Persian Gulf oil-producers.

After the first oil price shock, demand slackened because of conservation efforts and the economic recession induced by the shock. But, after a number of years, as the world economy pulled out of the recession, oil demand soared again, creating the tight market conditions that made it possible for the Organization of Petroleum Exporting Countries (OPEC) to increase the price of oil by a factor of two (from $17 a barrel in 1978 to $34 a barrel in 1980), in the aftermath of the Iranian revolution.

The second oil price shock, like the first, has been followed by a softening of the world price of oil, a decline in oil demand, and modest increases in non-OPEC production. In other words, 1981 and 1982 have been years of oil glut—a condition that has led to many news reports that the OPEC cartel has been broken.

The current glut may well continue, but the balance of oil power still lies with OPEC and the Persian Gulf (see table 12.1). As recently as 1982, OPEC and the Persian Gulf accounted for 47 and 28 percent, respectively, of crude oil production in non-Communist countries. Moreover, the importance of OPEC and the Persian Gulf will probably grow because they control, respectively, two-thirds and more than half of the world's proven reserves.

Hence, the outlook for oil supplies in the decades ahead is (1) constant OPEC production capacities, (2) declining oil reserves in industrialized countries, (3) at best, modest increases in oil production in the rest of the world, and (4) increasing OPEC internal consumption. The net effect is almost sure to be less oil available for the oil-importing world. In fact, the impact of the oil price increases has been

TABLE 12.1. Global patterns of production of crude oil and natural gas liquids (million barrels per day).

	1978	1979	1980	1981	1982
Persian Gulf	—	20.8	17.8	15.0	11.7
Total OPEC	29.8	30.8	27.6	23.5	19.3
Non-OPEC West	16.6	17.7	20.5	21.2	22.2
Communist countries	13.7	14.0	14.3	14.2	14.4
World totals	60.1	62.5	62.4	58.9	55.9

Source: *Petroleum Intelligence Weekly.*

mainly on the industrialized countries and on the rich in poor countries. The poor in developing countries have a long-standing energy problem of their own—they are in the grip of a fuelwood crisis. Biomass (mainly fuelwood) is the main source of energy for at least half the world's population. In the developing countries, it provides on the average about 43 percent of the total energy used, which amounts to about 14 percent of the world's total energy consumption, the equivalent of about 20 million barrels of oil per day. This is slightly more than the daily oil consumption of the United States.

In many developing countries, the fuelwood resource base is disappearing rapidly. The Food and Agriculture Organization estimates that about 100 million human beings experience "acute scarcity" of fuelwood, and about 1 billion persons, a "deficit."

The human consequences of this situation are profound: backbreaking drudgery for women and children who gather fuelwood, missed schooling by children who must contribute to this family survival task, and the inhibition of progress for women who must spend long hours procuring cooking fuel. In addition to this human suffering is the tremendous ecological damage from deforestation.

Hence, whether energy is viewed from the standpoint of the developed or developing countries, a global energy crisis exists today.

The Energy Aspect of Other Global Problems

Energy, however, is not the only global problem. The world is plagued with many others, such as North-South conflicts, the poverty of majorities in developing countries and of minorities in the industrialized countries, environmental degradation in both developed and developing countries, the possibility of world-scale climatic changes from the buildup of atmospheric carbon dioxide, global insecurity and proliferation of nuclear weapons that increase the danger of nuclear war, undernutrition and scanty food supplies, and population growth. These issues cannot be decoupled from energy problems. Attempts to implement an energy strategy inevitably affect other global crises. Indeed, their linkages with energy have major implications with regard to the design of energy strategies.

NORTH-SOUTH CONFLICTS—THE IMPORTANCE OF MEETING THE REQUIREMENTS OF DEVELOPING COUNTRIES. The North-South issues of commodity trade, the financial and monetary system for handling this trade, the control exercised by transnational corporations, and the distribution of resources are intimately related to energy problems in general and to the oil problem in particular. Oil is the leading traded commodity, accounting for about one-eighth of the world trade. The widespread use of oil has resulted in huge monetary flows, which in turn help determine the stability of the world's financial and monetary system. In the past, the oil industry was almost completely controlled by a small number of transnational corporations. The situation has changed with the increasing control exerted since the 1970s by the oil-producing countries, but even the producers have to deal largely with the corporations. Finally, against a growing realization of the rapid depletion of the world's oil resources, there is a tremendous North-South imbalance in the use of oil—the developed countries account for about 85 percent of the world's oil consumption. Thus, the oil problem is central to the North-South issue.

The oil-importing countries face special difficulties arising from the impact of oil prices on their mounting balance-of-payments problems. At present, these countries confront simultaneously huge oil import bills, low commodity prices due to a worldwide recession, and urgent developmental needs. The large increase in the debts that many oil-importing countries incurred during the 1970s to maintain economic growth has become intolerably burdensome, because real interest rates are at record high levels and world commodity markets are severely depressed. Since failure to service these debts can lead to a collapse of the global financial system, the problem has become as much a problem of the creditor as of the debtor countries.

The fundamental solution to the problem of North-South conflicts consists in accelerating the development of poor countries, but this requires that energy not be a constraint. Energy in all requisite forms and for all necessary services must be accessible to the developing countries. Since oil is a depletable resource, developing countries must move away from oil, but the transition cannot be accomplished overnight, and during the transition period, adequate oil resources are required.

Energy for Basic Human Needs in Developing Countries

An important part of the solution to the problem of poverty in developing countries is a concerted effort to meet basic human needs, including the need for productive employment, particularly among the poorest people. To fulfill these basic needs requires the deployment of resources and capital, as well as new technologies that depend on inputs of energy. Thus, the prevalence of poverty in developing countries demands that the energy required to satisfy basic human needs be provided directly and immediately.

SPREADING IMPROVEMENTS IN ENERGY EFFICIENCY TO THE POOR IN DEVELOPED COUNTRIES. Quite distinct from the absolute poverty of the masses in the poorest countries (a problem of inadequate goods and services aggravated by inequality) is relative poverty in industrialized countries, which results mainly from skewed distribution of goods and services.

In the developed countries, relative poverty is being transformed into absolute poverty by the rise in energy prices. The poor suffer more than others from increases in energy prices, because the services for which they use energy—for example, heating and transportation —are essential for survival, but they cannot make the investments needed to use energy more efficiently. The obvious remedy is the dissemination of improvements in energy efficiency in space heating, household appliances, and automobiles.

Environmental Degradation in the Developed Countries

Acid deposition in the developed countries has become a matter of public concern. It is not only a major national problem in many countries, but it is also becoming an awkward international issue because the acid rain produced by some countries is deposited on other countries.

The principal sources of acid rain are thermal power plants burning high-sulfur coal. Technical measures, such as scrubbers (flue-gas desulfurization systems), are now able to prevent 90 percent or more of the sulfur dioxide in flue gas from being released into the atmosphere. However, these measures are expensive, and therefore alternate solutions must be adopted in the long term. Fortunately, new ways of burning coal, such as fluidized-bed combustion and coal gasification, are becoming available and are capable of eliminating the acid rain problem.

The environmental aspects of nuclear power have also been the subject of intense public debate during the past two decades. Of the large number of concerns relating to this subject, there are two outstanding, but fundamentally different, issues: reactor safety and disposal of radioactive wastes.

Reactor safety is a serious problem but is amenable to technical solutions—a reactor can, in principle at least, be designed to be safe. No solution yet exists, however, for the permanent disposal of spent fuel elements and the related radioactive fission products that will remain active for thousands of years.

Environmental Degradation in the Developing Countries

The main environmental problems in developing countries are deforestation, erosion, and desertification. In each of these processes, the unsustainable exploitation of forests is a crucial factor. The direct relation between deforestation and energy is seen in the use of firewood as a cooking fuel in low-efficiency wood-stoves by more than 1.5 billion people in developing countries. Therefore, if energy strategies do not assign the highest priority to the problem of meeting the cooking-fuel needs of people in developing countries, it is inevitable that these problems will worsen.

Atmospheric Carbon Dioxide and the Importance of Minimizing Fossil Fuel Consumption

The major cause of carbon dioxide buildup is the combustion of fossil fuels. In 1978, carbon released as carbon dioxide in fossil fuel combustion amounted to about five billion tons worldwide, of which about 80 percent was due to fossil fuel use by the industrialized nations.

Considering the present mix of fossil fuels, an estimated doubling of the atmospheric carbon dioxide level could occur by 2030 if fossil fuel use grows at its present rate of 4 percent per year or by 2060 if the growth rate is cut in half. The obvious approach, therefore, is to limit the use of such fuels, particularly coal, through increased use of other energy sources and to increase the efficiency with which fossil fuels are used.

The Danger of Nuclear War and the Importance of Reducing Dependence on Oil

The immediate cause of global insecurity and the danger of nuclear war are superpower conflicts, which in turn are invariably the result of vital interests in external territories. President Reagan illustrated this when asked how the United States would respond to the closure of the Strait of Hormuz: "There [is] no way that we . . . could stand by and see that sea-lane denied to shipping, and particularly the tankers that are so essential to Japan, to our Western Allies in Europe, and to a lesser extent ourselves." Thus, the dependence on external territories for oil, currently a vital energy source, is a major source of global insecurity and a potential trigger of nuclear war.

One straightforward approach to the problem is for countries to maximize reliance on their indigenous resources and to reduce imports of materials such as oil which come from sensitive areas of the world.

Nuclear Weapons Proliferation, Alternatives to Nuclear-Generated Electricity, and a Safer Nuclear Fuel Cycle

The developing countries are, by and large, passive spectators in the debate over the vertical proliferation of nuclear arms in the weapons systems of the superpowers, but they are closely involved in the possible spread of nuclear weapons to many states that do not now have them. In principle, whatever facilitates the development of nuclear weapons is a potential source of this horizontal proliferation. Since nuclear power plants discharge enormous quantities of fissile plutonium, a material that can be used in weapons, as spent fuel, there is an indissoluble bond between nuclear-generated electricity and nuclear weapons proliferation. The international safeguards covering the operation of nuclear power plants in countries without nuclear weapons provide only a partial and transitory barrier to proliferation.

If, in the long run, nuclear power produces a significant fraction of the world's energy, safeguarding fissile material will become still more difficult, for techincal as well as political reasons. In the "once-through" fuel cycle on which civilian nuclear power is now based, weapons-grade material is never isolated from radioactive fission products. But reprocessing and recycling would for the first time give nations virtually instantaneous access to material that could be used in weapons.

Several nations are already trying to develop plutonium breeder reactors as well as reprocessing plants to separate plutonium from spent fuel. Although these new developments are concentrated in the industrialized countries, it is clear that the developing countries will eventually demand the same advanced nuclear technologies. With this ill-starred convergence, the principal technical barrier to proliferation will be shattered in developed and developing countries alike.

If the threat of nuclear weapons proliferation is to be curbed, nuclear fuel cycles that involve reprocessing (and hence, plutonium breeder reactors) must be avoided or internationally controlled. Energy strategies should therefore encourage alternatives to nuclear-generated electricity where such alternatives are feasible. Where there are no viable alternatives, policy should favor those nuclear fuel cycles that preclude reprocessing. In any case, nuclear power should be the energy source of last resort.

The Importance of Energy for the Domestic and Agricultural Sectors

Undernutrition is a grave problem even at present population levels, but by the end of this century the world may have to feed as many as two billion additional people. The prevalence of malnutrition requires a special emphasis on increasing food production and availability in the developing countries where most of the population increase will occur. The FAO study *Agriculture: Toward 2000* calls for a doubling of food production in developing countries by the year 2000. The achievement of this goal implies nearly a fivefold increase in the commercial energy needed, if, in addition to the direct energy requirements of farm machinery to prepare land and perform other agricultural operations and of irrigation pumps, the energy required to make fertilizers, pesticides, and machinery for use in food storage and preservation is included.

An increase in food production, particularly in the developing countries, is a necessary but not sufficient condition for solving the problem of undernutrition. Even if food supplies were adequate, the problem of distribution remains, and the distributional problem is related to income inequalities and the inadequate purchasing power of the poorest households. Thus, apart from increasing the production and supply of food in developing countries, many other measures are necessary. These include raising incomes through generation of employment, providing a healthy environment and supplementary nutrition, and supplying water for domestic use, cooking fuel, and efficient stoves. The energy components of these measures must be built into energy strategies.

Population Growth and the Importance of Energy for the Needs of Women, Households, and a Healthy Environment

Almost every one of the socioeconomic conditions for reducing fertility—for example, increased life expectancy, improved living conditions, education of women and children, and diversion of children away from life-support tasks and employment—depends on energy-using technologies. Reducing infant mortality depends on adequate and safe water supplies and a clean environment. Educational opportunities for girls are improved only if the drudgery of their household chores is reduced through use of efficient energy sources, cookstoves, and water supplies. The deployment of energy in industries that generate employment and income for women can help delay marriage. Availability of energy use reduces the need for child labor in crucial household tasks, an important rationale for large families is eliminated. In short, energy can contribute to a reduction in the rate of population growth if it is directed preferentially toward the needs of women, households, and a healthy environment.

The Indifference of Conventional Energy Strategies to Other Global Problems

There have been three major official studies addressing global energy problems:

- The 1977 report of the Workshop on Alternative Energy Strategies (WAES)
- The 1977 and 1983 versions of the World Energy Conference (WEC) report on world energy demand
- The 1981 Report of the Energy Systems Program Group of the International Institute for Applied Systems Analysis (IIASA).

The basic approach in these studies consists of two steps: estimating future energy demand through energy-GDP "correlations," and matching this demand with a mix of energy supplies. The mix is chosen to be compatible with estimates of the energy resources available and, in the case of new energy supply technologies, with judgments about how much energy could be produced by these supply technologies at various future dates. The WAES, WEC, and IIASA studies all envision that worldwide growth in energy demand will be slower in the future than it has been historically, that energy demand will grow much more rapidly in developing countries than in industrialized countries, and that it will grow more slowly after the turn of the century in industrialized countries. On the supply side, these energy studies envisage *a shift from energy dependence on oil to reliance on more abundant energy resources—coal and nuclear power.*

Even though these studies all envision slower energy growth in the future than in the past, they are still basically supply-oriented: the solution to the energy problem, they say, is to produce even more energy. Because the present level of global energy demand is already so high, even the slower growth envisioned in these studies implies a herculean production effort.

In view of the sixfold increase in the world oil price since 1972 and the substantial increase in other energy prices, improvements in energy efficiency must be a key part of any global strategy. Indeed, all three of the global energy studies under consideration here claim to emphasize energy efficiency. However, they hardly take account of the real opportunities for improving energy efficiency.

In addition to overestimating growth in energy demand, overemphasizing the supply aspects of the energy problem, and failing to deal adequately with opportunites for improving end-use efficiency, there is a far more serious defect in all these studies. By approaching the problem of energy primarily as a challenge to produce more energy, *they fail to consider the relationships between the energy problem and other major global problems.* Indeed they imply a future in which, even if the energy problem is solved, almost all the other major global problems will be aggravated.

The inescapable conclusion is that even if conventional global energy strategies could yield a system of energy production that is sustainable, the world of which the energy system is a part would become unsustainable. Thus, it is not enough for an energy strategy to provide a solution only to the energy problem—it must either facilitate solutions to other global problems or at the very least not aggravate them.

The imposition of this new condition upon an energy strategy implies the need for a totally different and much larger perspective for energy analyses. From this larger perspective, many apparently "perfect technical solutions" to the energy problem may have to be set aside because they aggravate one or more other global problems. Alternative energy goals, strategies, and policies are required.

FUNDAMENTAL GOALS FOR ENERGY STRATEGIES

Energy Strategies as Instruments of Development in the Third World

The crucial goal of satisfying basic human needs emerges from four global problems: mass poverty in developing countries; environmental degradation through deforestation, soil erosion, and desertification; undernutrition; and population growth. The experience of the past thirty years shows clearly that growth must not be equated with development. Far more important than the sheer magnitude of growth is its structure and content and the distribution of its benefits. Once a growth process benefiting the elite has taken place, the material output of that process (for example, processed and packaged foods, expensive cloth, luxury houses, universities, and private cars) cannot be transformed easily into growth for the masses (cheap food and cloth, low-cost housing, mass health care, education, and transportation). The scarce resources available for development can go much further in eliminating human suffering if targeted on meeting a limited set of well-defined basic human needs.

This approach has been criticized on the grounds that it conflicts with, and even inhibits, economic growth. However, cross-country multiple regression studies show a significant correlation between economic growth and basic-needs variables. In general, countries that successfully provide for basic needs tend to enjoy higher-than-average economic growth, which suggests that emphasizing basic needs can actually increase growth. Improved nutrition, health, education, and the like enhance the productivity of otherwise underfed, sickly, and illiterate workers, and thereby increase production.

If, therefore, the satisfaction of basic human needs is accepted as a direct immediate objective of development, then the provision of energy for this purpose should be assigned a high priority in energy strategies. But even if basic needs are satisfied, the quality of life is eroded unless work is meaningful and people have a voice in their destiny. The concept of development must therefore include the way in which basic needs are satisfied and emphasize social participation in decision making so that people can exercise and have confidence in their own efforts, abilities, powers, and judgment.

Emphasis on self-reliance has important energy implications. It is preferable that people have energy sources and end-use devices that they can operate, maintain, and manage themselves, rather than be at the mercy of fragile and complex systems. But this preference should not override other considerations to the point that large systems are necessarily excluded. The argument is more for indigenous sources of energy that strengthen self-reliance.

The environmental implications of energy strategies are also of crucial importance. Since development must be sustainable over the long run, the process of satisfying basic needs must not result in a society destroying its resource base and its environment. Dependence on fast depletion of exhaustible, polluting resources must be curtailed. Renewable energy sources must be given immediate and serious consideration.

It is self-evident that attempts should be made to minimize, if not avoid, those energy sources that are a potential threat to peace—imported oil and nuclear-generated electricity. Adopting this viewpoint toward development is tantamount to abandoning the notion that development goals can be met by increasing the supply of energy without scrutinizing its end uses and how society will benefit from this energy. If energy is to facilitate development, it must become a means to satisfying basic needs and to self-reliance and environmental harmony. Thus development must become the goal of energy strategies.

Economically Stable, Environmentally Safe, and Strategically Secure Industrialized Societies

The industrialized countries have been moving from energy-intensive to low-energy industries. Most of the reductions in energy expenditures have been associated with shifts from basic material processing to finishing industries accompanied by increasing automation. Structural changes and automation have reduced employment opportunities in the old materials-processing industries and have created a growing service sector. However, retraining and relocation of low-skilled workers cannot easily keep pace with changes in the structure of industry. Therefore, there is unemployment (of the order of 10 percent), concentrated in pockets originally dominated by old industries, giving rise to hardship, hunger, crime, and economic suffering.

The United States today is paying roughly twice what it was paying for energy before the oil price shocks. The technologies that are sensitive to energy prices are becoming obsolete. Enormous industrial assets have suddenly become liabilities, yet they cannot be dismantled overnight. The problem has been compounded by the instability and uncertainty of oil prices, which have made planning extremely difficult. All this has increased the importance of economic stability as a goal of developed countries.

A Sustainable World—The Goal for Global Energy Strategies

For convenience of presentation, the discussion so far has treated the developing and developed countries separately. Energy strategies in developing countries should be need-oriented, self-reliant, environmentally sound, and in the interests of world peace; in industrialized countries, economically stable, environmentally safe, and strategically secure. This does not imply, however, that these goals are independent. In fact, North-South interrelationships demonstrate the interdependence of the two goals. Further, they can be combined and unified into a global goal of *a sustainable world*. The theme of a sustainable world necessarily implies concern for all the major problems that threaten the stability of the world.

From the perspective of the goals described above, an energy strategy can be judged in terms of equity, economic efficiency, interests, self-reliance, and peace. On the basis of these criteria, there have been some dramatic energy "successes."

The Decoupling of Energy Consumption from Growth in GDP

The importance of estimating future energy demand has grown with the increase in lead times for constructing large-scale energy-generation facilities and the lengthening time scale for energy-supply investment planning. After the first oil price shock, government agencies with broad energy-planning responsibilities, such as the US Department of Energy and the OECD's International Energy Agency, began making energy forecasts using sophisticated models. Nevertheless, these models are still largely extrapolations of aggregated trends involving correlations of energy consumption, GNP, and energy prices.

Insofar as the future differs from the past, these forecasts leave much to be desired. Official projections have been continuously revised downward because energy demand is growing more slowly than previously anticipated. The most recent projections envisage energy demand levels for the year 2000 that are roughly half the levels that were projected in the mid-1970s. Moreover, projections of future electricity demand do not appear to have stabilized. Between 1974 and 1983, the projection of *Electrical World* (a utility publication) for installed generating capacity needed in the United States by 1995 went down, on average, by 56 Gw(e) each year. The point is that basic changes are taking place in the pattern of actual energy consumption in the industrialized countries.

Before the 1970s, demand for electrcity grew twice as fast as both total energy use and the economy in most countries. This rapid growth was expected to continue well into the twenty-first century. Energy planners now realize that a future with "electricity too cheap to meter" was a dream and have drastically reduced projections of future electricity demand. For instance, the most recent US Department of Energy projection of installed nuclear generating capacity in 2000 is just 130 Gw(e), or about one-tenth of the level projected in 1974 by the US Atomic Energy Commission.

As for oil, before the crises of the 1970s the industrialized countries had become increasingly dependent on imports. In 1950, in OECD countries, oil accounted for 29 percent of total energy use, of which 29 percent, or 2 million barrels per day, was imported. By 1973, the situation had changed dramatically: oil had soared to 53 percent of total energy use, of which 67 percent, or 26 million barrels per day, was imported.

The energy price increases of the 1970s have flattened the growth of net energy demand in OECD countries. On average, between 1973 and 1982, energy demand fell by 0.3 percent per year, while GDP grew by 2.1 percent per year. Between 1979 and 1982, OECD countries reduced oil use by one-sixth and oil imports by nearly 10 million barrels per day—more than the total oil consumption of oil-importing developing countries.

The changes in the pattern of energy consumption in the industrialized countries are due in part to changes in energy intensity (joules per dollar) produced by *technical* improvements in efficiency and in part to *structural* changes in the economy affecting the relative energy-using activities to the GDP. These structural changes correspond to changes in the "product-mix" in the economy (that is, its composition of goods and services). Recently, the industrialized countries have shown abundant evidence of both technical and structural changes.

The success of the industrialized countries in decoupling energy consumption from GDP shows that energy demand projections based on energy-demand correlations have to be viewed with skepticism.

Further, the decoupling compels a shift from a supply bias in energy strategies to a focus on demand, end uses, energy devices, and above all, the services that energy performs. Finally, it indicates that improvements in the quality of life in developing countries can be achieved without significant growth in energy consumption.

Improvements in the Efficiencies of Energy End-Use Technologies

The growing ability to provide tremendously improved energy services from a given level of energy input is another success of energy systems. This success is revealed by the serious discrepancies between the improvement in energy efficiency projected in the IIASA study and *what has already been achieved and implemented*. In crucial energy sectors, IIASA projected that energy efficiencies would be no better half a century hence (in 2030) than they are today, and that trends established since 1973 for improvement in energy efficiency would be sharply curtailed. But, in fact, reality has outstripped IIASA dreams.

For space heating and water heating, for instance, which together account for 80-90 percent of final energy use in the residences of North America and Western Europe, IIASA projected that by the year 2030 North American households would attain efficiency standards that have already been achieved in the average US gas-heated house of 1980. The present downward trend in energy intensity for heating can be expected to continue, because fuel use for space heating in the United States can be reduced by a factor of two or three in existing houses and by a factor of four or five in new houses through investments in insulation, storm windows, air leakage reduction, and so forth.

In developing countries, energy needs for cooking dominate residential energy budgets. Although IIASA analysts envisaged that the use of noncommercial energy for cooking would not increase, they did project that the efficiency of using this resource would increase from 7.5 percent on the average in 1975 to about 13 percent in 2030. In fact, improved fuelwood stoves already being field-tested are three to four times as efficient as those IIASA projected for use fifty years from now.

In the transportation sector, IIASA projected an increase in demand equal to 32-61 million barrels per day of oil equivalent, which is 50-100 percent of total world oil consumption in 1980. In doing so, IIASA analysts considered some improvement in energy efficiency for the automobile, which today accounts for more than 40 percent of global energy use for transportation. Average automotive fuel efficiency is expected to increase from 17 mpg in 1975 to 30 mpg by 2030.

By comparison, Brazil's efforts to shift to biomass-based ethanol fuels for automobiles have already been accompanied by marked improvement in automotive fuel economy. The alcohol cars that will be produced in Brazil in 1985 are expected to average the equivalent (on a fuel heating value basis) of 31 mpg of gasoline. In Brazil, therefore, alcohol cars have already reached the fuel economy targets IIASA analysts envisaged for industrialized nations in 2030. Moreover, automotive energy performance is capable of even more dramatic improvements—to more than 60 mpg and probably to 90 mpg.

In the IIASA analysis, industry accounts for more than half of the total increase in global energy demand over the period 1975 to 2030. The IIASA analysts expected industrial energy requirements to increase by 6-17 times in various developing regions and by 1.7-3.5 times in industrialized areas in the period 1975-2030. But, in fact, there was a 6-percent decline between 1973 and 1981 in primary energy use by industry in OECD countries, even though their GDP increased by 20 percent during that time. The problem with the IIASA analysis is that it ignores a wide range of technical opportunities for making improvements in energy efficiency.

Much can be accomplished by such simple housekeeping measures as direct metering of major energy-using sections of industrial facilities, charging energy costs to production departments instead of general overhead, using sophisticated inspection and maintenance equipment such as infrared scanners, establishing training programs in energy conservation techniques for the operation of energy-intensive equipment, and using automatic control systems for such equipment.

Since new processes are more likely to displace existing processes if they simultaneously improve several factors of production, energy requirements have often been reduced through technological innovation even during periods of declining energy prices. Thus, process innovations can improve energy efficiency to a greater extent than simply retrofitting an existing process with an energy conservation device.

There are also major opportunities for introducing new products that can accomplish the same tasks more effectively with much less energy by facilitating the recycling of materials, prolonging product life, substituting materials, and reducing product weight.

Finally, there are opportunities for introducing new energy conversion and conservation technologies, which typically yield savings on the order of 20-50 percent. Although such relative savings may not be so dramatic, the aggregate savings can be significant. The opportunities here include the use of more insulation on furnaces, radiation reflectors, heat recovery devices, induction heating of metals, microwave heating, and better mechanical drive sytems.

Perhaps the most important possibility however, is cogeneration, the combined production of electricity and heat in small-scale installations.

The Brazilian Example

Like most other developing countries, Brazil has shifted away from traditional biomass fuels and become a petroleum-based economy. In the absence of adequate domestic oil, Brazil's import bill escalated with the oil price increases despite a vigorous export drive. As heavy borrowing from abroad continued, the foreign debt climbed to more than $50 billion, and this, togther with high interest charges for debt servicing, threatened to lead the country into bankruptcy.

The extreme gravity of the situation led Brazil to reduce the consumption of petroleum derivatives by the two-pronged strategy of raising prices and producing large quantities of an alternative fuel (ethanol) from biomass sources (sugarcane), thereby replacing an imported fossil fuel with an indigenous renewable fuel.

Even before ethanol production became significant, price increases played a major role in reducing gasoline consumption between 1975 and 1979. However, the policy of "getting the prices right" had limited effectiveness. Even if the relative consumption of petroleum derivatives can be altered, pricing policies cannot by themselves reduce total consumption of oil products in a rapidly expanding economy such as Brazil's. In fact, between 1975 and 1980, petroleum consumption overall did not decrease. Only the combination of increased availability of an indigenous alternative—namely, ethanol —for one of the petroleum derivatives—namely gasoline—coupled with a change in the output of refineries could lead to this decrease in oil imports.

Although the energy content of ethanol is only about 60 percent that of gasoline, the mileage per liter of fuel decreases by only 25 percent when Brazilian automobiles are converted to hydrated ethanol (91-93 percent ethanol and water). Further, since ethanol is sold at a price that may be only 65 percent that of gasoline, a shift to ethanol results in a net benefit to the consumer of about 20 percent.

In 1975, Brazilian production of ethanol from sugarcane was only 903 million l/yr, mainly for industrial purposes. But, benefiting from government subsidies, the program picked up speed, and all gasoline used in the country was rapidly converted to "Brazilian gasohol," a mixture of up to 20 percent ethanol and 80 percent gasoline. In 1979, the Iraq-Iran war threatened Middle Eastern oil supplies, and automobile manufacturers, stimulated by the government, took the bold step of producing cars with new engines adapted for the use of pure ethanol.

In 1981, Brazilian production of ethanol reached a total of 4.08 billion liters, of which 1.88 billion were consumed as hydrated ethanol in more than 300,000 out of 8 million automobiles. The remainder of the fleet used 2.2 billion liters of anhydrous ethanol mixed with gasoline in the proportion 10-20 percent ethanol.

The cost of production of ethanol from sugarcane is approximately $58 per barrel of gasoline equivalent, taking into account both the heating values and the higher efficiency of ethanol in motors. In Brazil, one barrel of gasoline from petroleum crude (at $35 per barrel) costs approximately $52 to produce. Hence, although still subsidized, ethanol is close to becoming economically competitive.

However, the real impact of the Brazilian ethanol program is that in 1985 the value of imports is expected to be only 46 percent of that in 1979. Further, to produce the alcohol, about 300,000 direct jobs in agricultural and industrial activities will be generated in 1985 and another 100,000 indirect jobs in commerce, services, and government.

The first lesson from the Brazilian strategy worth emulating in most developing countries is that indigenous renewable biomass resources can be used to produce liquid fuels for the transportation sector, thereby reducing oil imports. The second lesson is that a developing country can, acting on its own, establish in a short period a major industry as the basis of a modern renewable resource strategy for the transition away from petroleum.

Energy Strategies

By analogy with an ecological system, in which every species has a niche, in an energy system too, it is likely that each renewable energy source will find the niche for which it is best suited. Energy strategies that include the goals of environmental soundness and long-term interests must necessarily emphasize renewable sources of energy and identify these niches.

Energy demand and supply problems are usually dealt with separately, and important relationships among energy-using activities are ignored. Yet, armed with a detailed understanding of energy end uses in different economic sectors, analysts can often identify opportunities for "synergisms." For example, cogeneration can simultaneously address consumer needs for heat and electricity and provide a more viable basis for electric utility planning than the present independent approach to these problems.

The benefit of an end-use approach to energy analysis is that it extends to the generation and supply of energy too. The goal is to identify economical ways of providing specific energy services with smaller and more efficient energy inputs, since it is usually cheaper to save energy than to generate it. These potential savings are overlooked in most conventional energy strategies, which focus on supply.

Lowering energy demand widens supply options. Many energy sources incapable of meeting large demands can meet demands that are scaled down through synergism and increased efficiency. In particular, direct solar energy, wind, biomass, and other renewable energy sources can seldom compete widely with fossil fuels when energy demands are high, but they become competitive when supply targets are scaled down. In addition the larger the number of competitive energy sources, the easier it is to do without those that aggravate other global problems.

National Policy Instruments

Many analysts believe free markets will lead to the most efficient allocation of energy resources, but direct and indirect subsidies for particular energy sources, suppliers, and consumers mean that the prices consumers see do not reflect the costs of additional energy supplies. Also, consumer energy investment decisions are made on the basis of short-term considerations. Indeed, lack of awareness about the opportunities for making improvements in energy efficiency and about longer-term considerations obstructs rational decision making, and consumers sorely need better information on energy conservation. Hence, governments often resort to administrative allocation of energy carriers, capital, and technology.

Many governments also rely on subsidies to influence the market. Some governments give more favorable tax treatment or other direct subsidies (including loan guarantees and loans at below-market rates) to oil and gas producers, electric and gas utilities, and other energy supply industries than to other industries. The energy supply industry generally argues that without special incentives, it cannot guarantee that enough oil will be drilled or power plants built. But generating new energy supplies is not the only way to provide needed energy services. In fact, investments in energy efficiency are often more cost-effective. Producer subsidies hold energy prices below costs, and they attract to the energy supply industries much scarce capital that would be better invested in energy efficiency and other activities.

In most developing countries, the price of kerosene ("poor people's oil") is kept well below the equivalent world price so that the poor can afford it. However, the price of diesel fuel, which kerosene can replace in trucks, must then also be kept low; thus truck freight is subsidized and expands rapidly at the expense of rail freight. As a result, the nation's oil import bill rises and, with it, the need for foreign exchange to pay for the extra oil.

Another subsidy that insulates selected consumers from true costs is the electricity rate structure that gives enormous discounts to large-volume consumers, such as the primary aluminum industry. In this case too, major economic inefficiencies can arise, since energy-intensive industries are excessively encourraged.

Taxes and duties have become effective policy instruments for reducing energy consumption. However, the use of the revenues that thereby accrue to the government poses a problem. If they are used as general revenues and added to the common pool, the dislocations and inequities that they cause are ignored, and the resulting price increases are borne disproportionately by the poor. This problem can be avoided, however, if users' rebates are given in ways that are not directly related to consumption. Revenues might be used, for example, to help finance investment in improved energy productivity, with priority given to the poor and to energy-intensive industries.

The regulation of performance is particularly attractive to energy planners because it appears to reduce uncertainty about future use. There have been regulatory success stories, such as the 1975 US law mandating that auto-producers double their corporate average automobile fuel economies by 1985. In practice, however, regulations can be applied only to a limited set of energy-using activities, and they tend to be weak stimuli for promoting technological innovation. In general, regulations are best suited for energy-using activities that can be characterized by an energy performance index that is easily measurable, readily understood, and widely applicable and for problems that defy alternative solution.

One such problem is the landlord-tenant impasse. Because neither party has sufficient incentive to invest in energy efficiency, prescriptive standards may be required to promote cost-effective energy strategies for renter-occupied buildings.

Another regulatory device is to modify the charters of publicly regulated energy suppliers, which typically originated in an era of supply obsession. These charters can be enlarged to require utilities to give equal attention to consumption and supply, thus forcing them to deal with energy end uses and conservation.

Concrete policies have to be initiated in developing countries to meet basic human needs. Energy supplies should be channeled toward end uses related to food, shelter, clothing, health, education, transportation, communication, and so on. Among these end uses, special emphasis must be placed upon cooking, lighting, and the supply of sufficient and safe water for domestic purposes. Specific policies must also be implemented to provide energy services for the poor, women, and other underprivileged groups.

The suffering of the poor has often been given as a reason to keep energy prices low. However, instead of relying on inefficient price controls to protect the poor, it is far preferable to complement an economically efficient pricing system with ambitious programs specifically targeted at meeting the needs of the poor. One way to help protect them from the burden of energy taxes would be to shape the tax so that it is not regressive. In the case of a gasoline tax, for example, even in the United States, where the automobile is ubiquitous, rebating the revenues from such a tax on a per adult basis would result in a net gain by poor people since they are less dependent on the automobile than average Americans. Alternatively, energy tax revenues might be used to offset a regressive existing tax, such as the social security tax, or energy tax revenues might be used to help the poor to invest in energy efficiency.

In the United States, only modest federal assistance is provided to help the poor pay their fuel bills or winterize their homes. Far more aggressive programs may be necessary. Although assistance in paying fuel bills is needed to reduce short-term suffering, the greatest need is subsidies for investments to reduce fuel bills—especially for space heating. Large one-time investment subsidies to the poor are more economically efficient than fuel bill subsidies, and they avoid the demoralizing aspects of continuing dependence on fuel assistance programs.

In most countries, electricity is produced by monopolies and sold at average cost. New electricity supplies are generated from coal or nuclear thermal power plants, and costs are considerably higher than present electricity prices. When expensive new power plants are brought into operation, consumers rarely see these higher costs in their utility bills because they are averaged together with the costs of older, much cheaper sources of electricity. Accordingly, consumers tend to use far more electricity than they would if prices were based on marginal costs.

A policy aimed at bringing energy prices in line with marginal costs would be an important step toward making markets work better than they do. It would also make the government's task of dealing with inherent market failures much easier by reducing unnecessary intervention.

Among the many effective instruments for improving energy pricing policies, two that merit emphasis are an elimination of subsidies to energy producers and a move toward marginal cost prices in markets regulated by government. These policies should not be carried out in isolation but in conjunction with complementary measures to address problems that the original policies were intended to solve and the dislocations and inequities that might be created by a shift to marginal cost pricing.

In developing countries, for example, removing subsidies on prices of kerosene and diesel fuel would adversely affect the poor and must be done only in conjunction with policies that would provide alternatives to kerosene for lighting and cooking (rural electrification for lighting, and improved fuelwood or charcoal stoves and biogas or producer gas for cooking). The excess revenues from sales of kerosene and diesel fuel might be used to help finance the implementation of these complementary policies.

Investments in new energy supplies are made by a few large energy companies only, but numerous consumers invest in energy efficiency improvements in buildings, transportation, and industry. In making these investments, the consumer would behave rationally if he chose the option with the least total life-cycle cost, where costs and benefits are discounted at the consumer's market rate of interest. In practice, this is not what happens. The discount rates implicit in actual consumer purchases that involve energy efficiency choices are far in excess of market interest rates, often by as much as several hundred percent.

There are many reasons why the discount rates used by consumers are so high. Often consumers are inadequately informed about the opportunities for energy savings and the cost-effectiveness of investments in energy efficiency, and often the opportunities also entail effort. Many individual and business consumers must forgo energy efficiency investments because capital is scarce, especially in developing countries. For some important uses in automobiles and buildings (which constitute significant fractions of society's energy consumption), expenditures on energy are such a small fraction of the total cost of the activity that consumers are indifferent to energy efficiency. Those who invest in or implement energy efficiency improvements, such as a building developer or landlord, are often not those for whom the energy-saving benefits are intended—the home-buyer or the tenant. Moreover, powerful interests have actively discouraged investment in promising alternative energy technologies such as cogeneration. Even though the most promising cogeneration technologies are those that involve the production of much more electricity than is produced at industrial sites, the export of electricity to the utility grid is discouraged by utilities in most countries. Finally, uncertainty about energy prices discourages long-term investment in energy efficiency.

Since the high implicit discount rates are caused by so many factors, what is required is the coordination of numerous policies to remove the obstacles consumers face and to close the gap between the interests of society and those of individuals in energy decisions.

Crucial among these policies is that of facilitating fair competition in the marketplace between investments in energy efficiency improvement and investments in energy supply, by providing targeted subsidies, regulating energy performance information, creating a more stable energy price environment, making capital more readily available, promoting the development of an energy service industry, and improving the flow of information. It is best to use subsidies only when the costs can clearly be justified and workable alternatives are not available. A good example of such a subsidy is a rebate that might be offered by a utility to consumers who purchase household appliances that are more energy-efficient than the average units being sold, with the rebate increasing in proportion to the expected energy savings. To the extent that such rebates allow the deferral of more costly new supplies, the consumer, the utility, and its other rate-payers would all benefit. A growing number of utilities in the United States offer such rebates.

Regulations that improve the flow of information regarding energy performance can be highly effective if the consumer can use the information easily and readily. In the United States, the appliance efficiency labeling program that went into effect in 1980 requires that all refrigerators, freezers, water heaters, dishwashers, clothes washers, and room air conditioners carry labels designating the expected yearly cost of operating them and the range of energy costs for all similar appliances. More recently, there has been considerable interest in requiring energy labels for new and existing buildings. For owner-occupied buildings, the labels could be affixed at the time of sale, and for rental properties, perhaps at the time of rental. Many parties, including the prospective buyer or tenant, would benefit. The seller or landlord would be better able to capture the value of investments in energy efficiency and would thus be more willing to make them, and builders would be better motivated to offer energy-efficient housing designs.

To provide investors with relatively unambiguous energy price signals, it is desirable to replace the zigzag oil price variations created by the natural fluctuation of the world oil market with consumer oil prices that increase slowly and smoothly as oil supplies approach depletion. This might be accomplished by an oil tax or oil import tariff that varies with world oil market conditions and is rebated to consumers directly or indirectly.

In countries that are major carbon dioxide polluters, special policies must be implemented to reduce fossil fuel consumption and to support international agreements for limiting the buildup of carbon dioxide. In countries that are major sources of acid deposition, stringent policies to cut down emissions from fossil fuel-burning power plants may include enacting mandatory emission standards, taxing emissions, encouraging the installation of scrubbers or flue-gas desulfurization systems, and facilitating the adoption of alternative coal-combustion technologies such as fluidized-bed combustion and coal gasification.

The problems of nuclear reactor safety and wastes argue for policies that will ensure the safety of nuclear power, and the problem of nuclear weapons proliferation suggests policies that will limit the expansion of nuclear power and discourage reprocessing. A policy of nuclear power as an energy source of the last resort would be consistent with these objectives. Such a policy would also ensure the interests of countries that have difficulty finding alternatives to nuclear power.

Developing countries are significantly dependent on biomass sources but use them with notoriously inefficient technologies. There are promising new biomass conversion technologies that offer striking improvements in efficiency. Promotion of these technologies would have to be sustained by research and development.

Energy policies that emphasize both supply and demand cannot be implemented unless there is a firm data base with detailed information on energy needs, end uses, and the resource potential of biomass and other energy sources. Hence, governments should generate and maintain such a data base.

Although major improvements in energy productivity can be made with available technologies, further improvement could be realized through appropriate research and development. Energy-efficient end-use technology is still at the start of its learning curve, much as thermal electricity-generating technology was at the turn of the century. Similarly, renewable energy technology, especially for the production of fluid fuels and electricity, is at an early stage of development. Hence it is crucial to formulate and implement policies to support research and development in many areas of potentially high payoff. The introduction of new energy-efficient technologies may prove easier in the developing countries, which do not have the problems that industrialized countries face in dismantling energy-inefficient technologies.

It is doubtful whether energy strategies focused on end uses can be carried out without intimate knowledge of the locale, detailed information on the socioeconomic factors associated with consumer demand for end-use technologies, and sustained commitment to formulate, implement, and see through energy solutions. Developing countries should be encouraged to acquire, largely through manpower training, capabilities for energy-related research and development, assessment, analysis, and planning. If this capability is to be sustained, then energy-related insitutions in developing countries must also be strengthened.

Energy conservation is so crucial that it should be highlighted by special policies. For rapid diffusion of energy-saving techologies, it is essential that complete packages be assembled, including hardware and software, whether for improved fuelwood stoves for villages in developing countries or for home insulation in industrialized countries. The development of these packages must constitute an important component of conservation policies.

Decentralized energy sources may prove more economical than centralized sources, particularly in scattered and remote villages in developing countries. Promoting these decentralized sources may require alterations in present laws, which often restrict electric utilities from providing other energy sources and which preclude agencies other than utility companies from generating electricity. Similarly, removing the legal obstacles that in many countries prevent the export of surplus electricity from cogeneration systems to electric utilities would encourage investment in cogeneration.

Promoting Energy Service Industries

It is easy for a consumer to purchase an energy carrier such as oil or electricity. A reliable system exists for making such transactions, the quantities exchanged are easy to measure, and both supplier and consumer understand the values of the commodities involved. This is not the case with investments in energy savings. Unlike conventional energy purchases, opportunities must be analyzed, and contracting and financing are complicated operations for the consumer.

New industries that market energy services in much the same way as energy companies today market energy carriers and supplies could markedly simplify consumers' decisions. Electric and gas utilities could easily market conservation technologies and services. Already, a number of the more progressive utilities have initiated energy conservation services that include advising on investments in energy efficiency, arranging for contractors to carry out such work, financing such investments with low- or zero-interest loans, providing rebates to consumers for the purchase of energy-efficient appliances, and so forth. It may be desirable to expand such efforts and convert utilities from purveyors of fuel and electricity to vendors of energy services because utilities, unlike the customers they serve, would be forced by this role to make investment choices between the expansion of energy supply and the improvement of energy efficiency. Accustomed to accumulating large quantities of capital, utilities would be in a good position to devote resources to energy efficiency investments. Moreover, the utility billing system offers the opportunity for customers to pay "life-cycle-cost bills" as an alternative to fuel or electricity bills: they could receive loans from the utility and pay them off through their utility bills.

Instead of requiring a utility to establish energy efficiency programs, regulators might consider rewarding the utility for cost-effective improvements in energy efficiency. One promising approach would be for the public utility commission to allow the utility to treat program costs as operating expenses and grant financial rewards for realized energy savings.

Making utilities responsible for vending energy services is even more important in developing countries. Investments in energy efficiency are often less capital-intensive than investments in the equivalent amount of new energy supply. Thus, capital-poor developing countries would be able to conserve scarce capital resources if utilities were able to provide energy services.

In some areas, utilities will be unable or unwilling to create needed energy conservation programs. Electric or gas utilities, for example, may not wish to offer a retrofit service for oil heated homes. In such circumstances, government energy policies could stimulate the creation of a new energy service industry that would market energy efficiency improvements by making loans or grants available to customers of service firms.

Promotion of energy sevices industries needs to be extended from the utility/industry level to the level of state and national governments. Governments are notoriously supply-oriented in energy matters, and they invariably prefer to assign the responsibility for supplying specific energy sources to particular ministries, departments, or agencies. The supply orientation and the fragmentation of responsibility for energy services prevent the identification and implementation of the most economically efficient technologies and measures that require coordinated action. It must therefore become a policy to set up interministerial/departmental/agency task forces for various energy services.

International Energy Policies

The global energy goal of a sustainable world can be jeopardized by national energy policies narrowly conceived to meet only short-term national goals. Conversely, national policies can be strengthened by international support. Efforts to cooperate on an international oil policy aimed at reducing the vulnerability of oil-importing nations to disruptions in supply, making oil more affordable to developing countries, and stabilizing oil prices would benefit all the countries concerned. Similarly, the work of international institutions devoted to the technical aspects of global cooperation in energy conservation would yield benefits for all.

However, many of the proposals for international energy cooperation are intended only to avoid negative-sum games in which all participants lose. International energy policies to reduce global insecurity, degradation of the environment, risks of major climatic change, and excessively rapid depletion of nonrenewable resources are all examples.

Although there are good reasons to continue the work started in recent years to reduce the use of oil, investments in energy efficiency and supply alternatives are discouraged by uncertainties about future energy prices. The onset of an oil glut following each oil price shock gives the misleading impression to investors that the oil crisis is over. It encourages increased consumption and thus sets the world on a course leading to still another shock. Moreover, the glut periods, which have extended over most of the last decade, have diminished the sense of urgency that is needed to induce oil-importers to reduce their long-run vulnerability to disruptions in supply. To create a stable investment climate for alternative energy sources, potential investors should be able to plan on future oil prices that remain constant in real terms or rise slowly over time.

Vulnerability to oil supply disruptions can be reduced by keeping oil demand low relative to global productive capacity and by increasing substitutability among energy sources in importing countries. Reducing oil demand would reduce payments for oil imports both because less oil would be imported and because the world oil market price would decrease. Oil-importing developing countries would probably benefit most from reduced oil import bills.

Most of the instruments of this policy have to be wielded at the national level, but there may be a need for supportive international policies. It may well be desirable for oil-importing countries to engage in cooperative efforts to reduce their demand for oil, perhaps under the terms of an international oil price agreement. A single country might be hesitant to tax the use of oil by its own industry, thus making it less competitive, unless other countries did the same. But each country participating in a cooperative agreement would benefit from every other country's efforts, since the world market price of oil is likely to go down in the face of reduced demands from each country. Also, a consensus on targets for reduction in demand may not only facilitate energy planning in these countries but also help in planning investments in oil production in the oil-exporting countries.

Limiting the Buildup of Atmospheric Carbon Dioxide

To prevent global climatic changes due to the buildup of carbon dioxide in the atmosphere, it is not necessary to eliminate carbon dioxide emissions. For instance, all the known reserves of oil and gas and some coal may be consumed without producing serious global climatic changes. Using coal and heavy oils last would yield the largest amount of energy at any given level of carbon dioxide emissions.

Although oil and gas resources are spread over the world, coal and heavy oil resources are concentrated in relatively few countries. Ninety-eight percent of the geological resources and 29 percent of the technically and economically recoverable reserves are located in only ten countries—the USSR, the United States, China, Australia, Canada, the Federal Republic of Germany, Poland, Great Britain, India, and South Africa—and the first three of these have 83 percent of the totals.

The few countries that control the world's coal production thus control the carbon dioxide problem. These countries should evaluate the potentially large climatic effects of continued high levels of fossil fuel use and limit fossil fuel combustion. International agreements on consumer coal prices and coal trade might be useful to avoid potentially disruptive effects on industrial competitiveness.

Denuclearizing the World

The main institutional deterrent today to nuclear weapons proliferation is the Non-Proliferation Treaty (NPT), which several states have not signed, however, and which does not even forbid the activities that will bring signatories ever closer to a nuclear weapons capability. The countries most closely allied to the United States and the USSR appear to have accepted the two-cast system underlying the NPT, in which the world is formally divided into weapon and nonweapon states. But many of the countries that have not signed the NPT—for example, Argentina, Brazil, India, Iran, Israel, Pakistan, South Africa, South Korea, Taiwan, and Yugoslavia—have a reasonable technological basis for nuclear energy and, in all likelihood, could build nuclear weapons if they so desired.

The groundwork for reprocessing and recycling plutonium in the industrialized countries has already created a demand for these technologies in Argentina, Brazil, Pakistan, South Korea, Taiwan, and several countries that have joined the NPT. Indeed, it is precisely the ambiguous character of the plutonium fuel cycle technologies that allows states to move toward a weapons capability without having to announce or decide their ultimate intentions in advance. This "latent proliferation" undermines the effectiveness of present nuclear safeguards, because the NPT permits the development of all types of civilian nuclear power "without discrimination." Indeed, in Article IV, parties to the treaty undertake to facilitate the "fullest possible" exchange of equipment, materials, and information for the peaceful uses of nuclear energy.

Plutonium in spent fuel is well surrounded by radiation and can be separated only through reprocessing. One reason for reprocessing is to develop breeder reactors (which require plutonium) to make efficient use of uranium. Another is that reprocessing is required for storage of nuclear wastes. Neither reason stands up to critical analysis, however. The nuclear power systems in the world will not be constrained for at least fifty years by limits on supplies of uranium, and it appears to be no less cumbersome to dispose of high-level waste than to dispose of spent fuel elements.

An important step toward reducing the risk of proliferation would be to avoid reprocessing spent fuel. This constraint on nonnuclear countries, whether they have signed the NPT or not, would be acceptable only if the nuclear weapons states accepted parallel obligations, certainly on their civilian power programs but probably on their weapons programs as well. The issues of horizontal and vertical proliferation of nuclear weapons are intimately linked. A global agreement on the part of civlian power programs to avoid reprocessing spent fuel may require an agreement by the nuclear weapons states not to reprocess spent fuel to produce plutonium for weapons. Such an agreement would not only require nonnuclear states to accept the present restrictions imposed on them by the NPT, as well as additional contraints on reprocessing, but it would also require nuclear states to make their programs conform to the strictest international safeguards.

Strengthening National Energy-Related Capability

Because of the scarcity of economic resources, the inadequacy of technical manpower, and lack of appropriate institutional infrastructure for energy-related activities, most developing countries have relied on international aid from bilateral sources, UN agencies and, especially, the World Bank. Energy supply has clearly dominated all energy aid programs, and among the various supply options, more than 90 percent of the investments have been for large electricity generation, transmission, and distribution systems. Fossil fuel exploration has accounted for about 5 percent of energy aid, new and renewable energy sources for about 3 percent, and conservation efforts in the industrial sector and other measures to limit demand for less than 1 percent.

It is unclear how much aid is needed to implement the energy strategies suggested in this paper, but many appropriate technologies have relatively modest "front-end" costs. These technologies include improved cooking stoves, biogas plants, producer gas generators and engines, biomass-fired gas turbine cogeneration systems, wood-to-methanol plants, more efficient light bulbs, and direct-injection stratified-charge engines for motor vehicles.

International aid should promote development through energy analysis and planning, selection and implementation of energy technologies, and establishment of the associated technical capability and institutional infrastructure. Such a policy would involve shifting the emphasis from project to program support, building and strengthening energy-related indigenous institutions and technical capability, and supporting "technological leapfrogging" efforts.

Project aid may be appropriate for large energy-supply plants but is inadequate for promoting diverse, small-scale technologies tailored to regional and local conditions. Accordingly, it is desirable to reorient aid from specific projects to broad programs in which the detailed allocation of resources is largely the responsibility of a capable, locally based institution acting in accord with overall program objectives. This requires building and strengthening relevant institutions. Although a time-consuming and often frustrating task, the long-term payoffs are enormous.

Indigenous technical capability can be strengthened by stipulating that foreign consultants be recruited only when capable local services are unavailable. Even then, local groups should be included in the work. Aid must also be available for spending in the recipient countries so that it can help build local technical capability.

Energy Demand

What changes in global energy demand are implied by the policies proposed in this paper? If recent experience in Sweden and the United States is extrapolated, energy demand for the industrialized world can be projected. Since widespread adoption of highly energy-efficient technologies is both technically and economically feasible, it is reasonable to expect that, despite a major increase in the consumption of goods and services, a 50-percent reduction from 4.9 to 2.5 kw per capita final energy use could be achieved in all industrialized countries by 2020.

Current energy demand is vastly different for the three-quarters of humanity who live in developing countries and account for only one-third of world energy use. At present, per capita final energy use averages about 0.9 kw, of which 0.4 kw is noncommercial energy consumed at about 10-percent efficiency by the two-thirds of the population that live in isolated rural areas. Basic human needs in developing countries could be satisfied and living standards raised dramatically with essentially the current per capita level of energy use through exploitation in all sectors of the enormous opportunities to improve energy efficiency. Per capita energy of the order of 1 kw is the amount required to meet basic human needs with today's energy technology and is close to IIASA and WEC projections, but that amount would provide amenities far beyond those required to meet basic needs if efficiency were increased.

What are the global implications of this projected energy demand? Although global population would nearly double in this period (increasing from 4.4 to 7.8 billion), global energy demand would increase only slightly, from 8.4 TW in 1980 to 8.8 TW in 2020. What is envisaged is a much more rapid per capita GDP growth in the developing countries than in the industrialized countries. In addition, energy demand would decrease at 1.4 percent per year in the North and increase at 1.7 percent per year in the South, tending to a convergence in energy amenities that does not emerge from any other global energy strategies.

If energy demand should evolve in this manner, it would not be necessary to rely heavily on coal or nuclear power as oil and gas production peak and eventually go into decline. Solar technologies and especially wind, hydropower, and biomass could play a small but significant role in meeting additional energy demands and in substituting for fossil fuels as the process of phasing out the latter begins. But such an energy future depends on greater end-use efficiency.

By contrast, at the higher demand growth rates projected on the basis of past experience, the world would be forced to adopt environmentally risky energy sources. Mahatma Gandhi would have understood clearly the desirability of pursuing the end-use approach to energy, for he said, "The earth has enough for every man's need, but not for every man's greed."

REFERENCES

Choucri, N., with D. S. Ross and the collaboration of B. Pollins. 1981. *International Energy Futures: Petroleum Prices, Power and Payment.* Cambridge, Mass.: Massachusetts Institute of Technology Press.

Darmstadter, J. 1971. *Energy in the World Economy: A Statistical Review of Trends in Output, Trade and Consumption Since 1925.* Baltimore: Johns Hopkins University.

Despairies, P. "Report on Oil Resources, 1985–2020." Included in the Executive Summary of the Tenth World Energy Conference held in London in 1977.

US Department of Energy, Energy Information Administration. 1982. *Residential Energy Consumption Survey: Housing Characteristics, 1980.* Washington, D.C.: US Department of Energy.

FAO. 1981. *Agriculture Toward 2000.* Rome: FAO.

Haffele, W., and the IIASA. 1981. *Energy in a Finite World.* Cambridge, Mass.: Ballinger.

Hall, D. O., *et al.* 1982. *Biomass for Energy in the Developing Countries.* Oxford: Pergamon Press.

Hoffman, T., and B. Johnson. 1981. *The World Energy Triangle.* Cambridge, Mass.: Ballinger.

Landsberg, H., and J. Dukert. 1981. *High Energy Costs—Uneven, Unfair, Unavoidable?* Washington, D.C.: Resources for the Future.

Ross, M. and R. Williams. 1981. *Our Energy: Regaining Control.* New York: McGraw-Hill.

Salant, S. 1982. *Imperfect Competition in the World Oil Market.* Lexington, Mass.: Lexington Books.

United Nations. 1979. *World Energy Supplies 1973–1978.* New York: United Nations.

———. 1979. *Yearbook of International Trade Statistics.* New York: United Nations. See esp. pp. 1076–1123.

US Congress, Office of Technology Assessment. 1980. *Energy from Biological Processes.* Washington, D.C: Office of Technology Assessment.

World Energy Conference. 1978. *The Future of World Natural Gas Supply.* United Kingdom: IPC Press.

CHAPTER THIRTEEN

Future Changes in the Atmosphere

STEPHEN H. SCHNEIDER and
STARLEY L. THOMPSON

GLOBAL ATMOSPHERIC POLLUTION

The Extent of the Problem

This paper examines three international atmospheric pollution issues
—stratospheric ozone changes, acid rain, and the carbon dioxide
"greenhouse effect." The problems differ in geographic scale and in
details but share certain causes, effects, and possible policy responses.

The first section of the paper discusses the depletion of
stratospheric ozone. The buring of fuel by high-flying supersonic
transport (SST) aircraft and the release of chlorofluorocarbons (CFCs)
into the atmosphere cause certain chemical compounds to reach the
upper atmosphere, compounds which have been implicated in the depletion and vertical redistribution of stratospheric ozone. Ozone is
important to life on earth because it filters out biologically harmful ultraviolet radiation and because the earth's climate is influenced by the
amount and distribution of ozone.

From the point of view of policy analysis, the ozone problem is of
special interest because it marks the first occurrence of a truly anticipatory response to a potential global environmental issue. Policies
that have already been implemented in several nations in partial response to the ozone problem include restrictions on the use of CFCs as

propellants in aerosol spray cans and the refusal of the US Congress in 1971 to allow further development of a large fleet of ssts to compete with the Anglo-French Concorde.

Release of oxides of nitrogen and sulfur that result from human activities, largely the combustion of fossil fuel, contributes to acid deposition (commonly called acid rain), to be discussed in the third section. Policy responses to this problem are currently being formulated and debated.

Increasing carbon dioxide and other man-made trace gases, mainly from fossil fuel burning and some land-use practices, increase the greenhouse effect, which is discussed in the fourth section of this paper. The climatic implications of this trend may necessitate a hierarchy of individual, business, national, and international policy responses because the problem is global. The fact that future carbon dioxide increases will depend on fossil fuel use means that the associated climatic problem is fundamentally part of the global debate on the distribution and growth of population and resource use. Moreover, from a policy perspective, the greenhouse effect is largely a problem of the future, because it is just now becoming widely known and its largest impacts will not be felt until the twenty-first century.

Each of the three atmospheric problems is global in some sense. Ozone changes would be global in effect, although perhaps not in cause—for example, ozone reduction from fleets of military ssts. Acid rain is regional and often transnational in effect but occurs in more than one region of the globe and thus is of global interest. The increase in atmospheric carbon dioxide is truly a global problem in that both cause and effect are global in extent.

Lessons from Natural Climatic Variability

Interest in long-term atmospheric changes induced by human activities sometimes leads to our overlooking the fact that natural variability of climate on much shorter time scales must also be considered in assessing the influence of climate on society. Average, or mean, conditions are not nearly a sufficient representation of the role climate plays in environmental and human affairs. Biological systems are strongly affected by extremes in weather and climate; thus, the character of climatic variability has an important effect on both plant and animal, including human, communities.

Obvious examples of damage from natural climatic variability in the United States include the following. In the winter of 1977, drought in the West and extreme cold in the East created economic disruptions estimated to have cost billions of dollars. In the hot summer of 1980, the elderly, poor, and infirm in the South Central states suffered abnormally high rates of mortality and morbidity; in addition, yields of summer crops such as corn and soybeans were greatly reduced. There has been no thorough analysis of benefits and losses from such climate fluctuations.

Possible policy measures to minimize our vulnerability to anthropogenic climatic changes and to take advantage of new climatic resources should be guided by experience with natural climatic fluctuations. Moreover, atmospheric impact assessment for the purpose of dealing with long-term problems usually involves an extrapolation of experience with the shorter-term effects of natural variability. But such experience suggests that population size and the distribution and availability of resources mediate the effects of natural climatic variability on society, regardless of the long-term climatic trends. Thus, it is necessary to project how both climatic and societal factors will evolve and interact.

Day-to-day variability is an important atmospheric factor, because society and the living environment respond nonlinearly to such variations. Freezing point, for example, is a threshold below which small changes may have major effects on vegetation. Similarly, above certain temperatures, plant, animal, and human vitality can be seriously threatened. Since present-day climatic variability could well be superimposed on long-term climatic trends, one of the most significant effects of a seemingly small shift in the "mean" climate could be a large change in the frequency of harmful extreme situations. The section on the greenhouse effect examines this possibility in the context of carbon dioxide warming.

Policymaking

The process of making policy to deal with global atmospheric probles can be considered in three, albeit overlapping, stages:

1. During technical analysis, scientific facts and other relevant information are assembled and analyzed. Technical analysis attempts to cover a range of probabilities and consequences of each problem so as to put subsequent policymaking on a firmer scientific basis. Such analysis is sometimes clouded by the tendency for partisan groups to quote facts out of context.

2. An effort is then made to examine scientifically the differential consequences of possible policies. A few such analyses will be mentioned in the context of the three atmospheric problems.
3. Then there is the action stage, which, of course, depends on value judgments. This paper surveys a number of policy options for the environmental problems that are explored.

All three stages are discussed, with major emphasis on the first. Although the final section enumerates many policy options, it includes few specific legislative and regulatory actions.

THE OZONE PROBLEM

Reduction of Stratospheric Ozone

The destruction of stratospheric ozone by the injection of anthropogenic gases into the atmosphere was a pioneering environmental issue for several reasons. First, it awakened people to the potential for human alteration of the envirnment on a global scale. Second, the public debate was punctuated by conflicting technical testimony and proposed policy responses. Third, for the first time there was an anticipatory problem—that is, a response was made before the effects could be observed unequivocally. The ozone problem therefore raised issues pertinent to other global environmental problems. For this reason, it is instructive to review the history of the ozone problem, in terms of both scientific and policymaking experience.

There is little doubt that removal of the earth's ozone shield would be a biological catastrophe, but there is much less consensus on the biological effects of merely reducing the amount of ozone in that shield. Studies of the effects of the biologically damaging component of solar ultraviolet radiation (UV-B) on plant and animal life have not been extensive, and, for obvious reasons, no direct experiments involving human beings can be performed. Thus, determination of health effects for human beings must rely on statistical studies (for example, using persons who are occupationally exposed to large amounts of UV-B) and inferences drawn from animal tests. Despite these limitations, enough is known about the biological effects of UV-B to cause concern, since even the small ozone reductions predicted by atmospheric chemists as a result of chlorofluorcarbons emissions (2-20 percent) could pose substantially increased health risks.

Another potentially serious environmental effect of ozone changes is altered climate. Ozone, like carbon dioxide, is a gas that has a substantial influence on the energy balance of the planet. Even redistribution of ozone concentration with altitude, a probable effect of certain anthropogenic trace-gas emissions, would probably have an effect on global climate.

Anthropogenic Destruction of Ozone

Simple so-called Chapman chemistry successfully predicts the existence and approximate vertical distribution of ozone in the atmosphere, but the actual amounts predicted are much too large. Thus, it became apparent that one or more natural trace substances in the stratosphere must be aiding the destruction of ozone. The first hypothesized candidates were oxides of hydrogen formed from water vapor. Through repeated reactions, a single molecule of hydrogen oxide can destroy many molecules of ozone. This multiplier effect of catalytic ozone-destroying chemical reactions is the principal reason why seemingly minuscule amounts of harmful gases can have a substantial impact on the ozone layer.

In 1970, it was realized that hydrogen oxide generated from water vapor emissions of the proposed fleet of high-altitude SSTs could pose a threat to the ozone layer. Concern about the potential damage from such emissions was quickly superseded, however, when Paul Crutzen and Harold Johnston discovered independently that oxides of nitrogen in the stratosphere can also destroy ozone catalytically.

The possible destruction of ozone by nitrogen oxide emissions from SSTs played a role in halting US development of the aircraft in the early 1970s, although economic considerations were probably the crucial factor. The absence of a planned US fleet of civilian SSTs has, at least temporarily, reduced the SST nitrogen oxide-ozone question to one of mainly academic interest. However, the publicity accorded the SST issue provided an important scientific and political warm-up for an even larger controversy: the impact of chloroflurocarbons on ozone.

In 1974, Mario Molina and F. S. Rowland published a landmark paper in which they theorized that CFCs used as propellants in aerosol spray cans could reach the stratosphere, release chlorine, and destroy ozone. Furthermore, they noted that CFCs (sometimes referred to by DuPont's trade name Freon) were being released at an increasing rate

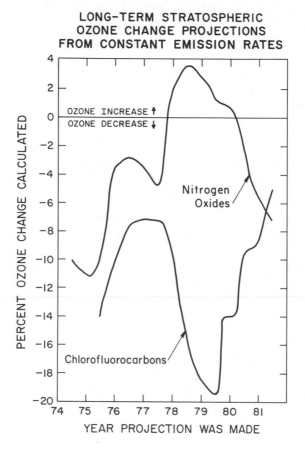

FIGURE 13.1. Long-term projections of stratospheric ozone change, based on constant emission rates provide an example of how complex, poorly understood processes can significantly affect the predictions of a mathematical model of man-made environmental changes. This graph shows stratospheric ozone changes estimates from a series of models developed to predict the effects in the next century of steady-state emissions of both CFCs and nitrogen oxides from a hypothetical fleet of SSTs. The calculations were made over a number of years at Lawrence Livermore National Laboratory. *Source: Schneider and Londer, 1984.*

and could, by their estimates, eventually destroy 20 percent of the ozone layer.

A fundamental problem in estimating ozone depletion by CFCs has been the lack of clear natural experiments. The complete chemistry is impossible to simulate adequately in the laboratory and is unprecedented in nature. Thus, estimates are made using computer models to simulate the reactions believed to be important in determining ozone concentration. Over the past decade, the incorporation in typical models of reactions involving new compounds and revised reaction rates has resulted in the fluctuating theoretical estimates of long-term ozone depletion shown in figure 13.1. The uncertainties inherent in the theory of ozone depletion have created exemplary conditions for policymaking.

Ozone Policy Experience: Determining Scientific Validity

A fundamental influence on the course of public scientific debate on an environmental issue is the determination of which side has the burden of proving its case. In the debate over ozone depletion, the question is whether CFC emissions should be banned until industry can prove that they are not harmful, or whether they should be allowed until it can be shown that they do indeed destroy ozone?

It was industry's position that CFCs should be presumed harmless until proved otherwise. However, invocation of the assertion "innocent until proven guilty" is not necessarily justified in this case. A fundamental principle in justice is that the consequences of a catastrophic error in judgment should be minimized. The values of our society typically dictate that "innocent until proven guilty" is the appropriate way of implementing this principle for criminal trials. With regard to the possible destruction of atmospheric ozone by CFCs, however, regulatory officials placed the burden of proof on industry. Thus, throughout the debate, most industry scientists and spokesmen were on the defensive. Clearly, governmental officials had decided that more harm could come from not regulating CFCs than from regulating them unnecessarily. (And the extent to which stratospheric ozone will be altered by CFC emissions is still not clear.) This decision was a value judgment that required the regulators, first, to understand the concept of marginality and, second, to separate known facts from implicit values.

Ozone Policy Experience: Making Value Judgments

The primary uses of CFCs are as propellants in aerosol spray cans and as working fluids in refrigeration systems. Because many uses are hardly frivolous and are difficult to supplant (especially in refrigeration), it would have been absurd to make policy solely on the basis of the potential risks to the ozone layer. The job of the regulators was to determine the acceptability of the risk of CFCs, using risk estimates supplied by experts, and, if the risks were not acceptable, to decide what emissions standards to impose. The decision-making process involved the weighing of marginal risks and benefits. The question was whether the incremental (or marginal) increase in individual or social benefits from allowing unabated CFC emission outweighed the potential incremental decrease in social benefit from depleting the ozone layer.

In 1973, spray cans (mostly for cosmetic uses) accounted for about 75 percent of all CFC emissions in the United States. Determining the value of the CFC-using spray-can industry at that time was problematical, but industry estimates placed the worth at nearly $3 billion. (Even this probably inflated figure is smaller than the value of the industries involved in acid rain disputes and is virtually insignificant in relation to the worldwide fossil fuel industry implicated in increasing atmospheric carbon dioxide.) Furthermore, the use of aerosol spray cans for cosmetics was regarded by the US public as a luxury rather than a necessity, especially since substitute propellants and other means of dispensing the contents of the cans were readily available. The combination of feasibility of regulating a major portion of emissions, limited economic dislocation, and public willingness to accept reductions in CFC emissions were important factors influencing the eventual regulatory decision. As stated in 1976 by Alexander Schmidt of the Food and Drug Administration (quoted in Dotto and Schiff, 1978), "It's a simple case of negligible benefit measured against possible catastrophic risk both for individual citizens and for society. Our course of action seems clear beyond doubt."

In 1976, many interested people, particularly those on congressional committees and in regulatory agencies, were awaiting the report of the National Academy of Sciences' Committee on Impacts of Stratospheric Change (CISC). The importance that the report had come to assume had grown over time as policymakers had essentially passed the buck by claiming that they must wait for the definitive statement of the National Academy of Sciences before making any decisions. The Federal Task Force on Inadvertent Modification of the Stratosphere had released a report the previous year (IMOS, 1975) stating that there was "legitimate cause for concern," and that regulatory actions should be started if the Academy committee report confirmed the IMOS assessment.

On account of some well-publicized uncertainties, publication of the CISC report was delayed, which served to heighten interest. The confusion had also made the Academy committee, consisting of thirteen physical scientists, more cautious than ever—it did not want to be burned by unforeseen scientific developments. As a result, the CISC report (NRC, 1976), while strongly endorsing the hypothesis that CFC emissions would deplete the ozone layer, included a recommendation "against decision to regulate at this time." Instead the committee recommended allowing up to two years to complete studies aimed at reducing uncertainties in the ozone depletion theory.

What the Academy committee disregarded was the difficult position in which its recommendation would place regulatory agencies. Since the regulatory process can be lengthy (on the order of several years), a delay of two years before even starting the process could have resulted in a regulatory delay much longer than the committee anticipated. Furthermore, industry invoked the prestige of the Academy to imply that there was no need for emissions controls in the interim. Russell Peterson, chairman of the President's Council on Environmental Quality at the time, complained that the Academy committee should be not have tried to assume the role of policymaker; it should have stuck to the scientific issues and left the value judgments to others. The recommendation of the CISC report is just one well-known example of the need for experts to avoid mixing facts and values, a pitfall that is common when dealing with complex technical issues.

Ozone Policy Experience: Regulatory Control

The initial phase of US emissions controls prohibiting nonessential uses of CFCs in aerosol cans was jointly announced in 1977 by the Environmental Protection Agency, the Food and Drug Administration, and the Consumer Product Safety Commission. This action marked the first time a substance suspected of causing global harm had been regulated before the effects had been demonstrated. (The earlier ban on atmospheric testing of nuclear weapons was implemented well after widespread contamination from radioactive fallout had ocurred.) Thus, a precedent was set that could prove important when similar issues (for example, carbon dioxide) are considered.

By late 1982, about twenty countries, including all major CFC-producing nations, had taken actions to control CFC emissions. In an analysis of the responses by Sweden, the United States, the Netherlands, West Germany, the United Kingdom, and France, Downing and Kates concluded that the factors most conducive to regulatory action were pro-environmental public attitudes, the presence of a strong regulatory authority, and the limited influence of CFC production on the national economy. Sweden and the United States, the nations having the strongest emissions controls, best satisfied the above conditions.

Probably as a result of the initial regulatory action, the CFC-ozone problem has faded from public view, at least in the United States. However, despite the precedent-setting regulations, by 1979 world production of CFCs had dropped by only 20 percent from its all-time high in 1974 (UNEP, 1981); and increased nonaerosol uses of CFCs will soon balance the production drop caused by decreased aerosol uses. There has been a movement toward international consensus that the ozone layer should be protected from human modification (for example, a proposed Global Framework Convention for Protection of the Ozone Layer is being considered under the auspices of UNEP). However, movement toward regulating global CFC emissions has not been rapid, particularly considering the relatively small global economic stake in CFCs compared to that in energy production and use. If the CFC-ozone problem is any indicator, it will be extremely difficult to achieve substantial international action to reduce carbon dioxide emissions.

ACID RAIN

The problem of acid rain differs from the problem of stratospheric ozone depletion in that (1) acid rain is regional (but also transnational), (2) it occurs in broad geographical areas, (3) there is a much greater uncertainty associated with the atmospheric transport of the precursor pollutants, (4) there is strong empirical evidence of serious environmental effects, and (5) the generation of the precursor pollutants is fundamental to the present global economic structure.

The report of increasing acidity of precipitation in the eastern United States between 1955 and 1972 essentially marked the first recognition of acid rain as a visible environmental issue in this country (Cogbill and Likens, 1972). In the past decade, data have confirmed that precipitation is substantially more acidic in the eastern United States than elsewhere in the country (figure 13.2a). This observation, coupled with the fact that the areas of highest rainfall acidity tend to lie over and downwind from the major suspected sources of pollution (figure 13.2b), has been taken as prima facie evidence of cause and effect.

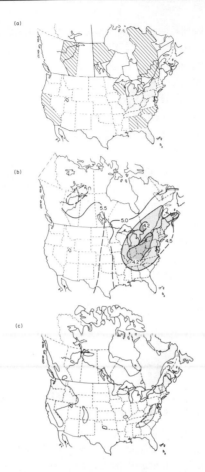

FIGURE 13.2. (a) Annual mean value of pH in precipitation weighted by the amount of precipitation in the United States and Canada for 1980. (b) Representative values of annual sulfur dioxide emissions in the United States and Canada in 1980. States and provinces emitting more than 800,000 mt are stippled; regions emitting more than 400,000 mt are hatched. (c) Regions of North America with a low geochemical capacity for neutralizing acid deposition. *Source:* NRC, 1983.

Causes

To follow the technical arguments in this debate in even cursory fashion requires some background on the causes of what is loosely referred to as acid rain. The degree of acidity of aqueous solutions is commonly measured on the pH scale. Because this scale is logarithmic, a change of one unit represents a tenfold increase or decrease in acidity. Distilled water, which is taken to be neutral, is assigned a pH value of 7. Acidity increases with decreasing pH; thus, acidic vinegar has a pH of 2.4, and alkaline solutions have pH values larger than 7. Rainwater tends naturally to be somewhat acidic from the carbon dioxide that dissolves in it to form a weak carbonic acid solution. The normal acidity of precipitation is often assumed to be 5.6 as a result.

Strong acids like sulfuric and nitric acids also occur naturally in precipitation. These acids can be created by the reaction of natural pollutants such as sulfur dioxide and hydrogen sulfide (from volcanoes) or oxides of nitrogen (generated by lightning) with atmospheric water. The commonly used term *acid rain* is actually a misnomer, however, because deposition of strong acids at the surface by *both* wet processes (precipitation) and dry processes (direct deposition) are important.

The acidity of precipitation and surface waters is also affected by the chemical composition of both atmospheric dust and the underlying bedrock. Alkaline dust in the air can act to increase the pH of precipitation, and the buffering capacity of soils and bedrock can act to neutralize the acidity of runoff into streams and lakes. Areas of North America thought to be particularly sensitive to acid rain (that is, having a low buffering capacity) are shown in figure 13.2c. Considering the natural sources of variability in rainfall acidity, it is perhaps not surprising that measured values of pH even in so-called pristine areas vary considerably—for example, in a remote spot in Hawaii, measured pH values ranged from 4.0 to 6.3, a substantial spread around the benchmark value of 5.6 (Siebel and Semonin, 1981).

The precursor pollutants contributing to acid rain are also generated by human activities. Power plants and smelters, for example, emit sulfur dioxide, while oxides of nitrogen are generated by internal-combustion engines as well as power plants. Although widespread public awareness of the acid deposition problem is fairly recent, the recognition of sulfur dioxide and nitrogen oxide emissions as undesirable is not. These gases are just two of the four main pollutants known to be important determinants of local air quality. Addition of volatile organic compounds (VOCs) and fine particulate matter (FPM) rounds out what Rhodes and Middleton (1983b) have termed the "gang of four" air pollutants (figure 13.3). Acid rain is just the latest in a continuing series of environmental insults deriving from the so-called gang. However, the fact that acid deposition is cumulative makes it fundamentally different from air quality problems in which the occurrence of transient pollutants is of most concern.

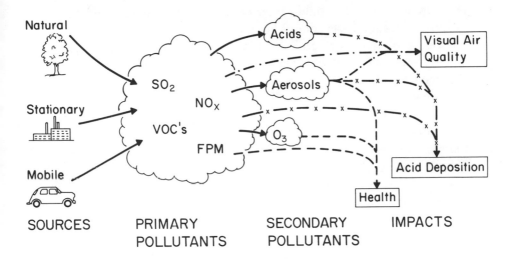

FIGURE 13.3. The "gang of four" primary air pollutants—their sources, chemical reaction products (secondary pollutants), and environmental impacts. *Source:* Rhodes and Middleton, 1983b.

The problem of acid deposition is clearly linked to older, more familiar forms of air pollution and their attendant control strategies. One of the ironies of pollution control is that, in the effort to meet stricter local air quality standards, taller smokestacks were built so that pollutants could be ejected at higher altitudes, from whence they could be more readily dispersed and transported away. But such long-range transport of pollution is one of the critical issues in the acid rain debate.

Ideally we would like to know for any given acid deposition site (the receptor) the relative fraction of acid deriving from each precursor source. This knowledge would be of great aid to policymakers wishing to implement the most efficient and economical emissions controls or mitigation strategies. Unfortunately, detailed understanding of relationships between sources and receptors is going to require more elaborate computer modeling of meteorology and chemistry than is yet possible. It may be possible, however, to use elemental "signatures" of pollutants to establish source-receptor relationships empirically (Rahn and Lowenthal, 1984). A recent National Academy of Sciences report (NRC, 1983) supports the hypothesis that reductions in precursor emissions over the entire eastern United States would result in linearly proportionate decreases in acid deposition over the same large area. However, reliable predictions about reducing acid deposition over smaller areas cannot be made at this time.

Some of the most obvious effects of acid deposition occur in aquatic ecosystems. The direct effects on fish in lakes have been well publicized and can be severe. Sensitive species of fish are affected at pH levels of less than 6; and the lower limit for the survival of most fish is around 5. Depletion of fish populations occurs over a range of pH values, depending on local conditions. In particular, it is known that acid leaching of aluminum from soils plays a fundamental role in fish deaths. The synergistic effect of a combination of aluminum poisoning and acidity is particularly harmful to fish at a pH of about 5. Moreover, the average pH of runoff does not tell the entire story of potential harm. Acid shock, a surge of low-pH runoff, occurs when high-acidity snow melts in the spring. Amphibians that use snowmelt pools for breeding can be devastated by such shock.

Acid deposition on terrestrial ecosystems can damage both vegetation and microorganisms. Aluminum leaching in soils can kill rootlets, thus stunting plant growth. Removal of nutrients by leaching and direct damage to foliage are other potential consequences of acid rain. Soil bacteria generally do not thrive in acidic environments. This is not a trivial consideration, because microbial decomposition is a crucial element in the flow of nutrients through the food chain.

The ways in which acid deposition can affect human health (other than effects due to local precursor pollutants) include potential metal poisoning from two sources (CEC, 1983): corrosion of lead and copper plumbing, and accumulation of mercury and cadmium in the aquatic food chain. Appropriate water treatment, particularly in centralized water distribution systems, can precipitate most of the harmful metals from drinking water.

A noteworthy policymaking concern is the question of irreversibility. The acid rain review panel appointed by the White House Office of Science and Technology Policy found that some effects may be irreversible—that is, the environment would take longer than one human generation to return to its original state once acid deposition was stopped. Of course, the corrosion of materials in buildings, statues, and metal structures is, left to itself, irreversible, since all remedies require human intervention.

Policy Arguments

Policy options for dealing with acid rain include more study, control of emissions, and mitigation of effects. Emissions control proposals have concentrated on dealing with the sulfur dioxide emitted by coal-burning power plants. Available techniques include the scrubbing of flue gas to remove this substance, washing coal to limit its generation, and switching to coal with a lower sulfur content. However, the contribution of nitrogen oxide emissions to acid deposition, thought to be about 30 percent in precipitation in the US Northeast, should not be ignored when developing emissions control policies. Controlling emissions of nitrogen oxide may be more difficult than controlling those of sulfur dioxide because, first, the former are not as localized as the latter—about half of US anthropogenic nitrogen oxide emissions derive from mobile sources (Rhodes and Middleton, 1983a)—and second, control technologies are not as well developed.

The only significant potential environmental countermeasure relies on distributing buffering material in area susceptible to acid deposition, a processed called *liming*. But the difficulty of doing this over large areas and the uncertain environmental effects of the liming operation itself limit the feasibility of this technique as a general strategy for dealing with acid rain.

All the options considered so far are expensive, although the question of who would bear the expense depends on the control strategy chosen. For example:

- The costs of scrubbing or washing coal would be expensive for electric utilities and rate-payers.
- Switching power plants to low-sulfur coal would be expensive for those regions and companies that mine high-sulfur coal.
- Costs of further limiting nitrogen oxide emissions from automobiles would probably be passed on to consumers.

Cogent risk-benefit analyses will be helpful in choosing an optimum suite of control tactics, but present technical uncertainties in all phases of the problem of acid deposition limit the utility of such analyses.

THE CARBON DIOXIDE GREENHOUSE EFFECT

Characteristics of the Carbon Dioxide Problem

It has long been known that carbon dioxide released by burning fossil fuel has the potential to generate a global warming by means of the greenhouse effect. Despite its potential environmental and societal significance, however, the prospect of carbon dioxide-induced climate change has generated little sense of crisis, primarily because the problem evolves slowly, albeit inexorably. Added to this are the many technical uncertainties surrounding both the causes and the implications of a carbon dioxide buildup. Thus, few people argue for immediate action other than further basic research.

The buildup of carbon dioxide in the atmosphere is the global-scale environmental problem most inextricably bound to present cultural and economic practices and plans for development. This is particularly true for Third World nations; their plans for economic development are so tied to future use of fossil fuels that any talk of restraint in fossil fuel burning is inherently divisive. Thus, dealing with the prospect of carbon dioxide increases is difficult and will require unprecedented degrees of international cooperation. In essence, the problem is part of a larger debate encompassing world population, resources, and economic equity.

The carbon dioxide level at Mauna Loa Observatory has been recorded for more than two decades and shows some 9-percent increase during that time. Although several large computer models of the earth's climate system which allow complex simulations of global climatic effects of carbon dioxide and other trace gases, differ by about a factor of two in their prediction of global average temperature increases, the problem has basically withstood the scientific test of time. No fatal flaws have been found in the basic arguments associating carbon dioxide buildup with increasing surface temperature despite intense study in many nations.

From an intellectual point of view, the problem is most interesting because it is in some respects the prototypical global environmental issue, for the following reasons:

- It is long-lasting—essentially irreversible on century time scales—and hence intergenerational.
- It has both perceived winners and losers.
- It is fraught with technical uncertainties.
- It can be proved to everyone's satisfaction only by "performing the experiment" on the real climatic system.

Components of the Carbon Dioxide Problem

For the purposes of discussion, it is helpful to break down the carbon dioxide-climate-society problem into a series of stages, each feeding into another, and then consider the principal issues associated with each stage.

BEHAVIORAL ASSUMPTIONS. At the very foundation of the problem are the behavioral assumptions that must be made in order to project future use of fossil fuels (or deforestation). The essence of the issue, then, is not chemistry or physics or biology, but social science. The amount of carbon dioxide that will be injected into the atmosphere over the next several decades is not precisely knowable. It depends upon projections of human population, the per capita consumpion of fossil fuel, deforestation and reforestation activities, and even countermeasures to remove carbon dioxide from the air. These projections depend on issues such as the likelihood that alternative energy systems or conservation measures will be available, their price, and their social acceptability. Furthermore, trade in fuel carbon (for example, a large-scale transfer of coal from coal-rich to coal-poor nations) will depend not only on energy requirements and available alternatives but also on the economic health of the potential importing nations. This, in turn, will depend on whether those nations are self-sufficient in food and have adequate capital resources.

Some analysts believe that energy end-use efficiency driven by economic necessity will virtually limit carbon dioxide increases to no more than about 50 percent or their present values. Figure 13.4 shows an example of alternative futures based on various assumed rates of growth in the use of fossil fuels.

THE CARBON CYCLE. Study of the interacting biogeochemical cycles that control the global distribution and stocks of carbon determines an important number, the airborne fraction. This is simply the fraction of carbon dioxide that remains in the atmosphere some given length of time after injection. Considering the contribution of fossil fuels only over the past twenty-five years, then the amount of carbon dioxide that must have been released into the air over this period is roughly twice that which has been observed in the atmosphere. This suggests an airborne fraction of about 50 percent, with oceanic sinks accounting for the other half. Nevertheless, primarily because of inadequate knowledge regarding biological sources of carbon, the cycle is not fully understood, and there is still considerable uncertainty over what the airborne fraction has been and will be. In particular, it is not known whether the airborne fraction will change with changing climate.

Finally, increasing the amount of carbon dioxide in the air enhances photosynthesis, which makes most plants grow faster. This

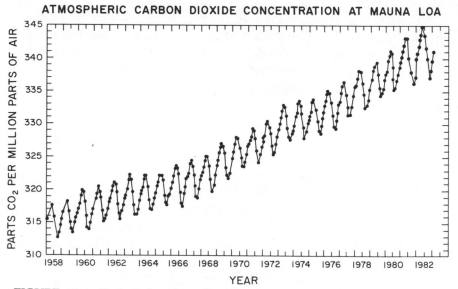

FIGURE 13.4. Projected carbon dioxide concentrations for different annual growth rates in fossil energy use, including the assumption that no increase in fossil energy use occurs (constant 1975 emission) and even a negative growth scenario in which annual energy growth after 1985 is assumed to be reduced by a fixed amouunt (0.2 TW, about 2 percent of present demand) each year. *Source* (negative growth line only): Lovins *et al.*, 1982.

would not only remove carbon dioxide from the atmosphere more rapidly than at present but might increase the overall productivity of the biosphere—with both positive and negative consequences, depending on the species and on the altered competitive balance of ecosystems.

GLOBAL CLIMATIC RESPONSE. After projection of the amount of carbon dioxide in the atmosphere, it is necessary to turn to either empirical methods or computer models to estimate potential climatic effects. This amounts to modeling the greenhouse effect, which is essentially the process by which the atmosphere allows solar radiation to penetrate to the earth's surface faster than it allows infrared radiation to escape from the surface and the atmosphere into space. In the earth's atmosphere, it works not so much by trapping radiation emitted from the surface as by reradiating infrared radiation in significant amounts downward to the surface, thereby causing a warming.

Heating of the surface leads to more evaporation of water, and water vapor contributes even more to the greenhouse effect than carbon dioxide. Thus, there is a strong positive feedback between increasing temperature and increasing water vapor in the atmosphere.

This feedback effect will significantly amplify the surface-temperature response caused initially by an increase in carbon dioxide. Many other climatic feedback processes (for example, the change in surface solar energy absorptivity as a function of snow cover and changes in cloud height and amount) must be considered when estimating the surface-temperature response to a carbon dioxide increase. It takes complex mathematical models to produce meaningful estimates of the climatic effects of an increase in carbon dioxide, simply because we have no unambiguous historical evidence for simultaneous increases in carbon dioxide and temperature.

The temperature of the earth's surface over the past hundred years has been estimated from thermometer and other instrumental data or proxy records. The data suggest a global warming of some 0.5°C from 1880 to about 1950, a cooling of about half that magnitude in the high latitudes of the Northern Hemisphere during the 1950s and 1960s, and a substantial rewarming during the 1970s. (Even these estimates of global temperature trends are uncertain to a few tenths of a degree centigrade, largely because data from remote land and oceanic areas is missing.) Thus, on average, the period from 1950 to 1980 was about 0.5°C warmer than the period from 1870 to 1900. This is consistent with predictions made on the basis of models for the consequences of a carbon dioxide increase of some 20 percent, the amount believed to have occurred over this time span.

Most global climatic models agree with a factor of about two both among themselves and with empirical data, but is this conclusive evidence that the carbon dioxide signal is in the climate records? Certainly it is strong circumstantial evidence, but whether it is conclusive depends upon one's criterion for acceptable evidence.

Terrestrial climate models are not completely invalid. For example, the most complex climate models, general circulation models, are able to reproduce with reasonable fidelity the largest climatic signal that has been observed since the Ice Ages: the annual cycle of the seasons. The fact that climate models can successfully simulate such a climate change certainly strengthens the arguments of those who believe that a global carbon dioxide-induced warming is already present in the system and that it will become even more obvious over the next two decades.

REGIONAL CLIMATIC RESPONSE. To estimate the societal importance of climatic changes, we need information about regional details and the evolving patterns of climatic change. Unfortunately, predicting regional responses of variables such as temperature and rainfall to carbon dioxide buildup requires climate models of greater complexity—and expense—than are needed to make globally averaged or equilibrium predictions. Some of the few models that have been used in dealing with this problem suggest that the following coherent regional features could occur:

- Wetter subtropical monsoonal rain belts
- Longer growing seasons in high latitudes
- Wetter springtimes in high and mid-altitudes
- Dry midsummer conditions in some mid- and high-latitude regions, a potential problem for future agriculture in some developed nations.

It must be stressed that considerable uncertainty remains, particularly since the regional effects inferred from models so far have been obtained on the basis of fixed increases in carbon dioxide—usually a doubling or quadrupling. What is needed is not a steady-state equilibrium response, but a response in which the smoothly varying increase in carbon dioxide over time is used to produce a time-varying set of regional climatic anomalies. It is quite possible that such a response will differ from that produced by present equilibrium models.

PHYSICAL IMPACT OF CARBON DIOXIDE-RELATED CLIMATE CHANGE. Given some scenario or set of scenarios for regional climatic change, we can estimate the physical impacts on environment and society. Most important are the direct and indirect effects on crop yields. Next is the potential for altering the range or population sizes of pests or disease sources that affect plant, animal, or human health. Also of interest are the effects on unmanaged ecosystems, in which both climatic change and direct influences of an increase in carbon dioxide on photosynthesis could alter productivity and species distribution.

Sea level could be altered, perhaps by some five meters over a 100- to 200-year period if there were a deglaciation in western Antarctica. Indeed, simply warming the oceans will cause the upper layers to expand, just as warming a thermometer causes fluid to expand up the tube. Roger Revelle's estimates (NCR, 1982, p. 433) of ocean expansion and the melting of small mountain glaciers in the mid-altitudes as a result of carbon dioxide warming suggest the possibility of a 0.5-1.0-m rise in sea level over the next 50-100 years. Recent evidence suggests that there has been a rise in sea level of about 0.1 m from the 0.5°C warming over the past century.

Increased evaporation over land could lead to decreased soil moisture, although increased oceanic evaporation would certainly increase precipitation on a global scale, but not necessarily locally. Soil moisture would undoubtedly change, but whether this would be for better or for worse, and where and when the change would occur, are still subject to speculation.

Temperature increases themselves can be serious, particularly if they occur in the warm months in already heat-stressed climates. It is important to examine extremes of temperature because the likelihood of extremes can increase greatly with a shift in mean temperature. Although little attention has been given to the issue of the increasing probability of extreme temperatures, this may prove to be one of the most important effects of carbon dioxide warming on biological systems, including humans.

Economic, Social, and Political Impacts. Estimation of the distribution of economic winners and losers, given a scenario of climatic change, involves more than simply looking at total dollars lost and gained. It also requires looking at the important equity questions of who wins and who loses, and how the losers can be compensated and the winners taxed. For example, if the Corn Belt in the United States were to move north by several hundred kilometers, then a billion dollars a year lost in Iowa could well be Minnesota's gain. Moreover, even the perception that the economic activities of one nation could create climatic changes that would be detrimental to another has the potential for disrupting international relations. In essence, carbon dioxide-induced environmental changes create a problem of redistributive justice.

Policy Responses. The last stage in dealing with the carbon dioxide-climate problem concerns the question of policy response. The appropriate response will depend not only on scientific information about both the probabilities and conseqences of physical, biological, and social impacts; it will also depend on the value judgments of individuals, groups, corporations, and nations as to how to deal with the potential distribution of gains and losses implied by carbon dioxide buildup. These issues are discussed further in the final section of this paper.

POLICY ISSUES

Relationships Among Atmospheric Problems

There are both fundamental commonalities and differences among the three problems discussed, namely, stratospheric ozone depletion, acid rain, and carbon dioxide-induced effects on climate. These pertain to geographic scale, fossil fuel dependence, uncertainties in risk assessment, and politico-economic inertia.

GEOGRAPHIC SCALE. The effects both of changes in stratospheric ozone and carbon dioxide increase are truly global in scale, whereas acid deposition effects are at present regional, although transnational. Expanded national and international development in the future, with concomitant increases in energy demand, will tend to increase the areas affected by acid rain in both size and number.

FOSSIL FUEL DEPENDENCE. Both acid rain and carbon dioxide buildup are directly related to the use of fossil fuels. The increase in fossil fuel burning that would be implied in a doubling of carbon dioxide in the atmosphere by the middle of the next century would greatly increase acid deposition as well, unless strong emissions controls are adopted.

The following are two examples of links between carbon dioxide and acid rain. First, synthetic fuels generated from coal can be given a low sulfur content as a by-product of the synthesis process, but more carbon dioxide per unit of available energy is released to the atmosphere by synfuels because of the energy penalty required to make them. Second, fundamental thermodynamic principles impose an efficiency penalty on low-temperature combustion techniques designed to minimize nitrogen oxide production. Furthermore, coal, the most abundant fossil fuel, produces two to four times as much nitrogen oxide per unit energy as fuel oil or natural gas. On the other hand, conservation and use of nonfossil energy sources generally alleviate both the acid rain and the carbon dioxide problems, quite possibly at least cost and least risk.

UNCERTAINTIES IN RISK ASSESSMENT. Risk is classically defined as the probability times the consequences of some event. With all these problems, assessments of such probabilities and their environmental and societal consequences are made difficult by large uncertainties associated with both the complexity of the natural environment and our limited ability to predict societal change.

- For acid rain, observations can be made to verify aspects of certain theories. However, the luxury of unambiguous empirical verification of CFC and carbon dioxide effects is not yet available to atmospheric chemists and climatologists, who must therefore

work with limited historical data and speculative projections of future releases of CFCs and carbon dioxide.
- Natural ecological and climatological systems include complex nonlinear thresholds that make predictions of impacts unreliable.
- The societal impacts of gradual environmental changes depend strongly on how society evolves. Therefore, scenarios of climatic impact assessment need to predict changes in both societal and environmental variables simultaneously. This limits the utility of specific risk-benefit methods applied to long-term atmosphere pollution problems.

POLITICO-ECONOMIC INERTIA. The acid rain and carbon dioxide problems in particular are inextricably caught up in the present fossil fuel-oriented global economy. Several features of society will make it difficult to deal with these problems that have time scales of decades or longer. The length of political cycles (for example, terms of office) largely determines which problems receive most governmental attention. This is characteristic of both market and centrally planned economies. In addition, the long-term planning and investments needed to address global environmental problems are hindered by the tendency to plan for the short term in an effort to maximize the short-term return on investments. In fact, since long-term environmental costs are hard to quantify, we often act as if they were zero.

Responses to Atmospheric Problems

These fundamental relationships among the global atmospheric issues affect the ways in which they can be dealt with as environmental problems. Three basic strategies are mitigation, adaptation, and prevention.

MITIGATION. The purpose of mitigating strategies is not to control pollution emissions but to control the consequences of emissions by some compensatory antidotal technique.

The various predictions shown in figure 13.1 indicate the complexity of the chemistry involved in estimating depletion of stratospheric ozone. It is irresponsible at this time to consider strategies that attempt to counteract ozone depletion through the addition of one or more other substances to the atmosphere. There simply is too much uncertainty.

In general, the technique of liming areas that suffer from acid rain reverses the environmental effects of acid deposition. The efficacy of liming depends on local conditions, such as water in lakes and streams having long residence times, and the ability to cover a large fraction of the runoff area with the liming agent. High-volume streamflow in spring and lakes with a high turnover rate are difficult to treat. Liming on a large scale is thus not a feasible response to acid deposition for both practical and environmental reasons. However, it can be used to defend some sensitive areas until adaptive or preventive strategies can be brought into play.

Several proposals have been made for reducing the amount of carbon dioxide in the free atmosphere as a means of moderating the greenhouse effect. Pumping the carbon dioxide produced at industrial plants into the deep ocean, as proposed by Marchetti (1977), would reduce and delay the rise of carbon dioxide in the atmosphere, but it would not prevent an eventual warming as some of it made its way back into the atmosphere. Reforestation as a form of carbon bank would also capture carbon from the atmosphere, but decay of the harvested trees would have to be prevented, by burial, for example, to avoid rereleasing carbon dioxide to the atmosphere. Furthermore, vegetational carbon banks would have to compete with other agriculture for land and nutrient resources.

Proposals for actually counteracting the global greenhouse effect must rely on extensive geoengineering. Russian climatologist M. Budyko has suggested that airplanes flying in the stratosphere could release aerosol particles that would reflect away part of the solar energy normally absorbed by earth, thus neutralizing a global warming trend. This could work, at least on a global-average basis, but the actual mechanisms of warming and cooling would be spatially and temporally different, implying that large regional climatic changes could still occur.

There are two major problems associated with environmental mitigation strategies: first, gaps in knowledge of environmental behavior may result in cures that are worse than the illnesses they are intended to combat, and second, anything that goes wrong may be blamed on the mitigation strategies. Considering this and the fact that it would be irresponsible to attempt mitigation on a global scale without at least some form of "insurance" for potential losers, it is doubtful that geoengineering strategies could be viable.

ADAPTATION. Adaptive strategies seek to adjust society to environmental changes without attempting to mitigate or prevent the changes. There are many different techniques of adaptation to changing environmental conditions on all geographic scales.

During the ozone debates of the 1970s, it was argued by industry supporters that living with reduced ozone protection from UV-B would simply be equivalent to moving a short distance toward the equator. This, of course, ignored the point that moving toward the tropics is a voluntarily assumed risk, whereas being forced to live with an ozone reduction is not. The concept of informed consent holds that individuals should be informed of, and be allowed to decline, risks to which they might be exposed for someone else's gain. Moving is clearly not a viable adaptation option for most people. Effective ultraviolet-blocking chemicals available over the counter can be applied to the skin, but even now they are not used heavily enough despite the high rates of skin cancer among susceptible people at low latitudes (for example, white Australians). Moreover, adaptive strategies designed for animals and plants are unavailable.

Adapting ecosystems to acid deposition will be difficult. In agriculture, it might be possible to use or develop more tolerant species, but native species would have to adapt on their own. Corrosion-resistant materials (for example, plastic pipes) could be used in new applications, but old materials (for example, marble used in buidings) would take a long time to replace, even if replacement were desirable.

One way of adapting to acid deposition would be by financially compensating "losers" (of both environmental and economic resources) to help them adjust to a degraded situation. (This use of compensation differs in intent from the compensation derived from penalty taxes. Such taxation would, in addition to providing funds that could compensate people harmed by acid deposition, also serve to reduce emissions and thus promote prevention.) However, without detailed knowledge of the relationships between sources and receptors, trying to make the individual polluting "winners" pay the "losers" would be divisive in itself. It is possible that a compensation fund supported by regional to national taxes or penalties could be a viable way of implementing compensation strategies.

Those who think that they are being injured by acid rain caused by someone else's pollution will not remain silent, witness the current debate both within and between the United States and Canada. Indeed, harsh words continue to pass between the United States and Canada regarding what should be done about transnational acid deposition. If prevention does not become a primary goal, then perhaps some form of compensation of the perceived losers might be used to moderate the political divisiveness of the problem.

An analogy for dealing with adaptations to carbon dioxide-induced climatic change is the experience of responding to the effects of natural climatic variablity on food-producing and food-distributing systems. Strategies, listed in Schneider and Londer, 1984, ch. 11, are as follows:

- Beware of generalizing from short-term records. Estimates of the likelihood or severity of climatic extremes should be based on as long a term as possible to maximize statistical reliability.
- Build diversity to provide stability. Maintaining diverse food, water, and energy sources is obviously a good hedge against large fluctuations in supplies. Development of diversity in crop strains can minimize vulnerablity to extreme climatic events or pest outbreaks.
- Improve genetic resources. Developing and testing a number of genetic varieties that can deal with a range of climatic, nutritional, or other conditions is an important component of crop diversity, which is essential to sustainable food production.
- Match agricultural practices to crop-climate timetables. Careful matching of irrigation, fertilization, and pest controls to the growth stages of crops can increase production with minimal resource use and environmental pollution.
- Maintain adequate storage. Keeping sufficient reserves of food, water, or energy to guard against some degree of climate-induced risk is time-worn wisdom.
- Match agricultural credit and climatic time scales . The threat of climatic variability often causes underinvestment in food production inputs such as fertilizer. This climate-defensive behavior is simply a way for food producers faced with fixed debt repayments to hedge against foreclosure should yields or prices fluctuate wildly in anomalous climatic years. By matching debt repayment to production variations, the consequences of production fluctuations could be shifted from the producers alone to a larger part of society. In essence, this is a generalized crop insurance strategy.
- Maintain future productive potential. Conservation of today's soil and wild genetic resources will be necessary if long-term production is to be greatly increased.
- Maintain a diversity of international economic ties. Trade is a principal means of adapting to regional imbalances caued by climatic anomalies.

A strategy more active than adaptation but short of prevention should be seriously considered in advance of major international efforts to control the carbon dioxide increase; it can be called anticipatory adaptation. (It has also been labeled build resilience.) Anticipatory adaptations are not the same as prevention; they are investments to make it easier to adapt to or to prevent, in this case, a carbon dioxide increase in the future. Such investments would result from strategic decisions to accelerate activities that would proceed more slowly with traditional economic decisions. Thus, anticipatory adaptation would tend to counteract the normal tendency to place a lower value on the future than the present.

Accelerated research (physical, biological, and social) is an obvious anticipatory adaptation strategy. Of course, delaying stronger actions in favor of research is a policy not without risk—namely, that of committing society to the necessity of adapting to a larger dose of carbon dioxide and its effects (good and bad) than if actions were taken earlier to reduce the impact. Accelerated research now, however, could minimize the need for crash research programs in the future were adverse climatic effects to occur sooner or in more extreme form than expected. Other adaptive strategies to carbon dioxide-induced climatic change could involve building dikes to protect property against a rise in sea level or improving the shelter of those who might hurt by an increase in the number of extremely hot days.

Further examples of anticipatory adaptation include:

- Building a diversity of political ties. Good rapport among nations will be absolutely necessary if an international consensus to limit the carbon dioxide increase is eventually to be sought.
- Accelerated development and testing of crop strains and agricultural practices for more efficient adaptation to higher carbon dioxide levels (recognizing, however, that pests and weeds may adapt in the same way).
- Starting work on possible compensation and mechanisms to adjudicate disputes between winners and losers. Examples of the kinds of problems in which climatic resources could be redistributed and for which redistributive justice might be required are movement of grain-growing belts, coastal flooding from sea-level rise, and altered crop productivity from carbon dioxide fertilization.
- Accelerated development of nonfossil fuel energy systems.
- Accelerated development and implementation of energy conservation methods and devices, particularly in those nations with high per capita use of fossil fuels.
- Accelerated population control efforts to minimize ultimate carbon dioxide emissions for a given per capita fossil fuel consumption standard, particularly in nations with high population growth rates.

These kinds of strategies to make future adaptation easier are sensible regardless of the eventual impacts of increases in carbon dioxide and other trace gases. Thus, the problem has links to other environmental and societal problems such as the impact of climatic variability on society or the problem of national energy self-sufficiency.

PREVENTION. Preventive strategies are, of course, those that act to control emissions of substances perceived to be environmentally harmful. The primary preventive strategy designed to avoid damage to the ozone layer is the reduction or banning of all nonessential uses of CFCs. Beyond this measure, preventive strategies become much more problematical (for example, finding substitutes for CFCs in such applications as refrigeration systems). More research into alternatives to CFCs and their efficient use will be needed.

Potential problems arising from a fleet of SSTs still exist, as do plans for new generations of aircraft. It is therefore important to continue research on effects of nitrogen oxide emissions in the stratosphere. The use of artificial fertilizers in agriculture also generates atmospheric nitrogen compounds that can reach the stratosphere and possibly destroy ozone. It is imperative to develop a better understanding of the global nitrogen cycle so that this potential problem and others we may yet uncover can be better assessed.

Attempting to control acid rain by limiting emissions of pollutants requires that we know enough about acid deposition and its environmental effects to give emissions controls a reasonable chance of success. Although detailed information about relationships between sources and receptors is not available, knowing that there would be a widespread decrease in acid deposition if there were a widespread decrease in emissions may be sufficient information to begin a prevention program. Several groups (including the Canadian-United States Memorandum of Intent Working Group on Impact Assessment) have set acid- or sulfate-deposition limits below which little cumulative damage to aquatic ecosystems would be expected.

If present theories of the origin of acid rain are correct, then technologies to limit acid rain are available today. Sulfur dioxide emissions can be reduced by switching to low-sulfur fuels. Unfortunately, only 20 percent of the world's petroleum reserves are low in sulfur, and these are currently being used at a disproportionately high rate. Switching US midwestern power plants to low-sulfur coal could, in the absence of compensation mechanisms, cause economic displacement, because much coal from the Midwest and Appalachia, the present fuel sources, has a high sulfur content. Nevertheless, not switching to low-sulfur coal allows more acid deposition in regions such as the Northeast, which typically follow more stringent sulfur dioxide emissions practices.

Sulfur dioxide can be prevented from reaching the atmosphere by washing the coal or by removing the sulfur dioxide from the flue gas. Simple washing can, at best, remove about 50 percent of the sulfur. Further removal, up to 90 percent, requires high temperatures and pressures and can cost ten times more than washing. Flue-gas desulfurization (scrubbing) by reacting the effluent gas with lime or limestone in water can remove 80-90 percent of the sulfur but generates large quantities of waste.

Techniques for minimizing emission of sulfur dioxide from coal-burning power plants have no effect on anthropogenic nitrogen oxide emissions. Oxides of nitrogen derive both from the burning of nitrogen impurities in fuel and from oxidizing the nitrogen normally found in combustion air. The percentage of nitrogen oxides generated by the burning of air, about 80 percent in the case of conventional coal-fired boilers, depends strongly on the temperature of combustion. Improved furnace design and combustion techniques can reduce nitrogen oxide emissions from stationary sources by 40-70 percent, although such methods are not in widespread commercial use now. Processes for removing nitrogeen oxides from flue gases are only in the development stage. Emissions from automobiles can be decreased to some extent by improvements in the design of combustion chambers and the control of combustion mixtures. Exhaust gas catalytic converters can be used to further limit emissions from mobile sources. Energy-efficient mass transit can also reduce mobile source emissions of nitrogen oxides as well as carbon dioxide.

There is no doubt that prevention of acid deposition would be costly. Cost estimates for US emission-control programs range from 2 to 20 billion dollars per year. Even the "small" $2-billion-per-year program that could reduce acid deposition in New York's Adirondack Mountains by, say, 25 percent is thought by some to be far too expensive. Office of Management and Budget director David Stockman reportedly estimates that the program would cost $6,000-$10,000 per pound of fish saved. However, Stockman's cost-benefit argument ignores the question of what might be fair to those affected by acid rain. More important, he concentrates on one particular visible form of damage from acid rain, apparently ignoring all the other environmental, agricultural, health, and materials damages. The quantitative assessments of these additional damages, given present uncertainties, cover a broad range. It would be folly at present to make policy decisions based solely on a few detailed risk-benefit studies for specific scenarios of control, mitigation, and compensation.

The divisiveness of the acid rain problem argues for some form of national cost sharing to finance preventive measures. It can also be argued, however, that it is only fair that polluters pay a large fraction of the costs of prevention. The height of smokestacks might be decreased, for example, so that more pollution would be deposited locally, with less being transported over long distances. Balancing the costs of prevention among the polluters, regions that are polluted, and those that are relatively unaffected is obviously a sensitive political task.

At present, there are large uncertainties in determining the effectiveness of taxes and fuel bans in limiting carbon dioxide. Thus, it appears that the single most important and effective means of preventing a rapid and large buildup of carbon dioxide in the atmosphere is to apply existing standards of efficiency for energy use as a strategic goal of nations, particularly those with high per capita use of fossil fuels. There are few more important national strategic options than energy conservation, since it helps in reducing the impact of many problems. Increasing energy efficiency can

- Reduce atmospheric pollution on nearly all scales
- Enhance national security through increased energy independence
- Reduce the environmental effects of carbon dioxide and acid rain, thereby reducing the effort required to adapt to such conditions
- Reduce risks of uncertain but plausible climatic catastrophes, such as coastal flooding or increases in the probability or severity of extreme heat-stress periods
- Buy time to study climatic change and climatic impact problems and to develop nonfossil energy sources, upon which ultimate prevention of carbon dioxide, acid rain, and local urban air pollution depend.

The development of nonfossil energy sources as well as improvements in efficiency for all energy sectors, should be viewed in part as high-priority strategic (rather than purely market) investments. Whether the mechanisms to accomplish this should be subsidized research and development (for example, solar photovoltaic cells or better nuclear reactor designs), tax incentives to reduce fossil fuel emissions, or elimination of existing hidden subsidies to fossil fuel technology are important tactical questions to be studied further by appropriate private, academic, and legislative institutions.

Even though nonmarket investments are possible and are already desirable at national levels, carbon dioxide is nonetheless fundamentally a problem that is global in both cause and effect. Moreover, it is inextricably interwoven with the overall problem of global economic development and cannot be removed from the debate over population, resources, environment, and economic justice. Rich nations cannot ask poor nations to abandon their development plans simply because of the potential carbon dioxide problem without making comparable sacrifices that will help provide international economic equity. Since developed countries are at present by far the major producers of carbon dioxide from use of fossil fuel, their disproportionate per capita use of energy must be part of the bargaining process to control global emissions. Therefore, any global strategies for preventing a carbon dioxide buildup will require international cooperation between rich and poor nations on the transfer of knowledge, technology, and capital.

A point of further contention in the dialogue between developed and developing countries will be the question of population growth rates. This is relevant to the carbon dioxide issue simply because total emission is the per capita emission rate times population size. If there is a future movement toward parity between rich and poor in per capita use of fossil fuels, then population growth (which is occurring predominantly in the Third World) will become as important a factor in the carbon dioxide climate problem as high per capita use of fossil fuels is today in the developed nations.

Schneider and Mesirow (1976) proposed a "global survival compromise" whereby developed countries would control their disproportionate use of natural resources and provide capital and technology to help developing countries improve their economic base. At the same time, the less developed countries would be expected to reduce population growth rates markedly and raise their standards of living. Of course, such negotiations would not be a simple or short-term process. If buildup of carbon dioxide is not viewed as part of the negotiation process for global development, however, it is extremely unlikely that substantially greater buildup will be prevented, except by fortuitous technological advances in alternative energy systems, major programs to increase energy efficiency, and population control.

Policy instruments to restrict carbon dioxide emission are, of course, at an early stage of discussion and study. Their ultimate viability on the national or international scale is unknown. At the national level, several bodies have suggested that taxing fossil fuel use might be effective, although only marginally so. At a grander, global level, Kellogg and Mead (1977) proposed the ultimate need for a "law of the air," whereby all nations would agree to limit carbon dioxide emissions to some negotiated level.

This discussion clearly suggests that global atmospheric problems can be prevented through a variety of mechanisms. Major immediate efforts to implement global prevention strategies are unlikely, however, given current political alignments, economic investment strategies, and prevailing philosophies of nations. Even if such atmospheric problems cannot be substantially prevented, a hierarchy of policy actions over the next few decades could help to minimize societal vulnerability to atmospheric changes and perhaps even help certain sectors to take advantage of altered conditions.

The atmospheric problems examined here represent in large part a fundamental challenge to the philosophy of individual, corporate, and state interests. These interests normally react to problems on time scales that are much shorter than those associated with the effects of ozone depletion, acid rain, and a buildup of carbon dioxide in the atmosphere. What may be needed before major policy initiatives are forthcoming is a reevaluation of the present balance between short-term, narrow economic interests and long-term national and global concerns. The development of strategic goals such as increased energy efficiency and development of nonfossil energy supplies seems of the utmost importance to help reduce the major atmospheric pollution problems. If short-term return on investment is the principal goal of individuals, organizations, or nations, then we are likely to be forced to adapt to the range of consequences, good and bad, that will inevitably be thrust upon us if present trends continue. It is questionable whether present market-driven forces alone will encourage sufficent investment to prevent—or even anticipate—the potentially serious long-term consequences of the increase in atmospheric pollution.

Finally, there is an ethical question associated with the atmospheric problems discussed here: Do we have the right to commit future generations to unprecedented atmospheric perturbations without actively attempting to prevent or at least anticipate them? We are insulting the atmospheric environment faster than we are coming to understand it. Some of the uncertain consequences of our insensitivity could be serious and irreversible.

To be sure, further institutional actions are needed to build a scientific consensus on physical, biological, and social aspects of atmospheric pollution issues. Perhaps even more important is the need for public awareness and understanding, which could lead to demands for political action. The prospects for alleviating most foreseeable atmospheric problems are good, but it is doubtful that anything more aggressive than research funding will be instituted before the atmosphere has itself performed the experiments that are now under way, with all of life on earth inside its laboratory.

REFERENCES

Ausubel, J. H. 1982. Review of *Least-Cost Energy: Solving the CO$_2$ Problem*, by A. B. Loving et al. *Climatic Change* 4:313–17.

Cogbill, C. V., and G. E. Likens. 1974. Acid precipitation in the northeastern United States. *Water Resources Research* 10:1133–37.

CEC. 1983. *Acid Rain: A Review of the Phenomenon in the EEC and Europe*. Report prepared by Environmental Resources Limited. London: Graham and Trotman.

Covery, C., S. H. Schneider, and S. L. Thompson. 1984. Global atmospheric effects of massive smoke injections from a nuclear war: Results from general circulation model simulations. *Nature* 308:21–25.

Dotto, L., and H. Schiff. 1978. *The Ozone War*. New York: Doubleday.

Downing, T. E., and R. W. Kates. 1982. The international response to the threat of chloroflourocarbons to atmospheric ozone. *American Economic Review* 72, no. 2.

Grier, P. 1983. A battle of charts and graphs on what to do about acid rain. *Christian Science Monitor*, 13 October, p. 4.

Hileman, B. 1983. Acid rain: A rapidly shifting scene. *Environmental Science and Technology* 17:401A–05A.

Houghton, J. T. 1977. *The Physics of Atmospheres*. Cambridge: Cambridge University Press.

IMOS. 1975. *Fluorocarbons and the Environment*. Council on Environmental Quality, Federal Council for Science and Technology. Washington, D.C.

Kellogg, W. W., and M. Mead, eds. 1977. *The Atmosphere: Endangered and Endangering*. Fogarty International Center Proceedings no. 39, Publication no. NIH 77-1065. Washington, D.C.: National Institutes of Health.

Lovins, A. B., L. H. Lovins, F. Krause, and W. Bach. 1982. *Least-Cost Energy: Solving the CO$_2$ Problem*. Andover, Mass.: Brick House.

Marchetti, C. 1977. On geoengineering the CO_2 problem. *Climatic Change* 1:59–68.

Molina, M. J., and F. S. Rowland. 1974. Stratospheric sink for chlorofluoromethanes: Chlorine atomic-atalized destruction of ozone. *Nature* 249:810–12.

NRC. 1976. Halocarbons: Environmental effects of chlorofluoromethane release. Report of the Committee on Impacts of Stratospheric Change. Washington, D.C.: National Academy Press.

————. 1982. *Causes and effects of stratospheric ozone reduction: An update.* Report prepared by the Committee on Chemistry and Physics of Ozone Depletion and the Committee on Biological Effects of Increased Solar Ultraviolet Radiation. Washington, D.C.: National Academy Press.

————. 1983. *Acid Deposition: Atmospheric Processes in Eastern North America.* Report of the Committee on Atmospheric Transport and Chemical Transformation in Acid Precipitation. Washington, D.C.: National Academy Press.

Rahn, K. A., and D. H. Lowenthal. 1984. Elemental tracers of distant regional pollution aerosols. *Science* 223:132–39.

Rhodes, S. L., and P. Middleton. 1983a. The complex challenge of controlling acid rain. *Environment* 25:7–38.

————. 1983b. Acid rain's gang of four: More than one impact. *Environmental Forum* 2:32–35.

————. 1983c. Canada, the U.S., and acid rain: Environmental and political degradation. *Environment* 25:34–35.

Schneider, S. H., and R. S. Londer. 1984. *The Coevolution of Climate and Life.* San Francisco: Sierra Club Books.

Schneider, S. H., and L. E. Mesirow. 1976. *The Genesis Strategy: Climate and Global Survival.* New York: Plenum.

Seidel, S., and D. Keyes. 1983. *Can We Delay a Greenhouse Warming?* U.S. Environmental Protection Agency. Washington, D.C.: U.S. Government Printing Office.

Siebel, E. P., and R. G. Semonin. 1981. *Acid Rain: What Do We Know?* Illinois Department of Energy and Natural Resources, State Water Survey Division.

UNEP. 1981. *Environmental Assessment of Ozone Layer Depletion and Its Impact as of November 1980.* Nairobi: UNEP.

CHAPTER FOURTEEN

Present and Future State of Living Marine and Freshwater Resources

ROGER REVELLE

PRESENT SIZE, VALUE, AND DISPOSITION OF THE WORLD CATCH OF LIVING MARINE AND FRESHWATER RESOURCES

The world catch of fish, shellfish, and marine algae from both marine and fresh waters increased by nearly 6 percent per year between 1950 and 1970, more than tripling in two decades from 21.9 to 70.6 million metric tons.[1] Around 12 percent of the world harvest in these years was obtained from rivers and lakes; the marine catch was 19.4 million mt in 1950 and 61.4 million mt in 1970. In 1981, the harvest of marine organisms was 66.7 million mt (see table 14.1). Thus, between 1970 and 1981, the rate of increase of the marine catch greatly diminished, to less than 1 percent per year. The catch of freshwater species was actually somewhat lower in 1981 (8.1 million mt) than in 1970 (9.2 million mt).

The sharp decline in the rate of increase can be ascribed to several causes, including the precipitous rises in the cost of fuel for fishing vessels after the oil shocks of 1973 and 1978, the generally depressed economic conditions of the 1970s, and the collapse of the Peruvian anchoveta fishery after the climatic perturbation caused by the hurricane El Niño, in 1972. In 1970, the Peruvian anchoveta fishery was the largest in the world, amounting to more than 13 million mt;

TABLE 14.1. Annual world fish landings (million metric tons).

	1948–52	1953–57	1953–57	1958–62	1963–67	1968–72	1973–78	1979	1980
Total, all species	21.9	29.0	39.0	53.9	67.1	68.2	71.3	72.4	74.8
Inland waters	2.5	3.8	5.8	7.3	8.9	7.1	7.3	7.6	8.1
Anchoveta	0.0	0.1	3.7	9.0	10.0	2.8	1.4	0.8	1.6
Marine, less anchoveta	19.4	25.1	30.3	37.6	48.2	58.3	62.5	64.0	65.1

Source: FAO Committe on Fisheries, "Review of the State of World Fishery Resources," (Paper read at the fifteenth session in Rome, October 10–19, 1983).

in 1973, only 1.7 million mt were taken. Since that time, it has never recovered to more than 20 percent of its former level. Its collapse was probably due in part to overfishing and in part to the catastrophic, though temporary, decline in the supply of plankton food for the young anchovetas in 1972 as a result of El Niño.

The principal cause of the decline in the annual rate of increase in the world catch, however, is the limited size of the stocks of fish species on which present-day fisheries are based. Some of these species are already overexploited, while several others are near the limits of sustainable yeild. The Food and Agriculture Organization (FAO) of the United Nations has estimated that the potential catch of all conventional marine species is less than 97 million mt, only about 30 million mt, or 45 percent, larger than the 1981 marine catch of 66.7 million mt.[2] This estimate does not include herring and anchovy, which are subject to wide natural fluctuations due to environmental changes (for example, the herring catch dropped by 75 percent between 1965 and 1977[3]). According to the FAO, most of the potential expansion in the catch of conventional species would come from increased fishing, which would require a large capital investment in fishing boats and gear and would probably entail sharply declining returns per unit of effort for all fishermen as the potential catch limits were approached.

Fish make up about 88.6 percent of the total weight of the world marine catch. Lobsters, crabs, shrimps, and prawns account for 3.2 percent by weight; mollusks, including clams, oysters, mussels, squid, and octopus, make up 6.3 percent, and marine algae 1.9 percent. Seven species of fish—anchoveta, Alaskan pollack, herring, cod, capelin, mackerel, and Japanese pilchard—constitute about one-third of the total marine catch. Other important species, largely because they are highly valued economically, are salmon, halibut, sole and other flatfish, redfish, and tuna.

Although more than a hundred countries—thirty "developed" and more than seventy "developing"—are listed in the fishery statistics of the FAO, 80 percent of the recorded world marine catch is taken by just nineteen countries. Japan and the USSR alone account for more than 30 percent of the total, and Norway, the United States, Denmark, Spain, Canada, Great Britain, Iceland, and France harvest an additional 20 percent. Norway and the United States each take about 3 million mt, and the remaining six developed countries take between 0.75 and 2 million mt. Peru, the Republic of Korea, the People's Republic of China, the Korean Democratic Republic, India, Thailand, Chile, the Philippines, and Indonesia together harvest 30 percent of the world catch. On a per capita basis, the marine harvest is very unevenly distributed. The share of the ten developed countries listed above is about 45 kg per capita per year, whereas that of the nine developing countries is less than 10 kg.

During the 1970s, all developed countries together harvested about 60 percent of the world marine catch, or close to 35 kg per capita per year, and developing countries took 40 percent, or about 10 kg per capita per year. The share of the developing countries may have been larger than these figures indicate because part of their catch was taken by "artisanal" fishermen (those using fixed, shallow-water fish traps and small traditional fishing boats operating relatively close to shore). The artisanal catch is only approximated in national fishery statistics and may be substantially underestimated.

In 1972, about 30 percent of the marine catch came from "distant-water" fishing vessels operating off the coasts of other countries.[4] The recent establishment of exclusive economic zones, in which fishing within 200 nautical miles of the shoreline is controlled by the coastal state, may be expected to lower drastically the catches of these world-ranging fishing boats and to increase the catches of the coastal state fishermen correspondingly. Insofar as these coastal states are developing countries, the share of these countries in the world marine catch may be expected to rise. As table 14.2 shows, however, this had not happened by 1981 in the east central Atlantic and southeast Atlantic territories of African coastal states.

Two ocean regions—the northwest Pacific, including the Bering Sea with a catch of 19.81 million mt in 1981, and the northeast Atlantic, with a 1981 catch of 11.65 million mt—account for 47 percent of the world marine catch. Another 10 percent of the 1981 harvest (6.85 million mt) came from the southwest Pacific off Ecaudor, Peru, and Chile. Overall, the portions of the Pacific and Atlantic oceans in the Northern Hemisphere contributed 78 percent of the world marine catch, whereas the southern Pacific and Atlantic and the Indian Ocean provided only 22 percent, even though the Southern Hemisphere contains 57 percent of the total area of the world's oceans. This seeming paradox can be explained at least in part on social and economic grounds: most of the world's people and an even larger fraction of the world's economic activity are concentrated in the Northern Hemisphere. The total value of the marine catch in 1978 has been estimated as 28 billion 1980 dollars, equivalent to an average of $450 per metric ton.[5] These data refer to the "landed value," or first sale, of the catch and do not include the value added in processing, distribution, and marketing. The landed value of the marine harvest was thus approxi-

TABLE 14.2. Fish catches (thousand metric tons) by local and long-range fleets in selected regions.

Area	1970–74		1975–79		1980		1981	
	Local	Long range	Local	Long range	Local	Long range	Local	Long range
N.W. Atlantic	2014.5	2209.0	2125.8	1040.2	2558.7	307.1	2510.7	270.4
% of total area catch	47.7	52.3	67.1	32.9	89.3	10.7	90.3	9.7
E.C. Atlantic	1122.7	1935.4	1243.5	2108.6	1270.3	2147.6	1320.6	1838.4
% of total area catch	36.7	63.3	37.1	62.9	37.2	62.8	41.8	58.2
S.E. Atlantic	1710.8	1039.8	1212.0	1539.0	927.3	1243.9	981.9	1348.2
% of total area catch	62.2	37.8	44.1	55.9	42.7	57.3	42.1	57.9
N.E. Pacific	509.7	1882.3	651.0	1407.3	783.9	1170.7	955.2	1365.7
% of total area catch	21.3	78.7	31.6	68.4	40.1	59.9	41.2	58.8

Source: FAO Committee on Fisheries, Review of the State of World Fishery Resources," (Paper read at the fifteenth session in Rome, October 10–19, 1983).

mately 0.7 percent of the total world economic product, but the contribution to GNP in different countries was highly variable, ranging from 37.2 percent for the Faeroe Islands to only 0.1 percent for the United States and the Federal Republic of Germany.[6] The contribution was 5 percent or more in ten countries—Thailand, the Philippines, Iceland, Indonesia, Vietnam, Malaysia, Senegal, the Faeroe Islands, Oman, and the Yemen Democratic Republic—and more than 2.5 percent in seven other countries—Norway, China, the Democratic People's Republic of Korea (North Korea), Burma, Ghana, Bangladesh, and the Republic of Korea (South Korea). All but Norway, Iceland, and the Faeroe Islands in this group of seventeen are developing countries.

About 12 percent of the world catch, or between 7 and 8 million mt, enters into international trade. The United States, the Federal Republic of Germany, Japan, and sixteen other developed countries are the principal importers, accounting for 80 percent of total imports. Exporting countries include Japan, Norway, Denmark, USSR, Iceland, Canada, the United States, Netherlands, and seven other developed countries, in addition to Peru, Chile, Malaysia, Thailand, Republic of Korea, Morocco, and Angola among developing countries. Except for Norway, Denmark, Iceland, and Canada, most of the developed countries are net importers.

During the 1970s, an average of some 50 million mt of the total world catch of more than 70 million mt were used for direct human consumption, and about 20 million mt were "reduced" to fish oil and fish meal.[7] Nearly all the oil was used in edible products for human consumption, and the fish meal was fed to livestock and poultry as a protein supplement. It is estimated that some 35 percent of the protein in fish meal was converted by domestic animals into milk, egg, and meat protein that was in turn used for human food.[8] Slightly more than 40 percent of the fish consumed directly was marketed as fresh fish, about 24 percent was frozen, 16 percent was salted and dried, and about 19 percent was canned.

In the inshore waters of developing countries, significant quantities of fish are captured in shallow-water fish traps. But in 1982 most of the world's marine catch was taken by more than 21,000 fishing vessels exceeding 100 gross registered mt as well as a large number (estimated by the FAO at three million) of smaller fishing boats engaged in artisanal fishing. Sixty-two percent of the fishing vessels were of more than 500 gross registered mt; the total of all registered vessels was 9,364,000 mt.[9] Besides these fishing boats, there were 845 factory ships and carriers grossing nearly 3.5 million mt. Assuming a construction cost of $1,000 per mt, the total cost of the world fishing fleet, not including artisanal vessels, was about $13 billion, approximately half the value of the annual marine catch.

Between 1979 and 1982, the number of registered fishing boats and mother ships increased by 7.7 percent, and the total tonnage by 4.5 percent. These rates of increase were probably approximately matched by the rate of increase in the marine catch. This was more than 4 percent between 1979 and 1982, the last year for which catch statistics are available.

MARINE PRODUCTS IN HUMAN NUTRITION

The nutritional value of fish and other seafood lies primarily in its high-quality, easily digestible protein. On the average, protein makes up 10 percent of the landed weight of fish and shellfish. Fats in marine fishes and the oil extracted from them also make a small contribution to human diets.

Although the proportion of total protein originating in fish and shellfish consumed directly by humans is small (about 5 percent) for the world as a whole, it is very substantial in some countries.[10] Japan's population of 118 million obtains 25 percent of its total dietary protein and more than half of its animal protein from marine fish and shellfish. In thirty-seven other countries, five developed and thirty-two developing, with a combined population of close to 300 million people, 10 percent or more of the total protein intake is obtained by direct consumption of fish and shellfish. Thirty to ninety percent of the animal protein in twenty-two of these thirty-seven countries is obtained from seafood. Portugal is one of this group. All the rest, including Ghana, the Ivory Coast, Sierra Leone, Senegal, Jamaica, the Philippines, Papua New Guinea, North and South Korea, East Malaysia, Vietnam, Thailand, and Singapore are developing coastal or island states. Outside the group of thirty-seven countries, direct consumption of fish protein accounts for 30-47 percent of animal protein in six countries—Indonesia, Sri Lanka, the Congo, Angola, Mauritius, and Togo—with a combined population of about 170 million. But this is less than 10 percent of total protein (animal and vegetable).

Because of its balanced protein content of amino acids, animal protein, including fish protein, has a much higher nutritional value than an equivalent amount of protein from cereals alone or from legumes alone. However, a combination of cereal and legume proteins from, for example, maize and beans—the diet of poor people in Mexico and Central America—has nearly the same nutritional value as fish or other animal protein but may not be as easily digested, particularly by children.

The requirement for high-quality protein in human diets averages about 30 g per person per day. More than this amount is needed by growing children, adolescents, and pregnant and nursing mothers, whereas most adults need less. Much more is needed when the protein comes from a single vegetable source such as a cereal. In Indonesia, the Philippines, Sri Lanka, Angola, Papua New Guinea, and the Congo, total protein intake in the absence of fish protein would be less than 40 g per person per day. Considering the main cereal or root-crop foods in these countries, the average diet of the poor might be especially severe if their intake of fish protein were curtailed. In Vietnam, Thailand, Ghana, East Malaysia, Sierra Leone, Surinam, Togo, and twelve other small island or coastal developing nations, the average protein intake, excluding fish, would be less than 50 g per person per day. Many of the poor in these countries suffer from protein deficiencies. It should be noted, however, that the average calorie intake in several of these twenty-eight countries is less than the food energy requirements; consequently, much of the ingested protein is used as a source of energy so that even an excess of protein would not prevent protein-calorie malnurition among the poor.

Because most of the population in China and India lives far from the sea, the average fish protein intake from capture fisheries in these two most populous countries is 1.2 and 0.5 g per capita per day, respectively—much below the world average of 3.6 g. In the remaining developing countries, with a population of 1.6 billion people, the average protein in fish consumed directly is 2.3 g per person per day, or 4 percent of the total protein intake of 57 g per person per day. In the developed countries, average fish protein consumed directly is 6.2 g per person per day, or 6.4 percent of the total daily protein intake of 96 g, about one and a half times the proportion in the poor countries, even though the weight is nearly three times as great.[11]

It has been pointed out that a large fraction of the marine harvest is reduced to fish meal and oil. Between 1974 and 1977, the average annual production of fish meal was close to 4.5 million mt. It was used as a feed supplement for livestock and poultry and to a minor extent for cultivated fish such as trout. The protein in meat and poultry in this tonnage was about 35 percent of the protein in the fish used for reduction, or 15 percent of the protein in the marine harvest. Most of this animal protein gained by conversion of marine fish protein was consumed in the developed countries.

As a result, the average daily protein consumption originating directly or indirectly from marine fish and shellfish in developed countries was 7.8 g per person, about 25 percent more than the fish protein consumed directly and 8 percent of total protein intake.

In the developing countries, excluding India and China, protein of marine origin consumed directly and indirectly by human beings was 2.6 g per person per day, or 4.6 percent of total protein intake. To bring protein intake from capture fisheries up to the level in developed countries, these poor nations, even with their present populations, would need to increase their fish catch by about 30 million mt per year.

Fats and oils together make up nearly 5 percent of the weight of average marine fish landings, or about 3 million mt. One million tons is extracted as oil products from the portion of the world fish catch that is reduced to fish meal and oil. Overall, the fats and oils in marine fishes, including extracted oil products, provide less than 1 percent of the calories in human diets and less than 5 percent of fat calories.[12] The share of marine fats and oils in the caloric intake of the populations of developing countries is less than 25 percent of the share per capita per year in the developed countries.

AQUACULTURE

Aquaculture is the farming and husbandry of freshwater and marine organisms. It is more closely related to farming and animal husbandry on land than to the capture fisheries described above. In some parts of the world, aquaculture (including mariculture, the cultivation of marine organisms) is an ancient occupation, but its worldwide potential as a source of food and industrial products has only recenttly been recognized.

In developing countries, aquaculture can provide protein, and if high-value species like shrimp and prawn are produced, much-needed foreign exchange. It can also furnish alternative or additional employment to underemployed fishermen and farmers. In developed countries, aquacultural production of oysters, mussels, shrimps and prawns, lobsters, abalones, trout, carp, and other fish species can provide a welcome diversity to human diets. Cultivation of pearl oysters in Japan is an important industry. Together with agriculture, aquaculture repesents a desirable way to make use of human and animal wastes and industrial waste heat.

Aquaculture production has been increasing rapidly during the past twenty years. In 1980, 8.7 million mt of finfish, mollusks, crustaceans, and edible or industrially useful seaweeds were produced, which compares with 6.1 million mt in 1975.[13] This represents a 43-percent increase in five years for an average annual rate of increase exceeding 7 percent. The aquacultural harvest in 1980 was nearly one-eighth of the catch of both freshwater and marine capture fisheries but in 1975 only a little more than one-twelfth. If this rate of increase continues, the projection made by FAO in 1976 will be realized: aquacultural yields will double in ten years, and a five- to tenfold increase could be achieved in thirty years.[14]

Aquaculture was practiced by sixty-six countries in Asia, Oceania, Africa, Europe, North America, Latin America, and the Caribbean in 1975, and by seventy-one countries in 1980. Of the latter, forty-four were low-income developing countries, and twenty-seven were relatively high-income countries. All but nine of the seventy-one countries had marine coastlines, and most of the production in both developing and developed countries came from marine species.

In contrast to the capture fisheries, in which the developed countries' catch and consumption are considerably larger than those of poor countries, the developing countries dominate in aquaculture. Of the total production of 8.7 million mt in 1980, only 2.2 million, or about 26 percent, were obtained in developed countries, 6.4 million (74 percent) being produced in developing countries. However, 4.2 million mt—two-thirds of the developing countries' share—was produced in China (including Taiwan), and the remaining developing countries, including India, produced 2.2 million mt, equal to the production in the developed countries. Because of their much larger populations, the per capita share of aquacultural production in all developing countries, excluding China, was considerably lower than in rich countries. It should be noted that various species of seaweeds made up more than one-third of the Chinese production. Consequently, per capita protein intake from aquacultural production of fish and shellfish in China was only about 0.7 per person per day, much less than the protein obtained from capture fisheries.

Unlike the capture fisheries, in which the size of the catch is ultimately limited by the size and availability of the populations of fish and shellfish, aquaculture is limited by the extent of suitable areas. It must be practiced close to shore, either in estuaries and semi-enclosed bays or in open ocean waters near shore. The land resource for aquaculture is therefore one-dimensional, and there is much competition from other users of the coastal zone for this resource. The greatest potential for expansion of aquaculture exists in archipelagoes such as Indonesia, the Philippines, Hawaii, and the southwest Pacific Islands and in countries such as Japan, Bangladesh, Nigeria and other West African countries, and northeast Brazil, where there are many estuaries, long and complex coastlines, and shallow offshore waters.

However, coral reefs, mangrove swamps, and other wetlands constitute a large fraction of the coastal zones in tropical developing countries. These make a very important contribution to the capture fisheries, but the net gain in production from the transformation of these areas to aquaculture might not be large.

It was estimated in 1976 that the area under aquaculture was on the order of 3 to 4 million ha.[15] Average yields were between 1.5 and 2.0 mt/ha, ranging from less than 1 to more than 20 mt/ha. With improved techniques, these yields could be increased as much as threefold, and a tenfold expansion of aquacultural areas to more than 30 million ha is considered feasible. But this will require accelerated transfer of technology and massive financial investment, suitable legislation, manpower training, development of institutions and other essential infrastructures, and intensive research.

Aquaculture is usually labor-intensive and is therefore most suitable for densely populated, low-income countries. Considerable capital investment is required, however, and capital is most scarce in just those countries that possess an abundant labor supply.

Among the scientific and technical problems of aquaculture are breeding and larval production (or, in the case of one commonly used fish, tilapia, prevention of frequent breeding to avert overpopulation of ponds and consequent stunting of adult fish); the need to reduce feed costs; improving management of ponds, pens, and cages; disease control; and harvesting technology. Chinese and Indian carp and gray mullet have been induced to breed by injections of pituitary hormones. Shrimps have been brought to reproductive maturity in the laboratory, and the spawn have been carried through the various larval stages of their life cycle. Controlled reproduction of oysters and hatchery production of oyster seed are developments of considerable importance because they have helped in genetic selection of strains for special qualities such as disease resistance.

Because future growth of aquaculture must involve development and transfer of technology on a large scale, regional and inter-regional cooperation assume special significance. The Consultative Group on International Agricultural Research has recognized the need for coordinated regional networks of research centers in Asia, Africa, and Latin America to undertake systems-oriented, interdisciplinary research. In the United States, the US Sea Grant Program is sponsoring a National Aquaculture Information System. A principal problem, however, is the shortage of adequately trained and experienced field personnel with the ability and knowledge to assist aquafarmers through national or international extension services. Educational programs for aquacultural scientists and technicians are thus urgently needed.[16]

Marine plant culture, one aspect of aquaculture, is practiced most extensively in China and also in Japan, Malaysia, Taiwan, Korea, Scotland, France, and the West Coast of the United States. The industry in the United States is primarily for production of nonfood substances such as algin and agar. In China, Japan, and other Asian countries, marine plants, although of little nutritive value, are a widely used table delicacy.

As in agriculture, where maize, which originated in Central America, is now an important crop in China, and soybeans have migrated in the reverse direction, international exchanges of cultivated fish and shellfish species have become widespread. But the possible adverse effects of imported species on local fauna and flora and in the transmisson of communicable diseases are perhaps much greater than in agriculture.

Of relevance to aquaculture are the research results obtained on genetic improvement and the homing adaptation of salmon, which have made "sea ranching" economically profitable. Loren Donaldson of the University of Washington has bred salmon varieties that reach full maturity after 18 months at sea and has "imprinted" young salmon in a saltwater bay on the coast of Oregon. The adults return directly to a processing plant on the bay shore and its contained saltwater ponds, where selected animals can be milked for eggs and sperm and a new generation can be produced.[17]

Carl Hodges of the University of Arizona and Emanuel Epstein of the University of California at Davis have been experimenting with halophytic crop plants.[18] Hodges has been working to increase the quantity of useful products from plants that thrive under marine conditions, whereas Epstein's approach has been to increase the salt tolerance of conventional crops by genetic manipulation. Both of these promising technologies, even at the present stage of development, could find wide applications in coastal regions of arid lands.

FUTURE DEMAND FOR FISH

The future demand for fish was estimated in 1970 by the FAO.[19] The basic data for the estimates are per capita consumption figures over a selected base period derived from commodity balance sheets. Projections for food-fish demand (fish consumed directly as food) were based on projected population increases and projected changes in per capita income, assuming a constant relationship between income and fish consumption and constant relative prices of food commodities. As with the FAO dietary data, the projections refer to total aquatic production and not only marine production. The projections for the years 1980 and 2000 are summarized in table 14.3.

The estimate of 60 million mt for world food-fish demand in 1980 is nearly 10 million mt above the quantity actually made available for human consumption (50.4 million mt), but it is 12.4 million mt less than the total world fish catch—both freshwater and marine—of 72.4 million mt in 1980. As we have already seen, more than one-third of the world catch was reduced to fish meal and fish oil. The tonnage of fish used for reduction consisted in part of 22 million mt of small, low-valued fish, such as anchovetas, capelin, and menhaden, and in part of food-fish residues from filleting or other processing. It is assumed in table 14.3 that the share of the world catch consumed directly as human food in both the developing market economy countries and in countries with centrally planned economies will increase between 1980 and the year 2000, whereas that of the developed market economies will decrease by nearly one-third.

In the light of present knowledge about resource availability, the projected demand for 113 million mt of food fish in the year 2000 goes beyond reasonable expectations. Simple extrapolation of the recent rate of increase of the world catch leads to projection of a total catch of about 100 million mt at the turn of the century. Assuming the proportion of fish used for reduction remains constant, the tonnage of

TABLE 14.3. Food-fish demand projections (million mt).

	1980	2000
Developed market economies	21	28
Developing market economies	18	40
All market economies	39	68
All centrally planned economies	21	45
World	60	113

fish used for direct human consumption can be between 65 and 70 million mt. A third projection can be made by assuming that the actual world demand for food fish will bear the same relation in the year 2000 to the demand projected by FAO as it did in 1980. The demand for fish for direct human consumption in the year 2000 would then be about 95 million mt. But the total demand for fish for both reduction and direct consumption would be on the order of 130-135 million mt, of which approximately 120 million would be of marine origin— assuming no change in the size of the freshwater catch. Such a large marine catch could be sustained only by a major increase in the exploitation of so-called unconventional species, such as Antarctic krill, squid, and other cephalopods, and mesopelagic fish species that are not now taken in substantial quantities.

The gap between projected demand and potential marine harvests could also be closed by a relative increase in food-fish prices, which would reduce demand. But price increases are likely to reduce the consumption of fish in many developing countries where they make an important contribution to the food supply. Measures that would increase the supply of food fish therefore seem more desirable. One such measure would be a tripling or quadrupling of aquacultural fish production, which seems to be well within the realm of possibility. A second would be technological and economic changes that would result in direct human consumption of larger quantities of the fish now used principally for reduction. Efforts to this end are being made and, if successful, would result in a net increment of animal protein to human diets, in contrast to the present use of fish meal as feed for livestock and poultry. These animals are able to convert only about 35 percent of the protein originally in fish into the protein of meat, eggs, and milk. A third step toward increasing the supply of food fish would be to reduce fish wastage, which occurs both in fishing and after the catch is taken.

In shrimp fisheries of tropical and subtropical waters, for example, several tons of "trash" fish are caught in the trawls and discarded at sea for every ton of shrimp caught and frozen. Because of the high economic value of shrimp, fishermen cannot afford to use any of the hold capacity aboard their vessels to store the lower-value fish. Similarly, in trawl fisheries where mixed species are taken, only the most valuable species are usually retained, the less valuable being sorted out and discarded.

It has been estimated that the quantity of fish discarded from shrimp boats alone is now about 4 million mt annually, and that total deliberate discards of fish may reach 6 million mt—more than 10 percent of the world's marine catch.[20] Fishing vessels using purse seines also waste considerable quantities of potential human food. If, for example, the haul of a pelagic schooling species such as mackerel is too large to be handled by the vessel or to be accommodated in the remaining hold space, the catch is "slipped," and none, or only a small part of it, is taken aboard. The fish that are slipped normally die from shock, suffocation, or mechanical damage. Likewise, unwanted fish brought up in trawls in deep water die as a result of rapid pressure change as well as mechanical damage. Slipping is also practiced when the purse-sein haul contains too many species other than the main target species, or even the wrong size range of the target species. Unfortunately, there are no estimates of the quantities of fish slipped or otherwise killed by fishing gear and hence never brought on board fishing vessels.

In less affluent countries, especially in the tropics, important losses occur during shortage and transfer of dried or salt- and smoke-cured fish, through bacterial action and from depredation by insects and other pests. In the Lake Chad fishery of northeastern Nigeria, it is estimated that half the total fish catch is lost to insects and bacteria before it has been brought to market.

THE NATURE AND LIMITS OF MARINE LIVING RESOURCES

Unlike agricultural production on land, which can be greatly expanded by the use of suitable technology, the productivity of the ocean is limited by the chemical and physical properties of ocean waters and by marine organisms' ability to adapt to these properties. On both land and sea, plants convert solar energy into the organic materials on which all animal life ultimately depends. The productivity of marine plants, like that of plants on land, depends on the amount of sunlight and on the availability of nutrients, including nitrogen compounds, phosphorus, potassium, and other mineral substances. Photosynthesis is possible only in the upper ocean layers where bright sunlight penetrates. Consequently, plants in the open sea are extremely small because they must be free-floating, and to maintain themselves in suspension in the upper ocean waters they require a large surface-to-volume ratio. These plants of the open sea have a short lifespan, usually only a few days, in contrast to land plants, which live for months or years. Because of this, the biomass of marine plants at any one time is two orders of magnitude smaller than the biomass on land. Owing to the small size of the plants, herbivorous animals in the open sea are also usually small, and there is a succession of carnivores of increasing size. Hence, the food web in the sea is complex, with several trophic levels. The animals useful to humankind make up only a small part of biological production in the open sea.

In shallower waters, less than a few tens of meters deep, the situation is more complicated. In some areas, large bottom-living plants furnish a primary food supply for the larger animals (for example, kelp for sea urchins). Elsewhere, herbivorous bottom-living animals, such as oysters, clams, and mussels, have developed special feeding mechanisms that enable them to filter large quantities of seawater and extract small suspended particles of organic matter, including phytoplankton.

Some of these generalities can be quantified. Total net plant production (photosynthesis minus plant respiration) on land corresponds to about 60 billion mt of organic carbon per year,[21] whereas in the ocean, the net biological production is believed to be only about 30 billion mt. (Some recent data suggest that this figure may be too low, perhaps by a factor of two or three, but in this discussion we shall use the more widely accepted value.) Since the ocean area is almost three times the land area where plants can grow, plant productivity per unit area in the sea is about 80 g/m², less than a fifth of the 460 g/m² on land. On average, plants on the land surface are able to convert about 0.2 percent of the incoming sunlight into chemical energy of organic materials.[22] In the sea, only about 0.04 percent is converted.

The *seasonal* plant production in the ocean can be calculated from seasonal changes in the concentration of phosphorus in the top 100 m, where sufficient sunlight usually penetrates for photosynthesis. In the regions in which relatively large quantities of nutrients are brought up from deep water or from the bottom by upwelling or turbulence (about 10 percent of the ocean surface area), the concentration of phosphorus in this top layer varies from 2 g/m² at the beginning of the spring and summer growing season to zero in the fall when vigorous organic production ceases. The ratio by weight of carbon to phosphorous in marine plants is called the Redfield ratio and is virtually constant throughout the ocean, with a value of about 50. Thus, 100 g/m² of carbon is fixed by photosynthesis during the course of the growing season and removed from solution in the surface water layers. In the fertile 10 percent of the ocean, this amounts to 3.6 billion mt. Probably, an equal quantity of carbon is fixed seasonally by plants in the remaining 90 percent of the ocean area. A large fraction of this amount is eaten by marine zooplankton that in turn are eaten by fish or other larger organisms. At each step, most of the organic material consumed and digested as food is oxidized to provide energy, and only a fifth to a tenth is converted to animal tissue. Thus, the biological productivity of fish and other organisms usable by man is roughly a few hundred million metric tons.

Before human beings intervened, biological production in the ocean was virtually a closed system. Small quantities of nitrogen, phosphorus, and other nutrients were brought to the sea each year by rivers, and small quantities of organic material were buried each year in marine bottom sediments. But the quantity of nutrients entering each year was only one ten-thousandth to one one-hundred-thousandth of the quantity in the ocean, and the leakage to the bottom sediments was of the same order of magnitude.

Considering this system in terms of its fish, a fish population under natural conditions had no yield. In other words, natural mortality was equal to natural reproduction and growth. A sustained yield can be obtained from such a population only by changing its age distribution or other characteristics or by changing the environment—that is, by creating a difference between the net production of organic matter in the fish population and natural oxidation by predators and microorganisms. This can be done in one or a combination of four ways: by reducing the average age of the population so that there is a preponderance of rapidly growing individuals; by removing predators to reduce natural mortality; by removing competitors to increase the food supply available to the fish population; or by genetic manipulation to produce faster-growing, more "efficient" fish. If the population consists mainly of older individuals, its food supply is utilized mainly for energy, not for growth. Rapid gowth is characteristic of a population of young fish, and the sustainable yield for a fishery to provide human food is basically equal to the growth rate of younger fish minus the predation by other marine organisms. Under proper conditions, establishment of such a fishery will reduce the proportion of older fish and thereby increase the weight of fish that can be taken on a sustained basis. If too many fish are taken, however, the numbers of spawning fish may be lowered to the point that not enough larval fish are produced and the population will become depleted. In practice, the weight of fish that can be taken on a sustained basis is usually less than half the rate of production of fish tissue.

THE ENCLOSURE MOVEMENT IN THE OCEANS

Fish populations have commonly been treated as open access resources—"fish belong to him who captures them." This treatment of the ocean as a common property did not appear to be uneconomic or inefficient when the resources of the sea were thought to be so large that they could not be affected by human actions. But with the great increase in the size of the fish catch during the past thirty-five years, it has become evident that the biological resources of the ocean are limited and can be gravely affected by unrestricted fishing. This realization is one of the underlying causes of the ocean enclosure movement, which is reflected in recent actions by many coastal states and in the new convention produced by the Third UN Conference on the Law of the Sea (which was ratified in 1982 by most maritime nations). This enclosure movement has brought the living resources within 200 nautical miles of the shoreline of each continental landmass and each inhabited oceanic island under national jurisdiction. The areas so enclosed—between 30 and 40 percent of the entire world ocean area—are called exclusive economic zones (EEZs) of the coastal states.

In the past, national enclosure of large ocean areas was thought to be neither possible nor desirable. Because of the uncertainties of navigation and the absence of recognizable "landmarks," it was difficult to establish boundaries in the ocean. The great depth of water in the open sea made it virtually impossible to build a fence. Because of the vast size and volume of the ocean and the opacity of the waters below the surface, it was difficult to estimate the size or nature of fish populations, and it was easy to believe that these resources were very large, if not inexhaustible. Little was known about the replenishment of fish stocks or the size of the populations required for successful recruitment. Except for certain sedentary species, fish populations move from place to place in the oceans without regard to the boundaries established by human beings. Societies accustomed to defining property rights in terms of specified land areas were not able to accommodate their concepts to resources that move in unpredictable ways.

The enclosure movement and the broad extent of the exclusive economic zones have been made possible by several technical developments: the greatly increased accuracy of navigation using satellites and radio; the capacity of nations for ocean surveillance using satellites, aircraft, radar, and acoustic detection and tracking; and their increased capacity for control through use of high-speed surface ships and aircraft. All these give coastal states the ability to "occupy" a much larger area of the ocean than previously. Enclosure has become desirable because of improvements in fishing technology that have made it possible to capture an increasingly large fraction of the world's fish and shellfish populations and to rapidly deplete these living resources. The technical changes include the rise of distant-water fishing fleets with mother ships for storing and processing the catch and resupplying the fishing boats (a development used in particular by the USSR and Japan, the two principal fishing nations). Other improvements include the development of acoustic detection methods for locating and tracking fish and fish schools; the use of inexpensive and long-lasting synthetic fibers for fish lines and nets; the use of power sheaves to haul large nets; development of "midwater trawls" that can fish well below the surface and well above the bottom, a region of the ocean that was previously not accessible to fishermen; the development of freezing and other processing technology; improved fishery science and better estimates of population size, recruitment, and mortality of year-classes; and the use of larger and faster fishing vessels for offshore fisheries. These developments have been accompanied during the past thirty-five years by the unprecedented rapid growth of human populations and income levels, which have greatly increased the demand for fish protein and other products of the living resources of the sea.

MANAGEMENT OF FISHERIES

In each exclusive economic zone, fish and shellfish remain open-access resources of the coastal state and its people. This open-access characteristic, in addition to the limited quantity of the resources and the ease with which they can be depleted, gives rise to a need for governmental management and regulation of fisheries.

Some highly migratory fish, such as tuna, wander over entire oceans and remain for only a short time within the exclusive economic zone of any particular coastal state. Indeed, they spend a considerable fraction of their lives in the high seas outside coastal-state jurisdiction. Special cooperative management measures among the several states in whose economic zones the tuna spend parts of their lifespan are necessary to make sure that stocks of these valuable fish are not depleted.

One of the basic objectives of modern fishery management is to estimate the optimum sustainable yield—the weight of fish that can be economically harvested on a sustained basis. This is usually less than the maximum sustainable yield, which is the weight of fish that can be caught without depleting the population. One reason for the difference is that the cost of the fishing effort required to capture the marginal increment of fish needed to reach the maximum sustainable yield is likely to be greater than the value of the fish taken.

In more general terms, the objectives of fishery management are to maximize the social and economic benefits from fisheries, to conserve marine populations and their habitats for present and future generations, and to improve international relations. Because the seas and their animal and plant populations are used by all peoples, they have often been a source of conflict among nations. Minimizing the reasons for conflicts must therefore be a major objective of fishery management. The subjects that fishery managers must address include commercial and recreational species of fish and marine invertebrates; marine mammals, including seals, sea lions, sea otters, porpoises, whales, and walruses; the facilities for capture, processing, transportation, distribution, and marketing—fishing boats and gear, canneries and freezing plants, fishing ports, and warehouses and markets for wholesale and retail distribution and marketing; and, finally, aquaculture facilities development.

Effective fishery management depends on the availability of adequate data and on their proper interpretation and use. These data are of several different kinds. Estimates of potential yield require biological data on the size and age distribution of the fish population, its "recruitment rate" (the rate at which young fish enter the fishery), natural and fishing mortality, and changes in its availability (location of the fish population). These data must be obtained year after year because changing climatic conditions in the ocean and changes in fishing patterns bring about marked interannual variations in the size and characteristics of fish populations. Competent fishery biologists equipped with the mathematical skills of population science and an intimate knowledge of the morphology, physiology, and life histories of the organisms being studied are essential for this work. Fishery biology is still far from an exact science. Inadequacy of data and uncertainties of interpretation tend to exacerbate conflicts among different interest groups and to weaken the making and enforcement of management decisions.

Economic studies are needed concerning the value and cost of the catch per unit of the fishing effort and the economic returns to fishermen. These data can be used, inter alia, to determine the allowable numbers of fishing vessels and the limits of entry of new vessels into the fishery. Sociological studies are needed to probe the factors affecting the welfare of artisanal fishing communities, which in developing countries are usually among the "poorest of the poor." Political information and judgment are needed to determine the strength and influence of different fishery groups, including sports fishing industries versus commercial fishermen, commercial fishermen versus processors and distributors; and consumers versus other interest groups.

Besides determining the size of the optimum sustainable yield (the total allowable catch, or TAC), the major problem of fisheries management is the appropriate allocation of the TAC among competing groups of users. In the new EEZs, for example, how can equity be achieved between the national fishermen of the coastal state and distant-water fishermen, who often have traditional fishing rights? (The Grand Banks off Canada and the United States have been fished for 500 years by Portugese, French, and other European fishermen.) Other problems of allocation arise between inshore fishermen, many of them artisanal fishermen using small traditional vessels, and offshore fishermen using more powerful fishing technologies on large fishing ships. This problem is often solved by preventing the larger fishing vessels from coming within a certain distance of the shore.

Special problems of artisanal fishing arise on the West Coast of the United States and Canada. Native American fishermen in the Pacific Northwest have been recognized as possessing traditional rights of subsistence fishing for salmon, and this cuts across management regulations imposed on commercial and sports fishermen. Alaskan Eskimos are allowed to fish in their traditional way for bowhead whales in the Bering and Beaufort seas despite the strictures of the International Whaling Commission.

A third kind of problem arises from the conflict between high-seas processing ships, usually under foreign flags, that cooperate in joint ventures with local fishermen and shore-based processors who would otherwise receive the local catch.

Sports fishermen repesent an economically powerful industry that is often in conflict with commercial fishermen and onshore processors. The former desire conservation of fish that serve as food for large sports fish, whereas commercial fishermen and onshore processors want to capture the feed species for canning or reduction to fish meal.

Another conflict is between people who consume fish directly as food and the operators of fish reduction plants, who want to extract oil and fish meal. Often the latter have an immediate economic advantage, but consumers who are poor may be worse off for the self-interested actions of plant operators.

Fisheries managers have a choice of many kinds of management technology. In the northeast Atlantic fishery, the size of the mesh in fishing nets has been regulated to ensure that small growing fish are not captured until they reach a suitable size. Quotas on the size of the catch for different species have been used by several international fish commissions, as have closed seasons for different species. In the Pacific Northwest halibut fishery, which was shared by Canada and the United States, catch limitations were managed by establishing closed seasons, limiting the size of fishing vessels, and prohibiting the use of highly efficient fishing gear. A management method that has been widely advocated by economists is to limit the entry of new fishing vessels into an established fishery.

Enforcement of management regulations is a continuing problem that has not been solved. It can be accomplished by monitoring fishing vessels and the size and composition of fish landings, but this must be supplemented by surveillance of entire EEZs to keep out foreign fishermen who will land their catch elsewhere. Managers must design enforceable penalties for violators and rewards for those who comply. Conservation is a major problem of fishery management. In the United States, the emphasis is on the conservation of marine mammals. From the fisherman's point of view, this is not very desirable, because seals and cetaceans compete directly for fishery resources.

In the eastern Pacific tuna fisheries, which are fished almost exclusively by large ships with huge purse-seine nets, fishermen locate schools of tuna by setting their nets on combined schools of porpoises and tunas. Hundreds of thousands of porpoises have been killed by being caught in the nets. Enforcement of measures to limit the kills of these long-lived and slow-to-reproduce animals requires the development of appropriate net patterns and enforcement by inspectors on the fishing vessels. In many developing countries, conservation of nearshore fish and shellfish habitats is of great importance. Coral reefs need to be protected against mining operations and pollution from eroding coastal lands. Mangrove swamps and coastal marshes and wetlands are the nursery grounds of many important fishes. These need to be protected from pollution and destructive exploitation for other purposes.

A beginning toward prevention of fish wastage can be made if fishery managers encourage and reward retention and use of the "by-catch," and if fish processing points are developed near landing points to lower postharvest losses.

In the past, fishery managers have tended to concentrate on individual species. In recent years, however, it has been recognized that management must take account of the ecology of many different species. Those under heavy fishing pressure, for example, are often replaced over large areas by other species. The decimation of the Peruvian anchoveta population was accompanied by a rapid increase in the abundance of Peru of sardines, mackeral, bonita, and hake. Even though the total Peruvian catches are now lower than those at the peak of anchoveta fishery, economic returns are probably greater, because it has been possible to use the incoming species for canning and other human food products.

Even with comparatively low fishing pressure, the relative abundance of different species may change markedly with time. Hence, future fisheries management can be expected to deal with fish ecosystems, not just single species. It may be useful to greatly reduce the population of unwanted species by heavy fishing in order to increase the population of more valuable kinds. An example is the low-value hake fishery off the West Coast of the United States versus the high-value fishery for pink shrimp. Since the hake prey on the shrimp, a large hake population tends to deplete the shrimp fishery.

Establishment of EEZs for all coastal states could lead to viable fishing industries in developing countries, more rational management of many coastal fisheries, and, possibly, an increase in both of the total world fish catch and of the proportion used for direct human consumption. But if these goals are to be attained, wise and effective management must be fostered by the coastal states. Large-scale training and adequate rewards for fishery scientists, engineers, technicians, economists, and administrators are required. Flexible and responsive governmental institutions must be established. Appropriate agreements must be reached with other fishing countries, and capital must be found for investing in fishing vessels and shore facilities. One developing country that has advanced a long way in these directions is Mexico.[23] In the four years after 1977, when the EEZ was established, the Mexican catch of fish and shellfish increased nearly fivefold, from 0.4 to 1.47 million mt/yr. During the process, the size of the Mexican fishing fleet was greatly expanded, and large capital expenditures were made. There is now danger of overcapitalization attended by a decline in the profitability of the fishery and possible overexploitation of the stocks.

In the United States, methods and institutions for fisheries policy and management were markedly changed in 1976 when the Fisheries Conservation and Management Act was passed by Congress. This act established seven regional fisheries councils consisting of public, industry, and state and federal representatives. These councils, acting on the recommendation of their scientific staffs and subject to approval by the National Marine Fisheries Service of the Department of Commerce, are responsible for annually setting total allowable catches for different commercial fish stocks (other than tuna and related species) and for allocating this catch among US and foreign fishermen. However, there are many other governmental agencies involved in establishing and enforcing US fishery policy, including state agencies that regulate fisheries and shore facilities in territorial waters (within the three-mile limit) and inland waters, the US Coast Guard, the Food and Drug Administration, the Environmental Protection Agency, the Fish and Wildlife Service, and the Department of State. The State Department is responsible for negotiating agreements with other countries concerning access of their fishermen to US waters and reciprocal access of the US fishermen to the EEZs of other coastal states.

For many years, the FAO, through nine international regional commissions, has provided technical assistance and advice to help advance the fisheries of developing countries. Unfortunately, these commissions have received little support or management authority from their member states. Recently the FAO has adopted a new strategy[24] and is organizing technical missions in response to requests from developing countries for assistance in the management of their EEZs. Advisory missions on fishery policy and planning have been set up in twenty-six countries. Assistance in drafting fishing legislation is being provided to forty-one countries, and advice on surveillance, fish marketing, and consumer issues is being given to a number of countries. It is not yet possible to judge the effectiveness of these measures.

NOTES

1. E. M. Borgese and N. Ginsburg, eds. *Ocean Yearbook 4* (Chicago: University of Chicago Press, 1983). Appendix C, tables 1C–6C, pp. 564–75.

2. FAO, *World Fisheries and the Law of the Sea* (Rome: 1981).

3. S. J. Holt and C. Vanderbilt, "Marine Fisheries," in *Ocean Yearbook 2*, ed. E. M. Borgese and N. Ginsburg (Chicago: University of Chicago Press, 1982), pp. 9–56.

4. K. C. Lucas, and T. Loftas, "FAO's EEZ Program: Helping to Build the Fisheries of the Future," in *Ocean Yearbook 3*, ed. E. M. Borgese and N. Ginsburg (Chicago: University of Chicago Press, 1978), pp. 38–76.

5. Lucas and Loftas, 1978.

6. Holt and Vanderbilt, 1982.

7. Borgese and Ginsburg, 1983.

8. Holt and Vanderbilt, 1982.

9. Borgese and Ginsburg, 1983.

10. Holt and Vanderbilt, 1982.

11. Protein derived from freshwater and saltwater aquacultural production in China provides 0.7 g per person per day, bringing the total per capita fish protein intake to 1.9 g per person per day, not much less than the average for the smaller developing countries. Similarly, in India, 0.3 g of fish protein per person per day comes from aquacultural production, bringing the total intake to 0.8 g per person per day.

12. Holt and Vanderbilt, 1982.

13. S. N. Dwivedi and N. P. Dunning, "Progress and Potential of Aquaculture: A Note on Developments in India," in *Ocean Yearbook 4*, ed. E. M. Borgese and N. Ginsburg (Chicago: University of Chicago Press, 1978), pp. 60–74.

14. T. V. R. Pillay, "Progress of Aquaculture," in *Ocean Yearbook 1*, ed. E. M. Borgese and N. Ginsburg (Chicago: University of Chicago Press, 1978), pp. 84–101.

15. Pillay, 1978.

16. R. R. Revelle, "Marine Technical Cooperation in the 1980s: An Overview," in *International Cooperation in Marine Technology, Science, and Fisheries: The Future U.S. Role in Development* (Washington, D.C.: National Academy Press, 1981), pp. 15–16.

17. Revelle, 1981.

18. E. Epstein, J. D. Norlyn, D. W. Rush, R. W. Kingsburg, O. B. Kelly, G. A. Cunningham, and A. F. Wrona, "Saline culture of crops: a genetic approach," *Science* 210 (1980):399–404.

19. FAO Committee on Fisheries, "Review of the State of World Fishery Resources" (Paper read at the fifteenth session in Rome, October 10–19, 1983).

20. Holt and Vanderbilt, 1982.

21. W. R., Emanuel, G. G. Killough, and J. S. Olson, "Modelling Circulation of Carbon in the World's Terrestrial Ecosystems," in *Carbon Cycle Modelling*, SCOPE 16, ed. B. Bolin (New York: Wiley, 1981), pp. 335–54.

22. The net conversion of sunlight by land plants varies widely from place to place and from time to time; it is more than 1.5 percent in some fields of tropical sugarcane and virtually zero in the Sahara. The variability in the ocean is probably somewhat smaller.

23. A. Szekely, "Implementing the New Law of the Sea: The Mexican Experience," in *Global Fisheries, Perspectives for the 1980s*, ed. R. J. Rothschild (New York: Springer-Verlag, 1983), pp. 51–72.

24. Lucas and Loftas, 1978.

CHAPTER FIFTEEN

Nonfuel Minerals and the World Economy

WILLIAM A. VOGELY

Minerals and materials (such as metals and ceramics) have not limited society's welfare in the past. Nor do they have the potential for limiting the welfare of mankind in the future, so long as certain institutional conditions are maintained. These conditions are the internalization of external environmental damages, worldwide trade access to raw materials, access to the earth's crust for exploration, and prevention of market control by either sellers or buyers. If these rules of the game are followed, mineral markets will provide supplies and ration use so that minerals and materials will be available to meet society's needs without significantly increasing costs for a very long time, probably forever.

EXHAUSTION AND DEPLETION OF MINERAL RESOURCES

There are two approaches to analyzing the exhaustion and depletion, one physical, the other economic. In the physical approach, mineral resources are thought of as a set of deposits in the earth that were formed in geologic time and that cannot be duplicated in human time. Removal of ore from this set of deposits reduces the remaining ore and depletes the resource. An elegant economic theory, the Pure Theory of Exhaustion, has been developed to fit this physical view, which is intuitively appealing and underlies much of the work on future supplies.

The economic view, which perhaps has less intuitive appeal, is strongly supported by history and by standard economic theory. In this view, reserves are thought of as the working inventory of the mineral-producing sector. They are provided efficiently by investment as needed. In this view, reserves are created from the underlying resource base by investing in exploration, technology, and mine development, just as capacity is generated in the nonmineral goods sector (see table 15.1). Minerals are scarce because they have production costs. The issue of future supply is whether they will become more scarce—that is, more expensive.

The physical approach and the Pure Theory of Exhaustion lead to the conclusion that minerals are certain to become more scarce in the future because the stock of reserves is finite and is thus exhausted by production. This view is widely held, but it is inconsistent with the behavior of prices and reserves over time. In the face of such behavior, should we still hold this view or should we try to understand the process better?

The simplest theory of exhaustion assumes that all reserves are known. Since the lowest-cost reserves are used first, costs rise as cumulative production increases. This is a correct model of a single deposit—say, a mine. A mine or an oil field will be depleted and then abandoned when, compared with other mines or fields, it no longer pays to mine or drill it. Such is the history of any mine or oil field. But the total of reserves does not behave this way, as many observers have noticed:

> By definition, reserves cover only those minerals contained in deposits that are known and that can be exploited profitably with existing technology and prices. Thus, reserves constitute

TABLE 15.1. World reserves and cumulative production of selected minerals, 1950–80 (million mt metal content).

Mineral	1980 reserve	Production 1950–80	1980 reserve
Copper	100	156	494
Iron	19,000	11,040	93,466
Aluminum	1,400	1,346	5,200
Lead	40	85	127

Source: Based on Tilton, 1977, p. 10; and "1980 Reserves from US Bureau of Mines," in *Mineral Facts and Problems*, 1980 ed.

only a subset, and typically an extremely small subset, of the resource base, the total amount of a mineral contained in the earth's crust.

While the resource base for a particular mineral commodity is a fixed stock, its reserves are not. Indeed, world production would have completely consumed copper reserves by the early 1970s had no new reserves been found. However, additions to reserves more than offset production, so that known copper reserves today are far larger than in the early postwar period.

As for iron, after World War II many feared that the world faced a serious shortage of this important mineral product, for wartime consumption had depleted the rich deposits of the Mesabi Range in Northern Minnesota. Since then major new deposits have been found in Canada, Brazil, Venezuela, Liberia, Australia, and other countries; and new technology has made the taconite deposits in Northern Minnesota and elsewhere viable sources of iron ore. These developments have added billions of tons to reserves. [Tilton, 1977, pp. 8–9]

A more formal statement is the following:

In any given mineral deposit and for all deposits taken together, there is a constant movement toward equating price with marginal cost in several stages:

1. The current operating margin, or rate of production, which is governed by the proportion of the reserve already depleted.
2. The intensive development margin, which includes investment costs for the already known deposits and is governed by the trade-off between rising investment requirements and quicker realization of revenue.
3. The extensive development margin, where exploitation is begun of known but previously uneconomic deposits.
4. The exploration margin, where a search for new deposits is conducted. The expected cost per unit is highly uncertain and the certain costs of many failures must be balanced against the chance of finding something worth finding, something with total marginal costs no higher than at margins 1-3.
5. The technology margin, which interacts with the first four.

The Gray-Hotelling [exhaustion] theory, it is apparent, is a special case because it covers only stages 1-3, setting 4 and 5 at zero. Yet, the last two are, in the long run, far more important. . . .

Reserves at any moment are by definition a stock, a fixed amount. But over time, both reserves and resources form part of a flow. [Adelman and Houghton, 1983, pp. 8-9, 15].

These quotations portray what has become the mainstream of economic thought, even though those who engage in resource assessments using an engineering or physical view of resources and reserves disagree. A less technical argument is presented by Julian Simon (1981) in *The Ultimate Resource*, chapter 3, "Can the Supply of Natural Resources Really Be Infinite? Yes!"

Stated simply, the argument is that primary mineral supplies produced from reserves will flow to the world economy at a cost that will support the demand for primary supplies as affected by supplies from scrap. Historically, primary minerals have become available when they have been demanded and at increasingly lower real prices. Energy price rises in the 1970s, however, caused mineral prices to rise to reflect energy's role in production. Also, external costs have been incorporated in mineral production costs. Yet, rises in energy cost came not from exhaustion but from market power. Even with these factors, real mineral prices rose less than 1 percent in the 1970s. Any sharp break will be quickly reflected in price and output behavior, as producers adjust to the margins listed above.

THE EVIDENCE

The argument that mineral supply as measured by reserves increases to meet demand at a price has been presented in theoretical terms, with the performance of reserves as the fundamental evidence. But what about prices? Table 15.2 shows the price history of minerals and fuels for more than a century. Only in the 1970s did general price increases occur. (US prices are used in table 15.2, since the United States is the major consumer and producer of many minerals.) Table 15.3 presents the picture in Europe. Table 15.4 compares US and European prices. The price data show a sharp break in the price trend for the 1970s.

Is this evidence that the reserve replacement process is now involving increased real cost? Perhaps not. The increases in fuel and energy prices are clearly traced to the exercise of market power, but these costs are incorporated into the cost structure for other minerals that are relatively energy-intensive. Equally important, in the United States and perhaps elsewhere, the environmental externalities have

TABLE 15.2. United States, relative price changes of minerals, 1950–70 and 1970–80 (minerals prices divided by GNP deflator; average annual rates of change, percent).

Mineral category	Trend 1950–70 "b"	Change in trend "c"	Trend 1970–80 "b" + "c"
Fuels[a]	−1.7[b]	13.8[b]	12.1[b]
petroleum	−1.4[b]	12.5[b]	11.0[b]
natural gas	2.6[b]	15.0[b]	17.6[b]
bituminous coal	−2.2[b]	11.7[b]	9.4[b]
Ores and metals[a]	−0.2	2.5	2.3
iron ore	−1.1[b]	1.5	0.4
steel	−0.3	4.7[b]	4.5[b]
manganese	−6.2[b]	10.6[b]	4.4[b]
aluminum	0.1	4.8[b]	4.7[b]
copper	0.3	−1.7	−1.3
lead	−2.8[b]	+8.8[b]	6.0[b]
mercury	3.9[b]	−14.1[b]	−10.3[b]
nickel	1.1[b]	2.5[b]	3.6[b]
tin	0.6	9.1[b]	9.8[b]
zinc	−2.1[b]	4.9[b]	2.7[b]

Source: Barnett and Myers, "Minerals and Economic Growth," in *Economics of Minerals Industries*, ed., Vogely, 4th ed. in press.
[a] Only selected components are shown separately.
[b] Significantly different from zero at the 5% probability level.

been internalized into production costs. Three factors can cause prices to rise in real terms:

1. The exercise of market power
2. The failure of technology to offset depletion of currently producing deposits
3. The incorporation of external social costs into product prices.

The price increases of the 1970s are clearly related to the first and third factors. The experience of the first half of the 1980s is that the trend of the century 1870-1970 has been resumed in the first four years of the decade. Table 15.5 presents selected price histories for 1980-1983 using year-average data, and table 15.6 shows the increase in mineral consumption underlying the price trends.

The dismissal of the problem of long-term adequacy of nonfuel mineral supplies does not mean that there are not mineral supply problems. The establishment of presidential commissions or

TABLE 15.3. Western Europe, relative price changes of minerals, 1950–70 and 1970–80 (minerals prices divided by GNP deflator; average annual rates of change, percent).

Mineral category	1950–70	1970–80
Fuels[a]	− 3.7	16.6
petroleum	− 4.2	18.3
natural gas	n.a.	6.6
bituminous coal	− 3.0	2.9
Ores and metals[a]	− 1.9	− 2.6
iron ore	− 3.0	− 4.4
steel	− 2.0	0.8
manganese	− 7.8	− 0.6
aluminum	− 1.9	− 0.2
copper	− 0.4	− 7.5
lead	− 5.2	1.5
mercury	1.8	− 14.1
nickel	− 0.4	− 1.3
tin	− 1.2	5.4
zinc	− 4.5	− 3.8

Source: Barnett and Myers, "Minerals and Economic Growth," in Economics of the Mineral Industries, ed. Vogely, 4th ed., in press.
[a] Only selected components are shown separately.
n.a. = not available.

congressionally mandated studies every few years clearly indicates that there are at least perceived supply problems. However, almost every commission or study team has concluded that these perceived problems do not require corrective action. The only exceptions were the implementation of national security stockpiles after World War II and the incorporation of environmental standards beginning in the 1960s and supported by the commission reporting in 1972.

The commission that was set up in response to the rise in materials prices after the removal of price controls in 1974 reported in 1976 that, as a result of certain US policies, including price controls, not enough was invested in metals during the late 1960s and early 1970s. The modest recommendations of this commission were not implemented by Congress or the Carter administration. In a study organized by the National Academy of Sciences, a committee of the Nonfuel Minerals Advisory Board found no evidence that mineral supply interruptions had ever cost the US economy enough to justify a government program to handle the problem.

The cobalt supply problem of the mid-1970s serves as an excellent case study of how economies can adjust to interruptions in supply without government interference in markets. Cobalt has many uses, some of which (especially its use in jet engine turbines and, at the time of the interruption, in high-temperature magnets) are considered vital to US national security. The United States gets most of its cobalt from Zaire, where the military cut off supplies. Consumers of cobalt turned to the strategic stockpile for supplies, but their applications were denied since there was no state of national emergency. As they scrambled for supplies, prices rose. Applications of less value uses diminished, and consumers who absolutely had to have cobalt were able to obtain it at a higher price. Meanwhile, the search for new technologies was spurred: cobalt-free magnets were developed, and research is continuing on other materials (ceramics, for instance) for turbine blades. Ceramics have replaced cobalt in automobile turbochargers.

A continuing concern that has global policy implications is that reserves at any given time are concentrated in relatively few areas, so trade is necessary if minerals are to be available to the world's econo-

TABLE 15.4. Relative price changes of minerals, OECD-Europe and United States, 1950–80 (average annual rates of change, percent).

Mineral category	1950–70		1970–80	
	Europe	US	Europe	US
Fuels	− 3.7	− 1.7	16.6	12.1
petroleum	− 4.2	− 1.4	18.3	11.0
natural gas	n.a.	2.6	6.6	17.6
coal	− 3.0	− 2.2	2.9	9.4
Ores and metals	− 1.9	− 0.2	− 2.6	2.3
iron ore	− 3.0	− 1.1	− 4.4	0.4
steel	− 2.0	− 0.3	0.8	4.5
manganese	− 7.8	− 6.2	− 0.6	4.4
aluminum	− 1.0	− 0.1	− 0.2	4.7
copper	− 0.4	0.3	− 7.5	− 1.3
lead	− 5.2	− 2.8	1.5	6.0
mercury	1.8	3.9	− 14.1	10.3
nickel	− 0.4	1.1	− 1.3	3.6
tin	− 1.2	0.6	5.4	9.8
zinc	− 4.5	− 2.1	− 3.8	2.7

TABLE 15.5. Selected prices of minerals for 1980 and 1983, in current and 1972 dollars.[a]

Commodity	Prices (average) 1980	In 1972 dollars (b)	1983		In 1972 dollars (c)
Coal	135.1 (cents per million Btu)	73.34	164.70	(Oct)	73.56
Oil (imported refiner acquisition cost of crude oil)	33.89 ($ per lb)	18.40	29.09	(Nov)	12.99
Copper (domestic producer cathode)	1.013 ($ per lb)	0.55	0.77		0.34
Pig iron	203.00 ($ per ton)	110.21	213.00		95.13
Lead (US)	0.425 ($ per lb)	0.23	0.22 ($ per lb)		0.10
Molybdenum (concentrate)	9.70 ($ per lb)	5.27	4.00		1.79
Nickel (fob Ontario)	3.41 ($ per lb)	1.85	3.20		1.43
Zinc (US)	0.374 ($ per lb)	0.20	0.42		0.19

[a] The figures for coal are taken from US Department of Energy, Energy Information Administration, *Monthly Energy Review*, (December, 1983), those for oil from ibid., p. 84; those for the other commodities from Janice L. W. Jolly, *Mineral Commodity Summaries 1984* (US Dept. of the Interior, Bureau of Mines).
[b] Deflation factor is 1.842.
[c] Deflation factor is 2.239.

mies. Influenced by proximity to markets, the world's major nonfuel production has been located in the industrialized countries, including the United States and western Europe. Least-cost supplies in the future, however, are likely to come from the current developing countries. This is already true of copper and is becoming true of iron. A multilateral nonbarrier trading system is fundamental to meeting these mutual needs.

A related concern is how technological change provides new supplies or alters material demands. Major new copper supplies were developed from the low-grade deposits of the southwestern United States in the 1920s. Supplies from the rich native copper deposits of the Midwest could not increase in response to growing demands from the electrical and automobile sectors. Although the copper deposits of the Southwest had long been known, two new technologies were needed for their development. First, the internal-combustion engine increased miners' ability to move large quantities of rock and earth in open-pit mining. Second, new means of concentrating the desired mineral contained in the ore were developed in the 1920s. In particular, froth-flotation techniques were developed to allow concentration of ores less than half the grade of ore concentrated by direct gravity methods (then the state of the art). Similar advances have greatly increased the reserves of nickel, by making the mining of large low-grade laterite deposits around the world economical.

SEABED MINERALS

Typically, there are large resource deposits that are not considered reserves because of the costs of extraction. Such resources attract research and commercial interest, however, because of their large total

TABLE 15.6. United States, mineral consumption, 1870–1970, at ten year intervals (physical quantities valued at 1967 prices in millions of dollars).

Year	Total	Fuels	Metals	Non metal, nonfuel minerals
1870	456	258	64	134
1880	964	510	172	283
1890	1,878	995	349	535
1900	2,635	1,551	584	500
1910	4,936	3,104	1,143	689
1920	6,716	4,533	1,511	673
1930	7,860	5,426	1,450	985
1940	9,669	6,627	2,136	906
1950	14,419	9,748	3,021	1,650
1960	18,669	13,181	2,788	2,700
1970	27,326	19,651	3,691	3,984
	annual average rate of change, percent			
1970–	+4.2	+4.4	+4.1	+3.5

Source: *Barnett and Myers, "Minerals and Economic Growth," in Economics of the Mineral Industries, ed. Vogely, 4th ed., in press.*

mineral content. Two examples of eventual movement of such resources into reserves are the taconite developments and the nickel laterites. Seabed nodules and the sea-bottom crust contain large quantities of nickel, copper, cobalt, manganese, and probably other minerals. Movement along the technology margin is necessary before these resources, even in part, become reserves. Also, political and legal issues must be settled before the required investments can be made. Because of their large potential, seabed minerals will continue to attract research investments in technology, as well as multinational attempts to settle the political and legal issues. Careful and scholarly work, as opposed to promotional work, does not foresee any likelihood of the needed technological or political developments for several decades, but, to emphasize a fundamental point of this paper, prophesying the future of technology, and thus mineral supplies and demands, is very risky. If any of the three factors of depletion, market control of supply, or high environmental costs of the land developments come into play, the seabed minerals might attract larger research interest and political motivation that could transform some part of these deposits into reserves sooner than expected. On the other hand, continued improvements in current production technology and successful exploration for other new deposits could delay development of seabed minerals indefinitely.

ESTIMATES OF FUTURE SUPPLIES AND CONSUMPTION

Almost all studies dealing with the future are based on the physical view of exhaustion. Most pay lip servie to technology and exploration but nevertheless estimate a stock of potential reserves, thus placing a finite limit on ultimate production. Such efforts add no information about future supplies. Not only are they useless, if believed by policymakers, but they can lead to bad, self-fulfilling policies. Such may be the case in the United States with its price controls and legislated end-use controls on natural gas.

This is not to say that there should be no further study of long-term resource assessment. Such work should be carried out as long as it leads to a better understanding of resource endowment and improves the efficiency of exploration. But work spent on puttng numbers in the various boxes on the unknown geologic side of the McKelvy box reproduced as figure 15.1 is useless and, unless it is clearly understood that the box applies to only a small area of the earth, misleading. Resource assessments are useful policy and invest-

RESOURCES OF (commodity name)
[A part of reserves or any resource category may be restricted from extraction
by laws or regulations (see text)]
AREA: (mine, district, field, State, etc.) UNITS: (tons, barrels, ounces, etc.)

Cumulative Production	IDENTIFIED RESOURCES			UNDISCOVERED RESOURCES	
	Demonstrated		Inferred	Probability Range (or)	
	Measured	Indicated		Hypothetical	Speculative
ECONOMIC	Reserves		Inferred Reserves		
MARGINALLY ECONOMIC	Marginal Reserves		Inferred Marginal Reserves		
SUBECONOMIC	Demonstrated Subeconomic Resources		Inferred Subeconomic Resources		

Other Occurrences	Includes nonconventional and low-grade materials.

Author   Date:

FIGURE 15.1. Major elements of mineral-resource classification, excluding the reserve base and inferred reserve base.

ment guides for small well-defined geologic and geographic areas, but they cannot be used for estimation of future world supply. (Examples of worldwide studies based on the physical view of resource supply include Ridker and Watson, 1980, and Leontief et al., 1982.)

Similar problems are associated with long-term consumption forecasts. A mineral is demanded because it embodies certain physical properties. All estimates of future demands for this mineral are on a commodity basis and thus do not consider switches among minerals in response to changes in technology or relative prices. Estimates of copper consumption for communication uses made several decades ago, for example, could not have foreseen the growth of satellite communications or the development of optic fiber cables for telecommunications. So the scenario studies of the future come out as the writer chooses.

The demand for minerals is derived from the technologies used to produce capital and consumer goods. Thus mineral demands are derived from final product demands. If real prices for any mineral increase, either because the exploration and investment needed to turn resources into reserves are inadequate or because the market is controlled, substitutes for that mineral will be found. Macro variables, such as commodity consumption per unit of GDP or per capita GNP, are usually the basis for consumption estimates. Typically, such trends show declines in a minerals ratio over a long time period. These declines represent not only mineral-for- mineral substitution but also increased efficiency in the use of a mineral in the production of a final product (see Tilton, 1983).

There are mineral issues and problems. The geographic distribution of reserves means that demands may be in areas where there is no production, so trade is vital. Political factors may create fears of supply interruption. Price volatility may create income difficulties for producers or nations that depend heavily on resource income to purchase other goods.

DIFFERENTIAL IMPACT OF PRICE VARIABILITY

The high price variability exhibited by metals has differential implications for consumers and producers. Producers can insulate themselves by holding stocks, hedging their inventories, and seeking substitute technologies for manufacturing their products. The alternatives for the developing country producer who is dependent on mineral production for foreign exchange earnings are less obvious and effective. Papua New Guinea has approached the copper price problem by establishing a fund into which government receipts from copper mining are placed as received, but expenditures are levied on an annual basis to avoid the wide swings in the national budget arising from price changes. To date, even with the depressed price of copper, the fund has remained in the black. Other producer countries try to maintain revenues by continuing high levels of production even at depressed prices. This practice has been cited as a contributing reason for the failure of copper prices to rise with the recent expansion in world economic activity. Attempts by the industrialized countries to adopt tariff structures to protect their refining and processing industries, a traditional policy, intensifies the adverse implications of primary metal price variability for developing country producers.

Since many such policies are based on arguments by the industrialized countries that they must protect themselves in times of political crises from the cutoff of needed raw material supplies, the difference between dependence on imported supplies and vulnerability to danger must be sharply drawn. The danger can be most cheaply avoided by stockpiles for emergency use or research on substitute materials, rather than protection of high-cost domestic industry capacity. The simple equation of import dependence with danger leads to policies that damage both developing country exporters and industrialized country importers.

Society often make decisions that can lead to bad results. The development of nuclear weapons is but the extreme example, whereas autarky and national drives for self-sufficiency and maintenance of domestic industries for regional or defense purposes are more common policies that can greatly diminish the global possible future. Market power can redistribute wealth as it has through the petroleum markets, though the income flows are much smaller from nonfuels that fuels, so the incentives are smaller. Just as it is in the self-interest of a producer to seek market power, it is in the short-teerm self-interest of a nation to protect domestic industry from world competition. But in both cases, consumers pay the price, and total income flow and wealth are diminished. The world, in short, is worse off. The challenge is to fight for policies that allow efficient production, trade, and use.

If we don't want nonfuel mineral resource supply to limit economic welfare, we must protect and provide flows from the resource base to reserves and efficiently ration use. Having rejected arguments that cite exhaustion or depletion as causes of interruption of the supply flow, what else remains? The necessary conditions for a functioning market remain. These can be laid out simply:

1. External costs should be internalized—that is, incorporated into the cost and price of every mineral. This can be done by many methods. Economists prefer to use taxes to reduce external damages at the least cost, but political decision-makers seem to prefer standards and regulations.
2. Relatively free international trade must be maintained, including capital flows.
3. Access to exploration markets must be maintained. This does not mean that some lands cannot be closed on the grounds

that exploration will entail relatively greater losses. It does mean that the cost of preventing exploration must be considered. If exploration damage could be internalized, there would be no need to close any lands. But, when damages can be irreversible, this policy may not be possible to implement.

4. Exercise of market power by either producers or consumers must be prevented—perhaps the most difficult condition to achieve on an international basis.

ACHIEVING THE GLOBAL POSSIBLE

The focus of efforts toward achieving the global possible should be on how to maintain the mineral supply process that has provided low-priced minerals for such a long time. In general, this means maintaining the necessary conditions for the market to operate. However difficult, governments and action organizattions must simply stay out of the way in most cases and not impose their own preconceptions upon market solutions. The job of those interested in the future of humankind is not to meddle but to act only to prevent governments and market participants from exerting control over markets or from transferring wealth to themselves by taking advantage of other producers. Yet, because the market works, albeit differently, regardless of who owns productive capacity, national ownership of minerals is not a fatal market failure.

To achieve the global possible through an unfettered market, several actions are necessary. Internalizing external costs requires solid data and a willingness to accept trade-offs. Further, efficiency requires that the marginal external damage reduction equal the marginal cost of damage mitigation—easier said than done. Those who would bear the cost of mitigation naturally tend to understate the damages, while those who experienece the damages just as naturally overstate them. Somehow, disinterested scientific research must be brought to bear. Similarly, there are many difficulties in carrying out the required cost-benefit or risk-benefit studies. But it must be understood that action to force mitigation always implies a cost-benefit finding or a risk-benefit judgment. Clearly, better knowledge can lead to better solutions, even though it hasn't always been this way.

A more difficult issue is that societies around the world and groups within each society make differing value judgments about external damages. Developing countries may feel that external costs are acceptable if they allow the use of local resources to generate wealth and perhaps to supply food. So, worldwide internalization might require imposing outside value judgments on such societies. The same holds true within a society if the external cost is borne by a different group from that which bears the internalized cost. The acid rain issue in the United States and elsewere in the world is a good case in point.

The discussion so far has called for internalization of environmental damage, so that the full social costs of production are reflected in mineral and all prices. Most economists believe that the tax system is the most effective way to internalize external cost, but most have chosen direct regulation, which has been successful but perhaps at excessive cost to society. Although efficient internalization has proved elusive, it must remain a top objective of worldwide policy.

Still, if governments and international organizations fail to impose external costs across the board, those who do not bear the cost will amass wealth from those who do. Efficiency will suffer and the global possible will be reduced.

Perhaps a multinational scientific examination of the external damages associated with the production-and-use cycle of nonfuel minerals should be directed to gather sound information without imposing value judgments. Perhaps a science court, where rules of evidence and cross-examination procedures, before a jury or judge of scientific competence could give a strong evaluation of the issues to political decision-makers. Failure to achieve this goal for a properly functioning supply process will recduce the global possible.

The key to guaranteeing worldwide trade access to raw materials and capital sources is to avoid autarky. The free-trade movement that started in the early 1930s has died. Protection of domestic industries is on the rise, centered in the developed nations of Europe and North America. If these countries decide not to let their economies adjust to the changing state of comparative advantage, the future of the world's productivity will be severely limited.

Nations should renew their dedication to free trade. Every nation sees the short-term advantage in protecting domestic industry and tends to ignore the longer-term implications of retaliation—overall inefficiency in the domestic economy, which will manifest itself as slower growth in real income. The political appeal of protection is strong, regardless of the form of government, but free trade should be a high priority.

Since resources are fed into the supply stream by exploration, and competition for land use grows as certain land-use values become increasingly important, mineral values created by exploration must be considered in land-use decisions. Unfortunately, some uses are not reversible, and many values (such as mineral potential and wildlife habitats) are difficult to measure. For nonfuel minerals, these difficulties will not become serious unless large percentages of geologically attractive regions are closed. Of course, forcing a shift of exploration activities does reduce the efficiency of exploration and could raise mineral costs. Society must weigh these costs against the gains in value from alternative land uses. If the external costs of exploration could be internalized, the problem could be solved.

Market control is illegal in some nations. Other nations deliberately establish market controls to shift wealth to themselves. Market power is self-limiting and can be mitigated if markets are allowed to work. For instance, world markets, when finally freed from government-imposed constraints, have moved to change the market shares of OPEC and to limit OPEC's power to set prices.

Market failures are less likely to occur with nonfuel minerals. There is less concentration of low-cost deposits on a regional basis, and substitutes for any particular mineral are more available and cheaper. Also, the possible gain from market control is much smaller, as the total value of mineral supplies is orders of magnitude smaller than that of oil. Nevertheless, producers still try to establish coordinated production policies through producer associations and through commodity agreements. Also, major consumers may attempt to coordinate purchases to take rents from producers. Such attempts at gaining market control, if successful, can reduce the global possible.

The main challenge for policy makers, therefore, is to find specific ways to reduce impediments to competitive market production and trade, to curtail market power and its harmful exercise, and, most difficult perhaps, to assess and internalize the inevitable tradeoffs between commercial and nonmarket environmental values.

REFERENCES

Adelman, M. A., and J. C. Houghton. Introduction of Estimation of Reserves and Resources. Part I of *Energy Resources in an Uncertain Future.* Cambridge, Mass.: Ballinger.
Leontief, W., J. Koo, S. Nasar, and I. Sohn. 1982. *The Production and Consumption of Nonfuel Minerals to the Year 2030 Analyzed Within*

an *Input–Output Framework of the U.S. and World Economy*. New York: New York University Press.

Ridker, R. G., and W. D. Watson. 1980. *To Choose a Future*. Baltimore: Johns Hopkins University Press, for Resources for the Future.

Simon, J. L. 1981. *The Ultimate Resource*. Princeton: Princeton University Press.

Tilton, J. E. 1977. *The Future of Nonfuel Minerals*. Washington, D.C.: The Brookings Institution.

Tilton, J. E., ed. 1983. *Material Substitution*. Baltimore: Johns Hopkins University Press, for Resources for the Future.

Tilton, J. E., and W. A. Vogely, eds. 1981. Market instability in the metal industries. In *Materials and Society*, vol. 5, no. 3. New York: Pergamon Press.

PART III

Policy Agenda and Implementation

CHAPTER SIXTEEN

The Global Possible: What Can Be Gained?

NORMAN MYERS

A wide range of resources and environmental concerns will be of increasing importance as we move toward the twenty-first century. Equally important will be a number of impressive opportunities to preserve our resource base and to manage it for sustained, higher productivity. A lengthy agenda of policy changes and other initiatives, mostly derived from positive experience, has been formulated in the Global Possible Conference.

The aim here is to foster the process of building commitment and forging a determined effort to carry out that agenda. This paper depicts, in broad strokes at least, what we can hope to gain through imaginative, as well as rapid, responses to our problems.

Detailed projections and scenarios have been avoided, however, because of the uncertainty and surprise inherent in human events. Simple extrapolations of present trends and the mere continuation of present policies in many cases are impossible because change is inevitable. Yet society lacks the capacity to foresee more than the dim outlines of the future, even a decade or two in advance. Nonetheless, we can see the direction in which certain paths will lead us, even though it is uncertain how long it will take to reach the destinations to which they lead. Yet the farther we travel, the more it becomes apparent that one path diverges from another, and thus the greater the importance of choosing the right direction at the start.

This is why it is vital to keep the payoffs clearly in mind. Even though investment initiatives, policy changes, and other proposed mechanisms are feasible, practical, and promise benefits well in excess of the costs, there are short-term obstacles—notably, political interests and institutional inertia—to be overcome. But these impediments seem formidable only when we consider the near future. By contrast, when we balance against them the enormous benefits possible in the long term and the immense cost of inaction, the short-term costs appear a small price to pay. For example, governments that delay in initiating policies and providing services to lower the rates of population growth will face much greater demographic pressures later on. Governments that wait to correct the pricing of energy, water, and other resources will find that future adjustments to the resulting shortages and inappropriate use patterns will be more onerous.

The challenges to be met in achieving the global possible are interconnected and transcend national boundaries. Common interests exist among the community of nations, which should induce governments to act in concert. It is essential, therefore, to establish common ground through coordinated assessment of our options—for example, through international discussion and negotiation of programs that will benefit all. Clearly the challenges reach far beyond sectoral limits.

It has been emphasized again and again that there are options for single-sector initiatives that will solidly enhance the prospects for a brighter future. Almost certainly, however, the biggest payoffs will lie not so much in a simple sector-by-sector approach. They will lie in those areas where an initiative in one sector generates benefits that spill over into other sectors. Even more important, it often happens that this intersectoral linkage operates to the synergistic advantage of the sectors in question. That is to say, simultaneous initiative in several sectors can generate benefits that, by virtue of dynamic interactions between the sectors, serve to amplify one another. It is in these areas, characterized by mutual compounding of impact, that we can expect the biggest payoffs of all.

MULTISECTOR PAYOFFS

Population Planning

The ultimate size of a population depends not only on growth rates at given times but also on the phenomenon of demographic momentum.

The more children born, the more potential parents there are for the future; and the longer the delay in bringing family size down to acceptable levels, the longer the inertia of population growth will persist.

In China, a case in point, even if family size were reduced to replacement level forthwith (that is, a little more than two children per reproductive couple), the population, with its "youthful profile," would continue to grow for almost another two generations, from just over one billion today to an eventual total of 8 billion.[1] So China is trying to establish the one-child family as the norm of 70 percent of its reproductive couples—and even this extraordinary measure will still mean continued population growth until the year 2000, before stabilization at an eventual total of 1.2 billion. These calculations indicate the immense gains to be derived from vigorous family planning campaigns.

The reverse side of this somewhat dismal picture[2] is that demographic momentum works to positive effect too, when once a decline in fertility rates is firmly under way. The UN median projection for our population future assumes that replacement fertility will be reached by the year 2025. Were it to be delayed by twenty years, there would be an extra 2.8 bilion people; and were it to be accelerated by twenty years, there would be 2.2 billion fewer people, a difference greater than the current world total.

Of course, replacement fertility will not be achieved by the year 2005. But if it were to be reached by the year 2015, an ambitious though not impossile goal requiring that the total number of women practicing contraception increase by 6.5 percent per year, the result would be at least a billion fewer people. If the initiatives proposed in this conference, especially those on population and poverty, were widely adopted in the next five years, the world's population could stabilize at about eight billion people.

This all points to a key conclusion, moreover. One dollar invested in birth control, basic health services, and the alleviation of poverty right now can achieve as much as several dollars invested for the same purpose ten years hence.

Without a sizable increase in population planning programs, it is difficult to see how most Third World nations can achieve their development goals. Of course, the situation is not a straightforward case of "fewer people means more socioeconomic advancement per head": a host of other factors impinge on the complex relationships involved. Nonetheless, the development prospects of Bangladesh, for instance, will surely be dim if its population continues to grow at projected rates, which would lead to 430 million people trying to survive in a country the size of Louisiana by late next century. Similar constraints must surely apply to Pakistan, whose popultion is projected to reach 411 million before stabilization; Brazil, 326 million; Indonesia, 416 million; Ethiopia, 244 million; Kenya, 127 million; and Nigeria, 623 million.[3]

The single most important factor in accelerating a fertility decline is the education of women. Education is also critical in reducing infant mortality, alleviating poverty, enchancing agricultural production, and improving energy use in most parts of the world. Yet outside of China and India, only 55 percent of primary school-age girls in low-income countries were enrolled in 1980, and, in low-income African countries, only 42 percent. Raising that figure close to 100 percent over the next fifteen years is feasible, albeit difficult, and it would have enormous returns.

It is surely not altogether coincidental that the region with the highest population growth rates since 1970, black Africa, is the region where per capita food production has declined by a full 10 percent, and where malnutrition is most widespread. According to strictly demographic projections (that is, projections that look at population dynamics in isolation from other factors such as the natural resource base), the population of Africa is projected to expand from its present total of 500 million people to five times that many before zero growth rate is reached early in the twenty-second century.[4] When impoverished peasants are starving, they will go to any lengths to sustain themselves: they will dig up marginal lands from one horizon to another, even though they realize that crop productivity in these areas will be short-lived at best. Without substantial changes in policies and programs, the outlook for Africa must surely be grim—a steady degradation of much of the natural resource base, with whatever that implies for the capacity of human communities to sustain themselves.

Hence, the payoff is large in all directions—food, health, education, employment, urbanization—if nations with rapidly growing populations undertake the policy initiatives and investments necessary to cut growth rates faster than is now anticipated. Fortunately, many of these nations have recently shifted their policy perceptions of population planning, and 90 percent of Third World people live in countries that have the avowed aim of meeting family planning needs and reducing growth rates. There is much motivation, not only on the part of governments but of citizenry as well. Yet only a quarter of married women of reproductive age practice contraception, and the fact that a huge need remains unmet is evidenced by the 50-70 million abortions performed each year. What is lacking is the funding and other resources to confront the challenge. We need to think in terms of outlays of $3 billion a year for family planning facilities, or three times more than is now expended—no great sum in comparison with the dividends to be enjoyed.

At the same time, we can take heart from some remarkable breakthroughs in reducing fertility rates. China has brought its birth rate down from 34 to 20 per 1,000 during just one decade, not only through vigorous family planning efforts and population policies but also through measures to reduce infant mortality, educate women, end sex discrimination, equalize economic opportunities, and eradicate mass poverty. Remarkable progress, not as extraordinary as China's but still far surpassing expectations, has recently been registered by such disparate countries as Thailand, Indonesia, Cuba, and Colombia. Plainly the job can be done if appropriate policies are designed, if these are backed by sufficient political commitment.[5]

Public Health in the Third World

Attention to the public health sector yields sizable payoffs, not only in physical welfare but also in worker productivity and the like—and most particularly in birth-control efforts.[6] Without greater progress in this field, the best population planning policies, let alone programs, will not be successful. Hence the linkage between public health and population planning, a salient instance of how benefits in one sector, public health, generate substantial spillover benefits for another sector, population planning.

Of 100 million children born in the Third World each year, an estimated 15 million do not survive beyond their first few years.[7] As long as child mortality rates remain high, Third World parents will feel little incentive to reduce their fertility rates. An immunization campaign to provide protection against six leading diseases and thus prevent some 5 million deaths each year can be achieved for a mere $5 per child, or $500 million per year—no great amount, yet much more than present funding of $70 million per year[8] The biggest single killer of all, whether through direct or indirect effects, is diarrhea, a problem that can be countered by simple oral rehydration therapy at a cost of under 10 cents per dose, or a total sum (including delivery charges) somewhere between $0.5 and $1 billion per year.[9]

Reducing the diarrheal diseases and parasitic infestations that debilitate hundreds of millions of children and adults would have enormous payoffs, some of which are little appreciated.[10] Nutrition would be immediately improved, with no increase required in agricultural production. Malabsorption of nutrients through the intestine robs sufferers from these diseases of the benefit of at least 20 percent of the food they consume, and acute cases of malnutrition in Third World children typically follow bouts of diarrheal disease. Learning would be immediately accelerated, with no increase necessary in the availability of teachers and schools. Illness, undernutrition, and absence from school are common causes of poor performance and early dropout, with lifelong consequences for the children. Encouraging mothers to continue breast-feeding and discouraging bottle-feeding except in cases of medical necessity would have an enormous impact.

Even more to the point, an entire package of primary health care for Third World people can be put together for a cost of only $2-4 per person per year.[11] This is no more than many Third World countries already spend on their health sectors. But a disproportionate amount goes to curative rather than preventive medicine, catering to the needs of a minority, usually an elite city-based minority, and thus bypassing the needs of the rural and disease-ridden majority. In the Philippines, a heart surgery unit has recently been installed at a cost of $50 million, or roughly $1 for every person in the country, yet able to help only a few hundred persons each year. Life expectancy in China is greater than that in Brazil, a country with a per capita income five times as high, yet China has achieved this with health spending of only about $4 per person per year.[12] A major initiative already attempted in the health sector is the UN Water and Sanitation Decade. To supply basic facilities for all Third World countries during the 1980s will cost $60 billion per year, about four times as much as was being allocated during the late 1970s by all funding sources—that is, by international development agencies and Third World governments. A more modest effort, aiming at 80 percent coverage, need cost only half as much. Yet we are nowhere near achieving even the second goal, even though dirty water and unhygienic environments are a prime source of water-borne diseases, with all that implies for child mortality, fertility rates, population planning, and development programs overall.

Genetic Resources

The earth's stocks of genetic resources constitute an abundant and diverse array of raw materials that serve our welfare in myriad ways.[13] Yet genetic resources in wild species of plants and animals are being eliminated at wholly unprecedented rates. By the end of the next century, we could lose anywhere between a quarter and a half of all species and a still greater proportion of the genetic materials they contain.[14] This will represent an irreversible loss of unique natural resources.

To gain an idea of the importance of genetic resources, consider that in the field of medicine and pharmaceuticals alone they generate products with over-the-counter sales worldwide on the order of $40 billion per year.[15] In agriculture, regular infusions of superior genetic materials into crop plants account for at least 1 percent of increased productivity each year, estimated to be worth $1 billion in the United States alone. A recently discovered form of wild corn, growing in the last four hectares of natural habitat in a Mexican forest, not only harbors perennial traits, but, by virtue of the dampness of its montane environment, could enable corn to be grown in soils that are too wet for conventional varieties, thus expanding the range of corn by more than one-tenth, with extra output worth $1 billion per year. In addition, the wild variety is immune to, or at least tolerant of, at least four of the eight leading viruses and mycoplasmas that now cause a loss of at least 1 percent in the world's corn harvest each year, worth more than $500 million. Thus, a single plant species can harbor potential for significant benefits—and in this case, it is an unusually threatened species.

The economic contributions of genetic resources to date derive from investigations of only a tiny fraction of all wild species, and a still smaller proportion of their genetic variability. Given our experience so far, we can fairly anticipate that genetic resources will yield an array of anti-cancer drugs, anti-viral products, genetically engineered crops for diverse environmental conditions, energy products, and a host of phytochemicals to substitute for ever-more-costly petrochemicals.

The principal way to safeguard genetic reservoirs and wild species is through protected areas. We need to expand our networks of protected areas several-fold, preferably by enough to include 10 percent of the area of each major biogeographical province, if we are to achieve a systematic spread of areas that represent all biotic provinces of the world.[16] The cost can be roughly estimated at some $1-2 billion per year for the next ten years—no great investment in view of the benefits to be generated in several prominent sectors. In the field of energy, a number of fast-growing plants offer potential for pyrolized fuels, and certain hydrocarbon-bearing plants open up the prospect of "growing gasoline." In agriculture, plant breeders are developing salt-tolerant strains of wheat, barley, tomatoes, and several other crops, thus allowing saline lands to be brought into production. Pioneer types of leguminous shrubs enable degraded lands to be rehabilitated. In the field of public health, plants offer not only a broad array of drugs but safe and effective contraceptive materials, for use by both women and men. If the buildup of carbon dioxide continues, we shall need a spectrum of crop varieties that can adapt to new climatic regimes and can exploit additional carbon dioxide without suffering water stress. Conversely, a world with vegetation boundaries migrating away from the equator will mean that many protected areas established now will no longer perform their intended function— which means that it is not too soon for conservation planners to anticipate a carbon dioxide-modified world.

Tropical Forests

Improved management of tropical forests will yield sizable payoffs, not only in the forestry sector itself but through spillover into other sectors, as Spears and Ayensu have shown.[17] Since the links between forestry and other sectors are so diverse, it is appropriate to review a number of them in detail.

Rationalized use of tropical forests will enable them to generate many products besides high-quality hardwood timber. For example, while covering only 7 percent of the earth's land surface, tropical forests harbor almost half of all species and thus offer abundant stocks of varied materials for medicine and other health products, for agriculture (improved forms of existing crops as well as entirely new crops), for industry (feedstocks of organic raw materials), and for energy. We have scarcely begun to make a systematic and comprehensive assessment of the myriad products we can expect to derive from tropical forests.

Still more important are the many environmental services provided by tropical forests. Through their "sponge effect," these forests soak up rainfall before releasing it slowly and steadily throughout the year. But in the wake of deforestation of catchment zones, there is frequent flooding during the rainy season, followed by months of drought. Two-fifths of the Third World farmers live in valley bottomlands that depend on watershed functions of forested catchments: hence there is a key link between forestry and agriculture. Irrigated-rice farmers are especially dependent on regular water flows for multiple cropping year-round. Yet in the Ganges river system, for example, dry-season water flows declined by almost one-fifth during the five-year period 1973-78. In southern Asia, the single biggest constraint on expanded food production now rests with inadequate supplies of irrigation water; yet major irrigation programs for the region, with proposed budgets at the $50 billion level, pay scant attention to safeguards for forested watersheds.

At the same time, too much water, even a little too much, can be as bad as too little. In one-third of the ricelands of southern Asia, rivers now flow at least half a meter higher during growing seasons, more than can be tolerated by green revolution varieties of rice with their short stems. Worse still, of course, is the severe flooding that increasingly occurs in the wake of deforestation. In the Ganges Plain, which is 1 million km² in area and supports 500 million people, flood damages regularly exceed $1 billion per year.[18]

As tropical forests mitigate flooding, so they control soil erosion. Java, for instace, with only a small fraction of its original forest cover remaining, loses at least 770 million tons of topsoil each year, worth more than 1.5 million tons in rice production, or enough to feed several million people—a further link with agriculture, offering positive payoff for those countries that safeguard their forests.

Washed-away topsoil causes sedimentation of downstream water systems. Again, let us look at the Ganges as illustrative of what is overtaking a good number of major rivers in the humid tropics. The riverbeds of the Ganges and several of its tributaries are rising at a rate of 0.25 m/yr, grossly aggravating the risk of flooding; at the river's mouth, the port of Calcutta now needs continuous dredging to clear it of sedimentation. Watershed erosion is causing the Panama Canal to become silted up; without widescale reforestation measures costing $35 million, the canal will forfeit its capacity to handle large freighters by the year 2000, with financial losses far greater than the required reforestation outlays.

Sedimentation also causes problems for hydropower facilities and other large water impoundments. There are a growing number, from the Tarbela Dam in Pakistan to the Poza Honda Reservoir in Ecuador, that are losing as much as half their planned operational life because of sedimentation caused by deforestation.

There is even a link between watershed functions and public health. Domestic water supplies to a number of metropolitan communities are becoming limited because both quantity and quality are inadequate. The consequence is an increased hazard of waterborne diseases in Manila, Bangkok, Abidjan, and Panama City.

Finally, there is a climatic connection. Burning of tropical forests, both by small-scale cultivators and large-scale ranchers, contributes to buildup of carbon dioxide in the global atmosphere. Deforestation also fosters the albedo effect, with potentially far-reaching impact on climatic patterns far beyond the tropics.

Thus, there is a host of interactions, especially environmental interactions, between forestry and several other sectors that justify expanded support for forestry. In thirty-one countries with critically eroding watersheds, 150 million ha can be protected through replanting, terracing, and the introduction of suitable farming systems, at an investment cost of $1.5 billion per year for fifteen years. Investments of this sort have been tested in several countries and yield economic rates of return to the practicing farmers—without taking account of the tremendous benefits that accrue to the economy as a whole. Yet, significant as they are, these spinoff benefits are rarely accorded realistic evaluation when economic planners carry out their cost-benefit appraisals of development projects in forestry and related sectors: it is difficult to put a dollar figure on the values that a forest represents through its mere existence—even though it is all too easy to put a dollar figure on the damages that ensue when forest cover and its environmental services are eliminated.

For an investment of about $1 billion per year over the balance of the century, fuelwood supplies can be expanded to serve the needs of more than one billion people in fifty-seven countries who face or are likely to face severe energy deficiencies. Successful models to involve individual farmers, village communities, and private entrepreneurs in these programs have been tested; and fast-growing, soil-enhancing multipurpose tree species are available. Rates of return on these investments are favorable as conventionally calculated, even before account is taken of the benefits of arrested erosion, improved soil quality, and savings of organic manures that would otherwise be burned.

What is needed to demonstrate the payoffs of these investments is an analytic methodology that takes all these further benefits of forestry into account—in short, a comprehensive and systematized methodology that takes explicit cognizance of the many interconnections at stake. Herein lies the principal deficiency of forestry as conventionally perceived—that is, as a discrete sector that goes its own way with indifference to its interaction with other sectors. But difficult as it will be to quantify the links, we can move ahead with a commitment to acknowledge them in qualitative terms, a marked advance over the present situation. Hence, a prime initiative surely lies with methodical measures to approach forestry within a broader policy framework.

The issue of forestry has been dealt with at some length since it seves to illuminate a basic conceptual problem. We shall tend to underestimate the value of policy initiatives and funding support in many sectors as long as we view these sectors as distinct entities. The world does not work in discrete, isolated spheres, even though we try to manage it through separate institutional devices such as departments of agriculture, energy, forestry, and the like, that do not always coordinate their activities so as to match the integrative workings of the "real world."

Of all areas of public policy, there is probably none that we understand less than this of intersectoral linkage. To this extent, then, the underlying problem is not so much one of economic outlays as of integrative policy, backed by institutional design.

ENERGY

The payoffs to the initiatives proposed in "Energy: Issues and Opportunities" in this volume illustrate the point of intersectoral linkage most strongly. Investments to conserve energy where it is now used most inefficiently are not only the least expensive means to meet additional demands but have the most far-reaching benefits in reducing environmental pressures, forestalling political and security threats, and improving living conditions for the world's disadvantaged. Energy conservation can be promoted in many countries at no cost simply by correcting policies, subsidies, tax codes, and regulations that discourage efficient use of the least-cost energy source. The substantial gains in energy efficiency achieved in the last decade illustrate the possibilities, but there are further opportunities that have scarcely been tapped. Greater energy efficiency in cars, appliances, homes, and industrial processes (through the application of known designs) can widely reduce life-cycle costs to the user and achieve energy savings of 30-40 percent.

In an increeasing number of applications, renewable energy sources are the least-cost supplies. Their importance during the past decade has grown beyond the expectations of most experts. When their broader advantages in environmental and social impacts are taken into account, the range of applications in which they are attractive expands. In many countries, biases in pricing structures, regulatory policies, and research priorities prevent the expansion of renewable energy sources from assuming a major role. The energy paper depicts a technically and economically feasible future in which total energy demand need grow at only 0.8 percent per year (much more slowly than GNP, nuclear power need not play a significant role, and the rate of fossil fuel consumption can be limited to levels below that prevailing now, to avoid adverse effects on climate and ecosystems. In this future, renewable energy sources and greatly improved energy efficiencies play the key roles.

AGRICULTURE, WATER, AND FISHERIES

The opportunities for resource conservation through improved efficiency are equally promising in agriculture, as Hrabovszky has shown. At present, for example, only 30 percent of the nutrients applied to farmers' fields by means of chemical fertilizers are taken up by the crops. Much of the rest runs off or leaches out into water bodies, often with adverse environmental effects. A one-third increase in efficiency would save 10 million mt of plant nutrients, worth $6 billion and sufficient to add 80 million mt of cereals to the world harvest, more than enough to eliminate undernutrition.

The efficiency of irrigation water use can be increased with similar dramatic results, as Revelle's paper indicates. In systems where farmers pay for the water themselves without subsidy, irrigation efficiencies are typically 50 percent higher than elsewhere. In India alone, where more than 50 million ha of cropland is irrigated, a 50-percent rise in irrigation efficiency, through more timely and reliable delivery as well as better on-farm use, could result in an additional production of 20-30 million mt of grain.

Overall, the scope for higher productivity in agriculture on existing irrigated and rain-fed croplands, especially in Third World countries, is enormous. Average yields could be doubled or tripled with existing technology; many of these gains are available through improved cultural practices and better use of currently available inputs. Gains of this magnitude would greatly reduce pressures on marginal land and reduce the need for extension of irrigation systems and cultivated area.

Impressive gains in productivity are available in fisheries as well. If we engage in more intensive exploitation of capture fisheries but do so without more effective national and international management, we shall not meet growing demands for fish protein, and we shall probably cause depletion of resource stocks. However, the potential for intensively managed aquaculture and mariculture production has scarcely been tapped. The present area of 3-4 million ha devoted to aquaculture worldwide could be increased tenfold if institutional obstacles were resolved and productive investments undertaken, and present average yields of 1.5-2.0 mt/ha could be doubled. These developments would not only provide an important source of protein in many Third World countries, they would also yield a fine return in additional income and employment.

In conclusion, several papers at this conference have come up with proposals for additional expenditures, some of them in the range of billions of dollars per year. At a time of financial stringency in certain citadels of power and in a political climate in which people are often disenchanted with still further public expenditures, it is perhaps inappropriate to promote the cause of hefty outlays over and above what have already been undertaken, even those that promise high returns. But as the background papers make plain, the true question is not "Can we afford to spend more?" but rather, "Can we afford not to?"

Nor do all the required initiatives involve money. Many relate to shifts in policy—fundamental modifications of political approaches to the challenges that we confront. Much more can be done within the limitations of current economic commitments overall, a salient instance lying in the public health sector in the Third World with its emphasis on curative rather than preventive medicine.

When we measure potential gains against required outlays, we must surely acknowledge that we possess the economic resources needed, and that what is lacking is political inclination.

Equally beyond doubt is the conviction that we can mobilize the political will if we develop a clear picture of the brighter future that can surely lie ahead of us. We do not face problems that daunt us beyond the point of response: we face challenges to call out the best in us. The resource in greatest demand is the creative insight to envisage the new era—call it "new century" or what you will—that we can jointly construct to our mutual advantage. True, the endeavor will be no simple matter, and no part of it can be tackled lightly. It will be a pioneering enterprise to surpass those undertaken by other segments of humankind in the past; partly because the problems are greater, the adverse repercussions of inaction will be greater, and the positive payoffs will be far greater. Appalling as the prospects of failure are, they give us hope insofar as they inspire us to a collective effort to relieve greater human suffering than has ever before afflicted mankind. Equally, we can take heart from the potential rewards that await us, in establishing an acceptable way of life for all humankind, on a planet whose sustaining capacity is enhanced through our stewardship.

We should count ourselves a privileged generation that we are allowed the chance to meet this unprecedented challenge.

NOTES

1. World Health Organization, *Heath for All* (Geneva, Switzerland: World Health Organization, 1983).

2. J. Rowley, and P. Harrison, *Human Numbers, Human Needs* (London: International Planned Parenthood Federation, 1984).

3. J. Grant, *State of the World's Children* (Geneva, Switzerland: UNICEF, 1983).

4. *Ibid.*

5. The World Bank, *World Development Report 1984* (Washington, D.C.: The World Bank 1984).

6. Rowley and Harrison, 1984.

7. E. J. Croll, "Production Versus Reproduction: A Threat to China's Development Strategy," *World Development* (June 1983).

8. *Ibid.*

9. R. S. McNamara, "Time Bomb or Myth: The Population Problem," *Foreign Affairs* (Summer 1984).

10. L. R. Brown *et al.*, *State of the World* (New York: Norton, 1984).

11. Population Reference Bureau, *1984 World Population Data Sheet* (Washington, D.C.: Population Reference Bureau, 1984).

12. Brown *et al.*

13. N. Myers, *A Wealth of Wild Species* (Boulder, Colorado: Westview Press, 1983).

14. Idem, "Genetic Resourcees in Jeopardy," *Ambio* 13 (1984):171–74.

15. Myers, 1983.

16. IUCN, *The Bali Action Plan* (Gland, Switzerland: International Union for Conservation of Nature and Natural Resources, 1983).

17. See also N. Myers, *The Primary Source: Tropical Forests and our Future* (New York: Norton, 1984).

18. N. Myers, "The Himalayas: An Influence on 500 Million People," *Earthwatch* (1984).

The Global Possible: Resources, Development, and the New Century

STATEMENT

At a time when bleak predictions are all too familiar, the Global Possible Conference was convened to reexamine the relationship between earth's resources and the human future. The Conference accepted that these predictions could be accurate. But its central and emphatic message is that they need not be—that it is possible to build a world that is more secure, more prosperous, and more sustainable both economically and environmentally.

This global possible will not happen automatically. It will require determined action to implement new policies. It will require new levels of cooperation among government, science, business, and groups of concerned people. It will require a global partnership between developed and developing countries with sustained improvements in the living standards of the world's poor. And it will require peaceful cooperation to remove the threat of nuclear war—the greatest human and environmental catastrophe of all.

The Need for Action

Many pressures on the human environment intensify daily. In the past, the most serious problems were localized in scale and obvious in their effects: urban smogs, lifeless rivers, or land sterilized by fumes. Today,

Published by World Resources Institute, Washington, D.C., 1984. The views expressed in this statement and the accompanying agenda for action are those of the participants in their personal capacities and not necessarily those of the governments or the organizations with which they are associated.

major components of man's life-support system are being changed slowly and insidiously. The buildup of carbon dioxide and other gases in the air threatens to change climate in ways we cannot predict. The deserts expand. The forests, with their immense wealth of life forms, retreat. The cities of many developing countries are growing faster than even the most basic services of clean water and sanitation can be provided. Hundreds of millions of people live in poverty, wasting enormous human potential and destroying the resources on which their future depends because no alternative is open to them. At the same time, many in developed countries use resources excessively and wastefully.

The Conference is confident that these trends can be reversed. We can stabilize human populations, improve people's quality of life, provide more food, save tropical forests and disappearing species, and protect the environment. We can do these things using means that are within our grasp and in ways that further other critical goals, both economic and humanitarian. But these goals will be realized only if a concerted effort is made, with some urgency, to change many current policies and to strengthen and multiply the successful initiatives that already have been undertaken.

Since the United Nations Conference on the Human Environment, held at Stockholm in 1972, many encouraging initiatives have pointed the way to a sustainable society. We have learned from both success and failure and have built many of the institutions needed for effective action internationally and locally.

We must mobilize now to achieve the global possible. If we do, the future can be bright. We have sufficient knowledge, skill, and resources—if we use them. If we remain inactive, whether through pessimism or complacency, we shall only make certain the darkness that many fear.

The Background to Action

During the past decade we have come to recognize some simple but fundamental truths about our world. It is interconnected in intricate ways. Air, water, land, and life form an interlocking system. Climate, shaping the fertility of the earth, is governed by both atmosphere and ocean. The elements vital to all life move in cycles between the rocks, waters, air, and bodies of animals and plants.

When we discharge pollutants or alter the pattern of vegetation on a large scale, we inevitably perturb these cycles. When we manage the environment wisely, we instead reap a series of reinforcing benefits. When we protect forests, for example, we not only secure important supplies of timber and fuelwood but also prevent soil loss, reduce the danger of flooding, protect vanishing species, and retain carbon that would otherwise augment that in the atmosphere.

Nature's systems operate as closed cycles that do not produce sustained surpluses. Therefore, exploiting natural systems alters them. People must use nature, but the global possible demands that we also leave natural systems of sufficient extent to sustain genetic richness and to maintain the supportive cycles of the biosphere. Modified and managed systems need occupy only a part of the surface of the planet. We must "travel more lightly" on the earth.

Our guiding philosophies for resource management must also mature—to improve our assessment of real costs and benefits and to regulate human activities so that we do not undermine our own futures. Voluntary transactions in competitive markets can help reconcile individual and social objectives provided that property rights encompass the environmental impacts of resource use on others, and provided that the distribution of property is equitable. Much can be done by governments and others to make these conditions realities and thereby enable business and individual initiative to promote wise resource use.

The interconnections extend to the world's economic and political systems, bound tighter than ever before by modern trade, communications, and finance, but stressed by the growing divergence of need, interest, and power among nations and groups at different stages of development. The adjustment of these systems so that they promote the sustainable development of the poorer regions of the world is essential to all. Without such development, populations will be less likely to stabilize, and both destructive pressures on the biosphere and political tensions must inevitably increase.

An Agenda for Action

Through its working groups, papers, and deliberations, this Conference has developed an agenda for action. This program of priorities could substantially improve globally important environmental and population trends, alleviate poverty, promote sustainable development, and help realize the global possible. Among its initiatives are significant ideas to shape national efforts, promote private sector involvement, and direct international undertakings.

Although we, as Conference participants, do not have identical opinions on all points, this statement and the accompanying agenda reflect a wide consensus among us, and we believe the ideas found here deserve prompt and intensive consideration.

Among the many urgent claims for action in this agenda, some stand out because of their synergistic effects across several resource sectors and on many aspects of human welfare. Successful pursuit of these initatives will simultaneously improve conditions in many realms and, because of these far-reaching implications, they deserve special attention.

The tasks outlined in the accompanying agenda are large, but the need is urgent and the rewards very great. Because so many opportunities for effective action are available, there is no cause for despair nor justification for rampant pessimism.

The Future

As we consider the contours of a brighter and sustainable future, its features become clearer. World population is stabilized before it doubles again, and the erosion of the planet's renewable resource base—the forests, fisheries, agricultural lands, wildlife, and biological diversity—is halted. Societies pursue management practices that stress reliance on the "income" from these renewable resources, not a depletion of the planet's "capital." Enlarging this income requires sophisticated management and more intensive use of prime farm and forest lands and fisheries, as well as the application of new technologies to improve agricultural yields, control pests and spoilage, and exploit new opportunities such as aquaculture, hydroponics, and salt-tolerant crops. People and resources are protected from the costly consequences of pollution and toxification and from disruptive climate change. Human activity becomes more "closed" in the ecological sense, so that it does not impair the functioning of natural systems. Manufacturing processes produce less waste, and what waste is produced is reused in other processes. Advanced technologies are widely applied to achieve high efficiencies, in the use of energy and in its production from solar, biomass, and other renewable sources. Broadly-based economic growth proceeds in ways that lessen the gap between rich and poor both within and among countries, and the door is increasingly opened to artistic and cultural pursuits in a world where the hard labor of survival is lessened.

Why Change Is Vital

Are world resource challenges serious enough, and broad enough in effect, to warrant the wide attention the Conference has urged? The answer is surely "yes."

Those of us now living allow natural systems to be abused, ignored, or destroyed at our children's peril. The resources under stress today are vital to tomorrow's economic development and growth in the many ways that the papers prepared for the Conference make abundantly clear. Sustainable development, in turn, by providing the means to earn a livelihood in a nondestructive manner, will reduce the pressures that people in poverty exert on natural resources. It can also stimulate the expansion of export markets and investment opportunities. Although much of the worst resource deterioration is occurring today in the Third World, the industrialized nations must come to terms with these issues and support better resource management around the globe: they are the dominant consumers of natural resources, and their economic futures are bound to the resources that the planet's thin envelope of land, air, and water provides.

International security is at stake too. There will be many more people on this earth soon. Without the changes urged here, a large portion will join the legions who alreaady live with constant hunger, illness, and illiteracy. If we allow their numbers to grow, if we allow economic development that is unsustainable, and the pressures of people on resources increase, political tensions and conflicts will rise. The effects will be felt in every sphere of political relations, from waves of "ecological refugees," to conflict over scarcer land and water, to increasingly isolationist trade and then foreign policies.

For all these reasons, the actions suggested in the accompanying agenda would make an enormous difference to the world's welfare over the next ten to thirty years. If we take the needed initiatives and take them now, widespread human suffering can be alleviated, threatened natural resources protected, and the vital groundwork laid for both international security and renewed—and sustained—economic growth. The new century can be much brighter than frequently supposed, but only if our actions match our aspirations.

Realizing the Global Possible

Realizing this future will require impressive international cooperation among governments, and larger roles for those outside government —for example, from private business, the scientific community, environmental organizations, and voluntary agencies—given the burdens that governments now face. Grassroots political movements and experimental programs should be encouraged to stimulate public and private bureaucracies to action. New patterns bringing forth more governance without more government must be found.

Additional financial resources will be needed to finance the transition to a brighter future. Both industrial and developing countries are today spending tragically large sums on competitive military preparations, far greater sums than they spend on education, on agriculture, or on any other sector. Even modest reductions in military budgets would release substantial funds.

As members of many communities, those of us who have participated in the Global Possible Conference recognize the contributions we
can make and pledge our best efforts to promoting these changes. As
one early step, we are establishing a task force to develop new mechanisms for communication and cooperation among business and other
nongovernmental groups, with a special emphasis on the participation
of such groups in developing countries.

Those of us in nongovernmental oganizations recognize the leadership role we must play in creating public awareness and political support for initiatives such as those proposed here. Widespread change in
perceptions and values is a key to action and will spring from people
united in passionate commitment to human betterment.

As scientists, we can create new understanding of human interaction with the environment at the largest and the smallest scale—from
the workings of global natural systems under human influence to the
technologies and production systems of relevance to impoverished villages. By launching its inquiries from a vision of a brighter future for
all, science can enormously expand mankind's possibilities.

Business, large and small, commands the management expertise,
the technology, and the enterprise to deploy human, financial, and natural resources efficiently to supply goods and services of value to society. We believe private business is ready to accept its stake in the solution of the issues addressed by the Conference.

Those of us from developing countries believe that it is possible to
manage the resources of the human environment for sustainable development by emphasizing the promotion of a better quality of life, basic
human needs, and a marked improvement in the living standards of
disadvantaged peoples. Developed and developing countries jointly
share responsibility for the status of the environment in developing
countries, and this shared responsibility should guide the development
of coordinated supportive policies.

Developed countries command greater influence and wealth and
have both a large stake in, and a large responsibility for, the well-being
of the global environment and its people. Recognizing the fundamental
interdependence of nature and society, and of countries rich and poor,
the industrial nations should strive to create conditions conducive to
peace, to conservation of resources and environment, and to the rapid
advancement of the world's poor.

AGENDA FOR ACTION

This agenda for action, developed by the Conference's working groups,
deserves wide and prompt consideration by governments, interna-

tional organizations, the business and scientific communities, and citizens. It calls for adoption of important initiatives and for an intensification of already successful efforts.

Although much of the agenda is organized here along sectoral lines one of the Conferences's points of departure was the view that complex linkages tie issues in one area to those in several others. Forest issues cannot profitably be considered in isolation from those of biological diversity, energy and fuelwood, and the management of agricultural lands and watersheds. In developing this agenda, the Conference laid special stress on policies and initiatives that have synergistic effects on critical problems across several sectors and tried to avoid apparent solutions that can create as many problems as they solve.

I. *Population, Poverty, and Development*

While many developing countries have experienced rapid declines in fertility, mortality, and population growth rates, and the rate of world population growth has turned down, the developing countries where most still live in conditions of poverty continue to face rapid population growth. This growth exacerbates resource and environmental pressures in all parts of the biosphere and aggravates the problems of achieving a poverty-free society. Perhaps a fourth of humanity now lives in what the World Bank calls "absolute poverty," a condition characterized by poor health, undernutrition, chronic deprivation, and shortened life expectancy. The human suffering and waste of talent and creativity implicit in these numbers is one of the great tragedies of the modern era.

Experience has shown that in countries where fertility and mortality have fallen rapidly, two mutually reinforcing strategies have been effective. First, broadly-based economic and social development has changed the conditions that perpetuate high rates of fertility and mortality. Second, services accessible to almost all households have provided basic health care and contraceptive supplies and information. Both of these strategies require government policies that reflect a strong commitment to the welfare of people, especially children. Precise approaches must spring from the values and direct involvement of communities and must give due account to the great diversity that exists both within and among nations.

Within this framework, policy and program initiatives are needed in three areas: actions to reduce poverty, actions to improve the position and employment of women, and actions to reduce mortality and fertility rates. With serious efforts in these areas, it should be *possible* to stabilize world population at about 8 billion by the middle of the next century.

To achieve these goals, developing-country governments, international organizations, aid agencies, and others* should take the following actions:

1. Adopt labor-intensive economic development strategies aimed at alleviating poverty by expanding employment opportunities more rapidly. These strategies should direct a larger share of development funds to dispersed and small-scale programs that employ more labor and provide quicker returns, should stimulate and encourage labor-intensive exports, and should give high priority to providing basic services and access to land, livestock, and other resources to the poor.

2. Expand greatly the educational and employment opportunities available to women, and establish and achieve a goal of universal primary-school and doubled secondary-school enrollment of women in this century. Business and industry can contribute importantly to these objectives by ensuring that recruitment, training, and compensation policies actively encourage the participation of women. Nongovernmental groups can also contribute by advocating needed change and establishing pilot programs to broaden economic opportunities.

3. Reduce death rates by making basic sanitary services and simple health care widely available (e.g., oral rehydration, expanded immunization programs, growth monitoring of infants, health education, pre-natal and post-natal care). Although these services cost only a few dollars per person per year, they are not available to three-quarters of the people in the developing world.

4. Set and achieve an international goal of doubling access to family planning services in the Third World over the coming decade, with a particular emphasis on program elements that have proven successful. These elements include building on local organizations and customs; promoting the welfare of children; using community workers to visit couples and stock and resupply contraceptives; and using socioeconomic incentives to encourage family planning and reinforce the benefits of a smaller family size.

A different set of considerations involves the economic policies of the industrial nations. The international economic setting strongly affects the ability of developing countries to reduce poverty and achieve sustainable development patterns. To accelerate sustainable growth in

---

*Nongovernmental groups—business, science, private voluntary organizations, church groups, environmental groups, and other citizens' organizations—that have essential roles in pursuing this agenda are also treated in XIII, *Business, Science and Citizens.*

the developing countries and attack world poverty in a meaningful way over the longer run, and ultimately to reap the benefits of increased economic growth and trade at home, the industrial countries should take the following steps:

1. Reduce quantitative restrictions on labor-intensive manufactures from the Third World, simplify import procedures, and rely on compensation and retraining of workers displaced by imports instead of on trade restraints.
2. Eliminate the escalation of tariff rates on processed materials to help developing countries expand their domestic processing of export commodities.
3. Increase official capital flows for development assistance to low-income countries through bilateral and multilateral channels.
4. Expand the share of international assistance made available through program and structural adjustment lending, which is linked to the pursuit of appropriate programs and policies rather than to the purchase of equipment.
5. Encourage mechanisms that reduce the risks to private lenders of investing in low-income countries, such as co-financing, expanded insurance facilities, and greater financial intermediation.
6. Pursue coordinated economic policies that reduce the current burden of developing-country debt and stabilize future real interest rates.

II. *The Urban Environment*

By 2000, most of the largest urban agglomerations will be in the Third World, and half the Third World population will be urban. In almost all Third World cities, lower income groups lack space, drinking water, sanitation, waste collection, drainage, lighting, other urban services, minimally adequate housing, and even the acknowledged right to be where they are. Morbidity and mortality rates among the urban poor often exceed rates in rural areas. Compounding these problems are largely uncontrolled industrial and vehicular emissions. The magnitude of the problem has not been widely recognized nor given the sense of urgency if deserves.

In countries with these problems, governments and international organizations should take the following actions:

1. Slow the rate of migration into the largest cities through policies that decentralize industries and provide employment op-

portunities in rural hinterlands and that improve rural living conditions by providing health, education, and other basic services.

2. Take advantage of self-help efforts by legalizing informal urban settlements and encouraging neighborhood improvement initiatives.

3. Provide the financial resources for basic environmental services in urban areas by strengthening cities' tax and rate systems, and by sharing national and regional revenue sources with urban governments. This marshalling of resources must be accompanied by a devolution of authority from the central government, a significant upgrading of municipal administrative capacity, and an intensive effort to develop and demonstrate low-cost sanitation and other technologies appropriate to densely populated areas.

Nongovernmental organizations should take the following steps:

1. Launch a concerted effort to raise international awareness of mounting urban problems and their implications.

2. Build institutions that focus specifically on developing solutions to Third World urban environmental problems. Initially through an organized effort to exchange successful techniques and measures already being taken by local groups and to encourage wider adoption of successful measures.

Many of the initiatives discussed under I. *Population Poverty, and Development* and under III. *Fresh Water* address the problems of the urban poor.

III. *Fresh Water*

The good news about fresh water is that, even after accounting for the large volume of water that is unavailable to people from the hydrologic cycle, there is enough on a global scale to support current and anticipated populations on a sustainable basis. However, there are areas, regions, and even nations that have experienced, or soon will, serious problems of water shortages or water pollution. Indeed, providing safe drinking water is a major challenge and expense for both developing and industrialized nations, and in many places the lack of safe water remains a chief obstacle to meeting basic standards of health. Some of the causes are geographical or climatological; some are the result of mismanagement; and some are the result of abuse. Three essential goals are dependable and safe supplies for people, protection and management of the environmental systems through which water moves, and efficient water use. Meeting these goals will require that fresh water not continue to be treated as a free good or as the principal means for disposing of human and industrial wastes.

To help provide adequate supplies of fresh water, governments, international organizations, and others should take the following steps:

1. Prepare national analyses of existing fresh water uses and supplies and likely future demands as a basis for sound future planning. Incorporate environmental and social factors and public participation into the planning of projects.
2. Ensure that water users are charged rates that encourage efficiency and reflect the costs of providing water on a sustainable basis.
3. Give greater attention to opportunities for ground water storage, as opposed to surface storage, for stabilizing inter-year variations in supply.
4. Achieve sharp increases (as much as 50 percent) in the efficiency of water use in irrigation by using readily available, cost-effective means such as pricing water to cover the true cost of supply, harmonizing cropping practices and water delivery, modifying water-application techniques, and managing water supply systems more reliably.
5. Emphasize both the construction of smaller, community-based irrigation systems (which can be locally managed and designed for local needs) and the rehabilitation, better operation, and maintenance of existing systems as alternatives to new, large projects.
6. Manage fertilizers and pesticides in a way that protects surface- and groundwaters. Nations that export agricultural chemicals and firms that manufacture them have an obligation to help educate users about prudent application rates and techniques.
7. Give precedence to the development and demonstration of simple, low-cost, decentralized urban water supply systems and sanitation technologies that minimize water conveyance, promote nutrient recovery, and reduce human exposure to pathogens.
8. Control potential industrial water pollutants at the source through required application of available and effective processes and technologies and through "chemically tight" management that recycles or contains hazardous industrial wastes.

IV. *Biological Diversity*

The maintenance of biological diversity is important for the functioning of natural systems, improvement of crops and livestock, development of new pharmaceuticals and other useful products, and for scientific and aesthetic reasons. Habitat destruction, especially in the tropics, is causing a historically unprecedented and accelerating loss of genetic resources and extinction of species, the total cost of which is unquantifiable because the lost species and varieties are mostly unknown to science. Ironically, this loss is occurring at a time when the new techniques of genetic engineering allow us for the first time to make full use of the vast genetic reservoir of wild species.

The most urgent threat to biological diversity is in the tropics, where about 40 percent of the earth's species live. The remedy can be found only within the context of development that meets the needs of human populations and at the same time relieves pressures on the environment. Considerable action has already been taken, including varying degrees of protection for over 3000 sites totaling about 450 million hectares in 120 countries. But major new initiatives are neeeded to ensure the preservation of a minimum network of tropical and other habitats and to manage effectively new and existing sites in the years ahead.

To halt the accelerating loss of our genetic heritage, cooperative efforts should be undertaken by governments, international organizations, and others to:

1. Complete a comprehensive international network of protected areas for *in situ* conservation of genetic resources, which current data indicate should total about 10 percent of the world's land area. Long-term management of the protected areas should be accorded equal priority to their creation.
2. Create, as one means of furthering this system of representative protected areas, a new international convention to provide funding by industrial countries for establishing and managing protected areas in developing countries. Funding for developing countries that would otherwise lack the necessary means to preserve biological diversity should also be provided by development aid agencies and by private firms in energy, agriculture, pharmaceuticals, and other industries that have a long-term stake in biological resources.
3. Launch an international effort to raise the level of awareness of the nature and importance of biological diversity, including the sponsorship by scientific and environmental organizations from around the world of a major international event designed to bring to the attention of policymakers in all countries both the links between biological diversity and other prominent concerns and the depth of public support for preservation efforts.
4. Develop national conservation strategies within the *World Conservation Strategy* framework for conserving biological diversity while achieving sustainable development. Among other things, these strategies should provide people living on lands

adjacent to protected areas with nondestructive employment opportunities and other means of meeting their basic human needs and should ensure effective management and protection of existing reserves.
5. Address the universal shortages of trained personnel in resource management, forestry, genetics, taxonomy, and ecology through a sharp increase in funds from national governments and international agencies going to university and mid-level training programs.
6. Enforce vigorously national laws and international treaties and conventions protecting wildlife and endangered species.

V. *Tropical Forests*

In contrast to the relatively stable forests in the developed world, the area of forests in the developing countries has declined by half during this century and is shrinking by about 11 million hectares per year, due primarily to agricultural settlement. The acccelerating loss of tropical forest cover is an extremely serious problem with immediate and long-range socioeconomic and ecological consequences:

- Some 150 million hectares of tropical watersheds are threatened by overgrazing and soil erosion, causing flooding, sedimentation of dams and reservoirs, disruption of downstream irrigation systems, and losses of crops, land, even human life.
- By the year 2000, a significant proportion of the unique genetic resources harbored by tropical forests—the most biologically diverse ecosystems on earth—will become extinct through the anticipated losses of a further 100 million hectares of forests.
- Already fuelwood is acutely scarce in some 57 developing countries containing more than 1 billion people, making it necessary for rural households to burn about 400 million tons of animal dung per year—enough to raise grain production by 20 million tons if used as manure.
- As a result of past overcutting and inadequate investment, 23 developing countries with climates and lands well suited to tree-growing now import forest products costing more than $50 million per year, and another 14 countries will soon exhaust exportable hardwood species.

The principal underlying causes of tropical deforestation include rural poverty and low agricultural productivity, inequalities in land tenure, population pressure, underinvestment in forestry and the general ineffectiveness of forestry agencies, and the lack of integrated planning of forestry, agriculture, energy, and other sectors.

Many of the socioeconomic measures to reduce tropical deforestation are already known. What is needed is a concerted international action plan directed toward five priority goals through which it should be possible to contain deforestation in the most critically affected developing countries by the turn of the century. These goals are as follows: to rehabilitate 150 million hectares of seriously degraded tropical watersheds; to preserve 100 million hectares of threatened forest ecosystems*; to increase fuelwood planting rates fivefold by the year 2000; to improve and expand industrial forestry; and to strengthen forestry research, education, and training. To meet these goals, governments, international organizations, and others should take the following actions:

1. Provide farmers in degraded watersheds with the necessary materials, credit, and technical support they need to improve farm productivity, control grazing and logging, and check runoff and erosion. These programs must recognize the watershed as the planning unit and involve the local community and private voluntary organizations.
2. Provide international assistance for ecological surveys to select conservation sites and for purchase and maintenance of conservancy areas. Conservation objectives should also be incorporated into project and country planning.
3. Create a new international fund to subsidize the establishment of protected forests through the leadership of the industrial countries, which will reap many of the benefits.
4. Channel land settlement projects into unforested lands and create buffer zones along the forest fringe by intensifying agricultural development, introducing land reform and employment programs, and helping forest-dwelling families to adopt proven agroforestry systems.
5. Lay the groundwork for large-scale fuelwood planting in the 1990s by greatly expanding the establishment of tree nurseries, credit and extension programs, and demonstration woodlots.
6. Encourage private-sector participation in tree farming through fiscal measures, including long-term leases of government forest land to cooperatives, village associations, and private companies.
7. Strengthen legislative, fiscal, and administrative policies aimed at encouraging private industrial forestry and at making more effective use of existing forests through less wasteful logging, greater use of secondary species, more effective control of log-

*This goal, and its implementing actions, complement and overlap those presented in IV. *Biological Diversity*.

ging company activities, and increased domestic processing.

8. Shift the emphasis in tropical forestry research toward the sociological aspects of forestry, increased biological productivity of trees and agroforestry systems, efficient use of fuelwood in rural areas, and forest management for the conservation of genetic diversity.

9. Use restructured education and training programs to reorient forest services from a "policing" mission to providing technical extension support to small farmers, village cooperatives, private companies, and others who use the forests.

The total cost of this action plan is estimated at $5.3 billion per year over the balance of the century.

VI. *Agricultural Land*

Much of the land currently in agriculture is deteriorating due to inappropriate soil and water management. Loss of topsoil through soil erosion is the most widespread form of degradation. Other serious problems include salinization, compaction, and waterlogging. Along with desertification, these reduce productivity and jeopardize long-range sustainability. However, there is no agreement as to how serious their overall effects are on agricultural production. Lack of data on current land uses, land capabilities and deterioration rates, and the demand for land for nonagricultural uses make it difficult to resolve disagreements over the earth's capacity to meet the food needs of future generations.

Agricultural modernization programs have bypassed the marginal regions of desert fringe and hilly upland. It is precisely in these marginal areas that erosion and deterioration are most severe, but farmers in these areas have remained among the poorest and the least able to invest in soil conservation. Without alternative sources of income and access to better land or improved technologies, farmers will continue to erode marginal lands in order to survive.

Agrarian policy that provides small and marginal farmers and landless laborers with greater access to credit, information, and other means of production and—in many countries—redistributes highly concentrated landholdings and regular tenancies would relieve much rural poverty, reduce the rates of migration to the cities, and reduce the land scarcity that drives peasant farmers into semiarid zones, up erosion-prone hillsides, or into remaining forested areas.

Governments, in concert with international organizations and others, should take the following steps:

1. Promote intensified production on existing good agricultural lands, rather than expanding agricultural activities into previ-

ously unused, usually lower-potential areas. Key elements include favorable producer incentives, improved management of irrigation and drainage systems, stronger agricultural research and expanded extension programs that close the gaps between farmer and researcher, and the promotion of balanced farming systems that do not rely excessively on chemical inputs or degrade soil fertility.

2. Give priority in international assistance to investments that improve existing irrigation works, promote smallholder agriculture rather than new plantation agriculture or large land settlement schemes, and strengthen rural infrastructure, especially in storage, transportation, and marketing. Local participation in all phases of planning is essential.

3. Increase sharply soil conservation programs targeted at the most critical areas through training the personnel and providing the finances to promote on-farm improvements, protecting critical watersheds, introducing sustainable mixed farming systems suitable to fragile environments, and reviewing commodity and water pricing and other agricultural policies to ensure their consistency with soil conservation goals.

4. Reduce the impacts of livestock overgrazing by supporting and modernizing nomadic lifestyles on arid and semiarid lands where these provide efficient and sustainable land use, and by intensifying underused grazing systems, especially in Latin America, so as to reduce conversion of forests and cropland to rangeland.

5. Relieve pressures on marginal lands by stimulating nonfarm rural employment and carrying out land-reform programs. Industrial country governments, international organizations, and others should provide consistent economic and political support for governments dedicated to agrarian reform.

6. Improve data on current land uses, land capabilities, and the extent of land degradation as the basis for long-range land use and investment planning. Governments should also strengthen legal, fiscal, and administrative mechanisms for land use control.

7. Establish closer working relationships between the international agricultural research centers and national research institutions in developing countries, and strengthen the scientific and technical skills of the latter. Higher priority in research programs should be given to high-productivity mixed cropping and husbandry systems for marginal areas, as well as to promising new biological means to intensify productivity on good soils.

VII. *Living Marine Resources*

The marine environment plays a central role in the biological, chemical, and physical cycles on which life depends. Until very recently, the prevailing view was that the marvelous absorptive and rejuvenating abilities of marine ecosystems would enable them to take care of themselves. But today it is clear that these capacities are often being surpassed, specially in coastal areas. A central goal of marine management must therefore be to educate the public and policymakers to recognize that the marine environment, including the polar regions, does play this critical role, that scientific understanding of the oceans is still rudimentary, and that the traditional view of the oceans as a huge area that can take care of itself is no longer valid.

Because of the low primary productivity of the oceans and related characteristics, increasing total fishery harvests much above the present level of 70 million metric tons per year will be difficult. Through better management of fish stocks in complete ecosystem units, reduction of waste due to spoilage and the discard of unmarketed secondary species, greater use of underexploited stocks (like squid, krill, and deep-water ocean species), and other means, it may be possible for the amount of protein actually reaching the table from the sea to keep pace with population growth in this century.

The creation of exclusive economic zones covering 40 percent of the ocean area presents new opportunities for improved management. Protection of critical spawning grounds and habitats like estuaries, reefs, mangrove swamps, and wetlands is fundamental. Overcrowded onshore fisheries in developing countries can be relieved by investment in hatcheries, preservation and processing plants, small-scale aquaculture, and especially, the creation of alternative employment opportunities.

In marked contrast to the limited expansion potential of traditional fisheries, marine resources can be increased significantly through the development of aquaculture, which can yield up to 10 metric tons of fish per hectare per year on as many as 20–30 million hectares. A fivefold increase in the aquaculture harvest by the end of the century is feasible, with research attention to problems of fish diseases and reproduction, removal of administrative and legal barriers to this use of the coastal zone, and adequate investment.

To preserve and enhance the harvest of living marine resources, governments, regional and international fishery organizations, and others should take the following steps:

1. Improve fisheries management by developing and adhering to an ecosystem conservation principle ("unit management")

whereby all associated species, the relevant habitat, and spawning and nursery areas are jointly managed; by effectively regulating catch, entry of fishing vessels, and mesh sizes; by helping coastal states to develop the indigenous capacity for effective fishery management; and by providing traditional (artisanal) fishermen with marketing and other services to increase their economic viability.

2. Prevent pollution and physical destruction of critical habitats, including estuaries, coral reefs, swamps and wetlands, and undertake research to address the impacts of habitat destruction or alteration of fish stocks.

3. Expand programs to help coastal developing countries effectively manage their exclusive economic zones (EEZs) through provision of technology for monitoring and research; training of scientific and technical personnel; advice on the development of legal and administrative structures; and help in realizing the economic benefits of the EEZ through such devices as the auctioning of harvesting rights and joint economic ventures with more technologically advanced nations.

4. Provide effective opportunities, including financial support where appropriate, for nongovernmental organizations to participate in decision-making processes, following such models as the London Dumping Convention, the International Whaling Commission, and the US Environmental Protection Agency's Ocean Dumping Advisory Committee.

5. Reduce the losses of fish taken and wasted as incidental catch by developing storage ships into which to transfer these fish and by promoting new markets for the incidental catch. Millions of tons of postharvest waste due to spoilage can be saved by promoting the construction of refrigeration and processing facilities near landing sites.

6. Accelerate aquaculture development through large-scale public and private planning, investment, technical assistance, and training programs, and modify legal and administrative systems to allow aquaculture enterprises to lease offshore areas, to protect aquaculture operations from pollution damage, and to balance conflicting uses of the offshore area. An aquaculture research unit should be added to the Consultative Group on International Agricultural Research.

VIII. *Energy*

A temporarily soft oil market, partly due to worldwide recession, has diverted attention from the central fact that sometime in the next 15–25 years, global oil production will begin to decline, as it already has in the non-OPEC oil-producing states. As a result, there will begin a gradual transition to a new energy era, one in which global energy use is no longer dominated by oil, and in which countries' national energy plans are far more individualistic and tailored to each nation's particular mix of needs, end uses, and domestic energy resources.

In the developing countries, noncommercial biomass fuels are a major source of energy, especially for domestic uses. Shortages of fuelwood and other biomass sources have caused serious deforestation in many countries, and the diversion of vegetative and animal manures from use in soil replenishment. Unless adequate and affordable supplies can be made available, environmental degradation and poverty will increase. At the same time, industralization and urbanization are proceeding rapidly in many developing countries. Those without indigenous energy resources have faced heavy, sometimes crippling, oil import bills. These have been a factor in the current international debt crisis. Unless commerciaal energy supplies are available to these countries at manageable prices, their economic development programs will falter.

Conventional energy strategies that focus mainly on fossil fuels and nuclear energy pay insufficient attention to (1) the environmental impacts of expanded fossil fuel use, (2) the threat of nuclear weapons proliferation implicit in widespread nuclear fuel enrichment and reprocessing, (3) the political and economic vulnerability of economies highly dependent on imported energy, (4) the pressing energy needs of the rural sector in developing countries, (5) the economic impact of expanding energy use in the industrial countries on the growth of developing countries, and (6) the imperative to meet the basic human needs of the poor, especially of women and households.

New energy strategies are needed that recognize these issues. These strategies must promote not just a sustainable energy supply, but also a sustainable world. To pursue these goals governments, international organizations, the energy industry, and others should:

1. Promote rapid gains in conservation and energy efficiency as the highest priority through raising domestic oil and natural gas prices to international levels, moving toward the goal of marginal cost pricing of electricity, setting energy efficiency standards and requirements, and providing consumer information and credit. Complementary policies should be used to offset the impacts of higher energy prices on low-income households.
2. Promote the development of renewable energy sources, including direct solar, wind, hydro, and biomass technologies, by

eliminating subsidies and other advantages enjoyed by fossil
and nuclear supply sources, by substantially increasing current
efforts to research and develop solar and biomass conversion
technologies, and by undertaking (with international assistance) major investments in fuelwood production.

3. Establish national and international mechanisms to reduce misleading world oil price signals by, for example, adopting an oil
import levy that would vary countercyclically to maintain gradually and predictably rising prices for oil.

4. Develop national and other energy plans and end-use analyses
that recognize the untapped potential of demand management,
energy efficiency, and renewable energy sources. The private
sector and international lending and aid institutions have major
roles to play in stimulating and supporting more sophisticated
long-term energy planning.

5. Insist upon control of pollution and other environmental impacts of energy production by requiring use of effective and
available pollution control techniques, using such innovative
regulatory approaches as "bubbles" and tradable emission permits, establishing international compacts for the reduction of
acid deposition and transboundary pollution, and giving detailed consideration to greater use of natural gas as a transi-
tional energy source.

IX. Nonfuel Minerals

Supplies of nonfuel minerals need not seriously limit world economic
growth or welfare, even in the long run, provided that market adjustments can readily take place and governments do not erect barriers to
exploration and exploitation of new deposits or to the flow of capital
and technology to producting countries.

Most mineral markets are subject to short-term price fluctuations,
which are usually more disruptive to producing than to consuming
countries. Management and financial reserves, including international
credit, can mitigate these impacts, which become less important as exports are diversified and as mineral producers expand their processing
and fabrication operations.

There are few countries that are truly vulnerable to interruptions of
supplies of strategic minerals, such as cobalt, chromium, manganese,
and the platinum group. Even in these, most uses are not strategic,
alternative supply sources exist (including recycling and substitution),
and properly managed stockpiles can reduce vulnerability.

Mineral exploitation causes environmental damage during extraction, processing, and disposal. The advanced industrial countries have

created regulatory structures to cope with such problems, albeit with difficulty, and developing countries are currently trying to devise comparable mechanisms. "Internalizing" these environmental side effects is possible without major changes either in the costs of end products or the location of production.

Recycling can both break up a highly concentrated supply situation and reduce environmental damage from nonfuel minerals use. Its potential benefits deserve greater recognition, especially through the removal of economic and institutional barriers that hinder its widespread use.

In order to ensure adequate supplies at stable prices, to enhance the benefits developing countries derive from mineral exploitation, and harmonize mineral development with wise environmental management, governments, international organizations, and others should take the following steps:

1. Ensure adequate flows of investment capital to developing countries for minerals exploitation and development by expanding the World Bank's and other institutions' co-financing and loan guarantee facilities, political risk insurance, and support for pre-investment studies. Developing countries can reduce investor uncertainty by avoiding unstable fiscal and regulatory climates.

2. Vigorously oppose cartelization of minerals markets and imposition of trade restrictions or price ceilings by importing countries. Private industry and international organizations such as the United Nations Conference on Trade and Development (UNCTAD) have an active role to play here, as well as governments.

3. Reduce the vulnerability of producing countries to market fluctuations by applying appropriate financial and foreign exchange reserve management and by encouraging export diversification through tax, exchange rate, and investment policies. Member countries of the International Monetary Fund's Compensatory Financing facility should support expansion of its capacity to stabilize exporting countries' balance of payments and budgetary positions when export prices fluctuate.

4. Enhance the benefits of mineral exploitation to developing economies by "unbundling" foreign direct investment (i.e., making separate supply agreements for capital, technology, management, and marketing), relaxing tariff and nontariff barriers by importing countries to imports of processed mineral products, and investing a reasonable fraction of producing countries' projected revenues in pre-investment studies, staff training, consulting services, and measures to avoid environ-

mental damage and to monitor performance under concession agreements.

5. Establish and enforce reasonable standards for restoration of mining sites and prevention of offsite pollution, create compensatory set-aside policies to preserve recreational and wilderness areas, and exclude highly sensitive or valuable areas from minerals development. The "polluter pays" principle provides sound guidance for environmental protection.

X. *Atmosphere and Climate*

Scientific investigations during the last decade have established the seriousness of potential changes to the global atmosphere, and climate due to human activities. Our understanding of the relationship among changes in the composition of the atmosphere, climatic change, and ecosystem disruption is still rudimentary, but it is known that changes within the range of possibility could produce enormous social and economic dislocation. Acid rain, stratospheric ozone depletion, and the "greenhouse effect"—climate change caused by the buildup in the atmosphere of carbon dioxide and other gases—are the most serious transnational atmospheric problems.

Local air quality problems due to industrial activity and use of liquid fuels for transportation are also important. Health problems and damages to crops and other resources due to air pollution are familiar concerns in the developed world, and similar concerns are emerging in developing nations along with urbanization and economic growth.

Our overriding objective ought to be preservation of the basic characteristics of the atmosphere and the avoidance of large and irreversible anthropogenic changes. The risks associated with a "wait and see" approach may be severe.

There exists sufficient knowledge on atmospheric problems to propose some immediate action. But large uncertainties remain. Thus, we should also strive to better understand the impact of human activities on the atmosphere as quickly as possible in order to minimize the danger of unanticipated harmful changes and to allow the longest possible lead time to change course.

Most of the steps required to deal with atmospheric issues are needed to deal with other problems, so atmospheric hazards make the need to take advantage of available opportunities all the more urgent. Specifically, governments, international organizations, and other should:

1. Pursue vigorously three policies previously advocated in this agenda; energy conservation and improvements in energy end-

use efficiency, rapid development of renewable energy sources, and forest conservation and reforestation. These measures could have positive effects on local air pollution problems, transboundary pollution such as acid deposition, and global issues such as the buildup of carbon dioxide.

2. Make the "greenhouse effect" a central feature of energy policy and planning and, in this context, carry out national and international energy analyses aimed at developing long-term energy strategies that meet the real energy needs of all countries while avoiding the grave risks of the buildup of carbon dioxide and other greenhouse gases. Nations should strive to maintain flexibility and diversity in supplying energy and to avoid policies that commit the world to the large-scale long-term use of coal or oil shale.

3. Prepare for the potential adverse impacts of climate changes, whether natural or man-made, by pursuing "anticipatory responses," such as more resilient crop strains and agricultural systems and improved water storage and management.

4. Achieve major reductions in sulfur dioxide and other pollutant gases over the next decade and seek to negotiate agreements to limit transboundary air pollution.

5. Adopt the proposed Framework Convention to Protect the Ozone Layer, ban all nonessential uses of chlorofluorocarbons (CFCs), and, by international agreement, impose an overall cap on CFC emissions.

6. Support substantial, coordinated research on these atmospheric issues, including a search for fundamental understanding of the nature and processes of the atmosphere, and a steady effort to produce a wider range of ideas about preventing problems and mitigating or adapting to those that do arise.

XI. *International Assistance and the Environment*

Actions needed to expand, improve, and target international assistance efforts are called for repeatedly throughout this agenda. In addition to the policies and measures already mentioned, multilateral and bilateral aid agencies should give high priority to adopting and implementing the following general policies that would have important cross-cutting benefits:

1. Give greater support to decentralized, small scale projects that provide services to all, such as low-cost sanitation measures and health care, village fuelwood plantations, and local watershed rehabilitation projects.

2. Provide the information, technical assistance, and training needed to achieve a rapid improvement in the capabilities of developing countries to assess and manage their own resource problems.
3. Place greater emphasis on agrarian reform and improvements in the productivity of smallholder agriculture.
4. Make long-run resource and environmental objectives an integral part of planning and operations. Major efforts should be undertaken to require environmental impact assessment, to encourage uniform standards for the evaluation of project costs and benefits, to estimate the value of ecosystem and natural resource services, and to supplement national income accounts with natural resource balance sheets so that economic growth based on mining natural resource stocks is not misrepresented as purely an income gain.

XII. *Assessment of Conditions, Trends, and Capabilities*

The era we are entering is new in human experience. For the first time the human species has the capacity to alter the environment on a global scale and within the span of a single generation. Wise management of the environment will require great improvements in our ability to measure and analyze environmental trends and assess the capabilities of land and water areas, at every level from the village to the remote-sensing satellite. A dramatically improved assessment capability will enable countries to plan land use in an integrated fashion, avoid irreversible environmental damage, anticipate and act quickly to correct emerging resource degradation, and allow for sustainable resource use.

We must also be able to coordinate data collection at the international level to avoid duplication of effort and to facilitate comparison and cross-calibration by using comparable units, time frames, and geographical reference systems. Lack of communication among different governments and official sources and in multidisciplinary research areas is still all too common. Research results need to be more widely disseminated and presented to policymakers in forms useful to them. Finally, there are few mechanisms available for sharing information on the success or failure of regulatory actions and other policies.

To fill the many existing gaps with reliable, timely, and usable data and to bolster the capabilities of developing countries to collect and interpret data, governments, international organizations, and others should take the following steps:

1. Agree on key "environmental indicators" and standard "geographical information systems" to be used by international organizations and governments.

2. Fully develop the Global Environment Monitoring System (GEMS), first proposed in 1972, providing sufficient support to enable the system to track the major changes in the physical and chemical, biochemical and physiological, resource and industrial, demographic and socioeconomic parameters that determine the quality of the human environment.
3. Undertake an international scientific research program to develop an understanding of the earth and its environs as a single physical, biological, and geological system and build a predictive capability based on that understanding.
4. Spur the development, in the public and private sectors, of computer applications that enable local, regional, and national governments to make use of international environmental data bases. Particular attention needs to be paid to ensure that the application of new technologies, especially remote sensing capabilities, narrows rather than widens the gap between the industrialized and the developing countries in resource and environmental management.

XIII. *Business, Science, and Citizens*

In each recommendation in this agenda calling for governmental action, there is an implicit call for action by others, particularly business, the environmental community, and science. These three, acting independently and together, can both reduce the need for governmental responses and make governmental responses viable and effective. Without an active partnership among government, business, science, and citizens, progress on the great and common issues facing us will prove impossible.

This agenda does not attempt to state explicitly the important roles these three communities must play in promoting each policy and initiative. But broad responsibilities and issues appropriate to each nongovernmental community are worthy of special note.

A. *Business and Industry*

Two points deserve emphasis. First, global resource and environmental issues in many parts of the world will probably not be successfully addressed without the support and cooperation of business and industry. Large international companies have the technology and management expertise for successful environmental and resource management and the financial resources for investment and growth. And, second, all businesses depend on adequate resources, social stability, and receptive markets for their services. Without these conditions, private business on any scale cannot prosper and may not survive.

From these premises, a consensus on goals can be reached among private business, environmentalists, and those most concerned with alleviating poverty. Briefly, each group seeks to promote a better standard of living in a way that limits adverse impact on the biosphere and the resources on which mankind's future depends. Over the long term, the goal of each must be an ecologically sustainable level of economic activity that satisfies the reasonable aspirations of the world's population. The experience of the last decade suggests that there is no necessary contradiction in these goals and that private business has much to contribute to achieving them. From this perspective, private business should:

1. Support governmental and private efforts that will help business managers understand more fully the environmental and social impacts of their actions and the relationship of these impacts to long-term economic survival and public acceptance of their organizations. More generally, a need exists for more information on the worldwide environmental effects of economic activity. Business should join with research centers and government in providing for the collection and evaluation of relevant data and in forecasting the long-term effects of developing trends and proposed actions.

2. Join with government and other stakeholders in the development of appropriate regulations and constraints on economic activity when the external social costs of production must be internalized. While the market mechanism is often imperfect in taking into account the external effects of economic activity, the forces of price and market are fundamental to the efficient creation of economic wealth, and private business becomes ineffective if these forces are rendered inoperative. To the extent that externalities can be incorporated into the market equation through pricing adjustments, business becomes more efficient.

3. Resist the tendency to support trade barriers that confer temporary local immunity from competition at the expense of long-term general benefit. Prosperity will be promoted by free trade among nations.

4. Encourage, in the context of direct foreign investment in developing countries, cooperation with host governments in establishing reasonable, effective, and stable environmental regulations and in solving other problems.

5. Direct an increased share of voluntary contributions to environmental awareness programs and institutions, support voluntary programs under which pollution control specialists and other experts are made available to developing countries, and partici-

pate in conferences and organizations seeking a sustained dialogue among business, government, and citizens.

B. *Environmental and Other Nongovernmental Organizations*

In creating public awareness of environmental problems and in generating policy options and political support, environmental groups,
policy study centers, and other nongovernmental organizations (NGOs)
can play critical rules. One key to action is widespread change in perceptions and values, to which in most countries governments respond.
Generally, NGOs are in the vanguard of these changes.

NGOs have also been remarkably successful in devising and
promoting innovative policies, technologies, production systems, and
organizational approaches. Organic farming, solar energy, the delivery
of family planning and basic health care services, and irrigation users'
associations are just a few of many important examples. Their ability to
assume risks and experiment with innovative ideas and their relative
independence from past technological and policy commitments put
NGOs in a key role.

In order to fill these roles more effectively, environmental NGOs
should:

1. Organize a series of international events designed to attract
   wide attention from the media, policymakers, business leaders,
   and others to a series of key issues: the loss of biological diversity, changes in climate and precipitation patterns, degradation
   of agricultural land, emergence of resistance to pesticides, and
   others. Reaching and involving young people, the leaders of the
   future, is especially important.
2. Publicize through the media and international networks instances of successful policies, programs, and demonstrations,
   and bring these success stories to the attention of policymakers.
3. Emphasize experiments and demonstrations of innovative technologies and approaches to sustainable development, including
   social mechanisms for the management of common resources.
4. Strengthen NGOs in developing countries by encouraging financial support from abroad, building links and collaborative projects among environmental organizations in industrial and developing countries, and preparing a world directory of NGOs
   concerned with environment and sustainable development.
5. Establish an international network of environmental NGOs,
   analogous to Amnesty International, with the ability to publicize activities that threaten world life-support systems and to
   mobilize expressions of international public concern.

Individuals and institutions committed to sustainable development and preservation of essential natural systems should consider increasing financial support for environmental and other NGOs. In order to promote NGOs in developing countries, they should:

1. Support the Environment Liaison Centre—a Nairobi-based, worldwide NGO network—including its program of small grants to competent Third World NGOs.
2. Institute an international program of awards for developing country NGOs active in promoting sustainability, thereby conveying prestige, legitimacy, and support.
3. Assist regional NGO networks around the world since these important linkage mechanisms, even in the richer regions, are severely underfunded.

C. *Science and Research*

In almost all sectors, there are critical gaps in understanding, sometimes sufficiently broad to deter action. The highest priorities for expanded research efforts appear, ironically, both at the largest scale of human interaction with the natural environment and the smallest. Much more needs to be done to understand global natural systems and the human impact on them. At the same time, more research is urgently needed on health, technologies, and production systems, mostly small-scale, of use to the world's poor.

In addition to support for specific research areas suggested elsewhere in this agenda, the scientific community should take the following more general steps:

1. Strengthen international scientific oganizations (such as the Consultative Group on International Agricultural Research, the Scientific Committee on Problems of the Environment, and the Coordinating Committee on the Ozone Layer) so that they can play a larger part in shaping and coordinating the research agenda on global resource problems and in obtaining consensus on priorities for both research and action.
2. Support the proposed Internaional Geosphere–Biosphere Program of research on global biogeochemical cycles.
3. Achieve greater consensus on important environmental and resource indicators for worldwide monitoring and on common units of measurement and geographical formats for international compatibility of data and their presentation.
4. Consider means such as an international joint venture modeled on Intelsat to stimulate the development and application of

remote-sensing technologies. These technologies have the potential to revolutionize environmental monitoring.

5. Focus more and larger efforts on the environmental and resource problems of the developing countries by educating funding sources and scientists on the importance of research into technologies relevant to the developing world and the poor, expanding scientific exchanges between industrial and developing countries, creating stronger links between research institutions in the two groups, and expanding the number of top scientific institutions in the developing countries.

6. Work closely with policy research centers focusing on global-scale resource and environmental issues to bridge the gap between basic research and policy.

Contributors

EDWARD S. AYENSU is a Senior Scientist at the Smithsonian Institution in Washington, D.C., secretary-general of the International Union of Biological Sciences, and chairman of the African Biosciences Network. He is author of *Jungles*, *Medicinal Plants of West Africa*, *Medicinal Plants of West Indies*, and coauthor of *Medicinal Plants of China*, and *Our Green and Living World*.

ROBERT DORFMAN is David A. Wells Professor of Political Economy at Harvard University. A founding member of the Center for Population Studies, he is coauthor of *Economics of the Environment: Selected Readings* and numerous publications on environmental economics, economic theory, and related fields. He has been editor of the *Quarterly Journal of Economics*, vice-president of the American Economics Association and vice-president of the Association of Environmental and Resources Economists.

JORGE E. HARDOY is a Senior Fellow at the International Institute for Environment and Development, Director of its Human Settlements Programme, and a member of the Centro de Estudios Urbanos y Regionales (CEUR) in Buenos Aires. He is author of many books on urban history in Latin America, and on contemporary problems in the Third World, including *Politicas Agrarias y Politicas urbanas en America Latina* and *Urban Planning in Pre-Columbian Cities*, and is coauthor with David Satterthwaite of *Shelter: Need and Response—Housing, Land and Settlement Policies in Seventeen Third World Nations*.

JANOS P. HRABOVSZKY is a Research Fellow at the International Institute for Applied Systems Analysis in Austria. Formerly, he was Senior Policy and Planning Coordinator of the Agriculture Department, UN

Food and Agriculture Organization, Italy. He has participated in the FAO study *Agriculture: Toward 2000* and numerous other large-scale interdisciplinary studies of agriculture in developing countries.

KENTON R. MILLER is director-general of the International Union for Conservation of Nature and Nature Resources (IUCN), Gland, Switzerland. Formerly, he was director of the Center for Strategic Wildland Management Studies and Associate Professor of Natural Resources at the University of Michigan. For ten years he was employed by the FAO and was responsible for activities related to resource management and conservation, principally in Latin America. He has carried out fieldwork throughout the developing world and written numerous books, including *Planning National Parks for Ecodevelopment*. In 1982, he was the secretary-general of the World National Parks Congress in Bali, Indonesia.

NORMAN MYERS is a consultant in environment and development. He is the author of *The Sinking Ark, A Wealth of Wild Species: Storehouse for Human Welfare, The Primary Source: Tropical Forests and Our Future*, and *An Atlas of Planet Management*. He has served as consultant with many development agencies and research bodies, including the Organization for Economic Cooperation and Development (OECD), the Royal Swedish Academy of Sciences, the US Office of Technology Assessment, the World Bank, and various UN agencies.

AMULYA K. N. REDDY is presently Senior Visiting Research Scientist at the Center for Energy and Environmental Studies at Princeton University, New Jersey, on leave from the Indian Institute of Science, where he is a professor in the Department of Inorganic and Physical Chemistry. He also has been Convenor of the Centre for the Application of Science and Technology to Rural Areas (ASTRA). He is the author of *Modern Electrochemistry* and coauthor of the forthcoming book *Energy for a Sustainable World*. He has served as Senior Scientific Affairs Officer of the UN Environment Programme (UNEP) in Nairobi.

ROBERT REPETTO is Senior Economist at the World Resources Institute, Washington, D.C. Formerly, he was an associate professor of economics in the School of Public Health at Harvard University and a member of the economics faculty and the Center for Population Studies. His writings include *Economic Incentive Arrangements for Environmental Protection* and *Economic Equality and Fertility in Developing Countries*.

ROGER REVELLE is professor of science and public policy at the University of California, San Diego. He was formerly director of the

Harvard Center for Population Studies and of the Scripps Institution of Oceanography. He is a member of the US National Academy of Sciences, the American Academy of Arts and Sciences, and the American Philosophical Society. A former president of the American Association for the Advancement of Science, he was the first president of the Scientific Committee on Oceanic Research of the International Council of Scientific Unions and of the Joint Committee on Climatic Changes and the Oceans of UNESCO's Intergovernmental Oceanographic Commission and the Scientific Committee on Oceanic Research.

PETER P. ROGERS is Gordon McKay Professor of Environmental Engineering and Professor of City Planning, Harvard University. He has served on the Water Resources and Environmental Management Committee of the American Geophysical Union and as visiting professor at the Indian Institute of Technology in New Delhi. He is coauthor of *Resource Inventory and Baseline Study Methods for Developing Countries,* published by the American Association for the Advancement of Sciences.

DAVID E. SATTERTHWAITE is Senior Research Associate, International Institute for Environment and Development, London, and Working Associate, Development Planning Unit, University College, London. He is coauthor of *Shelter: Need and Response* and the forthcoming *Small and Intermediate Urban Centers: Their Role in Third World Development Strategies.*

STEPHEN H. SCHNEIDER is Deputy Director, Advanced Study Program, National Center for Atmospheric Research, Boulder, Colorado. He is a member of the American Meteorological Society, American Geophysical Union, Federation of American Scientists, and other professional organizations and is a member of the Board on Atmospheric Sciences and Climate of the National Academy of Sciences. He is editor of *Climatic Change* and coauthor of *The Genesis Strategy: Climate and Global Survival, The Primordial Bond: Exploring Connections Between Man and Nature Through the Humanities and Sciences,* and *The Coevolution of Climate and Life.*

KRISTIN SHRADER-FRECHETTE is a professor in the Department of Philosophy at the University of Florida, Gainesville. She serves on the editorial boards of five professional journals and as senior editor of the Reidel series of monographs on Environmental Ethics. She is the author of *Risk Analysis and Scientific Method; Science Policy, Ethics, and Economic Methodology; Environmental Ethics; Nuclear Power and Public Policy Ethics* and *Science Policy, Ethics, and Economic Methodology*. She is a member of the American Philosophical Association and the Humanities and Technology Association. She is also vice-president of the Society for Philosophy and Technology.

JOHN SPEARS is Forestry Advisor to the World Bank in Washington, D.C. He was formerly with the World Bank's Cooperative Programme with the FAO in Rome. He spent ten years traveling extensively and working on investment and appraisal of forestry and forest industrial programs in thirty developing countries. Formerly, he also served as Conservator of Forests for Kenya.

HUGH THOMAS is best known for his books *The Spanish Civil War* (1961), *Cuba: The Pursuit of Freedom* (1971), and *History of the World* (1979). He was professor of history and chairman of the Graduate School of Contemporary Studies at the University of Reading, England, and has been chairman of the Centre for Policy Studies in London since 1979. His most recent work is a novel, *Havannah* (1984).

STARLEY L. THOMPSON is a research scientist at the National Center for Atmospheric Research, Boulder, Colorado. He has written articles for several scientific publications, including *Science* and *Nature*.

WILLIAM A. VOGELY is head of the Department of Mineral Economics at Pennsylvania State University, University Park, Pennsylvania. He has coedited *Energy Supply and Government Policy* and was editor-in-chief of *Economics of the Mineral Industry* (3rd edition). He is coeditor of the Journal *Materials and Society*. He is a member of the National Materials Advisory Board of the US National Academy of Sciences.

GEORGE M. WOODWELL is currently director of The Ecosystems Center, Marine Biological Laboratory, Woods Hole, Massachusetts. A past president of the Ecological Society of America and recent chairman of the board of the World Wildlife Fund (WWF) he has participated in founding several environmental oganizations, including the Environmental Defense Fund and the Natural Resources Defense Council. He is a Fellow of the American Academy of Arts and Sciences and a member of the board of trustees of the World Resources Institute. He is the author of more than two hundred scientific articles, books, and papers on ecology, science, and public affairs.

Attendance at the
Global Possible Conference

PARTICIPANTS

Abdulbar Al-Gain, Vice-President, Meteorology and Environmental Protection Agency, Saudi Arabia.

Robert O. Anderson, Chairman, Atlantic Richfield Company, Los Angeles, California.

A. T. Ariyaratne, President, National Central Council for Peace and Harmony, Sri Lanka.

Edward S. Ayensu, Senior Scientist, Smithsonian Institution, Washington, D.C.; Secretary-General, International Union of Biological Sciences; Chairman, African Biosciences Network.

William J. Baumol, Professor of Economics, Princeton and New York Universities; former president, American Economics Association.

Robert O. Blake, Senior Fellow, International Institute for Environment and Development; former ambassador.

Wallace D. Bowman, Vice-President for Operations, World Resources Institute, Washington, D.C.

Nyle C. Brady, Senior Assistant Administrator for Science and Technology, US Agency for International Development, Washington, D.C.

Lester R. Brown, President, Worldwatch Institute, Washington, D.C.

Gro Harlem Brundtland, Chair, UN Special Commission on Environmental Perspectives; former prime minister and former minister of environment of Norway.

William Clark, President, International Institute for Environment and Development, United Kingdom.

Douglas M. Costle, attorney, Wald, Harkrader, and Ross, Washington, D.C.; former administrator, US Environmental Protection Agency.

Ann Crittenden, writer, Washington, D.C.

Meinolf Dierkes, President, The Science Center, Berlin, Federal Republic of Germany.

Robert Dorfman, Professor of Political Economy, Harvard University, Cambridge, Massachusetts.

Marc J. Dourojeanni, Director, Program in Forestry Sciences, National Agrarian University, Peru; former director-general for forestry and wildlife, Peru.

John R. Eriksson, Deputy Assistant Administrator, Bureau for Science and Technology, US Agency for International Development, Washington, D.C.

John W. Firor, Director, Advanced Study Program, National Center for Atmospheric Research; former executive director of the center.

Richard B. Ford, Co-Director, Program for International Development and Social Change, Clark University, Worcester, Massachusetts.

Murray Gell-Mann, Professor of Physics, California Institute of Technology, Pasadena, California.

Arturo Gomez-Pompa, Director-General, National Institute for Biological Resources, Mexico.

Branislav Gosovic, Deputy Coordinator, Joint Economic Commission for Latin America/UN Environment Programme Unit, Chile.

Jorge E. Hardoy, Senior Fellow and Director, Human Settlements Program, International Institute for Environment and Development; Center for Urban and Regional Studies, Argentina.

Martin W. Holdgate, Chief Scientist and Deputy Secretary, Department of the Environment, United Kingdom.

Janos P. Hrabovszky, Research Fellow, International Institute for Applied Systems Analysis, Austria; Senior Policy and Planning Coordinator, Agriculture Department, FAO.

Thomas Jorling, Director, Center for Environmental Studies, Williamstown, Massachusetts.

Jacqueline Ki-Zerbo, Permanent Interstate Committee for Drought Control in the Sahel, Upper Volta.

James A. Lee, Environmental Advisor, The World Bank, Washington, D.C.

Liu Jingyi, Director, Institute of Environmental Chemistry, The Chinese Academy of Sciences, People's Republic of China

James MacNeill, Director of Environment, Organization for Economic Cooperation and Development, France.

Thomas F. Malone, former director, Holcomb Research Institute at Butler University; former foreign secretary, National Academy of Sciences.

Edwin M. Martin, Senior Fellow, Population Crisis Committee, Washington, D.C.; former US ambassador to Argentina.

Jessica T. Mathews, Vice President and Research Director, World Resources Institute, Washington, D.C.

William H. Matthews, Director, Environment and Policy Institute, The East-West Center, Honolulu, Hawaii.

Mihajlo D. Mesarovic, Professor of Engineering and Mathematics, Case Institute of Technology, Case Western Reserve University, Cleveland, Ohio.

Kenton Miller, Director-General, International Union for Conservation of Nature and Natural Resources, Switzerland.

George Mitchell, President, Mitchell Energy and Development Corporation, Texas.

Norman Myers, consultant in environment and development, United Kingdom.

Alvin Natkin, Manager, Environmental Affairs, Exxon Corporation, New York.

Matthew Nimetz, Chairman, World Resources Institute; partner, Paul, Weiss, Rifkind, Wharton and Garrison, New York; former Under-Secretary of State for Security Assistance, Science and Technology.

Letitia Obeng, Director, Regional Office for Africa, UN Environment Programme, Kenya.

Gordon Orians, Director, Institute for Environmental Studies, University of Washington, Seattle, Washington.

Frank Press, President, National Academy of Sciences, Washington, D.C.

Amulya K. N. Reddy, Senior Research Scientist, Center for the Application of Science and Technology to Rural Areas, Bangalore, India; Center for Energy and Environmental Studies, Princeton University.

Robert Repetto, Senior Associate, World Resources Institute, Washington, D.C.

Roger Revelle, Professor of Science and Public Policy, University of California at San Diego; former director of Scripps Institute of Oceanography.

Walter Orr Roberts, President Emeritus, University Corporation for Atmospheric Research, Colorado.

Peter Rogers, Professor of Environmental Engineering, Harvard University.

Emil Salim, Minister of State for Development Supervision and the Environment, Indonesia.

Armando Samper, Director-General, Sugar Cane Research Center of Colombia; former Minister of Agriculture, Colombia.

Vicente Sanchez, Senior Research Fellow and Head, Development and Environment Program, El Colegio de Mexico, Mexico.

Peter Schwartz, Head of Business Planning, Royal Dutch Shell Group, United Kingdom.

Stephen Schneider, Deputy Director, Advanced Study Program, National Center for Atmospheric Research, Colorado.

Kristin Shrader-Frechette, Professor of Philosophy, University of Florida, Gainesville.

S. Fred Singer, Professor, Department of Environmental Sciences, University of Virginia, Charlottesville, Virginia.

S. Bruce Smart, Jr., Chairman, Continental Group, Inc., Stamford, Connecticut.

John Spears, Forestry Advisor, The World Bank, Washington, D.C.; former Conservator of Forests for Kenya.

James Gustave Speth, President, World Resources Institute, Washington, D.C.; former Chairman, US Council on Environmental Quality.

Thomas B. Stoel, Jr., Director of International Programs, Natural Resources Defense Council; President, Global Tomorrow Coalition, Washington, D.C.

Maurice F. Strong, Chairman of the Board, Canada Development Investment Corporation, Vancouver, Canada; former executive director, United Nations Environment Programme.

M. S. Swaminathan, Director-General, International Rice Research Institute, Manila, Philippines; former Secretary of Agriculture and Irrigation; Director-General, Indian Council of Agricultural Research.

Peter S. Thacher, Distinguished Fellow, World Resources Institute, Washington, D.C., former Deputy Director, United Nations Environment Programme, Kenya.

Hugh Thomas, Chairman, Centre for Policy Studies; Professor Emeritus of History and Chairman of the Graduate School of Contemporary Studies at the University of Reading, United Kingdom.

Russell E. Train, President, World Wildlife Fund, US; former Administrator, US Environmental Protection Agency.

Jun Ui, President, Jishu-Koza Citizen's Movement; Professor of Urban Engineering, University of Tokyo, Japan.

William Vogely, Professor, Department of Mineral Economics, Pennsylvania State University.

Konrad von Moltke, Director, Institute for European Environmental Policy (Bonn, Paris, and London).

Martha Redfield Wallace, Director, American Can, American Express, Bristol-Myers, and other companies, New York.

Melissa Wells, Senior Staff Member, UN Development Programme, Geneva; former US ambassador and US Representative to the UN Economic and Social Council.

Casey E. Westell, Jr., Director, Industrial Ecology, TENNECO, Inc., Houston, Texas.

Gilbert F. White, Institute for Behavorial Science, University of Colorado, Boulder, Colorado; former chairman of the Commission on Natural Resources, National Academy of Sciences.

George M. Woodwell, Director, The Ecosystems Center, Marine Biological Laboratory, Woods Hole, Massachusetts.

SPECIAL GUESTS

Robert C. Barrett, Program Officer, The William and Flora Hewlett Foundation, Menlo Park, California.

Bill L. Long, Director, Office of Food and Natural Resources, US Department of State, Washington, D.C.

Joan M. Nicholson, Senior Liaison Officer, UN Environment Programme, Washington, D.C.

David Runnalls, Vice-President and Director, North American Office, International Institute for Environment and Development, Washington, D.C.

Robert Socolow, Director, Center for Energy and Environmental Studies, Princeton University, Princeton, New Jersey.

Lee M. Talbot, Visiting Fellow, World Resources Institute, Washington, D.C.

Index